T0181198

Communications
in Computer and Information Science 751

Commenced Publication in 2007
Founding and Former Series Editors:
Alfredo Cuzzocrea, Orhun Kara, Dominik Ślęzak, and Xiaokang Yang

Editorial Board

Simone Diniz Junqueira Barbosa
 *Pontifical Catholic University of Rio de Janeiro (PUC-Rio),
 Rio de Janeiro, Brazil*
Phoebe Chen
 La Trobe University, Melbourne, Australia
Xiaoyong Du
 Renmin University of China, Beijing, China
Joaquim Filipe
 Polytechnic Institute of Setúbal, Setúbal, Portugal
Igor Kotenko
 *St. Petersburg Institute for Informatics and Automation of the Russian
 Academy of Sciences, St. Petersburg, Russia*
Ting Liu
 Harbin Institute of Technology (HIT), Harbin, China
Krishna M. Sivalingam
 Indian Institute of Technology Madras, Chennai, India
Takashi Washio
 Osaka University, Osaka, Japan

More information about this series at http://www.springer.com/series/7899

Mohamed Sultan Mohamed Ali · Herman Wahid
Nurul Adilla Mohd Subha · Shafishuhaza Sahlan
Mohd Amri Md. Yunus · Ahmad Ridhwan Wahap
(Eds.)

Modeling, Design and Simulation of Systems

17th Asia Simulation Conference, AsiaSim 2017
Melaka, Malaysia, August 27–29, 2017
Proceedings, Part I

 Springer

Editors
Mohamed Sultan Mohamed Ali
Universiti Teknologi Malaysia
Skudai
Malaysia

Herman Wahid
Universiti Teknologi Malaysia
Skudai
Malaysia

Nurul Adilla Mohd Subha
Universiti Teknologi Malaysia
Skudai
Malaysia

Shafishuhaza Sahlan
Universiti Teknologi Malaysia
Skudai
Malaysia

Mohd Amri Md. Yunus
Universiti Teknologi Malaysia
Skudai
Malaysia

Ahmad Ridhwan Wahap
Universiti Teknologi Malaysia
Skudai
Malaysia

ISSN 1865-0929   ISSN 1865-0937 (electronic)
Communications in Computer and Information Science
ISBN 978-981-10-6462-3   ISBN 978-981-10-6463-0 (eBook)
DOI 10.1007/978-981-10-6463-0

Library of Congress Control Number: 2017952391

© Springer Nature Singapore Pte Ltd. 2017
This work is subject to copyright. All rights are reserved by the Publisher, whether the whole or part of the material is concerned, specifically the rights of translation, reprinting, reuse of illustrations, recitation, broadcasting, reproduction on microfilms or in any other physical way, and transmission or information storage and retrieval, electronic adaptation, computer software, or by similar or dissimilar methodology now known or hereafter developed.
The use of general descriptive names, registered names, trademarks, service marks, etc. in this publication does not imply, even in the absence of a specific statement, that such names are exempt from the relevant protective laws and regulations and therefore free for general use.
The publisher, the authors and the editors are safe to assume that the advice and information in this book are believed to be true and accurate at the date of publication. Neither the publisher nor the authors or the editors give a warranty, express or implied, with respect to the material contained herein or for any errors or omissions that may have been made. The publisher remains neutral with regard to jurisdictional claims in published maps and institutional affiliations.

Printed on acid-free paper

This Springer imprint is published by Springer Nature
The registered company is Springer Nature Singapore Pte Ltd.
The registered company address is: 152 Beach Road, #21-01/04 Gateway East, Singapore 189721, Singapore

Preface

The Asia Simulation Conference is an annual simulation conference organized by the following Asian simulation societies: the Korea Society for Simulation (KSS), the China Simulation Federation (CSF), the Japan Society for Simulation Technology (JSST), the Society of Simulation and Gaming of Singapore, and the Malaysia Simulation Society (MSS). This conference provides a forum for scientists, academicians, and professionals from around the world. With this goal in mind, the Federation of Asia Simulation Societies (ASIASIM) was formed in 2011. The main purpose of ASIASIM is to provide an Asian forum for regional and national simulation societies to promote the advancement of modeling and simulation. As a leading conference in the field of simulation, the 17th Asia Simulation Conference (AsiaSim 2017), held in Melaka, Malaysia, aimed to be the premier forum for researchers and practitioners from academia and industry in the Asia Pacific region to share their ideas, research results, and experiences, thus promoting research and technical innovation in these fields domestically and internationally.

The papers presented at this conference have been collected in this volume of the series Communications in Computer and Information Science. The papers contained in these proceedings address challenging issues in modeling and simulation in various fields such as embedded systems, symbiotic simulation, agent-based simulation, parallel and distributed simulation, high performance computing, biomedical engineering, big data, energy, society and economics, medical processes, simulation language and software, visualization, virtual reality, modeling and simulation for IoT, machine learning, as well as the fundamentals and applications of computing. This year, AsiaSim received 263 submissions. After a thorough reviewing process by the Technical Committee, 124 papers were selected for presentation as full papers, with an acceptance rate of 47.1%. This volume contains 60 full papers presented at AsiaSim 2017 and divided into 2 main tracks, namely: Modeling and Simulation: Algorithms and Methods; and Modeling and Simulation of Systems.

The high-quality program would not have been possible without the authors who chose AsiaSim 2017 as a venue for their publications. We are also very grateful to the Program Committee members and Organizing Committee members, who put a tremendous amount of effort into soliciting and selecting research papers with a balance of high quality and new ideas and applications.

We hope that you enjoy reading and benefit from the proceedings of AsiaSim 2017.

August 2017

Mohamed Sultan Mohamed Ali
Herman Wahid
Nurul Adilla Mohd Subha
Shafishuhaza Sahlan
Mohd Amri Md. Yunus
Ahmad Ridhwan Wahap

Organization

AsiaSim 2017 was organized by the Universiti Teknologi Malaysia and the Malaysian Simulation Society.

Patron

Wahid Omar	Universiti Teknologi Malaysia, Malaysia

Advisor

Johari Halim Shah Osman	Universiti Teknologi Malaysia, Malaysia
Rubiyah Yusof	Malaysian-Japan International Institute of Technology, Malaysia

General Chairs

Yahaya Md. Sam	Universiti Teknologi Malaysia, Malaysia
Zaharuddin Mohamed	Universiti Teknologi Malaysia, Malaysia
Md Nazri Othman	Universiti Teknikal Malaysia Melaka, Malaysia

Secretariat Chairs

Nurul Adilla Mohd Subha	Universiti Teknologi Malaysia, Malaysia
Shafishuhaza Sahlan	Universiti Teknologi Malaysia, Malaysia
Rozaimi Ghazali	Universiti Teknikal Malaysia Melaka, Malaysia
Raihatul Jannah Abdullah	Universiti Teknikal Malaysia Melaka, Malaysia

Financial Committee

Anita Ahmad	Universiti Teknologi Malaysia, Malaysia
Khairul Hamimah Abas	Universiti Teknologi Malaysia, Malaysia

Technical Committee

Hazlina Selamat	Universiti Teknologi Malaysia, Malaysia
Zaharuddin Mohamed	Universiti Teknologi Malaysia, Malaysia
Norhaliza Abdul Wahab	Universiti Teknologi Malaysia, Malaysia
Fatimah Sham Ismail	Universiti Teknologi Malaysia, Malaysia
Mohamed Sultan Mohamed Ali	Universiti Teknologi Malaysia, Malaysia
Zool Hilmi Ismail	Malaysian-Japan International Institute of Technology, Malaysia

Publication Committee-Proceeding Editors

Mohamed Sultan Mohamed Ali	Universiti Teknologi Malaysia, Malaysia
Herman Wahid	Universiti Teknologi Malaysia, Malaysia
Nurul Adilla Mohd Subha	Universiti Teknologi Malaysia, Malaysia
Shafishuhaza Sahlan	Universiti Teknologi Malaysia, Malaysia
Mohd Amri Md Yunus	Universiti Teknologi Malaysia, Malaysia
Ahmad Ridhwan Wahap	Universiti Teknologi Malaysia, Malaysia

Publication Committee-Program

Herlina Abdul Rahim	Universiti Teknologi Malaysia, Malaysia
Sallehudin Ibrahim	Universiti Teknologi Malaysia, Malaysia
Mohd Ridzuan Ahmad	Universiti Teknologi Malaysia, Malaysia
Ahmad Ridhwan Wahap	Universiti Teknologi Malaysia, Malaysia

Local Arrangements Committee

Abdul Rashid Husain	Universiti Teknologi Malaysia, Malaysia
Shahdan Sudin	Universiti Teknologi Malaysia, Malaysia
Mohamad Amir Shamsudin	Universiti Teknologi Malaysia, Malaysia
Sophan Wahyudi Nawawi	Universiti Teknologi Malaysia, Malaysia
Mohd Ariffanan Mohd Basri	Universiti Teknologi Malaysia, Malaysia
Mohd Hafis Izran Ishak	Universiti Teknologi Malaysia, Malaysia
Mohd Amri Md Yunus	Universiti Teknologi Malaysia, Malaysia
Norazhar Abu Bakar	Universiti Teknikal Malaysia Melaka, Malaysia
Saifulza Alwi@Suhaimi	Universiti Teknikal Malaysia Melaka, Malaysia
Mohd Shahrieel Mohd Aras	Universiti Teknikal Malaysia Melaka, Malaysia
Ahmad Zaki Shukor	Universiti Teknikal Malaysia Melaka, Malaysia
Muhamad Khairi Aripin	Universiti Teknikal Malaysia Melaka, Malaysia

Publicity Committee

Herman Wahid	Universiti Teknologi Malaysia, Malaysia
Leow Pei Ling	Universiti Teknologi Malaysia, Malaysia
Salinda Buyamin	Universiti Teknologi Malaysia, Malaysia
Rosbi Mamat	Universiti Teknologi Malaysia, Malaysia
Muhammad Nizam Kamarudin	Universiti Teknikal Malaysia Melaka, Malaysia
Chong Shin Horng	Universiti Teknikal Malaysia Melaka, Malaysia
Afnizanfaizal Abdullah	Universiti Teknologi Malaysia, Malaysia
Mohd Adham Isa	Universiti Teknologi Malaysia, Malaysia

International Program Committee

Abdullah Alshehri	King Abdul Aziz University, Saudi Arabia
Abdul Ghapor	National University of Sciences and Technology, Pakistan
Abul K.M. Azad	Northern Illinois University, USA
Axel Lehmann	Universität der Bundeswehr München, Germany
Bidyadhar Subudhi	National Institute of Technology Rourkela, India
Bo Hu Li	Beihang University, China
Emiliano Pereira Gonzalez	University of Alcala, Spain
Fredrik Ekstrand	Malardalen University, Sweden
Gary Tan	National University, Singapore
Guoping Liu	University of South Wales, UK
Hemanshu R. Pota	University of New South Wales, Australia
Herman Parung	Hasanuddin University, Indonesia
Jie Huang	Beijing Institute of Technology, China
João Reis	University of Lisbon, Portugal
Jorge M. Martins	University of Lisbon, Portugal
Kang Sun Lee	Myongji University, South Korea
Kashif Ishaque	Mohammad Ali Jinnah University, Pakistan
Kyoko Hasegawa	Ritsumei University, Japan
Lin Zhang	Beihang University, China
Md Sohel Rana	Rajshahi University of Engineering and Technology, Bangladesh
Mehmet Önder Efe	Hacettepe University, Turkey
Mohammad Hasan Shaheed	Queen Mary University of London, UK
Moh Khairudin	Yogyakarta State University, Indonesia
Md Nazri Othman	Universiti Teknikal Malaysia Melaka, Malaysia
Mohd Rizal Arshad	Universiti Sains Malaysia, Malaysia
Mustapha Muhammad	Bayero University, Nigeria
Ngo Van Thuyen	Ho Chi Minh City University of Technology and Education, Vietnam
Nordin Saad	Universiti Teknologi Petronas, Malaysia
Osamu Ono	Meiji University, Japan
Quang Ha	University of Technology Sydney, Australia
Raymund Sison	De La Salle University, Philippines
Rini Akmeliawati	Islamic International University Malaysia, Malaysia
Sarvat M. Ahmad	Ghulam Ishaq Khan Institute, Pakistan
Sasikumar Punnekkat	Malardalen University, Sweden
Satoshi Tanaka	Ritsumei University, Japan
Stephen John Turner	King Mongkut's University of Technology Thonburi, Thailand
Sumeet S. Aphale	The University of Aberdeen, UK
Teo Yong Meng	National University of Singapore, Singapore
Thasaneeya R. Nopparatjamjomras	Mahidol University, Thailand

Victor Sreeram	University of Western Australia, Australia
Walid Aniss	Aswan University, Egypt
Yun Bae Kim	Sungkyunkwan University, South Korea

Regional Program Committee

Ahmad Jais Alimin	Universiti Tun Hussein Onn Malaysia, Malaysia
Azlina Aziz	Multimedia University, Malaysia
Edwin Tan	Monash University, Malaysia
Hairul Azhar Abdul Rashid	Multimedia University, Malaysia
Haziah Abdul Hamid	Universiti Malaysia Perlis, Malaysia
Hazimi Hamzah	Universiti Teknologi Mara Penang, Malaysia
Hazlina Mohd Yusof	International Islamic University, Malaysia
Hezri Fazalul Rahiman	Universiti Teknologi Mara, Malaysia
Iqbal Saripan	Universiti Putra Malaysia, Malaysia
Ismail Saad	Universiti Malaysia Sabah, Malaysia
Kamarul Hawari Ghazali	Universiti Malaysia Pahang, Malaysia
Khisbullah Hudha	Universiti Pertahanan Nasional Malaysia, Malaysia
Muhamad Fahezal Ismail	Universiti Kuala Lumpur, Malaysia
Muralindran Mariappan	Universiti Malaysia Sabah, Malaysia
Nooritawati Md. Tahir	Universiti Teknologi Mara, Malaysia
Norfaradila Wahid	Universiti Tun Hussein Onn Malaysia, Malaysia
Norimah Yusof	University of Malaya, Malaysia
Raja Ahmad Kamil Raja Ahmad	Universiti Putra Malaysia, Malaysia
Rosli Omar	Universiti Tun Hussein Onn Malaysia, Malaysia
Rosmiwati Mohd Mokhtar	Universiti Sains Malaysia, Malaysia
Rozaimi Ghazali	Universiti Teknikal Malaysia Melaka, Malaysia
Saiful Azrin Zulkifli	Universiti Teknologi Petronas, Malaysia
Sazli Saad	Universiti Malaysia Perlis, Malaysia
Shahnourbanun Sahran	Universiti Kebangsaan Malaysia, Malaysia
Shahrum Shah	Malaysian-Japan International Institute of Technology, Malaysia
Siti Norul Huda Sheikh Abdullah	Universiti Kebangsaan Malaysia, Malaysia
Yvette Shanli	Asia Pacific University, Malaysia
Zuwairie Ibrahim	Universiti Malaysia Pahang, Malaysia

Organizers

Organized by

In Cooperation with

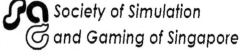

Contents – Part I

Contents – Part II

Modeling and Simulation Technology

Modeling and Simulation: Algorithms and Method

Simulation and Segmentation Techniques for Crop Maturity Identification of Pineapple Fruit

Muhammad Azmi Ahmed Nawawi and Fatimah Sham Ismail(✉)

Faculty of Electrical Engineering, Universiti Teknologi Malaysia,
81310 Skudai, Johor, Malaysia
mazmi34@live.utm.my, fatimahs@utm.my

Abstract. Image segmentation is the most important steps in image processing process, especially in detecting and segmenting the main focus object from its background or others unwanted image. The objective of this paper is to develop a segmentation technique for pineapple fruit from crop background at the plantation level. Hue value is used to remove the ground and sky from the image. Then, Adaptive Red and Blue chromatic (ARB) is implemented to segmenting the pineapple fruit from the background such as leaves. In this case, the ARB method is still produced misclassifies error. Further segmentation uses Ellipse Hough Transform (EHT) for results enhancement, so that the fruit's image is completely filtered from misclassify and background. The results obtained show that the proposed technique manages to identify the fruit from the background with better image output compared to conventional method.

Keywords: Adaptive Red and Blue Chromatic Map (ARB) · Ellipse Hough Transform (EHT) · Image processing · Pineapple segmentation

1 Introduction

Pineapple (*Ananas Comosus L.*) is one of the most consumption tropical fruits around the world. According to [1], pineapple has been ranked as third place after banana and citrus for most produced tropical fruit in the world. Besides Indonesia, Thailand, Philippine, South Africa and Brazil, Malaysia also has a large area of pineapple plantation especially at Pekan Nanas, Pontian, Johor. To increase the production of pineapple, government has allocated 7400 hectares land under East Cost Economic Region (ECER) program to encourage farmers [2].

Under ideal condition, swarm climate, optimum water and no infestation, the pineapple plant takes 24 to 39 months to yield fruit. Harvesting the fruit is quite difficult compared when growing it. This is because the quality of the pineapple is dependent on the time it be harvested. However, this process is still done manually and it is lack of efficiency. One of the indicators for the pineapple maturity is when the color change to yellow on the pineapples scale (*skin*). Figure 1 shows the pineapple anatomy. As fruit continues ripening, there is a notable change in the color of the fruit from the bottom to the top until the entire fruit turn yellowish green. When this happens, it is the right time to

© Springer Nature Singapore Pte Ltd. 2017
M.S. Mohamed Ali et al. (Eds.): AsiaSim 2017, Part I, CCIS 751, pp. 3–11, 2017.
DOI: 10.1007/978-981-10-6463-0_1

harvest the fruit. However, depending on the demand, pineapple is not necessarily harvested when it is fully turned yellowish green. Sometimes, it is necessary to be harvested in the early stage of maturity especially if the fruit was meant for export. Thus, to harvest on the correct time, the manual approach requires experience and it is time consumption. Moreover, even with an experienced worker, the quality of work can gradually decrease over time because of the human factor such as fatigue, emotional condition, personal preference and honesty. As a result, it will surely affect the quality of the pineapple [2].

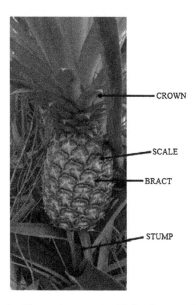

Fig. 1. Pineapple anatomy (Color figure online)

On the other hand, machine vision system has been proven can provide a huge advantage in automate process. Therefore, many researches have been conducted on the use of machine vision system to automate the process in agriculture especially in determining the fruit maturity index such as pineapple, mango, citrus, banana, strawberry, tomato, apple and dates. However, the current problem that limits the capability of machine vision system in agriculture is due to image pre-processing process. For image in plant, background can be classified as unwanted data such as ground, sky and leaves, while fruit is classified as foreground or interest data. To address this problem, researchers have studied an image pre-processing technique for segmentation process [2–8].

Mohammad et al. [2] used an image processing technique to categorize N36 pineapple. By using binary ellipse mask together with morphological normalized RGB to filter out the background, the research showed a promising result. However, the use of binary ellipse mask has its own drawback where the segment region did not include the entire region of interest. Zan et al. [3] has developed a method namely minimum symmetrical distance to overcome the problem mentioned in above. By using Josapine pineapple, the author managed to segment the entire region of interest from the background. Since the proposed method use symmetrical shape of the pineapple, it only works on Josapine pineapple.

Kamaruddin et al. [4] has chosen Otsu's Method as image pre-processing technique before applying morphological process. Otsu's Method assuming the image contains two classes of pixels following bi-modal histogram (*foreground and background*) and it calculate the optimum threshold separating the two classes. In this case, the Otsu's Method will segment the green pixels (*pineapple*) from blue pixels (*background*). Prabha and Kumar [5] also use threshold method to segment the banana from the black background. However, threshold method only works the best if the image contains two colors only. So, the accuracy will gradually decrease when the image contains more than two colors.

Most of the previous researches only considered the fixed position image, which cannot be implemented in real-time system. To improve this, Kaewapichai et al. [6] has developed a real-time automatic inspection system for Pattavia pineapple fruit. The system enables the sorting process to be carried out into each index, while pineapple still moving. It consists of two phases, namely learning and recognition phases. In learning phase, the system constructs a library of reference for pineapple skin color model, which can be used to segment the background in recognition phase. The system managed to sort the fruits within an appropriate time. Meanwhile, the use of g-r gray image was proposed by [7] in their real-time system for strawberry fruit. The author use the differentiation between g and r values to remove the background from the image.

Nandi et al. [8] has proposed a machine vision-based maturity prediction system to sort the harvested mangoes. The author proposed the use of moving conveyor to carry the fruit from starting place to the artificial illuminated image collection chamber before sorting the mangoes into maturity index. The use of controlled artificial illumination produces the captured image with constant illumination. Thus, it results in a simple segmentation process.

Based on the literature review, it is found that to extract fruit from background at the plantation level is very difficult. A few factors need to be considered. First, the algorithm must be robust for both immature and mature fruit. But to develop an algorithm for such it is quite difficult. Thus, most of the researchers only focusing on mature fruit because the intensity between mature fruit and background is easily to distinguished. On the other hand, the intensity between immature fruit and background is almost the same. Therefore, to apply the algorithm on immature fruit cannot be used without modifying the parameters. Second, the algorithm also must be robust against natural illumination. Compared to the artificial or constant illumination, natural illumination will affect the intensity of the pixels. Third, the fruit in plantation mostly cluster together or occlusion with other fruits, leaves or branches. Therefore, to improve the robustness of the algorithm, researchers have combine the process of color segmentation with other techniques such as feature extraction, edges detection, blob-based segmentation and others [9–11].

Edges detection method has been developed by [9] in detecting the citrus fruit. The author performs R-B chromatic on each pixel then applied edge detection to detect the fruit boundary because the use of R-B chromatic will result in some pixels to be misclassified. Yamamoto et al. [10] has developed a decision-tree based segmentation model (DTSM) and then applied blob-based segmentation. Zhao et al. [11] worked on identifying immature citrus fruit within tree canopy at plantation level by using Adaptive Red and Blue chromatic map (ARB). Similar to [11], this project will focus on the use of ARB to detect pineapple fruit from crop's background. The objective is to develop segmentation techniques for pineapple fruit at plantation level. However, ARB alone cannot detect fruit with high accuracy because of the intensity of the immature fruit is almost the same with the background. In this case, the Ellipse Hough Transform (EHT) is implemented for segmentation enhancement.

2   Methodology

Image pre-processing is a very important process before classifying the fruit. This is to ensure that the background is successfully removed from the image before the classification process. In this project, image pre-processing is involved with image segmentation. The overall procedure for this project is shown in Fig. 2. It consists of three step namely data acquisition, follows by color segmentation and lastly is feature extraction.

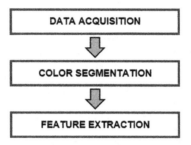

Fig. 2. The overall process

2.1   Data Acquisition

To develop an algorithm for pineapple image segmentation in real-time situation, sample of images were captured during daytime with various illumination conditions at pineapple plantation, Pekan Nanas, Pontian, Johor. Pineapple type MD2 is selected based on the suggestion from Malaysia Pineapple Industry Board (MPIB) to promote the MD2 pineapple in Malaysia. Figure 3 shows the sample of images used in this project.

There are several assumptions and limitations are applied to simplify the algorithm and to reduce the processing time especially for feature extraction, as follows:

(a) The horizontal axis must be at $0°$.
(b) The position of the pineapple is aligned with the vertical axis with $-5°$ to $5°$ tolerate from vertical axis.
(c) The position of the crown must be on the top of the image.
(d) The distance between camera and pineapple is between 1 m to 2 m.

Fig. 3. Sample images with different stage of maturity (*green = immature fruit, yellow = mature fruit*) and background (Color figure online)

2.2 Algorithm

The flowchart of the algorithm is shown in Fig. 4, which has two stages for segmentation and detecting the pineapple. Color segmentation is to remove background such as ground, sky and leaves, while keeping as many as possible pineapple pixels. Then, feature extraction process is conducted to completely segment the pineapple from misclassified background.

The proposed algorithm begins by acquiring the image from camera. Since the size of the captured image is too large, this project has conducted a few tests to find out suitable scale to resize the image. After that, the Hue in Hue, Saturation, and Value (HSV) color space is extracted and by setting threshold value obtained from the experimental test to detect ground and sky. Since image segmentation is quite difficult, it is necessary to remove any background that is easily to distinguished from fruit. As presented in Fig. 5, the Hue value for ground (*orange*) and sky (*white*) are easily differentiated from other colors. The threshold value has been selected based on these properties. Any value less than threshold value is removed (*pixel intensity becomes 0*), meanwhile, the value greater or equal than threshold value is maintained.

Adaptive Red and Blue chromatic map (ARB) are built to segment the pineapple fruit from the leaves. The ARB is defined in Eq. (2).

$$\text{Ratio} = \text{B}/\text{R} \tag{1}$$

$$\text{ARB} = \text{R} - \text{Ratio} \times \text{B} \tag{2}$$

Then, the threshold method is used in ARB to segment the potential pineapple fruit from the leaves. Similar to the HSV, any ARB value which less than threshold value is removed (*pixel intensity becomes 0*) from the image. This value is considered as leaves. On the other hand, ARB value for fruit is greater or equal than threshold value. Furthermore, the proposed ARB only works effectively for green pineapple fruit but the result still shows the misclassified pixels. Especially, for darker leaves, which have ARB value almost the same with fruit. However, the accuracy of ARB is gradually decreased when applied on yellow pineapple. This happens because many pixels in yellow

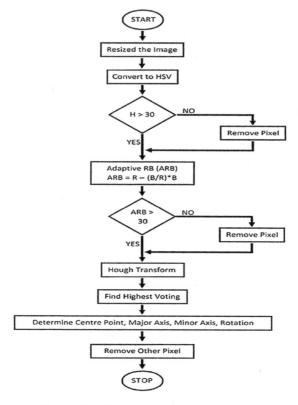

Fig. 4. Flowchart for the proposed algorithm

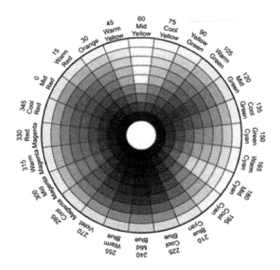

Fig. 5. HSV color space (Color figure online)

pineapple have blue intensity higher than red intensity. As a result, ARB will detect this pixel as background and will be removed. Therefore, to improve accuracy of the algorithm, this project has proposed the use of Ellipse Hough Transform (EHT) method for further segmentation process.

Hough Transform is a feature extraction technique in image analysis [12]. The purpose of this technique was to find the shape of pineapple by a voting procedure. This voting parameter was carried out in a parameter space. The parameter space and the voting procedure are defined in Eq. (3).

$$\frac{[(X - Xc)\cos\theta - (Y - Yc)\sin\theta]^2}{a^2} + \frac{[(X - Xc)\sin\theta - (Y - Yc)\cos\theta]^2}{b^2} = 1. \quad (3)$$

Where Xc and Yc represents the center of the pineapple, a represent the major axis and b represent the minor axis. By using Eq. (3), EHT will construct an accumulator and the highest vote in accumulator is chosen as a possible data. While other pixels from pineapple fruits are removed from the image.

3   Results and Analysis

This section presents the results and the analysis of the images' accuracy from various segmentation steps such as HSV to remove ground and sky, and the ARB for leaves removal and EHT for segmentation enhancement.

3.1   Hue Value Segmentation

First step, the Hue parameter has been selected to remove the ground and sky. The accuracy will increase due to the background in the image has been decreased. Refer to Fig. 6(a), the sky is successfully removed from the image and other objects are maintained. The ground also is removed as shown in Fig. 6(b). Finally, it has been found that the output image still can be considered as acceptable, even though a few interest pixels have been removed.

(a)   (b)

Fig. 6.   Result after applying HSV (*left = original image, right = result after HSV*). (a) Immature pineapple (b) Mature pineapple

3.2   Adaptive Red and Blue Chromatic Map (ARB)

Second step is to remove leaves from the image as shown in Fig. 7 using ARB method. It can be seen that, the ARB has successfully removed the leaves from the image. Even though the intensity between fruit and background in Fig. 7(a) is almost the same, ARB is still managed to remove almost all leaves, while the shape of the pineapple is still preserved. Similar to the image in Fig. 7(b), ARB only remove leaves while maintained the fruit area and shape.

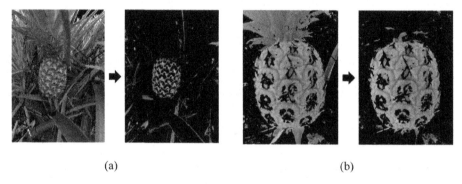

(a)   (b)

Fig. 7. Result after applying ARB (*left = result after HSV, right = result after ARB*). (a) Immature pineapple. (b) Mature pineapple (Color figure online)

3.3   Ellipse Hough Transform (EHT)

The result from ARB segmentation method has a few misclassified. Therefore, this project applies image enhancement process for further segmentation using Ellipse Hough Transform (EHT). The EHT process will detect the shape of the pineapple using ellipse approaches as shown in Fig. 8. The ellipse shape is constructed using the highest possible data and all the pixels outside this shape are eliminated.

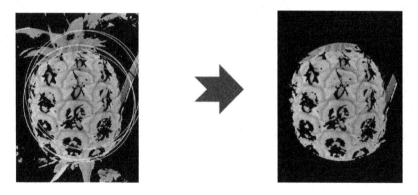

Fig. 8.   Result after applying EHT

4 Conclusion

The image segmentation and detection algorithms have been presented to detect pineapple fruit maturity based on color and shape. The results found show that the use of Hue value together with Adaptive Red and Blue chromatic map (ARB) in color segmentation is very effective and have good potential in detecting the fruit pixels and the implementation of Ellipse Hough Transform (EHT) has improved the accuracy of the algorithm by detecting the shape of the pineapple and then eliminated other pixels. Further research needs to be done using an intelligent optimization technique for optimal maturity algorithm. Also, further improvement is needed for algorithm to detect many fruits at the time. Furthermore, a method to reduce processing time in EHT is recommended.

Acknowledgement. The authors would like to thank for the support given to this project by Ministry of Higher Education (MOHE) and Universiti Teknologi Malaysia (UTM), under GUP grant: Q.J130000.2523.13H57.

References

1. Asnor, J.I., Rosnah, S., Wan, Z.W.H., Badrul, H.A.B.: Pineapple maturity recognition using RGB extraction. Int. J. Electr. Comput. Energ. Electron. Commun. Eng. **7**, 597–600 (2013)
2. Mohammad, S., Ghazali, K.H., Zan, N.C., Radzi, S.S.M., Karim, R.A.: Classification of fresh N36 pineapple crop using image processing technique. Adv. Mater. Res. **418–420**, 1739–1743 (2011)
3. Zan, N.C., Ghazali, K.H., Mohammad, S., Radzi, S.S.M., Jusof, M.F.M.: ROI segmentation using minimum symmetrical edges distance: a study on josapine pineapple. In: International Conference on Artificial Intelligence in Computer Science and ICT (AICS 2013), pp. 1–6 (2013)
4. Kamaruddin, S., Sunardi, K., Ghazali, K.H., Hamid, R.: Canned pineapple grading using pixel colour extraction. In: International Conference on Artificial Intelligence in Computer Science and ICT (AICS 2013), pp. 217–226 (2013)
5. Prabha, D.S., Kumar, J.S.: Assessment of banana fruit maturity by image processing technique. J. Food Sci. Technol. **53**, 1316–1327 (2015)
6. Kaewapichai, W., Kaewtrakulpong, P., Prateepasen, A.: A real-time automatic inspection system for pattavia pineapples. Key Eng. Mater. **321–323**, 1186–1191 (2006)
7. Liming, X., Yanchao, Z.: Automated strawberry grading system based on image processing. Comput. Electron. Agric. **71S**, S32–S39 (2010)
8. Nandi, C.S., Tudu, B., Koley, C.: Computer vision based mango fruit grading system. In: International Conference on Innovative Engineering Technologies (ICIET'2014), pp. 1–5 (2014)
9. Hui, P., Ruifang, Z., Shanmei, L., Youxian, W., Lanlan, W.: Edge detection of growing citrus based on self-adaptive canny operator. In: 2011 International Conference on Computer Distributed Control and Intelligent Environmental Monitoring, pp. 342–345 (2011)
10. Yamamoto, K., Guo, W., Yoshioka, Y., Ninomiya, S.: On plant detection of intact tomato fruits using image analysis and machine learning methods. Open Access Sens. **14**, 12191–12206 (2014)
11. Zhao, C., Lee, W.S., He, D.: Immature green citrus detection based on colour feature and sum of absolute transformed difference (SATD) using colour images in citrus grove. Comput. Electron. Agric. **124**, 243–253 (2016)
12. Changyi, X., Lihua, Z., Minzan, L., Yuan, C., Chunyan, M.: Apple detection from apple tree image based on BP neural network and Hough transform. Int. J. Agric. Biol. Eng. **8**, 46–53 (2015)

Multi-loop Damping and Tracking Strategy Emulating a Butterworth Pattern for Accurate Nanopositioning

Mohammed Altaher and Sumeet S. Aphale$^{(\boxtimes)}$

University of Aberdeen, Aberdeen, UK
{mohammed.altaher,s.aphale}@abdn.ac.uk

Abstract. Control schemes for nanopositioners typically combine damping and tracking. Due to the positioning performance requirements of the nanopositioning system, it is desirable for the closed-loop frequency response of the nanopositioner to mimic ripple-free pass-band low-pass characteristics. Earlier reports are available on simultaneous damping and tracking control emulating a Butterworth filter design, but this technique only incorporates a single integrator for tracking, which is inadequate for error-free tracking of the triangular and ramp-like signals typically used as input to nanopositioning systems. Double integral tracking guarantees error-free tracking, but is difficult to implement due to phase-related stability issues. In this work, a dual-loop integral tracking algorithm is proposed. Using simulation, it is shown that in the presence of hysteresis, the proposed dual-loop scheme delivers a more accurate positioning performance than the traditional single-loop integral tracking strategy.

Keywords: Butterworth pattern · Nanopositioner · Damping · Tracking

1 Introduction

A nanopositioner is a mechatronic system designed to deliver precise positioning with nano scale accuracy. In precise position control, there are many desired control objectives that aim to obtain a fast response with no overshoot and accurate set-point tracking, a very high travel range and a high bandwidth. All of these objectives can be improved by using a feedback controller; however, the complexity of the controller varies depending on which control objective is most important [6].

For systems that undergo parameter changes, such as a change in damping and resonance frequency due to loading, control designs offering good gain and

---

The original version of this chapter was revised: The figure 4 and 5 was corrected. The erratum to this chapter is available at https://doi.org/10.1007/978-981-10-6463-0_61

© Springer Nature Singapore Pte Ltd. 2017
M.S. Mohamed Ali et al. (Eds.): AsiaSim 2017, Part I, CCIS 751, pp. 12–26, 2017.
DOI: 10.1007/978-981-10-6463-0_2

phase margins are most suited. Nanopositioning systems exhibit various types of uncertainty due to a change in sample mass, mechanical ageing, sensors and actuator drifts. Furthermore, many control schemes have a tendency to exacerbate the high frequency out-of-bandwidth unmodelled dynamics [13]. In order to overcome these issues, control schemes have been employed to improve the performance of nanopositioners, which must be robust under the presence of parameter uncertainties. In addition to resonance and parameter uncertainty, nanopositioners are also marred by nonlinear effects such as hysteresis and creep due to the piezoelectric actuators that are popularly employed in these systems. Therefore, along with robust damping controllers and high gain, high-bandwidth tracking control is an essential component of the overall control scheme. For quite some time, damping and tracking controllers have been designed sequentially (damping first, tracking later) and implemented in an inner-outer loop fashion. It has been shown that the sequential design is sub-optimal in terms of obtainable positioning performance and simultaneous damping and therefore tracking control design has been proposed [8]. Using the Butterworth filter, which has the desirable properties of a flat, ripple-free passband and a quick roll-off at high frequencies as a motivation, simultaneous damping and tracking schemes that emulate a Butterworth filter have been proposed in [9].

In nanopositioning applications, the typical scanning pattern is a raster, generated by employing a slow ramp along one axis and a fast triangle wave along the other. Both the input signals therefore have non-zero velocity and it is impossible to track them error-free with a single integral tracking control. This paper provides a strategy to simultaneously design the damping and the multi-loop tracking controllers in order to mimic the Butterworth filter pattern. Simulations are presented to support the proposed theory.

The paper is organised as follows: Sect. 2 presents the linear model for axes on the nanopositioning platform, as well as the nonlinear Bouc-Wen model for the hysteresis exhibited by the actuator on this axis. The Butterworth filter pattern for the proposed multi-loop control strategy is presented in Sect. 3. Simulated open- and closed-loop, time-domain and frequency-domain results are given in Sect. 4, where the theoretical error analysis for the proposed control scheme is also presented. Robustness of the control scheme in the presence of resonance frequency shift is also examined in this section. Section 5 concludes the paper.

2   System Modelling

The dynamics of the nano axis has linear and nonlinear components; thus, the axis is modelled as a linear second-order transfer function and a Bouc Wen model for hysteresis.

2.1   Linear Dynamics Model

The mechanical system of the nanopositioning platform is shown in Fig. 1(a) [1], which can be characterised and simplified by a spring-damper system, as shown in Fig. 1(b) [10]. The axis of the nanopositioning platform is equipped with a capacitive sensor for position measurement. The equation of motion for this system is given by:

$$M_p\ddot{d} + c_f\dot{d} + (K_a + k_f)d = F_a \tag{1}$$

The system dynamics is regulated by the piezoelectric actuator force that moves the nanopositioning stage. The movement of the piezo actuators is manifested by expansion and contraction in response to an input voltage stimulus. Thus, (F_s) is the measured force acting between the actuator and the mass of the platform (M_p) in the vertical direction. The stiffness of the actuator is denoted by (K_a) and the force by (F_a). A force sensor is collocated with the actuator and measures the load force F_s. Equation 1 can now be rewritten as follows:

$$M_p\ddot{d} + c_f\dot{d} + k = F_a \tag{2}$$

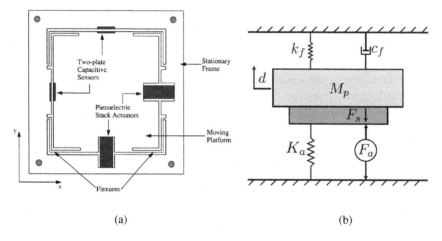

(a)   (b)

Fig. 1. (a) A simple schematic of a piezo-stack actuated two-axis nanopositioner; (b) The equivalent mass-spring-damper model for one axis of the nanopositioner

The relationship between the applied force (F_a) and the displacement d is described as in the following transfer function:

$$G_{dF_a}(s) = \frac{d}{F_a} = \frac{1}{M_p s^2 + c_f s + k} \tag{3}$$

This can be described in the frequency domain as a second-order system and the transfer function can be written in the form (4):

$$G(s) = \frac{\sigma^2}{s^2 + 2\zeta\omega_p s + \omega_p^2}, \tag{4}$$

where ζ is the damping ratio, ω_p is the natural frequency and σ^2 is the DC gain of the platform. The investigated system is represented by the linear dynamics transfer function below; this is characterised by its first resonant mode and given by:

$$G(s) = \frac{4.746 * 10^8}{s^2 + 910.1s + 2.927 * 10^8}, \tag{5}$$

where the value of the damping ratio (ζ) is 0.0266 and the natural frequency $f_n = 2\pi * \omega_p$, where the value of the ω_p^2 is $2.927 * 10^8$ and σ^2 is $4.746 * 10^8$.

Figure 2 shows that the modelled-based frequency response and the measurement-based, which have been superimposed, are almost identical.

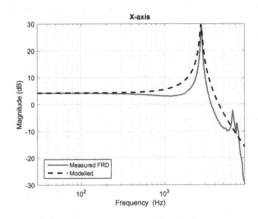

Fig. 2. Comparison between the measured- and model-based magnitude response for the x-axis of the system in. The slight mismatch in the width of the resonant mode is due to the sensor and amplifier dynamics, along with the nanopositioner axis dynamics included in the measured response

2.2   Hysteresis Model

Nonlinear effects are usually unmodelled and tracking is enforced to minimise the effect of nonlinearities on the actual trace. Hysteresis is a dynamic characteristic present in many physical systems such as piezo actuators. Hysteresis in piezo actuators can lead to problems such as an increase in undesirable inaccuracy or oscillation and instability [14]. Therefore, any control strategy must be designed to accommodate uncertain time-varying nonlinear systems.

The hysteresis in this work has been described by the Bouc Wen model [3, 11, 12]. The Bouc Wen describes the equation of motion for the nanopositioning platform using its nonlinear differential equations, as in Eq. (6):

$$\left\{ \begin{array}{l} m\ddot{x} + b\dot{x} + kx = k(du - h) \\ \dot{h} = \alpha d\dot{u} - \beta |\dot{u}| h - \gamma \dot{u} |h| \end{array} \right\} \tag{6}$$

where h represents the nonlinear relation between the lag force (applied voltage) u and the displacement x. The coefficients m, b, k and d denote the effective mass, damping coefficient, mechanical stiffness and effective piezoelectric
coefficients respectively. It is noted that hysteresis for the proposed system is
rate-independent, hence Bouc Wen has been selected as opposed to other models because it is rate-independent and simple. Its parameters, α, β, d and γ,
have been realised in MATLAB Simulink and determined so the hysteresis loop
produced by Bouc Wen can accurately match the experimental data on the
nanopositioning platform. The parameters of Bouc Wen are selected as follows
in (7):

$$\left\{ \alpha = 0.26, \beta = 0.005, \gamma = 0.00068, \mathrm{d} = 2\,\mu\mathrm{m} \text{ per volt} \right\} \tag{7}$$

The proposed hysteresis model is investigated by applying a 50 V peak amplitude sinusoidal signal of 10 Hz to the platform and the hysteresis cycle is thereby
generated. Figure 3 illustrates the generated hysteresis in the open-loop, which
is associated with a single axis of the nanopositioning platform. In Fig. 3, a comparison can be seen between the experimental and the modelling result, where
the x-axis represents the input voltage and the y axis is the generated displacement. It can be seen from Fig. 3 that the open-loop exhibits strong nonlinearity.
A system exhibiting such hysteresis is severely limited in its performance. The
hysteresis loop provides a rate-independent relationship between the applied
voltage and the generated displacement.

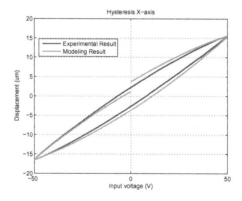

Fig. 3. Measured and modelled hysteresis loops show that the hysteresis model accurately captures the hysteresis of the piezo actuator

3   Control Strategy

Nanopositioning systems are lightly damped and highly likely to exhibit mechanical resonance when there is any sudden change in the voltage applied to the platform. Thus, the use of damping controllers is necessary, the damping to damp

resonance and the tracking controllers to treat nonlinearity. Consequently, minimising the error is considered the most important control object in the nanopositioning application. This section will explain the traditional approach and the proposed control strategy to control the nanopositioning platform.

3.1   Traditional Control Strategy

The traditional single-loop feedback scheme is shown in Fig. 4. In traditional tracking, nanopositioning tracking is achieved through the use of single-loop feedback. The tracking controller commonly used in this scheme is either a first-order integral (I), or a proportional integral (PI). Figure 4 also illustrates the method by which the tracking (Ct_1) and damping controllers (C_d) are combined and used together. This traditional approach can improve the positioning accuracy of the nanopositioning platform to some extent. However, feedback control law is limited in compensating for hysteresis. Due to stability issues, second-order controller in a single-loop is not directly applicable.

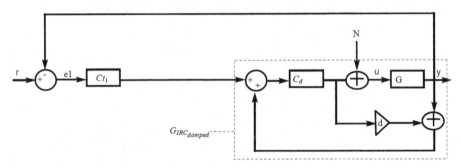

Fig. 4. Schematic of the traditional damping + tracking control scheme

3.2   Proposed Control Strategy

An attempt to apply second-order integral tracking to the nanopositioning platform has been proposed that will not affect the stability of the platform. In order to draw a comparison with a single-loop feedback controller, the multi-loop feedback control system is described by the scheme shown in Fig. 5. The overall control algorithm in Fig. 5 consists of two controllers for tracking: the outer-loop feedback uses a first-order integral tracking (Ct_1) with a transfer function of $\{\frac{K_{T2}(s)}{s}\}$, and the inner-loop feedback uses a first-order integral tracking (Ct_2) with a transfer function of $\{\frac{K_{T1}(s)}{s}\}$. The damped system ($G_{IRC_{damped}}(s)$) using the IRC controller has the following transfer function [2]:

$$G_{IRC_{damped}} = \frac{K_d * G}{1 - K_d * (G + d)} \tag{8}$$

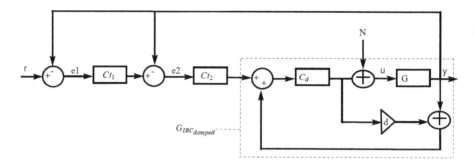

Fig. 5. Schematic of the proposed control scheme with dual-loop tracking + damping

The overall transfer function for the multi-loop scheme is given by:

$$\frac{Y(s)}{R(s)} = \frac{K_{T2}K_{T1}k_dG}{K_{T2}K_{T1}k_dG + 1 - dk_d - Gk_d + K_{T1}k_dG} \tag{9}$$

The transfer functions for $K_{T1}(s)$, $K_{T2}(s)$ and $K_d(s)$ are listed in (10):

$$\left\{ \begin{array}{l} K_{T1}(s) = \frac{K_{T1}}{s} \\[2mm] K_{T2}(s) = \frac{K_{T2}}{s} \\[2mm] K_d(s) = \frac{K_d}{s} \end{array} \right\} \tag{10}$$

The characteristics equation for the proposed multi-loop feedback scheme is specified by:

$$s^5 + (2\zeta\omega_p - dK_d)s^4 + (\omega_p^2 - 2\zeta\omega_p dk_d)s^3$$
$$+(-dK_d\omega_p^2 - K_d\sigma^2)s^2 + K_{T1}K_d\sigma^2 s + K_{T2}K_{T1}K_d\sigma^2 = 0 \tag{11}$$

The transfer function of the normalised fifth-order Butterworth filter is given by:

$$\frac{1}{s^5 + 3.236s^4 + 5.236s^3 + 5.236s^2 + 3.236s + 1} \tag{12}$$

Equation (12) can be rewritten for any given frequency by substituting s with $\frac{s}{\omega_c}$ and this is given by:

$$\frac{\omega_c^5}{\frac{s^5}{\omega_c^5} + 3.236\frac{s^4}{\omega_c^4} + 5.236\frac{s^3}{\omega_c^3} + 5.236\frac{s^2}{\omega_c^2} + 3.236\frac{s}{\omega_c} + 1} \tag{13}$$

The characteristics equation for the Butterworth filter at any given frequency is specified by:

$$s^5 + 3.236\omega_c s^4 + 5.236\omega_c^2 s^3 + 5.236\omega_c^3 s^2 + 3.236\omega_c^4 s + \omega_c^5 \tag{14}$$

In order to emulate the Butterworth pattern, the characteristics equation for the multi-loop control strategy must be equated to the characteristics equation for the Butterworth filter; this will determine the values for the feed-through term, damping gain and tracking gains. Thus, (11) must be similar to (14). The following quantities are obtained as a result of linking the two characteristics equations:

$$\begin{cases} 2\zeta\omega_p - dK_d = 3.236\omega_c \\ \omega_p^2 - 2\zeta\omega_p dk_d = 5.236\omega_c^2 \\ -dK_d\omega_p^2 - K_d\sigma^2 = 5.236\omega_c^3 \\ K_{T1}K_d\sigma^2 = 3.236\omega_c^4 \\ K_{T2}K_{T1}K_d\sigma^2 = \omega_c^5 \end{cases} \tag{15}$$

Substituting the above quantities, the value of ω_c can be estimated by solving the following equation using the quadratics polynomial formula:

$$\omega_c^2 - 1.23605806\zeta\omega_p\omega_c + \left(\frac{\omega_p^2(4\zeta^2 - 1)}{5.236}\right) \tag{16}$$

The value of the damping gain can be evaluated using the following formula:

$$k_d = \frac{3.236 * \omega_c * \omega_p^2 - 2 * \zeta * \omega_p^3 - 5.236 * \omega_c^3}{\sigma^2} \tag{17}$$

The value of the feed-through term can be calculated using the following equation:

$$d = \frac{2 * \zeta * \omega_p - 3.236 * \omega_c}{k_d} \tag{18}$$

The tracking gains can be valued as follows:

$$k_{T1} = \frac{3.236 * \omega_c^4}{k_d * \sigma^2}, \quad K_{T2} = \frac{\omega_c^5}{k_{T1} * k_d * \sigma^2} \tag{19}$$

Using (5), (16) can now be solved and the damped natural frequency ω_c can be determined as $7.7527 * 10^3$ Hz. Having calculated the damped natural frequency, all other variables can now be determined. Table 1 shows the values of the proposed scheme parameters required to achieve the Butterworth pattern.

Table 1. Controller parameters for the simultaneous damping and tracking strategy

Parameter	Value
d	−2.4746
k_d	9770.2
k_{T1}	2521.1
k_{T2}	2395.8

Further analysis to test the tracking performance of the proposed control strategy has been conducted, as will be clear in the following sections.

4   Simulation Results

In this section, the results are presented related to both the frequency and time domains, and error analysis is also conducted. Robustness of the proposed control strategy is also tested in this section.

4.1   Closed-Loop Positioning Performance

The simulated frequency response of the proposed multi-loop technique is presented in Fig. 6 and it can be seen that the Butterworth-based filter pattern has been obtained. The pattern is achieved as a result of the tuning method used in Table 1 based on the fifth-order Butterworth filter. The gain margin GM = 6.4 dB and phase margin PM = 600° are of optimal values for a robust stable system. An encouraging frequency response has been achieved with regards to better tracking performance as no ripple is exhibited in the passband or stopband and the closed-loop Butterworth-based bandwidth is observed at 1230 Hz. This bandwidth is of a sufficient level to cover the major harmonics that form the triangle wave, resulting in accurate tracking performance and reduced sensitivity to sensor noise.

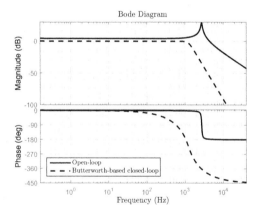

Fig. 6. Open-loop and closed-loop frequency response of the proposed multi-loop control strategy

Bandwidth in nanopositioning is defined as the point at which the closed-loop magnitude response of a given system is exhibiting (at any given point in the passband) a 0 dB gain, and this should not increase or decrease by ±1 dB [7]. The Butterworth-based magnitude response in Fig. 6 does not exceed 0 dB at any passband point; therefore, this is a useful characteristic in achieving accurate tracking performance of the nanopositioning platform.

The root locus has been investigated; it is shown that the poles of the system are at a significant distance from the imaginary axis. The Butterworth pattern is achieved as the tracking gain reaches its design value where the pole at origin with a $0°$ angle will be shifted further to the left of the imaginary axis. At this point, the distribution of the poles of the fifth-order Butterworth is achieved and the angles of the poles are $0°, \pm 36°$ and $\pm 72°$.

It is noted that stability is a critical concern when applying, for example, a double-integral tracking controller; applying a second-order integral without the use of the multi-loop feedback scheme causes instability. Hence, the proposed method preserves stability while applying two first-order integral controllers to avoid phase profile. It could be argued that adding another integrator would affect the bandwidth and increase the order of the system unnecessarily however, due to highly nonlinear hysteresis and sensitivity to noise, double integration is warranted. There are two common types of tuning method that provide compensation procedures, either to widen the bandwidth or reduce tracking error; this has been satisfied in this work. For the reasons given above, the multi-loop feedback controller scheme is therefore preferred.

In order to demonstrate the effectiveness of the proposed multi-path feedback controller, a 30 and 40 Hz triangles have been chosen to be tracked with a $20\,\mu m$ peak, and simulations performed in MATLAB Simulink. Results for the open- and closed-loop are presented in Fig. 7(a, b). It can be seen that in the open-loop the tracked signal deviates from the linear because of the presence of hysteresis. As is also clear from Fig. 7(a, b), in the open-loop the tracked signal is experiencing oscillatory behaviour because no damping controller is used. Neither resonance nor hysteretic behaviour is observed in the linear part of the tracked signal, as is shown in Fig. 7(a, b). The error plot is drawn to illustrate the linear part of the tracked signal, as is shown below. The error signal is directly proportional to the frequency of the tracked signal in a trade-off relationship. Therefore, as the frequency increases, there is a reduction in the linear part, which is an undesirable characteristics. Tracking of the high frequency signal is preferable in nanopositioning due to high speed scanning.

For the proposed dual-loop control strategy depicted in Fig. 4(b), the error is derived as in the following transfer function:

$$E_1(s) = \frac{R(s)(1 - dk_d(s) - G(s)k_d(s) + K_{T1}(s)k_d(s)G(s))}{1 - dk_d(s) - G(s)k_d(s) + K_{T1}(s)k_d(s)G(s) + K_{T2}(s)K_{T1}(s)K_d(s)G(s)} \quad (20)$$

For the system under consideration, the multi-loop control strategy is type 1; in order to ensure that the steady-state error is acceptable, steady-state error analysis is proposed. For the proposed system, the Butterworth-based controller design is considered; R(s) is for a ramp and the transfer functions are given by:

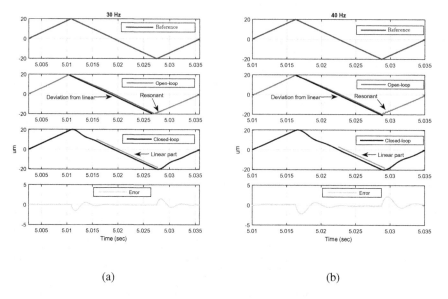

Fig. 7. The tracking performance of the platform for a triangle signal in the open- and closed-loop: (a) 30 Hz; (b) 40 Hz

$$
\left\{
\begin{aligned}
R(s) &= \tfrac{1}{s^2} \\[4pt]
K_d(s) &= \tfrac{kd}{s} \\[4pt]
K_{T1}(s) &= \tfrac{K_{T1}}{s} \\[4pt]
K_{T2}(s) &= \tfrac{K_{T2}}{s} \\[4pt]
G(s) &= \tfrac{\sigma^2}{s^2 + 2\zeta\omega_p s + \omega_p^2} \\[4pt]
& d
\end{aligned}
\right\} \tag{21}
$$

In order to find the steady-state error, the final value theorem is applied as in (22):

$$
e(\infty) = \lim_{s \to 0} sE(s) \tag{22}
$$

For any given second-order system, the steady-state error to track a ramp using the multi-loop scheme is given by:

$$
e_{1(steady\text{-}state)} = \frac{-\sigma^2 + \sigma^2 K_{T1} - d\omega_p^2}{-\sigma^2 + \sigma^2 K_{T1} + K_{T2}K_{T1}\sigma^2} \tag{23}
$$

Equation (23) can be minimised as in (24) below:

$$e_{1(steady-state)} = \frac{-d\omega_p^2}{K_{T2}K_{T1}\sigma^2} \equiv \frac{d\omega_p^2}{K_{T2}K_{T1}\sigma^2} \tag{24}$$

In order to achieve accurate tracking, $\forall G(s)|_{s=0} = 1$, it is assumed $\sigma^2 = w_p{}^2$ and then (24) can be approximated as in the equation below:

$$e_{1(steady-state)} = \frac{d}{K_{T2}K_{T1}} \tag{25}$$

In solving (25), zero steady-state error is almost achieved. For the system under consideration, after substantiating the quantities as in Table 1 and when the values of $\sigma^2 = 4.746 * 10^8$ and $\omega_n^2 = 2.927 * 10^8$ are known, the error at steady-state can now be estimated as e(∞) = 0.041735.

In nanopositioning, the raster scan trajectory is achieved by applying triangle wave in the x-axis and a ramp in the y-axis. The transient error occurs at the turn-around area of the triangular waveform at the end of each scan line, thereby promoting scanning speed (frequency) and amplitude of the driven signal. The error at the turn-around is relatively large due to the high frequency components of the triangle wave and hysteresis nonlinearity. The appearance of the transient error is due to system behaviour when encountering disturbance on attempting to track the triangle wave. The transient error can, however, be reduced by increasing the gain of the controller. Due to the fact that the controller design is simultaneously tuned for damping and tracking gains, changing the gain to reduce the transient error is difficult. Although the transient error at the turn-around adds some distortion to the raster scan image, its effect on the raster scan is limited because only the linear part is taken into account.

In order to demonstrate the strength and effectiveness of the proposed control strategy, a comparative error analysis of the multi-loop and single-loop feedback schemes, presented in [9], is examined in the following part.

In a single-loop feedback controller, the controller takes the tracking error $(r(t) - y(t))$ as input; this is called output feedback. In this case, the calculation of the control signal is based on the plant output and is subject to large control actions when the set-point undergoes a sudden change. On the other hand, in the multi-loop feedback control, the controller takes the error as input where the outer-loop defines the set point for the inner-loop; this is called error feedback.

Tracking a triangle wave (high frequency components) in nanopositioning generates significant positioning error at high frequencies, and the effect of hysteresis is also significantly more common at high frequencies. The RMS error plot is plotted across various frequency changes, as is clear in Fig. 8.

The positioning error is substantially improved by using the multi-loop feedback scheme in the presence of hysteresis; thus the use of this scheme in nanopositioning applications is preferred. To conclude, the performance of the multi-loop feedback scheme is better than that of the single-loop feedback scheme.

Further analysis to test the robustness of the proposed control strategy has been conducted, as will be clear in the following section.

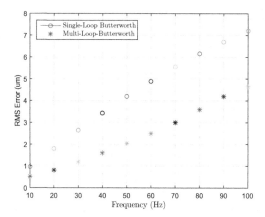

Fig. 8. A comparison of RMS error across various frequency changes

4.2   Robustness to Resonance Frequency Variation and Disturbance Rejection Profiles

Robustness refers to the ability of the closed-loop system to be insensitive to parameter variation. Disturbance rejection is another important performance index in nanopositioning applications that needs to be evaluated. This refers to the ability of a system to be insensitive to exogenous disturbances. In this section, both robustness to resonance frequency changes and the disturbance rejection profiles at these changed resonance frequencies are evaluated. Developing an accurate dynamic model in a positioning system is a difficult task because of the complex mechanical structure of the nanopositioning stage. In order to account for these uncertainties, designing a control algorithm capable of dealing with uncertainties is essential [4,5].

In order to test the capability of the proposed scheme to accommodate resonant frequency variation, a 5% and 10% reduction in the resonant frequency is considered. Resonance frequency changes can occur due to loading of the nanopositioners with different samples. The open-loop and closed-loop frequency response for all these changes is plotted in Fig. 9(a).

The sensitivity of the proposed method is reflected in Fig. 9(a). It can be seen that a 5% or 10% reduction in resonance frequency does not have a significant influence on the closed-loop; therefore, the proposed control scheme is robust to resonance frequency changes.

The disturbance rejection transfer function for the proposed system is given by:

$$\frac{Y(s)}{N(s)} = \frac{G(s)(1 - K_d(s)d)}{1 - K_d(s)d + G(s)K_d(s) + G(s)K_{T1}(s)K_d(s) + G(s)K_{T2}(s)K_{T2}(s)K_d(s)} \quad (26)$$

In order to test the ability of the controller to attenuate external disturbances, the bode plot for the transfer function in (26) is depicted in Fig. 9(b). From the figure, it can be seen that changing the resonant frequency by a 5% or

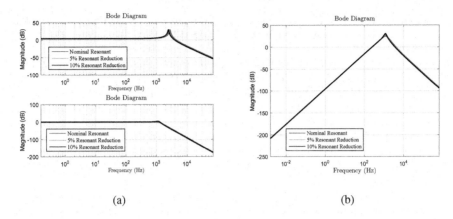

Fig. 9. (a) Open-loop and closed-loop magnitude response for resonant frequency changes (b) disturbance rejection across various resonant frequency changes

10% reduction does not have a significant influence on the disturbance rejection profile. Significant disturbance rejection is provided at a relatively low frequency up to 1000 Hz; nonetheless, the multi-loop feedback scheme does not exhibit significant disturbance rejection near the resonant frequency. Due to multiple integrals in the multi-loop feedback controller scheme, the steady-estate error is almost zero.

5   Conclusion

In this paper, a hybrid damping and tracking strategy with dual-loop tracking is proposed and its performance tested via simulation. The developed control strategy emulates the Butterworth pattern for maximally flat in-bandwidth response. Simulation results confirm the effectiveness of the proposed method in terms of high tracking accuracy in the presence of hysteresis and robust stability in the presence of resonance frequency changes.

References

1. Aphale, S.S., Bhikkaji, B., Moheimani, S.R.: Minimizing scanning errors in piezo-electric stack-actuated nanopositioning platforms. IEEE Trans. Nanotechnol. **7**(1), 79–90 (2008)
2. Aphale, S.S., Fleming, A.J., Moheimani, S.R.: Integral resonant control of collocated smart structures. Smart Mater. Struct. **16**(2), 439 (2007)
3. Bouc, R.: Forced vibration of mechanical systems with hysteresis. In: Proceedings of the Fourth Conference on Non-linear Oscillation, Prague, Czechoslovakia (1967)
4. Dong, J., Salapaka, S.M., Ferreira, P.M.: Robust control of a parallel-kinematic nanopositioner. J. Dyn. Syst. Meas. Control **130**(4), 041007–041007-15 (2008). http://dx.doi.org/10.1115/1.2936861

5. Eielsen, A.A., Vagia, M., Gravdahl, J.T., Pettersen, K.Y.: Damping and tracking control schemes for nanopositioning. IEEE/ASME Trans. Mechatron. **19**(2), 432–444 (2014)
6. Jain, S., Garg, M., Swarup, A.: Disturbance rejection of nanopositioner using internal model control. i-Manag. J. Electron. Eng. **2**(4), 1–7 (2012)
7. Namavar, M., Fleming, A.J., Aleyaasin, M., Nakkeeran, K., Aphale, S.S.: An analytical approach to integral resonant control of second-order systems. IEEE/ASME Trans. Mechatron. **19**(2), 651–659 (2014)
8. Russell, D., Fleming, A.J., Aphale, S.S.: Simultaneous optimization of damping and tracking controller parameters via selective pole placement for enhanced positioning bandwidth of nanopositioners. J. Dyn. Syst. Meas. Control **137**(10), 101004–101004-8 (2015). http://dx.doi.org/10.1115/1.4030723
9. Russell, D., San-Millan, A., Feliu, V., Aphale, S.S.: Butterworth pattern-based simultaneous damping and tracking controller designs for nanopositioning systems. Front. Mech. Eng. **2**, 2 (2016). http://journal.frontiersin.org/article/10.3389/fmech.2016.00002
10. Teo, Y.R., Russell, D., Aphale, S.S., Fleming, A.J.: Optimal integral force feedback and structured PI tracking control: application for high speed confocal microscopy. IFAC Proc. Vol. **47**(3), 11793–11799 (2014)
11. Wen, Y.K.: Method for random vibration of hysteretic systems. J. Eng. Mech. Div. **102**(2), 249–263 (1976)
12. Xu, Q., Tan, K.K.: Advanced Control of Piezoelectic Micro-/Nano-Positioning Systems. Springer, Cham (2015). doi:10.1007/978-3-319-21623-2
13. Yong, Y.K., Bazaei, A., Moheimani, S.O.R.: Control of a high-speed nanopositioner for Lissajous-scan video-rate AFM. In: 2013 3rd Australian Control Conference (AUCC), pp. 171–176 (2013)
14. Zhou, J., Wen, C.: Adaptive Backstepping Control of Uncertain Systems: Nonsmooth Nonlinearities, Interactions or Time-Variations. Springer, Heidelberg (2008). doi:10.1007/978-3-540-77807-3

Robust Control Design of Nonlinear System via Backstepping-PSO with Sliding Mode Techniques

Sahazati Md Rozali[1(✉)], Nor Syaza Farhana[2],
Muhammad Nizam Kamarudin[2], Amar Faiz Zainal Abidin[1,3],
Mohd Fua'ad Rahmat[1,3], Abdul Rashid Husain[1],
and Chong Chee Soon[2]

[1] Faculty of Engineering Technology, Centre for Robotics and Industrial
Automation (CeRIA), Universiti Teknikal Malaysia Melaka (UTeM),
Malacca, Malaysia
hazati@utem.edu.my
[2] Faculty of Electrical Engineering, Centre for Robotics and Industrial
Automation (CeRIA), Universiti Teknikal Malaysia Melaka (UTeM),
Malacca, Malaysia
[3] Faculty of Electrical Engineering, Universiti Teknologi Malaysia (UTM),
Skudai, Malaysia

Abstract. This research focus on designing controller for nonlinear system by integration of two robust controllers, back-stepping and sliding mode controller. The dynamics of the system is developed by consider its nonlinearities incorporating external disturbance injected to the system's actuator. The value of control and reaching law parameters are determined by using particle swarm optimization method such that these parameters are varying automatically according to the changes of the dynamics of the system. The tracking performance of the system yielded by integration of back-stepping and sliding mode controller is compared with its output performance produced by classical sliding mode controller. The results show that assimilation of back-stepping and sliding mode controller for the chosen system generates better performance than sliding mode controller itself which is evaluated in terms of tracking output and tracking error.

Keywords: Back-stepping · Sliding mode controller · External disturbance · Tracking error · Particle swarm optimization

1 Introduction

Back-stepping is a type of the recursive design controller which is designed by step back toward the control input starting with the scalar equation. The design process of this controller starts at the known-stable system because of this recursive structure and back out new controllers that progressively stabilize each outer subsystem. The process will terminate when the final external control is reached. The advantage of back-stepping is that is has the availability to avoid cancellations of useful nonlinearities and pursue the objectives of stabilization and tracking rather than that of linearization

© Springer Nature Singapore Pte Ltd. 2017
M.S. Mohamed Ali et al. (Eds.): AsiaSim 2017, Part I, CCIS 751, pp. 27–37, 2017.
DOI: 10.1007/978-981-10-6463-0_3

method [1]. In addition, back-stepping approaches relaxes the matching conditions on perturbations which means that the perturbation doesn't have to appear in the equation that contains the input of the system [1]. For tracking problem, usually, back-stepping will use the error between the actual and desired input to develop the design process [1]. The fundamental concept of back-stepping method is introduced in [1, 2]. This control method was used in numerous applications such as flight trajectory control [3], industrial automation systems, electric machines, and nonlinear systems of wind turbine-based power production and robotic system. It is also shown to be an effective tool in adaptive control design for estimating parameters [4] and optimal control problems. Besides, the observer based on back-stepping technique is also designed for force control of electrohydraulic actuator system [5] and guarantees the convergence of the tracking error. This control technique is also used as an observer to control DC servo motor by combining back-stepping observer with adaptive and sliding mode controller [6] and as controller for electro-hydraulic active suspension system [7].

Sliding mode control is a nonlinear control technique that changes the dynamics of a nonlinear system by introducing a discontinuous control signal which forces the system to slide along a cross-section of a system's normal behavior. It is a variable structure control method. The multiple control structures are designed so that trajectories always move toward an adjacent region with a different control structure. The ultimate trajectory will not exist entirely within one control structure. Instead, it will slide along the boundaries of the control structures. The motion of the system as it slides along these boundaries is called sliding mode. Sliding mode control has been applied for several systems such as coupled tanks [8], active suspension system [9], robotic system [10], underwater applications [11], electromechanical plant [12], induction motor [13] and hydraulic system [14].

Since both back-stepping and sliding mode controllers have their own strength and weakness, there are studies which integrate these two robust methods together as a single controller. Combination of back-stepping and sliding mode controller can be seen in [15] which have been applied to improve the speed dynamic tracking performance of permanent magnet synchronous motor control system. Combination of back-stepping and sliding mode controller has been proved that it has certain robustness with respect to the external disturbances and good adaptability with respect to parameter uncertainty of a coupled two tank system [16]. The assimilation of these two control method is also has been applied for tracking control of a vane-type air motor X-Y table motion system [17]. Besides, the integration of these two control techniques also has been applied to overcome chaotic problem [18]. In the paper, back-stepping is designed in order to achieve new equilibrium point while combination of back-stepping and sliding mode control techniques is used to control the system to another equilibrium point. In addition, the integration of these two control techniques also has been combined with neural networks in order to design controller for nonlinear systems in strict feedback form with unknown nonlinearities and uncertain disturbances [19]. Another assimilation of these two control methods also can be found in [20, 21].

This work presents a controller design for nonlinear system which combines two robust controllers, back-stepping and sliding mode controller in order to improve the tracking performance of the chosen system. Particle Swarm Optimization (PSO) is integrated to the designed controller such that it has the ability to adjust the control parameters automatically regarding to the dynamic changes of the system. The dynamic of the chosen system is considered by injecting constant force to the system's actuator. The assessment of the tracking performance of the system is presented by its tracking output and tracking error. Sum of squared error (SSE) is used as performance index of the system. This evaluation is compared with the design of classical sliding mode controller for the system in terms of similar index performance.

2 Dynamic Model of the System

Electro-hydraulic actuator (EHA) is a non-linear system with uncertain dynamics. The dynamics characteristic of the system comes from either the system itself or external environment such as disturbance. This research considers electro hydraulic actuator system (EHA) with external disturbance injected to its actuator as numerical example since the position tracking of this system is highly nonlinear [22].

The dynamic of the system's actuator is represented by

$$m\ddot{x}_p = SP_L - f\dot{x}_p - kx_p - F_L \tag{1}$$

where m is load at the rod of the system, x_p is the displacement of the piston, k is the coefficient of aerodynamic elastic force, f is the coefficient of viscous friction, S is the piston area and F_L is the external disturbance injected to the system's actuator. The control applied to the spool valve is proportional to the spool position [23] by assuming that high-response servo valve is used in the system. Its equation is given as

$$x_v = k_v u \tag{2}$$

with x_v is the opening of the valve, k_v is the coefficient of the servo valve and u is the input voltage. The dynamics of cylinder oil flow can be expressed as

$$Q_L = \dot{P}_L + \frac{2\beta S}{V}\dot{x}_p \tag{3}$$

where Q_L is the different between supplied flow rate to the chambers, P_L is the different pressure between two chambers, V is the volume of the chamber and β is the effective bulk modulus of the fluid. The difference of the flow rate to the chambers is given as

$$Q_L = \frac{2\beta}{V}\left[c_d w \sqrt{\frac{P_a - P_L}{\rho}} x_v - k_l P_L \right] \tag{4}$$

with c_d is the coefficient of volumetric flow of the valve port, P_a is the supply pressure, ρ is the oil density and k_l is the coefficient of internal leakage between the cylinder chambers. Based on these equations, the dynamics of electro hydraulic actuator servo system with external disturbance injected to its actuator is represented as

$$\dot{x}_1 = x_2 \tag{5}$$

$$\dot{x}_2 = -\frac{k}{m}x_1 - \frac{f}{m}x_2 + \frac{S}{m}x_3 - \frac{F_L}{m} \tag{6}$$

$$\dot{x}_3 = -\frac{S}{k_c}x_2 - \frac{k_l}{k_c}x_3 + \frac{c}{k_c}\sqrt{\frac{p_a - x_3}{2}}k_v u \tag{7}$$

x_1 is displacement of the load, x_2 is load velocity and x_3 is differential pressure $p_1 - p_2$ between the cylinder chambers caused by load. F_L is external disturbance given to the system and it can be constant or time varying signal. The parameter of electro hydraulic actuator servo system is shown in Table 1.

Table 1. Parameter of electro hydraulic actuator servo system

Load at the EHS rod, m	0.33 Ns²/cm
Piston area, S	10 cm²
Coefficient of viscous friction, f	27.5 Ns/cm
Coefficient of aerodynamic elastic force, k	1000 N/cm
Valve port width, w	0.05 cm
Supply pressure, P_a	2100 N/cm²
Coefficient of volumetric flow of the valve port, c_d	0.63
Coefficient of internal leakage between the cylinder chambers, k_l	2.38×10^{-3} cm⁵/Ns
Coefficient of servo valve, k_v	0.017 cm/V
Coefficient involving bulk modulus and EHA volume, k_c	2.5×10^{-4} cm⁵/N
Oil density, ρ	8.87×10^{-7} Ns²/cm⁴

3 Design of Robust Back-Stepping Sliding Mode Controller

A robust control for a plant with uncertainty might be designed by using a combination of back-stepping and sliding mode control techniques. In this section, a systematic design procedure is proposed to develop these two control techniques. The design process is started by defining the tracking error for each state x_1, x_2 and x_3 as

$$e_i = x_i - x_{id} \tag{8}$$

i is equal to 1, 2 and 3 which represent the state of the system, x_{1d} is the reference input and x_{2d} and x_{3d} are virtual control of back-stepping. The control objective is to have EHA track of a specified x_{1d} position trajectory so that $e_1 \rightarrow 0$. Let the Lyapunov function as

$$V_1 = \frac{1}{2}e_1^2 \tag{9}$$

$$V_2 = V_1 + \frac{1}{2}e_2^2 \tag{10}$$

$$V_3 = \dot{V}_3 + \frac{1}{2}s^2 \tag{11}$$

with sliding surface,

$$s = c_1 e_1 + c_2 e_2 + e_3 \tag{12}$$

with $c_1, c_2 > 0$. The vitual control signal, x_{2d} and x_{3d} and control signal, u are obtained as

$$x_{2d} = -k_1 e_1 + \dot{x}_{1d} \tag{13}$$

$$x_{3d} = \frac{m}{S}\left[-e_1 + \frac{k}{m}x_1 + \frac{f}{m}x_2 + \frac{F_L}{m} + \dot{x}_{2d} - k_2 e_2\right] \tag{14}$$

$$u = \frac{k_c}{ck_v}\sqrt{\frac{2}{p_a - x_3}}\left[k_3 s - c_1 x_2 + c_1 \dot{x}_{1d} + \frac{c_2 k}{m}x_1 + \frac{c_2 f}{m}x_2 - \frac{c_2 S}{m}x_3 + \cdots \right.$$
$$\left. \cdots \frac{c_2 F_L}{m} + c_2 \dot{x}_{2d} + \frac{S}{k_c}x_2 + \frac{k_l}{k_c}x_3 - e_2 - \eta \operatorname{sgn}(s)\right] \tag{15}$$

4   Sliding Mode Controller Design

Sliding mode controller design starts with defining its sliding surface, s as

$$s = x_2 + x_3 + c_1 e \tag{16}$$

With

$$e = x_1 - x_{1d} \tag{17}$$

Taking derivative of s,

$$\dot{s} = \dot{x}_2 + \dot{x}_3 + c_1 \dot{e} \tag{18}$$

Derivative of error, e is taking as

$$\dot{e} = \dot{x}_1 - \dot{x}_{1d} = x_2 - \dot{x}_{1d} \tag{19}$$

Sliding mode controller is designed by having $s = \dot{s} = 0$ and satisfies the condition of reaching law

$$\dot{s} = -\varepsilon \operatorname{sgn}(s) - k_1 s \tag{20}$$

with $k_1 > 0$. The following control law satisfies these conditions.

$$u = \frac{k_c}{ck_v}\sqrt{\frac{2}{p_a - x_3}}\left[-\varepsilon\text{sgn}(s) - k_1 s + \frac{k}{m}x_1 + \frac{f}{m}x_2 - \frac{S}{m}x_3 + \cdots\right.$$
$$\left.\cdots\frac{F_L}{m} + \frac{k_l}{k_c}x_3 - c_1 x_2 + c_1 \dot{x}_1\right] \qquad (21)$$

For stability analysis, let

$$V = \frac{1}{2}s^2 \qquad (22)$$

Derivative of V is given as

$$\begin{aligned}\dot{V} &= s\dot{s} \\ &= s(-\varepsilon\text{sgn}(s) - k_1 s) \\ &= -\varepsilon|s| - k_1 s^2 \leq 0\end{aligned} \qquad (23)$$

with ε is the parameter of reaching law. Equation (23) proves the stability analysis of the designed controller on the chosen system.

5 Particle Swarm Optimization

The particle swarm optimization (PSO) algorithm is a population based search algorithm based on the simulation of the social behavior of birds within a flock [24]. PSO had been used for tuning back-stepping controller of power systems [25]. An adaptive back-stepping controller is designed for stability enhancement of multi-machine power systems. In addition, PSO also is integrated with back-stepping technique to design speed controller for permanent magnet synchronous motor based on adaptive law [26]. Simulation results show that the controller has robust and good dynamic response. An adaptive back-stepping control technique with acceleration feedback is designed in order to reject the uncertainties and external disturbances for Dynamic Positioning System with slowly-varying disturbances [27]. The research shows that controller parameters and acceleration feedback parameters are optimized using PSO. PSO also has been implemented to optimize the sliding coefficient of sliding mode controller for a buck converter [28] control parameters of robotic system [29] and industrial application [30]. Another integration of PSO and sliding mode control technique also can be found in [31].

In this work PSO is integrated with the designed back-stepping sliding mode controller and sliding mode controller in order to acquire the suitable value for each control and reaching law parameters so that good tracking performance and smaller error will be achieved. In the process of designing controller for tracking performance, the tracking error is important. The tracking error, $e(t)$ represents the different between reference inputs and real output. This error signal is used in Lyapunov functions to develop controller for the chosen system. The same signal also being used in the optimization process. In this study, Sum of Squared Error (*SSE*) is used as an objective function in optimization of control and Lyapunov parameters. The formula of *SSE* is given by Eq. (24).

$$SSE = \sum_{i=1}^{n} \left(x_i - y_{ref} \right)^2 \tag{24}$$

where

SSE = sum of square error,
i = number of iteration,
x_i = system output iteration,
y_{ref} = reference input.

A good tracking response will give smaller SSE.

6   Simulation Results and Discussion

Analysis on the tracking performance of the designed controller is presented in this section.

The top plot in Fig. 1 illustrates the system's output produced by integration of back-stepping and sliding mode controller while the output of the system yielded by sliding mode controller is presented in the bottom plot of Fig. 1. Referring to Fig. 1,

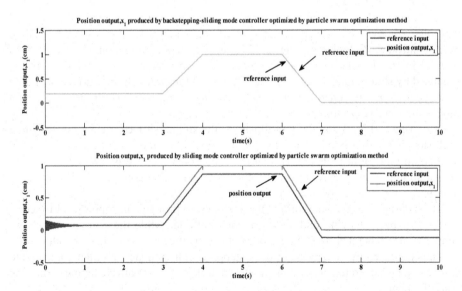

Fig. 1. Position output, x_1 yielded by back-stepping sliding mode controller and sliding mode controller

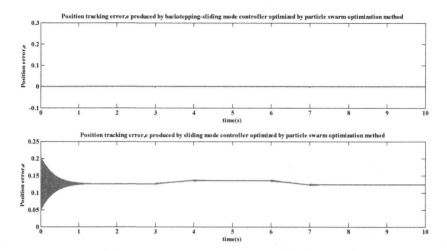

Fig. 2. Position tracking error produced by back-stepping sliding mode controller and sliding mode controller

integration of back-stepping and sliding mode controller produced good system's output with almost zero tracking error. The output of the system with sliding mode controller in the bottom of Fig. 1 also follows the shape of the reference input. However, its tracking error is bigger than the top plot. In addition, there is small oscillation in the early of the simulation process. This situation also can be seen in tracking error plot in Fig. 2.

Top graph in Fig. 2 shows the tracking error yielded by back-stepping sliding mode controller while the bottom graph demonstrates the similar signal generated by sliding mode controller. By looking at Fig. 2, it can be seen that assimilation of back-stepping with sliding mode controller produced zero tracking error while bigger tracking error is produced by sliding mode controller itself. Figure 3 illustrates sliding surface of sliding mode controller, s obtained for each back-stepping sliding mode controller and sliding mode controller respectively.

Referring to Fig. 3, the top plot illustrates the sliding surface, s used for designing back-stepping sliding mode controller while s for sliding mode controller is shown in the bottom plot. Both plots proved that the condition $s = \dot{s} = 0$ is fulfilled in order to design sliding mode controller for the chosen system. The control signal, u for each designed controller can be seen in Fig. 4.

By looking at Fig. 4, the top graph illustrates control signal, u produced by combination of back-stepping and sliding mode controller while the bottom plot shows similar signal generated by sliding mode controller. It can be seen that smooth control signal is produced by integration of back-stepping sliding mode controller compared to similar signal generated by sliding mode controller with small chattering along the control signal.

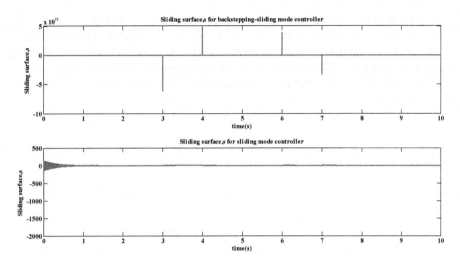

Fig. 3. Sliding surface of sliding mode controller, s for back-stepping sliding mode controller and sliding mode controller

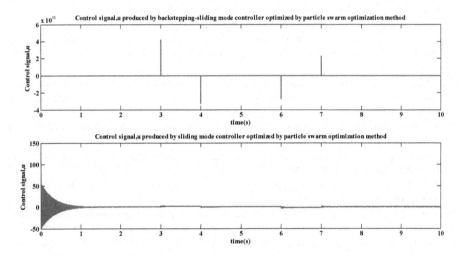

Fig. 4. Control signal, u for each designed controller on the chosen system

7   Conclusion

This research presents the design of robust controller for chosen nonlinear system by integrate back-stepping with sliding mode controller. Particle swarm optimization (PSO) technique is applied to search for optimum value of control and reaching law parameters such that these parameters of the designed controller varying automatically based on the nonlinearities of the system. The results are compared with nonlinear classical sliding mode controller designed for similar system. Based on the results, the tracking performance of the chosen system with back-stepping sliding mode controller is better than its performance with classical sliding mode controller. This is proved by smooth tracking output, small tracking error and zero chattering of the control signal. In addition, the stability of the controller was verified by proper selection of the Lyapunov function. As a conclusion, the designed back-stepping sliding mode controller with good adaptation ability of the changing of system's parameters produced better output than the classical sliding mode controller.

Acknowledgement. Highest appreciation to Universiti Teknikal Malaysia Melaka (UTeM) for sponsorship of this research through grant number PJP/2015/FKE(8C)/S01440.

References

1. Kristic, K.I., Ioannis Kanellakoupulos, M., Kokotovic, P.V.: Nonlinear and Adaptive Control Design. Wiley, New York (1995)
2. Khalil, H.K.: Nonlinear Systems, 3rd edn. Prentice Hall, Upper Saddle River (2002)
3. Fang, Z.E., Queiroz, M.S., Dawson, D.M.: Global output feedback control of dynamically positioned surface vessel: an adaptive control approach. Mechatronics **14**, 341–356 (2004)
4. Kamarudin, M.N., Rozali, S.M., Husain, A.R.: Observer-based output feedback control with linear quadratic performance. Procedia Eng. **53**, 233–240 (2013)
5. Rozali, S.M., Kamarudin, M.N., Rahmat, M.F.A., Husain, A.R.: Asymptotic tracking position control for nonlinear systems using backstepping technique. Procedia Eng. **53**, 255–263 (2013)
6. Kenne, J.P., Kaddissi, C., Saad, M.: Draw by wire control of an electro-hydraulic active suspension: a backstepping approach. In: IEEE Conference on Control Applications, pp. 1581–1587 (2005)
7. Karimi, A., Al-Hinai, A., Schoder, K., Feliachi, A.: Power system stability enhancement using backstepping controller tuned by particle swarm optimization technique. In: Proceedings of IEEE Power Engineering Society General Meeting, 12–16 June 2005, San Francisco, pp. 3055–3060 (2005)
8. Almutairi, N.B., Zribi, M.: Sliding mode control of coupled tanks. Mechatronics **16**, 427–441 (2006)
9. Sam, Y.M., Osman, J.H., Ghani, M.R.A.: A class of proportional integral sliding mode control with application to active suspension system. Syst. Control Lett. **51**, 217–223 (2004)
10. Liu, H., Gong, Z.: Upper bound adaptive learning of neural network for the sliding mode control of underwater robot. In: IEEE International Conference on Advanced Computer Theory and Engineering, pp. 276–280 (2008)
11. Bagheri, A., Moghaddam, J.J.: Simulation and tracking control based on neural-network strategy and sliding-mode control for underwater remotely operated vehicle. Neurocomputing **72**, 1934–1950 (2009)
12. Eker, I.: Sliding mode control with PID sliding surface and experimental application to an electromechanical plant. ISA Trans. **45**(1), 109–118 (2006)
13. Barambones, O., Alkorta, P., Garrido, A.J., Garrido, I., Maseda, F.J.: An adaptive sliding mode control scheme for induction motor drives. Int. J. Circ. Syst. Sig. Process. **1**(1), 73–78 (2007)

14. Chiang, M.H., Lee, L.W., Liu, H.H.: Adaptive fuzzy sliding-mode control for variable displacement hydraulic servo system. In: Proceedings of IEEE International Conference on Fuzzy Systems, pp. 1–6 (2007)
15. Qian, Y., Weiguo, L., Yongping, H.: Real time simulation study on backstepping sliding mode control of permanent magnet synchronous motor. In: International Conference on Electrical Machines and Systems, Beijing, China, pp. 1–5 (2011)
16. Benayache, R., Chrifi-Alaoui, L., Benamor, A., Dovifaaz, X., Bussy, P.: Robust control of nonlinear uncertain systems via sliding mode with backstepping design. In: Proceedings of American Control Conference, pp. 4695–4700 (2010)
17. Lu, C.-H., Hwang, Y.-R., Shen, Y.-T.: Backstepping sliding mode tracking control of a vane-type air motor X-Y table motion system. ISA Trans. **50**, 278–286 (2011)
18. Hu, P., Cai, G., Yao, L., Fang, X.: Recursive backstepping nonlinear control and sliding mode control of a novel hyperchaotic finance system. In: Proceedings of the 2nd International Conference on Computer and Information Application, pp. 777–780 (2012)
19. Liu, D., Yang, P., Wu, J.: A combined multiple sliding mode and backstepping design to robust adaptive neural control for uncertain nonlinear systems. In: Proceedings of 5th International Conference on Biomedical Engineering and Informatics, pp. 1221–1226 (2012)
20. Adhikary, N., Mahanta, C.: Integral backstepping sliding mode control for underactuated systems: swing-up and stabilization of the cart-pendulum system. ISA Trans. **52**, 1–11 (2013)
21. Khebbache, H., Tadjine, M.: Robust fuzzy backstepping sliding mode controller for a quadrotor unmanned aerial vehicle. J. Control Eng. Appl. Inform. **15**(2), 3–11 (2013)
22. Ursu, I., Ursu, F., Popescu, F.: Backstepping design for controlling electrohydraulic servos. J. Franklin Inst. **343**(1), 94–110 (2006)
23. Guan, C., Pan, S.: Adaptive sliding mode control of electro-hydraulic system with nonlinear unknown parameters. Control Eng. Pract. **16**, 1275–1284 (2008)
24. Engelbrecht, A.P.: Computational Intelligence an Introduction, 2nd edn. Wiley, Hoboken (2007)
25. Sirouspour, M.R., Salcudean, S.E.: On the nonlinear control of hydraulic servo-systems. In: Proceedings of the IEEE International Conference on Robotics and Automation, pp. 1276–1282 (2000)
26. Yang, M., Wang, X., Zheng, K.: Nonlinear controller design for permanent magnet synchronous motor using adaptive weighted PSO. In: Proceedings of IEEE American Control Conference, pp. 1962–1966 (2010)
27. Lin, X., Xie, Y., Zhao, D., Xu, S.: Acceleration feedback adaptive backstepping controller for DP using PSO. In: Proceedings of IEEE International Conference on Fuzzy Systems and Knowledge Discovery, pp. 2334–2338 (2012)
28. Erdem, H., Altinoz, O.T.: Implementation of PSO-based fixed frequency sliding mode controller for buck converter. In: Proceedings of IEEE International Symposium on Innovations in Intelligent Systems and Applications, pp. 531–535 (2011)
29. Yuhua, X., Chongwei, Z., Wei, B., Lin, T.: Dynamic sliding mode controller based on particle swarm optimization for mobile robot's path following. In: Proceedings of IEEE International Forum on Information Technology and Applications, pp. 257–260 (2009)
30. Sharaf, A.M., El-Gammal, A.A.: A variable structure sliding mode particle swarm optimization-PSO optimal regulating controller for industrial PMDC motor drives. In: IEEE International Electric Machines and Drives Conference, pp. 337–343 (2009)
31. Yu, K.W., Hu, S.C.: An application of AC servo motor by using particle swarm optimization based sliding mode controller. In: IEEE International Conference on Systems, Man, and Cybernetics, pp. 4146–4150 (2006)

The Capability of B-RISK Zone Modelling Software to Simulate BRE Multiple Vehicle Fire Spread Test

Mohd Zahirasri Mohd Tohir[1]([✉]) and Michael Spearpoint[2]

[1] Department of Chemical and Environmental Engineering,
Faculty of Engineering, Universiti Putra Malaysia, Serdang, Malaysia
zahirasri@upm.edu.my
[2] Department of Civil and Natural Resources Engineering,
University of Canterbury, Christchurch, New Zealand

Abstract. Building Research Establishment (BRE), United Kingdom have carried out several full-scale experiments of vehicle fire as to address the fire spread between vehicles. Thus, this paper aims to investigate the capability of the B-RISK zone modelling software to simulate the BRE multiple vehicle fire spread test. Using the information gathered from the work by BRE, series of simulations have been conducted. The results of the simulations are compared with the results from the experiments. Analysis shows that the predicted results from the B-RISK simulations give slightly faster time of ignition to the ones obtained using hand calculation. This could be due to B-RISK includes the radiation effect from the underside of the hot upper layer. As a conclusion, the analysis shows that using the B-RISK simulation software with additional radiation effects does not improve the result as compared to using the hand calculation considering the level of uncertainties which required to be assumed on some input parameters e.g. HRRPUA, heat of combustion, and/or latent heat of gasification.

Keywords: Zone model · Vehicle fire · Fire spread simulation

1 Introduction

Vehicle fires in car parking buildings can impact on the life safety of the vehicle occupants as well as the building occupants whom are in the vicinity of the fire. Vehicle fires in car parking buildings can also result in material losses in terms of the vehicles itself, to the building structure as well as to the neighbouring property. Recently, there have been several significant fires in car parking buildings involving multiple vehicles and in some cases these have led to fatalities. For example, in 2006 seven fire fighters were killed in a fire in an underground car park in Gretchenbach, Switzerland [1]. Also in 2006 there was a car park fire in Bristol, United Kingdom where 22 vehicles were destroyed in the incident and one person died in the occupancy above the car park [1]. Therefore it is prudent to understand the risks of vehicle fires

© Springer Nature Singapore Pte Ltd. 2017
M.S. Mohamed Ali et al. (Eds.): AsiaSim 2017, Part I, CCIS 751, pp. 38–51, 2017.
DOI: 10.1007/978-981-10-6463-0_4

and the need to potentially reduce their probability of occurring probability and/or mitigate the severity if a fire does occur.

In a performance–based engineering environment, it is still a question whether a car parking building should be designed differently based on the type and functionality of the buildings i.e. shopping center parking, airport parking, residential parking etc. or just use the generic design for all types of parking. Thus, this work is part of a larger research investigation into risk-based fire safety of passenger road vehicles in car parking buildings being undertaken at the University of Canterbury which will try to answer the prior question. The earlier part of the research has compiled 42 single passenger vehicle fire test data from available sources [2]. These data were then analysed to produce sets of distribution of heat release rate peak for single passenger vehicles which could be used for design purposes. Currently, in New Zealand, the specific design fire for car parking buildings from the verification method is medium t-squared fire [3]. In another earlier part of the research has produced a method of generating reasonable vehicle scenarios using fire risk analysis [4]. Thus, the question is then, how well these fire scenarios formed could produce reliable results for further use?

The previous research has led to this work, where the main objective is to investigate the capability of the B-RISK zone modelling software to simulate the Building Research Establishment (BRE) multiple vehicle fire spread tests. The B-RISK zone modelling software uses a probabilistic Monte-Carlo sampling technique with deterministic fire zone model calculation engine to automate repeat iterations of a fire scenario, each time sampling inputs from user-defined statistical distributions [5]. This zone model approach has been chosen here because of its relative simplicity as the creation of a risk-based approach is already complicated, so it is important to keep the level of detail consistent for each part throughout the whole research.

1.1   B-RISK Zone Modelling Software

The B-RISK zone modelling software is a part of a larger project that was funded by the Ministry of Science of Innovation (MSI) of New Zealand, Building Research Levy and Department of Building and Housing (DBH) of New Zealand involving Building Research Association of New Zealand (BRANZ) and the University of Canterbury. The main goal of the project was to produce a tool to support future risk-based building fire safety regulations and designing with B-RISK as one of the outcomes.

B-RISK is developed based on an existing deterministic fire zone modelling software named, BRANZFIRE. The development of B-RISK incorporates three primary areas of enhanced functionality as compared to BRANZFIRE [6, 7]. The three primary areas are; the ability to conduct probabilistic simulations rather than deterministic simulations, capability of incorporating fire safety systems reliability and efficacy into the B-RISK modelling predictions and the software is also capable of automatically generating unique designs of fire input for every loop iterations processes. After getting all the necessary input, the Design Fire Generator (DFG) can be either be randomly populated across the room or the user can enter the exact position of the items in the room. Once these item placements are done, the user can determine which item is to be ignited first. The DFG predicts the time of ignition of the second item to be ignited using ignition criterion and radiation models programmed in the software [7].

2 Full-Scale Multiple Vehicle Fire Experiment

Two full-scale multiple vehicle fire experiments identified as suitable for the purpose of simulation using B-RISK. Experiment H and Experiment I i.e., the identification number are used instead of 'Test 1' and 'Test 3' respectively from the original report which is by BRE [1]. The experiments were considered suitable due to the completeness of information as an input to perform simulation using B-RISK.

The experiments were conducted in a test rig that has a floor area of 72 m^2 with a height of 2.9 m from the floor. The structure of the rig comprised of a steel frame with breeze block infill and the roof was made of hollow-core concrete slabs. One end of the rig was open, but with a down stand of 0.5 m. Windows which allow ventilation were provided along one side and the back wall. At one end of the roof, a 1.6 m wide window channels the smoke via a deflector into the 9 m high calorimeter hood.

An example of the diagram and the instrument schematic of Experiment I is shown in Fig. 1. From the diagram, there were several instruments installed in the test rig for the purpose of results collection. The orange arrows in the diagram were the heat flux measurement gauges, the blue crosses were the slab temperature gauges, the yellow triangles were the gas samples collectors, the red stars were the thermocouple trees, and the green arrows refer to flow measurement and temperature gauges. The specific vehicles used in the experiments were also mentioned in the literature source whereas this piece of information is important for the simulation as input in recreating the experiment in the software.

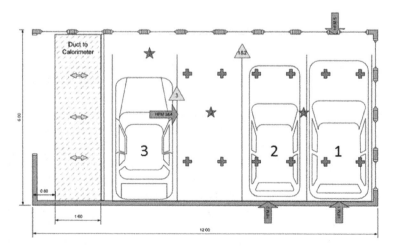

Fig. 1. The diagram and instrument schematic for Experiment I (Reproduced from BRE [1]) (Color figure online)

'No.' indicated in both tables corresponds with the number shown in Fig. 1. The vehicles used in the experiments were in full working order where all components such as gas struts, air bags, pressurised or pyrotechnic components were left in place except for the air condition gas which was removed. The fuel tanks for each of the vehicles were left with 20 litres of fuel.

2.1 Procedure

This section provides information in order to recreate of the experiments using the B-RISK software. The inputs, simplifications and assumptions in using the software are explained in detail.

2.1.1 Input – Room Design and Ventilation

In B-RISK, the user has to manually enter the information of the room and its ventilation in the room design tab. The test rig for the experiment is represented by a single room with certain dimensions. Also required by the software for the room is the surface material for wall, floor and ceiling. The inputs are: (Tables 1 and 2)

Table 1. Input for room design and ventilation

Attribute	Description
Room name	Test rig
Length	12 m
Width	6 m
Minimum height	2.9 m
Maximum height	2.9 m
Elevation	0 m

Table 2. Room surface materials

Attribute	Description
Wall material	Concrete
Wall thickness	100 mm
Ceiling material	Concrete
Ceiling thickness	100 mm
Floor material	Concrete
Floor thickness	50 mm

For the ventilation in the test rig, there are 13 windows, a main door and a ceiling vent on the test rig served as ventilation ports.

2.1.2   Input – Properties for the Burning Items

In the fire specification tab, the user is able to enter the details about the experiments. This includes the number of items in the room, the dimensions of the items, the position of the items, the material geometry and chemical properties, the Flux-time Product (FTP) properties and the heat release rate curves.

In the simulation, the vehicles, which are the main burning items, were considered a simple geometrical rectangle shape in which the heat source is fixed at the centre of the rectangle. The vehicles are treated as a single type of material, which represented the first component possibly to be exposed to the radiant heat flux. The dimensions and the position of the vehicles were obtained from the report [1]. However, the chemical properties of the vehicles have to be assumed due to being unreported in the literature. The best way to assume the chemical properties such as heat of combustion and latent heat of gasification is by estimation since there are no specific studies on mentioned properties of a vehicle.

A review by Taub [8] shows that in the 2000s, a typical vehicle usually consists of around $\sim 70\%$ metals and $\sim 30\%$ polymers, glass, rubbers, and ceramics. A study by Swift [9] shows that combustible materials in vehicles such as polymers take around 8.0–9.7% as the percent of the total weight of a vehicle from the 2000s while rubber ranges from 4.3–6.2% of the total weight of a vehicle. Large parts of the polymers are polypropylene, polyurethanes, and nylon.

The work by Harper compiles heat of combustions for selected polymers and states that the heat of combustions of polymers ranges from 6.4 MJ/kg to 44.0 MJ/kg. Polypropylene is listed at 42.6 or 44.0 MJ/kg, polyurethane at 24.7 MJ/kg, and nylon at 27.9 MJ/kg. Thus, for the simulation a minimum value of 24.7 and maximum value of 44.0 will be selected for the heat of combustion of a vehicle.

Mark [10] listed the latent heats of gasification of polymers where the latent heat of gasification for polypropylene is 2.0 MJ/kg and for nylon is 2.4 MJ/kg. There was no latent heat of gasification for polyurethane was found. Thus, for the simulation a range of values between 2.0 and 2.4 is estimated since there were only two available data on latent heat of gasification.

Finally, the averaged heat release rate per unit area (HRRPUA) for each of the vehicles are estimated using the probability distributions of design fire for different classifications introduced in the work by Tohir and Spearpoint [2]. The HRRPUA could not be obtained from the full-scale experiment heat release rate curves results due to complication of the curves which were a combination of three vehicles rather than one.

For the soot yield and the CO_2 yield, default values for a generic vehicle pre-programmed in the fire object database of the software are used. It was decided to use the generic values for the two parameters since at this stage, the focus on the results are on the prediction of time of ignition. The radiative fraction for all the vehicles are set at 0.3. With the dimensions known and the chemical properties have to be assumed for each vehicle in the simulation, the burning items properties for both experiments can be filled with attributes as follows: (Tables 3 and 4)

Table 3. Information for the 3 vehicles for Experiment H

Attribute	Vehicle 1	Vehicle 2	Vehicle 3
Detail description	Renault laguna	Renault clio	Ford mondeo
Length	1.8 m	1.6 m	1.8 m
Width	4.6 m	3.8 m	4.8 m
Height	1.4 m	1.4 m	1.5 m
Elevation	0 m	0 m	0 m
x-axis coordination	9.5 m	7.2 m	3.5 m
y-axis coordination	0.5 m	0.5 m	0.5 m
Combustible mass	1455 kg	975 kg	1357 kg
Heat of combustion	24.7 or 44 kJ/g	24.7 or 44 kJ/g	24.7 or 44 kJ/g
Soot yield	0.03 g/g	0.03 g/g	0.03 g/g
CO_2 yield	1.27 g/g	1.27 g/g	1.27 g/g
Latent heat of gasification	2.0 or 2.4 kJ/g	2.0 or 2.4 kJ/g	2.0 or 2.4 kJ/g
Radiative fraction	0.3	0.3	0.3
HRRPUA	248 kW/m^2	137 kW/m^2	168 kW/m^2

Table 4. Information for the 3 vehicles for Experiment I

Attribute	Vehicle 1	Vehicle 2	Vehicle 3
Detail description	Renault espace	Peugeot 307	Land rover freelander
Length	1.8 m	1.7 m	1.9 m
Width	4.4 m	4.4 m	4.5 m
Height	1.7 m	1.6 m	1.7 m
Elevation	0 m	0 m	0 m
x-axis coordination	9.5 m	7.1 m	3.5 m
y-axis coordination	0.5 m	0.5 m	0.5 m
Combustible mass	1660 kg	1070 kg	1425 kg
Heat of combustion	24.7 or 44 kJ/g	24.7 or 44 kJ/g	24.7 or 44 kJ/g
Soot yield	0.03 g/g	0.03 g/g	0.03 g/g
CO_2 yield	1.27 g/g	1.27 g/g	1.27 g/g
Latent heat of gasification	2.0 or 2.4 kJ/g	2.0 or 2.4 kJ/g	2.0 or 2.4 kJ/g
Radiative fraction	0.3	0.3	0.3
HRRPUA	258 kW/m^2	157 kW/m^2	248 kW/m^2

Work by Tohir [11] suggested that bumper trim to be used as the component to be ignited first in a multiple vehicle fires simulation. The FTP properties of bumper trim are 2.0 for power law index (Table 5).

Table 5. FTP properties for bumper trim

Component	Power law index	FTP $\left(\left(\frac{kW\,s^n}{m^2}\right)\right)$	$\dot{q}'_{cr}$ (kW/m^2)
Bumper trim	2.0	21862	3.1

2.1.3   Input – Heat Release Rate

In B-RISK, the user can choose the heat release rate from a generic item from the fire object database, or they can manually provide own heat release rate. The heat release rates from the experiments are used to predict the time of ignition of the secondary vehicle, thus manually entered in the fire specification section. The heat release rate curves from Experiment H and I exhibit the collective heat release rates for the whole three vehicles' fire. Therefore, for both experiments, only heat release rates for the first vehicle up until the second vehicle ignites are possible to be identified in isolation.

In both experiments, the heat release rates for the first vehicle are assumed to be the curve from the beginning of the experiment up until the observed time the secondary vehicle ignited. This is because that from the beginning of the experiment up until second vehicle ignites, during that time it was only one vehicle that was on fire and the recorded results should show the heat release rate for only a single vehicle. After the ignition of the second vehicle, it is assumed that the heat release rate is a combination of the first vehicle and the second vehicle. Finally, after the ignition of the third vehicle, it is assumed that the heat release rate is a combination of first, second and third vehicle.

However, it has to be considered that there will be uncertainty in the observed time of ignition due to human observational error. Thus, an error of ±30 s is taken into consideration for the observed time based on greatest possible error (GPE) calculation which is equal to one-half of the precision of the measure [12].

The input for the heat release rates of the vehicles in Experiment H are shown in Fig. 2 where the blue line represents the heat release rate of Vehicle 1 up until the observed time of ignition of second vehicle at 20 min, the red line is the combined heat release rates for Vehicle 1 and 2 up until observed time of ignition of the third vehicle at 22–25 min, and the green line represents the combined heat release rates for Vehicle 1, 2 and 3. The green line with black dash indicate the possible range of time of ignition which is from 22–25 min. Since the time of ignition of the second and third vehicle were uncertain, ±30 s time of ignition were added and indicated as error bars in Fig. 2.

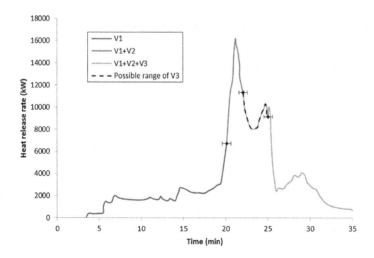

Fig. 2. Heat release rate for Experiment H B-RISK input. (Color figure online)

The input for the heat release rates of the vehicles in Experiment I are shown in Fig. 3 where the blue line represents the heat release rate of Vehicle 1 up until the observed time of ignition of second vehicle at 5 min, the red line is the combined heat release rates for Vehicle 1 and 2 up until observed time of ignition of the third vehicle at 10 min, and the green line represents the combined heat release rates for Vehicle 1, 2 and 3. Since the time of ignition of the second and third vehicle were uncertain, ±30 s time of ignition were added and indicated as error bars in Fig. 3.

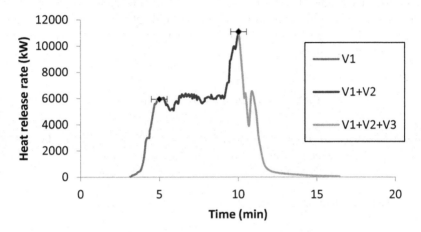

Fig. 3. Heat release rate for Experiment I B-RISK input. (Color figure online)

Other inputs which are needed for the simulation run are mainly in B-RISK CONSOLE where the information about how many iterations which for this simulation are set to be 1000 runs, how long is duration of the simulation, output intervals, and other options are asked to the user.

3 Results and Analysis

This section presents the results obtained from the simulation of the experiments using B-RISK software with the inputs mentioned in previous section. The results from the simulations were compared with the full-scale experiments results as well as with the ones obtained using hand calculation using the PSM and FTP methods in the work by Tohir and Spearpoint [11].

3.1 Experiment H and Experiment I

3.1.1 Variation of Heat of Combustion and Latent Heat of Gasification Input

Tables 6 and 7 shows the results of the simulation of Experiment H and Experiment I where four different simulations with a variation of combination of heat of combustion and latent heat of gasification. The brackets in the table imply what the minimum and maximum values of the possible range for heat of combustion and latent heat of gasification explained in Sect. 2.1.3.

From the results, it was shown from both of the simulations that increasing the heat of combustion (using both latent heat of gasification minimum and maximum range value) shortens the time it took to ignite the second and third vehicles. Though for most cases the time of ignition did not change by much, the prediction of time ignition could lead to a possible 23% change by varying the heat of combustion.

Also from the results, it was demonstrated from the simulation for both experiments that the increase of latent heat of gasification by 0.2 did not change the time of ignition. This signifies that the selection of latent heat of gasification from the available range does not give any changes.

Table 6. Simulation results of Experiment H

Simulation	1	2	3	4
Heat of combustion, ΔH_c (kJ/g)	24.7 (MIN)	44.0 (MAX)	24.7 (MIN)	44.0 (MAX)
Latent heat of gasification, L_g (kJ/g)	2.0 (MIN)	2.0 (MIN)	2.4 (MIN)	2.4 (MIN)
Time of ignition for second vehicle (min)	6.8	5.8	6.8	5.8
Time of ignition for third vehicle (min)	16.7	15.0	16.7	15.0

Table 7. Simulation results of Experiment I

Simulation	1	2	3	4
Heat of combustion, ΔH_c (kJ/g)	24.7 (MIN)	44.0 (MAX)	24.7 (MIN)	44.0 (MAX)
Latent heat of gasification, L_g (kJ/g)	2.0 (MIN)	2.0 (MIN)	2.4 (MIN)	2.4 (MIN)
Time of ignition for second vehicle (min)	5.0	4.5	5.0	4.5
Time of ignition for third vehicle (min)	8.6	6.8	8.6	6.8

3.1.2   Comparison of B-RISK and Hand Calculation Results

Figures 4 and 5 shows the comparison for the time of ignition between the observed time of ignition, the predicted time of ignition from B-RISK simulation, and predicted time of ignition performed using hand calculation for Experiment H and I respectively. In the figures, the bar with black diagonal pattern indicates the observed time of ignition from the experiment. In Fig. 4, the error bar for the third vehicle observed time of ignition indicates the possible range of ignition times.

For the predicted time of ignition from B-RISK simulation, the ranges of possible time of ignition using the variation of heat combustion and latent heat of gasification in Tables 6 and 7 were used, therefore the range is shown in the error bars in the figures. It has to be noted that in B-RISK, the heat source position is assumed to be at the centre of the burning object, hence, the result for heat source position '2-Centre' from the

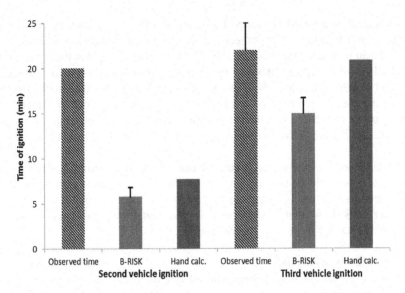

Fig. 4. Comparison of time of ignition for Experiment H

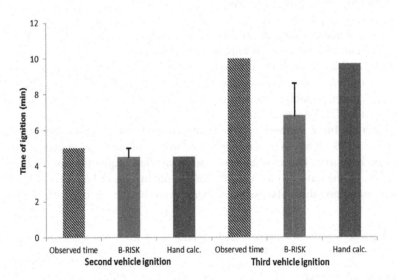

Fig. 5. Comparison of time of ignition for Experiment I

hand calculation is used for comparison. This is decided as to being consistent with the radial distance used in both methods, even though it was suggested that '2-Far' gave the best results for the hand calculation. For the third vehicle prediction, the result from '3-Centre' heat source position.

In Fig. 4, it can be seen that comparing the time of ignition predicted by using B-RISK for both second and third vehicle ignition are 0.9 and 4.2 min faster respectively than using hand calculation. The slight difference of results from the simulation and hand calculation could be due to the radiation effects from the underside of hot upper layer and burning rate enhancement feature in the simulation which provides additional heat flux to the targeted item. The analysis also shows that the predicted time using B-RISK gives bigger difference to the observed time as compared to the results from hand calculation. Figure 5 shows some consistency with the prediction of the results where the prediction of results using hand calculation is within the range predicted by using B-RISK. The third vehicle prediction again shows that the ranges of results calculated by B-RISK are faster than both observed time and the hand calculation time.

The analysis shows that the predicted time of ignition using B-RISK in both experiments gives quicker time of ignition for the second and the third vehicle. This could be due to B-RISK includes the radiation effect from the underside of the hot upper layer. This shows that hand calculation gives better match for the comparison on the observed time for these two experiments.

3.1.3 Sensitivity Analysis
Three sensitivity analyses have been carried out to assess the effects of changing parameters in the software.

3.1.3.1 Burning Rate Enhancement
As a sensitivity analysis, simulations for both experiments with the burning rate enhancement function being disabled were conducted. For the comparison with the predicted results with burning rate enhancement function turned on, heat of combustion at 44.0 kJ/g and latent heat of gasification of 2 kJ/g were selected. Table 8 shows the results of sensitivity analysis on burning rate enhancement function. It can be seen that in both simulations, disabling the burning rate enhancement function could delayed the time of ignition from 4.9% and up to 15%.

Although disabling the burning rate enhancement function could delay the time of ignition up to 15%, it has to be reminded that the heat of combustion and latent heat of gasification have to be known or at least made a justified assumption for the function to be working. In the case of the heat of combustion and latent heat of gasification are unknown and impossible to be assumed, then it would be better to disable the function.

Table 8. Results of sensitivity analysis on burning rate enhancement function.

Experiment	Experiment H		Experiment I	
Burning rate enhancement	ON	OFF	ON	OFF
Time of ignition for second vehicle (min)	5.8	6.1	4.5	5.3
Time of ignition for third vehicle (min)	15.0	15.6	6.8	7.5

3.1.3.2 Distance Change Between Vehicles
The distances between the first and second vehicle for both experiments taken from the literature were 0.7 m. In this sensitivity analysis, the consequences of varying the distances by ±0.1 m were assessed. This value was selected using the greatest possible error (GPE) method. Therefore for this purpose, the distance was increased by 0.1 m as

well as being decreased by 0.1 m to be 0.8 m and 0.6 m respectively. In this sensitivity analysis, other input parameters were fixed.

Tables 9 and 10 show the predicted time of ignition results from the simulations with different distances between the first and second vehicles and the percentage difference from the initial distance of 0.7 m. It is evident from both simulations that an increase of 0.1 m in the distance delays the time of ignition of the second vehicle to at least 4.2% and possibly up to 6.6%. Likewise, the decrease of 0.1 m in the distance speeds up the time ignition to at least 4.4% and possibly up to 5.1%. This sensitivity analysis concludes that it is important to have the exact position of the vehicles (if known) as an input for the simulation since a slight change on the distance will possibly affect the end results.

Table 9. Varied distance sensitivity analysis for Experiment H

Distance between first and second vehicle	d = 0.6 m	d = 0.7 m	d = 0.8 m
Time of ignition of second vehicle (min)	5.5	5.8	6.3
Percentage difference from 0.7 m	−5.1%	–	+6.6%

Table 10. Varied distance sensitivity analysis for Experiment I

Distance between first and second vehicle	d = 0.6 m	d = 0.7 m	d = 0.8 m
Time of ignition of second vehicle (min)	4.3	4.5	4.7
Percentage difference from 0.7 m	−4.4%	–	+4.2%

3.1.3.3 Variation of Radiative Fraction

Another sensitivity analysis conducted was on the variation of the radiative fraction as an input parameter for B-RISK. In this analysis, the consequences of varying the radiative fraction from the initial value of 0.3 by ±20% based on a study by Davis [13] was conducted. Therefore, for this analysis, the radiative fraction used in the simulation were 0.24, 0.30 and 0.36. For the simulations in this sensitivity analysis, other input parameters were fixed.

Tables 11 and 12 show the time of ignition of the second vehicle and the percentage difference from the initial radiative fraction of 0.3 for both experiment simulations. For both simulations, the decrease of 20% of the radiative fraction delayed the time of ignition by 7.9% for Experiment H and 10% for Experiment I. While increasing 20% of the radiative fraction sped up the time of ignition by 10.3% for Experiment H and 8.9% for Experiment I. In the end, the selection of sensible radiative fraction is important since a change of ±20% could lead to a possible 10.3% difference in the time of ignition.

Table 11. Varied radiative fraction sensitivity analysis for Experiment H

Radiative fraction	$\lambda_r = 0.24$	$\lambda_r = 0.30$	$\lambda_r = 0.36$
Time of ignition of second vehicle (min)	6.3	5.8	5.2
Percentage difference from $\lambda_r = 0.30$	−7.9%	–	+10.3%

Table 12. Varied Radiative fraction sensitivity analysis for Experiment I

Radiative fraction	$\lambda_r = 0.24$	$\lambda_r = 0.30$	$\lambda_r = 0.36$
Time of ignition of second vehicle (min)	5.0	4.5	4.1
Percentage difference from $\lambda_r = 0.30$	−10%	–	+8.9%

4 Conclusion

The main objective of this work is to examine the capabilities of B-RISK software in regards to whether it will be able to reproduce the time of ignition in the real experiments. The analysis in Sect. 3.1 shows that the predicted results from the B-RISK simulations give slightly faster time of ignition to the ones obtained using hand calculation. This could be due to B-RISK includes the radiation effect from the underside of the hot upper layer. As a conclusion, the analysis shows that using the B-RISK simulation software with additional radiation effects does not improve the result as compared to using the hand calculation considering the level of uncertainties which required to be assumed on some input parameters e.g. HRRPUA, heat of combustion, and/or latent heat of gasification. Another aspect that currently lacks on B-RISK is the ability to have probabilistic design fire as input hinders the usage of the software at this stage. Therefore, to keep the consistent level with the simple approach used in the fire risk tool in the work by Tohir [4], it is suggested that the application using hand calculation to predict time of ignition of subsequent vehicle is adequate at this stage.

From the sensitivity analyses, it was found that enabling the burning rate enhancement will speed up the time of ignition of the subsequent vehicle. However, assumptions and justifications have to be made for the heat of combustion and latent heat of gasification in order to enable the function. Also from the sensitivity analysis, it was found that it is better to have the exact position of the vehicles (if known) as an input for the simulation since a slight change i.e. 0.1 m on the distance will possibly affect the end results by up to 6.6%. Finally, from another sensitivity analysis, it was found that the selection of sensible radiative fraction is important since a change of ±20% could lead to a possible 10.3% difference in the time of ignition. It can be concluded that the analyses are able to give an indication that in a risk based research, wide range of inputs will possibly resulting in large range of answers.

References

1. Building Research Establishment: Fire Spread in Car Parks. Building Research Establishment (BRE), Eland House Bressenden Place London SW1E 5DU United Kingdom, BD2552 (2010)
2. Tohir, M.Z.M., Spearpoint, M.: Distribution analysis of the fire severity characteristics of single passenger road vehicles using heat release rate data. Fire Sci. Rev. **2**(5) (2013). http://dx.doi.org/10.1186/2193-0414-2-5

3. Department of Building and Housing: C/VM2 Verification Method: Framework for Fire Safety Design (2012)
4. Tohir, M.Z.M., Spearpoint, M.: Development of fire scenarios for car parking buildings using risk analysis. Fire Saf. Sci. **11**, 944–957 (2014)
5. Wade, C., Baker, G.B., Frank, K., Harrison, R., Spearpoint, M., Fleischmann, C.M.: B-RISK user guide and technical manual (2013)
6. Wade, C.: BRANZFIRE Technical Reference Guide. Building Research Association of New Zealand (BRANZ), Judgeford, New Zealand, BRANZ Study Report 92 (2004)
7. Baker, G., Collier, P.C.R., Wade, C., Spearpoint, M., Fleischmann, C.M., Frank, K., Sazegara, S.: A comparison of a priori modelling predictions with experimental results to validate a design fire generator submodel. In: 13th International Fire and Materials Conference, San Francisco, CA, pp. 449–460 (2013)
8. Taub, A.I.: Automotive materials: technology trends and challenges in the 21st century. MRS Bull. **31**(04), 336–343 (2006). doi:10.1557/mrs2006.74
9. Swift, K.: Chemistry and Light Vehicle Annual Report. Economics & Statistics Department. American Chemistry Council, Washington, D.C. (2012)
10. Mark, J.E.: Physical Properties of Polymers Handbook. Springer, New York (2007)
11. Tohir, M.Z.M.: Multiple vehicle design fire scenarios in car parking buildings, Ph.D. thesis, Department of Civil and Natural Resources Engineering, University of Canterbury, New Zealand (2015)
12. Leffin, W.W., Henderson, G.L., Van Beck Voelker, M., Janusek, F.C.: Introduction to Technical Mathematics: With Problem Solving, 3rd edn. Waveland Press, Long Grove (1998)
13. Davis, W.D.: Comparison of algorithms to calculate plume centerline temperature and ceiling jet temperature with experiments. J. Fire. Prot. Eng. **12**(1), 9–29 (2002). doi:10.1177/1042391502012001850

The Route Planning Algorithm Based on Polygon Fusion

Jing Luan[(⊠)], Yonglin Lei, Wenjie Tang, and Yiping Yao

College of Information System and Management,
National University of Defense Technology,
137 Yanwachi, Changsha 410072, Hunan, China
luanjing@mail.ustc.edu.cn,
{yllei,tangwenjie,ypyao}@nudt.edu.cn

Abstract. Route planning is widely used in public transportation, military and other fields. However, the mainstream algorithm adaptability is not comprehensive for the terrain, especially in barrier dense areas, such as A* algorithm, ant colony algorithm and so on. In these algorithms, time-consuming may be too high and planned route may be not optimal. To solve this problem, we propose a novel route planning algorithm based on polygon fusion (RABP). The basic principle of RABP is based on the plane geometry of the shortest line between two points, so the algorithm has strong guidance. Therefore, the algorithm has the advantages of low time-consuming and short route length. At the same time, because of the complex polygon fusion, too strong guidance would not make route planning cannot be accomplished. The algorithm needs to merge the barriers to avoid them and carry on route planning. Meanwhile, it will use the simplified operator to remove the redundant points on the planning route, so the final route is smoother and the route length is shorter. The experiment result shows that the RABP algorithm is more adaptive than A* algorithm and ant colony algorithm to dense barrier areas, the planning route is shorted and consumes less time.

Keywords: Polygon fusion · Route planning · Routing algorithm

1 Introduction

Route planning is to find an optimal collision free route from the starting point to the target point. It could provide an accessible and optimal route in complex terrain. It provides convenience for people to travel in the life, provides the basis for the commander's decision in the military, and meet the needs of the people.

Route planning depends directly on the routing algorithm. After decades of development, there have been a lot of mature routing algorithms, such as A* algorithm, ant colony algorithm and so on. However, there are some deficiencies in the existing routing algorithm, which are not comprehensive enough for terrain. Especially in dense barrier areas, the algorithms would have some problems such as low time efficiency, long planning route and so on. But the dense barrier area is a kind of common terrain, so it becomes more important to research the routing algorithm in dense barrier areas.

© Springer Nature Singapore Pte Ltd. 2017
M.S. Mohamed Ali et al. (Eds.): AsiaSim 2017, Part I, CCIS 751, pp. 52–60, 2017.
DOI: 10.1007/978-981-10-6463-0_5

Polygon fusion is a kind of technology to fuse many complex polygons in space [1, 2]. Therefore, we propose RABP algorithm. Compared with the traditional routing algorithm, it can be more adapted to barrier dense areas, and the planning route is shorted and less time-consuming.

The structure of this paper is as follows. The first section is the introduction. In Sect. 2, the related work is shown. In Sect. 3, RABP algorithm is described. In Sect. 4, the advantage is proved by experiments. In the last section, a summary is made for this paper.

2 Related Work

There are a lot of mature routing algorithms, such as A* algorithm, ant colony algorithm, and so on. These algorithms have been applied in many fields, but in some cases, the above algorithms may not be able to solve the problem well [3].

A* algorithm is an effective direct search algorithm for solving the shortest route in the static road network. By setting the appropriate heuristic function, A* algorithm can get the optimal solution. However, in barrier dense areas, it will be extremely difficult for A* algorithm to mapping the grid, and it could lead to a long route and low time efficiency [4, 5].

Ant colony algorithm is an ant colony foraging algorithm. The parameters such as heuristic factors are set according to different terrain, and different parameters have different effects on the performance of the algorithm. The search effect of the algorithm is very good, and under certain conditions, it can get the optimal solution. However, ant colony algorithm will fall into the optimal solution, but has strong randomness and requires a large number of iterations. Therefore, compared with A* algorithm, the time consuming of algorithm is higher [6–8].

In a word, although the mainstream algorithms have strong abilities of route planning, in barrier dense areas, there are still some problems to be solved, such as long route and high time consuming.

3 RABP Algorithm

In this paper, RABP algorithm is proposed to solve the problem of barrier dense area. The algorithm is divided into three stages: Pretreatment, route planning, optimization. The pretreatment consists of two parts: the construction of the chain and the fusion of the barrier trees. Route planning is based on the starting and the target point, and find a collision free routing after pretreatment. Optimization is to use the simplified operator to optimize the planning route. Therefore, the algorithm can also be divided into the following four process: construction of ring chain, obstacle fusion, route planning, simplified operator.

The basic principle of RABP is based on the plane geometry of the shortest line between two points. So the algorithm has strong guidance. It will go as far as possible from the shortest route of the target point. Compared to other intelligent algorithms, the planned path will be more optimized. Moreover, the algorithm only needs to preprocess the barrier trees, and achieves the fusion of intersecting obstacles. When planning route, it does not need to traverse the whole trees, so that the time efficiency of the algorithm becomes higher. At last, we use the simplified operator, and simplify the selection of inflection points on the route. Therefore, the final route is smoother and the route length is shorter (Fig. 1).

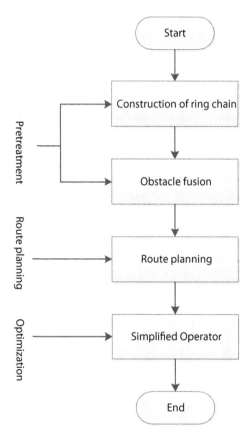

Fig. 1. RABP algorithm flow chart

3.1   Construction of Ring Chain

Since it is difficult to represent all points on the circular arc, an external polygon is used instead of the circle. At the same time, denote the polygon in the form of ring chain and determine the complete polygon with the chain order of vertexes (Fig. 2).

For each tree, there will be an external polygon. And each vertex of the polygon has an edge corresponding to it. So as long as the vertices of the polygon are in a certain order to express, it can only determine the polygon.

The use of the form of the ring chain on the polygon representation is applicable to the case of arbitrary polygon. And in the polygon shape change, the insertion of nodes and other operations, it is very easy to simplify the operation by using ring chain.

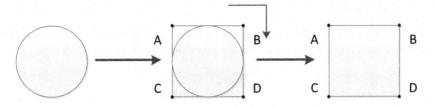

Fig. 2. Construction of ring chain

3.2 Obstacle Fusion

In order to avoid the mutual influence of the polygons, the polygons should be fused with each other, and the fused polygons will be independent from each other (Fig. 3).

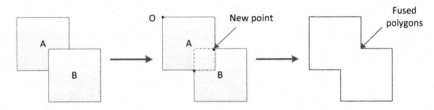

Fig. 3. Sketch of polygon fusion

```
For i = 1 to Point number of A
  For j = 1 to Point number of B
    If(IsIntersect(Connect(point(i),point(i+1)),
      Connect(point(j),point(j+1))
      Insert(Intersection point) -> Correspondent(A)
      Insert(Intersection point) -> Correspondent(B)
    End If
    End for
    End for
  Choose a datum point of A -> O
  Insert(O) -> route list
  NextPoint(O,A) -> Current point
  While(Current point !=O)
    Insert(Current point) -> route list
    If(Current point == Intersection point)
    A ⇔ B
    NextPoint(Current point,A) -> Current point
    End If
  End While
End
```

3.3 Route Planning

Mark the barrier trees and merge them with their own surrounding trees, and then, proceed with the route planning to get the planning route (Fig. 4).

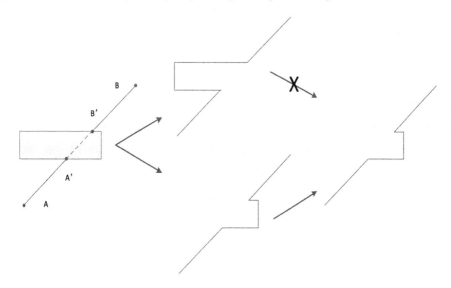

Fig. 4. Construction of ring chain

```
If(IsNotEmpty(A,B))
  Connect(A,B) -> Line L
    GetIntersectionPoint(L,rectangle close to A) -> A',B'
    Get two route lists along rect from A to B -> R1,R2
    ShorterRouteList(R1,R2) -> R
    Add(R) -> Final route list
    B' -> A
  End If
  End
```

3.4 Simplified Operator

The planning route, obtained through the above steps, will bring a large number of inflection points, and it will result in that the route is not smooth enough. So the simplified operator is used to optimize the planning route (Fig. 5).

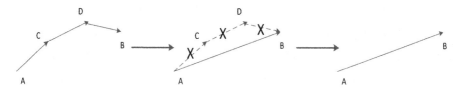

Fig. 5. Sketch of simplified operator

```
Choose start point -> A
  Choose end point -> B
    While(1)
      If(A==B)
        If(A==End Point)
          Break
        Else
          NextPoint(A) -> A
          End Point -> B
        End If
      Else
        If(HaveObstacle(A,B))
          BeforePoint(B) -> B
        Else
          Delete point from A to B
          B -> A
          End Point -> B
        End If
      End If
      End While
    End
```

Using the simplified operator to simplify the planning route, although it will consume a little time cost, the route obtained by the algorithm is highly optimized to eliminate a large number of path inflection points, and the final route length is shorter.

4   Test and Evaluation

Test data us a region of the 2D plan, in which the black circle represents the area of trees, the red line represents the planning route, the measured distance is the needless route length in order to avoid obstacles. The RABP algorithm is compared with A* algorithm and ant colony algorithm, and the effect is shown as follows (Figs. 6, 7 and 8 and Table 1):

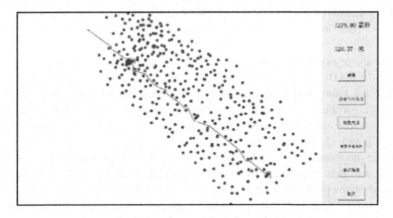

Fig. 6. RABP algorithm (Color figure online)

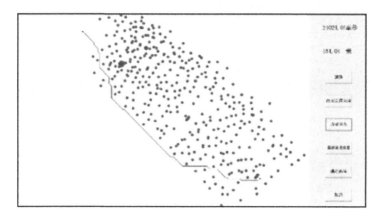

Fig. 7. A* algorithm (Color figure online)

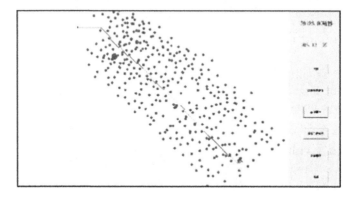

Fig. 8. Ant colony algorithm (Color figure online)

Table 1. Experiment data

	RABP algorithm	A* algorithm	Ant colony algorithm
Length (m)	120.57	154.01	105.13
Time (ms)	1279	24024	79123

In the above experiment environment, the density of trees is about 71%. It can be seen that the RABP algorithm has more advantages than the A* algorithm in the two aspects of the route length and time efficiency. Compared with ant colony algorithm, the RABP algorithm is much better than the ant colony algorithm, although the length of the route, the ant colony algorithm is slightly better, in terms of time efficiency (Figs. 9, 10 and 11 and Table 2).

Change the source point and the target point, and the density of trees is about 53%. It can be seen that the ant colony algorithm is trapped in the local optimal solution, which leads to the poor efficiency of the algorithm and the longer length of the planning route. However, the RABP still maintains a high performance, and the planning effect is better than the ant colony algorithm and the A* algorithm.

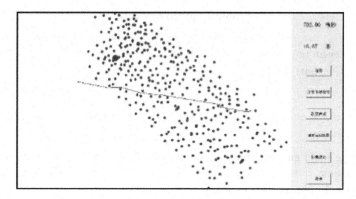

Fig. 9. RABP algorithm (Color figure online)

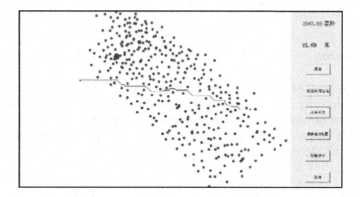

Fig. 10. A* algorithm (Color figure online)

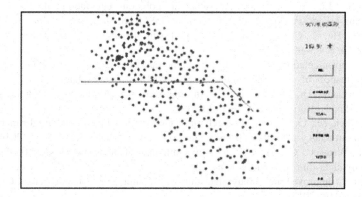

Fig. 11. Ant colony algorithm (Color figure online)

Table 2. Experiment data

	RABP algorithm	A* algorithm	Ant colony algorithm
Length (m)	16.67	91.69	143.97
Time (ms)	702	3947	80778

Through the above test results, we can see that the RABP algorithm has the following advantages:

1. The strong route guidance makes the final planning route as optimal as possible, at the same time, in the time efficiency, it will also reduce the avoidance of redundant barriers, and improve the efficiency of time.
2. The algorithm does not need to search the grid, and does not need to traverse a large number of grid maps, which makes the time efficiency greatly improved.
3. The stability of the algorithm is strong, so it can keep the high performance, not easy to fall into the local optimal solution.

5 Conclusion

In this paper, the RABP algorithm is proposed to solve the problem that the existing mainstream algorithms have poor searching results in barrier dense areas. Based on the polygon fusion of barrier trees, the algorithm does not need to be rasterized and large area search in the process of route planning. Therefore, not only the planning route is shorter, but also the time efficiency is greatly improved.

References

1. Meng, X.Q., Xue, Q., Long, L.: Convex polygon amalgamation algorithm used in real-time obstacle avoidance in virtual environment. J. Syst. Simul. (2006)
2. Wang, B., Li, J., Gao, L.: An efficient polygon integration algorithm in grid pathfinding-border crawling algorithm. Comput. Inf. Technol. **3**, 006 (2012)
3. Zhang, G., Hu, X., Chai, J., et al.: Summary of path planning algorithm and its application. Mod. Mach. **5**, 85–90 (2011)
4. Qiu, L.: Implementation of pathfinding on game maps based A-star algorithm and compare the performances of various algorithms. J. Shaanxi Univ. Sci. Technol. (2011)
5. Xin, Y., Liang, H., Du, M., et al.: An improved A* algorithm for searching infinite neighbourhoods. Robot **36**, 627–633 (2014)
6. Shi, E., Chen, M., Li, J., et al.: Research on method of global path-planning for mobile robot based on ant-colony algorithm. Trans. Chin. Soc. Agric. Mach. **45**(6), 53–57 (2014)
7. Li, L.-R., Wang, L., Gao, Y.B., et al.: A dynamic path planning model based on the optimal ant colony algorithm. J. Guangxi Univ. (2013)
8. Zhou, M.X.: Improved ant colony algorithm with planning of dynamic path. Comput. Sci. **40**(1), 314–316 (2013)

Gaussian Pedestrian Proxemics Model with Social Force for Service Robot Navigation in Dynamic Environment

Sheng Fei Chik[1], Che Fai Yeong[2(⊠)], Eileen Lee Ming Su[1],
Thol Yong Lim[3], Feng Duan[4], Jeffrey Too Chuan Tan[5],
Ping Hua Tan[6], and Patrick Jun Hua Chin[6]

[1] Faculty of Electrical Engineering, Universiti Teknologi Malaysia,
Johor Bahru, Malaysia
[2] Centre for Artificial Intelligence and Robotics, Universiti Teknologi Malaysia,
Johor Bahru, Malaysia
cfyeong@utm.my
[3] Malaysia Japan Institute of Technolgy, Universiti Teknologi Malaysia,
Johor Bahru, Malaysia
[4] Department of Automation, College of Computer and Control Engineering,
Nankai University, Tianjin, China
[5] Institute of Industrial Science, The University of Tokyo, Tokyo, Japan
[6] DF Automation and Robotics Sdn. Bhd, Skudai, Malaysia

Abstract. Pedestrian motion behaves stochastically, causing difficulties in modelling the appropriate proxemics for effective and efficient service robot navigation. Intruding the pedestrian social space can affect the social acceptance of a service robot. In this paper, a new proxemics model, Social-Force Gaussian Pedestrian Proxemics Model is presented to model the pedestrian social space and to improve the service robot navigation in dynamic human environment. This model was simulated and validated in a pedestrian simulator with both low and high pedestrian density environments. Results showed that the proposed model (i) improved proxemics representation of pedestrians, (ii) enhanced the robot performance in respecting the social norm and (iii) increased the efficiency in achieving a given task. This paper also presents the methods for parameter selections for the model without the requirement of complex tuning.

Keywords: Proxemics model · Social force model · Dynamic human environments · Service robot

1 Introduction

Robots start to co-exist in human environment, moving out from industry into populated restaurants, shopping malls and health care centers [1–3]. The design of service robot needs to consider the invisible social rules that govern the human social behaviors. Navigation framework of a service robot can be very complex, in which it involves knowledge from path planning, human tracking and detection, human-robot

© Springer Nature Singapore Pte Ltd. 2017
M.S. Mohamed Ali et al. (Eds.): AsiaSim 2017, Part I, CCIS 751, pp. 61–73, 2017.
DOI: 10.1007/978-981-10-6463-0_6

interaction to machine learning algorithms [4]. The proxemics model proposed by Hall [5] is another important component to be included in the navigation framework in order to respect the human management of social space. This paper focused on enhancing the pedestrian proxemics model that represents the social space around a pedestrian. A new proxemics model is presented in this paper, named as the Social-Force Gaussian Pedestrian Proxemics Model (SF-GPPM) which uses a Gaussian function with Social Force Model (SFM). The proposed model improves the robot navigation by following the human social rules and increases the efficiency in robot task completion. The rest of the article is organized as follows: Sect. 2 introduces previous works related to this study. Section 3 describes the design of SF-GPPM. Simulation results and discussion are presented in Sect. 4. The performance of the model is concluded in Sect. 5, with some suggestions for future works.

2 Related Works

Various researches were done by incorporating human social elements in constructing pedestrian proxemics model. Kirby et al. [6] used two Gaussian functions to represents the proxemics model [5] and also included pass-on-the-right social-convention into the model. Kollmitz et al. [7] assigned multiple layers of social space to capture the dynamic motion of human over time, but with the trade-off of larger memory required to store the information at different time. Nishitani et al. [8] used a similar concept by introducing an additional time axis to the x and y grid map to predict human motion and avoid intruding human personal space. Lu and Smart [9] used a linear model that assigned higher cost to human pathway which opposed robot navigation direction, and was able to demonstrate an effective social-aware navigation. In another study, Lu et al. [10] designed a semantically-separated layered costmap for an open source platform, the Robot Operating System (ROS) [11] and introduced a social costmap layer by applying the model from Kirby et al. [6], easing human-robot navigation implementation. However, these models are designed for less crowded scenarios such as single human encounter in corridors and hallways.

There were studies focused on Social Force Model (SFM) by Helbing and Molnar [12], that could capture the invisible force governing the human motion behavior. SFM is utilized to perform robot navigation amidst human environment. Ferrer et al. [13] proposed a navigation method based on SFM to accompany humans to their destinations. An improved SFM, the collision prediction SFM (CP-SFM) [14] was used by Shiomi et al. [15] to demonstrate a socially-acceptable navigation in a shopping mall. However, these methods required prior information about the available destinations in the test scenario and required pedestrian datasets for training.

SF-GPPM proposed in this paper improves the pedestrian proxemics model using SFM to adapt to different pedestrian motions and densities without the need for prior information on the environment and does not require complex parameter tuning.

3   Social-Force Gaussian Pedestrian Proxemics Model (SF-GPPM)

3.1   SF-GPPM

The proposed pedestrian proxemics model, SF-GPPM used to represent the pedestrian social space is as follow:

$$f_{SF-GPPM}(x, y, v, \varphi_{iq}, t) = f_{iq}(t) \cdot \omega(\varphi_{iq}) \cdot f_{ns}(x, y, v) \qquad (1)$$

where $f_{iq}(t)$ is the magnitude of the vector quantity, repulsive force $\boldsymbol{f}_{iq}(t)$ [16] while $\omega(\varphi_{iq})$ [17] is the anisotropic factor, where both terms are from the Social Force Model (SFM) [12]. $f_{ns}(x, y, v)$ is a non-symmetrical Gaussian function [6], these components are further described in Sect. 3.2. i and q represent pedestrian and robot respectively as shown in Fig. 1. The $f_{SF-GPPM}$ model is used to represent the pedestrian social space which the robot should avoid, with the larger the magnitude of $f_{SF-GPPM}$, the greater the need for the robot to avoid the social region. The amplitude dynamically varies based on the SFM components $f_{iq}(t)$ and $\omega(\varphi_{iq})$ to cater for pedestrians with various positions and orientations (Figs. 2 and 3).

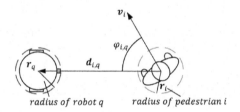

Fig. 1. A scenario where robot q encounters pedestrian i

3.2   Components of SF-GPPM

The main component of SF-GPPM is a non-symmetrical Gaussian function (Eq. 2) proposed by Kirby et al. [6].

$$f_{ns}(x, y, v) = \begin{cases} A \cdot exp\left(-\frac{x^2 + y^2}{2\sigma^2}\right), & x < 0 \\ A \cdot exp\left(-\left(\frac{x^2}{2(1 + \gamma v)\sigma^2} + \frac{y^2}{2\sigma^2}\right)\right), & x \geq 0 \end{cases} \qquad (2)$$

where A is amplitude, σ is variance, x and y is human position, v is the human velocity and γ is the velocity scaling factor.

Another component in $f_{SF-GPPM}$ is the SFM repulsive force $f_{iq}(t)$.

$$f_{iq}(t) = A_s e^{\frac{d-diq(t)}{B}} \tag{3}$$

where A_s denotes the strength of the repulsive force and B scales the interaction range, d is the sum of the "radii" of i and q while d_{iq} is the magnitude of distance vector between the pedestrian and the robot (d_{iq}) as shown in Fig. 1. Figure 2 demonstrates the effect of the component $f_{iq}(t)$ on the amplitude of $f_{SF-GPPM}$.

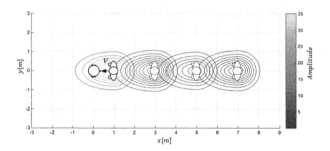

Fig. 2. The closer the pedestrian to the robot, the stronger the repulsive force $f_{iq}(t)$, the greater the need for the robot to avoid the region

$\omega(\varphi_{iq})$, the SFM anisotropic factor [17] is another component in $f_{SF-GPPM}$.

$$\omega(\varphi_{iq}) = \left.\left(\lambda + (1-\lambda)\frac{1+\cos(\varphi_{iq})}{2}\right)\right|_{0\le\lambda\le1} \tag{4}$$

where φ_{iq} is the angle between velocity vector v_i and distance vector $-d_{iq}$ as shown in Fig. 1, λ is used to scale the anisotropic factor. Figure 3 depicts various amplitude of $f_{SF-GPPM}$ affected by $\omega(\varphi_{iq})$.

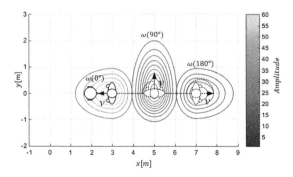

Fig. 3. The smaller the φ_{iq}, the larger the anisotropic factor $\omega(\varphi_{iq})$ which implies a greater avoidance is required

3.3   Parameter Consideration of SF-GPPM

The parameters in SF-GPPM include A, σ, γ, A_s, B, d and λ, can impact representation of the pedestrian proxemics which in turn affects the robot navigation in the pedestrian environment.

Considerations of A, σ and γ. Parameters A, σ and γ can be selected based on Eq. 5 proposed by Lu et al. [18].

$$\frac{P}{A_\gamma} = \sqrt{\frac{\pi}{2}} \frac{\hat{y}}{\sigma} \exp\left(-\frac{\hat{y}^2}{\sigma^2}\right) \tag{5}$$

where P is the constant cost of traverse of a path planning algorithm, $\hat{y}$ represents the closeness between a robot and a pedestrian, and A_γ is the amplitude of $f_{SF-GPPM}$.

Independent of A_s and d. To fulfilled the constraints of Eq. 5, $f_{iq}(t)$ should be kept within $0 \leq f_{iq}(t) \leq 1$, which results in the following equation:

$$A_s = e^{-\frac{d}{B}} \tag{6}$$

Combining Eqs. 6 and 2, $f_{iq}(t)$ is then independent of A_s and d.

$$f_{iq}(t) = e^{\frac{-d_{iq}(t)}{B}} \tag{7}$$

Consideration of B. According to Hall [5], when density increases, the social space of the pedestrians reduces. Hence, parameter B is proposed to be dynamically changing based on the pedestrian density to adjust the repulsive force $f_{iq}(t)$. A relationship between parameter B and pedestrian density ρ is introduced.

$$B(n) = e^{\frac{C_\rho}{p(n)}} \tag{8}$$

where C_ρ is the density coefficient that reflects the strength of the density ρ in affecting parameter B and $p(n)$ is the pedestrian density used by Vasquez et al. [19] with the following equation:

$$\rho(n) = \frac{n}{\pi r^2} \tag{9}$$

where n is the number of pedestrians in a circular area with radius r from the centre of the robot.

Consideration of λ. The term λ in the anisotropic factor $\omega(\varphi_{iq})$ is selected based on the implementation of the limiting safety distance d_{limit} of a robot approaching a pedestrian from behind before a detour is needed. λ can be selected based on the following constraint:

$$\lambda > \frac{cost_{min}}{A_\gamma} exp\left(\frac{d_{limit}^2}{2\sigma^2} + \frac{d_{limit}}{B}\right) \tag{10}$$

and should be kept within the range of $0 \le \lambda \le 1$.

4 Simulation and Discussion

4.1 Simulation Setup

Simulations were done to compare the performance of the SF-GPPM, $f_{SF-GPPM}$ with the non-symmetrical Gaussian model (f_{ns}) proposed and implemented in previous studies [6, 10]. The simulations were carried out using a 3D pedestrian simulator [19] on ROS [11] platform. A corridor scene was selected to have a fair comparison between SP-GPPM and previous works [6, 7, 9]. The corridor was 4 m wide and 20 m long. The pedestrian velocity was set to 1.26 ms^{-1} [20] and an average body radius of 0.25 m [21] was selected. The radius of the service robot was chosen based on a robotic platform for ROS, the Turtlebot2, with radius of 0.177 m, 0.25 m was used instead to account for possible extruded robot parts. In consideration of the limitation of robot dynamics, the robot maximum speed was set to the Turtlebot2 speed limit of 0.7 ms^{-1}. In the simulation, the robot had to complete of task of planning a path from point A to point B separated 10-m apart as shown in Fig. 4, under different variation of pedestrian densities. Standard non-modified A* global planner [22] and elastic band local planner [23] from ROS were used to eliminate experimental variation as suggested by a previous work [24]. Based on Sect. 3.2, the $f_{SF-GPPM}$ parameters used in the simulation are shown in Table 1 (Fig. 5).

Table 1. Parameter values of SF-GPPM for the performance comparison simulation

Parameters	Value
A_{set}	60
σ^2	0.25
γ	5
C_ρ	0.3
λ	0.26

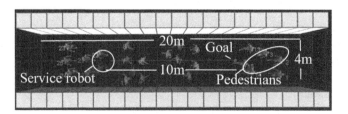

Fig. 4. Simulation setup (top view)

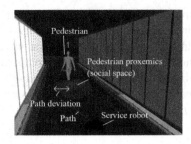

Fig. 5. Close view of the simulated environment

4.2 Performance Metrics

The performances of the pedestrian proxemics models are evaluated based on the metrics used in previous studies [7, 19, 25] (Table 2).

Table 2. Metrics to evaluate the efficiency of the robot in task completion and to quantify the robot social-awareness and understanding of the pedestrian motion behaviors

Metrics	Description
Distance travelled	Distance travelled by the robot
Maximum path deviation	Maximum y-coordinate deviation from the middle
Cumulative heading change (CHC)	Orientation change of the robot
Time	Robot task completion time
Zero crossing	Smoothness of the robot motion and detection of move-stop-move and freezing robot scenarios [26]
Number of stops	Total number of stops during the task
Maximum stop time	Maximum stop time during the task
Closest distance	Closest distance between the robot and pedestrian
Intimate intrusions	Number of times the robot enters the intimate space of the pedestrians based on the proxemics model [5]
Personal (close phase) intrusions	Number of times the robot enters the close-phase personal space of the pedestrians based on the proxemics model [5]

4.3 Results

Simulations were carried out with 1, 5, 10, 15, 20 and 25 pedestrians for 10 times each for both $f_{SF-GPPM}$ and f_{ns} which total up to 120 runs. The means of the performance metrics were plotted in Figs. 6a, b, c, d, e, 7a, b and 8a, b, c. Independent samples T-test (Tables 3 and 4) was carried out to check whether the difference in performance of $f_{SF-GPPM}$ and f_{ns} is significant.

The metrics in Fig. 6 are used to evaluate the efficiency of the service robot in task completion, a lower value in these parameters indicates higher efficiency. Figure 6a and Table 3 show improvement of distance travelled metric where the distance travelled using $f_{SF-GPPM}$ is significantly shorter ($p < 0.05$) as compared to f_{ns} when pedestrian density increases. Path deviation metrics (Fig. 6b) is improved where $f_{SF-GPPM}$ requires less path deviation as compared to f_{ns}. The number of stops and maximum stop time are greatly reduced by using $f_{SF-GPPM}$ (Fig. 6c, d). Figure 6e shows that $f_{SF-GPPM}$ has significant better completion time as compared to f_{ns} in different pedestrian density.

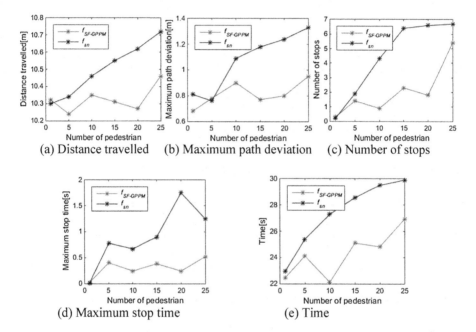

(a) Distance travelled   (b) Maximum path deviation   (c) Number of stops

(d) Maximum stop time   (e) Time

Fig. 6. Comparison of performance metrics distance travelled, maximum path deviation, number of stops, maximum stop time and time between $f_{SF-GPPM}$ and f_{ns}

For the metrics CHC and zero crossing, higher values indicate poorer path smoothness where the robot needs to perform more turning, accelerations and decelerations. Metrics CHC and zero crossing for both $f_{SF-GPPM}$ and f_{ns} increase as the pedestrian density increases (Fig. 7), and have no significant path smoothness improvements (Table 4) in all scenarios of pedestrian densities.

The metrics in Fig. 8 are used to evaluate the social-awareness of the service robot which the robot requires to distances itself away from pedestrians and avoid social-space intrusions. Larger values in closest distances and lower number of social-space intrusions indicates better social-awareness. Figure 8a, b, c show the when the pedestrian density increases, the distance between the robot and pedestrian reduces, and the number intrusions into the social space increases. Based on the independent samples T-test (Table 4), the intimate and personal space intrusions show significate

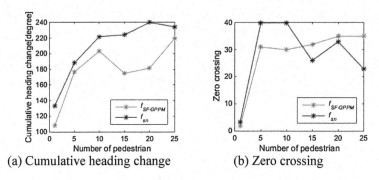

(a) Cumulative heading change   (b) Zero crossing

Fig. 7. Comparison of performance metrics cumulative heading change and zero crossing between $f_{SF-GPPM}$ and f_{ns}

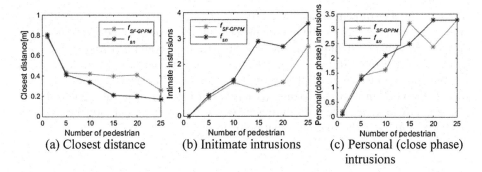

(a) Closest distance   (b) Intitmate intrusions   (c) Personal (close phase) intrusions

Fig. 8. Comparison of performance metrics closest distance, intimate intrusion and personal (close phase) intrusion between $f_{SF-GPPM}$ and f_{ns}

Table 3. The p-values of independent samples T-test to test for significant difference between $f_{SF-GPPM}$ and f_{ns} for the metrics path travelled, path deviation, time, number of stops and maximum stop time

Pedestrians	Path travelled	Path deviation	Time	Number of stops	Maximum stop time
1	0.33	0.00*	0.00*	0.63	0.8
5	0.01*	0.83	0.03*	0.54	0.21
10	0.02*	0.03*	0.00*	0.00*	0.02*
15	0.00*	0.00*	0.00*	0.00*	0.03*
20	0.01*	0.03*	0.00*	0.00*	0.01*
25	0.04*	0.09	0.01*	0.42	0.01*

improvements in certain density scenarios. For the closest distance metric, $f_{SF-GPPM}$ performed significantly better (p < 0.05) when the number of pedestrians is increased to 15, 20 and 25.

Table 4. The p-values of independent samples T-test to test for significant difference between $f_{SF-GPPM}$ and f_{ns} for the metrics cumulative heading change, zero-crossing, closest distance, intimate intrusion and personal (close phase) intrusion

Pedestrian	CHC	Zero crossing	Closest distance	Intimate intrusion	Personal (close phase) intrusion
1	0.00*	0.02*	0.22	n/a	0.56
5	0.48	0.34	0.62	0.8	0.77
10	0.07	0.24	0.08	0.84	0.36
15	0.00*	0.53	0.01*	0.01*	0.38
20	0.01*	0.84	0.00*	0.02*	0.18
25	0.18	0.09*	0.03*	0.23	1

4.4 Discussion

When the number of pedestrians increased, the amplitude of f_{ns} was maintained high, causing the social costmap to be over populated (Fig. 9a) with cost penalties, however $f_{SF-GPPM}$ was able to highlight the only social space that should be avoided (Fig. 9b). This enabled the robot using $f_{SF-GPPM}$ to travel a shorter distance, had a lesser path deviation and shorter task completion time by following the suitable pedestrian flow towards the goal, instead of avoiding all the pedestrians. $f_{SF-GPPM}$ also had a higher chance in providing feasible paths during the task with less stops and shorter maximum stop time to mitigate the freezing robot problem [26].

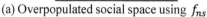

(a) Overpopulated social space using f_{ns} (b) Non-overpopulated social using $f_{SF-GPPM}$

Fig. 9. The social space (proxemics) formed based on f_{ns} and $f_{SF-GPPM}$.

CHC and zero crossing for both $f_{SF-GPPM}$ and f_{ns} increased as the pedestrian density increased, thus showing that $f_{SF-GPPM}$ was unable to address the path smoothness problem as the pedestrian density scaled up.

The overpopulated problem using f_{ns} caused the path planner ended up choosing a shorter path with a lower total travel cost and move closer to the pedestrians. The same scenario was captured by the metrics intimate intrusion and personal (close phase) intrusion where $f_{SF-GPPM}$ was able to avoid overpopulating the costmap, planning path further away from the pedestrians and thus has a lower number of intrusions as compared to f_{ns}.

5 Conclusions and Future Work

Service robot navigation in dynamic human environment is a multi-objective problem where the robot has to perform its task and at the same time abide to social rules. Understanding the pedestrian behavior can provide advantage in both increasing the navigation efficiency and respecting the social cues. The contribution of this paper is a new proxemics model - SF-GPPM that enables robot to perform better in its task completion and in following the social norm. The metrics (distance travelled, maximum stop time, closest distance) at pedestrian density of 0.83 m^{-2} (an environment of 25 pedestrians), showed significant improvements ($p < 0.05$), presenting the advantage of using SF-GPPM over the frequent employed non-symmetrical Gaussian model for navigations in human dynamic environments. This study also shows that the parameters of the SF-GPPM can be selected without the need of complex tuning method. Future work can consider designing a different model for local planner to improve the robot path smoothness. This model focus on human-robot collision-avoidance, future studies can include other social elements such as human-robot interaction.

Acknowledgement. The authors are grateful to Universiti Teknologi Malaysia for providing facilities to conduct this research. This work is supported by the Universiti Teknologi Malaysia Research Grant (00M81) and was supported in part by the Research Fellowship for International Young Scientists, National Natural Science Foundation of China (No. 61650110511). Authors also thank DF Automation & Robotics Sdn Bhd for providing useful robotic facilities, information and insights.

References

1. Zalama, E., García-Bermejo, J.G., Marcos, S., Domínguez, S., Feliz, R., Pinillos, R., López, J.: Sacarino, a service robot in a hotel environment. In: Armada, M.A., Sanfeliu, A., Ferre, M. (eds.) ROBOT2013: First Iberian Robotics Conference. AISC, vol. 253, pp. 3–14. Springer, Cham (2014). doi:10.1007/978-3-319-03653-3_1
2. Broadbent, E., Stafford, R., MacDonald, B.: Acceptance of healthcare robots for the older population: review and future directions. Int. J. Soc. Robot. **1**(4), 319–330 (2009)
3. Marchionni, L., Pages, J., Adell, J., Capriles, J.R., Tomé, H.: REEM service robot: how may I help you? In: Ferrández Vicente, J.M., Álvarez Sánchez, J.R., Paz López, F., Toledo Moreo, F.J. (eds.) IWINAC 2013. LNCS, vol. 7930, pp. 121–130. Springer, Heidelberg (2013). doi:10.1007/978-3-642-38637-4_13
4. Chik, S.F., Yeong, C.F., Su, E.L.H., Lim, T.L., Subramaniam, Y., Chin, P.J.H.: A review of social-aware navigation frameworks for service robot in dynamic human environments. J. Telecommun. Electron. Comput. Eng. **8**(11), 41–50 (2016)
5. Hall, E.T.: The Hidden Dimension. Anchor Books, New York (1966)

6. Kirby, R., Simmons, R., Forlizzi, J.: Companion: a constraint-optimizing method for person-acceptable navigation. In: 18th IEEE International Symposium on Robot and Human Interactive Communication, Toyama, Japan, pp. 607–612 (2009)
7. Kollmitz, M., Hsiao, K., Gaa, J., Burgard, W.: Time dependent planning on a layered social cost map for human-aware robot navigation. In: European Conference on Mobile Robots, Lincoln, UK, pp. 1–6 (2015)
8. Nishitani, I., Matsumura, T., Ozawa, M., Yorozu, A., Takahashi, M.: Human-centered X-Y-T space path planning for mobile robot in dynamic environments. Robot. Auton. Syst. 66(C), 18–26 (2015)
9. Lu, D.V., Smart, W.D.: Towards more efficient navigation for robots and humans. In: IEEE/RSJ International Conference on Intelligent Robots and Systems, Tokyo, Japan, pp. 1707–1713 (2013)
10. Lu, D.V., Hershberger, D., Smart, W.D.: Layered costmaps for context-sensitive navigation. In: IEEE/RSJ International Conference on Intelligent Robots and Systems, Chicago, Illinois, USA, pp. 709–715 (2014)
11. Quigley, M., Conley, K., Gerkey, B., Faust, J., Foote, T., Leibs, J., Wheeler, R., Ng, A.Y.: ROS: an open-source robot operating system. In: ICRA Workshop on Open Source Software, vol. 3, no. 3.2, p. 5 (2009)
12. Helbing, D., Molnar, P.: Social force model for pedestrian dynamics. Phys. Rev. E 51(5), 4282 (1995)
13. Ferrer, G., Garrell, A., Sanfeliu, A. (eds.): Robot companion: a social-force based approach with human awareness-navigation in crowded environments. In: IEEE/RSJ International Conference on Intelligent Robots and Systems, Tokyo, Japan, pp. 1688–1694 (2013)
14. Zanlungo, F., Ikeda, T., Kanda, T.: Social force model with explicit collision prediction. Europhys. Lett. 93(6), 68005 (2011)
15. Shiomi, M., Zanlungo, F., Hayashi, K., Kanda, T.: Towards a socially acceptable collision avoidance for a mobile robot navigating among pedestrians using a pedestrian model. Int. J. Soc. Robot. 6(3), 443–455 (2014)
16. Helbing, D., Johansson, A.: Pedestrian, crowd and evacuation dynamics. In: Meyers, R.A. (ed.) Extreme Environmental Events on Complexity in Forecasting and Early Warning, pp. 697–716. Springer, New York (2011). doi:10.1007/978-1-4419-7695-6_37
17. Johansson, A., Helbing, D., Shukla, P.K.: Specification of the social force pedestrian model by evolutionary adjustment to video tracking data. Adv. Complex Syst. 10(suppl. 02), 271–288 (2007)
18. Lu, D.V., Allan, D.B., Smart, W.D.: Tuning cost functions for social navigation. In: Herrmann, G., Pearson, M.J., Lenz, A., Bremner, P., Spiers, A., Leonards, U. (eds.) ICSR 2013. LNCS, vol. 8239, pp. 442–451. Springer, Cham (2013). doi:10.1007/978-3-319-02675-6_44
19. Vasquez, D., Okal, B., Arras, K.O.: Inverse reinforcement learning algorithms and features for robot navigation in crowds: an experimental comparison. In: IEEE/RSJ International Conference on Intelligent Robots and Systems, Chicago, Illinois, USA, pp. 1341–1346 (2014)
20. Azmi, D.I., Karim, H.A., Amin, M.Z.M.: Comparing the walking behaviour between urban and rural residents. Procedia-Soc. Behav. Sci. 68, 406–416 (2012)
21. Karmegam, K., Sapuan, S., Ismail, M.Y., Ismail, N., Bahri, M.S., Shuib, S., et al.: Anthropometric study among adults of different ethnicity in Malaysia. Int. J. Phys. Sci. 6(4), 777–788 (2011)
22. Hart, P.E., Nilsson, N.J., Raphael, B.: A formal basis for the heuristic determination of minimum cost paths. IEEE Trans. Syst. Sci. Cybern. 4(2), 100–107 (1968)

23. Quinlan, S., Khatib, O.: Elastic bands: connecting path planning and control. In: IEEE International Conference on Robotics and Automation, Atlanta, USA, pp. 802–807 (1993)
24. Okal, B., Arras, K.O.: Learning socially normative robot navigation behaviors with Bayesian inverse reinforcement learning. In: IEEE International Conference on Robotics and Automation, Stockholm, Sweden, pp. 2889–2895 (2016)
25. Kim, B., Pineau, J.: Socially adaptive path planning in human environments using inverse reinforcement learning. Int. J. Soc. Robot. 8(1), 1–16 (2015)
26. Trautman, P., Krause, A.: Unfreezing the robot: navigation in dense, interacting crowds. In: IEEE/RSJ International Conference on Intelligent Robots and Systems, Taipei, Taiwan, pp. 797–803 (2010)

Research on Parallel Ant Colony Algorithm for 3D Terrain Path Planning

Miao Zhang[1(✉)], Zhiwen Jiang[1], Lihui Wang[2], and Yiping Yao[1]

[1] College of Information System and Management,
National University of Defense Technology,
137 Yanwachi, Changsha, Hunan, China
{zhangmiao15,jiangzhiwen,ypyao}@nudt.edu.cn
[2] AllSim Technology Inc., Gwangju, Korea
285311226@qq.com

Abstract. Ant colony algorithm can be used for the automatic path planning of complex terrain. However, most of the current ant colony algorithms are based on 2D terrain, without considering the influence of terrain slope on path selection. In addition, the parallelism of the algorithm is not used, which makes the algorithm time-consuming. Aiming at the above problems, this paper proposes an improved ant colony algorithm 3D-PACA. First of all, we raster the map using bilinear interpolation method and translate the 3D terrain into 2D terrain according to the given slope threshold. And then we combine OpenMP parallel programming technology to accelerate this algorithm by mining the concurrency of ant colony algorithm using the idea of parallel computing. The simulation results show that compared with the traditional ant colony algorithm, the improved algorithm can effectively adapt to the three-dimensional terrain, and can get a speedup of about 3 times.

Keywords: Ant colony algorithm · 3D terrain · Path planning · Parallel acceleration

1 Introduction

With the rapid development of the unmanned vehicle, path planning technology, as one of the key techniques for unmanned vehicle control system has received great attention [1]. Among the existing algorithms [2], ant colony algorithm proposed by Dorigo et al. provides a good solution for us. This algorithm searches for a feasible path by simulating the foraging process of many ants in the nature. However, current ant colony algorithm is mainly aimed at the two-dimensional terrain, without considering the influence of the slope. In practical applications, different human and different machines have different adaptability for a given topographic gradient. If we ignore the influence of the topography on the path during the path planning process, we may obtain an unavailable result. At the same time, the traditional ant colony algorithm has some shortcomings in dealing with complex path problems, such as the long calculation time.

Grid modeling is one of the commonly used techniques for modeling the map, which can be used to abstract the target area effectively. In this paper, we use bilinear

© Springer Nature Singapore Pte Ltd. 2017
M.S. Mohamed Ali et al. (Eds.): AsiaSim 2017, Part I, CCIS 751, pp. 74–82, 2017.
DOI: 10.1007/978-981-10-6463-0_7

interpolation to raster the map and deal with the influence of topography on the path by estimating the height of grid vertex and the midpoint of each side. By computing the gradients between each inflection point, we can integrate the gradient information into the ant routing process, when the three-dimensional problem would be transformed into two-dimensional problem. As the traditional ant colony algorithm is time-consuming, we use the idea of parallel computing to mine the concurrent natural in ant colony algorithm. Through combining with OpenMP technology in the process of programming, we improve the efficiency of the algorithm and get a speedup of about 3 times.

The structure of this paper is as follows: The Sect. 2 is related work. The Sect. 3 is the 3D-PACA (Parallel Ant Colony Algorithm for 3D) algorithm. The Sect. 4 is the comparative analysis of the simulation results of the algorithm. The Sect. 5 is the summary of the whole article.

2 Related Work

Since the ant colony algorithm proposed by Dorigo, the domestic and foreign scholars have done a lot of work to improve the algorithm. Stutzle et al. proposed a max min ant system algorithm [2] to prevent the premature phenomenon; Botee and Bonabeau studied deeply on combinatorial optimization [5] of the parameters in ant colony algorithm using genetic algorithm; Liu et al. adjusted the heuristic function according to the target position in order to improve the convergence speed [6]; Aiming at the premature and local optimum problem prone to the traditional ant colony algorithm, Pan et al. fused genetic factor [9] in ACA and used crossover and mutation operators to expand the search space of [7] the solution.

But at present, most of the work focused on the improvement of the ant colony algorithm and the selection of parameters, without taking into account how the algorithm can optimize the path under the condition of three-dimensional terrain. At the same time, they did not consider the use of the complexity of the ant colony algorithm itself and [4, 8] idle computer resources to accelerate the process of calculating. At the same time, the concurrency of the ant colony algorithm was not fully utilized.

3 Parallel Ant Colony Algorithm for 3D Terrain

In this paper, an improved ant colony algorithm is proposed, called 3D-PACA, which can be applied to 3D terrain. The algorithm is divided into two parts: map modeling and parallel optimization. The purpose of map modeling is to abstract the terrain and the obstacles existing in the region, and provide the data basis for the next path optimization. The purpose of parallel optimization is to exploit the natural concurrency of ant colony algorithm and accelerate the computation process. The algorithm flow is shown in Fig. 1.

As showing in Fig. 1: PNG file stores the elevation information. XML file stores the obstacle information. M refers to the number of ants. Nc refers to the maximum number of iterations and the other parameters in the algorithm are explained in the third section.

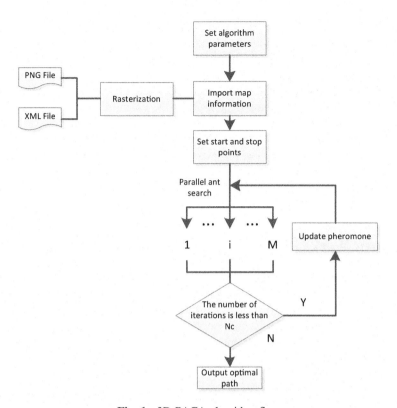

Fig. 1. 3D-PACA algorithm flow

3.1 3D Terrain Modeling Method

In the practical application of path planning, the terrain slope will have a great impact on the choice of path. Taking an unmanned vehicle as an example, it cannot cross a large mound slope or a big fissure. This puts forward a high demand for path planning in 3D Terrain.

For practical applications, we use PNG grayscale map to describe the terrain height and use XML documents to describe the distribution of trees and buildings. The adjacent pixels of PNG gray scale are sampled at 8 m, and the gray value of each pixel is from 0 to 255. 0 represents the actual lowest elevation of the region and 255 represents the actual highest point in the region above sea level.

In the process of map grid, we take each pixel as the center of the grid and label the grid from left to right, from top to bottom. The width of each grid is the sampling interval of the PNG file, that is, 8 m. The height of each pixel can be read from the PNG file, while the height of the four vertices of the grid cannot be read. In this paper, bilinear interpolation is used to approximate the height of the grid vertices and the edges.

As shown in Fig. 2, *A, B, C, D* are center points corresponding to the adjacent four grids and their heights are obtained from PNG file. In order to obtain the height of the

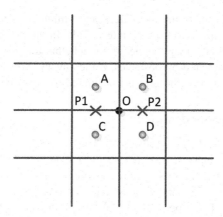

Fig. 2. Schematic diagram of bilinear interpolation

vertex O, we first need to use the linear interpolation method to obtain the height of the center point $P1$ of the AC segment and the height of the center point $P2$ of the BD segment. Calculating formulas are given as follows:

$$Height(P1) = (Height(A) + Height(C))/2 \tag{1}$$

$$Height(P2) = (Height(B) + Height(D))/2 \tag{2}$$

In the formula, $Height(P1)$ represents the height of the $P1$ point and the others are similar. Then the linear interpolation is used again to obtain the height of the center point O of the $P1P2$ segment.

$$Height(O) = (Height(P1) + Height(P2))/2 \tag{3}$$

After the completion of the map modeling process, it is necessary to introduce the information of the XML file into the map. In the XML file, trees are abstracted as cylindrical objects, and buildings are cuboids. The XML file format is shown in Fig. 3, where attributes X and Y represent the coordinates of the center of the building. The information of trees is similar.

```
<Info Z="9.1" Y="161.9" X="-97.7" radiusY="7.5" radiusX="19"/>
<Info Z="3.8" Y="110.3" X="-57.6" radiusY="7" radiusX="10"/>
<Info Z="3.1" Y="-26.6" X="35.3" radiusY="6.2 " radiusX="7.5"/>
<Info Z="9.1" Y="-95.5" X="74.2" radiusY="7.5" radiusX="19 "/>
<Info Z="7" Y="-157.4" X="112.7" radiusY="9.4" radiusX="23"/>
<Info Z="10" Y="-193.0" X="76.5" radiusY="14.3" radiusX="25"/>
<Info Z="10" Y="-226.5" X="14.3" radiusY="12.6" radiusX="28"/>
<Info Z="6.2" Y="-272.6" X="-65.7" radiusY="18.3" radiusX="18"/>
<Info Z="10" Y="-325.8" X="-142.3" radiusY="14.3" radiusX="25"/>
<Info Z="13" Y="-439.8" X="-273.8" radiusY="7.5" radiusX="19"/>
```

Fig. 3. Building information screenshot

In the XML file, the distribution of trees and buildings is without any rules and these obstacles may be not just in one or a few grids. In the process of introducing the obstacle information into the map, we determine whether the grid can be passed by the calculation of the area covered by obstacles. If the covered area of a grid is reached or exceeds 30% of the grid area, the grid is considered to be an obstacle grid.

3.2   Parallel Ant Colony Algorithm

The ACA algorithm proposed by Dorigo et al. is a random search algorithm which simulates the foraging behavior of ants in nature. The ants will choose the route of walking according to the pheromone left by foregoing ants. Based on the positive feedback mechanism and the parallel ability of the pheromone concentration, we can find an adoptable path. Traditional ant colony algorithm steps [2] are as follows:

ALGORITHM 1: Traditional ACA Algorithm

Initialize algorithm related parameters
While *number of iterations i* **is less than** *maximum number of iterations Nc,* **do**
        Generate M ants at the starting point
        For *k (k=1,2,...M),* **do**
            While *ant k* **does not reach the end and has an optional path,* **do**
                Calculate *the transition probability* $P_{ij}^k(t)$ according to *formula 4* and find *the next grid* to go
            End
                Record *the path of ant k* and *the length of the path*
            k=k+1
        End
        Update *the pheromone matrix* in accordance with *formula 5* and *formula 6*
End

Among them, $P_{ij}^k(t)$ represents the transition probability of ant k going to the neighboring grid j from the grid i at the time t. The calculation formula is as follows:

$$P_{ij}^k(t) = \begin{cases} \dfrac{\tau_{ij}^\alpha(t)\eta_{ij}^\beta(t)}{\sum_{s\in C}\tau_{is}^\alpha(t)\eta_{is}^\beta(t)} & j \in C \\ 0 & j \notin C \end{cases} \qquad (4)$$

In the formula,

$$\eta_{ij}(t) = \frac{1}{d_{ij}} \qquad (5)$$

$\tau_{ij}(t)$ is the pheromone value from grid i to j in the t iteration.
$\eta_{ij}(t)$ is the heuristic degree from grid i to j in the t iteration.
$d_{ij}(t)$ is the distance from grid i to grid j in the t iteration.
C is a set containing all the neighboring grids of grid i, in which each grid is accessible and has not been visited by ant k.

After one loop, the pheromone matrix is updated according to the following formulas.

$$\tau_{ij} = \rho\tau_{ij}(t) + \Delta\tau_{ij}(t, t+1) \tag{6}$$

$$\Delta\tau_{ij}(t, t+1) = \sum_{k \in V} \Delta\tau_{ij}^k(t, t+1) \tag{7}$$

$$\Delta\tau_{ij}^k(t, t+1) = \begin{cases} Q/L_k & (\text{ant } k \text{ passed}(i, j)) \\ 0 & (\text{ant } k \text{ did not pass}(i, j)) \end{cases} \tag{8}$$

In the above formula, Q is the total pheromone strength on the path left by the ant, and it can affect the convergence rate of the algorithm. L_k is the total length of path of ant k in this iteration.

V is a collection of ants that arrive at the end point.

When considering the effects of topography, ants need to not only consider whether the adjacent grid is obstacle grid or has been visited, but also consider whether the slope between current grid i to adjacent grid s exceeds the threshold. In Fig. 2, for example, B, C and D are adjacent to the current grid A. If the next grid is D, you must meet:

(1) D is accessible, that is, it is not the barrier grid.
(2) D has not been visited by current ant.
(3) The slope values of A-O and O-D are less than the given threshold value.

In the inner loop, M ants find the road independently based on pheromone and map information. There is no correlation between the ants and it is a highly concurrent behavior. The traditional ant colony algorithm is only a series of implementations of each routing process. In this paper, the idea of parallel computing is used to mine the natural concurrency of ant colony algorithm, and the OpenMP programming technology is introduced in the process of programming. OpenMP (Open Multi-Processing) is a technology that belongs to the shared memory programming model. Because of its advantages of simple structure, good portability, high scalability and support for parallel development, it has become the standard of parallel programming in shared memory system.

In the programming process in realizing the 3D-PACA algorithm, we use matrix τ_{ij} to characterize the pheromone between grid i and adjacent grid j. During an iterative process, each ant independently looks for the path, and determines the next step by reading the pheromone value and the map information. In the implementation of the operation to read the pheromone, it will not change its content, so it will not cause conflicts between the various threads access. Due to the randomness of the ants, some ants may end up in a dead end because of bad luck and end the search process early, while others will come to an end point after a lot of computation. If the thread is statically allocated to the task in parallel, the load is very likely to be unbalanced, which will affect the acceleration effect. To solve this problem, this paper uses the way of dynamic allocation. After the completion of the current task of each thread, they will get new tasks from the task pool, which can effectively avoid the problem of load imbalance.

4 Simulation Results and Analysis

In this paper, we use C++ programming language to implement the above algorithm on the VS2010 platform. The machine has 4 cores. In actual programming, we take the number of ants as 100, take the number of iterations as 10, take the slope threshold as 30°. A set of suitable values of other parameters of ant colony algorithm is found by using the control variable method. The specific values are as follows: the information elicitation factor is 1, the expected heuristic factor is taken as 8, the pheromone volatile factor is taken as 0.5, and the pheromone intensity is taken as 200. The map size is 100 × 100. The starting point is set to the upper left corner, and the end point is the lower right corner. The path planning results are shown in the following figure, where the black grid represents the obstruction and the white indicates the passage (Fig. 4).

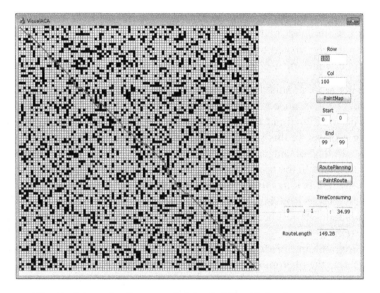

Fig. 4. Schematic diagram of path planning (Color figure online)

In the figure above, the red line is a feasible path based on the algorithm. It is obvious that the path is close to the connection between the starting point and the termination point. However, the planning time is too long, so it is necessary to introduce parallel. In the process of parallelization, we use the OpenMP statement to create 4 threads, and take 20 × 20, 50 × 50, 100 × 100, 200 × 200, 300 × 300 as the scale of the map. The corresponding time and acceleration ratio curves are as follows

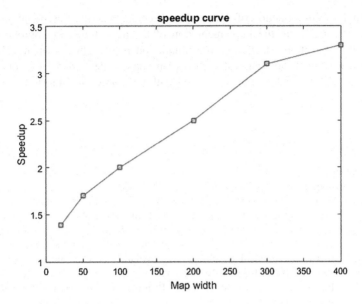

Fig. 5. Speedup curve

Table 1. Time comparison under different scales

Map scale	With parallelism/s	Without parallelism/s
20 × 20	5.18	3.71
50 × 50	46	27
100 × 100	181	95
200 × 200	840	336
300 × 300	2494	785
400 × 400	4177	1266

It can be seen from Table 1 and Fig. 5 that the parallel mechanism can significantly reduce the running time of the algorithm and improve the computing efficiency. At the same time, when the size of the map gradually increases, the cost of the time spent on the creation of the thread is gradually reduced and the acceleration ratio is slowly approaching 4. However, some parts of the algorithm can only be serially operated and the creation and destruction of the thread itself also takes time, so the speedup cannot reach 4.

5   Conclusions

In this paper, a modified ant colony algorithm (3D-PACA) is proposed and applied to 3D terrain. First of all, the bilinear interpolation method is used to model the 3D terrain, which provides the data base for the next step to deal with the terrain slope. At the same time, through the introduction of the parallel mechanism in the traditional ant colony algorithm, we accelerate the implementation of the algorithm and improve the efficiency of the algorithm effectively. The simulation results show that the 3D-PACA algorithm can be well applied to the path planning problem in 3D terrain, and can achieve speedup of about 3 times compared with the traditional algorithm.

References

1. Liu, C., Chang, J., Liu, C.: Path planning for mobile robot based on an improved probabilistic roadmap method. Chin. J. Electron. **18**(3), 395–399 (2009)
2. Dorigo, M., Maniezzo, V., Colorni, A.: Ant system: optimization by a colony of cooperating agents. IEEE Trans. Syst. Man Cybern. Part B (Cybern.) **26**(1), 29–41 (1996). doi:10.1109/3477.484436
3. Stutzle, T., Hoos, H.: MAX-MIN ant system and local search for the traveling salesman problem. In: IEEE International Conference on Evolutionary Computation, pp. 309–314. IEEE (1997). doi:10.1109/ICEC.1997.592327
4. Garcia, M.A.P., Montiel, O., Castillo, O., et al.: Path planning for autonomous mobile robot navigation with ant colony optimization and fuzzy cost function evaluation. Applied Soft Comput. **9**(3), 1102–1110 (2009). doi:10.1016/j.asoc.2009.02.014
5. Botee, H.M., Bonabeau, E.: Evolving ant colony optimization. Adv. Complex Syst. **1**(02n03), 149–159 (1998). doi:10.1142/S0219525998000119
6. Liu, C.A., Yan, X.H., Liu, C.Y., et al.: Dynamic path planning for mobile robot based on improved ant colony optimization algorithm. Acta Electron. Sin. **5**, 042 (2011)
7. Pan, J., Wang, X.S., Cheng, Y.H.: Improved ant colony algorithm for mobile robot path planning. Zhongguo Kuangye Daxue Xuebao (J. China Univ. Min. Technol.) **41**(1), 108–113 (2012)
8. Lim, K.K., Ong, Y.S., Lim, M.H., et al.: Hybrid ant colony algorithms for path planning in sparse graphs. Soft Comput. **12**(10), 981–994 (2008). doi:10.1007/s00500-007-0264-x
9. Xing, H., Pan, W., Zou, X.: A novel improved quantum genetic algorithm for combinatorial optimization problems. Acta Electron. Sin. **35**(10), 1999 (2007)

Cooperative PSOGSA Using Multiple Groups Approach for Functions Optimization

Zakariah Yusuf, Norhaliza Abdul Wahab$^{(\boxtimes)}$,
and Shafishuhaza Sahlan

Department of Control and Mechatronic Engineering,
Faculty of Electrical Engineering,
Universiti Teknologi Malaysia, 81310 Skudai, Johor, Malaysia
zakariah2@live.utm.my, {aliza, shafis}@fke.utm.my

Abstract. This paper presents the development and application of hybrid particle swarm optimization and gravitational search algorithm (PSOGSA) using cooperative technique (CPSOGSA). In this work, the algorithm is used for functions optimization problem. The CPSOGSA is developed with multiple groups using master-slave architecture. Six benchmark functions were tested to verify the effectiveness of the optimization algorithm. The developed algorithm was compared with the existing PSO, GSA and hybrid PSOGSA. The results indicate that the proposed technique produces better optimization solution compared to the conventional optimization algorithms.

Keywords: PSO · GSA · PSOGSA · Cooperative · Optimization · Functions

1 Introduction

In recent years many heuristic optimization algorithms were created based on the nature characteristic. These algorithms are become more attractive because its ability to solve many optimization problems. There are several well-known algorithms reported on the successful implementation of the heuristic optimization technique.

Particle swarm optimization (PSO) is well-known heuristic optimization technique. PSO algorithm is a proven technique to solve optimization problem in many fields. This algorithm originally was developed in [1], however the algorithm had some problem in balancing the exploration and exploitation capability. Since then, many modification of the algorithm have been made by researchers to enhance the PSO capability.

Gravitational search algorithm (GSA) [2] is another optimization algorithm that getting more attention in solving many optimization problems. This algorithm was inspired from the gravitational theory in space that attracted to each other. The Recently, many works were done to improve GSA algorithm such as in [3–5]. The combination of hybrid approach of GSA with other algorithms is among the best option to consider from various researchers. Khadanga and Satapathy [6] developed a hybrid GSA with GA algorithm to improve the original GSA technique. The authors applied the algorithm to tune the controller damping in a power system application.

© Springer Nature Singapore Pte Ltd. 2017
M.S. Mohamed Ali et al. (Eds.): AsiaSim 2017, Part I, CCIS 751, pp. 83–96, 2017.
DOI: 10.1007/978-981-10-6463-0_8

Work by Mirjalili et al. [7] investigated the application of hybrid PSO and GSA (PSOGSA) to train the feed forward neural network (FFNN). The authors find out the hybrid method can relatively give better solution compared with PSO and GSA individually. Mirjalili and Hashim in [8] compared the PSOGSA, PSO and GSA for optimized the benchmark functions. The propose PSOGSA is able to improve most of the functions minimization compared with the PSO and GSA.

Jayaprakasam et al. [9] proposed PSOGSA with new updated velocity equation which applied to beam pattern optimization in collaborative beam forming. The authors claim that their approach provides more explorative capability of the algorithm when combining the social thinking ability of PSO and the explorative capability of GSA.

This work presents the improvement of PSOGSA algorithm using the master –slave cooperative approach. The slaves are divided into a few groups and the best slave performance will have the opportunity to assist the master group. The equation for the master group is also proposed.

The organization of the paper as follow: In Sect. 2, the existing PSO and GSA algorithm is presented. Section 3 explains the development of the cooperative PSOGSA (CPSOGSA). Section 4 is where the optimization functions are explicated. The next section is the result and discussion of the finding. Finally, Sect. 5 is presents the conclusion of the paper.

2 Optimization Algorithm

2.1 Particle Swarm Optimization

The PSO used a linear function of weight in the velocity equation. The velocity $V_{id,}$ equation is presented in Eq. (1) where C_1 and C_2 are the constant, while *gBest* and *pBest* are the personal and global best solution respectively.

$$V_{id}(t+1) = wV_{id}(t) + C_1(pBest - X_{id}) \times rand_1 + C_2(gBest - X_{id}) \times rand_2 \quad (1)$$

The positions X_{id} update equation is given by:

$$X_{id}(t+1) = X_{id}(t) + V_{id} \quad (2)$$

The inertia weight w is represent by liner equation

$$w = (w_o - w_1)(max\_iter - iteration/iteration) + w_1 \quad (3)$$

where w_o is the initial weight, w_1 is the value of final weight, *max_iter* is the maximum iteration.

2.2 Gravitational Search Algorithm (GSA)

The algorithm system consists of N agent where the position of the agent is represented by Eq. (5)

$$X_i = \left(x_i^1, \ldots, x_i^d, \ldots, x_i^n\right), i = 1, 2, \ldots, N.$$ (4)

where x_i^d represents the ith agent in the dth dimensions. Equation (6) represents the force acting on mass i from mass j.

$$F_{ij}^d(t) = G(t)\left(\left(M_{pi}(t) \times M_{aj}(t)/R_{ij}(t) + \varepsilon\right)\right)\left(x_j^d(t) - x_i^d(t)\right)$$ (5)

where M_{aj} is the active gravitational mass related to agent j, M_{pi} is the passive gravitational mass related to agent i, $G(t)$ is agravitational constant at time t, ε is a small constant, and $Rij(t)$ is the Euclidian distance between two agents i and j.

$$R_{ij}(t) = \left\|X_i(t), X_j(t)\right\|_2$$ (6)

The total force on agent i is represents in Eq. (8).

$$F_i^d(t) = \sum_{j=1, j \neq 1}^{N} rand_j\, F_{ij}^d(t)$$ (7)

where $rand$ is the random function from 0 to 1. The acceleration of the agent i, is given by Eq. (8). $M_{ij}(t)$ is the inertial mass of agent ith.

$$\alpha_i^d(t) = F_i^d(t)/M_{ij}(t)$$ (8)

The velocity update of the agent is calculated from Eq. (9) where the updated velocity is obtained from current velocity multiply with random number 0 to 1 added with the mass.

$$V_i^d(t+1) = rand_i \times V_i^d(t) + \alpha_i^d(t)$$ (9)

Therefore, the position of the agent can be calculated using Eq. (10).

$$X_i^d(t+1) = X_i^d(t) + V_i^d(t+1)$$ (10)

The gravitational and inertial masses of the algorithm are updated using Eqs. (11) and (12).

$$M_{ai} = M_{pi} = M_{ii} = M_i, i = 1, 2, \ldots, N.$$

$$m_i(t) = fit_i(t) - worst_i(t)/best(t) + worst(t)$$ (11)

$$M_i(t) = m_i(t) / \sum_{j=1}^{N} m_j(t) \tag{12}$$

The fit_i (t) represent the fitness value of agent i at time t. For minimization problem the $best(t)$ and $worst(t)$ are calculated as follow:

$$best(t) = min_{j \in \{1,...,N\}} fit_j(t) \tag{13}$$

$$worst(t) = max_{j \in \{1,...,N\}} fit_j(t) \tag{14}$$

2.3 Hybrid PSOGSA

Hybrid PSOGSA optimization technique developed by Mirjalili and Hashim [8] has shown great improvement over the existing PSO and GSA in minimizing mathematical functions. The algorithm improves exploration and the exploitation capability in the evolvement equation where the best solution position is included in the velocity update equation. In hybrid PSOGSA optimization technique the velocity update equation is given by (15).

$$V(t+1) = wV(t) + c_1 rand_1 \, ac_i(t) + c_2(gBest - X_i(t))rand_2 \tag{15}$$

Position update for the PSOGSA is given by:

$$X_i(t+1) = X_i(t) + V(t+1) \tag{16}$$

3 Cooperative PSOGSA (CPSOGSA)

Decentralize cooperative technique has shown successful implementation in improvised the PSO algorithm [10]. The proposed CPSOGSA the fundamental approach of the algorithm allows more groups with different advantages to search for the best solution. Each of the groups can adopt any velocity update equations. The cooperative technique in this work is described by the interaction between master and slaves. The number of slave groups can be generated accordingly depending on the complexity of the optimization problem. Figure 1 shows the relation between master and slave

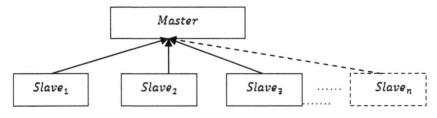

Fig. 1. CPSOGSA architecture

groups. Each of the slave groups will look for the best fitness and this fitness value will be compared among the slave group. The best fitness of the slave group will be compared again with the master group and the best fitness agent will be utilized for the velocity update calculation using Eq. (17).

The proposed master group velocity update equation is given by:

$$V_M(t+1) = wV_M(t)\ rand_1 + C_1\ a\ rand_2 + C_2\ \beta_1(gBest_{Slave} - X_{id})\ rand_3$$
$$+ C_3\ \beta_2(gBest_{Master} - X_{id}) \times rand_4 \tag{17}$$

Thus, the position of the master group is updated using:

$$X_M(t+1) = X_M(t) + V_M(t+1) \tag{18}$$

The competitive between the slave and the master which adopted in [10] is also applied in this algorithm, where the pseudo code of the algorithm are:

> **If** $(gBest_{Slave} > gBest_{Master})$
> $\beta_1 = 1, \beta_2 = 0;$
> **elseif** $(gBest_{Slave} < gBest_{Master})$
> $\beta_2 = 0, \beta_2 = 1;$
> **elseif** $(gBest_{Slave} = gBest_{Master})$
> $\beta_1 = 0.5, \beta_2 = 0.5;$
> **end**

The proposed framework of CPSOGSA can be described as the following steps:

Step 1. Initialize the population of the slave and master groups position.
Step 2. Evaluate the current fitness of the agents.
Step 3. Find the personal best and worst in each of the groups.
Step 4. Find β_1 and β_2 using competitive algorithm.
Step 5. Calculate and for groups with M and α using Eqs. (8) and (12).
Step 6. Update velocity and position for all groups with master group by using Eqs. (17) and (18).
Step 7. Compare if meet the optimization criteria. If not, return to step 2
Step 8. Return to the best solution.

In this work, two slave groups are used in the functions optimization. The first slave group is the GSA algorithm while the second slave group is used PSO algorithm.

4 Functions

In this work six benchmark functions were used to test the optimization algorithm. Each of the function has different difficulty and complexity. The functions also have been used in many optimization algorithm testing performance such as in [8, 11]. The dimensions for F_1 to F_4 are 30, while F_5 and F_6 are 4.

$$F_1(X) = \sum_{i=1}^{n} X_{i=1}^2 \tag{19}$$

$$F_2(X) = \sum_{i=1}^{n-1} \left[100(X_{i+1} - X_i^2)^2 + (X_i - 1)^2 \right] \tag{20}$$

$$F_3(X) = \sum_{i=1}^{n} \left[X_i^2 - 10\cos(2\pi X_i) + 10 \right] \tag{21}$$

$$F_4(X) = -20\exp\left(-0.2\sqrt{\frac{1}{n}\sum_{i=1}^{n} X^2}\right) - \exp\left(\frac{1}{n}\sum_{i=1}^{n}\cos(2\pi X_i)\right) + 20 + e \tag{22}$$

$$F_5 = \sum_{i=1}^{11} \left[a_i - \frac{x_1(b_i^2 + b_i x_2)}{b_i^2 + b_i x_3 + x_4} \right]^2 \tag{23}$$

$$F_6(X) = -\sum_{i=1}^{5} \left[(X - a_i)(X - a_i)^T + C_i \right]^{-1} \tag{24}$$

The iterations for the functions optimization are set to 1000 except for F_5 and F_6 where the iterations are set to 500. All functions (F_1–F_6) have a minimum value of 0 except for F_5 and F_6 where the minimum value are at 0.0003075 and -10 respectively. The functions are optimized with 10 independent runs.

5 Results and Discussion

The functions are tested by ten independent runs of the algorithms which are GSA, PSO, POGA and the proposed CPSOGSA. Generally, CPSOGSA algorithm performs better compared with others optimization method. The CPSOGSA algorithm produces the best result in all functions tested. Table 1 presents the full optimization results in term of its best, worst and average performances.

Table 1. Function optimization result

Func.	Algorithm	Average	Best	Worst
F1	GSA	2.5050e−17	1.7800e−17	3.1067e−17
	PSO	3.8600e−16	2.4320e−18	1.0700e−13
	PSOGSA	1.1979e−18	2.5745e−20	4.9519e−17
	CPSOGSA	**2.2165e−24**	**1.8697e−24**	**2.6935e−24**

(*continued*)

Table 1. (*continued*)

Func.	Algorithm	Average	Best	Worst
F2	GSA	26.4362	25.8364	28.1328
	PSO	49.2527	20.2521	133.8378
	PSOGSA	36.5722	24.2744	80.9237
	CPSOGSA	**13.9923**	**2.6541**	**19.4269**
F3	GSA	13.9318	13.4000	14.5000
	PSO	24.1035	10.9445	55.3184
	PSOGSA	22.4851	12.9345	28.8538
	CPSOGSA	**8.5569**	**2.9849**	**9.9496**
F4	GSA	3.5909e−9	3.8820e−9	3.8528e−9
	PSO	6.1121e−9	1.4113e−9	6.2568e−9
	PSOGSA	6.7992e−9	5.5301e−9	9.8094e−9
	CPSOGSA	**4.9048e−10**	**3.3755e−10**	**7.9484e−10**
F5	GSA	0.0044	0.0015	0.0067
	PSO	3.981e−4	**3.0750e−4**	3.3094e−4
	PSOGSA	4.343e−4	3.0707e−4	5.5090e−4
	CPSOGSA	**3.0706e−4**	**3.0750e−4**	**3.0800e−4**
F6	GSA	−6.4066	**−10.1532**	−2.6829
	PSO	−4.5893	−5.0552	−2.6828
	PSOGSA	−5.7686	**−10.1532**	−5.0552
	CPSOGSA	**−10.1532**	**−10.1531**	**−10.1532**

F1 minimization result it shows that the CPSOGSA perform far better that other tested optimization techniques. Comparison between with other techniques indicate that the CPSOGSA perform better with the best result is at 1.8697e−24. The average performance in minimizing F1 for CPSOGSA is at 2.2165e−24. The worst performance of CPSOGSA is at 2.6935e−24. The second best performance is the PSOGSA where the best performance is at 2.5745e−20, average is at 1.1979e−18 and worst is at 4.9519e−17. Figure 2 shows the convergent curve of the F1 minimization for all algorithms. In F1 minimization, the third best performance is given by the standard GSA followed by PSO algorithm.

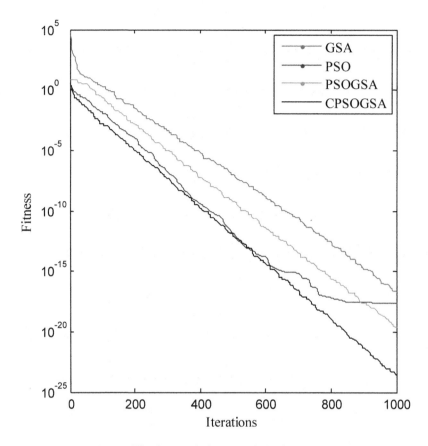

Fig. 2. Result for F_1 optimization

F2 minimization also indicates the CPSOGSA algorithms outperform the benchmark existing standard algorithms. The CPSOGSA algorithm performs best performance is at 2.654, the worst performance at 19.42 and average performance of this algorithm is at 13.9923. This performance is much better compared with the PSO, PSOGSA and GSA where the best performance is given by 17.2521, 24.2744 and 25.8364 respectively. Figure 3 shows the minimization performance from all algorithms.

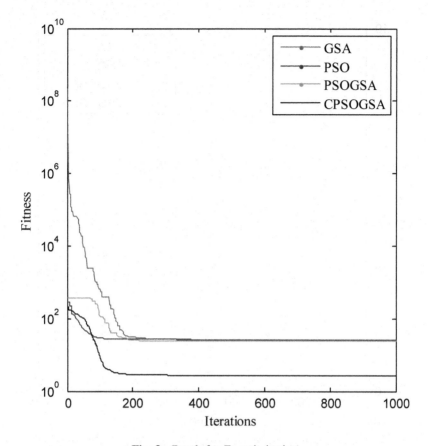

Fig. 3. Result for F_2 optimization

F3 function minimization indicate small different between the best performance of CPSOGSA and PSO after 10 independent runs. The best performance of CPSOGSA is at 2.9849 while the PSO is at 10.9445. The CPSOGSA also exhibits more consistent performance compare with the PSO. The average performance of CPSOGSA is 8.5569 and PSO is at 24.1035. Figure 4 presents the performance of F3 minimization performance after 10 runs.

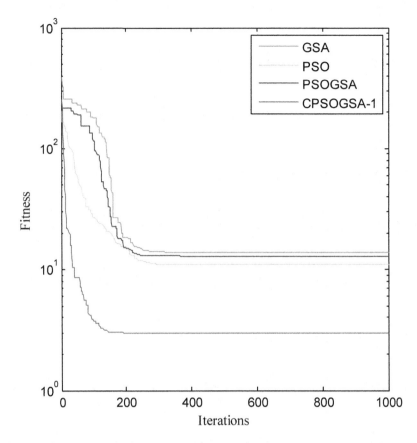

Fig. 4. Result for F_3 optimization

From the F4 minimization results, it can be observed the similar performances were achieved by the conventional PSO, GSA and PSOGSA. The best results from these three algorithms are at 1.4113e−9, 1.4113e−9 and 5.5301e−9 respectively. The proposed CPSOGSA shows better performance with the best result is at 3.3755e−10. The average and worst results are at 4.9048e−10 and 7.9484e−10 respectively. Figure 5 presents the minimization result for F6 function for all algorithms.

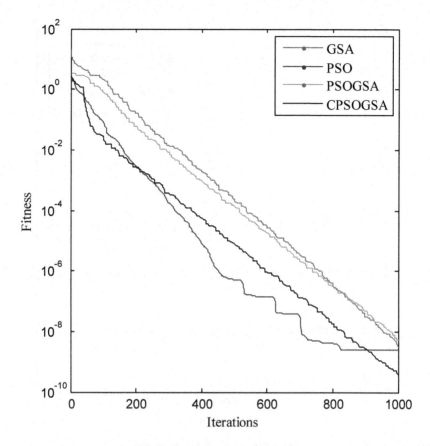

Fig. 5. Result for F_4 optimization

Performance of F5 minimization indicates that, three algorithms achieved the minimum fitness which are CPSOGSA, PSOGSA and PSO algorithm. This best result is achieved by CPSOGSA with 3.0750e−4; average performance is at 3.0786e−4 while the worst result is at 3.0800e−4. Figure 6 shows the minimization performance of F5 function.

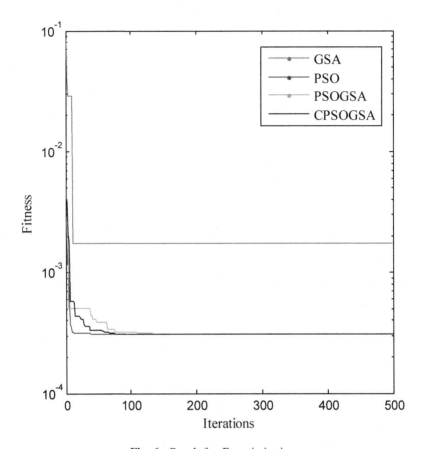

Fig. 6. Result for F_5 optimization

Result for F6 optimization shows three algorithms can achieve the minimum value which is 10.153. The algorithms are CPSOGSA, GSA and PSOGSA. From 10 runs, the results indicate the CPSOGSA can achieve minimum result for all 10 runs compare with the PSO and PSOGSA. The average result for PSO and PSOGSA are −5.7686 and −6.4066 while the CPSOGSA is at −10.1532. Figure 7 shows the minimization performance for all the algorithms.

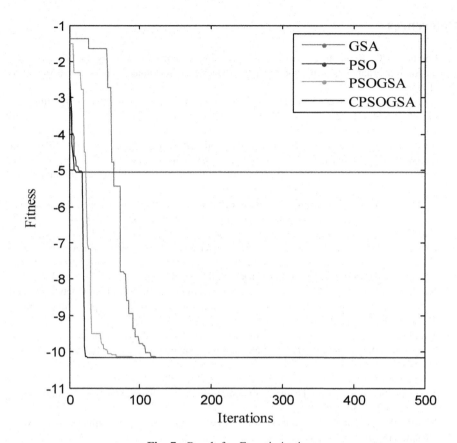

Fig. 7. Result for F_6 optimization

6 Conclusion

This paper presents the cooperative PSOGSA (CPSOGSA) in optimizing the mathematical functions. The algorithm adopted master-slave cooperative technique. In this work, PSO and GSA are used in the slave group. The results showed the proposed algorithm is able to improve the optimization result compared with the existing GSA, PSO and PSOGSA.

Acknowledgments. The authors would like to thank the Research University Grant (GUP) vote 13H70, Universiti Teknologi Malaysia for the financial support. The first author wants to thank the Universiti Teknologi MARA (UiTM) and the MOHE for the TPM-SLAI scholarship.

References

1. Eberhart, R.C., Kennedy, J.: A new optimizer using particle swarm theory. In: Proceedings of the Sixth International Symposium on Micro Machine and Human Science, vol. 1, pp. 39–43 (1995)
2. Rashedi, E., Nezamabadi-Pour, H., Saryazdi, S.: GSA: a gravitational search algorithm. Inf. Sci. (Ny) **179**(13), 2232–2248 (2009)
3. Jadidi, Z., Muthukkumarasamy, V., Sithirasenan, E., Sheikhan, M.: Flow-based anomaly detection using neural network optimized with GSA algorithm. In: 2013 IEEE 33rd International Conference Distributed Computing Systems Workshops, pp. 76–81, July 2013
4. Sarafrazi, S., Nezamabadi-Pour, H., Saryazdi, S.: Disruption: a new operator in gravitational search algorithm. Sci. Iran. **18**(3), 539–548 (2011)
5. Niu, P., Liu, C., Li, P.: Optimized support vector regression model by improved gravitational search algorithm for flatness pattern recognition. Neural Comput. Appl. **26**, 1167–1177 (2015)
6. Khadanga, R.K., Satapathy, J.K.: Electrical power and energy systems a new hybrid GA – GSA algorithm for tuning damping controller parameters for a unified power flow controller. Int. J. Electr. Power Energy Syst. **73**, 1060–1069 (2015)
7. Mirjalili, S., Hashim, S.Z.M., Sardroudi, H.M.: Training feedforward neural networks using hybrid particle swarm optimization and gravitational search algorithm. Appl. Math. Comput. **218**(22), 11125–11137 (2012)
8. Mirjalili, S., Hashim, S.Z.M.: A new hybrid PSOGSA algorithm for function optimization. In: International Conference on Computer and Information Application (ICCIA 2010), no. 1, pp. 374–377 (2010)
9. Jayaprakasam, S., Rahim, S.K.A., Leow, C.Y.: PSOGSA-Explore: a new hybrid metaheuristic approach for beampattern optimization in collaborative beamforming. Appl. Soft Comput. J. **30**, 229–237 (2015)
10. Niu, B., Wu, H.: MCPSO: a multi-swarm cooperative particle swarm optimizer. Appl. Math. Comput. **185**, 1050–1062 (2007)
11. Yao, X., Liu, Y., Lin, G.: Evolutionary programming made faster. IEEE Trans. Evol. Comput. **3**(2), 82–102 (1999)

A Proposed Framework for Massive MIMO Simulation Platform - 5G Systems

Olakunle Elijah$^{(\boxtimes)}$, Tharek Abdul Rahman, and Chee Yen Leow

Wireless Communication Center, Universiti Teknologi Malaysia (UTM),
81310 Johor Bahru, Malaysia
elij_olak@yahoo.com, {tharek,bruceleow}@fke.utm.my

Abstract. The study on 5G massive MIMO (maMIMO) systems has garnered a
lot of research interest. Several research works are ongoing and some of which
include, the development of mathematical models, performance evaluation,
algorithm development and basic prototyping work. However, the framework
for a unified simulation platform and methodology has not been established. The
need for a massive MIMO simulation platform that can be used for comparative
study and analysis purpose of different deployment scenarios of maMIMO
systems is envisaged. Hence, in this paper, a framework for massive MIMO
simulation platform (MMSP) for 5G cellular systems is proposed. To achieve
this, key research areas related to massive MIMO were identified from the
literature and a taxonomy which consists of three non-overlapping branches:
(1) System configuration, (2) System processing and (3) System analysis is
advocated. Preliminary results are presented using a developed prototype from
the proposed framework.

Keywords: 5G · Framework · Massive MIMO · Spectral efficiency ·
Simulation · Software tools

1 Introduction

The drive for increased capacity in wireless communications required to meet the
increasing demand for mobile wireless data has made massive multiple-input multiple
output (maMIMO) of great interest to researchers both in the academia and industry.
The maMIMO is a communication system where base station (BS) with a few hundred
arrays of active antennas simultaneously serves many tens of user terminals (UTs) with
lower number of antennas in the same time-frequency resource. See Fig. 1. The
maMIMO technology is an enabler for the development of future broadband (fixed and
mobile) networks, which will be energy-efficient, secure, robust, and will allow for
efficient utilization of the spectrum [1, 2]. The benefits of maMIMO have been discussed in detail in [3, 4]. In order to ascertain the potential of maMIMO systems,
several algorithms, analysis and performance evaluations, mathematical models based
on different scenarios, basic prototyping work have been widely carried out which
include the testbed jointly developed by Linköping University and Lund University [1],
a flexible 100-antenna testbed for maMIMO developed by Lund University [5],

© Springer Nature Singapore Pte Ltd. 2017
M.S. Mohamed Ali et al. (Eds.): AsiaSim 2017, Part I, CCIS 751, pp. 97–108, 2017.
DOI: 10.1007/978-981-10-6463-0_9

the Argos testbed developed at Rice University in cooperation with Alcatel-Lucent [6], and the Ngara testbed developed in Australia [7].

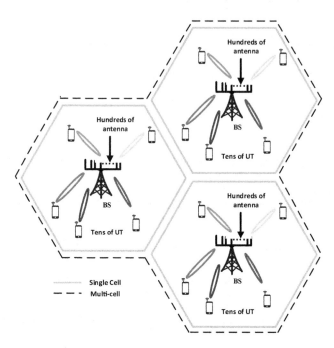

Fig. 1. Illustration of massive MIMO systems

The research areas regarding maMIMO systems include, but not limited to, propagation and measurement campaign, transmitter and receiver designs, pilot contamination, pilot allocation, spectral and energy efficiency, frequency spectrum, transmission and new air interfaces, backhauling and user association, security, mobility, and wireless energy transfer. Currently, there are no specified standards for maMIMO systems but as the work in maMIMO systems advances, there is a need for conceptual framework for a common simulation platform which can be used for comparative study and analysis purposes.

Simulations have been used extensively as an engineering tool for design, modelling and optimization of radio networks. Simulations enable investigations of much more complex, detailed and realistic scenarios, and facilitate comparison of different algorithms under identical conditions. Some simulation tools are identified in this paper, and a summary of their functions and limitations are presented. From our survey, there exists no simulation platform that accounts for all design aspect for research areas for maMIMO systems. The existing simulation platforms which are potential candidate for 5G system simulations identified are: the NYU open source 5G channel simulation software (NYUSIM), the Vienna LTE simulators (VLS), SystemVue, LTE system toolbox and LTE PHY Lab.

The NYUSIM [8] is a 5G channel simulation tool that covers extensive measurements and 5G millimeter wave channel models developed from 2 to 73 GHz. It consists of a complete statistical channel model and simulation code for generating realistic spatial and temporal wideband channel impulse responses. The VLS which is a simulation suite for link-level and system-level simulation aims to facilitate reproducibility of research results and to bridge the gap between researchers and standardization experts in LTE and LTE-Advance (LTE-A) [9]. Currently, the VLS can only support 4G systems simulations. SystemVue, a product of KEYSIGHT technologies, is a focused electronic design automation (EDA) environment for electronic system-level (ESL) design. It enables system architects and algorithm developers to innovate the physical layer (PHY) of wireless and aerospace/defense communications systems and is an invaluable tool to RF, DSP, and FPGA/ASIC implementers [10]. SystemVue consists of the 5G baseband exploration library and 5G forward baseband verification bundles, both of which are targeting to assist pre-5G investigations and research. This simulation tools are limited to specific research areas and can only be used to simulate certain aspects of physical level of maMIMO systems. However, there is a need for a platform that can be used to investigate and simulate different deployment scenarios of maMIMO systems especially at system levels. In view of this, we propose a simplified framework that can be used to develop a massive MIMO simulation platform that aims to reduce cost, time and provide a means to comparative analyses of different deployment scenarios of maMIMO technologies in 5G network.

Our major task in this paper is to establish a unified framework for simulation platform for maMIMO systems. To define the framework, first, an extensive survey of published works in maMIMO systems was carried out. Secondly, based on our survey, we categorize the research work into major areas. In addition, we propose a taxonomy which could serve as a framework that accounts for all design aspects of the MMSP. The advocated taxonomy consists of three non-overlapping branches: (1) System configuration, (2) System processing and (3) System analysis. This article also highlights the modules in the framework for system simulation and features of MMSP. Finally, we provide simulated results of possible case studies using the proposed MMSP.

The rest of this paper is organized as follows: Sect. 2 identifies the existing massive MIMO technologies, the taxonomy used in developing the framework for MMSP and key features of the proposed platform is discussed. Section 3 covers the prototype of the MMSP. In Sect. 4, the simulated results and analysis is presented. Section 5 concludes this paper.

2 Proposed Framework

In this section, the process for establishing a unified framework for a common simulation platform for maMIMO systems is presented. First, we identify the research areas in maMIMO technologies. Then the framework for a massive MIMO simulation platform (MMSP) is presented.

2.1 Massive MIMO Technology

The massive MIMO technology has attracted a lot of research interest and vast research area has been investigated. A survey of advances in massive MIMO technology was carried out to establish the key research areas. They included but not limited to, propagation and measurement campaign [6]; transmitter and receiver designs [7]; pilot contamination [11]; spectral and energy efficiency [12]; frequency spectrum – millimeter wave [13]; new air interfaces such as multiple access techniques (example, non-orthogonal multiple access) and various waveforms (examples, filter-bank based multi-carrier [14]); backhauling and user association [15]; security [16]; mobility [17]; and wireless energy transfer [18]. The details of our survey on these research areas are outside the scope of this paper. Each of these research areas requires extensive simulations for investigation of much more complex, detailed and realistic scenarios and to facilitate comparison of different algorithms under identical conditions.

2.2 Proposed Taxonomy

We develop a taxonomy, which could serve as a framework that accounts for all design aspects of the simulation platform and may be used for evaluating and simulating the performance of maMIMO systems. A high level abstraction of the top-down design systems is shown in Fig. 2. It illustrates the advocated taxonomy, which consists of three non-overlapping branches: (1) System configuration, (2) System processing and (3) System analysis.

System Configuration: The system configuration defines all the tuneable parameters that are needed for the maMIMO systems. The parameters can be selected based on the areas of maMIMO to be studied. We classify the systems configurations based on the following: simulation parameter, network topology, network distribution, transceiver design, transmission mode and user association. This system configuration abstraction allows for researchers to study the performance of maMIMO systems based on different system parameters and different scenarios.

System Process: The system process abstraction provides an avenue for researchers to engage with the system. At this level, the behaviour of the maMIMO systems can be explored under certain conditions such as the effect of pilot contamination, physical layer attacks and mobility of UT. In addition, measured data from propagation or prototypes can be imported into the system and analysed. New algorithms can be developed and compared with existing algorithms in the platform. In addition, the different optimization techniques can be explored using the MMSP.

System Analysis: In the system analysis, the performance of the maMIMO system can be evaluated based on selected metrics. This enables the users of the proposed platform to investigate how the system performs under certain preselected or defined scenarios. Key metrics are needed to access the performance of maMIMO systems. The system capacity, achievable rates, energy efficiency, energy efficiency and other performance metrics such as outage/coverage probability, QoS, and fairness [21] can be examined

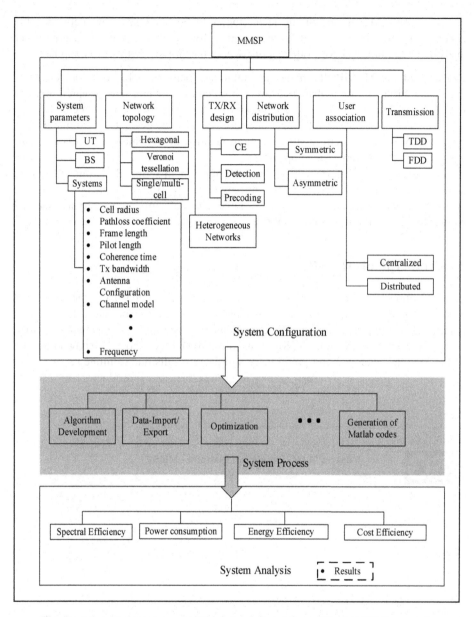

Fig. 2. Advocated taxonomy and high-level abstraction of the MMSP framework

using established information theory. In addition, the cost efficiency of deploying certain maMIMO technology can be compared as this would be useful not only to researchers but also to the industry.

Since maMIMO is one of the technologies to be featured in 5G networks, the results from the MMSP should be presented in formats that can be used for further analysis in combination with other 5G networks technology (where it is applicable).

Features of the MMSP: To make the simulation platform achieve its objectives of enabling reproducibility, enhancing research outcome, opening new research areas in maMIMO and engaging researchers, certain features need to be implemented in the platform. These includes graphic user interface (GUI), code generation and integration, parallel processing, system level simulation, detailed documentation, validation, cost analysis and collaborative development.

In addition, the platform will allow integration of m-script files from other open source simulations tools. Example, the investigation of performance analyses using the channel models from the NYU open source channel simulation software can be incorporated into the proposed platform.

3 Prototype of MMSP

In this section, we show example of use case scenario studied using the advocated MMSP. There are several scenarios in maMIMO which can be simulated such as spectral efficiency, the effect of pilot contamination, the effect of propagation factors, energy efficiency, and various deployments of maMIMO scenarios. We show prototype of the MMSP developed and preliminary simulated results due to limited space.

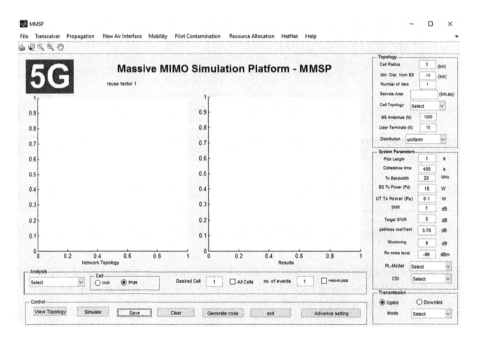

Fig. 3. Screen shot of the MMSP prototype

3.1 Graphic User Interface

The graphic user interface is developed to allow for simulations, selection and configuration of different system parameters. To achieve this, we developed a graphic user interface for the MMSP using Matlab 2014a. The Guide toolbox was used to design the layout of the system according to the system specification and requirements. Figure 3 shows the screen shot of the prototype.

The GUI allows user to select different systems parameters, simulate and visualize results. Example is selection of network topology i.e. distribution of UT and BS in either deterministic cells (hexagonal cells) or irregular cells (using poison point process). The prototype of the GUI in Fig. 3 consists of two axes that enable viewing of

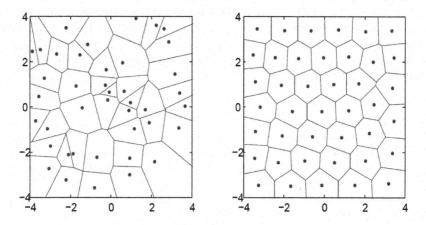

(a) BS in Voronoi tessellations cells (left) and BS in centroid of the cell using llyods algorithm (right)

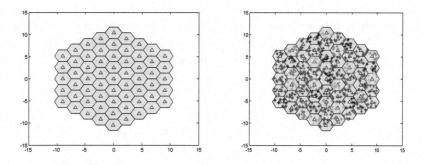

(b) BS in hexagonal cellular cells (left) and BS with UTs in hexagonal cellular (right)

Fig. 4. Example of network topology

the distribution of user terminals and mobile base stations, and results of performance analysis. There are panels that consist of the systems configurations parameters, and buttons that support different functions such as generation of m-script codes, advance settings, save, selection of different topologies and selection of different types of performance analysis as shown in Fig. 2. Due to limited space, the details and codes of this prototype are excluded from this paper but we hope to make it available in the future publication.

3.2 Network Topology

The different topology of the distributions of user terminals and base station can be explored using the proposed platform. Example in Fig. 4, the distribution of base station is presented. Figure 4(a-left) shows the Voronoi tessellation of point process for random distributed BS within a service area and Fig. 4(a-right) shows the BS placed in the center of the Voronoi cells using Llyod's method [19]. Figure 4(b-left) shows the distribution of BS in a hexagonal cell while Fig. 4(b-right) shows the distribution of BS and UTs in the hexagonal cell.

4 Simulated Results

In this section, the performance of the maMIMO systems using the developed prototype is presented. The system model and some simulated results are shown.

4.1 System Model

The system encompasses arbitrary UT location and distance-dependent pathloss, and considers varying number of UTs in each cell within a multi-cell system where each cell is assigned an index within a set $\mathcal{L}$, where the cardinality $|\mathcal{L}|$ is the number of cells. Each cell has a BS which is equipped with array of M active antennas and communicates with K UTs with single antennas. The UTs are distributed randomly in its serving cell $l \in \mathcal{L}$ with geographical position $\boldsymbol{b}_{lk} \in \mathbb{R}^2$ of UT $k \in \{1, \ldots, K\}$. The time-frequency resources are divided into frames with coherence time T_c and coherence bandwidth W_c. The coherence interval τ_c has the length $\tau_c = T_c W_c$. The uplink spectral efficiency for the multi-cell can be expressed as

$$\mathbf{y}_l^{(up)} = \sum_{l \in \mathcal{L}} \sum_{k=1}^{K} \sqrt{p_{u,lk}} \, \mathbf{h}_{lk} s_{lk} + \mathbf{n}_l, \tag{1}$$

where $\mathbf{y}_l^{(up)}$ is the receive signal in each cell l, $s_{lk}\mathbb{C}$ is the transmitted vector by UT k in cell l, $p_{u,lk} > 0$ is the uplink transmit power corresponding to signal that is normalized as $\mathbf{E}\left\{ |s_{lk}|^2 \right\} = 1$. The $\mathbf{n}_l \in \mathbb{C}^M$ is modeled as the additive noise $\mathbf{n}_l \sim \mathcal{CN}(0, \sigma^2 \mathbf{I}_M)$, where σ^2 is the noise variance. $\mathbf{h}_{lk}$ is the channel model which is considered to be independent.

The propagation factor from the kth UT of the lth cell (surrounding cell) to the mth antenna of the BS in the home cell or desired cell represented by jth cell is denoted as $h_{j,k,l,m} = \sqrt{\beta_{j,k,l}} g_{j,k,l,m}$. $\{g_{j,k,l,m}\}$ is the small scale fading factor which is independent and identical distributed (i.i.d) zero mean, and circularly-symmetric complex Gaussian $\mathcal{CN}(0, 1)$ random variables. The $\{\beta_{j,k,l}\}$ large scale fading coefficient and it accounts for geometric attenuation and shadow fading of each kth user that changes slowly and can remain constant over a coherence time interval.

The spectral efficiency for kth UT in a multi-cell system can be expressed as

$$R_{up,k} = \left(\frac{1 - \tau_p}{\tau_c}\right) \mathbb{E}_{\{b\}}\{log_2(1 + SINR_{jk}^{(ul)})\} \text{ [bit/s/Hz]}, \tag{2}$$

where $\mathbb{E}_{\{b\}}$ expectation with respect to UT position, τ_c the coherence interval while the τ_p is the fraction of samples in each coherence interval that are allocated for pilot transmission. The allocated pilot τ_p is determined by the number of K UTs and pilot reuse factor. The $SINR_{jk}^{(ul)}$ is the effective signal-to-interference-and-noise ratio for a multi-cell scenario for a UT k in cell j can be expressed as

$$SINR_{jk}^{(ul)} = \frac{p_{u,jk}\left|\mathbb{E}_{\{\mathbf{h}\}}\left\{\mathbf{a}_{jk}^H \mathbf{h}_{jjk}\right\}\right|^2}{\sum\limits_{l \in L}\sum\limits_{k}^{K} p_{u,lk}\mathbb{E}_{\{\mathbf{h}\}}\left\{\left|\mathbf{a}_{jk}^H \mathbf{h}_{jlk}\right|^2\right\} - p_{u,jk}\left|\mathbb{E}_{\{\mathbf{h}\}}\{\mathbf{a}_{jk}^H \mathbf{h}_{jjk}\}\right|^2 + \sigma^2 \mathbb{E}_{\{\mathbf{h}\}}\left\{\left\|\mathbf{a}_{jk}^H\right\|^2\right\}}, \tag{3}$$

where σ^2 is the noise variance and $\mathbb{E}_{\{\mathbf{h}\}}\{\cdot\}$ is the expectation of channel realization.

4.2   Simulated Results

The proposed MMSP can be used for investigation of different deployment scenarios of massive MIMO systems. Examples are the performance of massive MIMO systems with symmetric number of BS antenna, aggregate network performance in terms of spectral efficiency, energy efficiency and economic efficiency. The effect of systems parameters on network planning and scheduling and how this affect the aggregate network

Table 1. System parameters

Description	Values	Description	Values
Number of UTs (K)	25	Coherence time	2 ms
Number of BS antennas (M)	1000	Coherence bandwidth	210 kHz
Cell type	Hexagonal multi-cell	Coherence interval	420
Transmission	Uplink	Pilot reuse factor	1, 3, 4
No. of tiers	2	Number of cells	$L = 19$
Pathloss coefficient	3.76	Linear detector	MR and ZF
Cell radius	300 m	Minimum distance UT to BS	35 m
SNR	5 dB		

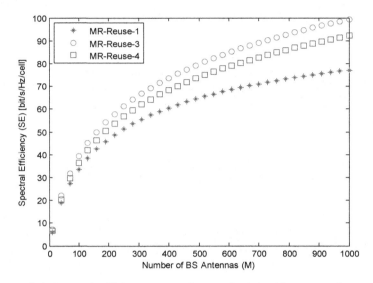

(a) Uplink Spectral efficiency, reuse factor of 1,3,4 with MR receiver

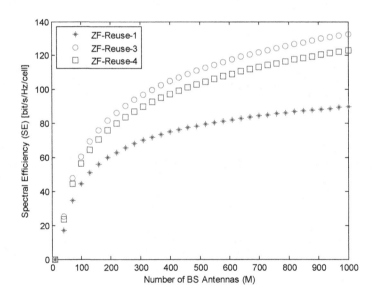

(b) Uplink spectral efficiency, reuse factor of 1,3,4 with ZF receiver

Fig. 5. Uplink spectral efficiency using the MR and ZF linear receivers with pilot reuse factor of 1, 3, and 4.

performance. Using the system several questions such as whether the massive MIMO should be deployed based on spectral efficiency or energy efficiency or spectral-energy efficiency trade-offs. Due to limited space, we present simulated result of spectral efficiency using two linear receivers which are maximum ratio (MR) and Zero-forcing (ZF) combining for uplink communication with different reuse factors. Using Eqs. (1–3), existing algorithm and system parameters identified in [20, 21] and we provide preliminary results using the proposed framework and MMSP prototype (Table 1).

The results in Fig. 5(a) and (b) shows the per-cell spectral efficiency for reuse factors of 1, 3 and 4 for a home-cell or desired-cell surrounded by interfering cells in a two-tier hexagonal network. In the first-tier, the home-cell is surrounded by 6 interfering cells while in the second-tier has 12 surrounding cells. The reuse factor of 1 delivers lowest spectral efficiency compared to reuse factors of 3 and 4. This is due to inter-cell interference from surrounding cells. Although it is expected that higher reuse factors should provider higher spectral efficiency, this is not necessary the case as shown in the Fig. 4. The inter-cell interference reduces but the number of UTs K that can be scheduled reduces due to the coherence interval. Hence, the reuse factor or 3 is delivers higher spectral efficiency compared to reuse factor 4. The ZF performance in Fig. 5(b) is better than the MR performance due to its ability to actively reject intra-cell interference reduction within the cell.

5   Conclusion

Research work in massive MIMO covers development of several algorithms, testbeds, physical level simulations, performance and evaluation of different technology and algorithms to explore the gains of maMIMO for the 5G network. Hence, we envisaged the need for a massive MIMO simulation platform that can be used for comparative study and analysis purpose. To achieve this, we proposed a framework for the MMSP. The development of a MMSP will allow 5G researchers to thoroughly validate new technology concepts, quantify baseband/RF performance margins, and develop new 5G proposals. In the future, further work will be carried out to on the MMSP prototype to allow for more complex simulations and analysis. More importantly, we hope that this proposed framework will result into a platform that will allow researchers to collaborate and share research outcome of maMIMO technology in the nearest future.

Acknowledgments. This research is supported by the Ministry of Higher Education (MOHE) in Malaysia and Universiti Teknologi Malaysia (UTM) through the HiCOE grant (R.J130000.7809.4J209). The grant is managed by Research Management Centre (RMC) at UTM.

References

1. Larsson, E.G., Edfors, O., Tufvesson, F., Marzetta, T.L.: Massive MIMO for next generation wireless systems. IEEE Commun. Mag. **52**(2), 186–195 (2013)
2. Lu, L., Li, G.Y., Swindlehurst, A.L., Ashikhmin, A., Zhang, R.: An overview of massive MIMO: benefits and challenges. IEEE J. Sel. Top. Signal Process. **8**, 742–758 (2014)

3. Persson, D., Lau, B.K., Larsson, E.G.: Scaling up MIMO: opportunities and challenges with very large arrays. IEEE Signal Process. Mag. **30**(1), 40–60 (2012)
4. Zheng, K., Zhao, L., Mei, J., Shao, B., Xiang, W., Hanzo, L.: Survey of large-scale MIMO systems. IEEE Commun. Surv. Tutor. **17**, 1738–1760 (2015)
5. Vieira, J., Malkowsky, S., Nieman, K., Miers, Z., Kundargi, N., Liu, L., Wong, I., Owall, V., Edfors, O., Tufvesson, F.: A flexible 100-antenna testbed for massive MIMO. In: 2014 IEEE Globecom Work, GC Wrkshps 2014, pp. 287–293 (2014)
6. Maccartney, G.R., Zhang, J., Nie, S., Rappaport, T.S.: Path loss models for 5G millimeter wave propagation channels in urban microcells. In: GLOBECOM - IEEE Global Communications Conference, pp. 3948–3953 (2013)
7. Tao, Y., Liu, L., Liu, S., Zhang, Z.: A survey: several technologies of non-orthogonal transmission for 5G. China Commun. **12**, 1–15 (2015)
8. NYU open source channel simulation software. http://wireless.engineering.nyu.edu/5g-millimeter-wave-channel-modeling-software
9. Mehlführer, C., Colom Ikuno, J., Šimko, M., Schwarz, S., Wrulich, M., Rupp, M.: The Vienna LTE simulators - enabling reproducibility in wireless communications research. EURASIP J. Adv. Signal Process. **2011**, 29 (2011)
10. SystemVue. http://www.keysight.com/en/pd-2410353/systemvue-201501?cc=US&lc=eng
11. Elijah, O., Leow, C.Y., Rahman, T.A., Nunoo, S., Iliya, S.Z.: A comprehensive survey of pilot contamination in massive MIMO-5G system. IEEE Commun. Surv. Tutor. **18**, 905–923 (2016)
12. Ngo, H.Q., Larsson, E.G., Marzetta, T.L.: Energy and spectral efficiency of very large multiuser MIMO systems. IEEE Trans. Commun. **61**, 1436–1449 (2013)
13. Pi, Z., Khan, F.: A millimeter-wave massive MIMO system for next generation mobile broadband. In: Conference Record - Asilomar Conference on Signals, System and Computers, pp. 693–698 (2012)
14. Farhang, A., Marchetti, N., Figueiredo, F., Miranada, J.P.: Massive MIMO and waveform design for 5th generation wireless communication systems. In: Proceedings of the 1st International Conference 5G Ubiquitous Connectivity, pp. 70–75 (2014)
15. Wang, N., Hossain, E., Bhargava, V.K.: Backhauling 5G small cells: a radio resource management perspective. IEEE Wirel. Commun. **22**, 41–49 (2015)
16. Kapetanovic, D., Zheng, G., Rusek, F.: Physical layer security for massive MIMO: an overview on passive eavesdropping and active attacks. IEEE Commun. Mag. **53**, 21–27 (2015)
17. Wu, J., Fan, P.: A survey on high mobility wireless communications: challenges, opportunities and solutions. IEEE Access **4**, 450–476 (2016)
18. Yang, G., Ho, C.K., Zhang, R., Guan, Y.L.: Throughput optimization for massive MIMO systems powered by wireless energy transfer. IEEE J. Sel. Areas Commun. **33**, 1640–1650 (2015)
19. Watson, D.: Spatial tessellations: concepts and applications of Voronoi diagrams. Comput. Geosci. **19**, 1209–1210 (1993)
20. Björnson, E., Sanguinetti, L., Hoydis, J., Debbah, M.: Optimal design of energy-efficient multi-user MIMO systems: is massive MIMO the answer? IEEE Trans. Wirel. Commun. **14**, 3059–3075 (2015)
21. Björnson, E., Larsson, E.G., Debbah, M.: Massive MIMO for maximal spectral efficiency: how many users and pilots should be allocated? IEEE Trans. Wirel. Commun. **15**, 1293–1308 (2016)

Amalgamating EC2 Theory and Holonic MAS to Design of Command and Control Architecture

Hua He$^{(\boxtimes)}$, Zhifei Li, Weiping Wang, Yifan Zhu, and Xiaobo Li

College of Information System and Management,
National University of Defense Technology,
Changsha Hunan 410073, China
Hehua3566@qq.com

Abstract. The process of C2 architecture design needs to consider the factors such as changeable battlefield environment, so the designed C2 architecture should be flexible, adaptive and so on. The theory of Enterprise Command and Control (EC2) concerns application of systems science collaborative processes of command and control. It can describe the C2 process and the entity function models of the organization, and analyze the performance of the architecture. However, in the simulation and optimization of the organizational structure is powerless. Multi-Agent Systems (MAS) has become a natural tool for modeling and simulating complex systems, these systems usually contain a great number of entities interacting among themselves, and acting at different levels of abstraction. In this context, it seems unlikely that MAS will be able to faithfully represent complex systems without multiple granularities. The holonic paradigm has proven to be an effective solution to several problems with such complex underlying organizations. The objective of this paper is to propose a preliminary framework of a holonic multi-agent model for the C2 architecture design. Which satisfies the characteristics of Holon's self-similarity, and combines the advantages of EC2, realized the mechanism of perception, decision-making and execution of C2 architecture and entity function models from different granularity.

Keywords: C2 architecture · Framework · Holonic MAS · Enterprise command and control

1 Introduction

The theory of EC2 is concerned with effective governance systems supporting value production in distributed intelligent enterprises, about increased institutional awareness and its ability to facilitate more effective, responsive and sustainable unilateral and multilateral action. Additionally, EC2 is about improved integration of human prerogatives and distributed computational systems that, acting in concert, are competent to establish and maintain viability of large-scale, dynamic and increasingly complex enterprise systems. The theory maintains that intelligent enterprises are not possible without a formal EC2 infrastructure, one based on a unified command and control

© Springer Nature Singapore Pte Ltd. 2017
M.S. Mohamed Ali et al. (Eds.): AsiaSim 2017, Part I, CCIS 751, pp. 109–120, 2017.
DOI: 10.1007/978-981-10-6463-0_10

framework. To this end, the theory of EC2 offers a framework for enabling collaborative, distributed and time-critical service-centric operations [1].

MAS has become a natural tool for modeling and simulating complex systems, these systems usually contain a great number of entities interacting among themselves, and acting at different levels of abstraction. In this context, it seems unlikely that MAS will be able to faithfully represent complex systems without multiple granularities. The holonic paradigm [2] has proven to be an effective solution to several problems with such complex underlying organizations [3–5]. Holons are defined as self-similar structure composed of holons as substructure. They are neither parts nor wholes in an absolute sense. The organizational structure defined by holons, called holarchy, allows the modelling at several granularity levels. Each level corresponds to a group of interacting holons. From the structure, the holonic and EC2 have a consistent form, are self-similar and progressive.

The objective of this paper is to propose a preliminary framework of a holonic multi-agent model for the C2 architecture design. Combining the holonic concepts that can be modeled at different levels of abstraction and EC2 on collaborative and organizational entity functional models. The next section summarizes the features of EC2 and holonic and lists some applications. Section 3 analyzes some common features of EC2 and holonic. Section 4, the two methods are briefly combined, and then the following section is dedicated to a case study. Finally, the paper concludes with a summary of the current results, and an outlook on future research activities.

2   Related Works

2.1   EC2 Theory and Applications

2.1.1   The Theory of Enterprise Command and Control

Bayne et al. Proposed the EC2 theory [6] in the 2003, followed public a number of articles and books [9, 12, 13]. EC2 theory is concerned with real-time enterprise governance and its requirements for a service-oriented C2 architecture (C2/SOA) capable of improving interoperability between and among interdependent enterprises. An EC2 framework comprising six key elements: (i) a coherent enterprise model, (ii) command (actor) interfaces, (iii) command services, (iv) control services, (v) performance measurement services and (vi) interfaces to legacy operational systems. The object of EC2's attention, includes operation of an enterprise, an abstract or virtual machine [7] is a value production unit (VPU). A VPU represents an object (service) encapsulating a well-defined and manageable capability [8].

An enterprise include a lot of VPU, called federated, every VPU introduces a naming (indexing) scheme that supports the requirement that each enterprise be uniquely identifiable. The focus of the figure is the central enterprise designated VPU [j, k, l]. Index "j" identifies the operational domain (i.e., federation, or community of interest), "k" denotes the horizontal position in the federation's collaboration network and "l" represents the location in its vertical command network. One of the more important context-sensitive issues for command to monitor in an enclave is the set of federation rules (policies) that constrain its prerogatives. Enterprises and the federations to which they belong may operate under a wide range of policies (rules of engagement, civil laws, military doctrines, etc.).

Inside the VPU, there is a control processing and a command processing, the left of Fig. 1 introduces three primary enterprise control processing stages: situation assessment, plan generation and plan execution. Situation assessment includes processes of observation (measurement), awareness (recognition) and analysis (understanding). Two functions define plan generation; they are responsible for policy compliance and resource allocation to proposed courses of action, respectively. Plan execution services (PES) of a VPU include two primary processes. Policy-validated and resource-allocated plans of record enter. The individual C2 service steps of a given VPU may participate in the C2 processing of other allied VPUs.

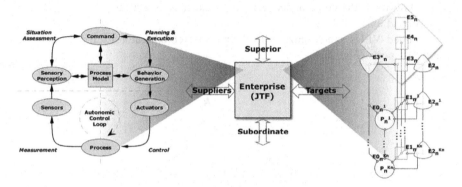

Fig. 1. Enterprise C2 services

The enterprise command structure, diagrammed in the right of Fig. 1 and enumerated in Table 1. Enterprise governance structures exist throughout a federated system [12]. Each VPU contains a command structure capable of self-governance. Command structures, typically co-located in mobile or fixed command "enclaves," are actor teams that operate semi-independently with a high degree of autonomy. These per-VPU actors list in Table 1.

Table 1. Principle EC2 actors

Label	Services	Roles and Responsibilities
E5	Command	Mission goals and objectives, policy and command authority
E4	Analysis/planning	Modeling, situation assessment and plan generation
E3	Operations	Plan execution and capability management
E3*	Audit	Program and process performance assessment
E2	Regulation	Plan (task) and resource synchronization
E1	Direction	Plan (task) execution management
E0/P	Process	Embedded [value] production process

The embedded enterprise command framework (ECF) C2 structure within VPU have more details:

1. Each VPU contains two or more embedded VPUs
   a. At least one supply chain process (VPUs)
   b. At least one asset chain process (VPUa)
2. Each VPU contains a regulator (E2) responsible for
   a. Regulating (synchronizing with) peers through its "C" port
   b. Regulating (synchronizing its) subordinates through its "H^a" and "J^a" ports
3. Each VPU communicates with its view of the "outside world" through its "U" and "V" ports
4. The navigator (E4) perceives the global context for the VPU through its "P" and "R" ports
5. Coupling the VPU commander (E5) to its superior is via the "A" and "B" ports (command axis)
6. Embedded VPUs synchronize with their peers (collaborators) through their "H^s" and "J^s" ports (Fig. 2).

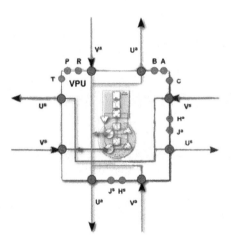

Fig. 2. VPU details

2.1.2 EC2 Related Applications

Bayne et al. present an enterprise command and control (EC2) framework designed to provide DOD enterprises, exemplified by a Joint Task Force (JTF) [9], with shared network-accessible C2 services. JTF EC2 includes a precise definition of enterprise, an associated enterprise command structure (ECS) and a specific set of control processing services (CPS). The proposed framework is consistent with the DOD's stated goal of migrating to network-centric (i.e., GIG-mediated) operations (NCO). In support of collaboration in jointly managed activities, agile JTF enterprises benefit from service-oriented capabilities along their vertical command (accountability) axes and along their horizontal production (logistics) axes, allowing them to support a wider range of NCO functions while simultaneously participating in and influencing behavior of multiple communities of interest (COIs).

The Joint Task Force is the organizational entity responsible for management of joint US warfighting activities, inherently collaborative affairs. Furthermore, JTF entities may operate in allied or coalition structures. Principal actors in the JTF model align with their EC2 model ounterparts as described in Table 2.

Table 2. Principle EC2 command actors in the JTF model

ECS element	JTF command element	Command function
E5	CJTF	Commander
E4	DCJTF + J5 JPG	Deputy Commander
E3	COS + J3	Chief of Staff
E3*	JOC	Joint Operations Center
E2	JFE	Joint Fires Element
E1-E0	JFACC	Joint Force Air Component Command
E1-E0	JFLCC	Joint Force Land Component Command
E1-E0	JFMCC	Joint Force Maritime Component Command
E1-E0	JSOTF	Joint Special Operations Task Force
E1-E0	JPOTF	Joint Psyops Task Force

Through the proposed model, can be performance measurement for JTF organization. The JTF ECS model includes a performance measurement framework (PMF) that includes two classes of metrics (ref. Fig. 3, "to-metrics").

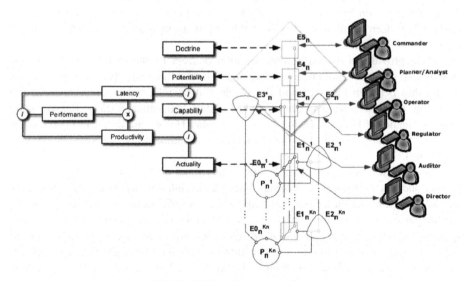

Fig. 3. JTF performance indices

The first class includes measures that define a JTF's performance in terms of its capability and actual performance. The second class of metrics defines a JTF's utility, its ability to meet plan completion-time requirements. Performance defines throughput (task completion rate); utility defines the value of the task to the overall mission. Both classes are required to scale vertically along the command axis and horizontally along the production axis. Table 3 summarizes the primary performance indices.

Table 3. JTF performance indices

Metric	Function
Potential	Design (architectural) limits
Capability	Deployed (e.g., funded) level of capacity
Actuality	Actual (instantaneous) performance
Latency	Latent potential (unused, unfunded) design potential
Productivity	Utility of deployed (used, funded) capability
Performance	Absolute performance of the enterprise as designed

2.2 Holonic Model and Specification

The concept of "Holon" is proposed by Koestler in the book "The Soul of the Machine." A holon is a whole-part construct that is composed of other holons, but it is, at the same time, a component of a higher level holon reflecting the entity at the same time with the overall autonomy and part of the collaboration, cannot simply as a whole, and cannot simply as part of it. Since the concept of Holon has been proposed, because of its self-similarity, autonomy, cooperation, the advantages of system analysis, design and implementation have been discovered and developed. In recent years the Holonic method has been applied in a wide fields, such as manufacturing system, virtual organization, MAS and so on.

Holon provides a recursive representation concept of the system, based on this method that part and whole is not considered to be a different entity. The dichotomous relationship between this part and the whole can be reflected at every level of the hierarchy, and it is evident in the biological system and human society. Based on the recursive nature of Holon, a Holon is part of another Holon, and it contains some other Holons, and these Holon form a Holon system, known as the Holonic system (Holarchy).

The Holonic system has the advantages that most of the holistic design methods lacked, such as robustness to internal and external interference have damaged, high efficiency of resource utilization, and adaptability to environmental changes. Holon's advantages have been effectively applied and embodied in flexible manufacturing systems, including stability, adaptability, flexibility and so on. A holon is a self-similar structure composed of holons as sub-structures and the hierarchical structure composed of holons is called a holarchy. Figure 4 shows a holonic system arranged in four holarchical levels [10].

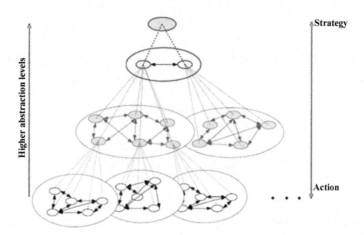

Fig. 4. A holarchy composed of four holarchical levels

Holonic systems offer the possibility to model a system from a high-level coarse-grained perspective to a low-level fine-grained one. On the other hand, using holons as modelling approach for a small close system may not always be recommended. If the system does not require multiple levels of granularity, holons will probably introduce an unnecessary overhead. Before applying any approach to model a system, the designer should analyse the adequacy of the under-lying concepts. Hence, holonic systems are well suited for analysing and modelling of large systems where multiple levels of abstraction exist. Another type of systems are those that can be decomposed recursively into smaller sub-components [11].

3 Some Common Features

Figure 5 is a typical, albeit simplified, view of the command or accountability hierarchy of the DOD enterprise. It reaches from the highest level ("L5") of the President to the lowest level ("L0") of a warfighter or semi-autonomous piece of warfighting equipment. The highest levels are primarily focused on policy (i.e., strategy), the middle levels on operations, and the lowest levels on mechanism (i.e. tactics) [12].

As diagrammed in Fig. 5, this C2 loop operates simultaneously at every node in the policy domain hierarchy, and is what is typically meant by the authority given to a manager of some activity. It implies a fundamental and critical requirement for distributed real-time C2 systems – their ability to synchronize (i.e., coordinate) along the federation's asset and supply chains. Synchronization requires that policy-based C2, in addition to its other objectives, be fundamentally about scheduling – both in time (e.g., rendezvous at a given deadline) and with respect to the effective sharing of resources (e.g., use of resource locks in implementing task resource scheduling) [13].

The system of systems (SoS) of C2 organization is relative to the hierarchical SoS, it has distribute, intelligent, diversity, self-organization and other characteristics [14]. Organizational entity coordination through the "contract network", "auction" and other

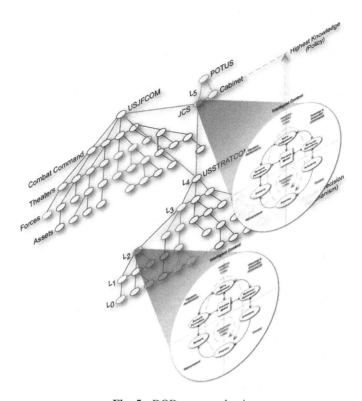

Fig. 5. DOD command axis

market mechanisms. Each VPU in the EC2 theory through publish - subscription way to coordinate [policy]. Similarly, Holon theory, but also through the contract network agreement and others assigned tasks.

To sum up, EC2 theory and holonic are similar in the following aspects:

1. Both of which have recursive features that provide a way to model the different granularity views. And are nestable and allow dynamic reorganization during runtime. That is both with the characteristics of flexibility.
2. Allocation of tasks are used on the market consultation mechanism, and through a specific role to complete the process (In EC2 is E2-E1 loop, and holonic is super-holon).

In addition, the two theories (methods) complement each other, EC2 provides a detailed description of the C2 architecture, the architecture can be tested and time analysis. HMAS features just conform to the characteristics of EC2, and can guide the modeling and optimization of C2 architecture.

4 Amalgamating EC2 and Holonic

In the face of increasingly complex, drastic changes and uncertain modern battlefield environment, flexible C2 organizational structure control SoS is the basis of establish and maintain the overall competitive advantage of the organization.

C2 organizational behavior includes two aspects: holistic behavior (organizational behavior) and local behavior (entity behavior). Our ultimate goal is to effectively control the overall behavior of the organization and to ensure that the local behavior of organization self-cognitive evolution. EC2 provides a good description, analysis and design approach for the C2 architecture, and makes the C2 architecture better measured. But the C2 architecture established by EC2 will be not easy to model and evolve.

In theory, the Holonic system is the same as the EC2 theory, a holon in the system is both a whole and a part. It is stable in the face of interference, adaptable in the face of change, and can make the most use of access to resources to maximize the comprehensive benefits.

Analyze the enterprise command framework (ECF) in each VPU through EC2 theory, specifying the possible input and output between VPUs. HMAS as means of modeling and simulation to avoid falling into the local optimal [13], according to the need to find the overall optimal C2 architecture. The C2-architecture simulation evolution model based on EC2 and Holonic will have the advantages of flexible, reliable and efficient, as shown in Fig. 6, which meets the requirements of HMAS in the form and inside the entity the C2 process is described in detail. As shown in the C2 architecture, can do some tests like time, performance through EC2 method.

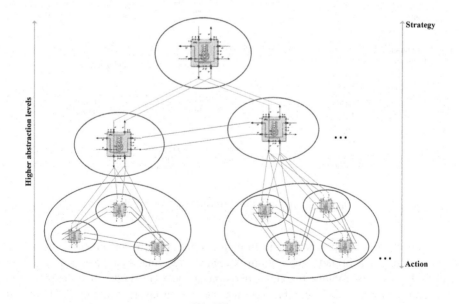

Fig. 6. Combine EC2 and holarchy

5 Case Study

Since the Gulf War, the US military has opened the new military revolution from the industrial age to the information age war with the guidance of the new military theory of "network-centric warfare". o achieve the transformed ability through army transform, trying to build the US Army to the most sophisticated equipment, the highest degree of modernization and strongest. The future force with adaptability, innovation, flexibility, versatility– "The army in 2020".

In this background, the US military combat force composition and combat equipment system is undergoing a comprehensive update, the main implementation of the way is transformation divisions to modular forces brigades, and its information technology network system and weapons systems supporting equipment molding.

The units of the long-range fire brigade include the brigade and the brigade headquarters company, target reconnaissance company, communication (signal) company, tactical unmanned aerial vehicle company, brigade security battalion and the rocket/missile battalion. During the combat readiness phase and the combat phase, the long-range fire brigade can also be programmed or assigned to 1 to 6 rockets/missiles and barrels battalion. Figure 7 is the basic structure of the US long-range fire brigade.

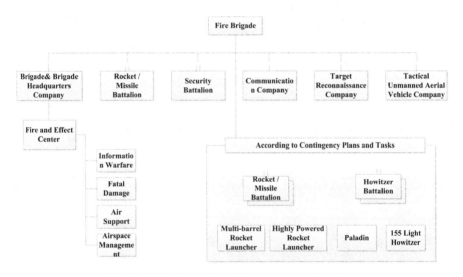

Fig. 7. US military Fire brigade organization chart

Figure 8, from top to bottom is from the strategy to action process, the top is control loop of the brigade, the bottom is combat, reconnaissance and other specific actions. Four layers from the functional division can be divided into: mission, planning, tasks and platform layer. It can be seen that the second layer, including the fight and protection holon, the third layer is subdivided of the second layer, the forth layer is specific combat unit (The lower part of the figure is L3 left holon magnification, we can see holon internal communication and holon communication with the outside).

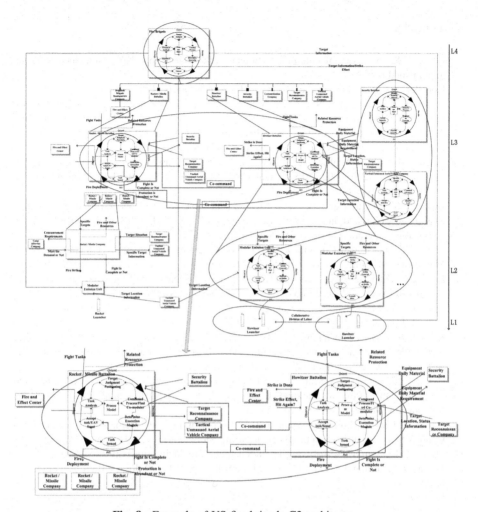

Fig. 8. Example of US fire brigade C2 architecture

6 Conclusions and Future Work

Based on the characteristics of Holon's self-similarity, the C2 architecture designed of this paper describe the perception, decision-making and implementation process mechanism at different levels, and based on the EC2 theory describes the organizational entity function model of each granularity Our ultimate goal is to get an optimized flexible C2 architecture. Therefore, the late work mainly has three aspects, one is the generation and decomposition of the task to drive the evolution of C2 architecture; the second is based on the existing EC2 theory, considering the constraints of resource allocation and the coordination strategy between the entities; the third is the cognitive evolution of the C2 architecture based on the description of models and tasks and constraints.

References

1. Bayne, J.S.: A theory of enterprise command and control, pp. 1–7, September 2006, an unpublished text
2. Koestler, A.: The Ghost in the Machine. Hutchinson, Paris (1967)
3. Maturana, F., Shen, W., Norrie, D.: Metamorph: an adaptive agent-based architecture for intelligent manufacturing (1999)
4. Tecchia, F., Loscos, C., Conroy, R., Chrysanthou, Y.: Agent behavior simulator (ABS): a platform for urban behaviour development. In: GTEC 2001 (2001)
5. Ulieru, M., Geras, A.: Emergent holarchies for e-health applications: a case in glaucoma diagnosis. In: IEEE 2002 28th Annual Conference of the Industrial Electronics Society, IECON 2002, vol. 4, pp. 2957–2961 (2002)
6. Bayne, J.S.: Mequon and WI (US) Method and System for Network-Based, Distributed, Real-Time Command and Control of an Enterprise. US,7,181,302,B2 [P], 3 October 2003
7. DOD: Joint Operations Concept (JOC), 19 August 2003
8. DOD: US Joint Forces Command (USJFCOM), Operational Concept for Global/Joint Battle Management Command and Control (GJBMC2) Working Paper, Draft Version 9N, Bedford
9. Bayne, J., Diggs, D.: C2 in the Joint Task Force (JTF) enterprise. In: 2006 Command and Control Research and Technology Symposium, San Diego, 20–22 June 2006
10. Abdoos, M., Mozayani, N., Bazzan, A.L.C.: Holonic multi-agent system for traffic signals control. Eng. Appl. Artif. Intell. **26**, 1575–1587 (2013)
11. Rodriguez, S.A.: From analysis to design of Holonic multi-agent systems: a framework, methodological guidelines and applications. Unpublished doctoral dissertation, Université de Technologie de Belfort-Montbéliard, Belfort, France (2005)
12. Bayne, J.S., Paul, R.: Scale-free enterprise command and control unified command structures. In: 10th International Command and Control Research and Technology Symposium, McLean, VA, 13–16 June 2005
13. Bayne, J., Paul, R.: Policy-based command and control. In: 10th International Command and Control Research and Technology Symposium, McLean, VA, 13–16 June 2005
14. Stark D.: Heterarchy: distributing intelligence and organizing diversity. In: The Biology of Business: Decoding the Natural Laws of Enterprise, pp. 153–179. Jossey-Bass, San Francisco (1999)

Optimal Formation Control of Multiple Quadrotors Based on Particle Swarm Optimization

Izzuddin M. Lazim, Abdul Rashid Husain$^{(\boxtimes)}$,
Nurul Adilla Mohd Subha, Zaharuddin Mohamed,
and Mohd Ariffanan Mohd Basri

Department of Control and Mechatronics Engineering,
Faculty of Electrical Engineering, Universiti Teknologi Malaysia,
81310 Skudai, Johor, Malaysia
izzuddin5585@gmail.com, rashid@fke.utm.my

Abstract. This paper presents the optimal formation control for a group of quadrotors based on particle swarm optimization (PSO) algorithm. This is motivated by the conventional approaches that still involve a certain degree of trial and error approach which may not give the optimal performance. The parameter optimization using PSO utilizes the linear quadrotor model obtained from feedback linearization technique. Simulations are conducted on the parameter optimization, followed by implementation of the optimal parameters for formation control of multiple quadrotors. The results show the effectiveness of the proposed technique.

Keywords: Formation control · Quadrotor · Quadcopter · Optimal control · Particle swarm optimization · UAV

1 Introduction

Quadrotor, also known as quadcopter is gaining popularity in the military and civilian applications due to the ability to take off and landing vertically, omnidirectional, and safer to interact in close proximity [1, 2]. This type of vehicle is being used in various applications including crop monitoring and spraying, surveillance, border patrol, photography, videography and much more. Although a single quadrotor can be utilized in these applications, it is believed that greater benefits can be achieved by a group of quadrotors that are working in a coordinated manner such as in a formation.

Rapid advancement on miniaturized computation, communication, sensing, and actuation technology have accelerated the study on cooperative control of multiple autonomous vehicles. As compared to the single agent system, autonomous vehicles that work cooperatively is more robust to single agent failure and flexible in performing the task required [3, 4]. Formation control is one of the main research areas in cooperative control of multiple vehicles. It is concerned with designing a controller that make a group of autonomous vehicles to form up and move in a desired geometrical shape [5]. Autonomous vehicles that are in formation will increase the robustness of the

© Springer Nature Singapore Pte Ltd. 2017
M.S. Mohamed Ali et al. (Eds.): AsiaSim 2017, Part I, CCIS 751, pp. 121–135, 2017.
DOI: 10.1007/978-981-10-6463-0_11

system and improve the communication properties. In addition, the reconfiguration ability and structural flexibility are also a favorable advantage of the system [6].

One straightforward way of implementing quadrotors' formation control is by using the leader-following approach as presented in [7–12]. However, the proposed works require the leader's state (e.g. position) to be known to all the followers, or every quadrotor knows the states of other quadrotors in the network. This requirement will impose communication constraint when the number of quadrotors in the network is large. Therefore, many researchers have turned to the formation control based on graph theory. This approach allows formation control of multiple vehicles in a distributed manner using local communications which can be described as a matrix via graph theory.

One of the common approaches in formation control of multiple quadrotors based on graph theory is by using simplified or linearized quadrotor model at the operating point as presented in [13–15]. However, since the quadrotor model is linearized at a certain operating point, this approach does not guarantee the stability of the quadrotor outside of the operating point. Thus, it is more desirable to implement a nonlinear controller for the quadrotor model as proposed in [16]. The authors obtained a linear decoupled model of the quadrotor system by using feedback linearization technique. Then, a controller based on graph theory is implemented for the formation. This approach simplified the overall control design by separating the single quadrotor design with formation control design, as opposed to the nonlinear single layer approach implemented in [17].

This paper proposes an optimal formation control for a group of quadrotors. The conventional approach of finding formation control parameters are by using pole assignment or linear-quadratic-regulation (LQR) approach. However, pole assignment approach still relies on trial and error to meet the desired response. Besides, the selection of weight matrices in the cost function of LQR still requires manual tuning to achieve the desired response. Therefore, both conventional approaches often require a few iterations before a desirable system response is obtained [18, 19]. These issues are more significant when the system has more degree. Therefore, the objective of this study is to optimize the control parameters to ensure the agents (quadrotors) optimally converge to the desired formation. Artificial intelligence based optimization using particle swarm optimization (PSO) is implemented to achieve this objective. The advantage of PSO is its simplicity in finding the optimal value without the need to have detail description of the system dynamics.

The main contribution of this paper is the utilization of PSO for optimal formation control of multiple quadrotors. A new algorithm is proposed for finding the fitness function of the formation based on the convergence time of the quadrotors' formation. To the authors' best knowledge, this is the first attempt of the PSO implementation for optimizing feedback gain in the formation control based on graph theory. This paper is organized as follows. Firstly, formation control of linearized quadrotor model using feedback linearization technique is presented in Sect. 2. Then, an overview of PSO technique and its implementation for optimizing formation control parameters are presented in Sect. 3. Simulations for the optimization and the implementation on quadrotor formation are discussed in Sect. 4. Finally, Sect. 5 gives some conclusions of the work.

2   Formation Control of Multiple Quadrotors

This section presents the linearization of a nonlinear quadrotor model using feedback linearization technique. Consequently, formation control algorithm and the configuration for the formation control of quadrotor are presented.

2.1   Feedback Linearization of Single Quadrotor System

Consider the configuration of a quadrotor shown in Fig. 1. The absolute position and the orientation of the quadrotor are denoted as (p_x, p_y, p_z) and (ϕ, θ, ψ), respectively, while (F_1, F_2, F_3, F_4) are the lift forces generated by the four rotors.

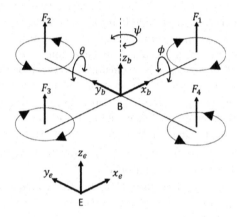

Fig. 1. Quadrotor configuration of a quadrotor with the earth fixed frame E and body fixed frame B.

By considering the translational and rotational components, the 6-DOF dynamics of a quadrotor are given as follow [13]:

$$\ddot{p}_x = D\frac{u^{\{1\}}}{M} \tag{1}$$

$$\ddot{p}_y = E\frac{u^{\{1\}}}{M} \tag{2}$$

$$\ddot{p}_z = -g + F\frac{u^{\{1\}}}{M} \tag{3}$$

$$\ddot{\phi} = \dot{\theta}\dot{\psi}\left(\frac{I_y - I_z}{I_x}\right) + \frac{1}{I_x}u^{\{2\}} \tag{4}$$

$$\ddot{\theta} = \dot{\phi}\dot{\psi}\left(\frac{I_z - I_x}{I_y}\right) + \frac{1}{I_y}u^{\{3\}} \tag{5}$$

$$\ddot{\psi} = \dot{\phi}\dot{\theta}\left(\frac{I_x - I_y}{I_z}\right) + \frac{1}{I_z}u^{\{4\}} \tag{6}$$

where

$$D = c\phi s\theta c\psi + s\phi s\psi$$
$$E = c\phi s\theta s\psi - s\phi c\psi$$
$$F = c\phi c\theta$$

with abbreviations $s(\cdot) = \sin(\cdot)$, and $c(\cdot) = \cos(\cdot)$, $u = \left[u^{\{1\}}, u^{\{2\}}, u^{\{3\}}, u^{\{4\}}\right]^T$ are the control input of the system, while $I_f (f = x, y, z)$, M and g denote the moment of inertia along each axis, the mass, and the gravitational acceleration, respectively. Notice that the quadrotor is an underactuated and highly unstable nonlinear system. This makes the controller design for the system is a challenging task. Fortunately, the dynamics of this system can be simplified by using feedback linearization approach.

In general, feedback linearization is a transformation method of a nonlinear system into the equivalent linear system. It can be achieved by using nonlinear coordinate transformation and nonlinear state feedback, rather than by linear dynamics approximations in Jacobian (conventional) linearization. In this paper, we are interested in controlling the formation of quadrotors in terms of relative positions and heading. Hence, absolute position of the quadrotor $\left[p_x, p_y, p_z\right]^T$ and the heading angle, ψ are selected as the desired output to be controlled.

Using the feedback control u given in [16] and [20] which renders a linear input–output map between the new input $\left(v^{\{1\}}, v^{\{2\}}, v^{\{3\}}, v^{\{4\}}\right)$ and the output $y = \left[p_x, p_y, p_z, \psi\right]^T$, the equivalent linear equation of the quadrotor system using the dynamic feedback linearization approach is given as follows:

$$\frac{d}{dt}\left(\overset{...}{p}_x\right) = v^{\{1\}} \tag{7}$$

$$\frac{d}{dt}\left(\overset{...}{p}_y\right) = v^{\{2\}} \tag{8}$$

$$\frac{d}{dt}\left(\overset{...}{p}_z\right) = v^{\{3\}} \tag{9}$$

$$\frac{d}{dx}\left(\dot{\psi}\right) = v^{\{4\}} \tag{10}$$

Block diagram which illustrates the configuration of the feedback linearized model is shown in Fig. 2. After using feedback linearization technique, each quadrotor in the formation can be treated as a linear decoupled sub-system. This allows the implementation of the well-established linear controller for the formation control layer which will be discussed in the next section.

Feedback Linearized Quadrotor Model (7)

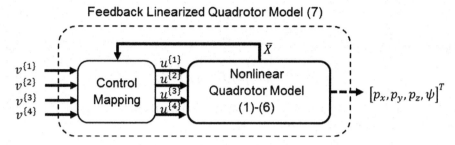

Fig. 2. Block diagram illustrating the feedback linearization of the quadrotor system.

2.2 Formation Control of Multiple Agents

This section presents the formation control algorithm using relative information from the neighboring agents. The objective of the algorithm is to ensure the states of each agent in the network converge to a predefined geometric pattern. Consider N agents i modelled by a linear dynamic in state space form given as follows:

$$\dot{x}_i = Ax_i + Bv_i, \qquad i = 1, 2, \ldots, N \tag{11}$$

where $A \in \mathbb{R}^{n \times n}$ and $B \in \mathbb{R}^{n \times p}$ are constant matrices, while $x_i \in \mathbb{R}^n$, $v_i \in \mathbb{R}^p$ are the state vector and control input of quadrotor i respectively which related to the positions (p_x, p_y, p_z) and heading (ψ) of the quadrotor presented earlier. It is assumed that the agents have identical dynamics. Therefore, the overall dynamics of the multi-agent system can be represented collectively as follows:

$$\dot{x} = (I_N \otimes A)x + (I_N \otimes B)v, \qquad i = 1, 2, \ldots, N \tag{12}$$

with $x = [x_1, x_2, \cdots, x_N]^T$, $v = [v_1, v_2, \cdots, v_N]^T$, $\otimes$ is a Kronecker product, and I_N is $N \times N$ identity matrix. Let the state errors for agent i is given as follows:

$$e_i = -\sum_{j \in \mathcal{N}_i} a_{ij}(x_{ij} - h_{ij}), \quad i = 1, 2, \cdots, N \tag{13}$$

with $x_{ij} = x_i - x_j$ and $h_{ij} = h_i - h_j$ (desired relative state), while $\mathcal{N}_i$ denotes the set of neighbors for agent i which it can communicate to. If the agent i receives the state of neighboring agent j, then $a_{ij} = 1$. Else, $a_{ij} = 0$. The interaction between the agents can be represented as a matrix using graph theory (brief overview of the graph theory is presented in the appendix). Then, Eq. (13) can be written collectively as follows:

$$e = -(L \otimes I_n)(x - h) \tag{14}$$

with $e = [e_1, e_2, \ldots, e_N]^T$, L is the Laplacian matrix which represent the interaction between agents, I_n is the $n \times n$ identity matrix, $x = [x_1, x_2, \cdots, x_N]^T$ and $h = [h_1, h_2, \cdots, h_N]^T$. To ensure the quadrotors achieve the desired geometric pattern, a formation control algorithm is implemented based on the work in [21] given as follows:

$$v_i = K_i e_i \tag{15}$$

Or collectively,

$$v = -(I_N \otimes K_i)(L \otimes I_n)(x - h) \tag{16}$$

with $v = [v_1, v_2, \cdots, v_N]^T$ and K_i is the feedback gain matrix to be designed. Hence, by substituting (16) into (12) yields

$$\dot{x} = (I_N \otimes A)x - (I_N \otimes B)(I_N \otimes K_i)(L \otimes I_n)(x - h), \quad i = 1, 2, \cdots, N \tag{17}$$

The agents are said to be in the desired formation h if and only if $\lim_{t \to \infty} e_i = 0, i = 1, 2, \cdots, N$. According to [21], the stability of the system which is associated with eigenvalues of (17) are the union sets of eigenvalues of the following:

$$A - \lambda_i B K_i, \quad i = 1, 2, \cdots, N \tag{18}$$

with λ_i is the eigenvalue of Laplacian matrix L. The interaction topology in this paper is assumed to be fixed. Hence, we are interested to identify the selection of matrix $K_i = [k_1, k_2, \cdots, k_n]$ on the convergence of the formation using PSO algorithm which will be presented in the next section.

3 Parameter Optimization in Multi-agent Formation Control

A brief overview of PSO algorithm is presented at the beginning of this section. Then, implementation of the algorithm for the parameter optimization of the formation control discussed earlier is described.

3.1 Overview of Particle Swarm Optimization

Particle swarm optimization (PSO) is an optimization technique based on Swarm Intelligence (SI). It was first introduced in [22] and inspired by the social behavior of bird flocking and fish schooling. In this optimization technique, each particle is a potential solution to the optimization problem. The particles move in the search space using adaptable velocity which is influenced by their current velocity, their previous experience and the experience of the neighbors. Basically, the implementation of PSO algorithm involve several steps given as follows [23]:

i. Generate random positions $\left(p_{id}^Q\right)$ and velocities $\left(v_{id}^Q\right)$ of the particles in the swarm at initial conditions within the specified minimum, p_{min} and maximum, p_{max} values, given as follows:

$$\begin{aligned} p_{id}^0 &= p_{min} + rand \cdot (p_{max} - p_{min}) \\ v_{id}^0 &= p_{min} + rand \cdot (p_{max} - p_{min}) \end{aligned} \tag{19}$$

with the subscript and superscript represent id^{th} particle at iteration Q respectively, while *rand* is a variable with a random value between 0 and 1.

ii. Update the particle velocity at iteration $Q+1$ based on the current position and current velocity. Besides, the velocity update also depends on the best position of each particle over the iteration (P_{best}) and the best global value in the current swarm (G_{best}) based on the fitness value. The velocity updates are given as follows:

$$v_{id}^{Q+1} = I_w \cdot v_{id}^{Q} + c_1 \cdot rand \cdot \left(P_{best} - p_{id}^{Q}\right) + c_2 \cdot rand \cdot \left(G_{best} - p_{id}^{Q}\right) \qquad (20)$$

where c_1 is the self-confidence factor, c_2 is the swarm-confidence factor, and I_w is the reduced inertia weight given as [24]

$$I_w = I_{w_{max}} - \frac{\left(I_{w_{max}} - I_{w_{min}}\right)}{Q_{max}} Q \qquad (21)$$

with $I_{w_{max}}$ and $I_{w_{min}}$ are the maximum and minimum inertia weight, respectively, while Q_{max} is the maximum number of iterations.

iii. Update the particle position at iteration $Q+1$ using the following equation

$$p_{id}^{Q+1} = p_{id}^{Q} + v_{id}^{Q} \qquad (22)$$

3.2   Optimal Formation Control of Multi-agent System

In multi-agent systems, one of the most important performance indexes is the convergence time which is when the agents get into the desired formation. Let the total square error between agents is $E = \mathbf{1} \cdot e^2$, where $\mathbf{1}$ is a matrix of ones with size $1 \times (N \cdot n)$. In this work, a new algorithm is proposed to obtain the convergence time, t_{conv} given as follows:

```
Initialize timer, t=0
Initialize simulation stop time, T
While t is less than or equal to T
   Calculate the total square error, E
   If E is more than σ
      Insert t into storage S
   Else
      Insert 0 into storage S
   End
      Increase t
End
Set t      with maximum value of storage S
    conv
```

with σ is the minimum convergence threshold. In this study, the optimization objective is find the value of gains that gives the minimum fitness value which is t_{conv}. This is obtained by executing the simulation of multi-agent formation for a period of T. Then, the fitness value which is associated with the particles are used in the PSO algorithm to find the optimal control parameter K_i. The optimization flow of the quadrotor formation carried out by PSO algorithm is shown in Fig. 3.

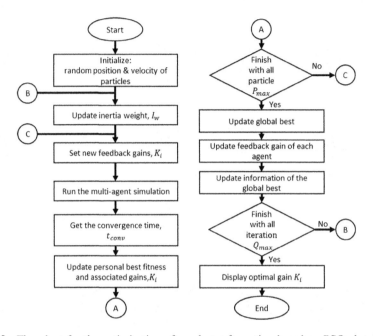

Fig. 3. Flowchart for the optimization of quadrotor formation based on PSO algorithm.

4 Simulations

The simulation results of the formation optimization using PSO algorithm is presented where the simulation setup are also described.

4.1 Optimization of the Formation Control

PSO is utilized to find the optimal parameters, K_i for the formation control of multiple quadrotors. To reduce the simulation time for finding the optimal control parameters, linear quadrotor models (7)–(9) are used instead of the nonlinear quadrotor model with feedback linearization controller. For the formation control in term of position (p_x, p_y, p_z), the optimization objective is to minimize the fitness function defined as $J_p = t_{conv}$. On the other hand, fitness function utilized by PSO algorithm to find the optimal feedback matrix for heading control, (10) is defined as $J_h = t_{conv}$.

The fourth-order integrator models in (7)–(9) can be represented in state-space Eq. (11) where matrix A and B are given as

$$A = \begin{bmatrix} 0 & 1 & 0 & 0 \\ 0 & 0 & 1 & 0 \\ 0 & 0 & 0 & 1 \\ 0 & 0 & 0 & 0 \end{bmatrix}, B = \begin{bmatrix} 0 \\ 0 \\ 0 \\ 1 \end{bmatrix} \tag{23}$$

Similarly, the second-order integrator model for heading (10) is transformed into state space equation with the following matrices

$$A = \begin{bmatrix} 0 & 1 \\ 0 & 0 \end{bmatrix}, B = \begin{bmatrix} 0 \\ 1 \end{bmatrix} \tag{24}$$

Based on the parameters adapted from [23], the following values are used for the controller optimization in this study:

   i. Dimension of search space
     a. Quadrotors' position: 4, i.e. $K_i = [k_1, k_2, k_3, k_4]$
     b. Quadrotors' heading: 2, i.e. $K_i = [k_1, k_2]$
  ii. Maximum iteration, $Q_{max} = 40$
 iii. Number of particles, $P_{max} = 20$
  iv. Simulation stop time, $T = 30\,s$
   v. Self and swarm confident factor, $c_1 = c_2 = 2$
  vi. Inertia weight with maximum, $I_{w_{max}} = 0.9$ and minimum $I_{w_{min}} = 0.4$
 vii. Search space with minimum $p_{min} = 0.1$ and maximum $p_{max} = 2$
viii. Minimum convergence threshold, $\sigma = 0.05$.

Figure 4(a) and (b) respectively, show the variation of fitness function with the number of iteration for the translation formation (p_x, p_y, p_z) and heading synchronization of the quadrotors ψ. In 40 iterations, both fitness functions decrease with the

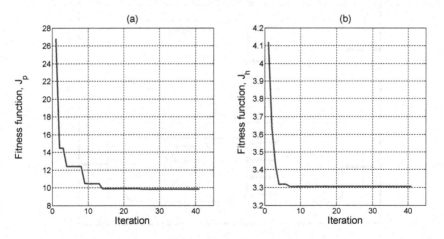

Fig. 4. Variation of fitness function with respect to iteration.

number of iterations until they reach the minimum values. The parameters that are associated with the minimum value of fitness function are tabulated in the Table 1. Optimization of the control parameters are conducted by using MATLAB/Simulink simulation tool in a computer with Intel i5-6200 2.4 GHz CPU and 4 GB RAM.

Table 1. Optimal parameters.

Control objective	Fitness	Optimization time (minutes)	Optimal control parameters
Position (p_x, p_y, p_z)	$J_p = 9.8286$	8.4167	$K_i = [k_1, k_2, k_3, k_4]$ $= [0.4380, 1.4665, 2, 1.3147]$
Heading (ψ)	$J_h = 3.3064$	4.23	$K_i = [k_1, k_2]$ $= [2, 1.7678]$

4.2   Implementation on Quadrotor Formation

Once the optimal formation control parameters have been identified, the values are used for the simulation of the quadrotor formation that uses nonlinear quadrotor model (1)–(6). The overall structure of the simulation is shown in Fig. 5, while Table 2 listed the simulation parameters [13].

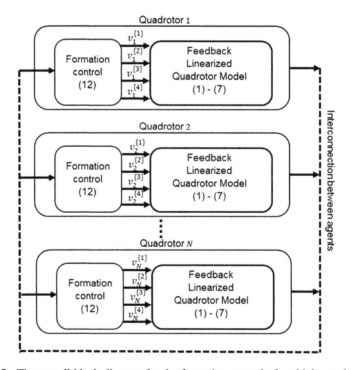

Fig. 5. The overall block diagram for the formation control of multiple quadrotors.

Table 2. Quadrotor parameters.

Parameter	Descriptions	Values	Units
M	Mass	0.6	kg
g	Gravitational acceleration	9.81	ms^{-2}
I_x	Roll inertia	0.005796	kg m^2
I_y	Pitch inertia	0.005796	kg m^2
I_z	Yaw inertia	0.010296	kg m^2

Let the number of quadrotors, $N = 5$. The communication between quadrotors in producing the formation is shown in Fig. 6. The desired formation (relative positions) between quadrotors are $h_x = \{0, 2, 2, 0, 1\}$, $h_y = \{0, 2, 2, 0, 1\}$, $h_z = \{0, 0, 0, 0, 0\}$ and $h_\psi = \{0, 0, 0, 0, 0\}$. Since the common task in formation control is to achieve desired geometric pattern with zero rates, the desired higher derivatives of the positions and headings are set to zero.

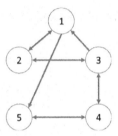

Fig. 6. Interaction topology between quadrotors.

Figure 7 shows that the quadrotors moved from their initial positions to the desired formation in the horizontal (x and y) plane. Meanwhile Fig. 8 shows that the quadrotors achieve consensus or formation with zero offsets on altitude and heading, respectively. Table 3 tabulates the performance comparison for the quadrotor formation optimized using parameters from PSO and LQR in [16]. Clearly, the quadrotor formation using parameters that have been optimized by PSO converge faster than the LQR.

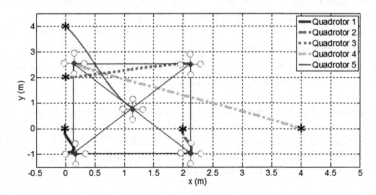

Fig. 7. Quadrotors achieve the desired horizontal formation where '*' indicate the initial positions.

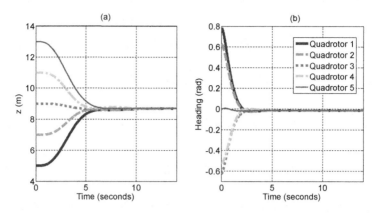

Fig. 8. Quadrotors (a) achieve a consensus on altitude, (b) synchronize to one heading.

Table 3. Comparison of the formation between LQR and PSO.

Output	Convergence time (s)	
	LQR	PSO
p_x	13.6600	8.6400
p_y	10.5800	7.9200
p_z	11.5800	9.3000
Heading (ψ)	6.4800	2.1800

5 Conclusions

This paper is concerned with the optimal formation control of multiple quadrotors. The quadrotor's nonlinear and underactuated model is transformed into linear decoupled equations using dynamic feedback linearization approach. Then, a linear formation control algorithm based on graph theory is implemented on the linearized quadrotor model. To find the optimal controller parameters for the formation control, optimization method based on PSO is proposed. A new algorithm for finding the fitness function based on the convergence time is presented. The simulation conducted on the parameter optimization, followed by implementation on the quadrotor formation show the effectiveness of the proposed optimization technique.

Acknowledgments. The first author would like to thank the Ministry of Higher Education (MOHE) and Universiti Sains Islam Malaysia (USIM) for their financial support under SLAB scheme, and all the authors acknowledge the support by Universiti Teknologi Malaysia in term of lab facilities. The project is supported under the Research University Grant No. Q. J130000.2608.14J62, Universiti Teknologi Malaysia.

Appendix: Graph Theory

The interaction topology in multi-agent system can be modeled using directed graph G, with the set of agents denoted as $V = \{V_1, V_2, \cdots, V_n\}$ and $\mathcal{E}$ is the set of edges E_{ij} connecting two neighboring agents. If agent i receives information from agent j, there will be an edge E_{ij} in $\mathcal{E}$. The set of neighbors of agent i which it can communicates to excluding itself is denoted by $\mathcal{N}_i$. The adjacency matrix $\mathcal{A} = [a_{ij}] \in \mathbb{R}^{n \times n}$ is defined such that $a_{ij} > 0$ if $E_{ij} \in \mathcal{E}$, and $a_{ij} = 0$ otherwise. Meanwhile the degree matrix is $\varepsilon = diag(d_1, \cdots, d_N)$ with d_i is the in-degree of the i-th agent. In multi-agent system, the frequently used matrix to represent the interaction topology is Laplacian matrix $L = \Delta - \mathcal{A}$. For example, consider the interaction topology given in Fig. 9.

Fig. 9. An example of interaction topology.

The unweighted Laplacian matrix of the interaction is given as follows:

$$
L = \Delta - \mathcal{A} = \begin{bmatrix} 2 & 0 & 0 & 0 & 0 \\ 0 & 2 & 0 & 0 & 0 \\ 0 & 0 & 2 & 0 & 0 \\ 0 & 0 & 0 & 2 & 0 \\ 0 & 0 & 0 & 0 & 2 \end{bmatrix} - \begin{bmatrix} 0 & 1 & 1 & 0 & 0 \\ 1 & 0 & 1 & 0 & 0 \\ 0 & 1 & 0 & 1 & 0 \\ 0 & 0 & 1 & 0 & 1 \\ 1 & 0 & 0 & 1 & 0 \end{bmatrix}
$$
$$
= \begin{bmatrix} 2 & -1 & -1 & 0 & 0 \\ -1 & 2 & -1 & 0 & 0 \\ 0 & -1 & 2 & -1 & 0 \\ 0 & 0 & -1 & 2 & -1 \\ -1 & 0 & 0 & -1 & 2 \end{bmatrix}
$$

(25)

References

1. Bouabdallah, S., Murrieri, P., Siegwart, R.: Design and control of an indoor micro quadrotor. In: Proceedings of the 2004 IEEE International Conference Robotics and Automation, ICRA 2004, vol. 5, pp. 4393–4398, April 2004
2. Mohd Basri, M.A., Husain, A.R., Danapalasingam, K.A.: Enhanced backstepping controller design with application to autonomous quadrotor unmanned aerial vehicle. J. Intell. Robot. Syst. **79**(2), 295–321 (2014)

3. Zhang, Y., Mehrjerdi, H.: A survey on multiple unmanned vehicles formation control and coordination : normal and fault situations. In: International Conference on Unmanned Aircraft Systems, pp. 1087–1096 (2013)
4. Hou, S.P., Cheah, C.C.: Can a simple control scheme work for a formation control of multiple autonomous underwater vehicles? Control Syst. Technol. IEEE Trans. **19**(5), 1090–1101 (2011)
5. Desai, J.P., Ostrowski, J.P., Kumar, V.: Modeling and control of formations of nonholonomic mobile robots. IEEE Trans. Robot. Autom. **17**(6), 905–908 (2001)
6. Arranz, L.B.: Cooperative control design for a fleet of AUVs under communication constraints. Universite de Grenoble (2012)
7. Mercado, D.A., Castro, R., Lozano, R.: Quadrotors flight formation control using a leader-follower approach. In: 2013 European Control Conference (ECC), pp. 3858–3863 (2013)
8. Abbas, R., Wu, Q.: Tracking formation control for multiple quadrotors based on fuzzy logic controller and least square oriented by genetic algorithm. Open Autom. Control Syst. J. **7**, 842–850 (2015)
9. Zhao, W., Go, T.H.: Quadcopter formation flight control combining MPC and robust feedback linearization. J. Franklin Inst. **351**(3), 1335–1355 (2014)
10. Ghamry, K.A., Zhang, Y.: Formation control of multiple quadrotors based on leader-follower method. In: 2015 International Conference on Unmanned Aircraft Systems, ICUAS 2015, pp. 1037–1042 (2015)
11. Davidi, A., Berman, N., Arogeti, S.: Formation flight using multiple integral backstepping controllers. In: 2011 IEEE 5th International Conference on Cybernetics and Intelligent Systems (CIS), pp. 317–322 (2011)
12. Vargas-Jacob, J.A., Corona-Sánchez, J.J., Rodríguez-Cortés, H.: Experimental implementation of a leader-follower strategy for quadrotors using a distributed architecture. J. Intell. Robot. Syst. **84**(1), 435–452 (2016)
13. Mahmood, A., Kim, Y.: Leader-following formation control of quadcopters with heading synchronization. Aerosp. Sci. Technol. **47**, 68–74 (2015)
14. Pilz, U., Popov, A.P., Werner, H.: Robust controller design for formation flight of quad-rotor helicopters. In: Proceedings of the IEEE Conference on Decision and Control, pp. 8322–8327 (2009)
15. Lara, D., Sanchez, A., Lozano, R., Castillo, P.: Real-time embedded control system for VTOL aircrafts: application to stabilize a quad-rotor helicopter. In: 2006 IEEE Conference on Computer Aided Control System Design, 2006 IEEE International Conference on Control Applications, 2006 IEEE International Symposium on Intelligent Control, pp. 2553–2558 (2006)
16. Mahmood, A., Kim, Y.: Decentralized formation control of quadcopters using feedback linearization. In: 2015 6th International Conference on Automation, Robotics and Applications (ICARA), pp. 537–541 (2015)
17. Wang, Y., Wu, Q., Wang, Y.: Distributed cooperative control for multiple quadrotor systems via dynamic surface control. Nonlinear Dyn. **75**(3), 513–527 (2014)
18. Wang, J., Brackett, B.T., Harley, R.G.: Particle swarm-assisted state feedback control: from pole selection to state estimation. In: 2009 American Control Conference, pp. 1493–1498 (2009)
19. Solihin, M.I., Wahyudi, Akmeliawati, R.: Self-erecting inverted pendulum employing PSO for stabilizing and tracking controller. In: 2009 5th International Colloquium on Signal Processing Its Applications, pp. 63–68 (2009)
20. Sabatino, F.: Quadrotor control : modeling, nonlinear control design, and simulation. KTH Royal Institute of Technology (2015)

21. Lafferrire, G., Williams, A., Caughman, J., Veerman, J.J.P.: Decentralized control of vehicle formations. Syst. Control Lett. **54**, 899–910 (2005)
22. Kennedy, J., Eberhart, R.: Particle swarm optimization. In: Proceedings of the IEEE International Conference on Neural Networks, vol. 4, pp. 1942–1948 (1995)
23. Basri, M.A.M., Danapalasingam, K.A., Husain, A.R.: Design and optimization of backstepping controller for an underactuated autonomous quadrotor unmanned aerial vehicle. Trans. FAMENA **38**(3), 27–44 (2014)
24. Ayob, M.N., Yusof, Z.M., Adam, A., Abidin, A.F.Z., Ibrahim, I., Ibrahim, Z., Sudin, S., Shaikh-Husin, N., Hani, M.K.: A particle swarm optimization approach for routing in VLSI. In: 2010 2nd International Conference on Computational Intelligence, Communication Systems and Networks, pp. 49–53 (2010)

Design of Component-Based CGF Modeling Framework

Yingqian Bao[✉], Qingjun Qu, and Yiping Yao

College of Information System and Management,
National University of Defense Technology,
137 Yanwachi, Changsha, Hunan, China
{baoyingqian15,fyao2015,ypyao}@nudt.edu.cn

Abstract. A well-designed modeling framework can improve the efficiency of modeling, which is of great significance to improve the reusability, scalability and combinability of model. The current popular simulation model representation specifications, such as BOM (Base Object Model) and SMP2 (Simulation Model Portability Standards 2), provide some modeling frameworks for modeling work. However, according to these modeling frameworks, either it is difficult to support the behavior description of model, or it is difficult to map the behavior description directly to the implementation of model, reducing the model development efficiency. To solve this problem, this paper presents a component-based modeling framework with hierarchical structure. This framework classifies the components according to their function. In addition, we propose a State Chart based on combined-actions in this framework to realize the mapping from the behavior description to the implementation of model directly. Analysis shows that the framework has good reusability, decoupling, scalability and combinability, which can greatly improve the development efficiency of model.

Keywords: Modeling framework · Component-based · CGF (Computer Generated Forces) · State chart · Behavior description

1 Introduction

In order to meet the construction of large-scale complex simulation application system, support the domain independence, platform independence, reusability, scalability, interoperability and combinability of simulation models, and provide simulation architecture description and simulation development approach, simulation experts has put forward a number of typical simulation model representation specifications, like HLA (High Level Architecture), BOM and SMP2, that provide us with some good modeling frameworks. Although these simulation model representation specifications have their own characteristics and have been widely used, however, HLA and SMP2 cannot support the behavior description of model. And BOM can just support model behavior description in the concept through the provision of state information table, which makes it difficult to be mapped to implementation of model automatically [1].

© Springer Nature Singapore Pte Ltd. 2017
M.S. Mohamed Ali et al. (Eds.): AsiaSim 2017, Part I, CCIS 751, pp. 136–145, 2017.
DOI: 10.1007/978-981-10-6463-0_12

For a long time, component-based modeling and simulation technology [2] has been the focus in the simulation domain. Based on the construction of component model, the component model is created through the component model code framework, and the component model that has been created can be re-customized according to the change of demand, which greatly improves the comprehensibility, scalability and modularity of the simulation model. In the aspect of model reuse, development efficiency, system maintenance and so on, it has obvious advantages. Since the granularity definition of a component is variable, a system, an object, a sub-model, or even a process, a function can be called a component. This paper defines the default component similar to the concept of "sub-model" [3], that is, each component only performs a single well-defined task.

In order to solve the problem that the behavior description of the model cannot be automatically mapped to the implementation of model, we design a component-based CGF simulation modeling framework. Firstly, we introduce the composition structure of the component-based modeling framework in detail. Secondly, we describe the behavior of the CGF based on the State Chart according to the modeling framework. Finally, we explain the automatically mapping from the behavior description of the CGF to the component-based modeling framework.

The rest of this paper is organized as follows. The second section discusses the related work. The third section introduces the structure of the component-based modeling framework. The fourth section explains how to complete the automatically mapping from the behavior description of the CGF to the component-based modeling framework based on State Chart. The fifth section summarizes the whole work of this paper.

2 Related Works

At present, the most commonly used modeling frameworks are provided by HLA [4], BOM [5] and SMP2 [6].

HLA is developed by the United States Department of Defense, used to solve the interoperability and reusable problems in the distributed simulation. HLA consists of three parts, namely, Framework and Rules, Federate Interface Specification, and Object Model Template-OMT. HLA owns the characteristics of distributed interactive heterogeneity, communication efficiency and efficient development specification. However, the degree of reusability of the model supported by HLA is relatively limited, and it does not support the behavior description of the model.

SISO organization in 2006 published the BOM (Base Object Model) to promote combinability, scalability, interoperability, manageability, and reusability of simulation model. The BOM template has four main template components: Model Identification Information, Conceptual Model Definition, Model Mapping and Object Model Definition, that provides a standard description specification for simulation model. The simulation model is designed as a component with high cohesion and low coupling characteristics by component method, which can be reused and interoperable in various simulation systems. However, BOM can just support behavior description of models conceptually through the provision of state information table, which makes it difficult to be mapped to the model implementation automatically.

SMP2 is a new generation of simulation model introduced by the European Space Agency. It has absorbed many advanced achievements in many fields of software engineering and simulation engineering, such as MDA [7] (Model Driven Architecture) and CBD (Component-Based Development). SMP2 aims to improve the portability, maintainability and reusability of the simulation model, and to realize platform independence and cross-simulation platform reuse and integration. Compared with HLA and BOM, SMP2 has stronger reusability, support model design, model integration description and dynamic model integration, but SMP2 also does not support the behavior description of the model.

3   Modeling Framework

This paper presents the component-based CGF modeling framework which has hierarchical structure, as shown in the Fig. 1. It needs to be emphasized once again that each component only performs a single well-defined task. It can be seen that this modeling framework consists of the following categories of functional components:

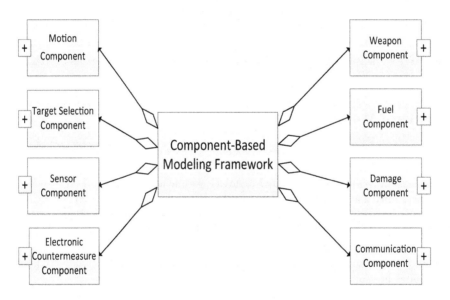

Fig. 1. The component-based CGF overall modeling framework.

3.1   Motion Component

The motion components provide the movement function and calculate the location and speed information for the CGFs when they are scheduled. Mainly include: ground 3D motion component, air 3D motion component, surface 3D motion component and submarine 3D motion component, as shown in the Fig. 2. (Air 3D motion component

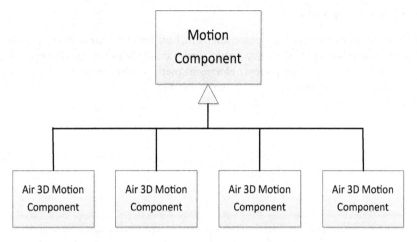

Fig. 2. The main compositive components of the motion component.

can also mainly include aircraft motion component, rocket motion component and so on. Due to the limited space, only one hierarchy expanded.) As we can see, air 3D motion component can be reused as submarine 3D motion component, because between their movement functions, the existing differences are just the different value of parameters (Also due to the limited space, the similar situations are no longer described).

3.2   Target Selection Component

The target selection components provide the target selection function for the CGFs. Mainly includes: navigation target selection component, electronic countermeasure target selection component, incoming weapon target selection component and incoming CGF target selection component, as shown in the Fig. 3.

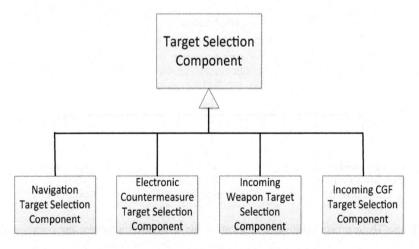

Fig. 3. The main compositive components of the target selection component.

3.3   Sensor Component

The sensor components provide perceptual function for the CGFs. Mainly includes: radar component, sonar component, visual sensor component, thermodynamic sensor component, laser sensor component, electromagnetic sensor component and enemy identification sensor component, as shown in the Fig. 4.

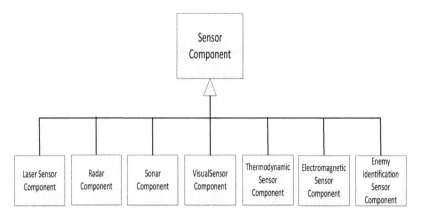

Fig. 4. The main compositive components of the sensor component.

3.4   Electronic Countermeasure Component

The electronic countermeasure components provide electronic countermeasure function for the CGFs. Mainly includes: electronic reconnaissance component, electronic interference component and electronic defense component, as shown in the Fig. 5.

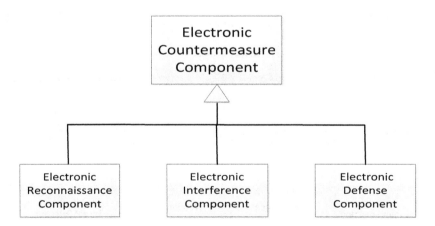

Fig. 5. The main compositive components of the electronic countermeasure component.

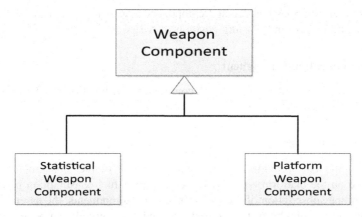

Fig. 6. The main compositive components of the weapon component.

3.5 Weapon Component

The weapon components provide weapon models for the CGFs. Mainly includes: statistical weapon component and platform weapon component, as shown in the Fig. 6. The statistical weapon component is designed to calculate the weapons impact point and impact time like gun, bomb and rocket. The platform weapon component is designed to generate a virtual platform (with the relevant body parameters such as size and detectability), like missile and torpedo (Clearly, missile's motion component can also reuse air 3D motion component).

3.6 Damage Component

The damage component provides damage calculation function for the CGFs. Mainly includes: collision damage component and blasting damage component, as shown in the Fig. 7. Collision damage component assesses the damage between CGF and CGF

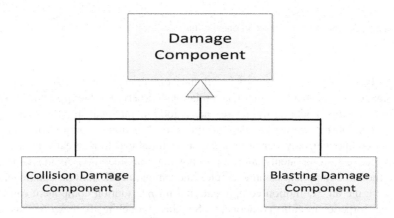

Fig. 7. The main compositive components of the damage component.

or CGF and terrain. Blasting damage component assesses the damage effect of the CGFs through the type and blasting position of weapons.

3.7   Communication Component

The communication component provides communication function for the CGFs based on different frequency channels.

3.8   Fuel Component

The fuel components provide the calculation function of fuel consumption for the CGFs based on the platform type and velocity and the fuel consumption parameters.

Through the subscription of the above functional components, the assembly of the CGF entity can be completed. For example, a fixed-wing aircraft can be assembled by subscribing the components, as shown in the Fig. 8.

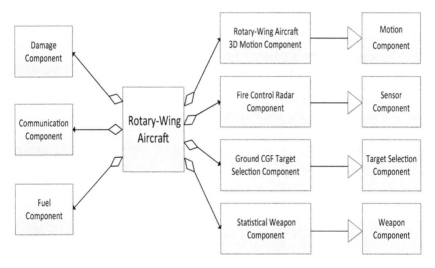

Fig. 8. Through the functional components, the assembly of fixed-wing aircraft can be completed.

It is obvious that each class of functional components also contains multi-layer sub-components, and there is inheritance relationship between the upper layer and the lower layer. So this modeling framework has a good hierarchical structure. There is no coupling relationship between different types of functional components for each functional component only performs a single well-defined task, greatly reducing the coupling between components, and improving the combinability. At the same time, take the motion component as an example. The submarine 3D motion component can easily reuse the air 3D motion component, and missile motion component can easily reuse the torpedo motion component. So this modeling framework has good reusability. When a new CGF class needs to be added and the currently existing component cannot fully meet its needs, for example, the existing motion component cannot satisfy the need of the rotary-wing aircraft. Under this circumstance, we only need to add the rotary-wing aircraft motion component in the specific level, and the others functional components of the rotary-wing aircraft can just reuse existing functional components. Besides, setting the subscription and publish relationship for the rotary-wing aircraft. In this way, the rotary-wing aircraft can be added into this framework easily. So the modeling framework has good scalability.

4   Behavior Description Based-on State Chart

State Chart [8] is a kind of object behavior description method proposed by Harel, which is an extension of FSM (Finite State Machine) [9]. The method can support nested state, guard condition, historical state, concurrency state, broadcast event and propagation transfer. In addition, it is easier to describe the concurrent and asynchronous behavior of system than FSM, especially reactive system. Therefore, State Chart is a better means of CGF behavior description. This section explains the mapping from the behavior description to the implementation of model directly according to a kind of specific State Chart. First, the specific State Chart needs to be introduced.

Action, which is atomic, cannot be interrupted. It is executed when the state enters, exits, or transfers. In this paper, each action corresponds to the functionality provided by a (class of) component. For example, the action "flying at a specified speed toward the target" of an aircraft is executed by one motion component.

State, which is a stage in the object's life cycle that satisfies certain conditions, performs certain actions, or waits for some events to occur. In this paper, we define the state as a stage of performing certain actions. For example, for an aircraft's "Fire to Enemy CGF" state, we can define the state corresponded to some actions, as shown in Fig. 9. It can be seen that each action of the state of aircraft corresponds to a certain types of functional component.

Transfer, which is a movement of an object that leaves from one state to another state.

Event, which changes the state of the CGF object once it happens. Events are generally divided into four categories: change events (a specified condition never set up to set up), signal events (receive asynchronous events of other objects), schedule events (scheduled by other object) and timed events (after a specified time interval). In this paper, the transition of the state is triggered by change events, and the execution of the actions is triggered by schedule event.

Actions corresponding to each state of CGF can be classified and designed according to the functional components, and then CGF objects can own complete description of behavior through the State Chart. In this way, the behavior of CGF can be directly mapped to the implementation of the CGF functional components, so as to construct a reasonable CGF object. At the same time, detailed behavior description in turn will help us to further enrich the modeling framework.

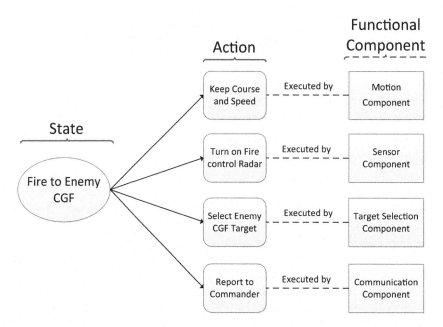

Fig. 9. A state is a stage that performs some actions, and these actions are executed by their corresponding functional component.

5   Conclusion and Future Work

This paper proposed a component-based CGF modeling framework. Firstly, we introduced the structure of the component-based modeling framework in detail. Then, we introduced the definition of specific State Chart and explained how to realize the automatically mapping from the behavior description of the CGF to the implementation of functional components. Analysis shows that the framework has good reusability, decoupling, scalability comprehensibility, and combinability, which can greatly improve the development efficiency of model.

In the future, we plan to research the interface specification of functional components and interactive relationship of functional components based on this modeling framework.

References

1. Lei, Y.L., Su, N.L., Li, J.J., et al.: New simulation model representation specification SMP2 and its key application techniques. Syst. Eng.-Theory Pract. **31**(4), 553–572 (2010)
2. OMG: OMG Unified Modeling Language (OMG UML) [EB/OL], 02 November 2007/11 February 2008. http://www.omg.org/spec/UML/2.1.2/Superstructure/PDF
3. Ya-Ping, M.A., Ke, L.I.: Architecture of military model in joint operations simulation system. Comput. Simul. **22**(1), 24–27 (2005)

4. IEEE: IEEE Standard for Modeling and Simulation (M&S): High Level Architecture (HLA) - Framework and Rules, 1–378. IEEE (2010)
5. SISO Base Object Model Product Development Group: Base Object Model (BOM) Template Specification. SISO-STD-003. 1-DRAFT-V0.12 (2005)
6. European Space Agency: SMP 2.0 Handbook Issue 1 Revision 2. EGOS-SIM-GEN-TN-0099 (2005)
7. Li, Q., Wang, C., Zhu, Y.F., et al.: Research on MDA based simulation model development and integration methodology. J. Syst. Simul. **19**(2), 272–276 (2007)
8. Liu, Z., Deng, S., Sha, J., et al.: Modeling object's behavior based on state chart. Comput. Eng. Des. (2001)
9. Liu, X.L., Huang, K.D., Zhu, X.J.: The application of finite state machine in the CGF's behavior modeling. Acta Simulata Systematica Sinica (2001)

An Evidence-Combination-Based Simulation Result Validation Method for Multi-source Data

Shenglin Lin, Wei Li, Ping Ma$^{(\boxtimes)}$, Ming Yang, and Ju Huo

Control and Simulation Center, Harbin Institute of Technology, Harbin, China
lin_44627079@yeah.net,
{frank,pingma,myang,torch}@hit.edu.cn

Abstract. Simulation result validation is a crucial work in simulation credibility assessment. The result validation metric is a measure of agreement between simulation output and experimental observations. Sometimes the observations maybe derive from different data sources such as the actual system output, credible hardware-in-the-loop simulation system output and the expert opinions and so on. Then the agreement analysis results of system response would be multiple certainly. To solve the simulation result validation with multi-source data, the paper proposes a result validation method based on evidence combination. First, the evidence representation methods for multi-source data on the structure of evidence space are proposed. Then the multiple evidence bodies are aggregated based on evidence combination rules and the integrated validation result could be achieved. In the end, the application process and effectiveness of this validation method is illustrated through a numerical example.

Keywords: Simulation result validation · Multi-source data · Evidence representation · Evidence combination

1 Introduction

Simulation models are increasingly being used to solve practical problems and to aid in decision-making. The developers and users of these models are all rightly concerned with whether a model and its results are "correct". This concern is mainly addressed through model validation. Simulation model validation is usually defined to mean "substantiation that a simulation model within its domain of applicability possesses a satisfactory range of accuracy consistent with the intended application of the model" [1]. The simulation model validation includes the conceptual model validation and simulation result validation which is accomplished by measuring the extent of agreement between the model output and experimental observations. Nowadays, the research on result validation method has become a frontier subject in simulation field.

The complexity of simulation models has increased during the last years, some result validation metrics have been proposed to measure the extent of agreement between the simulation output and the experimental observations.

© Springer Nature Singapore Pte Ltd. 2017
M.S. Mohamed Ali et al. (Eds.): AsiaSim 2017, Part I, CCIS 751, pp. 146–156, 2017.
DOI: 10.1007/978-981-10-6463-0_13

Existing validation metrics have been classified into five sorts such as classical hypothesis testing [2], Bayes factor [3], Mahalanobis distance [4], area metric [5] and Bayes network [6]. They are usually used to solve the multivariate validation, the validation and analysis of uncertain system responses and the reliability inference of complex simulation system. For instance, Zaman et al. researched the representation, quantification and propagation of data uncertainty in reliability analysis of engineering systems [7]. Zhan et al. proposed a multivariate result validation method based on Bayesian considering the uncertainty of dynamic Systems [8]. Jiang et al. developed a hierarchical result validation metric based on Bayes network [9].

However the experimental observations of system output of interest maybe derive from different sources such as the actual system, Hardware-in-the-loop (HITL) simulation system and expert opinions. Then the integration of multiple results of agreement analysis between simulation output and multi-source observations is necessary in the simulation result validation. The existing solution is just using the Weighted Sum Method (WSM) to achieve the comprehensive validation result [10], but the strong subjectivity involved in this method will cause the inaccurate validation conclusion. In this study, we propose a new result validation method to aggregate the multi-source validation results taking advantage of evidence combination.

This paper is organized as follows: Sect. 2 gives the problem description of multi-source simulation result validation and reviews the knowledge about evidence theory and evidence combination rules. A new result validation method based on evidence combination is proposed in Sect. 3. In Sect. 4, a numerical example is performed to verify the proposed method and an explicit comparison analysis between the proposed method and WSM is given. Finally, the conclusion and some thoughts for the future research are summarized.

2   Problem Description and Theoretical Background

In this section, we analyze the problem of simulation result validation with multi-source data and give the mathematical description firstly. Then the necessary theory background about the proposed validation method is given including the evidence theory and evidence combination rules.

2.1   Problem Description

In practical applications of simulation result validation, the experimental observations of system response usually derive from multiple sources such as the output of actual system and HITL simulation system, expert opinions and historical data. Then the agreement analysis result between the simulation output and experimental observations would be multiple certainly. So how to aggregate the multi-source data (i.e., multiple agreement analysis results) of system response and give a comprehensive validation conclusion need to be researched. An appropriate mathematical description of this issue is given as follows.

Let $\mathbf{X} = \{\mathbf{x}_1, \mathbf{x}_2, \ldots, \mathbf{x}_n\}$ stands for the common input of simulation model, S_s, and several referenced systems, $S_{ri}, i = 1, 2, \ldots, n$. And the corresponding system response under the same input condition are defined as $\mathbf{Y}_s$ and $\mathbf{Y}_{ri}$, $i = 1, 2, \ldots, n$ represent the ith referenced system. Then the extent of agreement between $\mathbf{Y}_s$ and $\mathbf{Y}_{ri}$ is defined as $\mathbf{C}_i(\mathbf{Y}_s, \mathbf{Y}_{ri})$. Besides, the experts could give the subject opinions which defined by $\mathbf{C}_j(\mathbf{Y}_s, \mathbf{Y}_{ri})$, $j = 1, 2, \ldots, m$ denotes the jth expert opinion. The main issue is that determining the ultimate validation result, C_u, through $\mathbf{C}_i(\mathbf{Y}_s, \mathbf{Y}_{ri})$ and $\mathbf{C}_j(\mathbf{Y}_s, \mathbf{Y}_{ri})$, i.e.,

$$\begin{cases} \mathbf{C}_i(\mathbf{Y}_s, \mathbf{Y}_{ri}) \\ \mathbf{C}_j(\mathbf{Y}_s, \mathbf{Y}_{ri}) \end{cases} \Rightarrow C_u \tag{1}$$

This paper develops a result validation method based on evidence combination to aggregate the multi-source data and determines the ultimate validation result. Evidence combination is a professional approach to meaningfully summarize and simplify a corpus of data whether the data is coming from a single source or multiple sources. The multi-source data are respectively represented as evidence bodies on the frame of evidence theory primarily. Then the multiple evidence bodies are aggregated as an evidence body that represents the ultimate validation result. The foundational information of evidence theory and evidence combination rules is introduced briefly in next section.

2.2   Evidence Theory

The theory of evidence also called Dempster-Shafer Theory (DST) has been originally developed by Dempster [11] in his work on upper and lower probabilities, and later on by Shafer [12]. Evidence theory belongs to an imprecise reasoning theory and is often used to solve the reasoning problem under uncertainty. We consider the problem of the identification of an object which can take N possible values. In traditional probability theory, evidence is associated with only one possible object. In DST, evidence can be associated with multiple possible objects, e.g., sets of objects [13]. As a result, evidence in DST can be meaningful at a higher level of abstraction without having to resort to assumptions about the objects within the evidential set.

Besides, the evidence is designed to cope with varying levels of precision regarding the information and no further assumptions are needed to represent the information. It also allows for the direct representation of uncertainty of system responses where an imprecise input can be characterized by a set or an interval and the resulting output is a set or an interval. The basic concepts of DST are introduced as follow.

Let Θ be the set of N elements corresponding to the N identifiable objects, i.e., the finite set of N mutually exclusive and exhaustive hypotheses [14]. This set is called the *frame of discernment*

$$\Theta = \{1, 2, 3, \ldots, N\} \tag{2}$$

The power set of Θ is the set containing all the possible subsets of Θ, represented by $P(\Theta)$. This set consists of 2^N elements A, each representing the event "the object is in A".

$$P(\Theta) = \{\varnothing, 1, \ldots, N, (1,2), (1,3), \ldots, (N-1,N), (1,2,3), \ldots \Theta\} \tag{3}$$

where $\varnothing$ denotes the empty set. The N subsets containing only one element are called singletons. A BPA (basic probability assignment) is a function from $P(\Theta)$ to $[0,1]$ defined by:

$$m: \quad P(\Theta) \rightarrow [0,1], \quad A \mapsto m(A) \tag{4}$$

And which satisfies the following conditions:

$$\sum_{A \in P(\Theta)} m(A) = 1, \quad m(\varnothing) = 0 \tag{5}$$

Because evidence theory considers the subsets of the set of N objects, it could then be stated: "$m(A)$ represents our confidence in the fact that all we know is that the object belongs to A". In other words, $m(A)$ is a measure of the belief attributed exactly to A, and to none of the subsets of A. So $m(A) = 1$ expresses the certainty that the object is in (A), but this alone does not allow to distinguish among the elements of (A) and identify the object. To obtain total certainty of an object's identity, the following two conditions must hold: (1) $m(A) = 1$ and (2) $|A| = 1$, where $|\cdot|$ denotes the cardinality function. Only then, it can be stated with certainty that $A = \theta^*$, where θ^* is the object to be identified. On the other hand, $m(A) = 1$ and $|A| = N$ correspond to total uncertainty.

The elements of $P(\Theta)$ that have a non-zero mass are called *focal elements*, and the union of all the focal elements is called the core of the m-function.

A body of evidence (BOE) is the set of all the focal elements, each with its BPA:

$$(B, m) = \{[A, m(A)]; A \in P(\Theta) \text{ and } m(A) > 0\} \tag{6}$$

Given a BPA m, a belief function Bel is defined as:

$$\text{Bel}: \quad P(\Theta) \rightarrow [0,1], \quad A \mapsto \text{Bel}(A) = \sum_{B \subseteq A} m(B) \tag{7}$$

Bel(A) measures the total belief that the object is in A. In particular, we have Bel($\varnothing$) = 0 and Bel($\varnothing$) = 1.

Given a belief function, a plausibility function Pl is defined as:

$$\text{Pl}: \quad P(\Theta) \rightarrow [0,1], \quad A \mapsto \text{Pl}(A) = \sum_{A \cap B \neq \varnothing} m(B) \tag{8}$$

It can also be stated that Pl(A) = $1 - \text{Bel}(A^c)$, where A^c is the complement of A. Pl(A) measures the total belief that can move into A. In particular, we have Pl($\varnothing$) = 0 and Pl($\varnothing$) = 1.

2.3 Evidence Combination Rules

Two BPAs m_1 and m_2 (i.e., two bodies of evidence or two belief functions) can be combined to yield a new BPA m, by a combination rule. The more classical one is the Dempster rule of evidence combination [11], also called orthogonal sum, noted by $m = m_1 \oplus m_2$ and defined by:

$$m(A) = \frac{\sum\limits_{B \cap C = A} m_1(B)m_2(C)}{1 - K} \tag{9}$$

With

$$K = \sum\limits_{B \cap C = \varnothing} m_1(B)m_2(C) \tag{10}$$

where K is a normalization constant, called *conflict* because it measures the degree of conflict between m_1 and m_2. $K = 0$ corresponds to the absence of conflict between m_1 and m_2, whereas $K = 1$ implies complete contradiction between m_1 and m_2. Indeed $K = 0$, if and only if no empty set is created when m_1 and m_2 are combined. On the other hand, $K = 1$ if and only if all the sets resulting from this combination are empty.

The Dempster rule of combination is not the only rule to combine two BPAs. Ferson proposed the Mixing (or p-averaging or averaging) rule, which describes the frequency of different values within an interval of possible values in the continuous case or in the discrete case, the possible simple events [13]. The formula for "mixing" combination rule is just

$$m_{1,\dots,n}(A) = \frac{1}{n} \sum\limits_{i=1}^{n} w_i m_i(A) \tag{11}$$

where m_i is the BPA for the ith belief structure being aggregated and the w_i is the ith weight assigned according to the reliability of the ith source. Insofar as averaging of probability distributions via mixing is regarded as a natural method of aggregating probability distributions, it might also be considered as a reasonable approach to employ with Dempster-Shafer structures, and that is why it is introduced here.

3 The Result Validation Method for Multi-source Data

In this Section, we present a new result validation method to conduct the multi-source validation results. The multi-source data is represented as the multiple evidence bodies. Then these evidence bodies are aggregated based on evidence combination rules as a single evidence body, and the ultimate validation conclusion is achieved naturally.

3.1   Evidence Representation for Multi-source Data

In this method, $C_i(\mathbf{Y}_s, \mathbf{Y}_{ri})$ and $C_j(\mathbf{Y}_s, \mathbf{Y}_{ri})$ need to be represented as evidence bodies on the frame of evidence theory primarily. Two types of evidence representation methods for multi-source data are developed according to the different sample sizes. The data sets are classified into two categories on the basis of the sample size: the large sample set is defined as the sample size is more than 30, otherwise is the small sample [15].

a. Evidence representation for large sample data

Let $X = \{x_1, x_2, \ldots x_n\}, n \geq 30$ be a set of large sample data set, $\hat{f}_n(x)$ be the estimate to the probability density function of variable x, $[a, b]$ be the interval of X. Then $[a, b]$ is divided into k sub-intervals which are shown as

$$\Omega = \{c_i = [a_i, b_i], i \in [1, 2, \ldots, k]\} \tag{12}$$

Assume that a frame of discernment Θ, includes a focal set $\Delta_i = \{A_i = (x \in c_i)\}$, Then the BPAs of the focal element A_i is calculated as

$$m(A_i) = \int_{x \in c_i} \hat{f}_n(x) dx = \int_{a_i}^{b_i} \hat{f}_n(x) dx \tag{13}$$

b. Evidence representation for small sample data

Suppose that $X = \{x_1, x_2, \ldots, x_n\}, n \leq 30$ be a set of small sample data set, $\bar{m} = (x_1 + x_2 + \ldots + x_n)/n$ be the mean value of X. Then the k minimum intervals focused on $\bar{m}$ are determined as $A_1, A_2, \ldots, A_k$, which could be represented by $[\bar{m} - \Delta_1, \bar{m} + \Delta_1]$, $[\bar{m} - \Delta_2, \bar{m} + \Delta_2]$, $\ldots [\bar{m} - \Delta_k, \bar{m} + \Delta_k]$. The probabilities that the test value dropped in the kth intervals are defined as $p_1, p_2, \ldots, p_{k-1}, 1$, where $\Delta_1 < \Delta_2 < \ldots < \Delta_k$ and $p_1 < p_2 < \ldots < p_{k-1} < 1$. Then $Bel(A_1) = p_1, Bel(A_2) = p_2, \ldots, Bel(A_{k-1}) = p_{k-1}, Bel(A_k) = 1$, and the BPAs of focal element A_i is defined as

$$\begin{aligned} m(A_1) &= Bel(A_1) \\ m(A_i) &= Bel(A_i) - Bel(A_{i-1}) \quad (2 \leq i \leq k) \end{aligned} \tag{14}$$

Then the sample data are represented in form of an interval and a corresponding probability.

3.2   Aggregation of Multi-source Evidence Bodies

The purpose of integration of the multi-source evidence bodies are to meaningfully summarize and simplify a corpus of validation results (i.e., $C_i(\mathbf{Y}_s, \mathbf{Y}_{ri})$, $C_j(\mathbf{Y}_s, \mathbf{Y}_{ri})$) and achieve the ultimate validation result, C_u. The validation result could be achieved by some agreement analysis methods such as classical and Bayes hypothesis test methods for static data, TIC, GRA and spectrum analysis methods for time series. After evidence representation of multi-source data, two types of evidence combination rules are used to aggregate the multi-source evidence bodies as follows.

Let (C_1, m) and (C_2, m) be the BOEs of $C_1(\mathbf{Y}_s, \mathbf{Y}_{r1})$ and $C_2(\mathbf{Y}_s, \mathbf{Y}_{r2})$ respectively, the BOE of ultimate validation result, C_u, is calculated based on Eq. (9).

$$m(C_u) = \frac{\sum\limits_{C_1 \cap C_2 = C_u} m_1(C_1) m_2(C_2)}{1 - K}, \quad K = \sum\limits_{C_1 \cap C_2 = \varnothing} m_1(C_1) m_2(C_2) \qquad (15)$$

where the denominator, $1 - K$, is a normalization factor. This has the effect of completely ignoring conflict and attributing any probability mass associated with conflict to the null set. Consequently, this operation will yield counterintuitive results in the face of significant conflict in certain contexts. So Eq. 8 will be used to aggregate two evidence bodies when no significant conflict among them.

Whereas, there are some significant conflicts between two BOEs, the Mixing rule will be used to aggregate the BOEs based on Eq. (11).

$$m_{1,\ldots,n}(C_u) = \frac{1}{2}(w_1 m_1(C_1) + w_2 m_2(C_2)) \qquad (16)$$

where w_1 and w_2 are the weights of two BOEs. This mixing operation provides different intervals and different BPAs than Dempster rule and could be used to aggregate the conflictive BOEs. The intervals are either equal to the Dempster intervals or in most cases wider. Then C_u is represented in form of BOE that indicates the true value of agreement extent between model output and experimental observations belongs to a certain interval with the corresponding probability.

4 The Numerical Example

A numerical example on multi-source simulation result validation is cited to verify the proposed validation method. Let $\mathbf{Y}_s$ be the simulation output, $\mathbf{Y}_{r1}$ and $\mathbf{Y}_{r2}$ denote the experimental observations of actual system and credible HITL simulation system which are regarded as the reference system. Now the multiple validation results such as $C_1(\mathbf{Y}_s, \mathbf{Y}_{r1})$ and $C_2(\mathbf{Y}_s, \mathbf{Y}_{r2})$ could be achieved based on the agreement analysis methods for static data and time series and are listed in Table 1.

Then the two teams of validation results are represented as the evidence bodies, $m(A)$ and $m(B)$, based on Eq. (14). The evidence representation forms are described in Table 2. Furthermore, Fig. 1 gives the cumulative belief and plausibility function of the two evidence bodies.

Next, the two evidence bodies are aggregated based on the Dempster rule and the ultimate validation result, C_u, is given as follows (Table 3).

Table 1. Multi-source validation results.

Experiment number	$C_1(\mathbf{Y}_s, \mathbf{Y}_{r1})$	$C_1(\mathbf{Y}_s, \mathbf{Y}_{r2})$
1	1.000	0.993
2	0.999	0.903
3	0.962	0.925
4	0.948	0.892
5	9.948	0.915
6	0.944	0.961
7	0.952	0.914
8	0.921	0.931
9	0.973	0.925
10	0.977	0.913

Table 2. Evidence representation for multi-source validation results.

$m(A)$		$m(B)$	
Focal element	BPA	Focal element	BPA
[0.948 0.973]	0.5	[0.925 0.931]	0.3
[0.944 0.977]	0.2	[0.913 0.961]	0.4
[0.921 1.000]	0.3	[0.892 0.993]	0.3

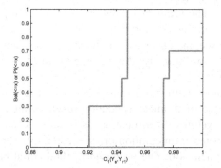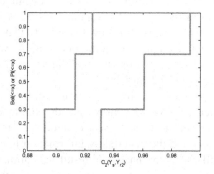

Fig. 1. Cumulative belief and plausibility function of $C_1(\mathbf{Y}_s, \mathbf{Y}_{r1})$ and $C_2(\mathbf{Y}_s, \mathbf{Y}_{r2})$ (*left and right*)

Table 3. Evidence representation of aggregation result, C_u.

Focal element	BPA
[0.925 0.931]	0.114
[0.948 0.961]	0.253
[0.944 0.961]	0.101
[0.921 0.973]	0.152
[0.948 0.973]	0.190
[0.944 0.977]	0.076
[0.921 0.993]	0.114

The cumulative belief and plausibility function of C_u are described in Fig. 2. Simultaneously the Cumulative Distribution Functions (CDF) of $\mathbf{C}_1(\mathbf{Y}_s, \mathbf{Y}_{r1})$ and $\mathbf{C}_2(\mathbf{Y}_s, \mathbf{Y}_{r2})$ are depicted to demonstrate the effectiveness of proposed method.

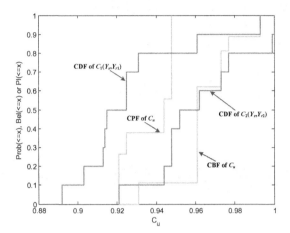

Fig. 2. Cumulative distribution function of $\mathbf{C}_1(\mathbf{Y}_s, \mathbf{Y}_{r1})$ and $\mathbf{C}_2(\mathbf{Y}_s, \mathbf{Y}_{r2})$, and the cumulative belief and plausibility function of C_u.

The uncertainty of multi-source validation results could be represented by the area surrounded by $\mathbf{C}_1(\mathbf{Y}_s, \mathbf{Y}_{r1})$ and $\mathbf{C}_2(\mathbf{Y}_s, \mathbf{Y}_{r2})$. The ultimate validation result C_u is represented as a rigorous evidence body that determines the probability of the agreement extent belonging to a certain interval. As we see, the uncertainty exist in C_u is less than the primary multi-source validation results. Consequently, the uncertainty interval of C_u is reduced further.

In the past, the simulation result validation with multi-source data is often conducted by WSM simply, and the single value of ultimate validation result could be achieved. But the subject opinion (i.e., the weights determination) is introduced naturally and the uncertainty information is ignored in integration process certainly. This will cause the inaccurate result validation conclusion. The proposed method could be used to tackle the aggregation of multi-source validation results objectively. The reduction of subject certainly causes the increase of data uncertainty. Consequently, the uncertainty exist in multi-source data is considered sufficiently taking advantage of the evidence representation method. And the precise intervals of true value of the ultimate validation result are achieved based on the evidence combination rules. In summary, the complete analysis result of validation with multi-source data could be calculated based on the proposed validation method.

5   Conclusion

In order to solve the simulation result validation with multi-source data, a validation method based on evidence combination rules is presented. The multi-source data are represented as evidence bodies on the frame of evidence theory firstly. Then the multiple evidence bodies are aggregated based on the evidence combination rules including the Dempster rule and the Mixing rule, and the ultimate validation result is achieved in form of evidence body. The numerical example shows that the uncertainty in multi-source data could be considered in the ultimate validation result using the proposed method instead of WSM.

It should be noted that the ultimate validation result is represented in form of evidence body (i.e., the focal elements and BPAs). The more validation information is necessary if we want to achieve the true value of validation result, and the interval of uncertainty will be decreased further. Moreover, this method is used to tackle the result validation with the multi-source data of univariate output, the multivariate simulation result validation problem still need to be researched in future work.

Acknowledgements. This research is supported by the National Natural Science Foundation of China (Grant No. 61403097).

References

1. Sargent, R.G.: Verification and validation of simulation models. J. Simul. **7**(1), 12–24 (2013)
2. Sornette, D., Davis, A.B., Ide, K., Vixie, K.R., Pisarenko, V., Kamm, J.R.: Algorithm for model validation: theory and applications. Proc. Natl. Acad. Sci. U.S.A. **104**, 6562–6567 (2007). National Acad Sciences, USA
3. Jiang, X., Yuan, Y., Mahadevan, S., Liu, X.: An investigation of Bayesian inference approach to model validation with non-normal data. J. Stat. Comput. Simul. **83**(10), 1829–1851 (2013)
4. Zhao, L., Lu, Z., Yun, W., Wang, W.: Validation metric based on Mahalanobis distance for models with multiple correlated responses. Reliab. Eng. Syst. Saf. **159**, 80–89 (2017)
5. Roy, C.J., Oberkampf, W.L.: A comprehensive framework for verification, validation, and uncertainty quantification in scientific computing. Comput. Methods Appl. Mech. Eng. **200**, 2131–2144 (2011)
6. Tien, I., Kiureghian, A.D.: Algorithms for Bayesian network modeling and reliability assessment of infrastructure systems. Reliab. Eng. Syst. Saf. **156**, 134–147 (2016)
7. Zaman, K., McDonald, M., Mahadevan, S.: Inclusion of correlation effects in model prediction under data uncertainty. Probab. Eng. Mech. **34**, 58–66 (2013)
8. Zhan, Z., Fu, Y., Yang, R.J.: Bayesian based multivariate model validation method under uncertainty for dynamic systems. J. Mech. Des. **134**, 034502(1–7) (2012)
9. Jiang, X., Mahadevan, S., Urbina, A.: Bayesian nonlinear structural equation modeling for hierarchical validation of dynamical systems. Mech. Syst. Signal Process. **24**, 957–975 (2010)
10. Huang, T.C.K., Chen, Y.L., Chang, T.H.: A novel summarization technique for the support of resolving multi-criteria decision making problems. Decis. Support Syst. **79**, 109–124 (2015)
11. Dempster, A.: Upper and lower probabilities induced by multivalued mapping. Ann. Math. Stat. **38**, 325–339 (1967)
12. Shafer, G.: A Mathematical Theory of Evidence. Princeton University Press, Princeton (1976)

13. Sentz, K., Ferson, S.: Combination of evidence in dempster-shafer theory. Technical report, Sandia National Laboratories (2002)
14. Jousselme, A.L., Grenier, D., Bosse, E.: A new distance between two bodies of evidence. Inf. Fusion **2**, 91–101 (2001)
15. Serfling, R.J.: Approximation Theorems of Mathematical Statistics, pp. 138–170. Wiley, Hoboken (1980)

Magnetic Force Model Approach with Path Finding Feature for an Improved Crowd Movement Simulation

Nurulaqilla Khamis[1], Hazlina Selamat[2(✉)], Rubiyah Yusof[1],
and Fatimah Sham Ismail[2]

[1] Centre for Artificial Intelligence and Robotics, Malaysia-Japan International
Institute of Technology, Universiti Teknologi Malaysia,
54100 Kuala Lumpur, Malaysia
[2] Centre for Artificial Intelligence and Robotics,
Faculty of Electrical Engineering, Universiti Teknologi Malaysia,
81310 Skudai, Johor, Malaysia
hazlina@utm.my

Abstract. Crowd model has been very important in the investigation and study of the dynamics of a crowd. Crowd analysis using simulation models such as the Social Force Model (SFM) in representing crowd dynamics is instrumental in this study where experiments with real humans are not practical. However, the SFM lacks features that can represent more detailed individual characteristics and realistic movement when dealing with multi-room environment. Therefore, in this paper, we propose some modifications to the original SFM with a magnetic model approach that also integrates a path finding feature to produce a more realistic simulation of individuals' movements in the crowd. Results show that common collective crowd behaviours have been produced by the modified crowd model in a multi-room environment.

Keywords: Crowd simulation model · Magnetic model · Path finding · Social force model

1 Introduction

Crowd is a collection of individuals that are present in a common environment at the same time [1], and usually share some common goals [2]. However, the definition of crowd is not simply a collection of individuals. Each of the individuals may exert collective types of behaviours such as physical, psychological and social characteristics that influence the crowd to behave dynamically [3]. How to predict and control the behaviour of a crowd in various events and in different situations (i.e. normal or emergency) are some of the intriguing questions faced by many psychologist, sociologist, physicists and computer scientists [3].

The development of crowd models has been very important in the investigation and study of the dynamics of a crowd. Crowd modeling is a simulation study where small to large number of movement of entities or individuals, including their physical, social, psychological behaviours factors and activities can be simulated. These works are

© Springer Nature Singapore Pte Ltd. 2017
M.S. Mohamed Ali et al. (Eds.): AsiaSim 2017, Part I, CCIS 751, pp. 157–168, 2017.
DOI: 10.1007/978-981-10-6463-0_14

particularly important in predicting crowd behaviours in the virtual environment where experiments with humans are too dangerous to be tested and experimented with [3]. Thus, crowd models are capable of giving insight into human movement pattern and used by, for example, architects, space designers or safety engineers, as a tool to assist them in buildings or facilities design before the actual implementation [4]. This is why, up to recent years, crowd modeling and simulation tools have been widely used in investigating crowd dynamics and behaviours. Various types of crowd simulation models have been developed with a variety of objectives and approaches.

In developing crowd models, the model type and the modeling approach must suit the modeling objectives [3]. Different environments (e.g. in a train station, a bus station, a concourse hall a platform area and a narrowed pathway) and situations (during normal or peak hours, panic or emergency) will produce different types of human behaviours, thus, requiring different modeling objectives and approaches. In general, there are two types of crowd modeling approaches reported in various previous works. They are the 'macroscopic' and 'microscopic' approaches. Each of these approaches carry different crowd modeling objectives and model representations. For the macroscopic approach, modelers treat the crowd as a continuous flow of elements and usually aims to look at the movement pattern of the crowd, as one unit [5, 6]. There are several models that apply this approach in their simulation models such as the flow tiles model [7] and the continuum model [8]. The objective of using this approach is to study the movement pattern of the crowd, for example, in the evacuation process for huge and dense crowds. The Evacnet4 is one of the most common crowd model applications that has been successfully developed using the macroscopic approach. This approach uses vector fields to represent the impact of environmental factors on the crowd movement. The crowd movement is described by using complex differential equations representation [9]. To form vector fields and differential equations, some hypothesis for crowd motion [8] and statistical assumption are needed [10]. However, their validity with complex mathematical representation is often debatable [3]. This approach also omits the internal and external characters of individual behaviours where, by including this factor into a crowd model may affect crowd decision movements and trajectories. Therefore, this approach is more suitable for modeling large or huge crowd, due to the computational cost involved. The main limitation of this approach is that it requires extensive computational and processing demand.

Meanwhile, in the microscopic approach, the modelers particularly focus on the heterogeneous character of an individual in the crowd that is integrated with a variety of individual behavioural factors [11]. Modelers are able to assign different levels of granularity details, such as the specified velocity, the current position, the destination and the field of view (FoV) of each individual. This approach is capable of supporting complex simulated environment (i.e. including the obstacle and barrier) [12]. This approach can be implemented using two methods, which are the Cellular Automata (CA) [13–15] and the physical force model [16–18]. CA has the limitation of not reflecting the real behaviour of the individuals as CA model is using heuristic approach in updating individual movement rules [19]. One of the physical force model is the Social Force Model (SFM) introduced by Helbing's [20]. In SFM, the individual motion was governed by the Newton's equations. Most recent works have applied the SFM in simulation analysis as it is capable of simulating medium-large scale of crowd that also include the socio-psychological behaviours, under emergency cases [21, 22]. Thus, various types of crowd behaviours under panic situations can be produced such as arching, clogging and the 'faster is slower' effect. However, most recent SFM models were applied to test for only simple rectangular rooms [23]. Hence, by involving more complex room design (i.e. multi-room or multi-floor) in the case studies, movement of crowd using the original SFM may not be properly captured and simulated. To overcome this problem and to reduce the complexity of the algorithm, this work will modify the original model by combining the magnetic force approach to reduce computational cost involved and an embedded path finding feature in the simulation model. Detailed analysis on multi-room environment will be included in the simulation analysis to study the effect of the path finding feature in the simulation model. Validation on modification of SFM with the magnetic force model will also be described in this paper.

2 Methodology

The SFM has been used to simulate interactions between crowd movements in complex systems. In developing the model for crowd basic movement, the mathematical model includes the individual movement that results in a motivational force ($F^0(t)$), the repulsion force with other individuals in the crowd ($F_{ij}(t)$) and the repulsion force with an obstacle ($F_{iw}(t)$).

Inspired by Helbing's SFM, in this work, the individual physical and socio-psychological interaction to move is described by the Newton Second Law [11], which has the following equation:

$$F(t) = m\frac{dv}{dt} \tag{1}$$

Based on Eq. (1) above, the movement of an individual is influenced by three main forces, as described in the following equation:

$$F(t) = F^0(t) + \sum_{i \neq j} F_{ij}(t) + \sum_w F_{iw}(t) \tag{2}$$

where $F^0(t)$ represents the motivational force for an individual in moving to its desired target, $F_{ij}(t)$ and $F_{iw}(t)$ are the repulsion forces to evade other individuals and obstacles, respectively.

2.1 Individual Movement Motivational Force

In Eq. (2), the motivational force, $F^0(t)$ is represented by the following equation:

$$F^0(t) = m\frac{v^0(t)e^0(t) - v(t)}{t} \tag{3}$$

where, m is the mass of the individual, $v^0(t)$ is the desired speed of the individual, $e^0(t)$ is the desired direction, which is obtained by normalizing the individual vector position with the destination point, and $v(t)$ is the current speed of the individual at time t.

2.2   Repulsion Force with Individual

As a modification to original SFM, the proposed model in this work utilizes the concept from the magnetic model, by including the individual Field of View (FoV) and the predefined boundary to repulse. Particularly, the modification was made by replacing, $F_{ij}(t)$ in the original SFM by the proposed magnetic model. Therefore, the new equation for a basic individual movement to repulse other individuals, $F_{ij}(t)$, is given by the following formula:

$$F_{ij}(t) = k_r \frac{M_i M_j}{x^2} . n_{ij} \qquad (4)$$

where, k_r is the repulsion constant, M_i and M_j are the social mass constant for the ith and j^{th} individuals, respectively. Thus, n_{ij} is a normalized vector perpendicular with the individual. The repulsion constant, k_r is represented by a positive number which can take any value between 0 and 10, i.e. $0 < k_r \leq 10$. This range has been selected as it was suitable to represent the amount of repulsive force to be exerted in the individual movement. As an initial assumption in this work, M_i and M_j are assumed to be unity in order to prove the similarity between the proposed and the original models. To calculate the distance, x, between two individuals in in Eq. (4), the Eqs. (5) and (6) are used:

$$D_{ij} = \sqrt{\left(x_i - x_j\right)^2 + \left(y_i - y_j\right)^2} \qquad (5)$$

$$x = D_{ij} - R_i - R_j \qquad (6)$$

where $\{x_i, y_i\}$ and $\{x_j, y_j\}$ are the position coordinates of the ith and j^{th} individuals, respectively, R_i and R_j are the radii of the ith and j^{th} individuals, respectively, and D_{ij} is the distance between the centres of the two individuals. In Fig. 1 shows how to calculate the distance between two individuals. From the modified model in Eq. (4), the condition for an individual to repulse is based on its navigation FoV as well as the pre-defined comfort area, as depicted in Fig. 2.

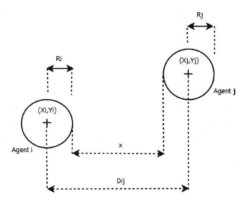

Fig. 1. Individual distance (from top view)

In the proposed method, if an individual underlies within FoV and the pre-defined boundary to repulse, denoted as A in Fig. 2, the latter will start to exert a repulsion force instantaneously. Otherwise, no repulsion force is exerted.

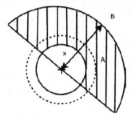

Fig. 2. Individual operation to repulse (FoV)

2.3   Repulsion Force with an Obstacle

In this section, the modification was made by replacing $F_{iw}(t)$ from original SFM model by the proposed magnetic model. Therefore, using the same strategy in calculating the repulsion forces among individuals described in section above, the repulsion force between an individual and an obstacle can be found in Eqs. (7) and (8):

$$F_{iw}(t) = \frac{k_w}{x_w^2} . n_{iw} \tag{7}$$

$$x_w = |r_i - r_w| \tag{8}$$

where k_w is a constant, r_w is the individual distance check based on the individual comfort area, x as described in Eq. (8). n_{iw} is the normalized vector perpendicular to the individual if the repulsion force is exerted, r_i, r_w are the positions of the individual and the obstacle, respectively. Similar to the range used for the repulsion constant, k_r, in Eq. (4), the range of k_w used in this work is given by $0 < k_w \leq 10$. In this work, the strategy adopted to avoid obstacles is depicted in Fig. 3 where additional normalized vector is introduced in calculating $F_{iw}(t)$ when an obstacle is encountered within the individual condition to repulse. More precisely, the normalized vector, which is perpendicular to the obstacle, is included in the calculation of the new repulsion force to evade. This modification will guarantee that no body contact will happen between the individual and the obstacle.

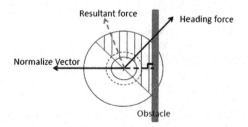

Fig. 3. Repulsion condition between individual and obstacle

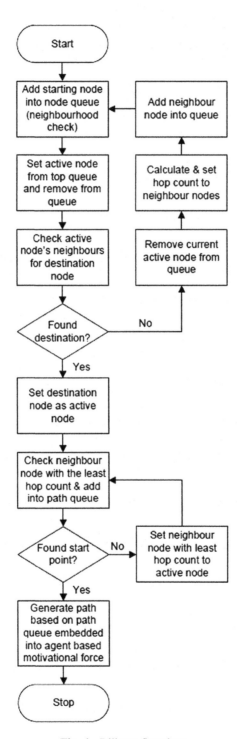

Fig. 4. Dijkstra flowchart

2.4   Path Finding Feature

Path finding feature is proposed in this work as a modification to the original model. The aim of this feature is to guide an individual in selecting the shortest route towards its target destination. For this purpose, the 'Dijkstra Algorithm' was adopted to achieve the path finding feature. This algorithm uses simplified nodes calculation in all directions of the individual movement. The Dijkstra Algorithm has been successfully applied in various applications. Furthermore, this algorithm is fast and the node's explorations propagate until the desired point is reached. Hence, it is adopted in this work. As depicted in Fig. 4, represent the flowchart of Dijkstra Algorithm integrated with the proposed model.

3   Results and Discussions

In this section we discuss the numerical simulation analysis based on two types which are:

(i) Qualitative analysis: through observing effect of collective behaviours.
(ii) Quantitative analysis: effect of path finding feature for multi-room environment.

3.1   Qualitative Analysis – Clogging Behaviour

Clogging behaviour are more likely to occur in a crowd of higher density. In this situation, when passing through a narrowed exit such as door, the more dense crowd will cause the slower individual can move. The exit door becomes clogged while the crowd will forms an arch-shape as depicted in Fig. 5.

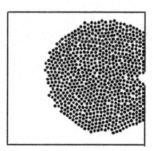

Fig. 5. Clogging and arching behaviour at a narrow exit door

We have constructed similar scenario of environment from the original model so that it can be directly compared with the approach in [20] to validate our proposed method. The environment of the simulation model is a single room of size 15 m × 15 m, with a single exit of width 1 m. A crowd of 50 individuals is considered in the room, and is randomly distributed using the parameters described in Table 1 below. The simulation is conducted in a 2-dimensional (2-D) space. Each individual in the crowd is positioned in (x, y) coordinates. The maximum desired speed of individual is set to 1.5 ms^{-1}, similar to that used in [20].

Table 1. Parameters used in the modified model

Symbol	Representation	Value
m	Individual body mass	80 kg
r	Individual body radius	0.25–0.35 m
τ	Reaction time	0.5 s
k_r	Repulsion force with individual	$0 < k_r \le 10$
k_w	Repulsion force with obstacle	$0 < k_w \le 10$
M_i and M_j	Social mass	1

By replacing the original mathematical model with the proposed magnetic approach for $F_{ij}(t)$ and $F_{iw}(t)$ in the SFM, qualitative type of analysis such as arching and clogging behaviour can be observed in the simulation results, which are as same as those produced in [20, 24, 25]. This can be shown through snapshots of the crowd movement at $t = 0$ s, $t = 10$ s, $t = 20$ s and $t = 30$ s in Fig. 6. The total time taken for the crowd to escape in the simulation analysis is $t = 34.5$ s. It shows that the proposed mathematical model provides a good representation for crowd movement, hence

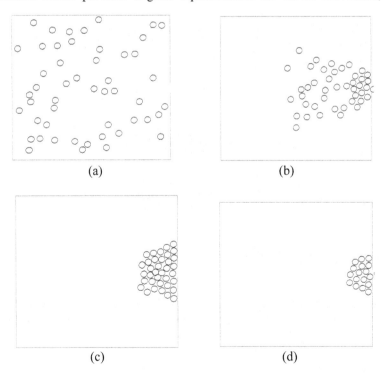

Fig. 6. Simulation snapshot for (a) $t = 0$ s (b) $t = 10$ s (c) $t = 20$ s (d) $t = 30$ s

allowing various details of individual characteristic such as the FoV (180°) and pre-defined boundary (2 m) to repulse other individual to be included.

This phenomena, arching and clogging, happens due to higher physical interaction between individuals to evacuate through a single narrow exit. This effect can also cause individual speed to slowly decrease, hence, the time duration for the individual to escape from the environment are delayed. Figure 7 shows the comparison of qualitative analysis for the benchmark test produced by the developed model, original models [20], Helbing's Model and previous works [24, 25].

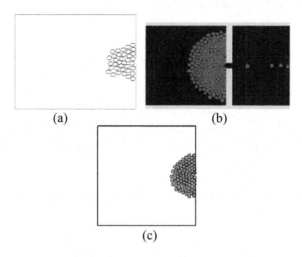

(a)   (b)

(c)

Fig. 7. Benchmark test for qualitative analysis (a) developed model, (b) SFM, (c) other model

3.2   Quantitative Analysis – Dijkstra Algorithm for Path Finding in Multi-room Environment

To test the effectiveness of the proposed path finding feature in the model where we have considered a multiple rooms on a single floor problem in the simulation environment. There are 6 rooms (5 m × 5 m) with 1 main exit constructed in the model as represented in Fig. 8.

Room 1	Room 2	Room 3	
Individual 1 ○	Individual 2 ○	Individual 3 ○	
			Main Exit
Individual 4 ○	Individual 5 ○	Individual 6 ○	
Room 4	Room 5	Room 6	

Fig. 8. Multi-room environment

All the individuals will escape from each room by moving towards the main exit door. Each of the rooms and main exit door sizes were assigned with 1 m, which is the standard door size in residential/office buildings. For initial testing, we used 6 number of individuals that are randomly placed in the room. The individual used the generated waypoint from the 'Dijkstra Algorithm' to move towards the main exit door. The total time taken and generated waypoints for them to move towards the exit door have been compared with the original SFM. The experiment was repeated for 5 times by changing the initial individual position in the environment randomly. The results are as depicted in Figs. 9 and 10 and tabulated in Table 2.

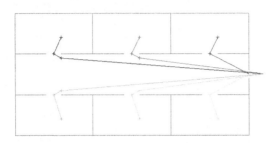

Fig. 9. Generated waypoint for the individual using Dijkstra algorithm

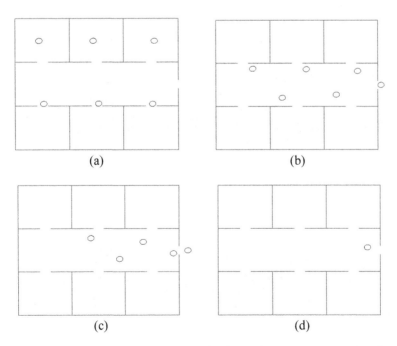

Fig. 10. Snapshot of the individual movement in the environment at (a) $t = 1$ s (b) $t = 4$ s (c) $t = 6$ s (d) $t = 10$ s

Table 2. Comparison total time taken to escape between the proposed and original model

Experiment	Proposed model	Social Force Model (SFM)
1	11.5 s	Task was not completed - no path finding feature
2	11.7 s	
3	11.9 s	
4	12.2 s	
5	12 s	

By using path finding feature integrated with the proposed model, the time taken for all individuals to evacuate through the main exit door is in between 11.5–12.2 s. Generated waypoint from the 'Dijkstra Algorithm' will guide the individual to the exit door. Hence, proposed 'Dijkstra Algorithm' will be benefit to be used in finding shortest path for the individual in selecting route to evacuate. Meanwhile, by using original SFM, the task for the individual to evacuate safely through main exit was not completed. This is due to individual waypoint for path finding feature to move in complex environment was not defined in the model. Other than that, individual movement was treated as a particle to move to search the target destination without guidance thus, will take longer time to end the simulation. Furthermore, it will not represent on how the real individual in the crowd will behave.

4 Conclusion

This paper presents a modified SFM with magnetic model and path finding feature in representing detailed characteristics of individuals in a crowd moving in a simulated environment. From the simulation studies presented, the proposed model has shown its effectiveness in producing realistic movement of individuals in the multi-room environment with waypoints to guide them towards the target destination. Furthermore, the modified SFM with the magnetic model has reduced the complexity of the mathematical model while including details characteristic (FoV and repulsion boundary) of the individual to represent more detailed real human characteristics. Eventhough the original model has been modified, common collective behaviours such as arching and clogging at the main exit door can still be produced from the proposed model. The main limitation of this model is that the values of individual parameters k_r, k_w, M_i and M_j need to be tuned in order to represent realistic crowd movement.

Acknowledgments. The authors would like to thank Universiti Teknologi Malaysia and the Ministry of Higher Education for their supports. This project is supported by Research University Grant Vote Q.K130000.2509.13H78.

References

1. Musse, S.R., Thalmann, D.: A model of human crowd behavior: group inter-relationship and collision detection analysis. Comput. Animat. Simul. **97**(9), 39–51 (1997)

2. Sharma, A.: Crowd-behavior prediction using subjective factor based multi-agent system. In: SMC 2000 Conference Proceedings of the 2000 IEEE International Conference on Systems, Man and Cybernetics. "Cybernetics Evolving to Systems, Humans, Organizations, and their Complex Interactions" (Cat. No. 00CH37166), vol. 1, pp. 298–300 (2000)
3. Simulation, C.: Review Paper : Crowd Modelling and Simulation Technologies (2009)
4. Khamis, N., Selamat, H., Yusof, R.: Simulation of agent movement with a path finding feature based on modification of physical force approach. Appl. Comput. Sci., 38–43 (2014)
5. Coscia, V., Canavesio, C.: First-order macroscopic modelling of human crowd dynamics. Math. Model. Methods Appl. Sci. **18**(Suppl. 01), 1217–1247 (2008)
6. Bellomo, N., Dogbé, C.: On the modelling crowd dynamics from scaling to hyperbolic macroscopic models. Math. Model. Methods Appl. Sci. **18**(Suppl. 01), 1317–1345 (2008)
7. Chenney, S.: Flow tiles. In: Flux, pp. 233–242 (2004)
8. Hughes, R.: A continuum theory for the flow of pedestrians. Transp. Res. Part B Methodol. **36**(6), 507–535 (2002)
9. Paris, S., Pettré, J., Donikian, S.: Pedestrian reactive navigation for crowd simulation: a predictive approach. Comput. Graph. Forum **26**(3), 665–674 (2007)
10. Hänseler, F., Farooq, B.: An aggregated dynamic flow model for pedestrian movement in railway stations. In: Proceedings of the 13th Swiss Transport Research Conference (2013)
11. Cohen, E., Cohen, E., Najman, L.: From crowd simulation to airbag deployment: particle systems, a new paradigm of simulation. J. Electron. Imaging **6**(1), 94 (1997)
12. Cristiani, E., Piccoli, B., Tosin, A.: Multiscale modeling of granular flows with application to crowd dynamics. Multiscale Model. Simul. **9**(1), 155 (2011)
13. Zheng, X., Li, W., Guan, C.: Simulation of evacuation processes in a square with a partition wall using a cellular automaton model for pedestrian dynamics. Phys. A: Stat. Mech. Appl. **389**(11), 2177–2188 (2010)
14. Aubé, F., Shield, R.: Modeling the effect of leadership on crowd flow dynamics. In: Sloot, P. M.A., Chopard, B., Hoekstra, Alfons G. (eds.) ACRI 2004. LNCS, vol. 3305, pp. 601–611. Springer, Heidelberg (2004). doi:10.1007/978-3-540-30479-1_62
15. Yuan, W., Tan, K.H.: Cellular automata model for simulation of effect of guiders and visibility range. Curr. Appl. Phys. **9**(5), 1014–1023 (2009)
16. Moussaïd, M., Perozo, N., Garnier, S., Helbing, D., Theraulaz, G.: The walking behaviour of pedestrian social groups and its impact on crowd dynamics. PLoS One **5**(4), e10047 (2010)
17. Yang, X., Dong, H., Yao, X., Sun, X.: Effects of quantity and position of guides on pedestrian evacuation. In: Proceedings of the IEEE Conferences on Intelligent Transportation Systems, ITSC, vol. 2015, pp. 1317–1322, October 2015
18. Yang, X., Dong, H., Wang, Q., Chen, Y., Hu, X.: Guided crowd dynamics via modified social force model. Phys. A: Stat. Mech. Appl. **411**, 63–73 (2014)
19. Teknomo, K.: Microscopic pedestrian flow characteristics: development of an image processing data collection and simulation model (2002)
20. Helbing, D., Farkas, I., Vicsek, T.: Simulating dynamical features of escape panic. Nature **407**(6803), 487–490 (2000)
21. Dong, H., Gao, X., Gao, T., Sun, X., Wang, Q.: Crowd evacuation optimization by leader-follower model. IFAC Proc. Vol. **19**(61233001), 12116–12121 (2014)
22. Hou, L., Liu, J.G., Pan, X., Wang, B.H.: A social force evacuation model with the leadership effect. Phys. A: Stat. Mech. Appl. **400**, 93–99 (2014)
23. Daoliang, Z., Lizhong, Y., Jian, L.: Exit dynamics of occupant evacuation in an emergency. Phys. A: Stat. Mech. Appl. **363**(2), 501–511 (2006)
24. Ha, V., Lykotrafitis, G.: Agent-based modeling of a multi-room multi-floor building emergency evacuation. Phys. A: Stat. Mech. Appl. **391**(8), 2740–2751 (2012)
25. Ma, Y., Yuen, R.K.K., Lee, E.W.M.: Effective leadership for crowd evacuation. Phys. A: Stat. Mech. Appl. **450**, 333–341 (2016)

Irregular Spatial Cluster Detection Based on H1N1 Flu Simulation in Beijing

Yitong Zhao[1](✉), Shan Mei[1], and Wei Zhang[2]

[1] College of Information System and Management,
National University of Defense Technology, Changsha 410073, China
poaa3414@163.com
[2] Institute of Telecommunication Satellite,
China Academy of Space Technology, Beijing 110101, China

Abstract. Spatial cluster detection of infected areas is widely used for disease surveillance, prevention and containment. However, the commonly used cluster methods cannot resolve the conflicts between the accuracy and efficiency of detection. We present an improved method for flexibly shaped spatial scanning, which can identify Irregular spatial clusters much more accurately and efficiently. First, we convert geographic information to a graph structure. Next, we approximately locate the disease regions. And then, based on the approximately located regions, we detect arbitrarily shaped and connected clusters in the graph based on likelihood ratio. Finally, we check the significance of the identified regions by Monte Carlo method. The algorithm is tested by an agent based simulation of H1N1 influenza data in Beijing. The results show that compared with the previous spatial scan statistic algorithms, our algorithm performs better in terms of shorter time and higher accuracy.

Keywords: Agent-based simulation · Graph mining · Cluster detection · Spatial statistics · Disease surveillance

1 Introduction

In the area of public health security, the space disease surveillance study was conducted to identify and predict the spatial distribution of disease transmission at the beginning of the disease outbreak, which can help disease containment.

To illustrate this scenario, Fig. 1 depicts the disease outbreak problem, which shows the cholera outbreak along a winding river floodplain. In the left part, each region represents a county. We convert the left part to a connected graph $G = (V, E)$ where nodes $v \in V$ represent the regions with features values x_v representing the patient number, which is shown in the right part. Our goal is to find the most possible outbreak regions over all connected sub-graphs.

Common spatial cluster detection algorithms search the epidemic regions by setting the scan window to a specific shape, such as circle [1, 2] (CircleScan), rectangle [3], and oval [4]. These algorithms are fast, but the outbreak regions can be irregularly shaped, many regions without decease outbreak are often included in detection, it has been recognized that this can result in loss of detection performance [5].

© Springer Nature Singapore Pte Ltd. 2017
M.S. Mohamed Ali et al. (Eds.): AsiaSim 2017, Part I, CCIS 751, pp. 169–179, 2017.
DOI: 10.1007/978-981-10-6463-0_15

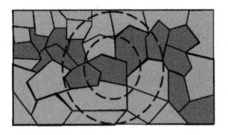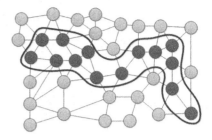

Fig. 1. Convert the real map to a connected graph.

In order to solve the problem of the above algorithms, Tango et al. proposed a spatial cluster algorithm that can detect arbitrary shape outbreak regions, called "flexibly shaped spatial scan statistic" [5] (FlexScan). Compared with the previous algorithms, the FlexScan algorithm detects the epidemic regions more accurate. However, since the FlexScan algorithm needs to traverse the entire region and its nearest $K-1$ regions, the computational efficiency of the algorithm will be very low when $K \geq 20$.

Some scholars hope to use the heuristic algorithm to accelerate the process of detection. Duczmal et al. used simulated annealing algorithms to check criminal clusters in large cities [6]. Neill et al. proposed a fast space scanning algorithm (LTSS) by build scoring functions to accelerate the calculation process [7]. Although the heuristic algorithms have fast computing speed, so far, most of the heuristic algorithms will detect regions which is much larger than the actual outbreak regions or get multiple non-connected outbreak regions, the accuracy is still lower than common algorithms.

In the field of disease surveillance algorithm test, it is difficult to distinguish between epidemic disease and general disease, for they have similar symptoms. Scholars always use simulation data for algorithm performance test. Neill et al., by assumed that the number of patients increases linearly within the duration of the outbreak but the range of disease transmission does not change over time [8], which is inconsistent with the real situation. While other data generation methods based on previous outbreaks of data require a lot of historical data support [9] and are complex for researchers in non-simulation areas.

The main contribution of this paper is to balance the accuracy of detection and the efficiency of computation, and use an agent-based simulation for algorithm performance test. We explore the improved flexibly shaped spatial scan statistic (IFlexScan) algorithm by combining the CircleScan algorithm and the FlexScan algorithm. And according to an agent-based simulation model of Beijing [10–12], the performance test data is generated.

2 Improved Flexibly Shaped Spatial Scan Statistic

Spatial cluster detection algorithms generate a large number of scanning windows, and the regions which are covered by the window are called candidate regions. We assume that the number of patients subject to Poisson distribution, and select the candidate region, which has the largest likelihood function of patients, as a predicted disease epidemic region.

For any given region i, the CircleScan algorithm generates a set of concentric circles as the scanning window. In order to improve the accuracy of detection, the FlexScan algorithm generates subsets of the candidate regions in the CircleScan algorithm, which can be arbitrarily shaped, as their candidate regions. For any given region i, we denote the maximum of neighbor regions is K, then the computational complexity of the FlexScan algorithm is $O(2^K)$, and the CircleScan algorithms is $O(K)$. Therefore, the FlexScan algorithm takes much more time than the CircleScan algorithm.

It is shown that in the case of K greater than 30, the operation time of FlexScan algorithm will more than a week [5]. Therefore, FlexScan algorithm is not suitable for discovering large epidemic regions.

2.1 Criteria for the Surveillance Epidemic Regions

If there is spatial clustering of the diseased population, then we believe that there is at least a region A in the candidate regions set Z, in which the proportion of the disease will be higher than outside. Then we can establish the following hypothesis test as shown in formula (1):

$$H_0 : E[N(A)] = \xi(A), \forall A \in Z, H1 : E(N(A)) > \xi(A), \exists A \in Z \qquad (1)$$

where N represents the observed number of patients in the region, and ξ represents the expected number of patients in region.

The test statistic is constructed by using the likelihood function according to the Poisson distribution, as shown in (2):

$$L = sup_{A \in Z} \left(\frac{n(A)}{\xi(A)}\right)^{n(A)} \left(\frac{n(A')}{\xi(A')}\right)^{n(A')} I(\frac{n(A)}{\xi(A)} > \frac{n(A')}{\xi(A')}) \qquad (2)$$

where A' represents the regions except region A, n represents the observed number of patients in region, $I(\frac{n(A)}{\xi(A)} > \frac{n(A')}{\xi(A')})$ denotes an instruction function.

To test the significance of A, we use Monte Carlo simulation to generate 999 groups of data, which obey the null hypothetical. Then we calculate the corresponding L value of each group, if the L value of A is greater than 95% of the simulation data, we can determine that the region A is the disease outbreak region.

2.2 Narrow the Scope of Surveillance and Precisely Identify Outbreak Regions

Figure 2 shows the spatial scanning process of the IFlexScan algorithm, where the circle regions represent the approximate range of the epidemics. Note that there must be intersecting nodes between the circle regions. The dark gray region represents the precise positioning of the epidemics. The criteria for determining the epidemic regions are described as above.

For the nodes inside the approximate range of the epidemics. We use a set of Boolean values to represent the scan window, where 0 indicates the node is outside the scan window, 1 indicates the node belongs to the scan window. Generate all possible combinations by traversing, and the connectivity of nodes is judged by the adjacency matrix.

As can be seen from Fig. 2, although the IFlexScan algorithm and FlexScan algorithm both used traversal search method, the surveillance scope of IFlexScan algorithm is significant reduction. In addition, CircleScan limits the search direction of the IFlexScan algorithm, so that the IFlexScan algorithm is more efficient than the FlexScan algorithm when the maximum of regions K is same.

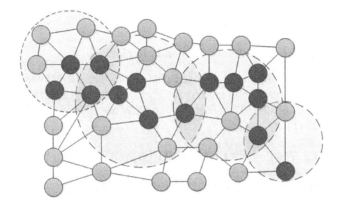

Fig. 2. IFlexScan algorithm spatial scanning process

3   The Generation of Simulation Data

Disease outbreak is hard to predict. In real situation, it is difficult to distinguish H1N1 from common cold, because they have similar symptoms. And we cannot evaluate the performance of detection algorithms. Simulation data can help us solve this problem. We use an agent-based simulation model to build artificial Beijing that contains 10 million people [10–12]. And then we set the initial patient of the H1N1 flu, and then carried out simulation for 100 days.

3.1   The Simulation Model of Beijing

We divided Beijing into 309 areas according to streets, use the distribution of residential buildings and corporations which we found on the internet, to simulate the population in Beijing [10–12], as shown in Fig. 3.

The generation of daily activity schedules depends on the daily activity pattern. According to literature [13–15] generate their daily activities schedule, as shown in Table 1. Based on a city survey, the percentage is derived from [15]. In the actual simulation, an entertainment or medical activity will replace O (others).

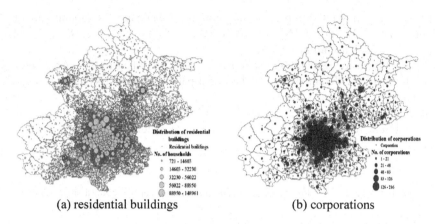

(a) residential buildings   (b) corporations

Fig. 3. Distribution of residential buildings and corporations.

Table 1. Agent activity schedule, where H means home, W means workplace, O means others.

Activity mode	Percentage
HWH	53.4
HWHOH	10.3
HWOWH	2.7
HWHWH	27.1
HWHWHOH	6.5

The required movement time can be dynamically estimated, taking into account starting point and end point. In addition, an agent's infectious status will affect their behavior and then be reflected in the activity schedule. For example, if agents were infected, it will be extended to stay at home time, reduce working hours, to avoid crowded places such as entertainment place. Therefore, the parameters of the generated activity can be adjusted to suit different situations.

3.2   The Simulation of H1N1 Flu

The contact between agents may cause H1N1 infection. The course of disease development can be described by SIR model, as the following stages shown:

(1) *Susceptible: Agents not infectious;*
(2) *Infected: Agents are infectious, and can infect others;*
(3) *Recovered: Remove agents from model.*

In stage 2, agents can transmit H1N1 flu to others, we assume that each agent in stage 2 has the same infectivity. We describe the infection process by basic regeneration number R_0, which means during symptom period, average number of agents can be infected by an infected agent. We introduce three parameters $D_{\text{incubation}}$, D_{symptom}

and $D_{vaccination}$ for stage 2, represent the duration of incubation, symptom and vacci-nation respectively. For H1N1 flu we can set $D_{incubation} = 1–2$, $D_{symptom} = 1–7$, $D_{vaccination} = 7–21$ according to [16].

We set the basic regeneration number $R_0 = 1.86$, according to [17]. And we chose 10 residents from different streets, as the initial patient of the H1N1, and then carried out simulation for 100 days. Recording the regions where all patients were located from the beginning of the simulation to the day which has largest patient growth rate, as the H1N1 outbreak regions. The detailed information of simulation is shown in Table 2.

Table 2. The detail information of agent-based simulation in Beijing H1N1 flu

No.	Initial patient's location	Record time (day)	Cumulative number of patients	Number of regions within H1N1
1	Ganjiakou	23	849	11
2	Chongwenmen	18	1136	15
3	Tiantan	25	1527	15
4	Qinglong bridge	31	462	12

The range of H1N1 influenza transmission is shown in Fig. 4, where the dark gray regions represents the street where the initial patients were located and the light gray regions represents the street under the H1N1 flu spread.

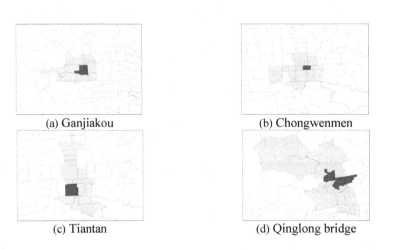

(a) Ganjiakou   (b) Chongwenmen

(c) Tiantan   (d) Qinglong bridge

Fig. 4. Influenza-transmitted regions of experiment (1)–(4), respectively.

We injected the simulated data into real-world fever data. This allows us to take into account the noisy nature of real world. The fever data were counted by 10 tertiary hospital in Beijing, from May 1, 2016 to July 31, 2016. The data had a daily mean of 35 case, and were analyzed by one-way ANOVA, the P value was less than 0.001. Therefore, there was no significant correlation between the number of patients and the time.

4   Experimental Results

We present empirical results of IFlexScan's detection power and running time, using the simulation data above. And we compare the results with CircleScan and FlexScan to show the advantages of our proposed algorithm.

4.1   Comparison of Algorithms Performance

We measured the performance of the algorithm by recall rate and precision. In order to illustrate the significance of the recall rate and precision, we set the outbreak regions as the positive samples, and no outbreak regions as the negative samples. The introduction of the relative conceptions is shown as below:

(1) *TP (True Positive): Indicates the number of positive samples correctly predicted by the algorithm.*

(2) *TN (True Negative): Indicates the number of negative samples correctly predicted by the algorithm.*

(3) *FP (False Positive): Indicates the number of negative samples that were incorrectly predicted by the algorithm as positive samples.*

(4) *FN (False Negative): Indicates the number of positive samples that were incorrectly predicted by the algorithm as negative samples.*

Let $recall = \frac{TP}{TP+FN}$, $precision = \frac{TP}{TP+FP}$. In the problem described in this paper, the number of positive samples are relatively small, which belongs to the class imbalance problem. To measure the performance of the algorithm, the above two indicators combined as an indicator, called F_1 value, which is defined as follows:

$$F_1 = \frac{2 * recall * precision}{recall + precision} \tag{3}$$

Table 3 shows the computational performance of the three algorithms for the four experiments when $K = 25$.

It is can be seen from Table 3, in experiment 1 and experiment 2, outbreak regions showed relatively regular shape, CircleScan algorithm has a higher F_1 value. In experiment 3 and experiment 4, outbreak regions showed a relatively irregular shape, CircleScan algorithm has a lower F_1 value. Therefore, CircleScan algorithm cannot accurately determine the epidemic regions for the irregular shape. FlexScan and IFlexScan algorithms have good performance for any shape of the epidemic regions.

Figures 5 and 6 show the results of the three algorithms in Experiment 3 and Experiment 4 when the F value is maximum respectively. The outbreak regions of the correct classification (TP) are colored by blue. The non-outbreak regions of the correct classification (TN) are colored by white. The outbreak regions which are incorrectly classified as non-outbreak regions (FN) are colored by yellow. The non-outbreak regions which are incorrectly classified as outbreak regions (FP) are colored by red.

Table 3. Comparison of algorithm performance

No.	Algorithm	TP	TN	FP	FN	Recall	Precision	F_1
1	CircleScan	11	296	2	0	1	0.85	0.92
	FlexScan	11	298	0	0	1	1	1
	IFlexScan	11	298	0	0	1	1	1
2	CircleScan	10	294	0	5	0.67	0.91	0.77
	FlexScan	13	294	0	2	0.87	1	0.93
	IFlexScan	15	294	0	0	1	1	1
3	CircleScan	11	280	14	4	0.73	0.44	0.55
	FlexScan	11	293	1	4	0.73	0.92	0.81
	IFlexScan	13	293	1	2	0.87	0.93	0.90
4	CircleScan	9	285	12	3	0.75	0.43	0.55
	FlexScan	10	297	0	2	0.83	1	0.91
	IFlexScan	12	296	1	0	1	0.92	0.96

Through Figs. 5 and 6, we find that for irregular outbreak regions, CircleScan's classification regions are approximately circular and therefore CircleScan has a high FP value which lead to a lower F_1 value. In contrast, FlexScan and IFlexScan classification regions are more consistent with the actual situation, and IFlexScan has a better surveillance effect.

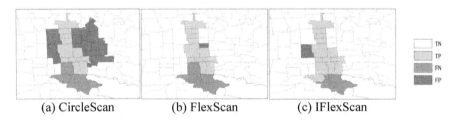

(a) CircleScan   (b) FlexScan   (c) IFlexScan

Fig. 5. The detection results of the three algorithms in experiment 3. (Color figure online)

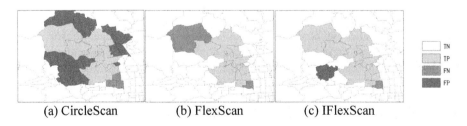

(a) CircleScan   (b) FlexScan   (c) IFlexScan

Fig. 6. The detection results of the three algorithms in experiment 4. (Color figure online)

4.2   Comparison of Algorithms Run Time

We use a personal computer (windows 8, CPU i5-5257U, 2.7 GHz) to compare the running time of IFlexScan, FlexScan and CircleScan, according to experiment 4. In Fig. 7, we present average run time for the three different algorithms.

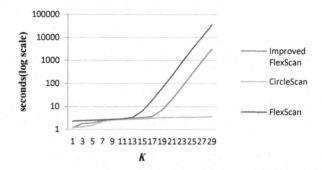

Fig. 7. Run time analysis for the three algorithm.

It can be seen from Fig. 7, when $K \leq 13$, the three algorithms can find outbreak regions within 10 s. The running time of CircleScan algorithm is level off with the change of K value. The running time of FlexScan algorithm and IFlexScan algorithm starts to increase rapidly when $K \geq 13$ and $K \geq 17$ respectively. But compared to the FlexScan algorithm, our proposed algorithm is about 10 times faster, when K is same. Therefore, our proposed algorithm can cover a larger range of monitoring when the run time is allowed.

Table 4 shows the best performance achieved by FlexScan and IFlexScan, as well as the required running time, in each experiment.

Through Table 4, we find that for the irregular regions in this article, compared to FlexScan, IFlexScan required much shorter running time.

Table 4. The best performances and running time

No.	Algorithm	K	F_1	Running time (seconds)
1	FlexScan	11	0.95	3
	IFlexScan	15	0.91	2
2	FlexScan	19	0.92	223
	IFlexScan	15	0.93	4
3	FlexScan	25	0.81	2616
	IFlexScan	25	0.9	382
4	FlexScan	23	0.91	741
	IFlexScan	19	0.91	6

5 Conclusion

We convert geographic information to a graph structure and present IFlexScan algorithm to detect the most possible outbreak regions over all connected sub-graphs. According to the agent simulation model to establish artificial Beijing [10–12], and generated H1N1 influenza simulation data, for algorithm test.

Compared with the FlexScan algorithm, the IFlexScan algorithm reduces the running time of the spatial clustering regions detection by narrowing the scope of surveillance. When the maximum neighborhood size $K \leq 20$, IFlexScan algorithm can get the operation result in 10 s. When the maximum neighborhood size $K > 20$, IFlexScan algorithm still has a relatively fast computational speed, which means IFlexScan can find a wide range of spatial clustering.

For irregular shape outbreak regions, our proposed algorithm also has a higher surveillance performance. For example, in experiment 3, the real epidemic regions present long strip shape, IFlexScan algorithm $F_1 > 0.9$, higher than the previous space scanning algorithms. This indicates that the IFlexScan algorithm can position the spatial clustering regions more accurate.

We believe, that in the field of disease surveillance algorithm test, compared with the previous data generation, the simulation model based on agent, has certain advantages. The agent-based simulation model data generation method is relatively simple, only researchers need to set a few parameters, can they can generate simulation data that similar to the reality. It has valuable reference for the future performance test of spatial clustering algorithm.

Acknowledgment. The authors wish to acknowledge the support of National Science Foundation of China under grant 71373282.

References

1. Kulldorff, M.: A spatial scan statistic. Commun. Stat.-Theory Methods **26**(6), 1481–1496 (1997)
2. Huang, L., Kulldorff, M., Gregorio, D.: A spatial scan statistic for survival data. Biometrics **63**(1), 109–118 (2007)
3. Neill, D.B., Moore, A.W.: A fast multi-resolution method for detection of significant spatial disease clusters. In: NIPS (2003)
4. Kulldorff, M., et al.: An elliptic spatial scan statistic. Stat. Med. **25**(22), 3929–3943 (2006)
5. Tango, T., Takahashi, K.: A flexibly shaped spatial scan statistic for detecting clusters. Int. J. Health Geograp. **4**(1), 11 (2005)
6. Duczmal, L., Assuncao, R.: A simulated annealing strategy for the detection of arbitrarily shaped spatial clusters. Comput. Stat. Data Anal. **45**(2), 269–286 (2004)
7. Neill, D.B.: Fast subset scan for spatial pattern detection. J. R. Stat. Soc.: Ser. B (Stat. Methodol.) **74**(2), 337–360 (2012)
8. Speakman, S., McFowland III, E., Neill, D.B.: Scalable detection of anomalous patterns with connectivity constraints. J. Comput. Graph. Stat. **24**(4), 1014–1033 (2015)

9. Buckeridge, D.L., et al.: Evaluation of syndromic surveillance systems—design of an epidemic simulation model. In: Morbidity and Mortality Weekly Report, pp. 137–143 (2004)
10. Ge, Y.: An agent-based framework and generation of an artificial society. National University of Defense Technology, Changsha, China (2014)
11. Zhang, P., et al.: The large scale machine learning in an artificial society: prediction of the Ebola outbreak in Beijing. Comput. Intell. Neurosci. **2015**, 6 (2015)
12. Chen, B., et al.: KD-ACP: a software framework for social computing in emergency management. Math. Probl. Eng. **2015**(5), 1–27 (2015)
13. Bhat, C.R., Singh, S.K.: A comprehensive daily activity-travel generation model system for workers. Transp. Res. Part A **34**(1), 1–22 (2000)
14. Roorda, M.J., Miller, E.J., Habib, K.M.N.: Validation of TASHA: a 24-h activity scheduling microsimulation model. Transp. Res. Part A **42**(2), 360–375 (2008)
15. Yang, M., Chen, X., Wang, W., et al.: Commuters' trip generation model based on activity patterns. J. SE Univ. (Nat. Sci. Ed.) **38**(3), 525–530 (2008)
16. Mei, S., Zhu, Y., Qiu, X., et al.: Individual decision making can drive epidemics: a fuzzy cognitive map study. IEEE Trans. Fuzzy Syst. **21**(6), 1–10 (2013)
17. Yang, Y., Sugimoto, J.D., Halloran, M.E., et al.: The transmissibility and control of pandemic influenza a (H1N1) virus. Science **326**(5953), 729–733 (2009)

Task Transfer in Software Agent Community with Sincerity Merit Point

Nur Huda Jaafar[1(✉)], Mohd Sharifuddin Ahmad[2],
and Azhana Ahmad[2]

[1] Faculty of Computer and Mathematical Sciences,
Universiti Teknologi MARA, KM 12, Jalan Muar,
85009 Segamat, Johor, Malaysia
nurhu378@johor.uitm.edu.my
[2] College of Computer Science and Information Technology,
Universiti Tenaga Nasional, Putrajaya Campus, Jalan IKRAM-UNITEN,
43000 Kajang, Selangor, Malaysia
{sharif,azhana}@uniten.edu.my

Abstract. The software agent technology is one of the human assistive tech-nologies that enables team working. In the process of achieving the team goals, an agent may need help from its teammate to perform its remaining task's activities in order to meet the task's deadline. However, certain conditions are needed to be fulfilled for the task transfer even though these would be a burden to the teammate. This paper shows the use of a Workload Manager for handling signals to allow the agent getting help from its teammate. It is also used to identify the available teammate agents that can really help. In this paper also, we simulate the transfer of the remaining task's activities from one agent to another and demonstrate the process of awarding merit points to the agent that sincerely helps its teammate.

Keywords: Task · Task transfer · Teammate agent · Workload · Sincerity

1 Introduction

The existence of intelligent technologies such as drones and robots which are autho-rized to make decisions at a certain level eases many burdens of humans especially in performing tasks. With these technologies, task performances are accelerated and at the same time are maintained at high quality of delivery and output. One of the autono-mous technologies that support these intelligent technologies is the software agent technology. A software agent is able to work individually or in a team to accomplish its assigned objectives [1]. The ability of a software agent to collaborate with its teammate and react to its environment is one of the keys that accelerate and improve task performance. It is also capable of performing multiple tasks at a certain time. This autonomous technology has proven its advantages in many fields such as healthcare, energy consumption, manufacturing and military [2–5].

While the advantages of software agent technology have been proven in many fields, the mechanism to avoid imbalance of task delegation among agents in a com-munity should be taken into account in designing the intelligent system. The situation

© Springer Nature Singapore Pte Ltd. 2017
M.S. Mohamed Ali et al. (Eds.): AsiaSim 2017, Part I, CCIS 751, pp. 180–188, 2017.
DOI: 10.1007/978-981-10-6463-0_16

is worst if the tasks involve deadlines which cause problems to an agent. One solution to this problem is for the agent to transfer some of its tasks to a teammate agent. However, in certain situation this can be a burden to the teammate agent, especially if it is having a heavy workload. The agent may face problem to identify a suitable teammate agent which is willing to cooperate in completing the task.

This paper discusses the method of designing the process of task transfer in a software agent community by considering the total workload of each agent. We propose a Workload Manager that calculates an agent's workload but also determines the right time for the agent to get help from a teammate agent. The Workload Manager also identifies a suitable agent which can offer help to the agent. This paper also shows the process of awarding merit points to an agent which helps its teammate to sincerely perform the task.

This paper presents the work-in-progress of our research in modeling sincerity for software agents. The rest of this paper is organized as follows: The next section discusses the related work in this area. We show the design of task transfer in a software agent community. We then animate the process as a simulation to validate the design. Finally, we conclude the paper.

2 Related Work

A software agent is a component that supports autonomous technology. It can work individually or in a group to meet some assigned objectives [1, 6]. The characteristics of software agent such as reactive, autonomous, communicative, goal-oriented, learning, mobile and flexible supports the software agent to work in dynamic environment [1, 6–9]. It also interacts with its community via negotiation, coordination and cooperation activities.

The ability of a software agent to work in a team is an advantage of this technology to deliver a much faster output and with higher quality. It can also build teams in dynamic environments. These advantages provide humans with the confidence to authorize agents in making decisions at certain levels and assist humans [4, 10].

Although working as a team brings many benefits to software agent in achieving the goals, the coordination among agents in a community should be designed properly. Since agents may have individual and shared goals, designers in agent-based systems should design the coordination of agents to avoid conflicts in achieving the individual or shared goals [1]. The situations of multi-agent systems' organization should be carefully studied because collaboration within the community depends so much on it [11].

Conflicts could become worst if the tasks that are handled by the agents involve tight schedules with deadlines. The problem of tasks with the deadlines involve issues such as resources problems that need to be managed to avoid conflicts in performing tasks individually or in groups [12]. The agents may face with issues in managing to achieve individual or team goals. In this situation, the agents should find ways to balance the effort of fulfilling the individual and the team goals [11]. Here, agents' workloads could be considered in solving this problem. The workloads could be an indicator to identify the percentage of burden for each agent, which enforces community awareness between the agents and their environments [13].

In order to motivate the agents to take action ethically, the ethical behaviour such as human sincerity should be instilled in software agent environments. Machine ethic is one of the applied ethics that is created to ensure the machine such as robot, drone or autonomous system to function ethically. The increasing of autonomous machines usage in taking over humans' tasks is a signal to us to include the machine ethics in autonomous machines, especially in the role of decision making [4, 14, 15]. Adapting human behaviour to the machine environment is a solution to develop ethical machine behaviour that is more human user-friendly. Previous researches had proven that adapting human behaviour to machine environment brought a lot of advantages to human livelihoods [16, 17].

3   Task Transfer Between Agents

The process of task transfer involves a group of agents that consist of worker agents and their teammate agents. In this environment, we propose a Workload Manager (WM) that computes a workload for each agent. This Workload Manager will monitor the each task under every agent and also the performance of overall tasks. The monitoring activity of each task is to identify the needs of favour completing it before the deadline. From here, the Workload Manager will be able to use the signal to worker agent to get help from another teammate agent. While monitoring the overall task performance of all agents, the Workload Manager, at the same time, will be able to identify the teammates that could offer help to worker agent. The details of Workload Manager processes have been discussed in the previous research [18].

Figure 1 shows the process of transferring a remaining task from a worker agent to its teammate agent. Based on the workload of each agent, the Workload Manager broadcasts a signal when a worker agent is allowed to get help from its teammate

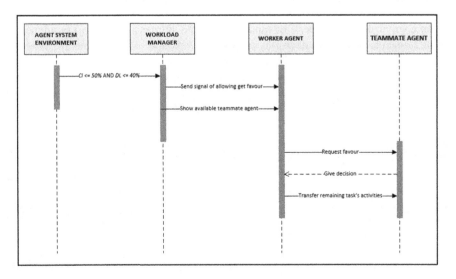

Fig. 1. Sequence diagram of transferring remaining task from one agent to another

agents. We constrain this signal to avoid a worker agent from overly depending on its teammate agents in performing tasks. In this research, the system broadcasts the signal when a worker agent achieves the percentage of a task completion; $CT <= 50\%$ and the remaining deadline of the task; $DL <= 40\%$.

In order to avoid the burden to the other agents which are having heavy workloads, the Workload Manager calculates all agents' workloads to identify their availabilities. In this system, a worker agent can only get help from a teammate agent which does not have a heavy workload. The system considers an agent as having a heavy workload if the total workload of all tasks assigned to it exceeds 100%. The current task, T_c, and the incoming task, T_i, (the task that will be transferred to the agent) is summed up to determine whether the workload exceeds 100%. The agent with a heavy workload is considered as an indispensable agent.

From the list of available agents, a worker agent chooses a teammate agent, which would give a supportive response to the request. If the available agent is more than one, the worker agent chooses the one with the lowest workload among the available agents. The worker agent then sends a request and waits for the decision from the selected teammate agent. The teammate agent decides whether to accept or reject the request. Once the teammate agent agrees to help, the worker agent transfers its remaining task's activities to the teammate agent.

In this system, we implement the awarding of merit points to a teammate agent and Fig. 2 shows the sequence diagram of the process. Merit points are used to analyze and gauge the sincerity of a teammate agent when it gives help to a worker agent. We use the point system as a mechanism to formulate the sincerity of agents in the environment [18–20].

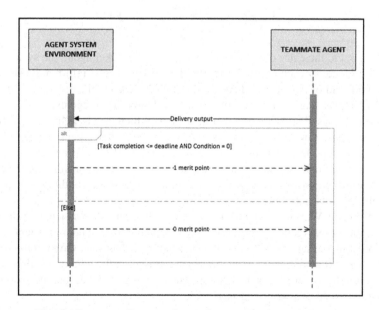

Fig. 2. Sequence diagram of awarding merit point to the agents

The system starts to analyze the merit point gains when a teammate agent delivers the output of a task it has agreed to help. Two criteria are considered when giving the merit point; (i) fulfilling the deadline, and (ii) the condition from the teammate agent. The teammate agent gets 1 merit point if the task is completed on time or earlier and the teammate agent does not give any condition for performing the task completely. The agent is considered as sincere agent if it fulfills these criteria. However, the agent gets 0 merit point if it fails to meet these criteria, which shows the agent's insincerity.

4   Simulating Task Transfer Between Agents

To validate the design, we create a simulation using Java and the JADE platform. We exploit the POSTGRESQL as a database for this system.

In the simulation, we create three agents: Agent_1, Agent_2 and Agent_3 that are involved in production works such as printing and packaging of products. In this simulation Agent_1 and Agent_2 have two tasks while Agent_3 is free. The tasks' information for Agent_1 and Agent _2 is stated in Table 1. Figure 3 is an example of an interface for inserting the task's information.

Table 1. The tasks' information for Agent_1 and Agent_2

Agent	Task	Task deadline	No. of activities
Agent_1	Printing	4/7/2017	3 activities
	Packaging	4/13/2017	5 activities
Agent_2	Printing	4/7/2017	3 activities
	Packaging	4/13/2017	5 activities

Subsequent to the entry of the task assigned to each worker agent, the system shows the total workload for each agent. Currently, the worker agents' information shows that the total workload of Agent_1 and Agent_2 is 17.77% each while the total workload of Agent_3 is 0.00%. Figure 4 shows the total workloads for all agents.

Figure 5 shows that there is a worker agent, which needs help to perform and complete its task. On 2017-04-04, the system detects that Agent_1 needs help to perform the printing task. The deadline for this task is 2017-04-07 and the completion status is 0/3, which shows that the activities are not completed for this task. Agent_1's workload also increases to 44.44%. These situations fulfill the condition for the agent to get help from its teammate.

Based on the Workload Manager, the available agent that can give help is displayed. In this case, Agent_2 and Agent_3 are available to give help to Agent_1. If the number of available agents that can offer help is more than one, the system compares the total workload among these available agents. Based on the communication between the agents as shown in Fig. 6, the system chooses Agent_3 because its workload is 0.00% while Agent_2's workload is 17.77%.

Task FormAgent_1@192.168.1.246:8888/JADE

Add New Task

Task Name	Packaging
Task Priority	3
Task Deadline	4/13/2017

Add Task Activities

Activity Type

+

Activity 1
Check all parts
Activity 2
Assemble
Activity 3
Final checking before packing
Activity 4
Packing
Activity 5
Send product to delivery department

Submit

Fig. 3. An example of interface for inserting a task

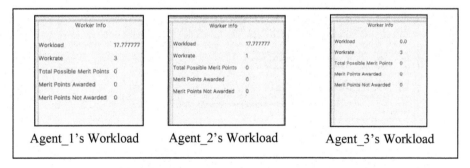

Agent_1's Workload   Agent_2's Workload   Agent_3's Workload

Fig. 4. Workload of agents

Then, the remaining task's activities are transferred to Agent_3. The workload of Agent_1 is reduced and the Agent_3's workload is increased. Figure 7 shows the changes to both workloads of Agent_1 and Agent_3 after the task transfer.

As mentioned earlier, the teammate agent gets 1 merit point if it completes the task on time or earlier without putting any condition and is considered as a sincere agent. In this case, Agent_3 successfully completes the task on time without putting any condition.

Fig. 5. Agent_1 needs help for performing its task

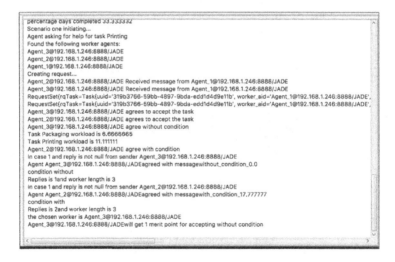

Fig. 6. The communication of agents at the time of choosing the available agent

Thus, Agent_3 gets 1 merit point because it actions shows that it is a sincere agent. Figure 8 shows the merit point earned by Agent_3.

The simulation shows that the Workload Manager works well in delegating tasks and managing help. The simulation also shows the validity of the task transfer design to streamline the imbalances of workloads among agents.

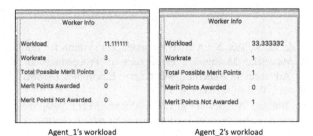

Fig. 7. The changes of workload for Agent_1 and Agent_2

Fig. 8. The Agent_3 gets 1 merit point from the system

5 Conclusion and Future Work

Team working is one of the keys for agents in accomplishing shared objectives. It provides many benefits in supporting autonomous agents to perform tasks faster and with higher quality. However, the problem of workload imbalances among agents can be a serious one. Indirectly, it would negatively affect the accomplishment of the objectives to perform scheduled tasks. Consequently, the transfer of the remaining task's activities from one agent to another should be crucially designed, which this research has attempted to achieve.

The implementation of the Workload Manager in this process somewhat eases this problem and at the same time ensures that the agents are able to deliver the tasks' output as scheduled. The use of merit points for awarding teammate agents which help the worker agents sincerely presents a positive strategy in motivating agents to help each other in its community.

However, the enforcement of sincerity behavior in software agents should be formulated properly to ensure that it works in its environment. As a perspective for further research, we plan to integrate all formulation of instilling sincerity in software agents and simulate it to study the effectiveness of this formulation. In future, the cumulative of sincerity merit point will be used to calculate the sincerity level of agent. This sincerity level will be used to identify how the agent will react to its environment when its teammate facing problems while performing the task.

References

1. Liu, H., Shao, Z., Li, S., Tan, X.: A study of multiagent systems for resource allocation. In: Advances in Materials, Machinery, Electronics I: Proceedings of the International Conference on Advances in Materials, Machinery, Electronics (AMME 2017). American Institute of Physics, Wuhan, China (2017)
2. Eldabaa, P.N., Bahgat, A., Seddawy, E.L., Ahmed, M.H.: Adaptive framework using intelligent system to enhance total quality management in pharmaceutical industry. Int. J. Adv. Sci. Res. Manag. **2**, 1–15 (2017)
3. Malibari, A.A., Gamlo, A.H., Metro, A.E.: Application of agents for efficient energy consumption: coalition formations approach; a systematic review. Int. J. Comput. Acad. Res. **5**, 279–289 (2016)
4. Hellström, T.: On the moral responsibility of military robots. Ethics Inf. Technol. **15**(2), 99–107 (2013)
5. Wallach, W., Allen, C.: Framing robot arms control. Ethics Inf. Technol. **15**, 125–135 (2013)
6. Wooldridge, M.: An Introduction to Multiagent Systems. Wiley, United Kingdom (2009)
7. Franklin, S., Graesser, A.: Is it an agent, or just a program?: A taxonomy for autonomous agents. In: Müller, J.P., Wooldridge, M.J., Jennings, N.R. (eds.) ATAL 1996. LNCS, vol. 1193, pp. 21–35. Springer, Heidelberg (1997). doi:10.1007/BFb0013570
8. Green, S., Hurst, L., Nangle, B., Cunningham, P., Somers, F., Evans, R.: Software agents: a review (1997)
9. Jennings, N.R., Sycara, K.P., Wooldridge, M.: A roadmap of agent research and development. Auton. Agents Multi-agent Syst. **1**, 7–38 (1998)
10. Anderson, M., Anderson, S.L.: Toward ensuring ethical behavior from autonomous systems: a case-supported principle-based paradigm, pp. 19–28 (2014)
11. Golpayegani, F.: Goal-based multi-agent collaboration community formation: a conceptual model. In: 4th Workshop on Goal Reasoning at IJCAI 2016, New York, USA (2016)
12. Ahuja, P., Sethi, P., Juneja, D., Mukherjee, S.: Task allocation strategy for multi agent: a review. J. Netw. Commun. Emerg. Technol. **7**, 18–21 (2017)
13. Bradshaw, J.M., Hoffman, R.R., Johnson, M., Woods, D.D.: The seven deadly myths of "autonomous systems". IEEE Intell. Syst. **28**, 2–9 (2013)
14. Allen, C., Wallach, W., Smit, I.: Why machine ethics? IEEE Intell. Syst. **21**(4), 12–17 (2006)
15. Anderson, M., Anderson, S.L.: Robot be good. Sci. Am. **303**(4), 72–77 (2010)
16. Liu, W., Zhou, L., Xing, W., Yuan, B.: Modeling human-like autonomous behaviors and movements of virtual humans in real-time virtual environment. In: IEEE Symposium on Computer and Communication, pp. 546–549 (2010)
17. Signoretti, A., Feitosa, A., Campos, A.M., Canuto, A.M., Xavier-Junior, J.C., Fialho, S.V.: Using an affective attention focus for improving the reasoning process and behavior of intelligent agents. In: 2011 IEEE/WIC/ACM International Conferences on Web Intelligence and Intelligent Agent Technology, pp. 97–100. IEEE (2011)
18. Jaafar, N.H., Ahmad, M.S., Ahmad, A.: The rationality of sincere software agent in task completion. In: The International Symposium on Agents, Multi-agent Systems and Robotics 2016 (ISAMSR 2016), Selangor, Malaysia (2016)
19. Jaafar, N.H., Basir, N.M., Ahmad, M.S., Ahmad, A.: Human sincerity factors for adaptation in software agents. In: 2014 IEEE International Conference on Control System, Computing and Engineering (ICCSCE 2014). IEEE, Penang, Malaysia (2014)
20. Jaafar, N.H., Ahmad, M.S., Ahmad, A.: The influence of human blaming or bragging behaviour towards software agent sincerity implementation. In: Omatu, S. (ed.) Distributed Computing and Artificial Intelligence, 13th International Conference. AISC, vol. 474, pp. 239–246. Springer, Cham (2016). doi:10.1007/978-3-319-40162-1_26

Neural Networks for Eye Height and Eye Width Prediction with an Improved Adaptive Sampling Algorithm

Chan Hong Goay and Patrick Goh$^{(\boxtimes)}$

School of Electrical and Electronic Engineering, Universiti Sains Malaysia,
14300 Nibong Tebal, Pulau Pinang, Malaysia
eepatrick@usm.my

Abstract. This paper discusses the application of artificial neural networks (ANN) in terms of eye diagram modeling, where ANN models are trained to predict the eye height and eye width, which are useful information for signal integrity inspection. This paper also presents an improved version of the adaptive sampling method which is used in the data collection process. The proposed adaptive sampling manages to reduce the number of training and testing samples needed to train the neural model, thus reducing the time needed to simulate the data. In addition, the proposed adaptive sampling can generate training and testing samples more evenly across the whole design space, reducing the risk of oversampling and undersampling.

Keywords: Neural network · Eye diagram · Transmission line · Adaptive sampling

1 Introduction

Recently, neural networks have been used in modeling signal integrity (SI) issues [1–4]. As the signal rate increases, signal integrity evaluation based on eye height (EH) and eye width (EW) requires a huge amount of computational power. Neural network can be used as a fast and accurate solution to the problem. One of the most widely used neural network structure for microwave modeling is the multi-layered perceptron (MLP) [5]. Theoretically, a 3-layered MLP is capable of modeling any highly non-linear function [6]. However, for a function with a high non-linearity and high dimensionality, a large amount of training data might be needed.

In [3], the design of experiment (DOE) technique is used to train an MLP model to model a high-speed interconnect system. However, using the DOE technique does not prevent the number of training samples from growing rapidly when the dimension starts to increase. An approach called the reduced training set (RTS) is presented in [4]. RTS only uses samples that contribute to the values of maximum, minimum, and nearest to the median of that of the frequency response at selected frequencies. Thus, RTS has its number of training samples independent of the dimension of the design space. Despite that, RTS still requires an initial generation of a large sample set before reduction, and this can be prohibitive if sample set generation is computationally expensive.

© Springer Nature Singapore Pte Ltd. 2017
M.S. Mohamed Ali et al. (Eds.): AsiaSim 2017, Part I, CCIS 751, pp. 189–201, 2017.
DOI: 10.1007/978-981-10-6463-0_17

Another method to reduce the amount of training samples is the adaptive sampling technique [7]. This technique starts the training process of the neural network with a small amount of training data, and then computes the accuracy/performance of the model at each region of the design space to identify the regions with high non-linearity. Then, more training samples are added to the non-linear regions. However, the adaptive sampling can sometimes focus on generating too many samples in the already identified non-linear region while completely missing the other regions. A simple modification is proposed in this work to improve the original adaptive sampling by dividing the errors of every region with weights where their values are dependent on the volume of the regions.

2 Multilayer Perceptron

Artificial neural networks (ANN) is a computational model consisting of a number of simple, highly interconnected processing units called neurons or nodes. The main advantage of a neural network is its ability to learn and adapt during the training process, and then store the acquired knowledge in the form of an interconnection strength between neurons known as the weights. Multilayer perceptron (MLP) is a type of neural network with an input layer, an output layer, and one or more hidden layers. In this work, MLPs with one hidden layer are used (Fig. 1). Usually, hidden neurons have non-linear activation functions which are continuously differentiable such as the *tansig* function as shown in Fig. 2, whereas the output neurons have linear transfer functions. In this work, the Levenberg-Marquardt backpropagation algorithm [8] is used to create and train neural network models. The purpose of the training process is to adjust the weights of a neural network so that the errors between the desired outputs from the training samples and the modelled outputs by that neural model are minimized. More details on neural network computation and its training process can be found in [9], while [10] presents a survey on applications of neural network in microwave and RF design modeling.

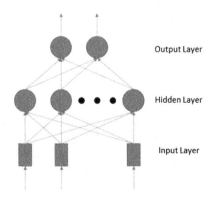

Fig. 1. An example structure of a 3 layer MLP.

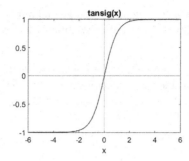

Fig. 2. *Tansig* activation function of hidden neurons.

2.1   Selection of the Number of Hidden Neurons

A trial-and-error approach is used to find the optimum number of hidden neurons. First, a total of N_{trials} neural models with H_{min} hidden neurons are created and trained. Then, this process is repeated by creating N_{trials} neural models with their number of hidden neurons, H increase by dH until $H = H_{max}$. The Nguyen-Widrow method is used to generate initial weight and bias values for a layer so that the active regions of the layer's neurons are distributed approximately evenly over the input space. All neural models are trained using the Levenberg-Marquardt backpropagation algorithm. During training, early stopping with a validation set is used to improve the generalization capability of the neural model. Each time a neural model is created, it is evaluated based on its test performance. The neural model with the best test performance is selected as the final design. The pseudo-code in MATLAB for implementing the trial-and-error method is shown below:

```
for H = Hmin:dH:Hmax
  for index = 1:Ntrials
    net = neural model with H hidden neurons;
    train net with training samples;
    test net with testing samples;
  end
end

bestNeuralModel = neural model with lowest test error
```

3   Eye Diagram Measurement

An eye diagram is a representation of high-speed signals that allows SI engineers to examine and determine the quality of the signal. An eye diagram is constructed by slicing the time-domain (TD) signal waveform into sections that are a small number of symbols in length, and overlaying them. Then, signal metrics such as the height of the eye opening and width of the eye opening are extracted from the eye diagram.

A MATLAB script is developed to generate an eye diagram and measure its eye height and eye width. The steps involved in the generation of the eye diagram are presented below.

Step 1. Use 1 dimensional interpolation to generate more points for the voltage waveform. This has the same effect as increasing the sampling rate by a factor of 4. Thus, the resolution of the eye diagram is improved.

Step 2. Overlay the sliced TD signal waveform on top of each other to form a matrix with a size of $N_T \times N_S$ as shown below:

$$
\begin{pmatrix}
V_{1,1} & \cdots & V_{1,N_S} \\
\vdots & \ddots & \vdots \\
V_{N_T,1} & \cdots & V_{N_T,N_S}
\end{pmatrix}
\tag{1}
$$

Step 3. The matrix is then binned to 1000 levels. Level 1 represents the minimum voltage of the TD waveform, V_{min}, whereas level 1000 represents the maximum voltage of the TD waveform, V_{max}.

Step 4. The binned matrix is then mapped onto another matrix with a size of $1000 \times N_T$, where each of its members represents a pixel in an eye diagram.

Step 5. Image processing techniques such as morphological closing are then used to join any disconnected line and thicken the line so that the eye diagram is completed.

This method allows us to quickly generate the eye diagram and makes integration between data collection and neural model generation easier. Image processing techniques are then used to analyze and measure the eye height and eye width of the eye diagram. Figure 3 shows the eye diagram before and after morphological closing. First, the maximum horizontal eye opening is identified as the eye width. Then, the vertical eye opening is measured based on the user defined option. There are two measurement options which the user can define. The first option named "MidPoint" defines the eye height measurement time axis marker at the midpoint between the left and right eye

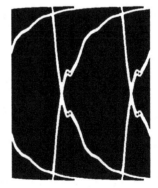

Fig. 3. Eye diagram before (left) and after (right) morphological closing

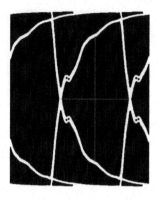 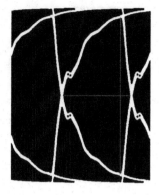

Fig. 4. Eye diagram measurement using the "MidPoint" option: eye height = 0.3457 V, eye width = 0.96 ns (left). Eye diagram measurement using the "BestHeight" option: eye height = 0.4328 V, eye width = 0.96 ns (right).

crossings while the second option named "BestHeight" defines the eye height measurement time axis marker at the sampling time that gives the largest eye height. The difference in both methods is visualized in Fig. 4. In this paper, the "MidPoint option is used.

4   Adaptive Sampling

The original concept on adaptive sampling is first proposed in [7] and is used in [11]. The main advantage of adaptive sampling is that the highly non-linear regions can be identified easily, and training and testing samples can be generated depending on the linearity of the regions. Thus, redundant training and testing points can be avoided, saving precious simulation time. This is especially important when the generation of training/testing samples involves computationally expensive simulations such as the eye diagram with a long bit sequence.

The sampling algorithm considers the original bounded n-dimensional input space as a group of 2^n regions of equal-volume. Training and test data are systematically generated for each region in a pre-defined way, for example, using a star distribution [12]. In this work, the training points are generated using a star distribution whereas the testing points are generated using a rotated star distribution, which is done by rotating the training points by $45°$ at the center of the region. A total of $(2n + 1)$ training points and $2n$ testing points are generated. The training process starts with a small amount of training data, and then slowly adds more samples to the non-linear regions as the training continues. The training process usually starts with $2n$ regions, and then samples within these regions will be used to create an intermediate neural model. The intermediate neural model is used to determine the degree of the non-linearity of each region using the testing samples. After that, the region with the worst performance will be identified and it will be split into 2^n new regions. Figure 5 shows the splitting process of a region, R* into 4 new regions, R. Each time a region is split, the total

Fig. 5. Worst performing region, R* is split into 4 new regions, R.

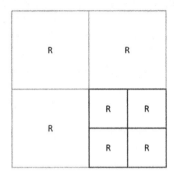

Fig. 6. Regions after the first splitting process.

number of regions will be increased by $(2n - 1)$. Figure 6 shows the regions after the first splitting process. The algorithm will be terminated once the desired accuracy of the neural model is reached.

4.1 Weakness of Adaptive Sampling

The original adaptive sampling does not take the volume of the regions into consideration during the selection of the worst performing region. Regions with large volumes usually mean that the amount of uncertainty about its non-linearity is large as well. Adaptive sampling would focus in generating more samples in already identified non-linear regions and can actually provide very good representations of that region [13]. However, it can easily miss other non-linear regions as well. For example, the algorithm might be 'trapped' inside a highly non-linear region, in a case where there is a large change in the electrical properties when small changes are made to its geometrical parameters. This problem can also happen if the measurement or simulation error is large for a certain set of design parameters. If this happens, the algorithm is very likely to generate large amount of samples around the area with the erroneous measurement, while completely ignoring other regions. Figure 7 shows the distribution of the training samples when the sampling algorithm is 'trapped' around the circled area for a microstrip line modeling problem (where its width and length are varied).

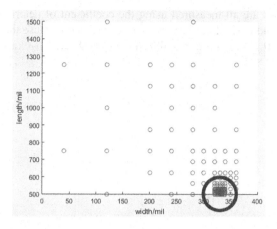

Fig. 7. The sampling algorithm generates a large amount of training points around the circled area resulting in oversampling, but completely ignores other regions.

4.2   Proposed Adaptive Sampling

This paper proposes a simple modification to the adaptive sampling so that the algorithm takes the volume of the regions into consideration when determining the worst performing region. A term named region error, E_r is defined as below:

$$E_r = \frac{mse\left(y_{N,r} - t_{N,r}\right)}{n_r} \tag{2}$$

where $mse(y_{N,r} - t_{N,r})$ is the mean squared error between the normalized outputs of the neural model $y_{N,r}$ and the corresponding normalized desired outputs $t_{N,r}$ respectively, and n_r is the weight given to a region r according to its volume. The value of n_r can be computed as follows.

$$n_r = \log_{2^n}\left(\frac{\text{volume of entire design space}}{\text{volume of region } r}\right) + 1 \tag{3}$$

$$\text{volume of region } r = \prod_{i}^{n}\left(x_{\text{max},i} - x_{\text{min},i}\right), x_i \in r \tag{4}$$

where $x_{max,i}$ and $x_{min,i}$ are the maximum and minimum values of the ith design parameter or the ith ANN input in the region r.

Figure 8 shows the value of n_r for each region. The original region (before any splitting) has n_r value of 1. The region with the largest E_r would be identified as the worst performing region. This simple modification allows the adaptive sampling algorithm to split the region more evenly in terms of volume, thus preventing it from being "trapped". In addition, the whole process will not terminate immediately when the desired accuracy is achieved, but it will be terminated only if the desired accuracy is reached continuously for a certain amount of iterations. The performances of neural models in this work are all measured using the coefficient of determination. Both the predicted outputs and desired outputs are also normalized because the value of the eye height (as high as 0.35 V) and eye width (as high as 1 ns) have varying ranges.

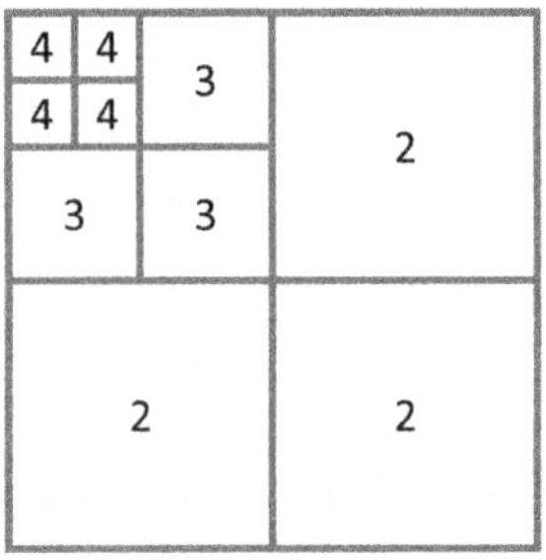

Fig. 8. The values of n_r for each region for a 2-dimensional problem

The pseudo-code for implementing the proposed modified sampling is presented below:

```
define regions;
passIteration = 0;
while(passIteration < numOfpassIterationNeeded)
  generate training points;
  generate testing points;
  create and train a neural model;
  compute testPerformance;
  if testPerformance >= desiredAccuracy
    passIteration++;
  end
  compute Er using the neural model and testing points;
  identify worst performing region R* using Er;
  split R* into 2^n new regions;
  update regions;
end
```

5   Examples

In this paper, the proposed adaptive sampling is tested on eye height and eye width prediction problems with the geometrical parameters of a microstrip line as the variables using neural networks. This can be visualized in Fig. 9. A circuit consisting of a microstrip transmission line in a 50 Ω system (50 Ω source and load impedances) with an additional 10 pF capacitor at the load is used in the simulation of the output signal waveform, which is used to generate the eye diagram. Some of the geometrical parameters of the microstrip line are kept constant such as the relative permittivity of the dielectric (4.4), dielectric thickness (12 mils), physical thickness of microstrip (1.2 mils), loss tangent of dielectric (0.02) and conductor conductivity (58000000 S/m).

The voltage source used in the circuit is a pseudo-random pulse train defined at discrete time steps with a symbol rate of 1 GHz and a sampling rate of 100 samples per symbol. Each eye diagram is generated using 5000 symbols. MATLAB RF toolbox [14] is used to create the circuit and carry out the transient simulation, while the neural models are created using the MATLAB Neural Network Toolbox [15]. All of the simulations are done using MATLAB R2016a, on a PC with Intel(R) Xeon(R) CPU E5-2603 v2 (1.8 GHz) with 8 GB of RAM.

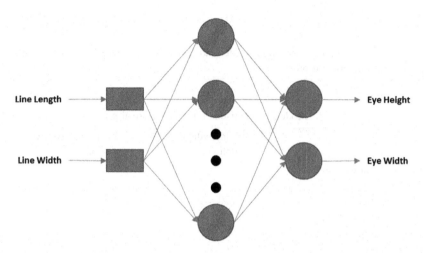

Fig. 9. MLP with geometrical parameters as input and eye height and eye width as outputs.

5.1   1-Dimensional Problem

In this example, the width of the microstrip is fixed at 80 mils and the length is varied from 600 mils to 2000 mils. Two equal-volume starting regions are used. Additionally, 141 samples are generated separately to evaluate our neural models. Figure 10 shows

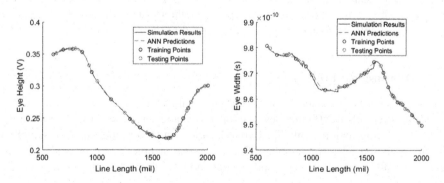

Fig. 10. Correlation of the simulation results and ANN predictions using original adaptive sampling for 1-dimensional problem.

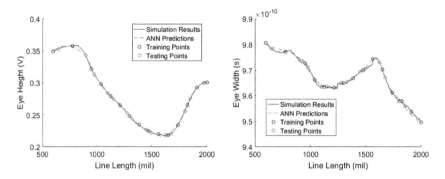

Fig. 11. Correlation of the simulation results and ANN predictions using proposed adaptive sampling for 1-dimensional problem.

Table 1. Models comparisons for 1-dimensional problem.

	Original adaptive sampling	Proposed adaptive sampling
Number of iterations before termination	7	6
Test performance	0.9970	0.9953
Number of training samples	17	15
Number of testing samples	16	14
ANN structure	1:8:2	1:6:2
Simulation time	240.66 s	213.35 s
Training time	425.00 s	309.77 s

the distribution of the training and testing samples, the simulation results and the ANN predictions of the eye height and eye width using the original adaptive sampling. The results obtained using the modified adaptive sampling are presented in Fig. 11 and the comparisons between both methods are tabulated in Table 1. In this table, the ANN structure is presented in the form of *number of input: number of hidden neurons: number of outputs*. It is shown that the proposed method reduces the amount of training and testing samples, thus reducing the time needed to train the neural model.

5.2   2-Dimensional Problem

In this example, both the length and width of the microstrip are varied. The width is varied from 60 mils to 100 mils and the length is varied from 600 mils to 2000 mils. We use 4 starting regions with equal volumes for both the original adaptive sampling and the proposed adaptive sampling. 705 additional samples are generated independently and are used to evaluate both neural models. Table 2 compares the models

Table 2. Models comparisons for 2-dimensional problem.

	Original adaptive sampling	Proposed adaptive sampling
Number of iterations before termination	8	7
Test performance	0.9913	0.9952
Number of training samples	122	104
Number of testing samples	100	88
ANN structure	2:15:2	2:12:2
Simulation time	1667.80 s	1206.80 s
Training time	1878.80 s	1334.70 s

generated using the original adaptive sampling and the proposed adaptive sampling. It is shown that the proposed adaptive sampling can achieve a similar level of accuracy as the original adaptive sampling but with fewer training and testing samples, thus reducing the time needed for the simulation and training process. This is especially helpful when the samples are expensive in terms of computational power and time. From Fig. 12, it can be seen that the samples are more evenly generated when the proposed adaptive sampling is used. Also, there exist a single region with a large volume (80 mils < Line Width < 100 mils, 1400 mils < Line Length < 2000 mils) when the original adaptive sampling is used. This indicates that the risk in under-sampling is increased, which means that the samples might not be adequate to accurately represent the problem in the entire design space. Figure 13 confirms this problem where the neural model cannot accurately predict the outputs in the region noted above. Figure 14 shows that the neural model created using the proposed adaptive sampling can successfully model the entire design space.

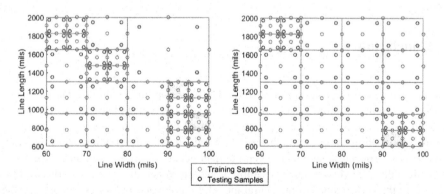

Fig. 12. Distribution of training and testing samples for original adaptive sampling (left) and proposed adaptive sampling (right). The blue colored lines are borders of the regions. (Color figure online)

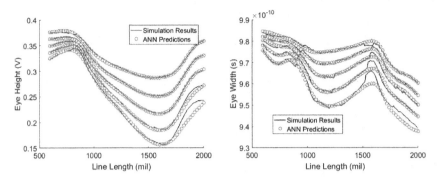

Fig. 13. Correlation of the simulation results and ANN predictions using original adaptive sampling. Five different values of line width are shown (top to bottom: 60, 70, 80, 90, and 100 mils).

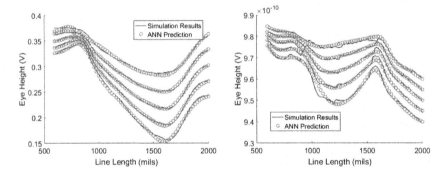

Fig. 14. Correlation of the simulation results and ANN predictions using proposed adaptive sampling. Five different values of line width are shown (top to bottom: 60, 70, 80, 90, and 100 mils).

6 Conclusion

In this paper, artificial neutral networks are used to predict the eye height and eye width of the eye diagram by using an improved adaptive sampling technique. The proposed method takes the volume of the region into account when determining the worst performing region. Results show that the proposed method can reduce the amount of training and testing samples which leads to a reduction in the training and simulation time. This is especially beneficial when the data generation process is time expensive. Other than that, the chances of oversampling and undersampling are also reduced, thus improving the performance of the neural model. Future work will focus on applying the proposed method on more complex systems and other real word design problems.

Acknowledgments. This work is supported by the Universiti Sains Malaysia under the Research University Grant (RUI) grant no. 1001/PELECT/8014011.

References

1. Ambasana, N., Gope, D., Mutnury, B., Anand, G.: Application of artificial neural networks for eye-height/width prediction from S-parameters. In: 2014 IEEE 23rd Conference on Electrical Performance of Electronic Packaging and Systems (2014)
2. Ambasana, N., Anand, G., Mutnury, B., Gope, D.: Eye height/width prediction from S-parameters using learning-based models. IEEE Trans. Compon. Packag. Manuf. Technol. **6**, 873–885 (2016)
3. Beyene, W.: Application of artificial neural networks to statistical analysis and nonlinear modeling of high-speed interconnect systems. IEEE Trans. Comput. Aided Des. Integr. Circuits Syst. **26**, 166–176 (2007)
4. Ambasana, N., Gope, D., Mutnury, B., Anand, G.: Eye-height/width prediction from S-parameters using bounded size training set for ANN. In: 2014 IEEE Electrical Design of Advanced Packaging and Systems Symposium (EDAPS) (2014)
5. Zhang, Q., Gupta, K., Devabhaktuni, V.: Artificial neural networks for RF and microwave design-from theory to practice. IEEE Trans. Microw. Theory Tech. **51**, 1339–1350 (2003)
6. Hornik, K.: Approximation capabilities of multilayer feedforward networks. Neural Netw. **4**, 251–257 (1991)
7. Devabhaktuni, V., Zhang, Q.: Neural network training-driven adaptive sampling algorithm for microwave modeling. In: 30th European Microwave Conference (2000)
8. Hagan, M., Menhaj, M.: Training feedforward networks with the Marquardt algorithm. IEEE Trans. Neural Netw. **5**, 989–993 (1994)
9. Haykin, S.: Neural Networks and Learning Machines. Prentice Hall, Upper Saddle River (2009)
10. Koziel, S., Yang, X., Zhang, Q.: Simulation-Driven Design Optimization and Modeling for Microwave Engineering. World Scientific Publishing Company, Singapore (2013)
11. Devabhaktuni, V., Yagoub, M., Zhang, Q.: A robust algorithm for automatic development of neural-network models for microwave applications. IEEE Trans. Microw. Theory Tech. **49**, 2282–2291 (2001)
12. Rayas-sanchez, J., Gutierrez-Ayala, V.: EM-based statistical analysis and yield estimation using linear-input and neural-output space mapping. In: 2006 IEEE MTT-S International Microwave Symposium Digest (2006)
13. Eason, J., Cremaschi, S.: Adaptive sequential sampling for surrogate model generation with artificial neural networks. Comput. Chem. Eng. **68**, 220–232 (2014)
14. RF Toolbox - MATLAB. https://www.mathworks.com/products/rftoolbox.html
15. Neural Network Toolbox - MATLAB. https://www.mathworks.com/products/neural-network.html

A D Number-Goal Programing Integrated Method for Evaluating Credibility of Complex Simulation Systems

Gengjiao Yang[1,2(✉)], Lin Zhang[1,2], Longfei Zhou[1,2], and Jin Cui[1,2]

[1] School of Automation Science and Electrical Engineering,
Beihang University, 100191 Beijing, China
{yanggengjiao,jincui}@buaa.edu.cn,
johnlin9999@163.com, zlfstudy@126.com
[2] Engineering Research Center of Complex Product Advanced
Manufacturing Systems, Ministry of Education, 100191 Beijing, China

Abstract. For a complex simulation system with little or no simulation data, the credibility evaluation of simulation system is mainly based on the expert experience to grade the simulation system. However, the existing evaluation methods do not take into account the uncertainty of the evaluation result. To this end, a D number-goal programming method is proposed for complex simulation systems. This method not only handles the uncertainty, but also simplifies the whole evaluation procedure. Finally, the proposed evaluation method is validated by a practical system to illustrate the effectiveness of the proposed method.

Keywords: Credibility evaluation · Complex simulation systems · D number · Goal programing

1 Introduction

Simulation systems has been widely used in various fields, such as industrial, agricultural, commercial, military [1–3]. The credibility evaluation of simulation system plays an important role in modeling and simulation. The simulation system credibility refers to the degree to which the simulation system adapts to the simulation purpose, which is determined by the similarity between the simulation system and the prototype system [4]. For a specific simulation system with a clear purpose, the credibility of simulation system is certain, and will not change with the attitude of the evaluators and the evaluation methods. For complex simulation systems, the credibility assessment process is very complicated, involving the construction of evaluation indicators system, the measurement and evaluation of a large number of qualitative and quantitative indicators, the judgment of individual expert as well as the integration of expert evaluation opinions. A specific evaluation method is required to manage and aggregate such measurements and evaluations for obtaining the final evaluation result.

© Springer Nature Singapore Pte Ltd. 2017
M.S. Mohamed Ali et al. (Eds.): AsiaSim 2017, Part I, CCIS 751, pp. 202–212, 2017.
DOI: 10.1007/978-981-10-6463-0_18

Over the past few decades, many evaluation methods are proposed to evaluate the credibility of simulation systems. Delphi Method [5] is a method used to evaluate complex simulation system, which is mainly prepared by investigators, questionnaires, in accordance with established procedures, respectively, the members of the expert group are consulted by letter and their views are submitted anonymously (letters). After repeated consultation and feedback, the opinions of the members of the expert group gradually became centralized, and finally the collective judgment results with high accuracy were obtained. The chief drawback of Delphi method is that it is easy to ignore the opinions of a few people, which may lead to the result of prediction deviating from reality; BP network [6] is a multilayer feedforward network trained by error back propagation, which adjusts the network structure according to the existing integrated samples, and thus the indicator synthesis mechanism is determined. However, the training of neural networks requires a large number of integrated samples while it is often difficult to obtain these training data for complex simulation systems due to the difficulty of simulation data acquisition or the absence of reference systems. Analytic Hierarchy Process (AHP) [7] is a complicated multi-objective decision making problem as a system, the target is decomposed into multiple objectives or criteria, and then divided into multi indicator (or criterion, some constraints) level, through qualitative indicator fuzzy quantitative method to calculate the level of single weight and the total order for the target, which is characterized by making the decision-making process mathematically based on less quantitative information so as to provide a simple decision-making method for complex decision problems with multiple objectives. Because the data available of complex simulation system is less, AHP is applicable to the credibility evaluation of complex simulation systems, like underwater vehicle simulation system [8], missile simulation system [9], guidance simulation system [10].

However, AHP has strong subjective, the group AHP(GAHP) [11] are developed to overcome this drawback. However, GAHP is only used to calculate the weights of indicators, and the credibility scores of the indicators are mainly determined by expert consultation in [11]. There are three limitations for the evaluation method in [11] as follows: (1) The determination of indicator credibility score is very subjective. (2) Because each expert has different experience and knowledge, which leads to the uncertainty of the evaluation result. which is not considered in [11]. (3) The determination of the indicator weight and the indicator credibility score is independent, which is not consistent with the actual evaluation process. For the first limitation, multiple experts are invited to evaluate the credibility score of the indicators independently to reduce the subjectivity. For the second limitation, D number [12], a new mathematic tool to deal with uncertainty, was proposed by Deng Yong in 2012, which has been widely used to describe the uncertainty of expert opinions [12, 13]. In addition, D number can also link the weights of the indicators with the credibility scores of the indicators so as to overcome the third limitation. After that, the deviation function between the credibility obtained by expert evaluation and the true credibility is constructed. The smaller the deviation, the closer the evaluation results to the true credibility. Finally, the credibility of the simulation system is obtained by goal programming method. The proposed method has three main advantages: (1) it is also applicable to the previous evaluation procedure. (2) the evaluation opinions of all experts are retained as far as possible, which is helpful to avoid the consensus of expert opinions. (3) the original evaluation opinions of the indicators are aggregated directly, without integrating the evaluation opinions of the indicator weight and the indicator credibility score respectively, which reduces the uncertainty of the evaluation results.

The remainder of the article is arranged as follows. Section 2 introduces foundation theory of the D number. In Sect. 3, the credibility evaluation model of complex simulation system is presented. In Sect. 4, three evaluation procedures are introduced including the proposed evaluation method based on D number. In Sect. 5, a real system is evaluated to illustrate the effectiveness of the proposed method. And the conclusion and future research are discussed in Sect. 6.

2 Preliminaries

2.1 D Number

Let Ω be a finite nonempty set, D number is a mapping formulated by [12]

$$D : \Omega \to [0, 1] \tag{1}$$

with

$$\sum_{B \in \Omega} D(B) \leq 1 \text{ and } D(\varphi) = 0 \tag{2}$$

where, φ is an empty set and B is a subset of Ω.

Furthermore, for a discrete set $\Omega = \{b_1, b_2, \cdots, b_i, \cdots, b_n\}$, $b_i \in R$ and $b_i \neq b_j$ if $i \neq j$, a kind of special D number can be expressed as follows [12]:

$$
\begin{aligned}
D(\{b_1\}) &= v_1 \\
D(\{b_2\}) &= v_2 \\
&\cdots \\
D(\{b_i\}) &= v_i \\
&\cdots \\
D(\{b_n\}) &= v_n
\end{aligned}
\tag{3}
$$

which is denoted by $D = \{(b_1, v_1), (b_2, v_2), \cdots, (b_i, v_i), \cdots, (b_n, v_n)\}$ with $v_i > 0$ and $\sum_{i=1}^{n} v_i \leq 1$.

2.2 Integration of D Number

For D number $D = \{(b_1, v_1), \cdots, (b_i, v_i), \cdots, (b_n, v_n)\}$, the integration of D number is defined as [12]

$$I(D) = \sum_{i=1}^{n} b_i v_i \tag{4}$$

where,

$$b_i \in R, v_i > 0, \sum_{i=1}^{n} v_i \le 1. \tag{5}$$

3 General Evaluation Procedure in AHP

In AHP, the general evaluation procedure mainly consists of 3 parts: the construction of hierarchical evaluation indicator system, the determination of indicator weight as well as the determination of indicator credibility score. The previous evaluation procedure is mainly concentrated in the indicator weights, ignoring the effects of the indicator weight on the indicator score. The proposed evaluation procedure considers the influence between the indicator weight and the indicator score.

3.1 Previous Evaluation Procedure

In the previous evaluation methods, the weight of the indicator and the credibility score of the indicator are respectively determined, then the credibility score of the simulation system are obtained by the integration of the weight and score. The whole evaluation procedure is shown in Fig. 1.

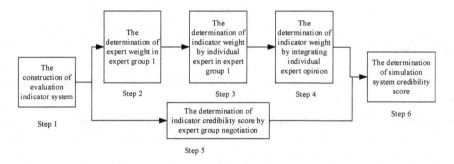

Fig. 1. Traditional credibility evaluation procedure

The detailed evaluation process is as follows.

Step 1. Construct hierarchical evaluation indicator system

Following the general principles of indicators system establishment, the simulation model user, simulation model developers as well as domain experts construct hierarchical simulation system credibility evaluation indicator system in terms of the purpose of simulation system through repeated communication and consultation. It is worth noting that the bottom indicators in the indicator system can be quantified, either measured directly or scored by experts.

For the convenience of statements, we will use three-layer evaluation indicator system, which is shown in Fig. 2.

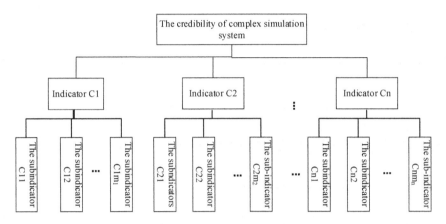

Fig. 2. The evaluation indicator system of complex simulation systems

Step 2. Determine expert weight

The invited experts should cover all aspects of the problem domain and the whole life cycle of simulation system development. Because experts have different background knowledge and experience level, experts should endow different weights.

Step 3. Determine indicator weight by individual expert

In terms of the influence degree of the indicator to the simulation purpose, every expert makes a pairwise comparison of indicators by Saaty's rating scale, then calculate indicators' weights using AHP.

Step 4. Integrate expert opinion to determine final indicator weight

Integrate all expert opinions into a group opinion. Then based on group opinion, the final indicator weight is determined.

Step 5. Determine indicator credibility score

The indicator credibility score is determined by expert group negotiation according to the analysis results of the verification and validation of the simulation models.

Step 6. Calculate the credibility score of complex simulation system

Combine the weight of the indicator with the credibility score of the indicators to obtain the credibility score of complex simulation system.

3.2   The Proposed Evaluation Procedure

The proposed evaluation procedure does not calculate the weight and score of indicators respectively but achieve them simultaneously based on raw evaluation opinion of experts.

The whole evaluation procedure is shown in Fig. 3.

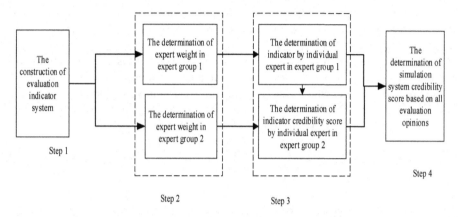

Fig. 3. A novel credibility evaluation procedure

The first three steps are the same as the previous evaluation procedure, the remaining steps are as follows:

Step 4. Individual expert provides the credibility score of indicators from according to the weight of indicators independently based on verification and validation of simulation system.

Step 5. Integrate indicator weights and indicator credibility scores to obtain the credibility score of the simulation system.

4   A Method Based on D Number-Goal Programing (DNGP)

For the novel evaluation procedure, we proposed a method called DNGP to evaluate the credibility of complex simulation systems, which is elaborated below.

4.1   Description of Expert Opinion

The following is an introduction to the evaluation method of indicator C1, which is the same as that of other indicators.

The credibility scores of the sub-indicators of indicator C1 are determined by l experts according to the evaluation score scale (as shown in Table 1), which are denoted by vectors $s_1, s_2, \cdots, s_l$.

Table 1. Evaluation score scale

Credibility level	Very credible	Relatively credible	Credible	Relatively uncredible	Uncredible	Very uncredible
Evaluation score	0.9–1	0.7–0.9	0.6–0.7	0.5–0.6	0.3–0.5	0–0.3

The weights of the sub-indicators of indicator C1 are evaluated by k experts using AHP independently, which are represented by vectors $v_1, v_2, \cdots, v_k$, respectively. where, $v_i = \{v_{i1}, v_{i2}, \cdots, v_{im_i}\}, i = 1, 2, \cdots, k$.

Any expert opinion on indicators' weight is combined with any expert opinion on indicators' credibility score to obtain $l*k$ evaluation opinions about the simulation system credibility score, which can be described by D number as follow:

$$D_{11} = \{(v_{11}, s_{11}), (v_{12}, s_{12}), \cdots, (v_{1m_1}, s_{1m_1})\}$$
$$D_{12} = \{(v_{11}, s_{21}), (v_{12}, s_{22}), \cdots, (v_{1m_1}, s_{2m_1})\}$$
$$\vdots$$
$$D_{1l} = \{(v_{11}, s_{l1}), (v_{12}, s_{l2}), \cdots, (v_{1m_1}, s_{lm_1})\}$$
$$D_{21} = \{(v_{21}, s_{11}), (v_{22}, s_{12}), \cdots, (v_{2m_1}, s_{1m_1})\}$$
$$D_{22} = \{(v_{21}, s_{21}), (v_{21}, s_{22}), \cdots, (v_{22}, s_{2m_1})\}$$
$$\vdots$$
$$D_{2l} = \{(v_{21}, s_{l1}), (v_{2m_1}, s_{l2}), \cdots, (v_{1m_1}, s_{lm_1})\}$$
$$\vdots$$
$$D_{k1} = \{(v_{k1}, s_{11}), (v_{k2}, s_{12}), \cdots, (v_{km_1}, s_{1m_1})\}$$
$$D_{k2} = \{(v_{k1}, s_{21}), (v_{k2}, s_{22}), \cdots, (v_{km_1}, s_{2m_1})\}$$
$$\vdots$$
$$D_{kl} = \{(v_{k1}, s_{l1}), (v_{k2}, s_{l2}), \cdots, (v_{km_1}, s_{lm_1})\}$$

$$(6)$$

where,

$$\sum_{p=1}^{m_1} v_{ip} = 1, i = 1, 2, \cdots k,$$
$$0 \leq s_{jq} \leq 1, j = 1, 2, \cdots, l, q = 1, 2, \cdots, m_1$$

$$(7)$$

4.2   Construction of Goal Programming Function

Assuming that the true credibility score of the simulation system is z^*, according to the integration operation of D number, $k*l$ evaluation opinions can be obtained, which is denoted by $z_1, z_2, \cdots, z_{kl}$.

where,

$$z^* = I(D^*)$$

$$D^* = \{(d_1^*, s_1^*), (d_2^*, s_1^*), \cdots, (d_{m_1}^*, s_{m_1}^*)\}, \sum_{i=1}^{m_1} d_i^* = 1, 0 < s_j^* < 1, j = 1, 2, \cdots, m_1 \tag{8}$$

where, $d_i^*(i = 1, 2, \cdots m_1)$ are indicators' weight determined by expert group, and $s_j^*(j = 1, 2, \cdots m_1)$ are indicators' true weight credibility score by expert group.

We define the total deviation between individuals and groups as follows:

$$e = \sqrt{\frac{1}{kl} \sum_{t=1}^{kl} (z_t - z^*)^2} \tag{9}$$

d_i^*, s_j^* can be worked out from (9). z^* can be obtained by D number integration.

5   Illustrative Example

Take the credibility of the data unit of the model algorithm in the equipment level combat simulation system for example, evaluation indicator system is shown in Fig. 4.

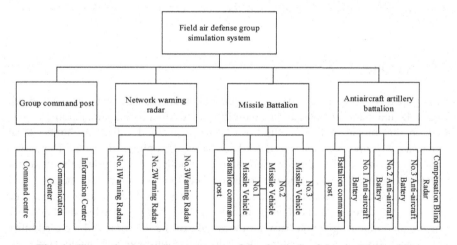

Fig. 4. The evaluation indicator system of the data unit of the model algorithm

We invite two expert groups to evaluate the weights of indicators and the credibility score of indicators and the original evaluation opinions of experts are shown in the appendix.

Combine the i-th indicator weight opinion with the j-th indicator credibility score opinion to obtain an evaluation opinion on simulation model credibility, which is expressed by D_{ij}. For example, D_{11} is an evaluation opinion on simulation model credibility which combine the 1-st indicator weight opinion with the 1-st indicator credibility score opinion, which is written as $D_{11} = \{(0.44, 0.95), (0.39, 0.8), (0.17, 0.97)\}$.

Finally, 225 evaluation opinions on simulation model credibility is obtained.

(4) Calculate $I(D_{11}), I(D_{12}), \cdots, I(D_{1,15}), \cdots, I(D_{15,1}), I(D_{15,2}), \cdots, I(D_{15,15})$ and the approximate true value of simulation model credibility is 0.9035, which can be worked out by the formula (9).

The evaluation results of DNGP and the method in [13] are as shown in Table 2.

Table 2. Comparison between DNGP and the method in [13]

	The method in [13]	DNGP
Indicator weight integration	Yes	No
Indicator score integration	Yes	No
Integration of indicator weight and indicator score	No	Yes
Evaluation result	0.8699	0.9035

From Table 2, we can be seen that there are two integrations in [13], which result in greater deviation between the evaluation result and the true credibility value of simulation system because each integration leads to deviations from the original evaluation opinion. In addition, comparing with the verified simulation system which has been proved to be very credible, the evaluation result of the proposed method is closer to the true evaluation result since $0.9035 > 0.8699$. Therefore, the proposed method is more reasonable.

6 Conclusion

In this paper, we presented a novel evaluation model considering the relationship between the indicator weight and the credibility score for complex simulation systems. Based on this model, a new credibility evaluation method called D Number-Goal Programing is proposed. First, we described the expert opinion using the D number through synthesizing all evaluation opinion on the indicator weight and the indicator credibility score, then constructed the deviation function between evaluation score and true score of complex simulation system credibility and worked out approximate true credibility score through the goal programming method. The proposed method not only considers the influence relation between the weight of the indicator and the credibility score of the bottom indicator, making the evaluation result more reasonable. However, when the real system does not exist, the proposed method is not available. In the future work, we will develop a specific theory to validate the effective of the suggested approach for evaluating the credibility of complex simulation systems.

Acknowledgements. This work was supported by the National Natural Science Foundation of China (No. 61374199) and the National High-Tech Research Development Plan of China (No. 2015AA042101)

Appendix

The opinions of expert group on the weight of indicators are as follows.

$$A_1 = \begin{pmatrix} 1 & 1 & 3 \\ 1 & 1 & 2 \\ 1/3 & 1/2 & 1 \end{pmatrix}, A_2 = \begin{pmatrix} 1 & 2 & 3 \\ 1/2 & 1 & 2 \\ 1/3 & 1/2 & 1 \end{pmatrix}, A_3 = \begin{pmatrix} 1 & 1/2 & 3 \\ 2 & 1 & 3 \\ 1/3 & 1/3 & 1 \end{pmatrix}, A_4 = \begin{pmatrix} 1 & 3 & 5 \\ 1/3 & 1 & 2 \\ 1/5 & 1/2 & 1 \end{pmatrix},$$

$$A_5 = \begin{pmatrix} 1 & 2 & 5 \\ 1/2 & 1 & 3 \\ 1/5 & 1/3 & 1 \end{pmatrix}, A_6 = \begin{pmatrix} 1 & 3 & 3 \\ 1/3 & 1 & 2 \\ 1/3 & 1/2 & 1 \end{pmatrix}, A_7 = \begin{pmatrix} 1 & 1 & 5 \\ 1 & 1 & 3 \\ 1/5 & 1/3 & 1 \end{pmatrix}, A_8 = \begin{pmatrix} 1 & 1 & 4 \\ 1 & 1 & 3 \\ 1/4 & 1/3 & 1 \end{pmatrix},$$

$$A_9 = \begin{pmatrix} 1 & 3 & 1/4 \\ 1/3 & 1 & 1/5 \\ 4 & 5 & 1 \end{pmatrix}, A_{10} = \begin{pmatrix} 1 & 4 & 3 \\ 1/4 & 1 & 1 \\ 1/3 & 1 & 1 \end{pmatrix}, A_{11} = \begin{pmatrix} 1 & 4 & 3 \\ 1/4 & 1 & 1/2 \\ 1/3 & 2 & 1 \end{pmatrix}, A_{12} = \begin{pmatrix} 1 & 4 & 5 \\ 1/4 & 1 & 1 \\ 1/5 & 1 & 1 \end{pmatrix},$$

$$A_{13} = \begin{pmatrix} 1 & 1/4 & 3 \\ 4 & 1 & 5 \\ 1/3 & 1/5 & 1 \end{pmatrix}, A_{14} = \begin{pmatrix} 1 & 1/3 & 2 \\ 3 & 1 & 5 \\ 1/2 & 1/5 & 1 \end{pmatrix}, A_{15} = \begin{pmatrix} 1 & 1/2 & 3 \\ 2 & 1 & 5 \\ 1/3 & 1/5 & 1 \end{pmatrix}.$$

The weight of the indicator is obtained by AHP as follows.

$$w_1 = [0.4434 \quad 0.3874 \quad 0.1692], CR_1 = 0.0158 < 0.1$$
$$w_2 = [0.5396 \quad 0.2970 \quad 0.1634], CR_2 = 0.0079 < 0.1$$
$$w_3 = [0.3325 \quad 0.5278 \quad 0.1396], CR_3 = 0.0462 < 0.1$$
$$w_4 = [0.6483 \quad 0.2297 \quad 0.1220], CR_4 = 0.0032 < 0.1$$
$$w_5 = [0.5816 \quad 0.3090 \quad 0.1095], CR_5 = 0.0032 < 0.1$$
$$w_6 = [0.5936 \quad 0.2493 \quad 0.1571], CR_6 = 0.0462 < 0.1$$
$$w_7 = [0.4806 \quad 0.4054 \quad 0.1140], CR_6 = 0.0251 < 0.1$$
$$w_8 = [0.4579 \quad 0.4161 \quad 0.1260], CR_6 = 0.0079 < 0.1$$
$$w_9 = [0.2255 \quad 0.1007 \quad 0.6738], CR_6 = 0.0739 < 0.1$$
$$w_{10} = [0.6337 \quad 0.1744 \quad 0.1919], CR_{10} = 0.0079 < 0.1$$
$$w_{11} = [0.6250 \quad 0.1365 \quad 0.2385], CR_{11} = 0.0158 < 0.1$$
$$w_{12} = [0.6908 \quad 0.1603 \quad 0.1488], CR_{12} = 0.0048 < 0.1$$
$$w_{13} = [0.2255 \quad 0.6738 \quad 0.1007], CR_{13} = 0.00739 < 0.1$$
$$w_{14} = [0.2297 \quad 0.6483 \quad 0.1220], CR_{14} = 0.0032 < 0.1$$
$$w_{15} = [0.3090 \quad 0.5816 \quad 0.1095], CR_{15} = 0.0032 < 0.1$$

The opinion of expert group on the credibility scores of indicators are as follows.

$$S_1 = [95 \quad 80 \quad 97]; S_2 = [97 \quad 85 \quad 90]; S_3 = [75 \quad 70 \quad 85]; S_4 = [96 \quad 92 \quad 96];$$
$$S_5 = [78 \quad 90 \quad 76]; S_6 = [85 \quad 75 \quad 96]; S_7 = [84 \quad 92 \quad 91]; S_8 = [73 \quad 79 \quad 86];$$
$$S_9 = [92 \quad 89 \quad 98]; S_{10} = [91 \quad 90 \quad 99]; S_{11} = [90 \quad 89 \quad 92]; S_{12} = [75 \quad 88 \quad 90];$$
$$S_{13} = [96 \quad 89 \quad 78]; S_{14} = [85 \quad 87 \quad 93]; S_{15} = [84 \quad 89 \quad 94]$$

References

1. Towill, D.R., Naim, M.M., Wikner, J.: Industrial dynamics simulation models in the design of supply chains. Int. J. Phys. Distrib. Logist. **22**, 3–13 (1992)
2. Schreinemachers, P., Berger, T.: An agent-based simulation model of human–environment interactions in agricultural systems. Environ. Model. Softw. **26**, 845–859 (2011)
3. Lin, G.: Credibility evaluation of warship combat simulation system based on TFN-FAHP. Comput. Eng. Des. **31**, 2815–2818 (2010). (in Chinese)
4. Zhang, W., Wang, X.: Simulation credibility. J. Syst. Simul. **3**, 312–314 (2001). (in Chinese)
5. Ahn, J., Weck, O.L., Steele, M.: Credibility assessment of models and simulations based on NASA's models and simulation standard using the Delphi method. Syst. Eng. **17**, 237–248 (2014)
6. Sun, S., Yang, J., Qiu, X., Huang, K.: Credibility evaluation method based on BP network for large-scale complex system simulation. J. Syst. Simul. **18**, 2037–2041 (2006). (in Chinese)
7. Yang, H., Kang, F., Yan, J.: A methodology of simulation credibility evaluation based on AHP. J. Syst. Simul. **18**, 52–54 (2006). (in Chinese)
8. Yang, H., Kang, F., Li, J.: The application of AHP in integrative process of assessing the credibility of underwater vehicle system simulation. J. Syst. Simul. **14**, 1299–1301 (2002). (in Chinese)
9. Zhang, S., Ye, M.: Simulation credibility evaluation method for missile weapon system. Comput. Simul. **23**, 48–52 (2006). (in Chinese)
10. Jiao, P., Zha, Y.: Application of AHP in integrative process for assessing the credibility of guidance system simulation. Comput. Simul. **22**, 68–72 (2005). (in Chinese)
11. Zhang, Z., Fang, K., Yang, M.: Method for complex simulation credibility evaluation based on group AHP. J. Syst. Eng. Electron. **33**, 2569–2572 (2011). (in Chinese)
12. Deng, Y.: D numbers: theory and applications. J. Inf. Comput. Sci. **9**, 2421–2428 (2012)
13. Xiao, F.: An intelligent complex event processing with numbers under fuzzy environment. Math. Probl. Eng. **2016**, 1–10 (2016)

A Moment Independent Based Importance Measure with Hybrid Uncertainty

Xiaobing Shang, Tao Chao, and Ping Ma[✉]

Control and Simulation Center, Harbin Institute of Technology, Harbin, China
Shangxiaobing1992@126.com, chaotao2000@163.com,
pingma@hit.edu.cn

Abstract. Input uncertainty always exists in most engineering problems and leads to output response uncertainty for model predictions. Several global sensitivity analysis methods are utilized to measure the importance of input aleatory uncertainty which influence output the most. However, the aleatory uncertainty often involves epistemic uncertainty in the distribution parameters due to the lack of knowledge. In this paper, an improved moment independent approach coupled with auxiliary variable method is presented to separate aleatory and epistemic terms of hybrid uncertainty. The importance measure is derived to compute the individual contributions of aleatory and epistemic parameters to model output's uncertainty. Considering the high computation costs of moment independent method, a double loop sampling method is applied in the numerical codes to alleviate simulation. A modified Ishigami function is take for instance for demonstrating the effectiveness and rationality of proposed method and high efficiency of sampling algorithm.

Keywords: Hybrid uncertainty · Global sensitivity analysis · Moment independent method · Latin hypercube sampling

1 Introduction

Sensitivity analysis (SA), especially for global SA, is frequently used in the high critical engineering problems, such as structural mechanics, aerospace science and material engineering, [1, 2]. SA, also termed as importance measure, aims at estimating the contribution of model output uncertainty sourced from the uncertainty in the model input. In other words, SA methods are used to determine which element of input variables influence output the most [3]. Methods to efficiently represent and propagate from input to output uncertainty is of vital importance, which including the probability theory, fuzzy set, possibility theory, and evidence theory [4]. The probabilistic approach is the most widely known and regarded as the most rigorous approach in engineering design due to its consistency with the theory of decision analysis. Input uncertainty is always formulated by a random variable based on the mathematics of probability theory. Besides, input uncertainty, also called aleatory uncertainty, irreducible or stochastic uncertainty, is derived from the variation that aroused in physical system or surrounding environment. This type uncertainty cannot be reduced or eliminated with the restriction of certain condition [5].

© Springer Nature Singapore Pte Ltd. 2017
M.S. Mohamed Ali et al. (Eds.): AsiaSim 2017, Part I, CCIS 751, pp. 213–224, 2017.
DOI: 10.1007/978-981-10-6463-0_19

SA techniques, dealt with the uncertainty problems, should satisfy three requirements: global, quantitative, and model free. Three types of SA approaches including variance based methods, non-parametric techniques and moment independent methods, share the requirements mentioned above [3]. With respect to these methods, some researchers pointed out some non-parametric methods (regression based methods and Spearman rank correlation coefficient) depends on the model from. The variance based methods take a priority compared with the rest two type methods in efficient and computation costs which consisting of Sobol' method, Extended Fourier Amplitude Sensitivity Test (EFST), and high dimensional model representation (HDMR) [6–8]. In these methods, the output variance is decomposed into assembles of individual input variable and interaction terms, which make it easy to identify their contributions. However, the variance based methods rely on the assumption of independent input. To tackle with correlated variable, several works have been conducted to obtain the sensitivity index for models, see [9–11] for more detail.

In fact, variance based method implicitly assume that the low central moment or variance is sufficient to describe output variability. An alternative way for sensitivity measure is the moment independent methods which take the entire distribution of the output response into account. The moment independent index refers to the entire distribution and not to one of its moments. Several of works, including Chun-Han-Tak (CHT) importance measure [12], Entropy-Based Importance Measure [13], Borgonovo method [3] and Kullback-Leibler divergence based method [14], have been established to identify the sensitivity indicator. The high computation costs to estimate the indicator is biggest obstacle to prevent the prevalent of these methods. Some useful techniques are investigated to avoid the "curse of dimensionality" problem, which involves modified estimation of indicator, screening method to reduce the insensitivity variables and efficient sampling methods.

These methods all take the input variables as pure aleatory uncertainty with ignoring epistemic uncertainty. Nevertheless, epistemic uncertainty, which also referred to reducible uncertainty and subjective uncertainty, always aroused with sparse or imprecise system data in the real engineering problems due to the lack of state of knowledge. Taking knowledge the state of the staff into consideration, the input variable is always represented by hybrid uncertainty, which consists of aleatory and epistemic uncertainty. Here the hybrid uncertainty is modeled as a family of known distribution with unknown parameters in a given interval. The traditional methods mentioned above cannot afford to compute the sensitivity where the uncertainty is described as a family of distributions. In this work, an improved moment independent approach is proposed, coupling with auxiliary variable method to depart aleatory and epistemic uncertainty from hybrid uncertainty. The improved method can measure the importance of individual uncertainty and hybrid one. Meanwhile, a double loop sampling (DLS) method based on Latin hypercube sampling (LHS) is adapted to alleviate the computation in the importance measure.

This paper is structured as follows: Sect. 2 reviews some traditional sensitivity analysis methods including variance based method and moment independent method. Section 3 proposes a moment independent method to solve the hybrid uncertainty problem. In Sect. 4, a numerical example is performed to demonstrate the effectiveness and rationality of proposed method. Finally, the conclusion and future work are summarized.

2   Global Sensitivity Analysis

The variance based and moment independent methods are discussed in this section, while the non-parametric one is not considered. For the variance based methods, Sobol' made a clear understanding of the meaning of global SA, and gave a widely acceptable definition of sensitivity indices [15]

$$S_i = \frac{\text{Var}_{X_i}[\text{E}_{\mathbf{X}_{\sim i}}(Y(\mathbf{X})|X_i)]}{\text{Var}[Y(\mathbf{X})]} \tag{1}$$

where, S_i is the sensitivity value of input parameter X_i, Y and $\mathbf{X}_{\sim i}$ denotes the output response and input vector $\mathbf{X}$ from which X_i has been deleted, notation Var_{X_i} and $\text{E}_{\mathbf{X}_{\sim i}}$ represent the mathematical expectation and variance with respect to probability density of X_i and $\mathbf{X}_{\sim i}$, respectively. Besides, for the parameters X_i and X_j, importance measure S_{ij} is defined as

$$S_{ij} = \frac{\text{Var}_{X_{i,j}}[\text{E}_{\mathbf{X}_{\sim i,j}}(Y(\mathbf{X})|X_{i,j})]}{\text{Var}[Y(\mathbf{X})]} \tag{2}$$

where, $X_{\sim i,j}$ denotes the vector X from which X_i and $X_{i,j}$ have been deleted. The notation S_{ij} represents the contribution of output uncertainty with respect to parameters X_i and X_j. An alternative measure of SA is the total sensitivity index, which is given by

$$S_i^T = \frac{\text{E}_{\mathbf{X}_{\sim i}}[\text{Var}_{X_i}(Y(\mathbf{X})|\mathbf{X}_{\sim i})]}{\text{Var}[Y(\mathbf{X})]} = 1 - \frac{\text{Var}_{\sim X_i}[\text{E}_{X_i}(Y(\mathbf{X})|\mathbf{X}_{\sim i})]}{\text{Var}[Y(\mathbf{X})]} \tag{3}$$

The variance based methods aim at exploring individual or interaction contribution of the output variance. Thus, it's necessary to assure the input variables are independently distributed, which determines the uniqueness form of variance decomposition. Meanwhile, the moment independent method concentrates on the entire probability distribution of output response. Chun et al. [12] proposed a famous moment independent based sensitivity indicator, which is represented by

$$\text{CHT}_i = \frac{\left[\int (y_\alpha^i - y_\alpha^0)^2 d\alpha\right]^{1/2}}{\text{E}[Y^0]} \tag{4}$$

where, y_α^i is the αth quantile of output Y for the sensitivity case, and y_α^0 is the αth quantile of Y for the base case. Indicator CHT_i denotes the area related to a shift in cumulative distribution function of output response from the base case to the sensitivity case. Hence, CHT_i concerns on the parameter that provokes the greatest change in the distribution of output Y. Besides, some similar indicators or improved methods can be found in the moment independent methods. In the next section, an improve moment independent method is proposed to deal with hybrid problems.

3 Importance Measure Under Hybrid Uncertainty

3.1 Hybrid Uncertainty Model Formulation

A discipline-independent mathematic model is considered here in the form of: $\mathbf{Y} = f(\mathbf{X})$, where $\mathbf{Y} = [Y_1, Y_2, \ldots, Y_n]$ is the output vector of the model. It's note that the single output is considered since the requirement of sensitivity analysis. Notation f corresponds to simulator, e.g. an algebraic equation, Partial differential Equation, or even some surrogate models. $\mathbf{X} = (X_1, X_2, \ldots, X_m)^T$ is a m-dimensional vector of input with parameter set $\boldsymbol{\theta} = (\boldsymbol{\theta}_1, \boldsymbol{\theta}_2, \ldots, \boldsymbol{\theta}_m)^T$. $\boldsymbol{\theta}_i = \left(\theta_{i,1}, \theta_{i,2}, \ldots, \theta_{i,m_i}\right)^T$, $(i = 1, 2.., m)$ is the distribution sub-parameters of random variable X_i with sub-parameters number m_i.

In the domain of uncertainty quantification, the random input X_i is also called aleatory uncertainty due to the irreducible property determined by model itself. If these distribution sub-parameters $\boldsymbol{\theta}_i = \left(\theta_{i,1}, \theta_{i,2}, \ldots, \theta_{i,m_i}\right)^T$ are precisely recognized, then each input variable has a precise probability density function (CDF). However, due to the lack of knowledge or sparse data, sub-parameters $\theta_{i,j}(i = 1, \ldots, m, j = 1, .., m_i)$ cannot be determined accurately. The uncertainty in $\theta_{i,j}$ is referred as epistemic uncertainty. Many representations, such as interval theory, probable theory and fuzzy theory, are widely used to characterize epistemic uncertainty. Here, epistemic uncertainty in sub-parameter $\theta_{i,j}$ is measured by a uniform random variable within interval $\left[\theta_{i,j}^L, \theta_{i,j}^U\right]$. The random variable X_i of input satisfies a family of distributions, which also term hybrid uncertainty, consists of epistemic uncertainty and aleatory uncertainty [16]. Some most widely known importance measure methods, especially variance-based moment techniques cannot be applied to measure the importance of input random variable X_i, since the output variance is unknown. The traditional moment independent method is based on the aleatory uncertainty without considering the epistemic part. Hence, an improved moment independent method is proposed to solve the problem.

3.2 Uncertainty Operation with Auxiliary Variable Method

For an input variable X_i with hybrid uncertainty, the initial step is to separate the aleatory and epistemic part from the mixed uncertainty. Let $f_{X_i}(x|\boldsymbol{\theta}_i)$ and $F_{X_i}(x|\boldsymbol{\theta}_i)$ denote the probability distribution function (PDF) and cumulative of input variable X_i with hybrid uncertainty in the given sub-parameters $\boldsymbol{\theta}_i$, U_i is taken as an auxiliary variable to represent the aleatory uncertainty in X_i. A novel auxiliary variable method is introduced to separate the aleatory and epistemic parts from the mixed uncertainty [17]. According to probability integral transform theorem, $U_i \in [0, 1]$ is uniform distributed and written as

$$U_i(x) = F_{X_i}(x_i|\mathbf{\theta}_i) = \int_{-\infty}^{x_i} f_{X_i}(x|\mathbf{\theta}_i)dx \tag{5}$$

where, x_i is a realization of random variable X_i. With the auxiliary variable U_i, the individual contributions of aleatory uncertainty and epistemic uncertainty in X_i is distinguished in the form of

$$x_i = F_{X_i}^{-1}(u_i|\mathbf{\theta}_i) \tag{6}$$

where, x_i and u_i is the realizations of random variable X_i and U_i, respectively. $F_{X_i}^{-1}(u_i|\mathbf{\theta}_i)$ is the inverse function of X_i's CDF. Then the model input $\mathbf{X}$ is transformed into a general form

$$\mathbf{X} = \left(F_{X_1}^{-1}(u_1|\mathbf{\theta}_1), F_{X_2}^{-1}(u_2|\mathbf{\theta}_2), \dots, F_{X_m}^{-1}(u_m|\mathbf{\theta}_m) \right)^T = F_X^{-1}(\mathbf{U}|\theta) \tag{7}$$

where $U = (U_1, U_2, .., U_m)^T$. Note that pure aleatory uncertainty U_i can be treated as a special case of which the interval of sub-parameter $\theta_{i,j}$ reduces to a fixed point and corresponding U_i becomes insignificance.

3.3 An Moment Independent Based Importance Measure

As aforementioned, the aleatory and epistemic uncertain in X_i can be represented by the auxiliary variable U_i and sub-parameters θ_i. For a given realization u_i^* of aleatory parameter U_i, the input of model $\mathbf{X} = F_X^{-1}(\mathbf{U}|\theta)$ is changed into the form of $\mathbf{X} = F_X^{-1}(U_1, U_2, ..U_{i-1}, U_i = u_i^*, .., U_m|\mathbf{\theta})$, corresponding conditional PDF and CDF of output Y are respectively denoted by $f_{Y|U_i=u_i^*}(y)$ and $F_{Y|U_i=u_i^*}(y)$. As shown in Fig. 1, the red and green lines respectively denote the model output's unconditional PDF $f_Y(y)$

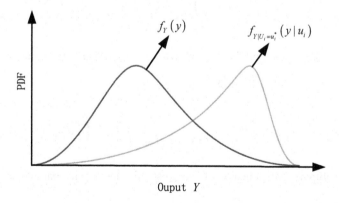

Fig. 1. Unconditional PDF $f_Y(y)$ and conditional PDF $f_{Y|U_i=u_i^*}(y)$ (Color figure online)

and conditional PDF $f_{Y|U_i=u_i^*}(y)$ in any arbitrary distribution. The difference between $f_Y(y)$ and $f_{Y|U_i=u_i^*}(y)$ can be measured by the area shown in Fig. 1, which is expressed by

$$V(u_i^*) = \int \left| f_Y(y) - f_{Y|U_i=u_i^*}(y) \right| dy \tag{8}$$

Equation (8) shows that $V(u_i)$ depends on u_i, and is a function of random variable. Thus, the expectation of $V(u_i)$ is measured by

$$E\left[V(u_i)\right] = \int_0^1 f_{U_i}(u_i) \int \left| f_Y(y) - f_{Y|U_i=u_i^*}(y) \right| dy du_i \tag{9}$$

As the auxiliary variable U_i is uniformly distributed with $f_{U_i}(u_i) = 1$, the expectation of $V(u_i)$ is simplified in the form of

$$E\left[V(u_i)\right] = \int_0^1 \int \left| f_Y(y) - f_{Y|U_i=u_i^*}(y) \right| dy du_i \tag{10}$$

It's obviously that the larger value of $E\left[V(u_i)\right]$, the more importance of auxiliary variable U_i with respect to the output Y. According to the study of Borgonovo [3], $E\left[V(u_i)\right] \in [0, 2]$, then the importance metric S_{U_i} is defined as

$$S_{U_i} = 1/2 \int_0^1 \int \left| f_Y(y) - f_{Y|U_i=u_i^*}(y) \right| dy du_i \tag{11}$$

Similarly, for the epistemic sub-parameters $\theta_{i,j}$, the importance metric $S_{\theta_{i,j}}$ can be constructed as

$$S_{\theta_{i,j}} = 1/2 \int_{\theta_{i,j}^L}^{\theta_{i,j}^U} f_{\theta_{i,j}}\left(\theta_{i,j}\right) \int \left| f_Y(y) - f_{Y|\theta_{i,j}=\theta_{i,j}^*}(y) \right| dy d\theta_{i,j} \tag{12}$$

Generally, the input variable X_i includes several distribution parameters $\theta_i = \left[\theta_{i,1}, \theta_{i,2}, \ldots, \theta_{i,m_i}\right]^T$ with joint probability density

$$f_{\theta_{i,1},\ldots,\theta_{i,m_i}}\left(\theta_{i,1}, \ldots, \theta_{i,m_i}\right) = \int K \int f_\theta(\theta) \prod_{j=1}^{m_i} d\theta_{i,j} \tag{13}$$

Then the importance indicator of the epistemic uncertainty parameter θ_i is constructed as

$$S_{\theta_i} = 1/2 \int_{\theta_{i,1}^L}^{\theta_{i,1}^U} \cdots \int_{\theta_{i,m_i}^L}^{\theta_{i,m_i}^U} f_{\theta_{i,1},\ldots,\theta_{i,m_i}}\left(\theta_{i,1},\ldots,\theta_{i,m_i}\right) \int \left| f_Y(y) - f_{Y|\theta_{i,1},\ldots\theta_{i,m_i}}(y) \right| dy \prod_{j=1}^{m_i} d\theta_{i,j}$$

(14)

Furthermore, since a realization x_i of X_i is $x_i = F_{X_i}^{-1}(u_i|\theta_i)$, the distribution of input X_i is determined by random variable U_i and θ_i. The sensitivity or importance of input variable X_i is also calculated by

$$S_{X_i} = 1/2 \int_0^1 \int_{\theta_{i,1}^L}^{\theta_{i,1}^U} \cdots \int_{\theta_{i,m_i}^L}^{\theta_{i,m_i}^U} f_{\theta_{i,1}\ldots,\theta_{i,m_i}}\left(\theta_{i,1},\ldots,\theta_{i,m_i}\right) \int \left| f_Y(y) - f_{Y|\theta_{i,1}\ldots,\theta_{i,m_i}}(y) \right| dy \prod_{j=1}^{m_i} d\theta_{i,j} du_i$$

(15)

3.4   Numerical Computation

After deriving the importance measure for aleatory and epistemic uncertainty, the most challenge is to code numerical method to compute the multiple integral in indicator S_{μ_i}, $S_{\theta_{i,j}}$ or S_{θ_i}. Take epistemic uncertainty parameter θ_i for instance, the importance metric S_{θ_i} is generally estimated by a Monte Carlo (MC) method

$$\widehat{S}_{\theta_i} = \frac{1}{2N} \sum_{j=1}^{N} \int \left| f_Y(y) - f_{Y|\theta_i^j = \theta_i^*}(y) \right| dy$$

$$= \frac{1}{2N} \sum_{j=1}^{N} \sum_{k=1}^{K} \left| \widehat{f}_Y(y_k) - \widehat{f}_{Y|\theta_i^j = \theta_i^*}(y_k) \right| \Delta y$$

(16)

where, N and K are the sampling number for parameter θ_i and density estimation, respectively. $f_{Y|\theta_i^j = \theta_i^*}(y)$ is the conditional output density with given parameter $\theta_i^j = \theta_i^*$ at the lth sampling. Notation y, referred to a realization of output Y, is computed by $y = f\left(F_X^{-1}(u|\theta)\right)$ with given parameters u and θ. Δy is the interval distance to compute the integral part. Density functions $f_Y(y)$ or $f_{Y|\theta_i^j = \theta_i^*}(y)$ is replaced by its kernel density estimation in the form of

$$\widehat{f}(y) = \frac{1}{Ph} \sum_{p=1}^{P} K(y - y_p)$$

(17)

where, K is one dimensional Gaussian kernel [18]. Some other analogous density estimate, like Rosenblatt estimation, Nearest Neighbor estimate or histogram estimate, can also be applied in this process.

However, the simulator model f is usually by a large computer code and the cost of MC method is quite high. Some studies have proved that LHS performs better than Monte Carlo in efficiency and convergence [19, 20]. Hence, a DLS method based on

LHS is proposed in this paper to compute importance metric S_{θ_i}. The DLS based importance measure process is given as follows:

(1) Define the input parameters sampling space $\Omega = (\mathbf{U}, \boldsymbol{\theta})$.
(2) Latin hypercube sampling is conducted to get P sampling points in the entire space Ω, then unconditional probability density $f_Y(y)$ is calculated through Eq. (1) after running simulator f.
(3) The next step is aiming at computing the conditional probability density $f_{Y|\theta_i}(y)$. Similarly, in the outer loop, LHS is used to generate N realizations of sub-parameter $\boldsymbol{\theta}_i = \left[\theta_{i,1}, \theta_{i,2}, \ldots, \theta_{i,m_i}\right]^T$, which make up sub-parameters set. Meanwhile, for a specified sub-parameter point $\theta_i = \theta_i^*$, P samples of parameters U and $\theta_{\sim i}$ is also obtained by LHS in the inner loop, where $\theta_{\sim i}$ denotes the vector θ except for θ_i. After DLS process, the conditional probability density $f_{Y|\theta_i}(y)$ is determined.
(4) Samples with K numbers are considered to measure the shift between $f_Y(y)$ and $f_{Y|\theta_i=\theta_i^*}(y)$ through MC methods. Repeat step 3 for N times until the whole realizations θ_i are ran in the simulator. Then the importance metric S_{θ_i} is completed by the process above.

4 Case Study

To illustrate the process and application of proposed importance measure, the Ishigami test function sourced from [3, 21] is taken for instance. Due to nonlinearity and non-monotony, this function is always regarded as an efficient function to assess the performance of importance metrics. A modified Ishigami function expression is

$$Y = f(X) = \sin(\pi X_1) + a\sin^2(\pi X_2) + b(\pi X_3)^4\sin(\pi X_1) \qquad (18)$$

where a and b are constants assumed to be 5 and 0.1, respectively. The distribution and parameters of input variables is shown in Table 1.

Table 1. Input variable parameters

Input variable	Distribution	Parameter
X_1	$X_1 \sim \beta(a_1, b_1)$	$1 \le a_1 \le 3, 2 \le b_1 \le 4$
X_2	$X_2 \sim \beta(a_2, b_2)$	$2 \le a_2 \le 4, 1 \le b_2 \le 3$
X_3	$X_3 \sim \beta(a_3, b_3)$	$3 \le a_3 \le 5, 2 \le b_3 \le 4$

The input parameters X_{1-3} are independently and beta distributed between 0 and 1, where the distribution parameters are represented by an unknown element of a given interval due to imprecise knowledge. Considering the difficulty of traditional sensitivity analysis method to tackle hybrid uncertainty, the proposed importance measure with the LHS method can be used to compute the epistemic and aleatory uncertainty, respectively. In this case, the inner loop takes LHS with 500 sampling points to yield the unconditional and conditional output PDF $f_Y(y)$ and $f_{Y|a_1=2,b_1=3}(y)$ as shown in Fig. 2.

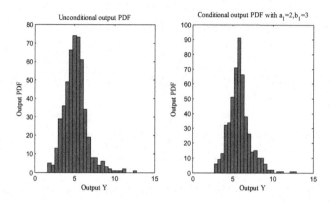

Fig. 2. Output PDF $f_Y(y)$ and $f_{Y|a_1=2,b_1=3}(y)$

In the outer loop, the conditional PDF is repeated for 100 times to compute aleatory and epistemic parameters with LHS method. The Gaussian kernel is used to estimation the density with the given value of output response Y, which is a key point to compute the area enclosed by unconditional and conditional PDF. Figures 3, 4 and 5 gives out the comparison of sensitivity indicator error between MC and DLS methods in variable $X_i, i = 1, 2, 3$.

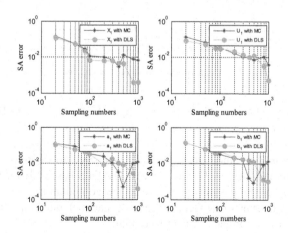

Fig. 3. Aleatory and epistemic sensitivity for X_1

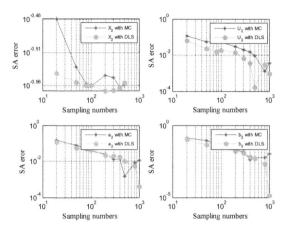

Fig. 4. Aleatory and epistemic sensitivity for X_2

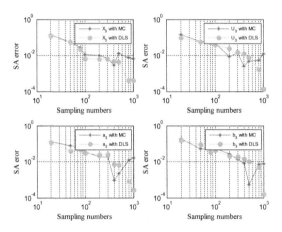

Fig. 5. Aleatory and epistemic sensitivity of X_3

The importance measure of uncertainty input $X_i(i = 1, 2, 3)$ is demonstrated in Figs. 3, 4 and 5. For the comparison between MC and DLS methods, DLS trend to get a higher accuracy than MC in the same sample sizes and perform better in the convergence. The sensitivity indicators gradually converge to certain values with the increased sampling numbers in the three charts. The DLS based LHS method is proved to be an efficient sampling strategy to reduce the computation costs. The proposed method also gives the sensitivity value of each sub-parameter and ranks their order with the consideration of importance respect to output.

5 Conclusion

Due to the epistemic uncertainty with insufficiency of knowledge is introduced into model's aleatory input. An improved moment independent method is presented in this paper to solve the hybrid problem. The auxiliary variable method distinguishes the aleatory and epistemic term from the hybrid uncertainty, respectively. The importance indicators of aleatory and epistemic uncertainty are derived based on the distance between unconditional and conditional output PDF, respectively. Furthermore, a DLS method based on LHS is proposed to ease the computation challenge. The test function shows that the DLS method performs well in sampling convergence and computing accuracy. The aleatory and epistemic importance indicators can be efficiently obtained by improved method, and the corresponding hybrid indicator is fitted with the reference value, which approve the validity of the proposed method.

In the future work, more test functions and engineering examples will be taken to investigate the property of this method. Besides, considerable attention will be also given to the sampling strategy for improving sampling efficiency.

References

1. Guidance on the Development, Evaluation, and Application of Environmental Models, Council for Regulatory Environmental Modeling. Technical report, U.S. Environmental Protection Agency, Washington, D.C. (2009)
2. Rumpfkeil, M.P.: Optimizations under uncertainty using gradients, hessians, and surrogate models. AIAA J. **51**(2), 444–451 (2013)
3. Borgonovo, E.: A new uncertainty importance measure. Reliab. Eng. Syst. Saf. **92**(6), 771–784 (2007)
4. Chaudhuri, A., Waycaster, G., Price, N.: NASA uncertainty quantification challenge: an optimization-based methodology and validation. J. Aerosp. Inf. Syst. **12**(1), 1–25 (2015)
5. Oberkampf, W.L., Deland, S.M., Rutherford, B.M.: Error and uncertainty in modeling and simulation. Reliab. Eng. Syst. Saf. **75**(3), 333–357 (2002)
6. Rabitz, H., Alis, O.F., Shorter, J., Shim, K.: Efficient input-output model representations. Comput. Phys. Commun. **117**, 11–20 (1999)
7. Tarantola, S., Gatelli, D., Mara, T.A.: Random balance designs for the estimation of first order global sensitivity indices. Reliab. Eng. Syst. Saf. **91**, 717–727 (2006)
8. Tarantola, S., Koda, M.: Improving random balance designs for the estimation of first order sensitivity indices. Procedia Soc. Bahav. Sci. **2**, 7753–7754 (2010)
9. Xu, C., Gertner, G.Z.: Uncertainty and sensitivity analysis for models with correlated parameters. Reliab. Eng. Syst. Saf. **93**(10), 1563–1573 (2008)
10. Fang, S., Gertner, G.Z., Anderson, A.: Estimation of sensitivity coefficients of nonlinear model input parameters which have a multinormal distribution. Comput. Phys. Commun. **157**(1), 9–16 (2004)
11. Iman, R.L., Davenport, J.M.: Rank correlation plots for use with correlated input variables. Commun. Stat. Simul. Comput. **11**(3), 335–360 (1982)
12. Chun, M.H., Han, S.J., Tak, N.I.: An uncertainty importance measure using a distance metric for the change in a cumulative distribution function. Reliab. Eng. Syst. Saf. **70**(3), 313–321 (2000)

13. Tang, Z., Lu, Z., Jiang, B.: Entropy-based importance measure for uncertain model inputs. AIAA J. **51**(10), 2319–2334 (2013)
14. Park, C.K., Ahn, K.I.: A new approach for measuring uncertainty importance and distributional sensitivity in probabilistic safety assessment. Reliab. Eng. Syst. Saf. **46**, 253–261 (1994)
15. Sobol', I.M., Tarantola, S., Gatelli, D., Kucherenko, S., Mauntz, W.: Estimating the approximation error when fixing unessential factors in global sensitivity analysis. Reliab. Eng. Syst. Saf. **92**, 957–960 (2007)
16. Oberkampf, W.L., Helton, J.C., Joslyn, C.A.: Challenge problems: uncertainty in system response given uncertain parameters. Reliab. Eng. Syst. Saf. **85**(1–3), 11–19 (2004)
17. Sankararaman, S., Mahadevan, S.: Separating the contributions of variability and parameter uncertainty in probability distributions. Reliab. Eng. Syst. Saf. **112**(112), 187–199 (2013)
18. Jourdan, A., Franco, J.: Optimal latin hypercube designs for the Kullback-Leibler criterion. Adv. Stat. Anal. **94**(4), 341–351 (2010)
19. Helton, J.C., Davis, F.J.: Latin hypercube sampling and the propagation of uncertainty in analyses of complex systems. Reliab. Eng. Syst. Saf. **81**(1), 23–69 (2003)
20. Fang, K.T., Ma, C.X., Winker, P.: Centered L2-discrepancy of random sampling and latin hypercube design, and construction of uniform designs. Math. Comput. **71**(237), 275–296 (1999)
21. Iman, R.L.: A matrix-based approach to uncertainty and sensitivity analysis for fault trees. Risk Anal. **7**(1), 21–33 (1987)
22. Xu, X., Lu, Z., Luo, X.: A kernel estimate method for characteristic function-based uncertainty importance measure. Appl. Math. Model. **42**, 58–70 (2016)

Flood Water Level Modeling and Prediction Using Radial Basis Function Neural Network: Case Study Kedah

Mohd Anuar Abu Bakar[✉], Fathrul Azarshah Abdul Aziz,
Shamsul Faisal Mohd Hussein, Shahrum Shah Abdullah,
and Fauzan Ahmad

Malaysia-Japan International Institute of Technology,
Universiti Teknologi Malaysia Kuala Lumpur, 54100 Kuala Lumpur, Malaysia
mohdanuar.abubakar@gmail.com

Abstract. Natural disasters are common nowadays and a major adverse event resulting from natural process of Earth. Most of the natural disaster are beyond control of human beings and cannot be predicted accurately when it occurs. For instance, prediction of a river water level is essential for flood mitigation in order to save people's lives and property. However, it is very difficult to predict river water level accurately since it is influenced by many factors and the fluctuations are highly non-linear. To address this problem, a river water level predictor utilizing the Radial Basis Function Network (RBFN) is proposed in this study. The goal of this project is to design a neural prediction algorithm that can forecast river water level prediction 7 h ahead with lower error. Result shows Best Fit value of 82.43% and Root Mean Square Error (RMSE) of 1.571.

Keywords: Flood water level prediction · Artificial neural network · Radial basis function network · Kedah river

1 Introduction

Flood are the most common occurring natural disasters that affect human and its surrounding environment [1]. Floods are often cited as being the most lethal of all natural disaster [2–4]. It is more vulnerable to Asia and the Pacific regions. It affects social and economic stability of a country.

Floods become a huge effect around the world especially in Malaysia because it causes suffering to human live and property loss [5]. Two major type of flood occur in Malaysia are monsoon flood and flash flood. The monsoon flood occurs mainly from Northeast Monsoon which prevails during the month of November to March with heavy rains to the east coast states of Peninsula, northern part of Sabah and southern part of Sarawak. Some of the recorded flood experiences in the country occur in 1926, 1931, 1947, 1954, 1957, 1963, 1965, 1967, 1971, 1973, 1983, 1988, 1993, 1998, 2001, 2006, 2007, 2010, 2013 and 2014. Report from Department of Irrigation and Drainage stated that about 29,000 km^2 or 9% of total land area and more than 4.92 million

© Springer Nature Singapore Pte Ltd. 2017
M.S. Mohamed Ali et al. (Eds.): AsiaSim 2017, Part I, CCIS 751, pp. 225–234, 2017.
DOI: 10.1007/978-981-10-6463-0_20

people (22%) is affected by flooding annually. Damage caused by flood is estimated about RM 915 million.

While monsoon flood is governed by heavy and long duration rainfall, more localized flooding which covers a large area has been reported in recent years. Most countries in Malaysia suffer from floods during monsoon season especially Kedah, Kelantan, Terengganu, Pahang and Johor. Flood of October 2–6, 2003 that affected a large area in the north-western part of the Peninsula covering states of Kedah, Penang and northern Perak. Flash flood is reportedly occurring quite rapid such as two events occur in April 2002 and October in Kuala Lumpur which has been recognized due to uncontrolled development and activities within the catchment and flood plain [6]. Large flood had damaged properties, public utilities, cultivation, loss of lives and caused hindrance to social economic activities. Average annual flood damage is as high as RM 100 million. Recently, 2014–2015 Malaysia floods hit Malaysia from December 15, 2014 until January 3, 2015. More than 200,000 people affected while 21 killed on the flood [7]. Thus, flood prediction system is very important to help people to evacuate prior to flood occurrence.

In recent years, the applications of Artificial Neural Network (ANN) has been widely used for modelling and forecasting in various area. The Artificial Neural Network (ANN) concept with neuron model was first developed by McCulloch and Pitts [8]. Then, the ANN has become extremely popular around the world after the first ANN training algorithm was introduced by Rosenblatt [9]. ANN models have the ability to solve and estimate nonlinear system and hence become important tools to solve diverse water resources problems [10, 11].

Several attempts to predict river water level in Malaysia has been done and the model used are normally Artificial Neural Network based such as Neural Network Autoregressive with Exogenous Input (NNARX), Elman Neural Network (ENN), Adaptive Neuro Fuzzy Interface System (ANFIS) and Autoregressive Integrated Moving Average (ARIMA). In this study, a river water level predictor utilizing the Radial Basis Function Network (RBFN) is proposed.

The applications of RBFN models have been widely used for prediction and forecasting. For example, Arora and Singhal [12] presented a study of application of RBFN. It has been used in various real time application for making accurate prediction such as weather forecasting, load forecasting, market analysis and many such application. Santhanam and Subhajini [13] used RBFN to predict the weather conditions of a place with an improvement in basic model.

RBFN has advantages of easy design, good generalization, strong tolerance to input noise, and online learning ability. The properties of RBFN make it very suitable to design flexible control systems. With this advantages of RBFN, this paper proposed a 7 h ahead flood water level prediction using RBFN structure. This paper is organized in the following manner: Sect. 2 states the related theory, Sect. 3 explains the methodology, experimental result using RBFN and discussion are presented in Sect. 4 and finally, Sect. 5 is conclusion.

2   Related Theory

A Radial Basis Function Network (RBFN) is a special type of neural network that uses a radial basis function as its activation function. RBFNs are very popular for function approximation, curve fitting, time series prediction, control and classification problems [14]. The RBFN is embedded into a 3-layered feedforward neural network comprised of input layer, hidden layer, and output layers. It possesses only a single hidden layer rather than multilayer structure, despite of this RBFN can solve complex problems similar to a neural network with multiple intermediary layers. In RBFN, determination of the number of neurons in the hidden layer is very important because it affects the network complexity and the generalizing capability of the network. In the hidden layer, each neuron has an activation function. The Gaussian function, which has a spread parameter that controls the behavior of the function, is the most preferred activation function [15]. A general block diagram of an RBFN is illustrated in Fig. 1.

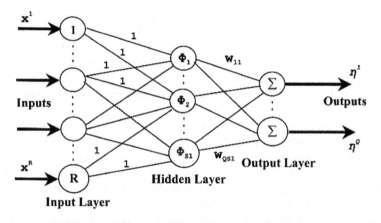

Fig. 1. A radial basis function network.

The network consists of three layers: an input layer, a hidden layer, and output layer. If the number of output, Q = 1, the output of the RBFN in Fig. 1 is calculated according to

$$n(x, w) = \sum_{k=1}^{M} w_{1k} \phi \left(\|x - c_k\|_2 \right) \tag{1}$$

where $x \in \Re^{Rx1}$ is an input vector, $\emptyset\,(-)$ is a basis function, $\| - \|_2$ donates the Euclidean norm, w_{1k} are the weight in the output layer, M is the number of neurons (and centers) in the hidden layer and $c_k \in \Re^{Rx1}$ is the RBF centers in the input vector space.

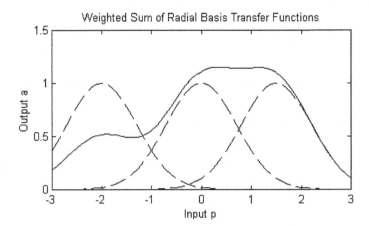

Fig. 2. Effects of different centers

The center c_k are defined point that are assumed to perform an adequate sampling of the input space. Effects of different centers is shown in Fig. 2. From this figure too, observe that the output is the weighted sum of the basis functions.

Thus, it is really important to find the correct second layer weight values so that the weight sum of the basis functions can approximate the given training output samples data.

Like Neural Networks and fuzzy interference system, Radial Basis Function Network (RBFN) [16] were also proven to be universal approximator [14]. Radial Basis Function Network (RBFN) and Multi-Layer Perceptron Network (MLPN) have different properties. First, RBFN is simpler than MLPN which usually have more complex architectures. Second, RBFN are often easier to be trained than MLPN because of the simple and fixed three-layer architecture. Third, RBFN act as local approximation networks and the network output are determined by specified hidden units in certain local receptive fields, while MLPN work globally and the network outputs are decided by all the neurons. Fourth, it is essential to set correct initial states for RBFN, while MLPN use randomly generated parameters initially. Last and most importantly, the mechanisms of classification for RBFN and MLPN are different: RBFN clusters are separated by hyper spheres, while in Neural Network, arbitrarily shaped hyper surfaces are used for separation.

3   Methodology

3.1   Data Collection

Water level at flood location is influenced by many factors such as upstream river water level, rainfall, water flow, and temperature. The flood location in this paper is Muda River, located at Syed Omar Bridge. The most substantial influence for flood location comes from four stations, water lever at two upstream rivers, Ketil River at Kuala Pegang and Muda River at Jeniang and rainfall at two stations, Pulai and Jeniang Klinik as shown in Fig. 3. Data used for developing this model were obtained from the Department of Irrigation and Drainage Malaysia by their Supervisory Control and Data Acquisition (SCADA) system. Water level at flood location was measured in real-time of water level and rainfall data.

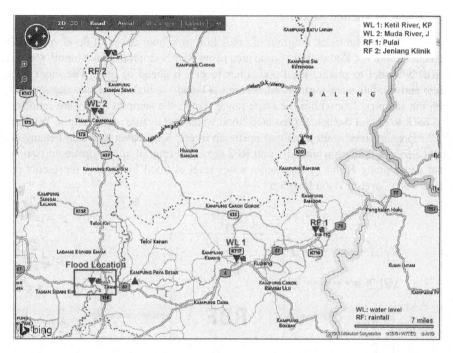

Fig. 3. The flood location stations for case study at Kedah. (Retrieved September 2016, http://infobanjir.water.gov.my/ve/vmapkdh.cfm)

3.2 Data Used

For RBFN modelling, data used were divided into two sets namely: training and testing samples data. In this study, prediction time starts from 1 h ahead, 3 h ahead, 5 h ahead and 7 h ahead. Firstly, the RBFN model was train by training samples data. Then, in order to evaluate the performance of RBFN model, testing samples data was used to fed the model. For each prediction time hours ahead, the samples data used for RBFN model training was in meters (m) for water level and millimeters (mm) for rainfall from, 1/9/2012 00:00:15 till 20/9/2012 24:00:00 in 15 min time interval with the total of 1920 samples data. These samples data were chosen because flood event was occurring during this period of time and providing reliable water level and rainfall data.

After training the samples data, the testing samples data were fed into the model to verify and evaluate the performance of the RBFN model. These testing data samples starting from 21/9/2012 00:00:15 till 30/9/2012 24:00:00 with 15 min time interval and the total of 920 samples. Hence, with reliable condition of training and testing samples data, optimal performance result was expected at the end of this study. The water level at flood location was also consider as one of input parameter.

3.3   Flood Prediction Model

Figure 4 showed the block diagram of prediction time hour ahead of flood water level prediction model at Kedah flood prone area using RBFN structure. Five inputs were fed to RBFN model to predict the flood water level 7 h ahead of time. The input water levels and rainfall were normalized between +1 and −1 before fed into the model to keep the samples data within the same range. Later, the samples data were renormalized back to obtain the actual predicted flood water level value at the output. WL1 and WL2 represent river water level two upstream rivers; Ketil River at Kuala Pegang and Muda River at Jeniang while RF1 and RF2 represent rainfall at two upstream stations; Pulai and Jeniang Klinik. y represents water level at flood location. $\hat{y}$ represents predicted water level at flood location.

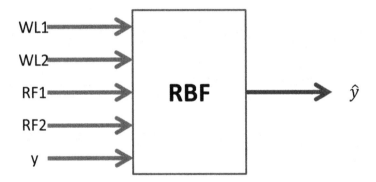

Fig. 4. RBFN for prediction time hours ahead of flood water level.

In this study, we optimized the RBFN by fixed center selected at random. The simplest and quickest approach for setting the RBFN parameters is to have their centers fixed at M point selected at random from N data points, and to set all their widths to be equal and fixed at an appropriate size for the distribution of data points. Specifically, we can use normalized RBFN's center at $\{c_k\}$ defined by

$$\phi_k(x) = \exp\left(-\frac{\|x - c_k\|}{2\beta_k^2}\right) \tag{2}$$

where

$$\{c_k\} \subset \{x^p\} \tag{3}$$

And the β_k are all related in the same way of the maximum or average distance between the chosen center c_k. Common choice are

$$\beta_k = \frac{d_{max}}{\sqrt{2max}} \tag{4}$$

or

$$\beta_k = 2d_{ave} \tag{5}$$

Which ensure that the individual RBFs are neither too wide, nor too narrow, for given training data. For large training sets, this approach gives reasonable results.

4   Result and Discussion

Using the RBFN model, all the data were training and testing to predict 1 h, 3 h, 5 h, and 7 h ahead of water level at flood location. The range of spread is 1 to 500 and centers is 1–1920. The lowest RMSEs for every hour obtained result are summarized in Table 1 for comparison purpose. From this table, it is concluded that the lowest Root Mean Square Error using RBFN model is prediction at 7 h ahead of water level at flood location with RMSE value is 1.5710. At this point, the center is 3 and spread is 10.

Table 1. Root Mean Square Error of prediction of water level at 1 h, 3 h, 5 h and 7 h ahead.

Time (hour ahead)	Root Mean Square Error (RMSE)
1	3.0423
3	2.6947
5	2.2645
7	1.5710

Figure 5 showed water level at two upstream rivers, Ketil River at Kuala Pegang and Muda River at Jeniang, while Fig. 6 showed rainfall at Pulai and Jeniang Klinik. Figure 7 showed the water level at flood location which is Syed Omar Bridge at Muda River. Figure 8 showed the prediction result when center is 3 and spread is 10 using RBFN model. The prediction result demonstrated optimal result with Best Fit value of 82.43%.

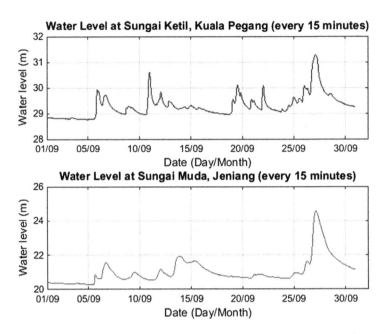

Fig. 5. Water level at Ketil River, Kuala Pegang and Muda River, Jeniang.

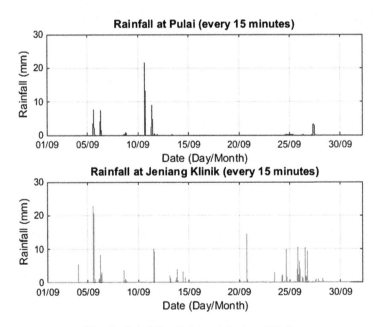

Fig. 6. Rainfall at Pulai and Jeniang Klinik.

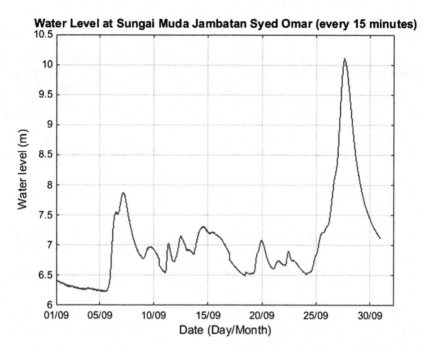

Fig. 7. Water level at flood location, Sungai Muda Jambatan Syed Omar.

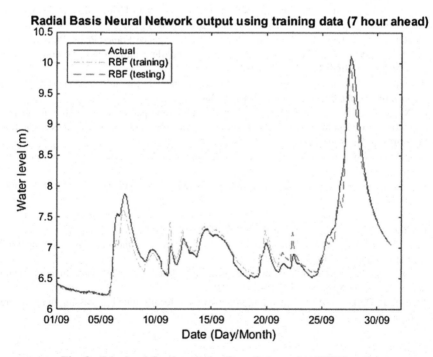

Fig. 8. 7 h ahead flood water level prediction using RBFN model.

5 Conclusion

The main goal of this study is to develop and design a neural prediction algorithm that can forecast river water level prediction 7 h ahead with higher Best Fit value and lower error. From this study, it showed that Radial Basis Functions Network model can predict up to 7 h ahead river water level. Hence, this study provides a lot of time and allows people to evacuate and save property before the flood occur. However, further modifications are needed to give better result. For future work, it will be best to test for one year data sample. In addition, comparison with other prediction model.

References

1. Hewitt, K.: Region of Risk: A Geographical Introduction to Disaster. Longman Ltd., Essex (1997)
2. Noji, E.K.: The Public Health Consequences of Disaster, 1st edn. Oxford University Press, Oxford (1997). ISBN-10:0195095707
3. Alexander, D.E.: Natural Disaster, 1st edn. Springer Science and Business, New York (1993). ISBN-10: 0412047411
4. Jonkman, S.N., Kelman, I.: An analysis of the causes and circumstances of flood disaster death. Disaster **29**, 75–97 (2005)
5. Department of Hydrology, Yearly Rainfall Data, Department of Irrigation and Drainage (DID) Malaysia, Kuala Lumpur (2011)
6. Hassan, A.J., Ghani, A.A.: Development of Flood Risk Map Using GIS for Sg Selangor Basin (2006). http://redac.eng.usm.my/html/publish/2006_11.pdf
7. AsiaOne: Floods Kill 21 in Malaysia, Water Recede, Agence France-Press, Paris (2014)
8. McCulloch, W.S., Pitts, W.: A logical calculus of the ideas immanent in nervous activity. Bull. Math. Biophys. **5**, 115–133 (1943)
9. Rosenblatt, F.: The perceptron: a probabilistic model for information storage and organization in the brain. Psychol. Rev. **65**, 386 (1958)
10. Li, X., Zecchin, A.C., Maier, H.R.: Selection of smoothing parameter estimators for general regression neural networks – applications to hydrological and water resources modelling. Environ. Model. Softw. **59**, 162–186 (2014)
11. Xiong, Y., Wallach, R., Furman, A.: Modelling multidimensional flow in wetable and water-repellent soil using artificial neural networks. J. Hydrol. **410**, 92–104 (2011)
12. Arora, Y., Singhal, A., Bansal, A.: A study of applications of RBF network. Int. J. Comput. Appl. **94**, 17–20 (2014)
13. Santhanam, T., Subhajini, A.C.: An efficient weather forecasting system using radial basis function neural network. J. Comput. Sci. **7**, 992–996 (2011)
14. Park, J., Sandberg, I.W.: Universal approximation using radial basis function network. Neural Comput. **3**, 246–257 (1991)
15. Ajeel, S.A.: A novel carbon steel pipe protection based on radial basis function neural network. Am. J. Appl. Sci. **7**, 248–251 (2010)
16. Moody, J., Darken, C.J.: Fast learning in networks of locally-tuned processing units. Neural Comput. **1**, 281–294 (1989)

Polygon 3D Surface Reconstruction Using IR Scanner

Siti Asmah Daud[1(✉)], Nasuha Mohd Shaber[1],
Nasrul Humaimi Mahmood[2], and Muhammad Hanif Ramlee[3,4]

[1] Department of Electrical and Electronics Engineering, Faculty of Engineering,
Universiti Teknologi PETRONAS, 32610 Seri Iskandar, Perak, Malaysia
sitiasmah.daud@utp.edu.my
[2] Faculty of Electrical Engineering, Universiti Teknologi Malaysia (UTM),
81310 Skudai, Johor, Malaysia
[3] Medical Devices and Technology Group (MEDITEG),
Faculty of Biosciences and Medical Engineering,
Universiti Teknologi Malaysia (UTM), 81310 Johor Bahru, Johor, Malaysia
[4] Sport Innovation and Technology Group (SITC),
Institute of Human Centered Engineering (IHCE),
Universiti Teknologi Malaysia (UTM), 81310 Johor Bahru, Johor, Malaysia

Abstract. Polygon model scanner is developed to reconstruct a three-dimension image of an object's surface. Amongst is by installing five infrared sensors in the sensor array as a medium to harvest data. All components used in the device then are installed in a closed box to avoid any source of light. Next is ellipse, hemisphere, cylinder and rectangle shapes were used to be tested in the developed device. Results from the experiment showed that the device is capable to reconstruct an image of a polygon model. As a whole, it requires 60 min to scan the whole model which covers 10 cm of the height with a diameter of 5 cm. Finally, Butterworth, Mean, Median filters and point fitting were used to determine which filters gives accurate dimension compared to the reference shape.

Keywords: Infrared sensor · Butterworth filter · Mean filter · Median filter · Point fitting

1 Introduction

Advancement in radiological imaging techniques is pivotal in the medical fields especially men are exposed to new illness which were not common before. Three-Dimension (3D) image reconstruction for example is far more informative compared to Two-Dimension (2D) image. It provides image(s) with x-, y- and z-axis data. Device that capable to provide the 3D image of an object is a good choice for the researcher or user to complete a task. Devices in the market offer a high resolution of an image, able to reconstruct a complex shape of an object but high in cost.

Some of the device requires an expert to operate the system. These drawbacks lead to the new development of a shape detector sensor that offers simpler operation at lower cost but many similar functions with the existing devices in the market. Ultrasound

© Springer Nature Singapore Pte Ltd. 2017
M.S. Mohamed Ali et al. (Eds.): AsiaSim 2017, Part I, CCIS 751, pp. 235–244, 2017.
DOI: 10.1007/978-981-10-6463-0_21

(US), infrared (IR), 3D sensor and photo-diode are the sensors that usually used to be installed in a device. It depends on the function and needs of the device itself. Combination of sensors in the same device helps to overcome the weaknesses of each other to obtain accurate results.

YAIR is a device developed by Benet *et al.* installed with US rotary sensor and 16 pairs of IRs. The device enables to draw a map accurately with a quick response. YAIR only takes 2.5 s to scan the circular area with a 15 ms response time for a single measurement. Figure 1 shows the installation setup of the YAIR device.

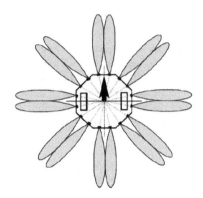

Fig. 1. YAIR is installed with two types of sensors, IR and US are used to perfectly draw a map with a fast response time [1].

The US rotary sensor rotates every 1.8° with a precision less than 1 cm. The rotation of the US sensor is to cover the whole circular area. The accuracy of the device is 2.5 mm for every 11 cm of a distance measurement. Unfortunately, US sensor has its drawbacks that leads to an error to the output data. Some of the disadvantages of the US sensor are poor angulation resolution [2], wide beam-width, and sensitive to certain surfaces [3].

The most suitable sensor to reconstruct the 3D geometry image is using 3D sensor [4, 5]. Dugan *et al.* used this sensor to calculate the surface angle of an object from multiple light sources [6]. However, it requires high computational power and data from the camera to avoid any obstacle [2, 7]. The cost to operate the 3D sensor is very expensive, and it is the main reason why researchers try to avoid using it.

Other than that, IR sensor can be combined with US, laser diode, 3D sensor and Position Sensing Detector (PSD) for a better result in the experiment. Basically, researchers used IR and US to avoid an obstacle accurately due to the ability of both sensors to measure distance for a short and long range. US sensor has a frequency of 20,000 Hz, which is above human hearing range. Easy to operate and low in cost are the main reasons why it has been used widely in a robotic system [8].

There are a number of researches that used IR sensors as a medium to harvest data and display results. However, the function or objective of each research is different in order to achieve the desired output. IR sensor can be used to measure distance [3], detecting movement of a target [9, 10], draw a map [11, 12], object's detection [13, 14], and localization purposes [8, 15]. Other than that, IR was combined with other sensors to gain more accurate data and to overcome the drawback of the IR itself. IR is limited to a certain distance; it is divided into two different type of sensors to detect a short and long range.

Nurmaini [16] used five IR sensors installed in the device to detect an obstacle in front of the device. All the IR sensors installed in a circular-shaped, and each sensor is placed 45° respectively. The objective of this research is to detect an obstacle in a complex corridor environment and to avoid any collision with the wall.

Meanwhile, Park *et al.* in their research used 12 pairs of IR sensor to detect any open area between the obstacles. Time taken to scan the whole area for 360° is shortened when using more than one IR in the device. Moreover, any small obstacles can be noticed by rotating the sensor due to the narrow detection of the IR. Each IR has the same detection area, since the sensors are installed in circular, the overlapping area exist helps in detecting the obstacle accurately. Figure 2 shows the arrangement of 12 IR sensors installed in the device.

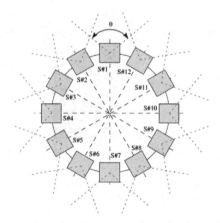

Fig. 2. Multiple rotating range sensors to detect any open area exist between the obstacles [17].

The overlapping area of each IR sensor confirmed that it could react to maximize an area during the scanning process. An accurate data of an obstacle location was obtained in the overlapped area. Lee *et al.* also applied the same concept of rotating and used more than one IR in a device for shorter and faster scanning [18].

Based on the explanation regarding IR sensor and all of its advantages, this research installed five sensors in a shape detector device to reconstruct the 3D image of an object. Various shapes of a polygon model were designed and tested using the sensor device. Distances between IR and the model surface were measured, and data were then used in Matlab algorithms to reconstruct the image. Results and accuracy for each model were displayed.

2   Shape Detector Sensor Device Specifications

Shape detector sensor device developed in the experiment is capable to reconstruct the 3D image of an object's surface. The device consists of IR sensor array, model plane, motor drive, Arduino microcontroller, stepper motor and control board. During the scanning process, an object is placed underneath the sensor array and on top of the model plane. Figure 3 illustrates the position of an object in the sensor device.

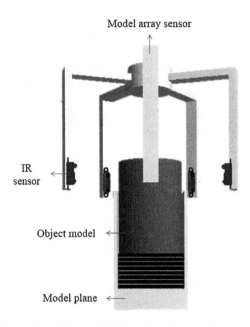

Fig. 3. Position of an object model placed underneath the sensor array [19].

The model plane rotates every 2° for the scanning purposes, meanwhile IR sensors measure data between sensor and object surface. The idea to rotate the model plane is to minimize a blind spot of the object surface when there is a curve or band exists on the surface [17, 18]. In order to increase the height, a cardboard was slotted underneath the object. A total of 50 cardboard layers were required to cover 10 cm height of an object.

The components in a sensor device are set up in a closed box with no light source when the device is turned ON. Each component installed in the sensor device has its own function. The control boards itself is responsible to monitor the ON and OFF condition of the IR sensors and transmit the output data to a microcontroller. Meanwhile, the sensor array holds the IR sensor to a fixed position during the experiment. Motor driver is a driver to control the function of a stepper motor to rotate every 2° after 20 s. The model plane is a casing to place the object to be reconstructed. Other than that, the cardboard layer acts as an actuator to increase the height of the object. Arduino UNO is a microcontroller in the sensor device to transfer data to a PC [19].

2.1   Conversion Equation

Data received by the sensor output is converted using Eq. (1), a smooth algorithm is applied to filter the unnecessary signal. Point fitting technique is used in the smoothing purpose. In this technique, both robust smooth and spline data were used to eliminate a small fraction of outliers and connect each point between x- and y-axis.

$$D = 9 - \left[\frac{2914}{V+5} - 1 \right] \tag{1}$$

From Eq. (1), coefficient 9 is distance length between IR sensor and the center of the model plane [20]. Meanwhile, coefficient 2914 is a constant value for GP2D12 sensor. V is the output sensor value. Some experiments have been conducted to test the accuracy of the Eq. (1). Where an object was placed in front of the IR sensor, and data were then collected. After the conversion equation was applied to the sensor value, results showed the actual distance was equal to the conversion. It showed that, Eq. (1) could be used in the experiment to convert sensor output to distance in *cm*.

3   Result and Discussion

Four different filters were used to determine which filter gives higher accuracy from the reconstructed image. Median, Butterworth, Mean, and point fitting filters were used in the experiment. Results from the reconstructed image are displayed in a figure format, and the accuracy for each model is calculated. Figures 4, 5, 6, and 7 shows the reconstructed 3D image for cylinder object.

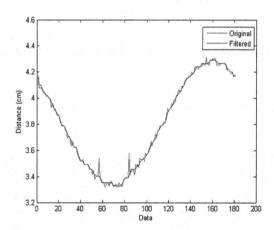

Fig. 4. Cylinder object data filtered using Median filter.

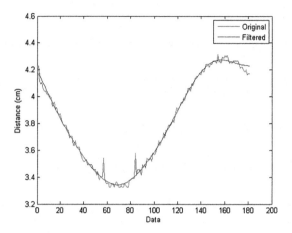

Fig. 5. Cylinder object data filtered using Butterworth filter.

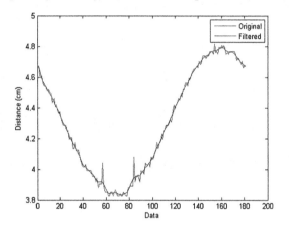

Fig. 6. Cylinder object data filtered using Mean filter.

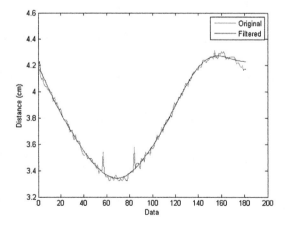

Fig. 7. Cylinder object data filtered using point fitting.

Result shows that, data filtered by Median, Butterworth, and Mean filters unable to produced smooth line data compared to point fitting filters. Point fitting techniques capable in providing smooth data to the captured sensor value. Smooth line data is required to increase accuracy of a 3D reconstructed image of a polygon model. Results from different filters were used to reconstruct 3D image as shown in Figs. 8, 9, 10, and 11.

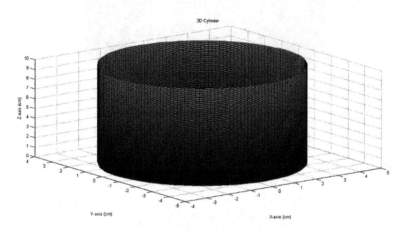

Fig. 8. 3D reconstructed of a cylinder object using Median filter.

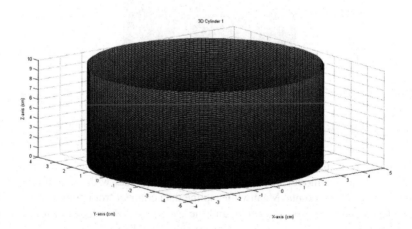

Fig. 9. 3D reconstructed of a cylinder object using Butterworth filter.

3D image surface were reconstructed using 3D plot in Matlab. The high for each image were fixed into 10 cm since the size of the object high did not change throughout the experiment. The diameter for each polygon were varies based on the size of the reference object. In this experiment, the x and y-axis of the 3D image were fixed into 5 cm due to the maximum and minimum size of the reference object itself.

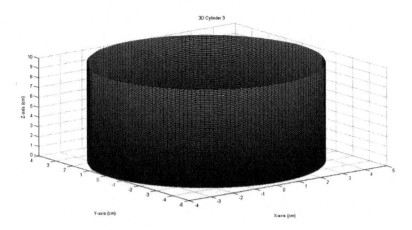

Fig. 10. 3D reconstructed of a cylinder object using Mean filter.

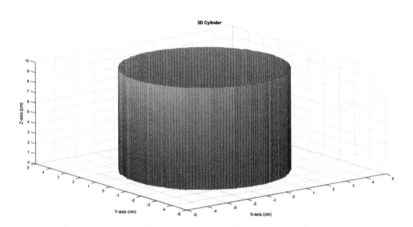

Fig. 11. 3D reconstructed of a cylinder object using point fitting.

From the reconstructed image, Point fitting technique contain of robust smooth and spline data. Robust smooth can be used in smoothing data with an outliers without changing the adjacent points. Meanwhile, spline data connect from point to a point. It is specified to a *smoothing parameter p,* and the *weights* w_i. Results from four different filtered used to determine the best filter were shown in Table 1.

Results from Table 1 showed that the accuracy for all polygon shapes. The highest accuracy percentage is the cylinder, which is 98.37%. Meanwhile, for ellipse, the average accuracy is 60%. For hemisphere, the average accuracy is 60% and higher accuracy was using point-fitting technique, 92.85%. Last but not least, the percentage accuracy when using point fitting is 89.05%. It shows that the shape detector device has successfully reconstructed 3D image of an object's surface when using point-fitting technique with the accuracy is above 95% in average.

Table 1. Accuracy percentage for four different polygon model with four different filter used to reconstruct 3D image of an object surfaces.

Polygon	Filter	Accuracy (%)
Cylinder	Butterworth	74.83
	Median	74.09
	Mean	74.31
	Point fitting	98.37
Ellipse	Butterworth	58.15
	Median	59.43
	Mean	59.58
	Point fitting	94.48
Hemisphere	Butterworth	62.14
	Median	60.57
	Mean	62.00
	Point fitting	92.85
Rectangle	Butterworth	74.00
	Median	73.57
	Mean	74.14
	Point fitting	89.05

4 Conclusion

Shape detector sensor device in the experiment could reconstruct the 3D image of various polygon models, and the accuracy is above 95% in average. However, several steps need to be considered, for example, during the scanning process, the surrounding area cannot be exposed to any light source due to the sensitivity of the IR sensor.

Other than that, a total time requires to scan an object with 10 cm in height is 60 min. By applying more infrared sensor to the device could reduce the total time required to scan an object. Slotting cardboard underneath an object during the experiment requires extra attention from the researcher to avoid any delay. The installation of an actuator to control the up and down movements of the model plane can help to increase the height of an object.

A developed algorithm could filter unwanted signals and smooth the surface area of a polygon model. Compared to Butterworth, Median and Mean filter, point fitting gives better result in terms of accuracy to the 3D surface image reconstruction. Since the entire object used in the experiment is polygon shape, an additional experiment is required to use more complicated model for the image reconstruction purposes. By doing this, the device can be claimed as a multipurpose shape detector device other than focusing on the reconstruction of a polygon model.

Acknowledgments. This work have been supported by Universiti Teknologi PETRONAS (UTP) and Universiti Teknologi Malaysia (UTM).

References

1. Benet, G., Blanes, F., Simo, J.E., Perez, P.: Using infrared sensors for distance measurement in mobile robots. Robot. Auton. Syst. **40**(4), 255–266 (2002)
2. Tar, A., Cserey, G.: Object outline and surface-trace detection using infrared proximity array. IEEE Sens. J. **11**(10), 2486–2493 (2011)
3. Mohammad, T.: Using ultrasonic and infrared sensors for distance measurement. Int. Sch. Sci. Res. Innov. **3**(3), 269–274 (2009)
4. Murray, D., Little, J.: Using real-time stereo vision for mobile robot navigation. Auton. Robot. **8**(2), 161–171 (2000)
5. Oike, Y., Ikeda, M., Asada, K.: A 375 × 365 high-speed 3-D range finding image sensor using row parallel search architecture and multisampling technique. IEEE J. Solid-State Circuits **40**(2), 444–453 (2005)
6. Dugan, U., Dongseok, R., Myungjoon, K.: Multiple intensity differentiation for 3-D surface reconstruction with mono-vision infrared proximity array sensor. IEEE Sens. J. **11**(12), 3352–3358 (2011)
7. Guivant, J., Nebot, E., Baiker, S.: Localization and map building using laser range sensors in outdoor applications. J. Robot. Syst. **17**(10), 565–583 (2000)
8. Do, Y., Kim, J.: Infrared range sensor array for 3D sensing in robotic applications. Int. J. Adv. Robot. Syst. **10**, 1–9 (2013)
9. Yang, B., Juo, J., Liu, Q.: A novel low-cost and small-size human tracking system with pyroelectric infrared sensor mesh network. Infrared Phys. Technol. **63**, 147–156 (2014)
10. Zappi, P., Farella, E., Benini, L.: Tracking motion detection and distance with pyroelectric IR sensors. IEEE Sens. J. **10**(9), 295–300 (2010)
11. Bloss, R.: Simultaneous sensing of location and mapping for autonomous robots. Sens. Rev. **28**(2), 102–107 (2008)
12. Jenkin, M., Dymond, P., Wang, H.: Graph exploration with robot swarms. Int. J. Intell. Comput. Cybern. **2**(4), 818–845 (2009)
13. Borse, H., Dumbare, A., Gaikwad, R., Lende, N.: Mobile robot for object detection using image. Glob. J. Comput. Sci. Technol. Neural Artif. Intell. **12**(11), 13–14 (2012)
14. Kim, S., Lee, S., Kim, S., Lee, J.: Object tracking of mobile robot using moving colour and shape information for the aged walking. Int. J. Adv. Sci. Technol. **3**, 59–68 (2009)
15. Djurovic, Z.M., Kovacevic, B.D., Dikic, G.D.: Target tracking with two passive infrared non-imaging sensors. IET Signal Process. **3**(3), 177–188 (2009)
16. Nurmaini, S.: Intelligent low cost mobile robot and environmental classification. Int. J. Comput. Appl. **35**(12), 1–7 (2011)
17. Park, H., Baek, S., Lee, S.: IR sensor array for a mobile robot. In: Proceeding of IEEE/ASME International Conference on Advance Intelligent Mechatronics, pp. 928–933. IEEE, Monterey (2005)
18. Lee, G., Chong, N.Y.: Low-cost dual rotating infrared sensor for mobile robot swarm applications. IEEE Trans. Ind. Inf. **7**(2), 277–286 (2011)
19. Daud, S.A., Mahmood, N.H., Leow, P.L., Harun, F.K.C.: Model sensor device used to reconstruct 3D image of an object. J. Teknol. Spec. Ed.-Biomed. Signal Image Technol. **74**(6), 109–113 (2015)
20. Daud, S.A., Mahmood, N.H., Leow, P.L., Harun, F.K.C.: The used of infrared sensor for 3D image reconstruction. J. Teknol. **73**(3), 127–132 (2015)

Pros and Cons of a Non-enclosed Community in Congested Traffic Networks: Braess Paradox-Based Analysis

Wei Shi[1], Jinghan Sun[2], Jiahui Liu[1], and Xiao Song[3(✉)]

[1] School of Electronic and Information Engineering, Beihang University,
Beijing, China
swl995@buaa.edu.cn
[2] School of Computer Science and Technology, Beihang University,
Beijing, China
sunjinghan1999@163.com
[3] School of Automation Science, Beihang University, Beijing, China
songxiao@buaa.edu.cn

Abstract. This paper focuses on the impact of an opened or enclosed residential community on a congested road network. The two-dimensional cellular automata-based model (CA) is used, combined with vehicle behavior such as left-turning and waiting. Also, the traffic controller is an employed model in the intersection. We divide the whole network into several basic modular structures, which could be combined to simulate typical residential communities. Based on these models, simulation of the real-world scenario is carried out. The results include the average traffic density of the network and the running time of probe cars. It is observed that, when we enclose the community during congested traffic, the density is diminished. This means a Braess paradox emerges. However, the average travel time of probe cars with a solid OD (origin and destination) pair will decrease for the reason that added roads give probe cars more choices.

Keywords: Enclosed residential community · Cellular automata · Microscopic traffic simulation · Braess paradox

1 Introduction

With the increasing number of cars on the road, the requirement for a high capacity of traffic networks is on the rise as well. We can see the compact-ordered traffic networks, of Western-developed cities, in the picture below (Fig. 1).

After analyzing the structure of the majority of traffic networks as well as residential communities, we find several typical features: broad roads, enclosed residential communities, and prohibited car entrance into those communities. This is because the geomantic omen is taken into account when designing buildings. Therefore, the ordered pattern of a building with the broad-long-straight road style creates lot of rectangular residential communities in China. Further, these buildings are expected to serve some functional activities as a whole, which lead to a continuous distribution of

© Springer Nature Singapore Pte Ltd. 2017
M.S. Mohamed Ali et al. (Eds.): AsiaSim 2017, Part I, CCIS 751, pp. 245–258, 2017.
DOI: 10.1007/978-981-10-6463-0_22

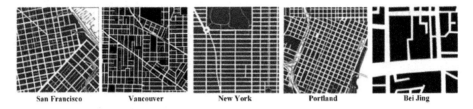

Fig. 1. Compact community pattern of the developed city.

these building. In other words, it is not easy to divide them. The big-size building pattern and road style reduce the connectivity of traffic networks in China. This makes people have to pay extra cost to get to their destination, which may be difficult to achieve by main road. The following pictures show the general enclosed residential community from the Baidu map.

Fig. 2. General enclosed residential community.

From the above comparison, it is clear that the open residential community and rising density of the road might be helpful to reduce the congestion. This is the critical problem we try to solve in this paper, i.e., evaluating the travel efficiency of traffic networks, when we take the opening enclosed residential community policy. Currently, most China communities are designed as enclosed residential communities (ERC). However, as more cars are on the road, drivers' adverse feelings are intensified due to increased traffic jams. One suggestion from the public is to make better use of the road resources in community, i.e., reconstructing the ERC to the open residential communities (ORC).

Adding new links to an existing traffic network is related to Braess paradox studies [1]. In Braess's settings, each agent routes selfishly, thus intending to minimize travel time. This results in a so-called user equilibrium [2, 3]. Based on this assumption, we try to formulate one typical type of road network topology surrounding a residential community (RC) and simulate with CA (cellular automata) microscopic simulation [8]. CA was first proposed by Von Neumann, and it is used to simulate the self-replicating function-in-life system [10]. Then it was applied to solve traffic problems via traffic simulations [11–14]. Based on the former research, Nagel and Schreckenberg proposed a stochastic discrete automaton model (NS model) to simulate freeway traffic [7].

This model was then expanded to a two-dimensional cellular automata model (BML model) [9]. In this paper, we improve upon the BML model as our basic model. In order to obtain a comprehensive view of the result, we try to analyze from two aspects. The average traffic density and the average speed of probe cars. Probe cars are always used to solve traffic problems [4, 5], especially in analyzing road congestion [6].

The main contributions are as follows. First, typical networks adjacent to RCs are generalized and analyzed, which represents the vast majority of RCs in China. Thus, we can draw upon useful and practical results for developing traffic networks. Note that we use modular road structure to combine different traffic networks, which means we can intelligently and flexible form more general traffic networks. Second, CA-based microscopic models are designed to simulate the effect of adding RCLs. Because a CA model could exactly reflect an agent's behavior when a new road is added, we use it to achieve basic metrics and calculate it in the SL model. Third, for one certain scene, we provide several practical scenarios, which are simulated with the CA model. Conclusions are drawn with respect to different scenarios.

The paper is structured as follows. In Sect. 2, we present the related works in recent years. In Sect. 3, CA-based microscopic models are prosed and formulated. Section 4 studies one typical network adjacent to RCs, which are generalized and analyzed, and several practical scenarios are simulated. In Sect. 5, conclusions are drawn and future works are generalized.

2 Brief Review of CA Model

All the notations used in this paper are summarized in the Table 1. In this paper, the CA model is the basic model. Each cell is 4 m long and 4 m wide. One vehicle is considered one cell. The vehicle state is updated by its behavior, speed, and the rule of movements. The behavior determines the location where the vehicle will go, and the speed and rule of movements determine the process of location changing. Each iteration in the experiment represents an increase in the actual time. The abstract description of the algorithm is as follows.

$$X_i(t) \xrightarrow{G} X_i(t+1), \quad V_i(t) \xrightarrow{G} V_i(t+1) \tag{1}$$

If the position is occupied by another vehicle, the speed of the current moving vehicle will drop to zero and remain at the current place and wait:

$$X_i(t+1) = X_i(t), \quad V_i(t+1) = 0. \tag{2}$$

For facilitating the discussion and analysis, all assumptions are listed below:

All agents drive on the right-hand side of the road. Non-motorized vehicles, which have highly flexibility, make no contribution to the model used in this paper: these vehicles include bicycles, motorcycles, etc. Vehicle preference difference and environment condition are ignored in this paper. In other words, in our model, an SUV is equal to a bus, and community of the same pattern in Beijing is equal to the one in Shanghai. Inherent vehicles in the community are ignored in our model because they

Table 1. Notations used in this paper.

Notation	Definition
t	Time in the model
i	Number of vehicles in the model
j	Different location in CA
G	The movement behavior of CA
X_i	The current location of CA
V_i	The speed of CA
T	Time of experiment
T'	Time of a position with a vehicle
$\overline{T}$	The average travel time of probe cars
S	Path length of OD pairs
$\overline{\rho}$	The average traffic density
V_0	Initial speed in CA model
V^*	The speed of probe cars
$\overline{V^*}$	The average speed of probe cars
$n(t)$	The number of moving probe cars
N	The number of probe cars

have a relative less quantity. Because of the limited dimension in the community, we only consider that the two-way, two-lane road will be built inside the community. Initial velocity is set at the same value for all agents in our model, i.e., CA model. The CA model, in this paper, rules that agents running on the outer lane must turn right when they reach the cross road. In other words, lane change reflects turning-right behavior. In this paper, a two-way four-lane road means a two-way road with two lanes in each direction, and a two-way two-lane road means a two-way road with one lane in each direction. Basic constant set in our model (see Table 2).

Table 2. Basic constant set in CA model.

Notation	Name	Units
Initial velocity in CA model	50	Km/h
Waiting time of the controller	60	s

3   Agent-Based Traffic Flow Simulation Model

The general road network structure is composed of roads and intersections. Thus, any structure of a road network can be combined by different types of roads and intersections. Based on this notion, we separate road networks into five parts. There are two kinds of road: two-way, two-lane road; two-way, four-lane road. There are three kinds of intersection: 2 * 2 cross road; 4 * 2 cross road; 4 * 4 cross road.

3.1   Road Simulation

3.1.1   Two-Way Two-Lane Road

Modular structure is the notation of a dual carriageway with one lane in each direction. In accordance with the real-world rules, vehicles in such a road could only go straight, without making a turn, and the agents could decide whether to move or to be stopped by the occupation of next apace. The representation of road and CA model is shown in Fig. 3.

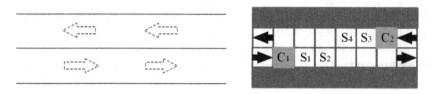

Fig. 3. Two-way two-lane road abstract and CA model.

Vehicles can only go straight on the two-way two-lane road. When C1 and C2 are at their position, as shown in Fig. 2, C1 could only move from S1 to S2 and C2 could only move from S3 to S4.

3.1.2   Two-Way Four-Lane Road

Modular structure m_2 is the notation of dual carriageway with two lanes in each direction, which is common around residential communities. The outer lane provides the chance of lane change, which provides more choices for an agent in the case of congestion and demand of making a turn. Note that the agent running on the outer lane can only turn right when it reaches a cross road. Only the agent running on the inner lane can either turn left or go straight. The probability of lane change is noted P_{23}. The process is shown in Fig. 4.

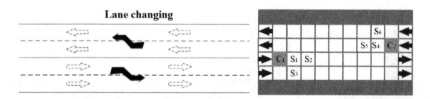

Fig. 4. Two-way four-lane road abstract and CA model.

There are two lanes in the same direction on the two-way four-lane road. According to the driving rules, an agent could only turn right when it is on the right lane. Thus, if the agent on the left lane wants to turn right, he has to change to the right lane, such as S1→S3 and S4→S6. And S1→S2, S4→S5 represent going straight.

3.2   Intersection Simulation

A cross road connects the linear road in different directions, which complicates agent behavior. We also define agent behavior in the CA model according to the real situation in different cross roads. The categories of cross road are 4 * 4 size cross road, 2 * 4 size cross road, and 2 * 2 cross road. For example, a 4 * 4 cross road means that two two-way two-lane roads converge in one point. We have to illustrate that we add controller in the 4 * 4 cross road, and the remainder do not due to size restrictions.

3.2.1   2 * 2 Cross Road

Intersection I is a crossing of two two-way two-lane roads. S1→S2→S3 means C1 passing through this intersection. If a vehicle wants to turn left, it needs to take the step of S1→S2→S5→S6 and S1→S4 is turning right. Vehicles from the other direction obey the same rule (Fig. 5).

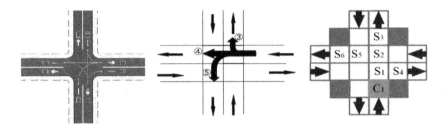

Fig. 5. 2 * 2 cross road and CA model.

3.2.2   4 * 2 Cross Road

When connecting the road network, we usually add a two-way two-lane road between the two two-way four-lane. Thus, there will be T-intersection such as in Fig. 6. According to the rule of driving, under this circumstance the vehicle from the two-way four-lane can only turn right to go into the two-way two-lane road, so does the vehicle from the two-way two-lane. If the vehicle C1 is at the position as shown in Fig. 6, it can take the step of

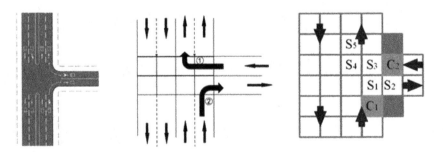

Fig. 6. 4 * 2 cross road abstract and CA model.

S1→S2. If the vehicle C12 at such position, it can take the step of S3→S4→S5. If the vehicle wants to go straight, it needs to obey the rule at the road simulation part.

3.2.3   4 * 4 Cross Road

Modular structure m_3 is the notation of the 4 * 4 cross road, which is common in residential communities. A 4 * 4 cross road means that two two-way four-lane roads converge in one point. According to the definition of the agent behavior on a two-way four-lane road, we will give the permitted behavior in a cross road.

We define every permitted move for each grid. As shown in Fig. 7, the No. 6 route presents the agent turning right. It is worth noting that the agent makes a turn to the inner lane of the road instead of the outer lane; No. 7 routes show the agent going straight to pass the cross road; No. 8 route presents the agent turning left.

The corresponding probabilities are:

Going straight: P_{31}
Turning left: P_{32}
Turning right: P_{33}

Agent possible route and behavior in the CA model are shown in the following pictures:

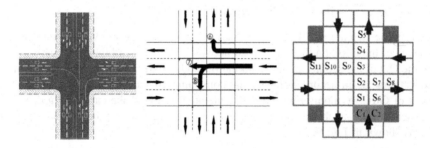

Fig. 7. 4 * 4 cross road abstract and CA model.

3.3   Road Network Under Consideration

The typical road network is shown in Fig. 8. The road network is divided into five parts: two kinds of road and three kinds of intersection. Road I is the two-way two-lane road, and Road II is the two-way, four-lane road. Intersection I is the crossing of the two two-way two-lane road. Intersection II is a T-intersection of a two-way, two-lane road and a two-way four-lane road. Intersection III is the crossing of two two-way four-lane.

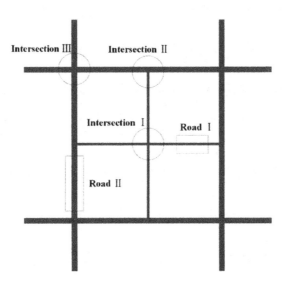

Fig. 8. Typical road network reconstructed by traffic simulation agents.

4   Road Network Simulation

4.1   Probe Cars with OD Pairs Setting

Based on the two angles of the whole network flow and the individual, we study the influence of the ORC on the whole road network. Thus, we use the probe cars, and we give the OD of the probe cars in each kind of road network. Let these probe cars in the road network be in accordance with the constraints of the OD pair. We evaluate the impact of ORC by monitoring the data generated by the probe cars during driving.

After creating an abstract of the selected road network, we set the OD pairs of probe cars, as shown in Fig. 9.

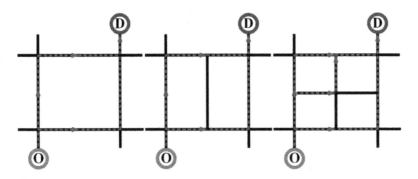

Fig. 9. OD pair settings of probe cars in different road networks.

4.2   Simulation and Results Analysis

We select the Wuzhong city Litong district Yuming community as a standard rectangular traffic network example. This traffic network could be reconstructed by four 4 * 4 intersections and some two-way four-lane roads. We use the CA model to simulate the environment. A bird's-eye view of the area and the surrounding road structure are shown in Fig. 10 (left); the abstract graph is on the right.

Fig. 10. Standard rectangular traffic network example and simulation result with CA model

Through the investigation of the real-world data in this community, we find the relevant parameters of the auto vehicle driving behavior at the intersection of the cell structure, as shown in the following figure. These data are our model input parameters (Table 3).

Table 3. Relevant parameters used in the CA model.

Parameter	Data	Units
Turning left probability	18.2	%
Turning right probability	51.45	%
Going straight probability	30.35	%
Width of community	376	m

We will take two steps to perform the simulation experiment.

First, we add one road to the community. This road connects the two main roads, allowing the driver to drive through the community. This makes the road network more complex.

The second step simulation is to open two roads in a residential community, which connects the main road. The road network abstract is shown in Fig. 11. Such a structure gives drivers more routes to choose for the destination. There will be a 2 * 2 intersection inside the residential community and four 4 * 2 intersections at the connection area of main road and added road.

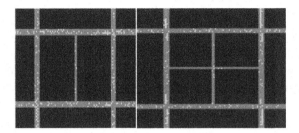

Fig. 11. Standard rectangular traffic network with road added.

4.2.1 Analysis from the Environment

According to the previous setting, we use the CA model to simulate. We will focus on two aspects: the average traffic density and the average speed of probe cars. These values can be calculated during the simulation process; the average traffic density is calculated by formula (3):

$$\overline{\rho_j} = \frac{T_j'}{T} \tag{3}$$

By plotting the density map of the road network under the condition of 25% input traffic density in Fig. 12, we can analyze ERC opened before and after.

We can clearly see, at the intersection of road in the traffic density map, the density is larger, which indicates that most of the road congestion occurs at the intersection. This is because of the traffic light influence. The traffic lights coordinate vehicles in all directions; thus, vehicles have to wait behind the intersection. The average traffic density is lower, which is also reflected in the traffic density map. The traffic density on the road is much lower on the road in the community. That is to say that most drivers pretend to drive on the main road. Traffic jams are less likely to happen in the community. However, opening ERC could have an influence on the main road in the road network.

The color bar shows the traffic density change in different situations. Before we open ERC, the maximum traffic density in the traffic network is 0.6; after adding one road, the maximum traffic density becomes 0.7 with an increase of 0.1. That is to say, a Braess paradox appears. After opening ERC, two 4 * 2 cross roads appear at the same time; thus, some drivers tend to choose the road inside the community, which means that drivers spend more time at intersections. When opening two roads with two 4 * 2 cross roads and one 4 * 4 intersection added, we can see the average traffic density maximum to 0.8. Such negative effect has a progressive effect: the more road it adds, the less efficient it will be. Rather than relieve the stress on the road, with more intersections added, vehicles take more time on the road, thereby making the road network more congested. Thus, we can say it is unwise to open ERC for the reason it has a negative impact on the road network. Such a result also reflects a Braess paradox.

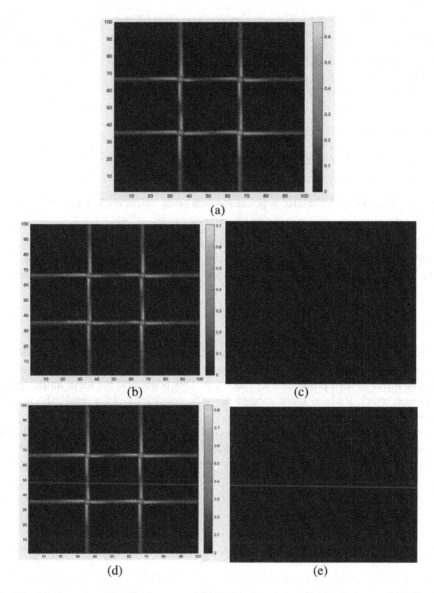

Fig. 12. (a) Average traffic density map of ERC. (b) Average traffic density map of ORC with one road added. (c) Traffic status inside ORC with one road added in detail. (d) Average traffic density map of ORC with two roads added. (e) Traffic status inside ORC with two roads added in detail. (Color figure online)

4.2.2 Analysis from the Individual

After that, we analyze probe cars from the individual point of view. We acquire simulation results of probe cars with a specific OD pair. Then we could perform an analysis from a micro-level. The simulation scene is shown in Fig. 13.

Fig. 13. Simulation procession with probe cars in black dots.

We set the experiment to loop 2084 times, which means 500 s in the real world. We monitor the average speed of probe cars and then analyze this speed based on these data. The average travel time of probe cars is calculated by the following formula:

$$V^*(t) = V_0 * \frac{n(t)}{N} \,,\; \overline{V^*} = \frac{\int V_{(t)}^* dt}{T} \,,\; \overline{T} = \frac{S}{\overline{V^*}} \tag{4}$$

Figure 14 shows that, for different road networks, when the road traffic density increases, the average speed of probe cars with a fixed OD pair will decrease. Thus, the average travel time of probe cars will increase. This is because the input traffic density increases, which leads to more congested traffic conditions. As a result, the average speed of vehicles will decrease.

In the actual traffic situation, vehicles could not turn left into the community with an added road. Thus, when one road is added to the residential community, probe cars could not turn into the ORC but drive on the main road, which accords with traffic

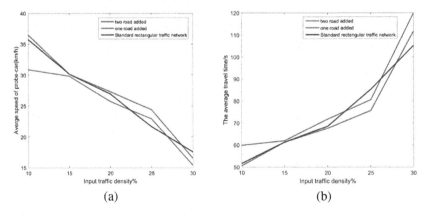

Fig. 14. (a) Relationship between average speed of probe cars and input traffic density. (b) Relationship between average travel time of probe cars and input traffic density.

regulations. Thus, we can see from the speed-density map that the average speed of probe cars on the road network with one road added is lower than previously. More road means more intersection added, which leads to congestion in the intersection, which is analyzed above.

However, if the added road gives drivers more routes to choose, the average speed of probe cars will increase, which will reduce the travel time. Because, relatively speaking, the traffic density inside the community is much lower. Although the maximum average traffic density is larger. For individual vehicles, its average speed increases. Under such circumstance, a vehicle achieves optimal speed.

5 Conclusion

We established the optimized CA model of different traffic modules (intersections and roads), with extended cellular behavior, and made it more similar to the actual road. At the same time, we develop the traditional road simulation model and create agent-based traffic flow simulation. The combination of different modules can simulate different road network structures, thus making the road simulation more convenient.

This paper analyzes from the two aspects of overall and individual. On the whole structure of the road network, we use the average density of road network traffic to measure, which can reflect the impact of ORC on a surrounding road network. At the same time, we use probe cars to analyze individual speed. From the average speed and the average travel time of probe cars with a solid OD pair, we can know the ORC's impact on an individual vehicle.

From the simulation result, the opening residential community will decrease the efficiency of a surrounding traffic situation, which reflects the Braess paradox. Adding a new road to the road network will make it become more congested and inefficient. Such negative effect has a progressive effect: the more road it adds, the less efficient it will be. However, for an individual, if the added road gives vehicles more routes to choose from, an individual's average speed will increase, which helps to achieve an individual's optimal speed.

References

1. Braess, D.: Über ein Paradoxon aus der Verkehrsplanung. Unternehmensforschung **12**, 258–268 (1968)
2. Zhao, C., Fu, B., Wang, T.: Braess paradox and robustness of traffic networks under stochastic user equilibrium. Transp. Res. Part E **61**, 135–141 (2014)
3. Di, X., He, X., Guo, X., Liu, H.X.: Braess paradox under the boundedly rational user equilibria. Transp. Res. Part B **67**, 86–108 (2014)
4. Kinoshita, A., Takasu, A., Adachi, J.: Real-time traffic incident detection using probe-car data. In: 2014 IEEE International Conference on Big Data, pp. 43–45. IEEE Press (2014)
5. Liu, B.: Study on the evaluation method of probe car system. In: 2010 IEEE Intelligent Vehicles Symposium, pp. 555–559. IEEE Press, San Diego (2010)

6. Li, M., Zhang, Y., Wang, W.: Analysis of congestion points based on probe car data on the Tokyo Metropolitan expressway. In: Proceedings of the 12th International IEEE Conference on Intelligent Transportation Systems, pp. 232–236. IEEE Press, St. Louis (2009)

7. Nagel, K., Scheckenberg, M.: A cellular automaton model for freeway traffic. J. Phys. I France **2**, 2221–2229 (1992)

8. Benjaafar, S., Dooley, K., Setyawan, W.: Cellular Automata for Traffic Simulations. Phys. A **263**, 438–451 (1999)

9. Rickert, M., Nagel, K., Schreckenberg, M., Latour, A.: Two lane traffic simulations using cellular automata. Phys. A: Stat. Mech. Appl. **231**(4), 534–550 (1996). Elsevier

10. Von Neumann, J., Burks, A.W.: Theory of Self-reproducing Automata, pp. 64–87. University of Illinois Press, Urbana (1966)

11. Wolfram, S.: Statistical mechanics of cellular automata. Rev. Modern Phys. **55**(3), 601–644 (1983)

12. Song, X., Zhang, S., Qian, L.: Opinion dynamics in networked command and control organizations. Phys. A: Stat. Mech. Appl. **392**, 5206–5217 (2013)

13. Xu, Y., Song, X., Weng, Z., Tan, G.: An Entry Time-based Supply Framework (ETSF) for mesoscopic traffic simulations. Simul. Model. Pract. Theory **47**(6), 182–195 (2014)

14. Song, X., Xie, Z., Xu, Y., Tan, G.: Supporting real-world network-oriented mesoscopic traffic simulation on GPU. Simul. Model. Pract. Theory **74**(3), 46–63 (2017)

15. Song, X., Ma, L., Ma, Y., Yang, C., Ji, H.: Selfishness- and selflessness-based models of pedestrian room evacuation. Phys. A: Stat. Mech. Appl. **447**(4), 455–466 (2016)

16. Song, X., Shi, W., Ma, Y., Yang, C.: Impact of informal networks on opinion dynamics in hierarchically formal organization. Phys. A: Stat. Mech. Appl. **436**(10), 916–924 (2015)

17. Yulin, W., Song, X., Gong, G.: Real-time load balancing scheduling algorithm for periodic simulation models. Simul. Model. Pract. Theory **52**(1), 123–134 (2015)

Assessment of Turbulence Model Performance Adopted Near Wall Treatment for a Sharp 90° 3-D Turning Diffuser

Normayati Nordin[1(✉)], Zainal Ambri Abdul Karim[2], Safiah Othman[1],
Vijay R. Raghavan[3], Sharifah Adzila[1], Suzairin Md Seri[1],
Ishkrizat Md Taib[1], and Yahaya Ramli[1]

[1] Flow Analysis Simulation and Turbulence Research Group,
Center for Energy and Industrial Environment Studies,
Faculty of Mechanical and Manufacturing Engineering,
Universiti Tun Hussein Onn Malaysia, Parit Raja, Malaysia
mayati@uthm.edu.my
[2] Department of Mechanical Engineering, Universiti Teknologi PETRONAS,
Teronoh, Malaysia
[3] OYL R&D Centre Sdn Bhd, Sungai Buloh, Malaysia

Abstract. The primary aim of this paper is to assess the performance of k-ε turbulence models by means of adopting various near wall treatments to simulate the flow within a sharp 90° 3-D turning diffuser. The Computational Fluid Dynamics (CFD) results were validated quantitatively and qualitatively with the experimental results (using Particle Image Velocimetry (PIV)). The standard k-ε adopted curvature correction and enhanced wall treatment of $y^+ \approx 1.2$–1.7 appears as the best validated model, producing minimal deviation with comparable flow structures to the experimental cases.

Keywords: Diffuser · Turbulence modeling · Near wall treatment · CFD · PIV

1 Introduction

Flow through a 90° turning diffuser is complex, apparently due to the expansion and sharp inflexion introduced along the direction of flow. The inner wall is subjected to curvature-induced effects where under a strong adverse pressure gradient, the boundary layer on the inner wall is likely to separate, and the core flow tends to deflect toward the outer wall region [1–6]. Despite extensive literatures on diffusers are available, less attention has yet been given to three-dimensional (3-D) diffuser type [7–9]. A 3-D turning diffuser is used widely in flow industries on account of its design flexibility offering various ranges of outlet-inlet configuration [10, 11]. Nevertheless, the performance of 3-D turning diffuser has never been scientifically justified and is commonly estimated using the guideline specifically established by Fox and Kline [1] for 2-D turning diffuser, or even often without a sound theoretical basis merely based on rule of thumb.

Computational Fluid Dynamics (CFD) has been used to examine the performance of diffusers since many years [7–9, 12–17]. The k-ε turbulence model along with

© Springer Nature Singapore Pte Ltd. 2017
M.S. Mohamed Ali et al. (Eds.): AsiaSim 2017, Part I, CCIS 751, pp. 259–273, 2017.
DOI: 10.1007/978-981-10-6463-0_23

appropriate setting of grid and wall boundary conditions managed to predict the flow within various type of diffusers [7, 8, 12–17]. There are also improved versions of k-ε turbulence models available for instance the model adopted by Mohamed et al. [18] which took into account the extra strain rate produced by curvature. In addition, ANSYS code Fluent provides other two improved k-ε models namely renormalization group k-ε and realizable k-ε. Both models are likely to deliver exceptional performance for flows involving adverse pressure gradient, separation and recirculation [19].

Involving significant change of variables, the inner wall of turning diffuser should be cautiously examined. The standard wall function was successfully applied by Ibrahim et al. [17] to predict the performance of S-shaped diffuser. The first grid point off the wall, $30 < y^+ < 300$ managed to adequately capture boundary layer separation within the respective diffuser [17]. On the other hand, relatively dense mesh, $30 < y^+ < 60$ was prescribed for axisymmetric curve diffuser in order to reflect the rapid change or much sharper gradient of flow field [14]. The non-equilibrium wall functions were applied to improve the results for flows with higher pressure gradients, separation and reattachment [19]. The enhanced wall treatments of $y^+ = 0.8$ and 4.6 were respectively prescribed to cope with highly complex three-dimensional near-wall flow phenomena of diffusers, i.e. 3-D diffuser and combined bend-diffuser [8, 9].

In the present work, the performance of k-ε turbulence models namely standard k-ε (ske), renormalization group k-ε (rngke) and realizable k-ε (rke) by means of adopting standard wall functions, non-equilibrium wall functions and enhanced wall treatment to simulate the flow of a 90° 3-D turning diffuser is assessed. A 3-D turning diffuser of area ratio ($AR = 2.16$), outlet inlet configurations ($W_2/W_1 = 1.50$, $X_2/X_1 = 1.44$) and inner wall length ($L_{in}/W_1 = 3.99$) operated at inflow Reynolds numbers, $Re_{in} = 5.786 \times 10^4 - 1.775 \times 10^5$ is considered.

2 Experimental Work

The rig was assembled as shown in Fig. 1 to incorporate with a settling chamber, four unit square-mesh screens and a contraction cone of 1:6. No fittings were introduced throughout the test section and the applied hydrodynamic entrance length, $L_{h,\ turb} \approx 28D_h$. The actual outlet turning diffuser was extended 10 cm, as recommended by Chong et al. [4] to obtain accurate measurements of velocity and pressure. The rig was proven to provide steady, uniform and fully developed flow entering the diffuser [20, 21].

The flow was admitted continuously to the system and measurement was taken after 5 min, when the system reached a steady state. As shown in Fig. 2, a Pitot static probe connected differentially to a digital manometer of resolution 1.0 Pa was used to measure the central dynamic pressure (P_{dync}) that subsequently was employed to obtain the mean inlet air velocity (V_{in}) [22]:

$$V_{in} = 0.9 \left(2P_{dync}/\rho\right)^{1/2} \tag{1}$$

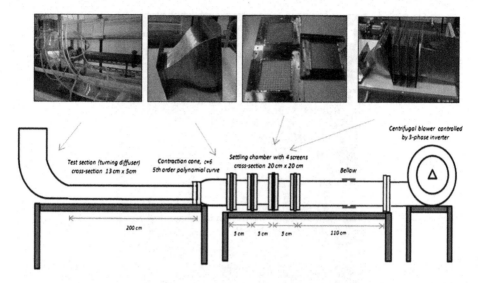

Fig. 1. Experimental test rig

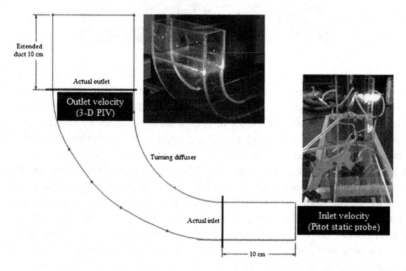

Fig. 2. Mean inlet (V_{in}) and local outlet (V_i) air velocity measurement planes

The local outlet air velocity (V_i) were obtained by means of a 3-D stereoscopic PIV. As shown in Fig. 3, two CCD cameras were mounted according to Scheimpflug rules at 30° angle on top of the target plane. The system was successfully calibrated via aligning the 200 mm × 200 mm standard calibration target board at five different positions and adopting image model fit (IMF)-Pinhole [23]. Seeding particles (Eurolite smoke fluid, 1 μm diameter) were injected into the system and measurements were made after 5 min to allow complete mixing between the air and the seeding particles. The laser light was illuminated the target plane at the thickness of 20 mm and the

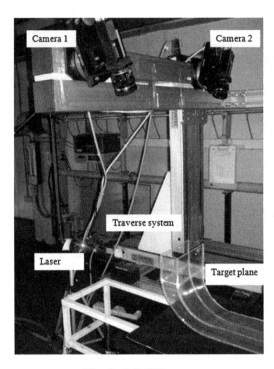

Fig. 3. 3-D PIV setup

intensity of 10. The cameras were run in double frame mode with time between pulses, $\Delta t = 30 - 90$ μs. 100 images per camera were captured and divided into interrogation areas of 128×128 pixels. As shown in Fig. 4, the third velocity component, v (represented by colour-code contour plot) was determined by correlating the 2-D velocity vectors, u and w obtained by camera 1 and 2 via stereo PIV processing.

A 2-D PIV was applied to visualise the flow structure at centre-longitudinal section of the turning diffuser. The camera was arranged to be perpendicular to the target plane (illuminated by the laser of thickness 2 mm) within a satisfied-calibrated distance that the plane could be entirely captured. The system was calibrated via positioning the calibration board exactly at the target plane and adopting image model fit (IMF)-DLT. 100 images per camera were captured and divided into interrogation areas of 64×64 pixels. Images captured were masked in order to get the best covered flow structure within the turning diffuser as shown in Fig. 5.

As shown in Fig. 6, static pressure tappings of 2 mm diameter were located 5 cm before and after the actual inlet and outlet turning diffusers respectively, and connected to a digital manometer of resolution 1.0 Pa using a triple T-design tube piezometer to provide the average static pressures at the inlet (P_{in}) and outlet (P_{out}). The outlet pressure recovery coefficient, C_p was calculated as follows:

$$C_p = 2(P_{out} - P_{in})/\rho V_{in}^2 \tag{2}$$

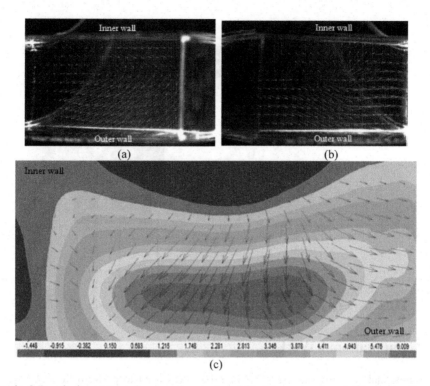

Fig. 4. 2-D velocity vectors, i.e. u and w captured by (a) camera 1 and (b) camera 2 were correlated using stereo PIV processing to obtain (c) the third velocity component v (represented by colour-code contour plot) (Color figure online)

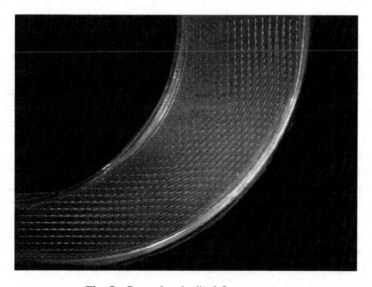

Fig. 5. Centre-longitudinal flow structure

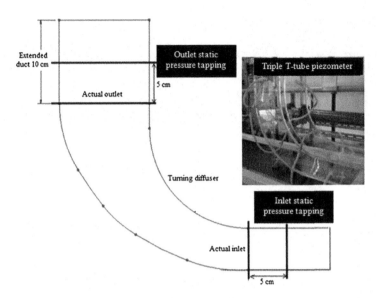

Fig. 6. Average inlet (P_{in}) and outlet (P_{out}) static pressure measurement planes

3   Computational Work

A commercial software package, ANSYS 14.5 was used to perform the CFD works including project and data management (Workbench), modelling (DesignModeler), grid generation (ICEM CFD) and flow analysis (Fluent). Several experimental tests by means of PIV were initially conducted to establish the actual data for the use of CFD validation.

3.1   Geometrical Domain and Boundary Conditions

As shown in Fig. 7(a), the inner-wall and centre curves were constructed using quarter circles of radii r_{in} = 12 cm and r_m = 15.6 cm respectively. The outer-wall curve was shaped using circular-arcs tangent to the sequence of circles, thus an even area propagation between the inner and outer wall passages could be established relative to the centre [4]. A three-dimensional flow domain in Fig. 7(b) was created by extruding the base object, i.e. solid line in Fig. 7(a) within angle of diffusion, θ = 15.154°. The actual outlet was extended by a length equal to the centre curve length, L_m to remedy the flow, after which the pressure could be considered as atmospheric pressure.

Three types of boundary conditions were imposed. The V_{in} was varied in the range 12.92 to 39.66 m/s corresponding to the Re_{in} = 5.786 × 10^4 − 1.775 × 10^5. This represented to a turbulent intensity, I_{in} of 3.5–4.1%. At the outlet boundary, the pressure was set at atmospheric pressure (0 gage pressure). At the solid wall, the velocity was zero due to the no-slip condition.

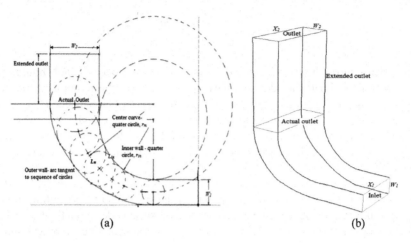

Fig. 7. (a) Construction lines, i.e. dashed line of a 90° 3-D turning diffuser (b) Isometric view of a 90° 3-D turning diffuser

3.2   Governing Equations and Turbulence Modeling

The following three-dimensional steady-state Reynolds Averaged Navier Stokes (RANS) equations were numerically solved for a Newtonian, incompressible fluid.

Continuity equation:

$$\frac{\partial u}{\partial x} + \frac{\partial v}{\partial y} + \frac{\partial w}{\partial z} = 0 \tag{3}$$

x - momentum equation:

$$u\frac{\partial u}{\partial x} + v\frac{\partial u}{\partial y} + w\frac{\partial u}{\partial z} = -\frac{1}{\rho}\frac{\partial P}{\partial x} + v\left[\frac{\partial^2 u}{\partial x^2} + \frac{\partial^2 u}{\partial y^2} + \frac{\partial^2 u}{\partial z^2}\right] + \frac{1}{\rho}\left[\frac{\partial(-\rho\overline{u'^2})}{\partial x} + \frac{\partial(-\rho\overline{u'v'})}{\partial y} + \frac{\partial(-\rho\overline{u'w'})}{\partial z}\right] \tag{4}$$

y - momentum equation:

$$u\frac{\partial v}{\partial x} + v\frac{\partial v}{\partial y} + w\frac{\partial v}{\partial z} = -\frac{1}{\rho}\frac{\partial P}{\partial y} + v\left[\frac{\partial^2 v}{\partial x^2} + \frac{\partial^2 v}{\partial y^2} + \frac{\partial^2 v}{\partial z^2}\right] + \frac{1}{\rho}\left[\frac{\partial(-\rho\overline{u'v'})}{\partial x} + \frac{\partial(-\rho\overline{v'^2})}{\partial y} + \frac{\partial(-\rho\overline{v'w'})}{\partial z}\right] \tag{5}$$

z - momentum equation:

$$u\frac{\partial w}{\partial x} + v\frac{\partial w}{\partial y} + w\frac{\partial w}{\partial z} = -\frac{1}{\rho}\frac{\partial P}{\partial z} + v\left[\frac{\partial^2 w}{\partial x^2} + \mu\frac{\partial^2 w}{\partial y^2} + \mu\frac{\partial^2 w}{\partial z^2}\right] + \frac{1}{\rho}\left[\frac{\partial(-\rho\overline{u'w'})}{\partial x} - \frac{\partial(-\rho\overline{v'w'})}{\partial y} - \frac{\partial(-\rho\overline{w'^2})}{\partial z}\right] \tag{6}$$

Boussinesq proposed that the Reynolds stresses ($\tau_{ij} = -\rho\overline{u_i'u_j'}$) are proportional to mean rates of deformation:

$$\tau_{ij} = -\rho \overline{u_i' u_j'} = \mu_t \left(\frac{\partial \overline{u_i}}{\partial x_j} + \frac{\partial \overline{u_j}}{\partial x_i} \right) - \frac{2}{3} \rho k \delta_{ij} \qquad (7)$$

In order to close the RANS equations, the turbulence model applied should enable to satisfactorily estimate the eddy viscosity, μ_t. The ske was the commonest turbulence model used by previous researchers to examine the diffuser performance [7, 8, 12–18]. With appropriate setting of grid and near-wall treatment, this model managed to sufficiently predict the flow within various types of diffusers. In the present work, the ske along with two improved versions of k-ε turbulence model namely, rngke and rke were considered.

All these models solved transport equations for turbulent kinetic energy, k and total energy dissipation rate, ε. Due to insensitivity of the ske model to streamline curvature and expecting further improvement of both the rngke and rke models, the curvature correction option available in ANSYS Fluent was enabled. The empirical function suggested by Spalart and Shur [24] to account for streamline curvature was defined as:

$$f_{curvature} = (1 + c_{r1}) \, 2r^* / (1 + r^*) \left[1 - c_{r3} \tan^{-1}(c_{r2} r) \right] - c_{r1} \qquad (8)$$

The function was limited in the range from 0 corresponding to a strong convex/concave curvature with stabilized flow and no turbulence production, up to 1.25 (strong convex and concave curvature with enhanced turbulence production).

3.3   Solver Details

Each governing equation was independently solved using a double precision pressure-based solver. A robust pressure-velocity coupling algorithm, SIMPLE which uses a combination of momentum and continuity equations to derive an equation for pressure (or pressure correction) was applied. To reduce numerical diffusion, the QUICK scheme was employed for the discretization of the momentum equations, the turbulent kinetic energy equation and the turbulent dissipation rate equation. A PRESTO discretization scheme was applied for the continuity equation and a default scheme, i.e. Green-Gauss Cell-based, was employed for the solution of the gradient. Under-relaxation factors were kept as default, except several cases where under - relaxation factors of 0.005 were prescribed mainly to stabilise the solutions to achieve convergence. The solutions were considered converged when the scaled residual of all simulated variables dropped to 10^{-6} and the conservation of overall mass balance through the domain boundary exceeded 99%. Typical compute times of about a day was consumed (PC used was Intel Core- i7 Processor 2.40 GHz, 8.00 GB of RAM).

3.4   Grid Independence Study

Involving significant change of variables, the near wall region of the turning diffuser was cautiously examined by means of adopting three types of near wall treatments namely standard wall functions, non-equilibrium wall functions and enhanced wall treatment. The first grid point off the wall, y^+ should be respectively placed for the wall functions and enhanced wall treatment within the range of $60 < y^+ < 300$ and $y^+ \approx 1.0$ [19]. The location of the first grid point off the wall was determined by:

$$y^+ = \frac{y\,u_\tau}{\nu} \tag{9}$$

The friction velocity, u_τ was given by:

$$u_\tau = \sqrt{\frac{\tau_w}{\rho}} = V\sqrt{\frac{C_f}{2}} \tag{10}$$

The skin friction coefficient for duct, C_f was empirically estimated:

$$\frac{C_f}{2} \approx 0.039 \mathrm{Re}^{-1/4} \tag{11}$$

As depicted in Table 1, the first grid points of $y^+ \approx 63$ and $y^+ \approx 1.2$–1.7 were respectively specified for the wall functions and enhanced wall treatment. High quality numerical results for the wall boundary layer shall only be obtained if sufficient resolution of mesh normal to the wall (10–20 cells within the inner layer) is all through provided [19]. In the present work, the number of cells around 10 was prescribed for the wall functions and 27 cells for the enhanced wall treatment.

Table 1. The first grid point off the wall, y^+

Re_{in}	Wall functions		Enhanced	
	y (m)	y^+	y (m)	y^+
5.786×10^4	1.51×10^{-3}	63	2.94×10^{-5}	1.2
6.382×10^4	1.43×10^{-3}	63	2.80×10^{-5}	1.2
1.027×10^5	9.40×10^{-4}	63	2.10×10^{-5}	1.4
1.397×10^5	7.18×10^{-4}	63	1.85×10^{-5}	1.6
1.775×10^5	5.82×10^{-4}	63	1.60×10^{-5}	1.7

The grid independence study was conducted at five different Re_{in}. The ske model adopted standard wall functions and enhanced wall treatment was applied for three kinds of grid, i.e. coarse, medium and fine. As shown in Fig. 8, in order to account the effect of three-dimensional turning expansion, the grid for the 3-D turning diffuser was sufficiently refined at the entire wall sides. The quality of the grid was inspected by keeping the grid to be evenly distributed throughout the domain and the equiangle skewness to be less than 0.3 for more than 95% of the control volumes. For highly skewed cells above the specified tolerance, they would be converted to polyhedra. As presented in Table 2, medium mesh provides relatively less percentage of error of C_p in each case. In fact, there is insignificant change in the velocity profiles obtained by medium mesh relative to fine mesh, as shown in Fig. 9. Therefore, the present work chooses medium mesh as a final meshing to be adopted in future intensive simulations.

Fig. 8. Hybrid grid, i.e. tetrahedral and wedge elements

Table 2. Grid independency check

Re_{in}	Mesh	Standard			Enhanced		
		Cells	C_p	Error (%)	Cells	C_p	Error (%)
5.786×10^4	Coarse	96465	0.560	0.5	276553	0.246	12.3
	Medium	106356	0.558	0.2	293402	0.216	1.4
	Fine	149004	0.557	–	344568	0.219	–
6.382×10^4	Coarse	96421	0.567	1.1	277332	0.250	18.5
	Medium	107173	0.565	0.7	294838	0.221	4.7
	Fine	203461	0.561	–	324801	0.211	–
1.027×10^5	Coarse	101058	0.586	0.9	280896	0.235	22.4
	Medium	120557	0.581	0.0	302809	0.205	6.8
	Fine	186031	0.581	–	331442	0.192	–
1.397×10^5	Coarse	104871	0.604	1.9	276568	0.260	23.8
	Medium	126719	0.598	0.8	299924	0.224	6.7
	Fine	195299	0.593	–	331861	0.210	–
1.775×10^5	Coarse	108347	0.618	1.8	272953	0.239	37.4
	Medium	131521	0.612	0.8	296726	0.192	7.9
	Fine	199830	0.607	–	323982	0.178	–

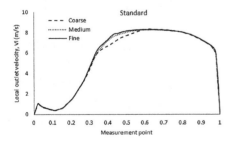
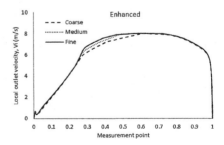

Fig. 9. Velocity profiles by refining the grid at $Re_{in} = 5.786 \times 10^4$

4 Results and Discussion

Validation of the CFD method was performed by quantitatively and qualitatively comparing the simulation results with the experimental results. Parameters considered for the validation purpose are local velocity on the centre-longitudinal axis of the actual outlet plane, V_i and C_p. In addition, outlet velocity profiles on the centre-longitudinal axis of the actual outlet plane and flow vectors throughout the centre-longitudinal plane are also examined. Figure 10 shows the planes considered for the validation purpose.

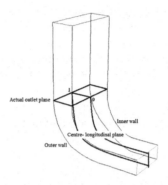

Fig. 10. Validation planes

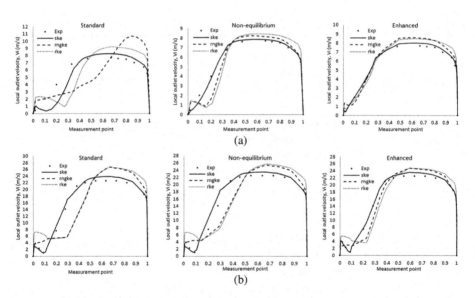

Fig. 11. Outlet velocity profiles of 3-D turning diffuser by applying various turbulence models and near wall treatments (a) $Re_{in} = 5.786 \times 10^4$ (b) $Re_{in} = 1.775 \times 10^5$

As shown in Fig. 11, overall there is a promising resemblance between the ske model and the actual velocity profiles while the other two models, rngke and rke overestimate the scale of flow disruption within the inner wall region (Point 0–1 on the *x*-axis referring to the inner - outer wall sides of the actual outlet). Enabling the curvature correction option absolutely helps to improve the sensitivity of the ske model to streamline curvature. Nevertheless, it overrates the performance both of the rngke and rke models due to the redundancy of including the effect of curvature which they already have in their own terms.

Applying enhanced wall treatment further improves the velocity profiles particularly in the vicinity of the inner wall. In the enhanced wall treatment, the near wall region was subdivided into viscous sublayer (*Re* < 200) and fully turbulent layer (*Re* > 200), where the turbulent viscosity of each region was defined differently. This so-called two-layer zonal model together with the blended-law of the wall that were applied in the enhanced wall treatment respectively to blend up the turbulent viscosities from the two regions and to incorporate the pressure gradient effect absolutely helps to improve the prediction of the near-wall flow. In brief, the ske model adopted enhanced wall treatment satisfies qualitatively the experimental data. However assessing the discrepancies quantitatively is more important.

The predictions of the inner wall region's flow are notably improved by applying the enhanced wall treatment in relative to the wall functions, with the optimal reduction of deviation from 139% to 0% taking place at the closest point to the inner wall. Table 3 presents the overall deviation of velocity distribution by applying ske model with various near wall treatments. Specifying a fine resolution mesh, $y^+ = 1.2$–1.7 really benefits the enhanced wall treatment to resolve any physical change of variables on the near wall region.

Table 3. Average deviation of velocity distribution (ske model + various near wall treatments)

Re_{in}	Near wall treatment	Average deviation of V_i (%)
5.786×10^4	Standard	25.7
	Non-equilibrium	3.2
	Enhanced	2.0
6.382×10^4	Standard	25.4
	Non-equilibrium	9.0
	Enhanced	2.2
1.027×10^5	Standard	11.6
	Non-equilibrium	8.1
	Enhanced	4.6
1.397×10^5	Standard	7.9
	Non-equilibrium	11.6
	Enhanced	4.0
1.775×10^5	Standard	16.7
	Non-equilibrium	2.1
	Enhanced	4.3

The most optimum turbulence model is finalised by quantitatively assessing another parameter, C_p when adopted enhanced wall treatment as depicted in Table 4. It is proven that the ske model provided applying enhanced wall treatment and curvature correction appears as the most optimum model, producing the least discrepancy range of 1.0–2.9%. Comparisons of flow structures between experiment and CFD (ske + enhanced wall treatment) are shown in Figs. 12 and 13. Similar flow structures obtained for both methods further prove the reliability of the CFD methodology applied in the current work.

Table 4. Deviation of c_p (various CFD models + enhanced wall treatment)

Re_{in}	Model	C_p	Deviation (%)
5.786×10^4	Exp	0.210	–
	ske	0.216	2.9
	rngke	0.150	28.6
	rke	0.151	28.1
6.382×10^4	Exp	0.217	–
	ske	0.221	1.8
	rngke	0.132	39.2
	rke	0.155	28.6
1.027×10^5	Exp	0.203	–
	ske	0.205	1.0
	rngke	0.168	17.2
	rke	0.149	26.6
1.397×10^5	Exp	0.219	–
	ske	0.224	2.3
	rngke	0.117	46.6
	rke	0.168	23.3
1.775×10^5	Exp	0.194	–
	ske	0.192	1.0
	rngke	0.158	18.6
	rke	0.147	24.2

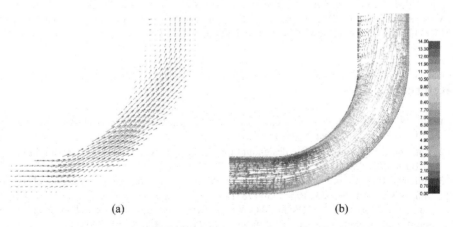

(a)   (b)

Fig. 12. Flow structure within the turning diffuser operated at $Re_{in} = 5.786 \times 10^4$ (a) PIV and (b) CFD (ske + enhanced wall treatment)

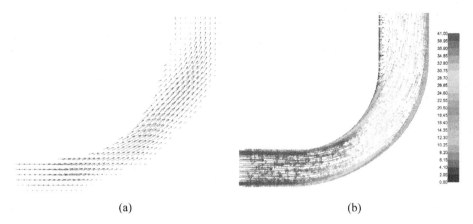

(a)   (b)

Fig. 13. Flow structure within the turning diffuser operated at $Re_{in} = 1.775 \times 10^5$ (a) PIV and (b) CFD (ske + enhanced wall treatment)

5   Conclusion

In conclusion, the ske adopted curvature correction and enhanced wall treatment of $y^+ \approx 1.2$–1.7 appears as the best validated model, producing minimal deviation with comparable flow characteristics to the actual cases. Therefore, this model is reliable to be used in future to intensively simulate the performance of a sharp 90° 3-D turning diffuser.

Acknowledgements. This work was financially supported by the Fundamental Research Grant Scheme (FRGS) of the Ministry of Higher Education, Malaysia and was conducted in Universiti Tun Hussein Onn Malaysia (UTHM). Immeasurable appreciation is extended to Head of Department of Energy and Thermofluid Engineering of UTHM, Dr. Azmahani Sadikin and Head of Center for Energy and Industrial Environment Studies, Dr. Mohd Faizal Mohideen Batcha for all provided research supports. A sense of gratitude is also devoted to Mr. Zainal Abidin Alias (Assistant Engineer of PIV Laboratory, UTHM) and Mr. Rosman Tukiman (Assistant Engineer of CFD Laboratory, UTHM) for the technical-lab assist.

References

1. Fox, R.W., Kline, S.J.: Flow regime data and design methods for curve subsonic diffusers. J. Basic Eng. ASME **84**, 303–312 (1962)
2. Sagi, C.J., Johnson, J.P.: The design and performance of two-dimensional curved diffusers. J. Basic Eng. ASME **89**, 715–731 (1967)
3. Sullerey, R.K., Chandra, B., Muralidhar, V.: Performance comparison of straight and curved diffusers. J. Def. Sci. **33**, 195–203 (1983)
4. Chong, T.P., Joseph, P.F., Davies, P.O.A.L.: A parametric study of passive flow control for a short, high area ratio 90° curved diffuser. J. Fluids Eng. **130**, 1–12 (2008)

5. Nordin, N., Karim, Z.A.A., Othman, S., Raghavan, V.R.: The performance of turning diffusers at various inlet conditions. Appl. Mech. Mater. **465–466**, 597–602 (2014)
6. Seth, N.H.N., Nordin, N., Othman, S., Raghavan, V.R.: Investigation of flow uniformity and pressure recovery in a turning diffuser by means of baffles. Appl. Mech. Mater. **465–466**, 526–530 (2014)
7. Gan, G., Riffat, S.B.: Measurement and computational fluid dynamics prediction of diffuser pressure-loss coefficient. Appl. Energy **54**(2), 181–195 (1996)
8. El-Askary, W.A., Nasr, M.: Performance of a bend diffuser system: experimental and numerical studies. Comput. Fluids **38**, 160–170 (2009)
9. Jakirlic, S., Kadavelil, G., Kornhaas, M., Schäfer, M., Sternel, D.C., Tropea, C.: Numerical and physical aspects in LES and hybrid LES/RANS of turbulent flow separation in a 3-D diffuser. Int. J. Heat Fluid Flow **31**, 820–832 (2010)
10. Nordin, N., Karim, Z.A.A., Othman, S., Raghavan, V.R.: Effect of varying inflow reynolds number on pressure recovery and flow uniformity of 3-D turning diffuser. Appl. Mech. Mater. **699**, 422–428 (2015)
11. Nordin, N., Raghavan, V.R., Othman, S., Karim, Z.A.A.: Compatibility of 3-D turning diffusers by means of varying area ratios and outlet-inlet configuration. ARPN J. Eng. Appl. Sci. **7**(6), 708–713 (2012)
12. Nordin, N., Raghavan, V.R., Othman, S., Karim, Z.A.A.: Numerical investigation of turning diffuser performance by varying geometric and operating parameters. Appl. Mech. Mater. **229–231**, 2086–2093 (2012)
13. Yang, Y.T., Hou, C.F.: Numerical calculation of turbulent flow in symmetric two-dimensional diffusers. Acta Mech. **137**, 43–54 (1999)
14. Xu, D., Leschziner, M.A., Khoo, B.C., Shu, C.: Numerical prediction of separation and reattachment of turbulent flow in axisymmetric diffuser. Comput. Fluids **26**, 417–423 (1997)
15. Gopaliya, M.K., Kumar, M., Kumar, S., Gopaliya, S.M.: Analysis of performance characteristics of S-shaped diffuser with offset. Aerosp. Sci. Tech. **11**, 130–135 (2007)
16. Gopaliya, M.K., Goel, P., Prashar, S., Dutt, A.: CFD analysis of performance characteristics of S-shaped diffusers with combined horizontal and vertical offsets. Comput. Fluids **40**, 280–290 (2011)
17. Ibrahim, I.H., Ng, E.Y.K., Wong, K., Gunasekaran, R.: Effects of centerline curvature and cross-sectional shape transitioning in the subsonic diffuser of the F-5 fighter jet. J. Mech. Sci. Technol. **22**, 1993–1997 (2008)
18. Mohamed, M.S., Djebedjian, B., Rayan, M.A.: Experimental and numerical studies of flow in a logarithmatic spiral curved diffuser. In: ASME Fluids Engineering Summer Conference, Boston (2000)
19. ANSYS FLUENT User's Guide, release 14.0, Canonsburg, USA (2011)
20. Nordin, N., Karim, Z.A.A., Othman, S., Raghavan, V.R.: Design and development of low subsonic wind tunnel for turning diffuser application. Adv. Mater. Res. **614-615**, 586–591 (2013)
21. Nordin, N., Karim, Z.A.A., Othman, S., Raghavan, V.R.: Verification of fully developed flow entering diffuser and particle image velocimetry procedures. Appl. Mech. Mater. **465-466**, 1352–1356 (2014)
22. Kim, J., Moin, P., Moser, R.: Turbulence statistics in fully developed channel flow at low Reynolds number. J. Fluid Mech. **177**, 297–302 (1987)
23. Nordin, N., Karim, Z.A.A., Othman, S., Raghavan, V.R.: Verification of 3-D stereoscopic PIV operation and procedures. Int. J. Eng. Technol. **12**(4), 19–26 (2012)
24. Spalart, P.R., Shur, M.L.: On the sensitization of turbulence models to rotation and curvature. Aerosp. Sci. Tech. **1**(5), 297–302 (1997)

A Deep Reinforcement Learning Based Intelligent Decision Method for UCAV Air Combat

Pin Liu[✉] and Yaofei Ma

School of Automation Science and Electrical Engineering,
Beihang University, Beijing, China
{liu0pin, mayaofeibuaa}@163.com

Abstract. Based on deep reinforcement learning, an intelligent tactical decision method is proposed to solve the problem of Unmanned Combat Aerial Vehicle (UCAV) air combat decision-making. The increasing complexity of the air combat environment leads to a curse of dimensionality when using reinforcement learning to solve the air combat problem. In this paper, we employed the deep neural network as the function approximator, and combined it with Q-learning to achieve the accurate fitting of action-value function, which is a good way to reduce the curse of dimensionality brought by traditional reinforcement learning. In order to verify the validity of the algorithm, simulation of our deep Q-learning network (DQN) is carried out on the air combat platform. The simulation results show that the DQN algorithm has a good performance in both the reward and action-value utility. The proposed algorithm provides a new idea for the research of UCAV intelligent decision.

Keywords: UCAV · Intelligent decision · Deep reinforcement learning · Combat simulation

1 Introduction

For the purpose of ensuring pilots' zero casualty in the future air combat, Unmanned Aerial Vehicle (UAV) will be gradually transformed into the protagonist of directly implementing the air combat mission from battlefield's supporting role, and Unmanned Combat Aerial Vehicle (UCAV) may even become the main force of air combat replacing manned aircraft [1]. At present, the man-in-the-loop ground station control system cannot meet the needs of increasingly complex and changeable environment of modern air combat [2], so it is necessary to study an intelligent decision method for UCAV air combat, which can evaluate the air combat situation and generate the corresponding maneuver command to perform combat missions autonomously. Expert system, one of the traditional methods in intelligent air combat maneuvering decision, can only be used to solve the known problems, but still need people involved when encountering the unknown problems, which is not fully autonomous decision-making [3]. In addition, the influence diagram [4], differential game [5], genetic algorithm [6], artificial neural network [7], which are widely used in the study of air combat

© Springer Nature Singapore Pte Ltd. 2017
M.S. Mohamed Ali et al. (Eds.): AsiaSim 2017, Part I, CCIS 751, pp. 274–286, 2017.
DOI: 10.1007/978-981-10-6463-0_24

maneuvering decision, are mostly applied to fighter's assistant decision or the UAV decision of ground station control mode. It remains to be verified whether these methods meet the requirements of UCAV online decision-making.

Recently, the successful application of machine learning techniques in many fields, such as games [8, 9], intelligent driving [10, 11], robots [12, 13], etc., has provided a new idea for the research of intelligent air combat decision-making. It is a powerful way to apply reinforcement learning (RL) in air combat domain since it can interact with the environment through trial and error, and obtain the optimal strategy through iteration [14].

However, traditional RL approach is not suitable for solving the large-scale Markov decision processes (MDP) like air combat due to computational overload caused by the curse of dimensionality. The approximate learning method, combining approximate technology with reinforcement learning, can alleviate the problem by curse of dimensionality to a certain extent, in which the key operation is to approximate the value function or the state space through a function approximator, to avoid accurate solution [15, 16]. The performance of the approximate learning method is determined by the ability of function approximator, including linear fitting function [17], nonlinear fitting function [18], classifier [19], neural network [20], etc., but these methods may not accurate enough to identify the complex state space. In this paper, a multi-layer stacking deep neural network (DNN) is employed as the function approximator to represent the complex state space accurately, due to its robust and accurate capacity. A number of typical researches using the combination of deep learning and reinforcement learning in Atari game and AlphaGo [8, 9], provide a good thinking for applying this approach to air combat missions.

In addition, for the purpose of maximizing the cumulative reward, the tradeoff of exploration and exploitation is the content we need to study. On the one hand, it is necessary to choose the action of highest reward using the learned experiences, so that the system moves to a better state. On the other hand, what we need is to fully grasp the environmental information and avoid falling into local optimum. Only by fully exploring the environment and using what we have learned can we maximize the cumulative reward. Consequently, we improved the algorithm by combining the deep learning with reinforcement learning and verify the feasibility of the algorithm by the battle in the air combat simulation platform. It lays the foundation for the further realization of UCAV autonomous air combat capability.

In this paper, the 1 versus 1 UCAV air combat scene is modeled in Sect. 2, including aircraft dynamics equation, states, actions, features and rewards. In Sect. 3, the reinforcement learning method is briefly reviewed, and the deep Q-learning network is built using some measures, such as experience replay and $\varepsilon - greedy$ policy. In Sect. 4, the experiment results validate the effectiveness of the proposed algorithm.

2   UCAV Air Combat Model

UCAV air combat platform involves two opponent planes (the roles of red and blue; red is the side that applies the approach proposed in this paper). The aircraft dynamics equation is shown as follows.

$$\dot{\psi} = \frac{g}{v_{xy}}\tan(\varnothing)$$
$$\dot{x} = v \cdot \cos(\psi)$$
$$\dot{y} = v \cdot \sin(\psi) \qquad (1)$$
$$\dot{h} = v_z,$$

where v is the velocity of the aircraft, and $v = \sqrt{v_z^2 + v_{xy}^2}$, in which v_z is in the vertical direction and v_{xy} is in the horizontal direction. $\psi \in [-\pi, \pi]$ is the yaw angle at which the flight of the aircraft deviates from north (along the y axis). $\varnothing \in [-\pi, \pi]$ is the roll angle of clockwise direction, whose value is changed to add or subtract change rate following the left or right scrolling of the aircraft. g is the gravitational acceleration.

Firstly, we can get each state in the air combat model, described with 12-dimension vectors.

$$s = \{x_r, y_r, h_r, \varnothing_r, \psi_r, v_{zr}, x_b, y_b, h_b, \varnothing_b, \psi_b, v_{zb}\}, \qquad (2)$$

where subscript r and b represent red and blue respectively. And state moves from s to s' after executing action of red and blue (u_r, u_b) with Eq. (1).

$$s \underset{u_r, u_b}{\longrightarrow} s'. \qquad (3)$$

The actions taken in the simulation model consist of five single actions. The move list is shown as follows.

$$movelist = [turn_{left_{up}}, turn_{right_{up}}, turn_{left_{down}}, turn_{right_{down}}, maintain]. \qquad (4)$$

Secondly, the features were extracted by preprocessing the state data for the purpose of making the convergence of approximate function faster and closer to the real utility. The chosen features in this paper are related to pilot's experience of determining the air combat situation, shown in Table 1.

$$state \overset{\varnothing(s)}{\rightarrow} feature, \qquad (5)$$

where aspect angle (AA) is the angle between the connecting line from target to attacker and the tail direction in body longitudinal axis of the target plane. Antenna train angle (ATA) is the angle between the direction of nose in body longitudinal axis of attacking plane and its radar's line of sight (LOS). Relative range (R) is the relative distance [21]. Their geometric description is shown in Fig. 1.

Table 1. Feature vectors

Features	Description
AA^+	Symbol of AA
$\lvert AA \rvert$	Absolute value of AA
ATA^+	Symbol of ATA
$\lvert ATA \rvert$	Absolute value of ATA
R	The relative distance between the two planes
$\dot{A}A$	The changing ratio of AA
$A\dot{T}A$	The changing ratio of ATA
ϕ_r	Red roll angle
ϕ_b	Blue roll angle

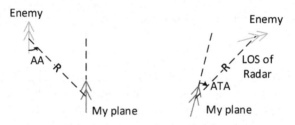

Fig. 1. The description of AA and ATA (Color figure online)

The reward function is also defined according to features.

$$R' = \left[\frac{\left(1 - \frac{\lvert AA \rvert}{\pi}\right) + \left(1 - \frac{\lvert ATA \rvert}{\pi}\right)}{2} \right] e^{-\left(\frac{\lvert R \rvert - R_d}{k\pi}\right)}, \tag{6}$$

where R_d is the best shooting distance of airborne weapon. The constant k is used to adjust the weight of the distance factor in the reward function (unit is m/rad).

3 Method

3.1 Reinforcement Learning

Reinforcement learning (RL) is one of machine learning methods that agent learns a mapping from environmental state to behavior by interacting with the environment, whose goal is to maximize the cumulative reward. The schematic diagram of the basic principle is shown in Fig. 2.

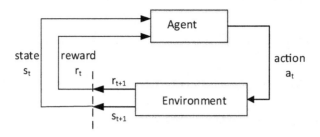

Fig. 2. Reinforcement learning framework

RL's mathematic model is Markov decision process (MDP), and air combat can be described with five-tuples $\{S, A, P, R, V\}$ in MDP. S is the set of states, $S = \{s\}$. A is all optional actions in aircraft flight, $A = \{a\}$. $P(s; a; s') \in [0, 1]$ is the state transition probability from s to s' by performing action a. $R(s)$ is the reward of the current state s. $V(s)$ is the utility function of the state s [22]. The goal of agent is to obtain optimal policy to maximize the total expected reward:

$$V(s) = max_\pi E\left[R(s_0, a_0) + \gamma R(s_1, a_1) + \gamma^2 R(s_2, a_2) + \cdots\right], \tag{7}$$

where $\gamma \in (0, 1)$ is the discount factor to make sure V converges eventually, which indicates that the latter state has a smaller impact on the total reward. The state-to-action mapping is defined as policy function $\pi : S \to A$. In order to evaluate the quality of policy, a value function $V(s)$ or state-action value function $Q(s, a)$ is defined as the expected discounted cumulative reward when performing policy π at the state s.

$$V(s) = E\left[R(s_0) + \gamma R(s_1) + \gamma^2 R(s_2) + \cdots | s_0 = s, \pi\right] \tag{8}$$

$$\begin{aligned} V^\pi(s_0) &= R(s_0) + \gamma\left(E\left[R(s_1) + \gamma R(s_2) + \gamma^2 R(s_3) + \cdots\right]\right) \\ &= R(s_0) + \gamma V^\pi(s') \end{aligned} \tag{9}$$

$$V^\pi(s) = R(s) + \gamma \sum_{s' \in S} P^a_{s,s'} V^\pi(s'). \tag{10}$$

There is an optimal policy π to get an optimal $V^*(s)$:

$$V^*(s) = max_\pi V^\pi(s). \tag{11}$$

The Bellman equation of the above formula is as follows.

$$V^*(s) = R(s) + max_{a \in A} \gamma \sum_{s' \in S} P^a_{s,s'} V^*(s'). \tag{12}$$

Then the optimal policy $\pi^* : S \to A$ is as follows.

$$\pi^*(s) = \arg\max_{a \in A} V^*(s) \tag{13}$$

The relationship between value function and RL is shown in Fig. 3. RL updates the value function by evaluating the policy, and uses the value function to determine the policy. The optimal value function and policy can be found step by step through this iteration.

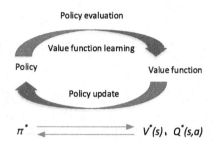

Fig. 3. The relationship between value function and RL

In this paper, we select Q-learning, one of off-policy RL algorithms, to interact with air combat environment, which replaces the value function $V(s)$ with the state-action value $Q(s,a)$ and update $Q(s,a)$ with $Q^*(s,a)$.

$$Q(s,a) = r + \gamma \sum_{s' \in S} P^a_{s,s'} \max_{a'} Q(s',a' \,|\, a' \in A) \tag{14}$$

$$Q^*(s,a) \leftarrow Q(s,a) + \alpha(r + \gamma \max_{a' \in A(s)} Q\left(s',a'\right) - Q(s,a)) \tag{15}$$

where α is the learning rate, and $\alpha = 1.0$ in this paper so that the iterative formula is shown as follows.

$$Q^*(s,a) \leftarrow r + \gamma \max_{a' \in A(s)} Q\left(s',a'\right) \tag{16}$$

3.2   Deep Q-Learning Network

In this paper, we built a deep Q-learning network (DQN) to approximate the action-value function, which combines deep neural network with Q-learning algorithm. The deep neural network (DNN) is a multi-layer structure and the connections between layers are realized by the weights of multiple neurons. In the supervised learning, DNN provide a complex and nonlinear hypothesis function $h_{w,b}(x)$ to fit the data by training the sample set $(x^{(i)}, y^{(i)})$. The parameters of model are recorded as (W, b), in which W represents the connecting weights between neurons and b is offset vector. In this paper, activate function $f : \mathbb{R} \to \mathbb{R}$ is described as Rectified Linear Unit (ReLU) because of its quick convergence velocity. And fully-connected layer is used to achieve the connection between the layers. And in the back propagation, we need define a loss function to evaluate the difference between the output value of the network and the real value, and optimize the objective function by parameter optimization, such as stochastic gradient descent, to update the weights of the network. Dropout is used as a measure to prevent overfitting. The parameters of function approximator are shown in Table 2.

Table 2. The parameters of function approximator

Name	Description
Input layer	A feature vector of 18 dimensions
1st-hidden layer	The neuron number of 90 dimensions
2nd-hidden layer	The neuron number of 36 dimensions
Output layer	The Q-value of 5 actions
Activate function	ReLU
Loss function	MSE
Optimization function	RMSProp
Dropout	The probability is 0.2

Some problems will be faced when combining deep learning with reinforcement learning, including the strong correlations between the samples, noisy and delayed reward signal and the changing data distribution with the new behavior. The method of experience replay is proposed to overcome these problems, in which a replay memory is established as $M_t = \{e_1, \cdots, e_t\}$ to store the agent's experiences $e_t = \{s_t, a_t, r_t, s_{t+1}\}$ at each-time step in each training epoch (where the end of an epoch occurs when a terminal state is reached). Then we obtain the experiences <s, a, r, s'> from the pool of stored samples using uniform random sampling and use them to do mini-batch update. During the experiment, we did not store all experiences due to memory limitations, but maintained an experience queue M of length N following the rules of first in first out, sampling samples from the queue when the update was performed. This approach improves the utilization of data and avoids falling into local minimum.

In addition, $\varepsilon - greedy$ policy is proposed to balance the exploration and exploitation by randomly selecting action. When selecting possible actions, agent will select a best action from the current model with a probability of $1 - \varepsilon$, and select a random action with probability ε. The value of ε will gradually decrease over time. Initial value of ε is 1.0.

$$\varepsilon = max\left(\varepsilon - \frac{1}{total\_steps}, 0.1\right) \tag{17}$$

$$action = \begin{cases} randint(0,5) & random() < \varepsilon \\ argmaxQ & others \end{cases} \tag{18}$$

where the value of ε will remain when reduced to 0.1. Action is selected from all possible actions to collect environmental information for follow-up learning at the beginning of ε close to 1. With the value of ε decreasing, agent performs its learned strategies when having more accurate prediction.

The process of DQN algorithm is shown below.

```
Deep Q-learning Algorithm
Initialize replay memory M to capacity N
For epoch=1,T do
   Initialize state s₁ = {x₁} and feature f₁ = Ø(s₁)
   While (status == 1)
      Initialize action-value function Q with random weights
      With ε − greedy policy to select an action aₜ
      Execute action aₜ in simulation and observe reward rₜ and
      next state s'and preprocessed feature sequence Ø(s')
      Sample random mini-batch of transitions from M
      Set yᵢ = { r              terminal state
               { r + γmaxQ(s',a')  non − terminal state
      Transform sampled data into training tuple of the model
      < xₖ,yₖ > xₖ = {Ø(s)}, yₖ = yᵢ
      Performs RMSProp on MSE to update the network weights
      with < xₖ,yₖ >
      Save model weights
   Break when step_to_stop <=0
End for
```

In this paper, we applied DQN approach to air combat scenario to evaluate our agent. The overall framework of air combat model is shown in Fig. 4. With the agent's action, the UCAV Air Combat Model can generate a series of continuous states

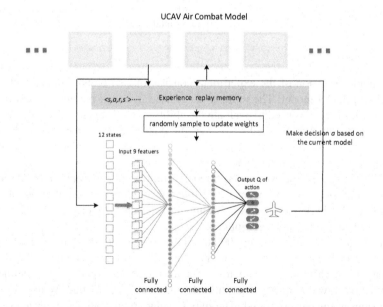

Fig. 4. The framework of air combat model

preprocessed as the inputs. The network is able to output the Q values of five actions, only receiving the 9-dimension features. Then observed variables (current state, action, reward, next state) are stored in the experience queue, from which the empirical samples are sampled. These samples are transformed into tuples of training network to update the weights according to the gradient information.

4 Experiment

To verify the validity of the algorithm, we take advantage of DQN agent fighting with an enemy using the Min-Max algorithm in the air combat platform. The Min-Max algorithm can make decisions by looking into future for steps [17]. Its depth is set as 3 steps in the simulation experiment taking into account the factors of computation time and decision-making effect. We use the belligerent results of two agents at the same simulation model, to demonstrate that our approach robustly learns more successful policies with the following minimal prior knowledge: features and all possible actions.

The experiments are arranged as follows. The initial states are selected randomly in Table 3.

Table 3. Initial states

State	Value
x_r, x_b	[−20, 20]
y_r, y_b	[−20, 20]
h_r, h_b	[−10, 10]
$\emptyset_r, \emptyset_b$	0, horizontal fly
ψ_r, ψ_b	[−π, π]
v_{zb}, v_{zr}	0, horizontal fly

The implementation of the experiment consists of two parts, training and testing, after building DQN model. The training set is used to adjust parameters and improve design, and testing set is used to evaluate the ability of DQN agent's decision. Winning or losing is determined by whether to enter the dominant area (that is $0.1 < R < 3$ and $|AA| < 1.105$ and $|ATA| < 0.523$). The value of *is_win* is set to 1 when red is dominant position and is set to −1 when blue is dominant position.

In the training section, we trained 5000 air combat epochs, each of which consists of one hundred steps, which means the Q-function is approximated after 500000 steps of sampling. All hyperparameters in training model are provided in Table 4, which consists of their values and descriptions.

In the testing section, we train 100 air combat epochs of 100 steps using the model of every 5000 sampling steps to observe the merits of the strategy. The decision performance is measured with 3 metrics: The average reward per epoch is defined that the cumulative rewards of all steps in each war round are divided by the number of fighting steps at the current round; The max Q-value, represents the expected discount

Table 4. List of hyperparameters and their values in training model

Hyperparameters	Value	Description
γ	0.9	Discount factor used in Q-learning update
ε	(0.1, 1.0)	The range of ε
Epochs	5000	The number of war rounds (where the end of an epoch occurs when a terminal state is reached)
Batch size	500	The bitch of random sampling from experience replay memory
Buffer size	50000	The length of replay memory
Observe	2000	The start size of replay
Total steps	5000 * 100	The number of all states

reward using the best action to the state S under the current model parameters; and the total number of winning, losing and drawing in each epoch are recorded.

In order to observe the stability of the algorithm, the average reward in the training process is represented through the broken line graph in Fig. 5. We use the weight parameters of model every 5000 steps to test 100 air combat epochs and get average reward of each model. It can be seen that the value of average reward is gradually increasing with the optimization of model parameters, though there is still noise due to random action selection of $\varepsilon - greedy$. This demonstrates that the level of agent's decision-making is generally improved as the training epoch increases.

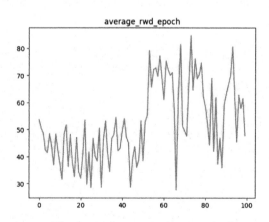

Fig. 5. Average reward per epoch

In order to evaluate the strategy more effectively, we observe the learning process through another metric, that is action-value function. Before testing, a fixed set of air combat states is collected to sample with 1 versus 1 air combat. Then we observe the decision making of sampling states with the weight parameters of model every 5000 steps, which can be represented by the max Q value. The changes of this variable is shown in Fig. 6. It can be seen that the max Q value is gradually increasing with the improvement of air combat results. At the same time, the max Q value is gradually converged to stability to demonstrate the feasibility of the learning model using deep neural network to fit Q function.

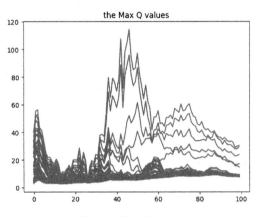

Fig. 6. Max Q value

The numbers of winning, losing and drawing are represented with red solid line, blue dotted line, and green point broken line in Fig. 7, respectively. It is clear that the numbers of winning and losing are almost the same at the beginning and the numbers of winning are gradually increasing with the optimization of model parameters.

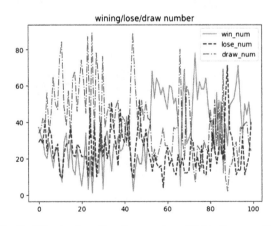

Fig. 7. Winning/lose/drawing numbers (Color figure online)

These results show that the approach combining deep neural network with reinforcement learning is effective and of high performance to resolve air combat problem. The plane using DQN approach has a better ability of air combat decision-making comparing with the plane using Min-Max approach.

5   Conclusion and Future Works

This paper studied the problem of UCAV air combat and employed an improved Q-learning approach to interact with environment of 1 versus 1 air combat. The deep neural network (fully connected layer) was used as the function approximator of DQN approach. The selections of features and reward function depend on the pilot's empirical indicators judging air combat situation in the real world. The DNQ approach involves the iteration of fitting functions and design of deep neural network. To break the strong correlation between samples and improve the stability of fitting function, we used experience replay, $\varepsilon - greedy$ policy, dropout, etc., to optimize the model structure and get a better convergence. According to the simulation results, the decision-making performance of DQN approach is quicker and more effective than Min-Max recursive approach.

In the future work, we plan to employ the features extracted by convolution neural network to replace artificial features for which the current features are too dependent on subjective experience. It is worthy looking forward to extract better features automatically by adding convolution neural network into the current network structure. And one of the follow-up works is to compare with other methods of decision-making.

References

1. Schmitt, M.N.: Unmanned combat aircraft systems (Armed Drones) and international humanitarian law: simplifying the oft benighted debate. J. Soc. Sci. Electron. Publish. **2**, 1006–1013 (2012)
2. Tsach, S., Peled, A., Penn, D., et al.: Development trends for next generation of UAV systems. In: AIAA Infotech@Aerospace 2007 Conference and Exhibit, Rohnert Park, California (2007)
3. Burgin, G., Sidor, L.B.: Rule-based air combat simulation. Technical report, TITAN-TLJ-H-1501, Titan Systems Inc., La Jolla, Calif, USA (1988)
4. Virtanen, K., Raivio, T., Hamalainen, R.P.: Modeling pilot's sequential maneuvering decisions by a multistage influence diagram. J. Guidance Control Dyn. **27**(4), 665–677 (2004)
5. Perelman, A., Shima, T., Rusnak, I.: Cooperative differential games strategies for active aircraft protection from a homing missile. In: AIAA Guidance, Navigation, and Control Conference, Toronto, Ontario, Canada (2010). J. Guidance Control Dyn. **34**(3), 761–773 (2010)
6. Nohejl, A.: Grammar-based genetic programming. Department of Software and Computer Science Education (2011)
7. Schvaneveldt, R.W., Goldsmith, T.E., Benson, A.E., et al.: Neural Network Models of Air Combat Maneuvering. New Mexico State University, New Mexico (1992)
8. Mnih, V., Kavukcuoglu, K., Silver, D., et al.: Human-level control through deep reinforcement learning. J. Nature **518**(7540), 529–533 (2015)
9. Silver, D., Huang, A., Maddison, C.J., et al.: Mastering the game of Go with deep neural networks and tree search. J. Nature **529**(7587), 484–489 (2016)
10. Liu, H.L., Taniguchi, T., Takano, T., et al.: Visualization of driving behavior using deep sparse autoencoder. In: IEEE Intelligent Vehicles Symposium, pp. 1427–1434 (2014)

11. Liu, H.L., Taniguchi, T., Tanaka, Y., et al.: Visualization of driving behavior based on hidden feature extraction by using deep learning. J IEEE Trans. Intell. Transp. Syst. **99**, 1–13 (2017)
12. Levine, S., Wagener, N., Abbeel, P.: Learning contact-rich manipulation skills with guided policy search. In: Proceedings of the IEEE International Conference on Robotics and Automation, pp. 156–163. IEEE, Seattle (2015)
13. Levine, S., Pastor, P., Krizhevsky, A., et al.: Learning hand-eye coordination for robotic grasping with deep learning and large-scale data collection. arXiv preprint arXiv:1603.02199 (2016)
14. Roessingh, J.J., Merk, R.J., Huibers, P., et al.: Smart Bandits in air-to-air combat training: combining different behavioural models in a common architecture. In: 21st Annual Conference on Behavior Representation in Modeling and Simulation, Amelia Island, Florida, USA (2012)
15. McGrew, J.S., How, J.P., Williams, B., et al.: Air-combat strategy using approximate dynamic programming. J. Guidance Control Dyn. **33**(5), 1641–1654 (2012)
16. Teng, T.H., Tan, A.H., Tan, A.H., et al.: Self-organizing neural networks for learning air combat maneuvers. In: The 2012 International Joint Conference on Neural Networks (IJCNN), pp. 1–8. IEEE (2012)
17. Ma, Y., Ma, X., Song, X.: A case study on air combat decision using approximated dynamic programming. Math. Probl. Eng. **2014** (2014)
18. Maei, H.R., Szepesvári, C., Bhatnagar, S., et al.: Convergent temporal-difference learning with arbitrary smooth function approximation. In: Advances in Neural Information Processing Systems, pp. 1204–1212. MIT Press, Vancouver (2009)
19. Duan, H., Shao, X., Hou, W., et al.: An incremental learning algorithm for Lagrangian support vector machines. J. Pattern Recogn. Lett. **30**(15), 1384–1391 (2009)
20. Lange, S., Riedmiller, M., Voigtländer, A.: Autonomous reinforcement learning on raw visual input data in a real world application. In: Proceedings of the International Joint Conference on Neural Networks, pp. 1–8. IEEE, Brisbane (2012)
21. Yang, D., Ma, Y.: An air combat decision-making method based on knowledge and grammar evolution. In: Zhang, L., Song, X., Wu, Y. (eds.) AsiaSim/SCS AutumnSim -2016. CCIS, vol. 644, pp. 508–518. Springer, Singapore (2016). doi:10.1007/978-981-10-2666-9_52
22. Ma, Y., Gong, G., Peng, X.: Cognition behavior model for air combat based on reinforcement learning. J. Beijing Univ. Aeronaut. Astronaut. **36**(4), 379–383 (2010)

Modeling and Simulation of Systems

Selection of Positive Position Feedback Controllers for Damping and Precision Positioning Applications

Rahul J. Moon[1]([✉]), Andres San-Millan[2], Majid Aleyaasin[1], Vicente Feliu[2], and Sumeet S. Aphale[1]

[1] School of Engineering, University of Aberdeen, Kings College Aberdeen, Aberdeen AB24 3FX, UK
{r01rjm15,m.aleyaasin,s.aphale}@abdn.ac.uk
[2] Escuela Tecnica Superior de Ingenieros Industriales, University of Castilla-La Mancha, Campus Universitario S/n, 13005 Ciudad Real, Spain
{andres.sanmillan,vicente.feliu}@uclm.es

Abstract. Positive Position Feedback (PPF) is a widely used control technique for damping the lightly damped resonant modes of various dynamic systems. Though PPF controller is easy to implement any rigorous mathematical optimization is not possible due to the controller structure. Therefore, almost all PPF designs reported in literature use a trial-and-error approach to push the closed-loop system poles adequately into the left-half plane to achieve adequate damping. In this paper, a full parametric study of the PPF controller based on the closed-loop DC gain vs achievable damping relationship is carried out. It is shown that the PPF controller best suited to only damp the resonance is not the best if both damping and tracking control is required (as is the case in most precision positioning systems). This leads to a more systematic and goal-oriented selection of appropriate PPF controller for specific applications, hitherto unreported in literature. Experiments performed on a piezoelectric-stack actuated nanopositioning platform are presented to support this conclusion.

Keywords: Positive Position Feedback · Damping · Tracking · Nanopositioning

1 Introduction

The PPF control design was first introduced in [1] for the vibration control of the space structures. In [2] it shows that PPF is capable of controlling several vibration modes. In [3] the Modal PPF (MPPF) controller is used to control the independent modal space of an undamped flexible structure. [4] demonstrated optimal control methods to design PPF controllers. Adaptive PPF (APPF) is suggested for the vibration control of frequency-varying structures (multi-modal

© Springer Nature Singapore Pte Ltd. 2017
M.S. Mohamed Ali et al. (Eds.): AsiaSim 2017, Part I, CCIS 751, pp. 289–301, 2017.
DOI: 10.1007/978-981-10-6463-0_25

control) in [5]. Further authors of [6] presented that PPF controller has global stability and which is verified with the help of negative imaginary theory. It has since been successfully implemented in nanopositioning stages to damp the dominant resonant mode of nanopositioner in conjunction with integral tracking controller with suitable gain [7–9]. It is known that the tracking controller changes the location of damped poles [8] and hence the characterized PPF controller for damping tracking application is essential.

PPF controller is popular and show adequate robustness under parameter uncertainties, its design is based on pole-placement via trial-and-error. As such, a systematic design strategy of the controller design against certain application-specific indices has remained elusive. Consequently, the selection of the closed-loop pole-location that delivers best damping performance has proved difficult. It is also noticed in several cases that increased damping comes at the cost of increased closed-loop DC sensitivity. In positioning applications such as nanopositioning, increased DC sensitivity is undesirable, but inherently unavoidable if positive-feedback damping controllers are incorporated [7].

In this work, the PPF controller is parametrically analyzed for closed-loop damping versus closed-loop DC gain. A method for selecting PPF controllers for best positioning performance is presented. It is shown that for a given open loop system, infinitely many PPF controllers can be designed. Yet, there is only one controller that delivers maximum closed-loop damping (ζ_{max}). For any other closed-loop damping value (ζ_{cl}), two controllers with different DC gains exist. Simulation and experimental analysis shows that choosing the PPF controller with a DC gain higher of the two possible controllers for the same closed-loop damping (ζ_{cl}), results in best overall positioning performance.

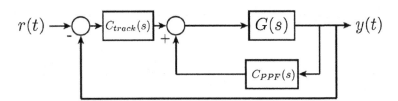

Fig. 1. Typical closed-loop combined damping and tracking control implementation. $r(t)$ is the reference input, $y(t)$ is the output.

1.1   Organization

The paper is organized as follows. In Sect. 2, background theory for second-order resonant systems is presented. In Sect. 3, the full parametric analysis of the PPF damping controller is presented along with the parametric relationships between the achievable closed-loop damping vs DC gain. In Sects. 4 and 5, an experimental setup, method of identification of the experimental platform is explained, further closed-loop combined damping and tracking experimental results for each of the controller implementations are presented and discussed. Section 6 concludes the paper.

2   Background Theory

Structural dynamics of flexible structures are very intricate to model with accuracy and high precision because of boundary conditions. Hence, there will always be uncertainty and unmodeled dynamics present in the models of flexible structures [6]. Such flexible structures are best described using a number of methods viz: partial differential equations, ordinary differential equations, Finite Element Method (FEM) or with hybrid models and hence they are infinite dimensional systems [10].

The best suited mathematical model for analyzing the vibration suppression problem in practical applications is the Finite Element Method (FEM) model which is of the form:

$$M\ddot{d} + C\dot{d} + Kd = Bu, \tag{1}$$

where d is the vector of generalized displacements, M is the symmetric positive definite mass matrix, C is the symmetric positive semi-definite damping matrix, K is the symmetric positive (semi-)definite matrix, u is the vector of control variables, B is the input matrix, which transforms control variables of the generalized actuator forces.

For the purpose of control design, however, one typically tends to include only a small finite number of modes in the modeling of such systems, which results in spillover unmodeled dynamics. Most techniques focus on damping the first resonant mode of the system as it tends to dominate the overall system dynamics at low frequencies and subsequently, controller designs are based on a plant model consisting of a second-order transfer-function modeling the first dominant resonant mode.

The single axis of a nanopositioning platform can be modeled as a mass-spring-damper system, having equation of motion:

$$M_p\ddot{d} + c_f\dot{d} + kd = F_a, \tag{2}$$

where M_p is the mass of the platform, c_f is the damping coefficient of the flexures, k is the sum of the spring stiffness of the flexures, k_f, and the actuator, k_a, and F_a is the force applied by the actuator.

Taking the Laplace transform of (2), and after rearrangement, the transfer function measured from the applied force, F_a, to the displacement, d, is

$$G_{dF_a}(s) = \frac{d(s)}{F_a(s)} = \frac{\gamma^2}{s^2 + 2\zeta_p\omega_p s + \omega_p^2}, \tag{3}$$

where ζ_p is the damping ratio for the first mode and ω_p is the resonant frequency.

The force generated by the actuator can be related to the unconstrained piezoelectric expansion, δ, by

$$F_a(s) = K_a(s)\delta, \tag{4}$$

and δ can be related to the reference input voltage, $r(s)$, by

$$\delta = g_{\delta_r} r(s) = d_{33} n g_a r(s), \tag{5}$$

where g_{δ_r} is a constant gain which is the product of the piezoelectric strain constant, d_{33}, the number of actuator layers, n, and the amplifier gain, g_a. Likewise, the displacement, d, can be related to the measured voltage, $y(s)$, by

$$d = g_s y(s). \tag{6}$$

where g_s is the sensor gain. The transfer function from the reference input, r, to the measured voltage, y, is then

$$G(s) = \frac{y(s)}{r(s)} = \frac{\frac{k_a g_{\delta_r}}{g_s}}{M_p s^2 + c_f s + k} = \frac{\frac{k_a g_{\delta_r}}{g_s M_p}}{s^2 + \frac{c_f}{M_p} s + \frac{k}{M_p}}. \tag{7}$$

substituting standard variables, becomes

$$G(s) = \frac{\gamma^2}{s^2 + 2\zeta_p \omega_p s + \omega_p^2}. \tag{8}$$

3   Positive Position Feedback Control Design

An important property of PPF controllers is that to suppress one dominant resonant mode it requires only one second-order term. PPF controllers are implemented in positive feedback as shown in Fig. 1 and their generic structure is given by:

$$C_{PPF}(s) = \frac{\kappa}{s^2 + 2\zeta\omega s + \omega^2} \tag{9}$$

where ζ and ω are the damping ratio and natural frequency of the controller and κ is a positive scalar gain. The underlying principle of the PPF control design is to push the closed-loop system poles further in to LHP (Left Hand Plane), thereby imparting additional damping.

3.1   Strategy and Design

Using the plant model given by (8) and the controller transfer-function given by (9), the overall transfer-function of the closed-loop damped system can be computed as follows:

$$G^{cl}_{damp}(s) = \frac{G(s)}{1 - G(s)C_{PPF}(s)} \tag{10}$$

The characteristic polynomial of the closed-loop damped system is given by:

$$P(s) = s^4 + [2\zeta_p\omega_p + 2\zeta\omega]s^3 \tag{11}$$
$$+ [\omega_p^2 + 2\zeta_p\omega_p(2\zeta\omega) + \omega^2]s^2$$
$$+ [2\zeta_p\omega_p\omega^2 + \omega_p^2 2\zeta\omega]s$$
$$+ \omega_p^2\omega^2 - \gamma^2\kappa = 0$$

Further (11) can be written as:

$$P(s) = s^4 + K_1's^3 + K_2's^2 + K_3's + K_4' = 0 \tag{12}$$

where the resulting coefficients K_i' are:

$$K_1' = 2\zeta_p\omega_p + 2\zeta\omega \tag{13}$$
$$K_2' = \omega_p^2 + 2\zeta_p\omega_p 2\zeta\omega + \omega^2$$
$$K_3' = 2\zeta_p\omega_p\omega^2 + 2\zeta\omega\omega_p^2$$
$$K_4' = \omega^2\omega_p^2 - \gamma^2\kappa$$

In the following subsection, the ideal pole-placement technique is briefly revisited. Then, using the closed-loop damping and the closed-loop DC gain as the desired performance metrics, controller parameters K_i' are computed in an iterative fashion to identify best suited PPF controller designs for (i) Damping only and (ii) Precision Positioning (combined damping and tracking) applications.

3.2   Ideal Pole-Placement

Let the ideal pole-placement for the 4th-order closed-loop damped system whose characteristic equation is given by be given by (11) be given by:

$$P_1, P_2 = \sigma_c \pm j\omega_c \qquad P_3, P_4 = \sigma_c \pm j\omega_c \tag{14}$$

Then, the desired characteristic polynomial, $P_d(s)$, that has as its roots, the poles as given in (14) is:

$$P_d(s) = s^4 - 4\sigma_c s^3 + (6\sigma_c^2 + 2\omega_c^2)s^2 - 4\sigma_c(\sigma_c^2 + \omega_c^2)s$$
$$+ (\sigma_c^2 + \omega_c^2)^2 = 0 \tag{15}$$

The abbreviated form of this desired characteristic polynomial is:

$$P_d(s) = s^4 + K_{d_1}' s^3 + K_{d_2}' s^2 + K_{d_3}' s + K_{d_4}' = 0 \tag{16}$$

where

$$K_{d_1}' = -4\sigma_c \tag{17}$$
$$K_{d_2}' = (6\sigma_c^2 + 2\omega_c^2)$$
$$K_{d_3}' = -4\sigma_c(\sigma_c^2 + \omega_c^2)$$
$$K_{d_4}' = (\sigma_c^2 + \omega_c^2)^2$$

In order to locate the closed-loop poles of the actual system (8) in the exact location as desired (14) the following equality must be satisfied:

$$P(s) \equiv P_d(s) \tag{18}$$

Combining (13) and (17) to satisfy (18) results in the following equalities:

$$
\begin{aligned}
K_1' &= -4\sigma_c \tag{19} \\
&= 2\zeta_p\omega_p + 2\zeta\omega \\
K_2' &= (6\sigma_c^2 + 2\omega_c^2) \\
&= \omega_p^2 + 2\zeta_p\omega_p 2\zeta\omega + \omega^2 \\
K_3' &= -4\sigma_c(\sigma_c^2 + \omega_c^2) \\
&= 2\zeta_p\omega_p\omega^2 + 2\zeta\omega\omega_p^2 \\
K_4' &= (\sigma_c^2 + \omega_c^2)^2 \\
&= \omega^2\omega_p^2 - \gamma^2\kappa
\end{aligned}
$$

By setting the controller parameters $\kappa = \Gamma_1$, $2\zeta\omega = \Gamma_2$ and $\omega^2 = \Gamma_3$, (19) can be restructured to result in (20). This set of equations will be utilized in identifying the best choice of parameters for the PPF controller design. In (19) there are more equations than unknowns and hence no exact solution exists in this.

$$
\begin{aligned}
\Gamma_2 &= (-2\zeta_p\omega_p + K_1') \\
2\zeta_p\omega_p\Gamma_2 + \Gamma_3 &= (K_2' - \omega_p^2) \\
\omega_p^2\Gamma_2 + 2\zeta_p\omega_p\Gamma_3 &= K_3' \\
-\gamma^2\Gamma_1 + \omega_p^2\Gamma_3 &= K_4'
\end{aligned} \tag{20}
$$

$$
\begin{bmatrix}
0 & 1 & 0 & 0 \\
0 & 2\zeta_p\omega_p & 1 & 0 \\
0 & \omega_p^2 & 2\zeta_p\omega_p & 0 \\
-\gamma^2 & 0 & \omega_p^2 & 0
\end{bmatrix}
\begin{bmatrix}
\Gamma_1 \\
\Gamma_2 \\
\Gamma_3 \\
\Gamma_4
\end{bmatrix}
=
\begin{bmatrix}
(K_1' - 2\zeta_p\omega_p) \\
(K_2' - \omega_p^2) \\
K_3' \\
K_4'
\end{bmatrix} \tag{21}
$$

3.3   Family of PPF Controllers for a Second-Order Resonant System

As the system of Eq. (21) is over-determined, ideal pole-placement cannot be achieved using the PPF control scheme. This is a well-known limitation of the technique. Therefore, controller parameters are identified via a least-squares approach by using the generalized inverse of the coefficient matrix. The details of this procedure are as follows: Let (21) be written as:

$$A\Gamma = K', \tag{22}$$

where $A = \begin{bmatrix} 0 & 1 & 0 & 0 \\ 0 & 2\zeta_p\omega_p & 1 & 0 \\ 0 & \omega_p^2 & 2\zeta_p\omega_p & 0 \\ -\gamma^2 & 0 & \omega_p^2 & 0 \end{bmatrix}$, $\Gamma = \begin{bmatrix} \Gamma_1 \\ \Gamma_2 \\ \Gamma_3 \\ \Gamma_4 \end{bmatrix}$ and $K' = \begin{bmatrix} (K_1' - 2\zeta_p\omega_p) \\ (K_2' - \omega_p^2) \\ K_3' \\ K_4' \end{bmatrix}$.

Then,

$$\Gamma = A^T(AA^T)^{-1}K' \tag{23}$$

Using the parameters computed in (23) will result in a new set of coefficients given by (24).

$$\begin{bmatrix} K_1'' \\ K_2'' \\ K_3'' \\ K_4'' \end{bmatrix} = A\Gamma + \begin{bmatrix} 2\zeta_p\omega_p \\ \omega_p^2 \\ 0 \\ 0 \end{bmatrix} \tag{24}$$

Therefore, the $P_d(s)$ as given in (12) will change to:

$$P_d'(s) = s^4 + K_1''s^3 + K_2''s^2 + K_3''s + K_4'' = 0 \tag{25}$$

There are two combination of roots possible: (i) The desired polynomial has two pairs of complex conjugate roots (ii) The desired polynomial has one pair of complex conjugate roots and one pair of negative real roots. If the poles of the closed-loop system are $P_1, P_2 = \sigma_c' \pm j\omega_c'$ and $P_3, P_4 = \sigma_c' \pm j\omega_c'$. The closed-loop damping can be approximated by:

$$\zeta_{cl} \cong \cos\left(\tan^{-1}\left(\frac{\omega_c'}{\sigma_c'}\right)\right) \tag{26}$$

A parametric search is carried out over a wide range of σ_c' and the closed-loop damping approximation given by (26) is monitored. Due to the over-determined nature of the system of equations, no control can be exerted over the closed-loop DC gain of the system. The trajectory followed by the PPF controllers in the closed-loop damping vs closed-loop DC gain space is plotted in Fig. 2.

Remarks: Once the second-order resonant system parameters are fixed, the plot of the closed-loop DC gain vs closed-loop damping (ζ_{cl}) achieved using PPF control demonstrates the following:

(i) Closed-loop DC gain is greater than the open-loop DC gain for any increase in damping.
(ii) There exists only one unique controller that achieves maximum closed-loop damping ζ_{max}.
(iii) For any other value of achievable closed-loop damping (ζ_{cl}), two distinct controllers exist. Each of the two controllers results in a different value for closed-loop DC gain.

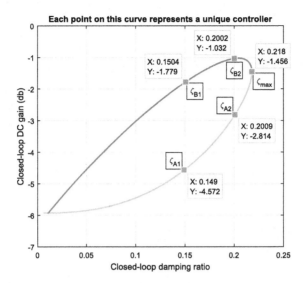

Fig. 2. Plot of the DC gain of the damped closed-loop vs the damping achieved using the PPF controller. Each point on the upward convex curve (green) and downward convex curve (red) represents a unique PPF controller. (Color figure online)

4   Experimental Setup and System Identification

In the following subsections, a brief description of the experimental setup is provided, followed by the details of the system identification carried out to model the dynamics of one axis of the piezoelectric-stack actuated nanopositioner within the bandwidth of interest.

4.1   Experimental Setup

Figure 3 shows the experimental setup used in this work. It consists of a two-axis piezoelectric-stack actuated serial kinematic nanopositioner designed at the EasyLab, University of Nevada, Reno, USA. It has an input range of ± 100 V resulting in a displacement range of $\pm 20\,\mu$m. Two low-noise, linear voltage amplifiers (PDL200) from Piezodrive, each with an output range of 0–200 V, a variable bias capability of 0–200 V and a fixed voltage gain of 20 are used to supply voltage inputs to the piezoelectric-stack actuators. The displacement is measured by a Microsense 4810 capacitive displacement sensor and a 2805 measurement probe with a measurement range of $\pm 50\,\mu$m for a corresponding voltage output of ± 10 V. A PCI-6621 data acquisition card from National Instruments installed on a PC running the real-time module from LabVIEW is used to interface between the experimental platform and the control design.

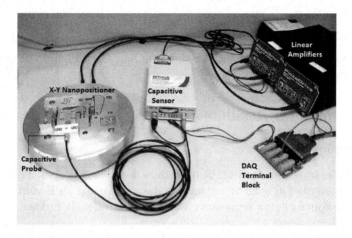

Fig. 3. A two-axis serial kinematic nanopositioner designed at the EasyLab, University of Nevada, Reno, USA.

4.2   Identification of the Experimental Platform

To identify the linear model of the plant, small signal frequency response functions (FRFs) were utilized. The FRFs are determined by applying a sinusoidal chirp signal (from 10 to 2000 Hz) with an amplitude of 0.2 V as input to the voltage amplifier of the x-axis and measuring the output signal in the same axis. Subsequently, the FRFs are computed by taking the Fourier transform of the recorded data. It should be noted that, using small amplitudes, the nonlinear effects of the Piezo Electric Actuators (PEAs) such as hysteresis can be considered negligible. In Fig. 4 the magnitude and phase responses (FRF) of G(s) are plotted for a sampling time of 50 μs. The x-axis of the platform is used to conduct the experiments presented in this work. However, the y-axis was set to 0 V as input to mimic a realistic platform operation. The platform axis shows a lightly-damped resonant mode at 716.2 Hz and open-loop damping coefficient of this resonant mode is $\zeta_{ol} = 0.011$. A second-order transfer-function that accurately captures the dominant resonant dynamics of this axis was procured using a least squares fit. The resulting transfer function is given by (27).

$$G(s) = \frac{1.024 \times 10^7}{s^2 + 99s + 2.035 \times 10^7}. \tag{27}$$

The experimental system has a significant delay. Hence, the theoretical model of the platform had to be modified in order to include the effects of the delay. The resulting system model is given by the following transfer function:

$$G(s) = \frac{1.024 \times 10^7 \times e^{-\tau s}}{s^2 + 99s + 2.035 \times 10^7}. \tag{28}$$

where the value of τ is determined by the following equation:

$$\tau = \frac{1}{2}T_s + 90 \times 10^{-6}. \tag{29}$$

where T_s is the sampling time. Both the sampling time T_s and the delay τ are expressed in seconds.

5   Experimental Results

5.1   Damping Only

PPF controller is designed using the procedure detailed in Sect. 3. The trajectory in Fig. 2 represents DC gain vs achievable damping using PPF controller. Each point on the convex curve represents a unique controller. It further shows that

(i) There is only one unique controller that achieves maximum damping ζ_{max} = 0.218 and DC gain = -1.456 dB.
(ii) For every other achievable closed-loop damping ratio, two distinct controllers with different DC gains are possible.

Minimal change in DC gain is usually desired in most damping applications. Thus for damping only application, It is advisable to choose the controller parameters resulting in low closed-loop DC gain (downward convex curve). Ideally, the PPF controller delivering the maximum closed-loop damping (ζ_{max}) would be chosen. However, if DC sensitivity or other implementations exist, for damping only applications the controllers represented by points on the downward convex (red curve) would be preferred over the upward convex (green curve) region for the same closed-loop damping ratio.

5.2   Precision Positioning (combined Damping and Tracking)

In precision positioning applications, it is popular practice to impart maximum damping to the resonant mode via a suitable damping controller first (in the inner loop) and then implement a suitably gained tracking controller (in the outer loop) to deliver precise positioning [7]. Tracking is usually effected by utilizing an integrator $(C_{track}(s) = \frac{K_t}{s})$ in feedback with the damped system [11].

To check if PPF controllers in downward convex region or upward convex region of the closed-loop DC gain vs closed loop damping curve result in better positioning performance, two ζ_{cl} values were arbitrarily selected viz: $\zeta_{cl} = 0.15$ and $\zeta_{cl} = 0.2$. For achieving closed-loop damping of $\zeta_{cl} = 0.15$, two distinct controllers at points denoted by ζ_{A1} and ζ_{B1} with different closed-loop DC gains can be designed. Similarly, for $\zeta_{cl} = 0.2$, there exist two distinct controllers denoted by ζ_{A2} and ζ_{B2} with different closed-loop DC gains respectively. For a full comparative analysis, the PPF controller that delivers the maximum closed-loop damping (ζ_{cl}) was also selected and the positioning performance of all five controllers was evaluated both via simulations and experiments. The overall block diagram for the combined damping and tracking scheme is shown in Fig. 1.

Both simulated and experimental results are in good agreement and show that for precision positioning performance (combined damping and tracking), controllers from the upward convex region deliver a superior positioning performance when compared with controllers from the downward convex region. The PPF controller transfer functions for the five selected cases, the respective closed-loop damping achieved and the corresponding closed-loop DC gains are given in Table 1.

Table 1. Damping performance of selected controllers

Controller	Transfer function	DC gain	Achievable damping
$C_{PPF_{\zeta A1}}$	$\dfrac{7.578 \times 10^6}{s^2 + 4.244 \times 10^3\,s + 2.629 \times 10^7}$	$-4.572\,\mathrm{dB}$	0.15
$C_{PPF_{\zeta A2}}$	$\dfrac{2.276 \times 10^7}{s^2 + 8.104 \times 10^3\,s + 3.867 \times 10^7}$	$-2.855\,\mathrm{dB}$	0.2
$C_{PPF_{\zeta max}}$	$\dfrac{4.999 \times 10^7}{s^2 + 1.446 \times 10^4\,s + 6.288 \times 10^7}$	$-1.456\,\mathrm{dB}$	0.218
$C_{PPF_{\zeta B1}}$	$\dfrac{1.329 \times 10^8}{s^2 + 4.751 \times 10^4\,s + 1.772 \times 10^8}$	$-1.779\,\mathrm{dB}$	0.15
$C_{PPF_{\zeta B2}}$	$\dfrac{8.995 \times 10^7}{s^2 + 2.59 \times 10^4\,s + 1.057 \times 10^8}$	$-1.038\,\mathrm{dB}$	0.2

The suitable tracking gain for each damped system is determined via the root-locus method. The respective tracking gains, maximum and RMS positioning errors for the five controllers are tabulated in Table 2. The closed-loop frequency responses are shown in Fig. 4.

The overall combined closed-loop damping and tracking transfer function is given by

$$G^{cl}(s) = \frac{C_{track}(s)G^{cl}_{damp}(s)}{1 + C_{track}(s)G^{cl}_{damp}(s)} \tag{30}$$

where $C_{track} = \frac{K_t}{s}$, K_t is tracking gain and $G^{cl}_{damp}(s)$ is given by (10).

Table 2. Closed-loop positioning performance (combined damping and tracking

	$G^{cl}_{\zeta A1}$	$G^{cl}_{\zeta A2}$	$G^{cl}_{\zeta max}$	$G^{cl}_{\zeta B1}$	$G^{cl}_{\zeta B2}$
Tracking Gain	1240	1590	1650	1435	1500
Maximum error (μm)	0.1407	0.3043	0.1314	0.1158	0.1133
RMS error (μm)	0.0398	0.1661	0.0834	0.0672	0.0373

A common input signal in nanopositioning is a triangle wave (used with a ramp or pseudo-ramp signal to generate a typical raster scanning pattern). For experimental validation, the nanopositioner axis was made to track a triangle wave at 50 Hz with an amplitude of 4 μm. The recorded time domain output trajectories as well as position errors are plotted in Fig. 5.

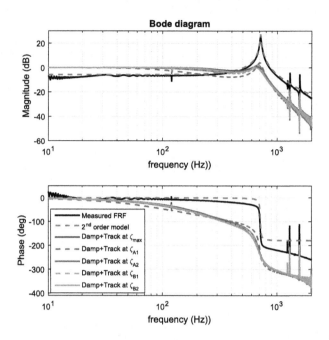

Fig. 4. Frequency responses for the combined damping and tracking closed-loop systems.

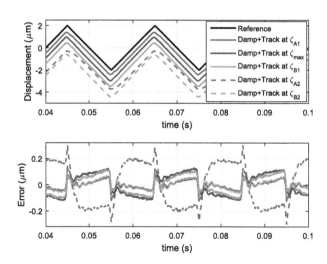

Fig. 5. Steady-state combined damping and tracking closed-loop time domain traces and respective position errors for a $4\,\mu\text{m}$ triangle wave at $50\,\text{Hz}$. Each trace is offset by $0.5\,\mu\text{m}$ for clarity.

6   Conclusion

In this paper, a systematic approach for selecting suitable PPF damping controllers for damping only as well as precise positioning applications is proposed and experimentally validated. Using the closed-loop DC gain vs closed-loop damping curve as a guideline, the following conclusions can be drawn.

(i) Only one unique PPF controller delivers maximum closed-loop damping $\zeta_{max} = 0.218$.

(ii) For all other $\zeta_{cl} < \zeta_{max}$, two possible PPF controllers can be designed. Both these controllers results in different DC gains.

(iii) For damping only applications, the best choice is the PPF controller results in lower DC gain (of the 2 possible controllers) for the same ζ_{cl}.

(iv) For precision positioning application (combined damping and tracking) the best choice is the PPF controller which results in higher DC gain (of the 2 possible controllers) for the same ζ_{cl}.

References

1. Goh, C.J., Caughey, T.K.: On the stability problem caused by finite actuator dynamics in the control of large space structures. Int. J. Control **41**(3), 787–802 (1985)
2. Fanson, J.L., Caughey, T.K.: Positive position feedback control for large space structures. AIAA J. **28**(4), 717–724 (1990)
3. Poh, S., Baz, A.: Active control of a flexible structure using a modal positive position feedback controller. J. Intell. Mater. Syst. Struct. **1**(3), 273–288 (1990)
4. Friswell, M.I., Inman, D.J.: The relationship between positive position feedback and output feedback controllers. Smart Mater. Struct. **8**(3), 285–291 (1999)
5. Rew, K.H., Han, J.H., Lee, I.: Multi-modal vibration control using adaptive positive position feedback. J. Intell. Mater. Syst. Struct. **13**(1), 13–22 (2002)
6. Petersen, I.R., Lanzon, A.: Feedback control of negative-imaginary systems. IEEE Trans. Control Syst. **30**(5), 54–72 (2010)
7. Aphale, S.S., Bhikkaji, B., Moheimani, S.O.R.: Minimizing scanning errors in piezoelectric stack-actuated nanopositioning platforms. IEEE Trans. Nanotechnol. **7**(1), 79–90 (2008)
8. Russell, D., San-Millan, A., Feliu, V., Aphale, S.S.: Butterworth pattern-based simultaneous damping and tracking controller designs for nanopositioning system. In: European Control Conference (ECC), Linz, vol. 2, No. 2, pp. 1088–1093 (2015)
9. Ratnam, M., Bhikkaji, B., Fleming, A.J., Moheimani, S.O.R.: PPF control of a piezoelectric tube scanner. In: Proceedings 44th IEEE Conference on Decision and Control, pp. 1168–1173 (2005)
10. Junkins, J.L., Kim, Y.: Introduction to Dynamics and Control of Flexible Structures. American Institute of Aeronautics and Astronautics, Reston (2000)
11. Namavar, M., Fleming, A.J., Aleyaasin, M., Nakkeeran, K., Aphale, S.S.: An analytical approach to integral resonant control of second-order systems. IEEE/ASME Trans. Mechatron. **19**(2), 651–659 (2014)

Artificial Neural Network for Anomalies Detection in Distillation Column

Syed A. Taqvi$^{(\boxtimes)}$, Lemma Dendena Tufa, Haslinda Zabiri,
Shuhaimi Mahadzir, Abdulhalim Shah Maulud, and Fahim Uddin

Chemical Engineering Department, Universiti Teknologi PETRONAS,
32610 Seri Iskandar, Perak, Malaysia
`aliammar884@gmail.com`

Abstract. Early detection of anomalies can assist to avoid major losses in term of product degradation, machines' damages as well as human health issues. This research aims to use Artificial Neural Network to recognize anomalies in the distillation column. The pilot scale distillation column for the ethanol-water system is selected for the study. Faults are generated by variation in feed rate, feed composition and reboiler duty using Aspen Plus® dynamic simulation. The effect of these faults on process variables i.e. changes in distillate and bottom composition, distillate and bottom temperature, bottom flow rate, and the pressure drop is observed. The network is trained using back propagation algorithm to determine root mean square error (RMSE). Based on RMSE minimization, the (6-8-6) net serves as the best choice for the case studied for efficient fault detection. The presented techniques are general in nature and easily applicable to various other industrial problems.

Keywords: Artificial neural network · Aspen Plus® dynamics · Back propagation algorithm · Distillation column · Fault detection

1 Introduction

Chemical plant designs and their control systems have been getting more complicated with the passage of time to attain the desired product quality, high productivity and maintaining environmental regulations [1–4]. The intricacy of process plants implies the necessity to assist the plant operators. This creates an interest in the development of fault detection strategies. Advantages of fault detection include the minimization of operator's efforts, improved effectiveness, safe operations, and continuous production. It is important to note that human errors cause approximately 70% of industrial accidents [5]. Early detection and isolation of these anomalies can be a worthy and promising area of research [6, 7].

Poor performance in the distillation column can lead to severe accidents and production loss. It can be caused by the malfunctioning of any sensor, valves sticking or blockage, and leaks in vent valves and connecting pipes, which can be over-sighted in the design stage [8].

Some other process faults such as the reflux failure affect both the column temperatures and purity. Similarly, the disturbance in steam flow rate in reboiler can

© Springer Nature Singapore Pte Ltd. 2017
M.S. Mohamed Ali et al. (Eds.): AsiaSim 2017, Part I, CCIS 751, pp. 302–311, 2017.
DOI: 10.1007/978-981-10-6463-0_26

deteriorate both top and bottom compositions and disrupt column pressure. The disturbance in feed rate on the column can change the column pressure profile and alter the top and bottom product purity [9, 10].

The principle objective of the control system is to sustain adequate operation by minimizing the disturbance level and transformation occurring in the process. The automatic control eased the operator's task from regulatory control task by developing an activity often known as the Abnormal Condition Management (ACM) or Abnormal Situation Management (ASM) or Abnormal Event Management (AEM).

Fault detection is generally designated to identify the occurrence of fault and its diagnosis is mainly performed for the identification of the cause and fault position. Methods for the fault diagnosis use causal fault-symptom-relationship using techniques from artificial intelligence, statistical decision, and soft computing [11]. However, the effective regulation, using Fault Detection and Diagnosis (FDD) is a demanding area. Moreover, fault management remains a key field to avoid plant shut down by detecting a fault on time. Fault diagnosis and process monitoring can be carried out by either first principle driven or data-driven models or by producing a model that deviates from the normal situation [12, 13]. However, due to unavailability of nonlinear process and complexity in the process control, there is an urge for data-based methods [14, 15]. Thus, numerous computer-aided approaches have been formulated to meet the requirement in previous years.

Over the past two decades, neural network has been in practice as the popular tool for the modeling and pattern classification of process systems. Currently, artificial neural network (ANN) has set a broad application in the chemical engineering for the development of FDD methods to meet the demand from industry regarding product quality, safety, and efficiency [16–19]. This approach has a great learning ability, which can approximate the pattern efficiently and easier to implement [20]. There are two different approaches to use neural networks for fault detection and diagnosis i.e. pattern classifier and process model. These are shown in numerous papers as an application of neural network in anomalies detection; process model approach has been shown in Fig. 1.

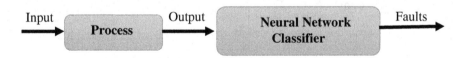

Fig. 1. Neural network for fault detection approach.

As distillation column shows nonlinear behavior, the neural network is the most promising model for its representation. Further, it is capable to capture the process dynamics and nonlinearity of input-output data modeling. Since Artificial Neural Networks (ANNs) are adaptive in nature, they can be conveniently employed for fault detection and classification techniques adequately [21–23]. The objectives of the current study are as follows:

- To generate normal and abnormal data using Aspen Plus® dynamic simulation.
- The training of neural network using generated data.
- To detect the anomalies/faults on the observed data.

2   Process Description

2.1   Aspen Plus® Simulation

The proposed fault detection scheme has been used for pilot plant distillation column in Universiti Teknologi PETRONAS. The feed contains a mixture (40% ethanol and 60% water). The system is brought to equilibrium under the total condenser to maintain the continuous operation. The feed with known temperature is pumped to the column. The above-mentioned process with specific input condition has been modeled using Aspen Plus®. The basic Aspen Plus® RADFRAC has been selected which consists of a condenser and a reboiler. RADFRAC columns allow being operated in rating or design mode. Non-Random Two Liquid (NRTL) thermodynamic property package has been used for the development of steady state simulation model [24, 25].

The schematic diagram of distillation column for application of ethanol-water mixture is shown in Fig. 2.

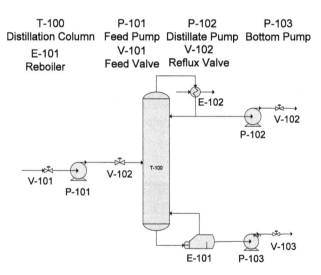

Fig. 2. Schematic of pilot scale distillation column.

The specifications of column and other feed conditions are described in Tables 1 and 2.

Table 1. Pilot scale distillation column specifications.

Specifications	Details
Column height	5.5 m
Colum diameter	150 mm
Number of trays	15
Type of tray	Bubble cap tray
Tray spacing	35 cm

Table 2. Feed condition for Aspen Plus® simulation.

Parameters	Values
Temperature	64.0 °C
Pressure	1.05 bar
Molar flow	3600 kmol/h
Reflux flow	2150 kmol/h
Reflux ratio	1.5

Further details of Aspen Plus® steady state simulation model can be found in our previous publications [6, 26].

The generation of dynamic data for network training is an essential step to generate ANN model. Training data must represent all the operating conditions along with possible fault occurrences. Aspen Dynamics® model has been used for the generation of data at normal and abnormal conditions. Flow, level, and composition controllers were installed in Aspen plus® dynamics simulation for the generation of steady state and faulty data.

3   Neural Network Model

The artificial neural network is a significant and dominant data modeling tool and can be used to represent a complex relationship of different chemical processes inputs and outputs [27, 28]. It has recently gained attraction due to its capacity to learn complex and nonlinear processes [3, 19, 22]. There are several existing models of neural networks, such as Multi-Layer Perceptron (MLP), Probabilistic Neural Networks (PNN), General Regression Neural Networks (GRNN) and Recurrent Network (RN). Among all the MLP types, the Back-Propagation Algorithm (BPA) has found most applications in chemical engineering. It is a supervised learning technique that can be used for the approximation of nonlinear maps. The back propagation uses the scheme in which the output is a feedback to input for the calculation of the alteration in weights by back propagation of errors. It uses the gradient search technique to minimize the RMSE by processing the data iteratively. The errors of each iteration at every point are calculated. Initiating from the last step by sending calculated error backward the generated output hence compared with the correct answer to compute error function. To reduce the error function to the minimum value, the BPA adjusts the weights of each connection. The fitness of network can be identified by the magnitude of RMSE.

3.1   Fault Selection

The input/output variable selection is very crucial for the ANN learning. It is imperative to choose input and output variables appropriately as the ANNs are trained based on input/output relationships. In the distillation column model, the input specifications signify its operating conditions. However, the output variables are normal conditions and the anomalies which can cause faults.

The process faults mentioned in Table 3 influence different output variables such as distillate composition (X_D), distillate temperature (T_D), bottom rate (B), bottom composition (X_B), bottom temperature (T_B), and the pressure drop (ΔP). The causes of faults in this work are considered due to the variation in reboiler duty, feed flow rate and reflux flow rate. Data generated from Aspen Plus® dynamic simulation is used for the fault detection in MATLAB® neural network.

Table 3. Distillation column fault category.

Symbol	Fault category
F_1	Decrement in feed rate
F_2	Increment in feed rate
F_3	Decrement in reflux flow rate
F_4	Increment in reflux flow rate
F_5	High steam flow rate
F_6	Low steam flow rate

3.2   Data Normalization

The generated data from Aspen Plus® dynamic simulation are normalized first. If the network is being trained with the raw data for training patterns, higher value inputs may lead to minimizing the effects of smaller values. It can also increase the chances that the simulated neurons may reach the saturated conditions, which results in very small changes or no change in the output values in case of changes in the input values. On the other hand, the rescaling or normalizing of an input vector can make the training faster and give equal value to all inputs. It can also trim the likelihood of getting stuck in local optima, leading to the optimal training of the system. The generated data are normalized between 0 and 1. The Aspen Plus® dynamic simulation data is normalized as follows;

$$\hat{a} = \frac{\bar{a}}{a_R} \tag{1}$$

Where,

$$\bar{a} = a - a_{min}$$
$$a_R = a_{max} - a_{min} \tag{2}$$

4   Results and Discussion

4.1   Neural Network Algorithm

The ANN has been modeled in the form of parallel distributed network model. These are based on the biological learning process as the human brain. ANNs comprises of several applications in pattern recognition, FDD, process control and data analysis. In this paper, the MLP has been used due to its fame as mentioned earlier. The proposed method for the fault diagnosis in the distillation column is established on back propagation in ANN for the detection of anomalies at given conditions, which results in various faults. The neural network toolbox in Simulink MATLAB® has been used for the data processing and it can be classified in two phases i.e., training and testing.

In training step, a relation has been established for chosen inputs and outputs by using the neural network. The training dataset is utilized to train the network by calculating the gradient and adjusting the weights until the networks converge to the minimum error. Subsequently, testing of the network is carried out with a test data. In the case of the network over-fitting on the data, the validation error increases until it crosses a particular value for which the number of validation process fails. This process stops here to avoid further over-fitting and the network is brought to the minimum number of the validation error. On completion of these two phases, the network becomes ready for the detection of faults at different operating conditions. The input and output to the neuron can be calculated by equations.

$$U_j = \sum_{i=1}^{N} w_{i,j} Y_j \qquad (3)$$

$$U_j = f(U_j + \theta_k) \qquad (4)$$

where w_{ij} connection is weight from i^{th} to j^{th} neuron, $f(U_j + \theta_k)$ represents the activation function, Y_j is the output of neuron j, θ_k and is the biases to the neuron.

4.2   Net-Training Scheme

The neural network is developed using six input nodes during the fault detection process. The network is trained on the data for input parameters caused by the malfunctioning or the fluctuation in feed flow rate, reflux flow and reboiler duty (based on steam flow rate). All values of different types of faults with normal and abnormal values have been considered during the development of data set. The data has been normalized before training. The 70% normalized data has been used for the training of network and 30% normalized data for the validation and testing of net. Six input nodes were selected for the training of neural network corresponding to the six indicators (X_D, T_D, X_B, T_B, B, ΔP), and six output nodes corresponding to the six potential faults (F_1, F_2, F_3, F_4, F_5, F_6). For training of network, the net examination has been limited to only one hidden layer since it is able to map all the data. The input/output measurements for a distillation column are shown in Fig. 3.

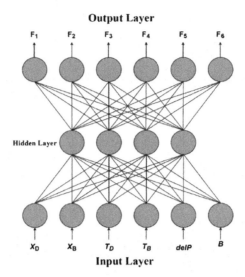

Fig. 3. Topology of back propagation feed forward neural network structure.

4.3 Performance Criteria

To analyze the performance and for the selection of appropriate net has been decided by results from RMSE.

$$RMSE = \sqrt{\frac{\sum_{i=1}^{N}(Y_{Sim} - Y_{ANN})^2}{N}} \tag{5}$$

where Y_{ANN} and Y_{sim} are the predicted values by ANN and by simulation from Aspen Plus® dynamics, respectively. Whereas N and i correspond to the total number of data-set and data-set number, respectively. The RMSE based performance criteria after 1000 iteration is shown in Fig. 4.

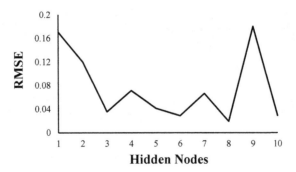

Fig. 4. Performance criteria based on RMSE.

4.4 Fault Detection

The net is first trained with the data with fault ranging from $\pm$ 2.5% to $\pm$ 10% using Levenberg–Marquardt algorithm as a training function. The desired outputs are discretized between 0 and 1 in the range of 0–20% faults. For instance a $\pm$ 2.5% deviation will result in $d_o = 0.125$. Similarly, for $\pm$ 5% and $\pm$ 7.5%, $d_o = 0.25$ and $d_o = 0.375$ respectively. Figure 5 shows the network prediction during the recall. Its ability to diagnose the fault severity is satisfactory except that of Fault No.1 (decrement in the feed flow rate) which can be caused by various reasons such as the nonlinear behavior of vapor-liquid equilibrium for ethanol-water system. It can also be examined that the network is capable of mapping the pattern efficiently. This net can also be utilized for the mapping of multiple faults simultaneously.

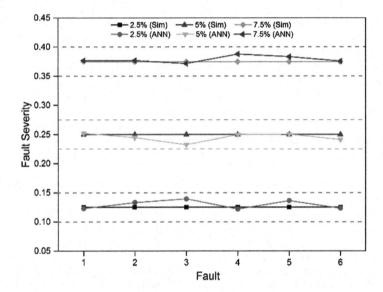

Fig. 5. Fault detection by neural network.

5 Conclusion

The main aim of this study is to develop an approach to the application of neural network for the detection of faults in the distillation column. The data required for ANN model development has been generated through real time dynamic simulation using Aspen Plus®. Six categories of disturbance i.e., feed flow rate, reflux flow rate and reboiler heat duty, were introduced in the simulation during data generation. Simulation results reveal that, for the detection of process fault, the neural network is a promising technique. The same model can be extended to further detect process faults, operational faults, actuator and sensor faults, and parameter faults in distillation column by considering appropriate parameters and faults. It can be observed that for the processes that are too sophisticated to model through first principle method, ANN is a promising tool for a staunch detection and precise diagnosing system.

Acknowledgment. The authors would like to acknowledge the support from Chemical Engineering Department, Universiti Teknologi PETRONAS.

References

1. Baratti, R., Vacca, G., Servida, A.: Neural network modeling of distillation columns. Hydrocarbon Process. **74**, (1995)
2. Behbahani, R.M., Jazayeri-Rad, H., Hajmirzaee, S.: Fault detection and diagnosis in a sour gas absorption column using neural networks. Chem. Eng. Technol. **32**, 840–845 (2009)
3. Rajakarunakaran, S., Venkumar, P., Devaraj, D., Rao, S.K.: Artificial neural network approach for fault detection in rotary system. Appl. Soft Comput. **8**, 740–748 (2008)
4. Tidriri, K., Chatti, N., Verron, S., Tiplica, T.: Bridging data-driven and model-based approaches for process fault diagnosis and health monitoring: A review of researches and future challenges. Annu. Rev. Control **42**, 63–81 (2016)
5. Chetouani, Y.: Change detection in a distillation column based on the generalized likelihood ratio approach. J. Chem. Eng. Process Technol. **2**(5), 1–7 (2011)
6. Taqvi, S.A., Tufa, L.D., Mahadzir, S.: Rigorous steady-state simulation of acetone production using Aspen HYSYS®. Aust. J. Basic Appl. Sci. **9**, 535–542 (2016)
7. Severson, K., Chaiwatanodom, P., Braatz, R.D.: Perspectives on process monitoring of industrial systems. Annu. Rev. Control **42**, 190–200 (2016)
8. Kesavan, P., Lee, J.H.: Diagnostic tools for multivariable model-based control systems. Industr. Eng. Chem. Res. **36**, 2725–2738 (1997)
9. Kister, H.Z.: Guidelines for designing distillation-column internals. Chem. Eng. **87**, 138–142 (1980)
10. Lieberman, N.: Troubleshooting Natural Gas Processing Wellhead to Transmission. Pennwell Books, Tulsa (1987)
11. Isermann, R.: Fault-diagnosis Systems An Introduction from Fault Detection to Fault Tolerance. Springer, Heidelberg (2006). doi:10.1007/3-540-30368-5
12. Qin, S.J.: Survey on data-driven industrial process monitoring and diagnosis. Annu. Rev. Control **36**, 220–234 (2012)
13. Uddin, F., Tufa, L.D., Taqvi, S.A., Vellen, N.: Development of regression models by closed–loop identification of distillation column-a case study. Indian J. Sci. Technol. **10**, 1–6 (2017)
14. Venkatasubramanian, V., Rengaswamy, R., Kavuri, S.N.: A review of process fault detection and diagnosis Part II: Qualitative models and search strategies. Comput. Chem. Eng. **27**, 313–326 (2003)
15. Venkatasubramanian, V., Rengaswamy, R., Yin, K.: A review of process fault detection and diagnosis: Part I: Quantitative model-based methods. Comput. Chem. Eng. **27**, 293–311 (2003)
16. Isermann, R., Ballé, P.: Trends in the application of model-based fault detection and diagnosis of technical processes. Control Eng. Pract. **5**, 709–719 (1997)
17. Korbicz, J., Koscielny, J.M., Kowalczuk, Z., Cholewa, W.: Fault Diagnosis: Models, Artificial Intelligence, Applications. Springer, Heidelberg (2012). doi:10.1007/978-3-642-18615-8
18. Chetouani, Y.: Detecting changes in a distillation column by using a sequential probability ratio test. Syst. Eng. Procedia **1**, 473–480 (2011)
19. Kialashaki, A., Reisel, J.R.: Development and validation of artificial neural network models of the energy demand in the industrial sector of the United States. Energy **76**, 749–760 (2014)

20. Uraikul, V., Chan, C.W., Tontiwachwuthikul, P.: Artificial intelligence for monitoring and supervisory control of process systems. Eng. Appl. Artif. Intell. **20**, 115–131 (2007)
21. Himmelblau, D.M.: Applications of artificial neural networks in chemical engineering. Korean J. Chem. Eng. **17**, 373–392 (2000)
22. Sharma, R., Singh, K., Singhal, D., Ghosh, R.: Neural network applications for detecting process faults in packed towers. Chem. Eng. Process. **43**, 841–847 (2004)
23. Samanta, B.: Gear fault detection using artificial neural networks and support vector machines with genetic algorithms. Mech. Syst. Sig Process. **18**, 625–644 (2004)
24. Lee, J.C., Yeo, Y.K., Song, K.H., Kim, I.W.: Operating strategies and optimum feed tray locations of the fractionation unit of BTX plants for energy conservation. Korean J. Chem. Eng. **18**, 428–431 (2001)
25. Luyben, W.L., Chien, I.L.: Design and control of distillation systems for separating azeotropes. Wiley, Hoboken (2011)
26. Taqvi, S.A., Tufa, L., Muhadizir, S.: Optimization and dynamics of distillation column using Aspen Plus®. Procedia Engineering **148**, 978–984 (2016)
27. Bishop, C.M.: Neural Networks for Pattern Recognition. Oxford University Press, Oxford (1995)
28. Haykin, S., Network, N.: A comprehensive foundation. Neural Netw. **2**, 41 (2004)

Modeling and Simulation of a Wireless Passive Thermopneumatic Micromixer

Marwan Nafea, Nasarudin Ahmad, Ahmad Ridhwan Wahap,
and Mohamed Sultan Mohamed Ali[(✉)]

Faculty of Electrical Engineering, Universiti Teknologi Malaysia,
81310 Skudai, Johor, Malaysia
nmmarwan3@live.utm.my,
{e-nasar,aridhwanwahap}@utm.my, sultan_ali@fke.utm.my

Abstract. This paper presents modeling and simulation of a wirelessly-controlled thermopneumatic zigzag micromixer. The micromixer is operated by selectively activating two passive wireless heaters with different resonant frequencies using an external magnetic field. Each heater is responsible for heating an air-heating chamber that is connected to a loading reservoir through a microdiffuser element, while the solutions pumped from each reservoir are mixed in a zigzag micromixing element that ends with an outlet hole. The performance of the micromixer is analyzed using finite element method, and mixing is investigated over a low range of Reynold's number $(Re) \leqslant 10$ that is suitable various biomedical applications. The optimal activation switching time of the heaters is 10 s, at which the micromixer achieves a maximum mixing efficiency of $\sim 96.1\%$, after ~ 65 s. The micromixer provides mixing-ratio controllability with a maximum flow rate and pressure drop of ~ 3.4 μL/min and ~ 385.22 Pa, respectively.

Keywords: Finite element method · Microfluidic · Micromixer · Thermopneumatic · Wireless actuation

1 Introduction

Micromixers play a core role in various biomedical applications, including point-of-care [1], lab-on-a-chip [2], and drug delivery systems [3]. These systems require precise transportation, mixing, and separation of miniature volumes of fluids within small (typically sub-millimeter)-scale geometries, which makes traditional methods of mixing fluids inapplicable. In addition, fluids flow is typically laminar in these systems, causing a low Reynold's number (Re) that consequently poses a challenge for sample mixing [4]. At low Re values, mixing is governed by molecular diffusion, which increases the length of the mixing channel and the time required to achieve a homogeneously mixed solution [5].

Micromixers are generally classified as active or passive, according to their mixing mechanisms [6]. Active micromixers require external forces to perform the mixing process, such as acoustics, pressure, temperature, electroosmosis, magnetohydrodynamics, electrohydrodynamics, and dielectrophoretics [5]. On the other hand, passive

© Springer Nature Singapore Pte Ltd. 2017
M.S. Mohamed Ali et al. (Eds.): AsiaSim 2017, Part I, CCIS 751, pp. 312–322, 2017.
DOI: 10.1007/978-981-10-6463-0_27

micromixers do not require external energy to mix the fluids. This makes passive micromixers more favorable in microfluidic systems due to their simple fabrication and implementation as compared to active micromixers [7]. Passive micromixers depend on molecular diffusion or chaotic advection principles, which are realized through the use of injection, droplet, parallel and serial lamination, and chaotic advection micromixers [7]. Chaotic advection micromixers are reported to perform efficiently over a wide range of Re values when compared to other types of passive micromixers [7]. Chaotic advection can be generated by modifying the shape of the microchannel in such a way that the laminar flow continuously splits, folds, stretches, and breaks over the cross-section of the microchannel. This can be realized using zigzag microchannels, intersecting microchannels, twisted microchannels, convergent–divergent microchannels, three-dimensional structures, staggered herringbone structures, Tesla structures, or by inserting grooves, obstacles, or embedded barriers in the microchannel walls [5].

Zigzag microchannel type has been widely investigated due to its high mixing index and ease of fabrication. Numerical and experimental studies of mixing in planar zigzag microchannels were performed by Mengeaud et al. [8]. The results indicated a transition in the mixing performance at a critical Re of ~ 10. Increasing Re led to form vortices at the corners of the microchannel, which therefore improved the mixing performance and reduced the diffusion length. In a recent work, a numerical study was performed on a micromixer that is composed of trapezoidal channels in a zigzag and split–recombine arrangement [9]. The optimal geometry had a mixing efficiency >85% for Re values in the range of 0.1–80, and reached up to 90% when Re ⩽ 0.9 and Re ⩾ 20.

Time-dependent pulsatile flows have been reported as a potential approach to achieve fast and efficient mixing. This approach was investigated by Glasgow et al. [10] using a low-frequency sinusoidal flow superimposed on a steady flow. The results indicated that the mixing performance with the pulsed sinusoidal flow was greatly improved as compared to the flow without pulsing.

However, these devices are limited to the use of on-board power supplies [1] or bulky magnetic cores [11], which limits the ability to implement these devices in portable or implantable systems. Passively actuated actuators can be utilized to address these issues while offering a smaller size, lower cost, higher robustness, and higher biocompatibility as compared to actively actuated actuators [12]. Wireless radiofrequency (RF) magnetic field actuation method has been utilized in several passively actuated microfluidic applications, such as multiple shape-memory-alloy actuators control of a microsyringe device [13], implantable drug delivery devices [14], and a thermopneumatic micropump for biomedical applications [15].

This paper presents an extended modeling and simulation study of a passive zigzag thermopneumatic micromixer that is wirelessly controlled using an external RF magnetic field [16]. Dynamic heat transfer, thermopneumatic actuation and mixing performance are analyzed using finite element method (FEM). The results suggest that the developed micromixer is able to provide mixing-ratio controllability and can be potentially implemented in biomedical applications.

2 Design and Working Principle

Figure 1 illustrates a schematic diagram of the developed the developed thermopneu-matic micromixer. The micromixer consists of two inductor–capacitor (LC) wireless heaters that have identical planar spiral inductors with dimensions of 5 mm × 6 mm, while the dimensions of each capacitor are 5 mm × 2 mm and 5 mm × 3 mm, respectively. Therefore, the heaters have different resonant frequency (f_r) values of ~100 and ~130 MHz, respectively. Each heater is located beneath two air-heating chambers that have similar dimensions to the spiral inductors. Each chamber is con-nected to a 5 mm-diameter loading reservoir through a 10° microdiffuser element to rectify the flow. The reservoirs are connected through a T-inlet with a width of 0.3 mm and a mixing length of 2 mm to a zigzag micromixing element that ends with a 1 mm outlet hole.

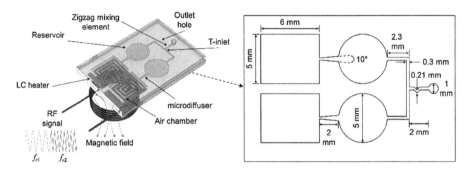

Fig. 1. Schematic diagram of the developed micromixer with an external coil (including a close-up view of the fluid-directing channel)

An AC current is generated in the LC circuit when it is exposed to an external AC magnetic field, due to the electromotive force induced by the magnetic field. Thus, the power, P, consumed in the LC circuit is given as [17]:

$$P(\omega) = \frac{Rv^2}{[R + j(\omega L - 1/\omega C)]^2} \tag{1}$$

where R is the parasitic resistance of the circuit, v is the electromotive force, ω is the angular frequency of the AC current, and L and C are the inductance and capacitance of the circuit, respectively. The maximum power transferred to the LC circuit when the field frequency is tuned to the resonant frequency of the circuit, $f_r = 1/2\pi\sqrt{LC}$. Therefore, the Joule heat generated in each LC circuit reaches its maximum value at the corresponding f_r of the LC circuit, and the steady state temperature, T_{SS}, can be expressed as [17]:

$$T_{SS} = \frac{R_T v^2/R}{1 + \alpha_R R_T v^2/R} \tag{2}$$

where R_T and α_R are the thermal resistance to the surroundings and the temperature coefficient of the resistance of the circuit, respectively. The generated heat is transferred by conduction from each LC circuit to the corresponding air-heating chamber through the polydimethylsiloxane (PDMS) layer. The rate of conductive heat transfer, q, is obtained using Fourier's law [18]:

$$q = kA\frac{\Delta T}{\Delta x} \tag{3}$$

where k is the thermal conductivity of the PDMS, A is the surface contact area between each LC heater and the corresponding air-heating chamber, and Δx and ΔT represent the thickness of the PDMS layer and the temperature difference across it, respectively.

As heat is transferred to the walls of the air-heating chamber, the temperature of the enclosed air rises, causing the volume of air to expand. This can be generally expressed by the ideal gas equation while assuming that the heating process is isobaric:

$$\Delta V = \frac{V_0}{T_0}\Delta T \tag{4}$$

where $\Delta V = V_1 - V_0$ is the amount of expanding volume, $\Delta T = T_1 - T_0$ is the elevation of the chamber temperature, V_0 is the volume of the gas at the room temperature, T_0 (23 °C in this work), and V_1 is the volume at the elevated temperature, T_1 [15]. Therefore, the expanded volume of air pushes the liquid from the loading reservoir to the T-inlet, causing them to mix at the zigzag mixing element.

The volume expansion of the air inside the air-heating chambers causes a deformation in their top walls. This is due to the fact that the high thickness of the side walls (Fig. 1), and that the bottom walls are attached to the LC heaters that are fabricated out of a polyimide film (~ 47 μm). This film is about three orders of magnitude stiffer than PDMS [19], making it rigid and greatly reducing the deformation of the bottom walls of the air-heating chambers. Thus, the deformation, s, of each top wall of the chambers can be approximated as:

$$s \approx \frac{3\Delta V}{A_W} \approx \frac{3V_0\Delta T}{A_W T_0} \tag{5}$$

where A_W is the area of the top wall of the chamber. The deformation is greatly reduced by increasing the thickness of the top walls of the chambers to 2 mm. Thus, the majority of the expanded volume of the air is applied on the inlet of the microdiffuser element, which significantly reduces the pumping loss.

3 Finite Element Analysis

Numerical simulation of a three-dimensional model of the developed micromixer was carried out using COMSOL Multiphysics®. Heat transfer, solid mechanics, laminar flow, and transport of diluted species physics were used in the simulation process. It was assumed that there was no thermal loss to the surroundings, and the initial air temperature was assumed to be 23 °C.

The temperature of the LC wireless heaters (heat source) was set according to their experimentally measured temperature [20]. FEM was implemented to solve the flow and mixing governing equations, which are the Navier-Stokes, continuity, and convection-diffusion equations, as follows:

$$\rho\left[\frac{\partial u}{\partial t} + (u.\nabla)u\right] = -\nabla p + \mu\nabla^2 u \tag{6}$$

$$\nabla u = 0 \tag{7}$$

$$\frac{\partial c}{\partial t} = D\nabla^2 c - u.\nabla c \tag{8}$$

where u is the fluid velocity, D is the diffusion coefficient, and c is the molar concentration. The fluid density, dynamic viscosity, and diffusion coefficient were set as 999.8 kg/m^3, 10^{-6} m^2/s (the kinematic viscosity of water at room temperature), and 10^{-10} m^2/s, respectively. The boundary conditions were set as follows: molar concentrations of 1 mol/m^{-3} at the inlet of reservoir 1 and 0 mol/m^{-3} at the inlet of reservoir 2, no-slip at solid walls, an equal volume flow rate at each microdiffuser inlet, and zero pressure at the outlet. The flow rate, Q, can be determined as a function of pressure using the Hagen–Poiseuille relationship:

$$Q = \frac{\Delta p A_C r^2}{8\mu L} \tag{9}$$

where A_C is the cross-sectional area of the channel, r is the diagonal length of the channel, and L is the length of the channel. The fluid dynamics in the microscale are characterized by a dimensionless parameter, Reynolds number (Re) that is defined as [8]:

$$Re = \frac{\rho u D_h}{\mu} \tag{10}$$

where D_h is the hydraulic diameter of the channel. The standard deviation, σ, of the molar concentration across the channel in a cross-section at any specific longitudinal location, and the mixing efficiency, η, at the outlet cross-section are calculated as follows [9]:

$$\sigma = \sqrt{\frac{1}{n}\sum_{i=1}^{n}(c_i - \bar{c})^2} \tag{11}$$

$$\eta = \left(1 - \sqrt{\frac{\sigma^2}{\sigma_{max}^2}}\right) \times 100 \tag{12}$$

where c_i is the molar concentration at a point i, $\bar{c}$ is the mean molar concentration of a fully mixed solution, n is the total number of sample points inside the cross-section, and σ_{max} is the maximum standard deviation at the inlet of the main channel. A mixing efficiency of 0% indicates completely separated streams ($\sigma = \sigma_{max}$), while a mixing efficiency of 100% indicates completely mixed streams ($\sigma = 0$) [20].

4 Results and Discussion

In this work, a time-dependent advanced multi-level multi-discretization GMRES solver was used to simulate the performance of the developed micromixer. Only heater 1 was activated with a power of 60 mW to demonstrate the heat transfer and thermal expansion behaviors. The heater was activated for 50 s until its temperature reached 50 °C (experimentally measured) [20] and then deactivated for 230 s until its temperature reached room temperature (23 °C). The temperature distribution profile of the simulated three-dimensional model of the micromixer after activating heater 1 for 50 s is illustrated in Fig. 2.

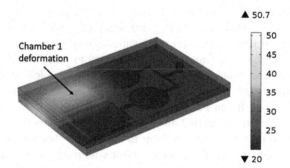

Fig. 2. A three-dimensional model of the micromixer showing the temperature distribution profile 50 s after activating heater 1.

The generated temperature in heater 1 is transferred by conduction to the bottom wall of air chamber 1, which therefore increases the temperature of the enclosed air. This behavior is demonstrated in Fig. 3, which shows that the temperature of the air chamber follows the change of temperature of the heater and reaches a maximum value of 42.5 °C after 50 s.

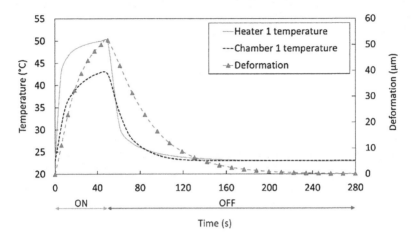

Fig. 3. The simulated temporal response of the temperature of heater 1 and the temperature and resultant deformation of air chamber 1 after 50 s from activating heater 1.

A deformation on the top surface of the air chamber occurred as the temperature of the enclosed air was increased, due to the expansion of the enclosed air. A maximum deformation of ~ 50 μm was generated after 50 s. Then it started to decrease after deactivating the heater until reaching its initial condition when the temperature of the air chamber returned to the room temperature.

To investigate the pumping and mixing performances of the micromixer, heaters 1 and 2 were operated using two different activation and deactivation patterns, as illustrated in Fig. 4(a). The resultant mixing efficiencies at the outlet when operating the micromixer for 140 s using these two activation patterns are presented in Fig. 4(b). It can be indicated that a maximum mixing efficiency of $\sim 96.1\%$ was achieved when using each activation pattern. However, activation pattern 1 generated a more stable mixing efficiency and a faster time (~ 65 s) required to reach the maximum mixing efficiency. On the other hand, activation pattern 2 showed a less stable mixing performance that fluctuated between $\sim 80.9\%$ and $\sim 96.1\%$ and required a higher response time (~ 70 s). It can be concluded that activation pattern generates a better performance than activation pattern 2 due to the fact that the latter one allows unwanted amounts of fluids to pass from one reservoir to the mixing channel without allowing a similar opposing amount from the other reservoir within a short period of time.

The mixing efficiency at the outlet and the pressure drop were examined over a range of $Re \leqslant 10$, as shown in Fig. 5. It can be indicated that the highest mixing efficiency was $\sim 96.15\%$ at $Re = 0.1$, while it was it its lowest value (81.14%) at $Re = 2$. Beyond that range, the mixing efficiency was improved up to 90.36% at $Re = 10$. This variance in the mixing performance is related to the transverse velocity components that are increasingly generated around the angle of the zigzag element at higher Re values. However, at low Re values, the transverse flow is negligible, which means that mixing is dominated by the molecular diffusion as a result of the low velocity and the high residence time. Further observations of Fig. 5 show that the pressure drop increased with Re, with a maximum pressure drop of ~ 385.22 Pa at $Re = 10$.

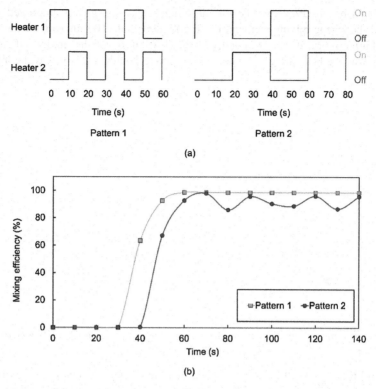

Fig. 4. Effect of activation patterns on the mixing efficiency. (a) Two activation patterns. (b) Numerical results of the mixing efficiency using the two activation patterns over 140 s.

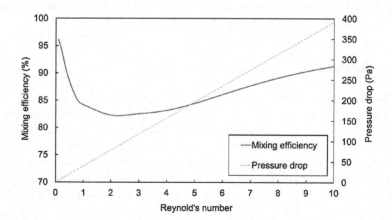

Fig. 5. Mixing efficiency and pressure drop at the outlet for different *Re* values.

The distribution of the mixing efficiency along the axial mixing length was investigated at three different *Re* values, i.e. 0.1, 1, and 10, as shown in Fig. 6. The results indicated that the three distributions of the mixing efficiencies follow the same trend. It can be observed that the mixing efficiencies were greatly improved at each corner of the zigzag mixing element, i.e. at 500, 800, and 1100 μm of the axial mixing length. Furthermore, it can be noted that the distribution of the mixing efficiency at $Re = 0.1$ was the best along the whole axial mixing length, while it was the lowest at $Re = 1$.

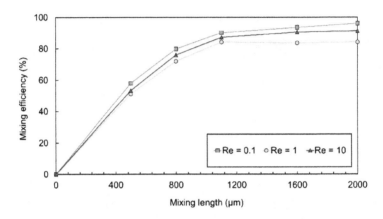

Fig. 6. Mixing efficiency along the axial mixing length for $Re = 0.1$, 1 and 10.

From Figs. 5 and 6, It can be indicated that the mixing efficiency can be improved beyond this range of Re values. However, the developed micromixer is intended to be used in typical microfluidic biomedical applications, where high flow velocities can cause rupture of cells, where the maximum flow rate generated at $Re = 10$ was ~ 3.4 μL/min. In addition, the operating temperature required to achieve higher Re values is limited to avoid any potential damage that might occur to the device.

5   Conclusion

A wirelessly-controlled thermopneumatic zigzag micromixer was demonstrated in this paper. The micromixer was operated using two passive heaters. Each heater generated heat when an external field frequency was tuned to its corresponding resonant frequency. Dynamic heat transfer, thermopneumatic actuation, and mixing performance were analytically presented and then verified using FEM as a demonstration of the proposed mixing technique. The proposed micromixer was able to achieve a maximum mixing efficiency of $\sim 96.1\%$, with a maximum flow rate and pressure drop of ~ 3.4 μL/min and ~ 385.22 Pa, respectively. Two activation switching patterns were investigated to find the optimal operating time of the two heaters. It was found that the optimal switching time is 10 s, at which the micromixer achieved a steady value of the maximum mixing efficiency after ~ 65 s.

The performance of the micromixer can be further improved by implementing metamodeling approach to find the optimal device design and activation pattern [21].

Acknowledgments. This work was supported by Research University Grant (10H40 & 14H31) from Universiti Teknologi Malaysia; and Fundamental Research Grant Scheme (FRGS) & Prototype Development Research Grant Scheme (PRGS) from Ministry of Higher Education Malaysia. M. Nafea acknowledges the financial support from the Malaysian Technical Cooperation Programme (MTCP).

References

1. Maleki, T., Fricke, T., Quesenberry, J., Todd, P., Leary, J.F.: Point-of-care, portable microfluidic blood analyzer system. In: International Society for Optics and Photonics, Microfluidics, BioMEMS, and Medical Microsystems X, pp. 82510C-82513, California (2012)
2. Rajabi, N., Bahnemann, J., Tzeng, T.-N., Platas Barradas, O., Zeng, A.-P., Müller, J.: Lab-on-a-chip for cell perturbation, lysis, and efficient separation of sub-cellular components in a continuous flow mode. Sens. Actuators, A **215**, 136–143 (2014)
3. Belliveau, N.M., Huft, J., Lin, P.J.C., Chen, S., Leung, A.K.K., Leaver, T.J., Wild, A.W., Lee, J.B., Taylor, R.J., Tam, Y.K., Hansen, C.L., Cullis, P.R.: Microfluidic synthesis of highly potent limit-size lipid nanoparticles for in vivo delivery of siRNA. Mol. Ther. -Nucl. Acids **1**, 37 (2012)
4. Hossain, S., Kim, K.-Y.: Mixing analysis of passive micromixer with unbalanced three-split rhombic sub-channels. Micromachines **5**, 913–928 (2014)
5. Lee, C.-Y., Chang, C.-L., Wang, Y.-N., Fu, L.-M.: Microfluidic mixing: a review. Int. J. Mol. Sci. **12**, 3263–3287 (2011)
6. Li, X., Chang, H., Liu, X., Ye, F., Yuan, W.: A 3-D overbridge-shaped micromixer for fast mixing over a wide range of reynolds numbers. J. Microelectromech. Syst. **24**, 1391–1399 (2015)
7. Nam-Trung, N., Zhigang, W.: Micromixers—a review. J. Micromech. Microeng. **15**, R1 (2005)
8. Mengeaud, V., Josserand, J., Girault, H.H.: Mixing processes in a zigzag microchannel: finite element simulations and optical study. Anal. Chem. **74**, 4279–4286 (2002)
9. Le Hai, T., Bao Quoc, T., Le Hoa, T., Tao, D., Trung Nguyen, T., Frank, K.: Geometric effects on mixing performance in a novel passive micromixer with trapezoidal-zigzag channels. J. Micromech. Microeng. **25**, 094004 (2015)
10. Glasgow, I., Lieber, S., Aubry, N.: Parameters influencing pulsed flow mixing in microchannels. Anal. Chem. **76**, 4825–4832 (2004)
11. Zhu, G.-P., Nguyen, N.-T.: Rapid magnetofluidic mixing in a uniform magnetic field. Lab Chip **12**, 4772–4780 (2012)
12. Joung, Y.-H.: Development of implantable medical devices: from an engineering perspective. Int. Neurourol. J. **17**, 98–106 (2013)
13. Mohamed Ali, M.S., Takahata, K.: Wireless microfluidic control with integrated shape-memory-alloy actuators operated by field frequency modulation. J. Micromech. Microeng. **21**, 075005 (2011)
14. Smith, S., Tang, T.B., Terry, J.G., Stevenson, J.T.M., Flynn, B.W., Reekie, H.M., Murray, A.F., Gundlach, A.M., Renshaw, D., Dhillon, B., Ohtori, A., Inoue, Y., Walton, A.J.: Development of a miniaturised drug delivery system with wireless power transfer and communication. IET Nanobiotechnol. **1**, 80–86 (2007)
15. Chee, P.S., Minjal, M.N., Leow, P.L., Mohamed Ali, M.S.: Wireless powered thermo-pneumatic micropump using frequency-controlled heater. Sens. Actuators A: Physical **233**, 1–8 (2015)

16. Nafea, M., AbuZiater, A., Faris, O., Kazi, S., Mohamed Ali, M.S.: Selective wireless control of a passive thermopneumatic micromixer. In: 2016 IEEE 29th International Conference on Micro Electro Mechanical Systems (MEMS), pp. 792–795. IEEE Press, Shanghai, China (2016)
17. Mohamed Ali, M.S., Takahata, K.: Frequency-controlled wireless shape-memory-alloy microactuators integrated using an electroplating bonding process. Sens. Actuators A: Physical **163**, 363–372 (2010)
18. Chee, P.S., Nafea, M., Leow, P.L., Mohamed Ali, M.S.: Thermal analysis of wirelessly powered thermo-pneumatic micropump based on planar LC circuit. J. Mech. Sci. Technol. **30**, 2659–2665 (2016)
19. Guo, L., Guvanasen, G.S., Liu, X., Tuthill, C., Nichols, T.R., DeWeerth, S.P.: A PDMS-based integrated stretchable microelectrode array (isMEA) for neural and muscular surface interfacing. IEEE Trans. Biomed. Circ. Syst. **7**, 1–10 (2013)
20. Nafea, M., AbuZaiter, A., Kazi, S., Mohamed Ali, M.S.: Frequency-Controlled Wireless Passive Thermopneumatic Micromixer. J. Microelectromech. Syst. **26**, 691–703 (2017)
21. Mohamed Ali, M.S., Abdullah, S.S., Osman, D.C.: Controllers optimization for a fluid mixing system using metamodeling approach. Int. J. Simul. Model. **8**, 48–59 (2009)

Novel Information Flow Topology for Vehicle Convoy Control

Mu'azu J. Musa$^{(\boxtimes)}$, Shahdan Sudin, Zaharuddin Mohamed,
and Sophan W. Nawawi

Department of Control and Mechatronics Engineering,
Faculty of Electrical Engineering, Universiti Teknologi Malaysia,
Johor Bahru, Malaysia
mjmusa@abu.edu.ng, {shahdan,zahar,e-sophan}@utm.my

Abstract. This paper analyzed a novel information flow topology (IFT) for vehicle convoy. The topology used two-vehicle look-ahead with an immediate rear-vehicle inclusive. Mass spring damper and Newton's second law were utilized to provide the behavior and basics for the vehicles motion respectively. The concept of homogeneous vehicle convoy and constant headway time (CHT) policy was in cooperated for the inter-vehicular spacing. The new IFT was compared with the conventional topology of the two-vehicle look-ahead to ascertain its improvement. The novel topology provides good inter-vehicular space of 0.42 m ahead of the conventional topology. Moreover, the proposed topology obeys the rate of change of speed throughout the vehicles journey than the conventional type. Low jerk of $0.44\,\mathrm{ms^{-3}}$ was achieved against $0.47\,\mathrm{ms^{-3}}$ of the conventional. Finally, the new topology is visible throughout the journey than the earlier, which discontinues after 117 s in all parameters.

Keywords: Jerk · Performance · Spacing · String-stability · Topology · Vehicle

1 Introduction

This paper focused to introduce a new version of information flow topology (IFT) of two-vehicle look-ahead and rear- vehicle. The concept of sting-stability would be used to tackle the issue of string instability in the convoy. String stability is the ability of the vehicle in the convoy to move without amplifying the errors of the lead vehicle downstream. In an effort to address this issue, researchers have been working on different techniques to maximize the usage of road transport to capacity and to enhance the safety and comfort of the road users. Levine and Athans [1] proposed the first mathematical model of a vehicle convoy system in the early 60 s. The study presented a system, in which the vehicle displacement and speed were regulated in a heavily dense convoy of possible number of vehicles moving in a single lane. The major features of the model includes; passengers comfort, safety measures, speed control and energy wastage. Moreover, Melzer and kuo [2] developed theory of linear systems for optimal regulation presented as a countably unlimited group of agents. The theory was used for an infinite size of string of vehicles. The shortcoming of the strategies is due to

© Springer Nature Singapore Pte Ltd. 2017
M.S. Mohamed Ali et al. (Eds.): AsiaSim 2017, Part I, CCIS 751, pp. 323–335, 2017.
DOI: 10.1007/978-981-10-6463-0_28

the used of centralized controller, in which each vehicle in the convoy has direct accessibility to all the state variables of the string. [3–5] reported IFT, in which only nearest neighbors were utilized in the topology. It was evident from the work that reduction in the number of utilized neighboring vehicles, leads to undesired convoy behaviors. The research work figures out the dependency of string stability to measurements of other vehicle (bi or unidirectional) within the convoy. Decentralized control for vehicle string strategies was investigated in [6] in which relative importance of different measurements were studied in the optimal control through minimization of the cost function.

More recently, number of convoy control methods where presented in real world for demonstration purposes, which include the Safe Road Trains for the Environment (SARTRE) in Europe [7], Intelligent Transport Systems (ITS) named Energy-ITS in Japan [8], and Grand Cooperative Driving Challenge (GCDC) in Netherlands [9] etc. The oldest convoy concentrates on the use of radar-based systems for sensing, which has limited communication exchange topologies [10]. The rapid growth in vehicle technology leads to the deployment of vehicle-to-vehicle (V2V) communications, like Dedicated Short Range Communications (DSRC) and Vehicular Adhoc Networks (VANET) [11] this however, permits more variety of topologies for convoy, such as the two-predecessor following and multiple-predecessor following configurations [10, 12] to achieve better convoy string stability. Due to the challenges that arise in different vehicle convoy information topologies [13], it is more preferable to take vehicle convoy systems as a group of dynamic systems, and to design an enhanced control strategy. Sudin and Cook [14] came up with an improved vehicle convoy strategy, were two-vehicle look-ahead control strategy was utilized to achieve string stability. Oncu et al. [15] examined the influence of convoy uniform delay and sampling-hold on string stability. Bernardo et al. [16] proposed techniques to analyse vehicle convoy string stability issues with more emphasis on dynamic network control. Wang et al. [17] studied the effect of time varying network architectures on convoy using discrete-time Markov chain.

All these makes the IFT a challenging control problem. There is the need for an enhanced and more realistic IFT; hence the interest of this paper is basically on the development of a novel IFT of homogeneous vehicle convoy system. Section 2 of this paper describes the mathematical modelling of the proposed topology. An analysis on the new IFT is shown in Sect. 3. Section 4 concludes on the obtained results.

2 Materials and Methods

MATLAB R2013b platform was used for both modelling and implementation in this paper. The proposed work used the assumption of a homogeneous convoy because it eases the investigation in various mathematical presentations of convoys [13, 18]. Furthermore, it has been proved in other researches that non-homogeneity does not instantly give an enhancement on experiment in the performance of the string [19]. Linear dependent spacing policy was utilized due to its simplicity to use; it as well reveals efficient and interesting results and also insight in some cases [3]. These encourage the selection of linear dependent spacing policy among the most confronting spacing policies; constant spacing (CS) which is the fixed time spacing policy and constant headway time (CHT) policy. The CS provides fixed inter-vehicular spacing that is independent of speed of the vehicles [20, 21]. It has been reported by [22] that such spacing policy suffers a lot to string instability due to the minimal inter-vehicular spacing used and hugely depends on V2V communication [23, 24]. The CHT is speed dependent, which was utilized in this work due to its ability to remain linear in nature [25]. This gives a greater chance to fully utilize the linearity involved and achieve one of the human driving habit [26]. Hence the speed dependent policy CHT is proposed as against the CS, which is prone to collusion. The mathematical modelling is presented in the subsequent sub-heading. The two-vehicle look-ahead and rear-vehicle formulation for the IFT is discussed in this section. The technique used is based on the fact that a driver can have much control of his/her vehicle if the driver has access to monitor the rear vehicle in addition to the two vehicles in front of him/her. The IFT for the control strategy is to simulate the human driving behaviour in a real convoy scenario, in which the following vehicle do not only relay on the information received from the preceding vehicle or leading vehicle but also the rear vehicle. The rear vehicle is necessary because of safety in the convoy, which is the primary function of mirrors in vehicle. This is to give adequate respond time for the control vehicle to changes in the leader, predecessor and rear vehicle's speed to avoid front and rear collusion and to enable passengers comfort. The strategy is designed to eliminate string instability in the convoy system. Therefore the new IFT to mimic human driving habit for safe convoy is proposed.

The novel topology of the two-vehicle look-ahead and rear-vehicle is presented in Fig. 1, while the Eq (1) presents the strategic equation derived from Fig. 1.

$$m\ddot{x}_i = K_{p1}(x_{i-1} - x_i) + K_{v1}(\dot{x}_{i-1} - \dot{x}_i) + K_{p2}(x_{i-2} - x_i) + K_{v2}(\dot{x}_{i-2} - \dot{x}_i) \\ + K_{p3}(x_{i+1} - x_i) + K_{v3}(\dot{x}_{i+1} - \dot{x}_i) \tag{1}$$

where: m is the vehicle mass, x_i, x_{i-1}, x_{i-2} and x_{i+1} are the instantaneous positions of the i-th, (i − 1)-th, (i − 2)-th and (i + 1)-th vehicle respectively along the X-axis, $\dot{x}_i$, $\dot{x}_{i-1}, \dot{x}_{i-2}$ and $\dot{x}_{i+1}$ are the correspoing velocities of the vehicles, $\ddot{x}_i$ is the acceleration of the i-th vehicle, $K_{p1}, K_{p2}, K_{p3}, K_{v1}, K_{v2}$ and K_{v3} are the constants.

The control signal ($\mathcal{U}_i$) has direct influence on the force applied to the vehicle, which was modelled as initial mass [14].

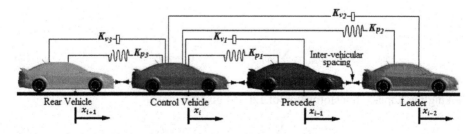

Fig. 1. Representation of the proposed control strategy.

$$\ddot{x}_i = f(\dot{x}_i, \mathcal{U}_i) \qquad (2)$$

The simplified model related to the problem can be expressed as in Eq. (3):

$$\ddot{x}_i = \mathcal{U}_i \qquad (3)$$

Hence, considering the fact that the following (i-th) vehicle has no influence on the three ((i − 1)-th, (i − 2)-th and (i + 1)-th) vehicles, Eq. (4) is obtained as:

$$\mathcal{U}_i = K_{p1}(x_{i-1} - x_i) + K_{p2}(x_{i-2} - x_i) + K_{p3}(x_{i+1} - x_i) + K_{v1}(\dot{x}_{i-1} - \dot{x}_i) \\ + K_{v2}(\dot{x}_{i-2} - \dot{x}_i) + K_{v3}(\dot{x}_{i+1} - \dot{x}_i) \qquad (4)$$

Equation (4) provides the control strategy of the two-vehicle look-ahead and rear vehicle using fixed spacing policy. [20–22, 27] reveal that the effect of string instability continues with such spacing policy. It is clear that different convoy speed required different inter-vehicular spacing [14]; this is to give enough time for the control vehicle to respond to changes in the leader, predecessor and rear vehicles' speed to avoid collusion. Hence, a more promising policy is required. Due to the fact mentioned here, the speed dependent policy is employed in this model. After incorporating the spacing policy CHT in the model equation, it yields to an improved control signal equation as presented in Eq. (5):

$$\mathcal{U}_i = K_{p1}(x_{i-1} - x_i - h\dot{x}_i) + K_{p2}(x_{i-2} - x_i - 2h\dot{x}_i) + K_{p3}(x_{i+1} - x_i - h\dot{x}_i) \\ + K_{v1}(\dot{x}_{i-1} - \dot{x}_i) + K_{v2}(\dot{x}_{i-2} - \dot{x}_i) + K_{v3}(\dot{x}_{i+1} - \dot{x}_i) \qquad (5)$$

where: $h\dot{x}_i$ is the speed dependent spacing from the adopted spacing policy. As the convoy speed increases, the inter-vehicular spacing increases and vice versa. When the vehicles in the convoy are moving with steady speed, it is assumed that the inter-vehicular spacing between the leader vehicle (x_{i-2}) to the control vehicle (x_i) is twice that of the rear vehicle (x_{i+1}) to the control vehicle or that of predecessor vehicle (x_{i+1}) to the control vehicle.

The realized strategy of the vehicle is based on the signals received from the two-vehicles ahead and one-rear. Hence Eq. (5) can be re-written as [28]:

$$\mathcal{U}_i = \sum_{m=1}^{n} \left[k_{pm}(\delta_{im} - mh\dot{x}_i) + k_{vm}\{(\dot{x}_{i-m} - \dot{x}_i) + (\dot{x}_{i+m} - \dot{x}_i)\} \right] \qquad (6)$$

where,

$$\delta_{im} = \sum_{l=0}^{m-1} \varepsilon_{i-l} = x_{i-m} - x_i - mL \qquad (7)$$

Taking the Laplace transformation of Eq. (6) gives:

$$X_i(s) = \sum_{m=1}^{n} G_m(s) X_{i-m}(s) X_{i+m}(s) \qquad (8)$$

Equation (8) yields,

$$s^2 X_i = K_{p1}(X_{i-1} - X_i - hsX_i) + K_{p2}(X_{i-2} - X_i - 2hsX_i) + K_{p3}(X_{i+1} - X_i - hsX_i)$$
$$+ K_{v1}s(X_{i-1} - X_i) + K_{v2}s(X_{i-2} - X_i) + K_{v3}s(X_{i+1} - X_i)$$

$$(9)$$

Re-arranging for X_i from Eq. (9) gives,

$$X_i = \frac{(K_{v1}s + K_{p1})X_{i-1} + (K_{v2}s + K_{p2})X_{i-2} + (K_{v3}s + K_{p3})X_{i+1}}{s^2 + \left[K_{v1} + K_{v2} + K_{v3} + (K_{p1} + 2K_{p2} + K_{p3})h\right]s + K_{p1} + K_{p2} + K_{p3}} \quad (10)$$

Further re-arranging Eq. (10) and reducing to a single pole system results to the following,

$$X_i = \frac{K_{v1}\left(s + \frac{K_{p1}}{K_{v1}}\right)X_{i-1} + K_{v2}\left(s + \frac{K_{p2}}{K_{v2}}\right)X_{i-2} + K_{v3}\left(s + \frac{K_{p3}}{K_{v3}}\right)X_{i+1}}{s^2 + (K_{p1} + 2K_{p2} + K_{p3})hs + K_{v1}\left(s + \frac{K_{p1}}{K_{v1}}\right) + K_{v2}\left(s + \frac{K_{p2}}{K_{v2}}\right) + K_{v3}\left(s + \frac{K_{p3}}{K_{v3}}\right)} \quad (11)$$

Hence:

$$X_i = \frac{K_{v1}\left(s + \frac{K_{p1}}{K_{v1}}\right)X_{i-1} + K_{v2}\left(s + \frac{K_{p2}}{K_{v2}}\right)X_{i-2} + K_{v3}\left(s + \frac{K_{p3}}{K_{v3}}\right)X_{i+1}}{s\left[s + (K_{p1} + 2K_{p2} + K_{p3})h\right] + K_{v1}\left(s + \frac{K_{p1}}{K_{v1}}\right) + K_{v2}\left(s + \frac{K_{p2}}{K_{v2}}\right) + K_{v3}\left(s + \frac{K_{p3}}{K_{v3}}\right)} \quad (12)$$

Several ways have been proposed by researchers to guarantee string stability to their developed control strategies [29]. To achieve stable string stability and reduce the complexity of the control law, the pole and zero cancellation is proposed. This aimed at reducing Eq. (12) to a single pole system (linear equation). To linearize Eq. (12) the pole and zero cancellation technique was used through the following constraint.

$$\frac{K_{p1}}{K_{v1}} = \frac{K_{p2}}{K_{v2}} = \frac{K_{p3}}{K_{v3}} = (K_{p1} + 2K_{p2} + K_{p3})h \quad (13)$$

This result to the simplification of Eqs. (12) to (14) as:

$$X_i = \frac{K_{v1}X_{i-1} + K_{v2}X_{i-2} + K_{v3}X_{i+1}}{s + K_{v1} + K_{v2} + K_{v3}} \quad (14)$$

Equation (12) is first order and the poles of the equation are on the left hand side of the s-plane since K_{v1} to K_{v3} are all positive. This implies that the mathematical model of the two-vehicle look-ahead and rear-vehicle system of Eq. (5) is string stable with respect to the constraint of Eq. (13) as shown in Eq. (14). Hence, the system response of the convoy depends to h and K_p's as seen from Eq. (15).

$$K_{v1} + K_{v2} + K_{v3} = \frac{K_{p1} + K_{p2} + K_{p3}}{(K_{p1} + 2K_{p2} + K_{p3})h} \tag{15}$$

2.1 Modelling Procedure

The model was built on MATLAB R2013b platform following the derived control strategy Eq. (5). The Simulink representation of the strategy is represented on Fig. 2. The model uses the CTH policy to provide the speed dependent spacing policy were the inter-vehicular spacing depends on the speed of the leader, predecessor and rear vehicles collectively. The novel topology with the adopted policy provides adequate spacing, minimises the chance of collusion and guaranteed stable string within the convoy.

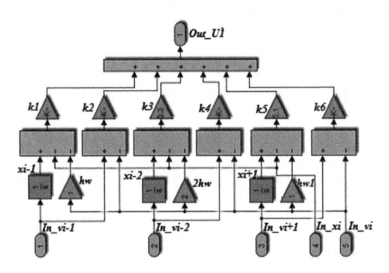

Fig. 2. Single car control strategy for the proposed convoy.

The control strategy was implemented in Fig. 2 and cascaded with a vehicle design by Sudin and Cook [14] to enable test the new topology with that of [14].

The top-level of the proposed model was shown in Fig. 3. This shows identical vehicles arrangement, were vehicle_1–4 represents the set of homogeneous vehicles in the order of leader, predecessor, control vehicle (vehicle_3) and rear vehicle respectively. The main input block in Fig. 3 provides the input speed to the independent vehicles in the convoy, initial position block gives an arbitrary position of each vehicle within the convoy, while position compare block compares the displacement of each vehicle with the control vehicle. This deliberate design provides a new knowledge in vehicle convoy IFT with more realistic human driving habit.

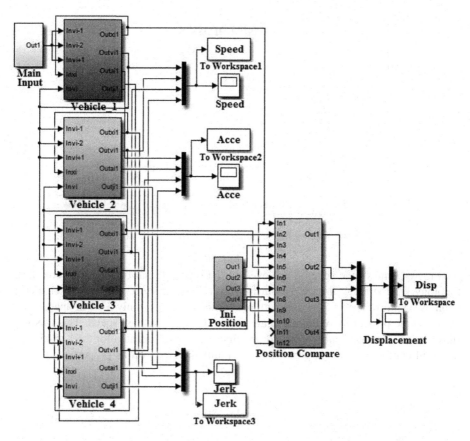

Fig. 3. Centralized control strategy for the proposed convoy.

3   Results and Analysis

The outcomes of the simulation of the proposed model were presented in this section and are used to compare with that of [14] to justify the improvements achieved with respect to the new topology. The model Eq. (5) was tested using the poles and zeros cancellation technique where proper cancellation was conducted with high convoy stability. The following simulations give an inside on the new topology as compare to that of Sudin and Cook [14].

Figure 4 shows a variable spacing of the proposed topology, where equal spacing was achieved among the vehicles with respect to any variation in speed of the vehicles. This indicator gives an improved and string stable IFT than that of Fig. 5. The new topology permits a smooth and free running of the vehicle over a period of 160 s of test with peak spacing of 150 m. This speed dependent policy gives a wider range of inter-vehicular spacing of maximum of 37.5 m apart; it also permits the control vehicle to react to sudden changes in speed of the other vehicles. As seen in Fig. 4, the maximum spacing from the new topology prevents collusion among the stream of the vehicle due to wide spacing apart when the vehicle accelerated and vice versa.

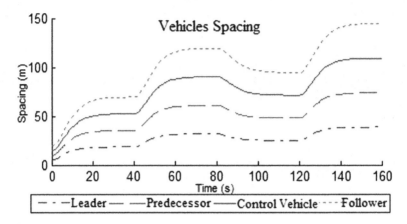

Fig. 4. Spacing of the proposed convoy control strategy.

Figure 5 shows the spacing achieved of the conventional two-vehicle look-ahead topology. The strategy uses CHT but has the following short comings of, chattering habit as seen for the first 70 s and with maximum spacing of only 33.3 m apart, which indicated the possibility of collusion among the vehicles on high speed. This topology runs for 160 s but was only visible for the first 115 s and truncated for the last 45 s due to the ill condition of the approach, which limits the study on its properties.

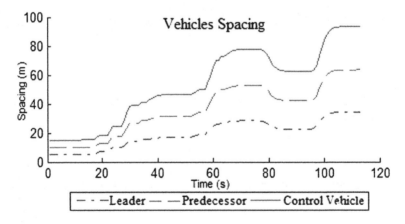

Fig. 5. Spacing of the two-vehicle look-ahead convoy control strategy.

Figure 6 reveals how the control vehicle of the proposed topology closely tracks the path of the leader, predecessor and follower vehicle speeds without collusion. This shows the ability of the control vehicle to depend hugely on the acceleration, deceleration and constant speed of the neighbouring vehicles within the convoy as compared to Fig. 7.

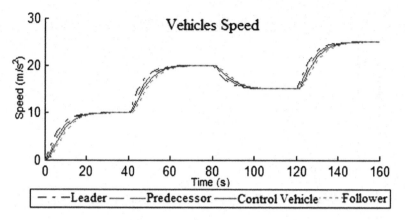

Fig. 6. Speed of the proposed convoy control strategy.

Figure 7 shows the lapses in the speed of the conventional against the novel topology. The speed is affected by the chattering effect within the first 70 s this shows an unrequired variation in speed, which caused an overlap in speed among the vehicles even at low speed of 30 ms^{-1}. Moreover, the convoy runs for 160 s but was only visible for 115 s due to the ill condition of the model, hence no account for the remaining 45 s is known.

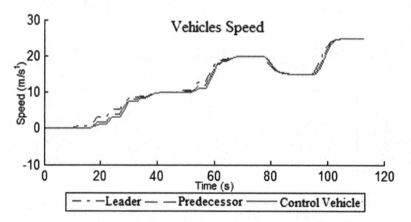

Fig. 7. Speed of the two-vehicle look-ahead convoy control strategy.

Figure 8 presents the acceleration of all the vehicles in the new topology. The rate of change of velocity in the control vehicle is maintained at maximum acceleration of 0.92 ms^{-2}, which is below the acceptable acceleration of 2 ms^{-2} [30]. The control vehicle's acceleration is between that of the predecessor and the follower, no single place where the control vehicle's acceleration overlaps that of other vehicles. This shows proper control of acceleration as compared to the conventional Fig. 9.

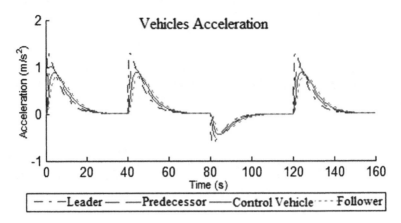

Fig. 8. Acceleration of the proposed convoy control strategy.

It is evidence that inconsistent acceleration is observed in Fig. 9. The control vehicle was controlled at a maximum acceleration of 1.0 ms^{-2}, which is however outstanding. The bone of contention to this acceleration is the chattering phenomena at the first 70 s of the journey and was discontinued at 115 s only during a journey of 160 s, moreover, the maximum acceleration of the control vehicle in Fig. 9 was high (1.0 ms^{-2}) as compared to the proposed topology (0.92 ms^{-2}). This slight difference in control vehicle acceleration in both cases has reasonable consequence on the final control vehicle's jerk, on which the overall passenger's comfortability depends.

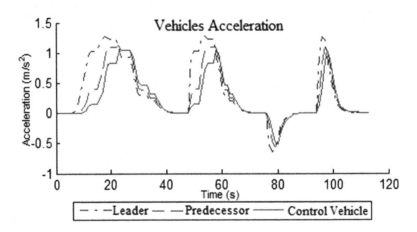

Fig. 9. Acceleration of the two-vehicle look-ahead convoy control strategy.

The smaller the jerk, the more comfortable is the vehicle and vice versa. The jerk of the control vehicle was found from Fig. 10 as 0.44 ms^{-3}, which is pretty well below the maximum accepted jerk of 5 ms^{-3} [31]. This 0.44 ms^{-3} proved that the control vehicle would be comfortable for passengers [14] compared to that of Fig. 11.

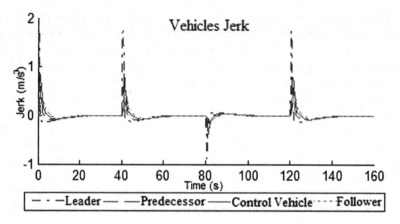

Fig. 10. Jerk of the proposed convoy control strategy.

The simulation result of Fig. 11 shows fast response with undesirable jerk of 0.47 ms^{-3}. The undesired oscillation produced in the simulation is due to the fact that small oscillation occurs as the vehicle is trying to settle down at its final speed in the two-vehicle look-ahead topology. The jerk is higher than that of the proposed topology with value of 0.03 ms^{-3}. This difference in jerk in addition to the oscillation would leads to passenger's discomfort.

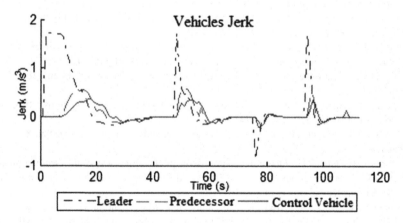

Fig. 11. Jerk of the two-vehicle look-ahead convoy control strategy.

4   Conclusions

The new topology gives an improved performance on the inter-vehicular spacing with no chattering effect and is visible throughout the journey. The spacing for the four vehicles is spread equally over distance of 150 m, i.e. 37.5 m apart. Sufficient inter-vehicular spacing of 37.5 m apart was achieved as against 33.3 m of the conventional topology. The large spacing of 37.5 m permits the control vehicle to react to any change in speed of the neighbouring vehicles within the convoy. The speed of the control vehicle is well arranged without an overlap as compared to that of the two-vehicle look-ahead, which was overlapped at some points within the journey. The overlap in speed results to collision of the vehicles. Rate of change of velocity is low on the control vehicle (0.92 ms^{-2}) as compared to that on the conventional topology (1.1 ms^{-2}). The lower the rate of changes of velocity, the better the control vehicle's jerk [14]. A jerk of 0.44 ms^{-3} was realised in the proposed topology as compared to that of the conventional topology (0.47 ms^{-3}). The low jerk provides passengers comfortability throughout the journey.

The proposed IFT is strictly based on centralized control, where the behaviour of each independent vehicle of the convoy is determined by a given input speed. The control vehicle used the collective behaviours of the neighbouring vehicles and make decisions on its movement and position. The novel topology prevents collusion, enhanced passengers comfort and improved the overall convoy's string stability.

Acknowledgments. The work is financially supported by Universiti Teknologi Malaysia (UTM) and Malaysia Government through the UTM Research University Grants (Vote number 12J52). We also appreciate the partial support from UTM IDF scholarship.

References

1. Levine, W., Athans, M.: On the optimal error regulation of a string of moving vehicles. IEEE Trans. Autom. Control **11**, 355–361 (1966)
2. Melzer, S., Kuo, B.: Optimal regulation of systems described by a countably infinite number of objects. Automatica Elsevia. **7**, 359–366 (1971)
3. Bender, J.G., Fenton, R.E.: A study of automatic car following. In: 19th IEEE Vehicular Technology Conference, pp. 134–400. IEEE Press, New York (1968)
4. Peppard, L., Gourishankar, V.: An optimal automatic car-following system. IEEE Trans. Veh. Technol. **21**, 67–73 (1972)
5. Peppard, L.: String stability of relative-motion PID vehicle control systems. IEEE Trans. Autom. Control **19**, 579–581 (1974)
6. Chu, K.C.: Decentralized control of high-speed vehicular strings. Transp. Sci. **8**, 361–384 (1974)
7. Robinson, E., Chan, E.: Operating platoons on public motorways: an introduction to the SARTRE platooning programme. In: 17th World Congress on Intelligent Transport System (ITS), Busan, Korea, pp. 1–11 (2010)
8. Tsugawa, S., Kato, S., Aoki, K.: An automated truck platoon for energy saving. In: IEEE/RSJ International Conference on Intelligent Robots and Systems, pp. 4109–4114. IEEE Press, San Francisco (2011)
9. Kianfar, R., Augusto, B., Ebadighajari, A.: Design and experimental validation of a cooperative driving system in the grand cooperative driving challenge. IEEE Trans. Intell. Transp. Syst. **13**, 994–1007 (2012)
10. Zheng, Y., Li, S.E., Wang, J., Wang, L.Y., Li, K.: Influence of information flow topology on closed-loop stability of vehicle platoon with rigid formation. In: 17th International IEEE Conference on ITSC, pp. 2094–2100. IEEE Press, Qingdao (2014)
11. Willke, T.L., Tientrakool, P., Maxemchuk, N.F.: A survey of inter-vehicle communication protocols and their applications. In: IEEE Communications Surveys & Tutorials, pp. 3–20. IEEE Press, Piscataway (2009)

12. Ploeg, J., Serrarens, A., Heijenk, G.: Connect & drive: design and evaluation of cooperative adaptive cruise control for congestion reduction. J. Mod. Transp. **19**, 207–213 (2011)
13. Li, S.E., Zheng, Y., Li, K., Wang, J.: An overview of vehicular platoon control under the four-component framework. In: 4th IEEE Intelligent Vehicles Symposium, pp. 286–291. IEEE Press, Seoul (2015)
14. Sudin, S., Cook, P.A.: Two-vehicle look-ahead convoy control systems. In: 56th IEEE Vehicular Technology Conference, pp. 2935–2939. IEEE Press, Milan (2004)
15. Oncu, S., Ploeg, J., Wouw, N., Nijmeijer, H.: Cooperative adaptive cruise control: network-aware analysis of string stability. IEEE Trans. Intell. Transp. Syst. **15**, 1527–1537 (2014)
16. Bernardo, M., Alessandro, S., Stefania, S.: Distributed consensus strategy for platooning of vehicles in the presence of time-varying heterogeneous communication delay. IEEE Trans. Intell. Transp. Syst. **16**, 102–112 (2015)
17. Wang, L., Syed, A., Yin, G., Pandya, A., Zhang, H.: Control of vehicle platoons for highway safety and efficient utility: consensus with communications and vehicle dynamics. J. Syst. Sci. Complex. **27**, 605–631 (2014)
18. Zheng, Y., Li, S.E., Wang, J., Cao, D., Li, K.: Stability and scalability of homogeneous vehicular platoon: study on the influence of information flow topologies. IEEE Trans. Intell. Transp. Syst. **17**, 14–26 (2016)
19. Kwon, J.W., Chwa, D.: Adaptive bidirectional platoon control using a coupled sliding mode control method. IEEE Trans. Intell. Transp. Syst. **15**, 2040–2048 (2014)
20. Fujioka, H.: Stability analysis for a class of networked/embedded control systems: a discrete-time approach. In: Proceedings of American Control Conference, Washington, USA, pp. 4997–5002 (2008)
21. Klinge, S., Middleton, H.: Time headway requirements for string stability of homogeneous linear unidirectionally connected. In: 48th IEEE Conference on Decision and Control and 28th Chinese Control Conference, pp. 1992–1997. IEEE Press, Shanghai (2009)
22. Marsden, G., McDonald, M., Brackstone, M.: Towards an understanding of adaptive cruise control. Transp. Res. Past C **9**, 33–51 (2001). Elsevier Science Ltd.
23. Jing, J., Kurt, A., Ozatay, E., Michelini, J., Filev, D., Ozguner, U.: Vehicle speed prediction in a convoy using V2V communication. In: IEEE Intelligent Transportation Systems, pp. 2861–2868. IEEE Press, Las Palmas (2015)
24. Yanakiev, D., Eyre, J., Kanellakopoulos, I.: Analysis, design, and evaluation of AVCs for heavy-duty vehicles with actuator delays. Technical report, California Partners for Advanced Transit and Highways (PATH), California, pp. 21–25 (1998)
25. Zhou, J., Peng, H.: Range policy of adaptive cruise control vehicles for improved flow stability and string stability. IEEE Trans. Intell. Transp. Syst. **6**, 229–237 (2005)
26. Van-Winsum, W.: The human element in car following models. Transp. Res. Part F: Traffic Psychol. Behav. **2**, 207–211 (1999)
27. Yang, T.C.: Networked control system: a brief survey. In: IEEE Proceedings of Control Theory and Applications, pp. 403–412 (2006)
28. Cook, P.A., Sudin, S.: Dynamics of convoy control systems. In: 10th IEEE Mediterranean Conference on Control and Automation, pp. 1–8. IEEE Press, Lisboa (2002)
29. Hassan, A.U., Sudin, S.: Road vehicle following control strategy using model reference adaptive control method stability approach. Jurnal Teknologi (Sci. Eng.) **72**, 111–117 (2015)
30. Li, P., Alvarez, L., Horowitz, R.: AHS safe control laws for platoon leaders. IEEE Trans. Control Syst. Technol. **5**, 614–628 (1997)
31. Godbole, D.N., Lygeros, J.: Longitudinal control of the lead car of a platoon. IEEE Trans. Veh. Technol. **43**, 1125–1135 (1994)

CFD Simulation of Two Phase Segmented Flow in Microchannel Reactor Using Volume of Fluid Model for Biodiesel Production

Afiq Mohd Laziz and Ku Zilati Ku Shaari[✉]

Universiti Teknologi PETRONAS, 32610 Seri Iskandar, Perak, Malaysia
afiq_laziz@hotmail.com, kuzilati_kushaari@utp.edu.my

Abstract. One of the advantages of using microchannel reactor in chemical process is enhancement of mass and energy transfer due to the high area-to-volume ratio created by the multiphase droplet. This total interfacial area can be varied by controlling the size of the droplet based on different volumetric flow ratio between continuous and disperse phase. CFD method is used to estimate the size of the droplet using VOF model. In many cases, there is always balance between simulation result accuracy and computational cost. In this study, the grid sensitivity analysis is investigated to see the result accuracy at different meshing quality. From this multiphase simulation, it was found that the simulation is highly dependent on grid size. The droplet size cases showing deviation ±5% and ±20% for highest and lowest meshing quality respectively, which the lowest meshing quality must have at least one layer of mesh refinement at the wall. By knowing this, one can have confidence on using lowest meshing quality for a lower computational cost but still at an acceptable level of result accuracy.

Keywords: Microchannel reactor · VOF validation · Meshing study · Multiphase droplet

1 Introduction

Microfluidic or specifically the microchannel reactor application has widely been studied for process intensification; for example in the transesterification process for biodiesel production [1–3]. Among many advantages of using microchannel is having high area-to-volume ratio which can increase the mass and heat transfer of a process [4]. In a liquid-liquid multiphase process, the interfacial area inside the microchannel can be controlled by varying the droplet size of the dispersed flow. According to Garstecki et al. [5], the size of the droplet is affected by the volumetric ratio between continuous and dispersed flow as shown in Eq. (1) below

$$\frac{L_d}{W_d} \approx 1 + \frac{Q_d}{Q_c} \qquad (1)$$

where L_d and W_d are the length and width of the droplet, and Q_d and Q_c are the volumetric rate of dispersed and continuous flow respectively. The correlation was later

© Springer Nature Singapore Pte Ltd. 2017
M.S. Mohamed Ali et al. (Eds.): AsiaSim 2017, Part I, CCIS 751, pp. 336–344, 2017.
DOI: 10.1007/978-981-10-6463-0_29

improved by Xu et al. by including fitting and wetting parameters in the correlation equation [6]. By using computational method such as computational fluid dynamics (CFD), the time and cost for predicting the droplet size inside microchannel could be significantly reduced. Few numerical models can be used for multiphase flow cases such as the level set [7], volume of fluid (VOF) [8], marker particle, lattice Boltzmann, and front tracking model [9]. In CFD simulation, there is always a balance between result accuracy and computational cost which is directly related to the grid size of the mesh. In theory, the finest mesh has the highest meshing quality and hence, produces the highest accuracy result. However, it requires high computational cost and computational time. But depending on any cases, there is an optimum or asymptotic meshing quality where further refinement of the mesh will not give any significant better accuracy. In this study, meshing study is investigated in terms grid sensitivity based on different quality of mesh in order to have balance between result accuracy and computational cost.

2 Methodology

2.1 Geometry Definition

The simulation is performed using ANSYS Fluent version 15.0 and the multiphase flow model chosen is volume of fluid (VOF) model. In order to validate the simulation results, the experimental result from Garstecki et al. [5] is used. The geometry of the microchannel used in the experiment is a T-junction made from polydimethylsiloxane (PDMS) and has a hydrophobic wetting property. Silicon oil is used as the continuous phase and water as dispersed phase. The diameter of microchannel is 100 µm and the inlet water has a width of 50 µm. The geometry of the microchannel is portrayed in Fig. 1.

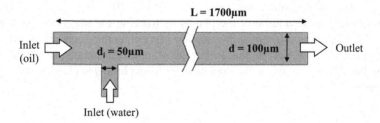

Fig. 1. Geometry description of the micro-channel as the simulation domain.

2.2 Boundary Conditions

Three different droplet sizes have been validated using computational method based on the ratio between the droplet length, L_d, to the channel width, w_c. Different droplet sizes are produced by injecting different volumetric flow rate ratios between water and oil. Table 1 shows the details of boundary conditions for all droplet size cases.

Table 1. Inlet boundary conditions.

Droplet name	Droplet size range	Inlet volume flow, μL/s		Water-oil flow rate ratio, Q_W/Q_O
		Q_{Oil}	Q_{Water}	
Short	$L_d \leq 2w_c$	0.028	0.010	0.36
Middle	$2w_c < L_d \leq 6w_c$	0.028	0.025	0.89
Long	$L_d > 6w_c$	0.028	0.111	3.96

In order to evaluate the grid sensitivity analysis, only the middle droplet size case is used and the grid size is varied by different meshing qualities. The detailed description on each meshing quality is presented in Table 2. The meshing size in the geometry is approximately constant throughout the boundary and the aspect ratio is very close to 1. Example of meshing studied for lowest (Mesh-1) and highest (Mesh-5) quality of meshing is shown in Fig. 2.

Table 2. Meshing sizing details.

Name	No. of nodes	No. of elements	Average cell size (μm)	Cell size (× ID)
Mesh-1	378	297	25.00	0.250
Mesh-2	731	618	16.67	0.167
Mesh-3	1404	1239	12.50	0.125
Mesh-4	2683	2459	8.30	0.083
Mesh-5	7402	7020	5.00	0.050

During the simulation running, Courant number, Cr, is kept below 0.1 in order to have a conservative and stable convergent value along the simulation. Therefore, the time step value taken is quite small in a range of 1×10^{-6} to 1×10^{-7} s. The VOF model estimates the separation of the phases by tracking the interface(s) between the phases [10]. It is accomplished by the solution of a continuity equation for the volume fraction of one (or more) of the phases. For the qth phase, this equation has the form as shown in Eq. (2); where, $\dot{m}_{qp}$ is the mass transfer from phase q to phase p and $\dot{m}_{qp}$ is the mass transfer from phase p to phase q.

$$\frac{1}{\rho_q}\left[\frac{\partial}{\partial t}\left(\alpha_q \rho_q\right) + \nabla \cdot \left(\alpha_q \rho_q \overline{V_q}\right) = \sum_{p=1}^{n}\left(\dot{m}_{pq} - \dot{m}_{qp}\right)\right] \tag{2}$$

A single momentum equation as shown in Eq. (3) is solved throughout the domain and the resulting velocity field is shared among the phases [10]. It is dependent on the volume fractions of all phases through the properties of ρ and μ.

$$\frac{\partial}{\partial t}\left(\rho\bar{v}\right) + \Delta \cdot \left(\rho\bar{v}\bar{v}\right) = -\nabla p + \nabla \cdot \left[\mu\left(\nabla\bar{v} + \nabla\bar{v}^T\right)\right] + \rho\bar{g} + \overline{F} \tag{3}$$

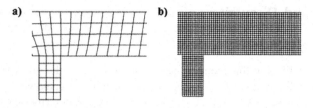

Fig. 2. Different mesh quality, (a) mesh-1, and (b) mesh-5.

The source term $\overline{F}$ in Eq. (3) is for the surface tension which in this study, the continuum surface force (CSF) model has been used. This model has been proposed by Brackbill *et al.* [11] and has been implemented such that the addition of surface tension to the VOF calculation results in a source term in the momentum equation. To understand the origin of the source term, the special case is considered where the surface tension is constant along the surface, and where only the forces normal to the interface are considered. It can be shown that the pressure drop across the surface depends upon the surface tension coefficient, σ, and the surface curvature as measure by two radii in orthogonal direction, R_1 and R_2 in Eq. (4) below:

$$p_2 - p_1 = \sigma \left(\frac{1}{R_1} - \frac{1}{R_2} \right) \tag{4}$$

where p_1 and p_2 are the pressures in the two fluids on either side of the interface. In Ansys Fluent, a formulation of the CSF model is used, where the surface curvature is computed from local gradients in the surface normal at the interface. Equation (5) show the surface normal, n, that is used to calculate the surface curvature, where α_q is defined as the gradient of the volume fraction of qth phase.

$$n = \nabla \alpha_q \tag{5}$$

2.3   Analysis Method

The size of the droplet is analysed qualitatively and quantitatively. For the qualitative method, contour plot of volume fraction is observed based on the two-dimensional contour plot of the droplet inside the microchannel in terms of the shape and the sharpness of the interfacial boundary between the two phases. For the quantitative analysis, the result is analysed from the line plot along axial direction of the microchannel. Along the axial direction, the exact value of droplet length can be measured where the volume fraction gives the value of 1. Subsequently, from both the analyses, the simulation result is evaluated by comparing it with the experimental result from Garstecki et al. [5] for validation of VOF model.

3   Results and Discussion

3.1   Geometry Definition

The meshing qualities of the geometry are varied to observe the grid sensitivity of the simulation. Five different meshing qualities have been investigated which vary in terms of the average cell size. Mesh-1 has the coarsest mesh which describes the lowest quality of mesh, while Mesh-5 has the finest mesh which describes the highest meshing quality. Figure 2 illustrates different meshing qualities between coarsest mesh from Mesh-1 and finest mesh from Mesh-5. Table 2 shows the detailed description of the grid size for each different mesh. It has been observed that at different meshing qualities, the shape and the length of droplet are changing as shown in Fig. 3 and Table 3. The droplet shape from highest quality Mesh-5 represents exactly like the shape of a droplet from the experimental observation which has a bullet-like shape. However, the droplet shape produced from Mesh-1 does not represent a real droplet shape from the experiment. In addition, it is observed that a thick diffusion layer at the phase boundary interface is observed for all meshing qualities. In reality, the interface between the two immiscible liquids is very sharp and the volume fraction should have sharp value either 0 or 1. The volume fraction value between 0 to 1 is only due to numerical diffusion which is due to numerical error by different meshing sizes. Low quality of mesh has the biggest grid size, hence showing highest numerical error where very thick diffusion layer can be observed at the liquid interfacial boundary layer of the droplet.

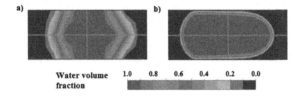

Fig. 3. Contour plot of droplet for (a) mesh-1, and (b) mesh-5.

Table 3 shows the detailed comparison of droplet length between simulation and experimental values at different meshing qualities for middle droplet case. It can be observed that, as the meshing quality increases, the length of the droplet also increases. By comparing with experimental value, the simulation result shows that the droplet length estimated in simulation is rather shorter than the real value. The highest quality meshing from Mesh-5 shows the best grid size condition where the deviation value compared between simulation and experiment is the lowest at −13% deviations. It must be observed that for the finest mesh-5, it took almost 14 days of calculation time until result is obtained which describes the augmented computational cost in terms of simulation time.

Table 3. Droplet length comparison with experimental value at different meshing qualities.

Name	Droplet length, (μm)		
	Simulation	Experiment [5]	Deviation (%)
Mesh-1	150	209	−28.2
Mesh-2	142	209	−32.1
Mesh-3	158	209	−24.4
Mesh-4	162	209	−22.5
Mesh-5	180	209	−13.9

3.2 Wall Boundary Mesh Refinement

According to literature [12], it was found that, there exists thin layer of continuous phase at the wall of microchannel encapsulating the droplet. This thin layer is also believed to be a factor that transforms the droplet into a bullet-liked shape inside a microchannel. Due to this, the mesh at the wall boundary is refined to create thin layer phenomenon inside a microchannel. Figure 4 illustrates one example of mesh wall refinement with 3 layers at both sides of the microchannel. Number of wall refinement layer has been varied from single to multiple layers to investigate an optimum number of layer/s required for the droplet case. In this wall refinement study, Mesh-3 has been used because it has moderate meshing quality between coarsest and finest mesh hence moderate computational cost.

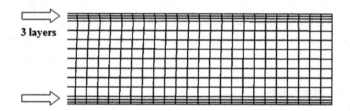

Fig. 4. Wall boundary mesh refinement with 3 layers.

From the result shown in Fig. 5, it can be observed that the shape of droplet has been significantly improved by adding even only one layer of wall refinement at the microchannel wall. The thin layer at the wall is very small, so for a coarse mesh like mesh-1, the grid size at the wall is still too big to simulate thin continuous phase layer near to the microchannel wall, hence giving inaccurate shape of the droplet. It can be understood here that there is a minimum size of grid that should be generated at the wall and in this case, it must be smaller than 6 μm thick.

Table 4 shows the quantitative analysis of the droplet length at different number of layers added for the wall refinement. The trend shows that, as the number of layers increases, the length of droplet will also increase and reaches the exact value from experiment. Although by adding many number layers at the wall, it must be noticed that adding more number of layer will also increasing the value of aspect ratio of total

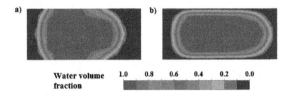

Fig. 5. Contour plot comparison between (a) without, and (b) with 1 layer wall mesh refinement.

Table 4. Droplet length comparison with experimental value for mesh-3 at different number of layers.

Number of layer	Droplet length, (μm)		
	Simulation	Experiment [5]	Deviation (%)
No-layer	158	209	−24.4
1-layer	182	209	−12.9
2-layers	180	209	−13.9
3-layers	184	209	−12.0
4-layers	186	209	−11.0
5-layers	194	209	−7.2

mesh. High value of aspect ratio bigger than 1 is not good because it gives numerical error and instability for example in the convergent issue. A good control of grid growth rate at the wall refinement is also important to avoid having high aspect ratio value. For example, in this case, the growth rate for the wall refinement was taken from 1.5 to 1.8 only.

3.3 Droplet Size Cases

After the best grid size and mesh condition has been found, all different droplet size cases are validated with experimental result using the lowest and highest quality of mesh with additional layers of mesh refinement at the wall. Only three layers of mesh wall refinement have been added at the wall to balance between accuracy and computational cost. As can be seen in Fig. 6, at different volumetric flow conditions (see Table 1), the size of the droplet formed is also different. As the water-to-oil ratio increases, the droplet size is also increases. This observation is exactly similar with the experimental observation from Garstecki et al. [5]. For a validation to be investigated more accurately, the quantitative measurement of the droplet length has been compared as shown in Table 5.

From this result, the highest meshing quality of Mesh-5 with three additional layers of mesh refinement at the wall gives almost similar length with the experimental value for all the droplet size cases. In general, the length deviations between the simulation and experimental values are ±5% and this shows very good agreement especially in

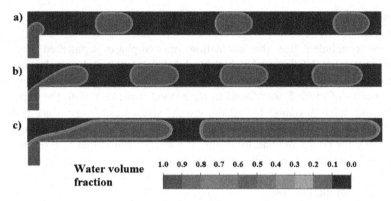

Fig. 6. Contour plot of droplet at different droplet sizes; (a) short, (b) middle and (c) long droplets.

Table 5. Summary of droplet length comparison at different droplet sizes and meshing qualities.

Droplet name	Meshing type	Droplet length, (μm)		
		Simulation	Exp. [5]	Dev. (%)
Short ($L_d \leq 2w_c$)	Mesh1 + 3L	130	161	−19.3
	Mesh5 + 3L	154		−4.3
Middle ($2w_c < L_d \leq 6w_c$)	Mesh1 + 3L	170	209	−18.7
	Mesh5 + 3L	214		+2.4
Long ($L_d > 6w_c$)	Mesh1 + 3L	506	1058	−52.2
	Mesh5 + 3L	1024		−3.2

micro scale measurement. It is also important to observe here that even at the lowest meshing quality, the deviation is still at an acceptable value of below ±20%. The only requirement for using the coarsest mesh is to have an additional layer of mesh refinement at the wall with at least 1 layer. This information is important because by understanding the acceptability of simulation result accuracy, one can have judgement of using coarse mesh in the simulation to have a fast result in the case of preliminary step analysis.

It has also been observed that the usage of coarse mesh for preliminary analysis is only applicable for short and middle size droplet and not for droplet longer than $6w_c$. This is because when the ratio of water-to-oil is higher than 4, it has been observed that in the current microchannel length, the droplet cannot be formed instead of creating a continuous parallel flow of lamellae structure. This can be due to the large velocity differences between the phases and the VOF model with CSF model for force term has the limitation of the shared-fields approximation to compute accurately near the velocity of phases at the interface [10]. All in all, the model is found to have a good agreement with the experimental value by using a right condition of grid size and meshing strategy. And by understanding the result accuracy level from a coarse mesh, one can have strategy in obtaining fast simulation results such as adding mesh refinement at the wall and still having an acceptable accuracy result.

4 Conclusion

It can be concluded that the simulation of two-phase segmented flow inside microchannel using VOF model is highly grid dependent simulation. No asymptotic value found even at the finest mesh of the smallest grid size generated. However, the highest quality of mesh-5 was found to have good agreement with the experimental result having ±5% deviation for all the droplet size cases. A necessary addition of mesh layer refinement must be made at the wall of the microchannel to improve the mesh quality for better simulation results. It was also found that at the lowest mesh quality, the simulation was still giving realistic result with an acceptable accuracy value. Therefore, an optimum grid size can always be strategized to balance between accuracy and simulation cost.

References

1. Wen, Z., Yu, X., Tu, S.-T., Yan, J., Dahlquist, E.: Intensification of biodiesel synthesis using zigzag micro-channel reactors. Bioresour. Technol. **100**, 3054–3060 (2009)
2. Aghel, B., Rahimi, M., Sepahvand, A., Alitabar, M., Ghasempour, H.R.: Using a wire coil insert for biodiesel production enhancement in a microreactor. Energy Convers. Manag. **84**, 541–549 (2014)
3. Rahimi, M., Aghel, B., Alitabar, M., Sepahvand, A., Ghasempour, H.R.: Optimization of biodiesel production from soybean oil in a microreactor. Energy Convers. Manag. **79**, 599–605 (2014)
4. Antony, R., Giri Nandagopal, M.S., Sreekumar, N., Rangabhashiyam, S., Selvaraju, N.: Liquid-liquid slug flow in a microchannel reactor and its mass transfer properties - a review. Bull. Chem. React. Eng. Catal. **9**, 207–223 (2014)
5. Garstecki, P., Fuerstman, M.J., Stone, H.A., Whitesides, G.M.: Formation of droplets and bubbles in a microfluidic T-junction-scaling and mechanism of break-up. Lab Chip **6**, 437–446 (2006)
6. Xu, J.H., Luo, G.S., Li, S.W., Chen, G.G.: Shear force induced monodisperse droplet formation in a microfluidic device by controlling wetting properties. Lab Chip **6**, 131–136 (2006)
7. Lan, W., Li, S., Wang, Y., Luo, G.: CFD simulation of droplet formation in microchannels by a modified level set method. Ind. Eng. Chem. Res. **53**, 4913–4921 (2014)
8. Soh, G.Y., Yeoh, G.H., Timchenko, V.: Improved volume-of-fluid (VOF) model for predictions of velocity fields and droplet lengths in microchannels. Flow Meas. Instrum. **51**, 105–115 (2016)
9. van Sint Annaland, M., Dijkhuizen, W., Deen, N.G., Kuipers, J.A.M.: Numerical simulation of behavior of gas bubbles using a 3-D front-tracking method. AIChE J. **52**, 99–110 (2006)
10. ANSYS Inc.: Fluent 15.0 Theory Guide, Canonsburg, PA (2011)
11. Brackbill, J.U., Kothe, D.B., Zemach, C.: A continuum method for modeling surface tension1. J. Comput. Phys. **100**, 335–354 (1992)
12. Arsenjuk, L., Kaske, F., Franzke, J., Agar, D.W.: Experimental investigation of wall film renewal in liquid–liquid slug flow. Int. J. Multiph. Flow **85**, 177–185 (2016)

A Framework of Multi-method Modelling Using System Dynamics and Enhanced Analytic Hierarchy Process Towards the Solution for Tobacco Endgame

Tisya Farida Abdul Halim[(⊠)], Hasimah Sapiri,
and Norhaslinda Zainal Abidin

School of Quantitative Sciences, College of Arts and Sciences,
Universiti Utara Malaysia, 06010 Sintok, Kedah, Malaysia
s96176@student.uum.edu.my

Abstract. Tobacco endgame is hotly debated worldwide as one of the effort by the World Health Organization Framework Convention on Tobacco Control (WHO FCTC) towards tobacco-free future. Tobacco epidemic involve dynamic interrelationships between multi-disciplinary elements. Hence, it become increasingly difficult to identify the root of the problem in order to solve the issues. System dynamics (SD) has been recognized with its ability to capture the flow and feedback as well as the dynamic relationships between components in a system under study. The holistic view offered by SD will portray the impact of anti-smoking strategies implementation. In order to identify the driving forces in tobacco epidemic, Enhanced Analytic Hierarchy Process (EAHP) has advantages over normal Analytic Hierarchy Process (AHP) based on its capability to eliminate inconsistency in prioritizing the driving forces in tobacco epidemic which is the initiation factors of smoking. SD and EAHP have different strengths and weaknesses, therefore, integrating both modelling approaches will provide more realistic projections of a tobacco control system. This paper uses SD and EAHP to model the complexity of the problem and to identify the dominant linkages between the initiation factors and anti-smoking strategies in assessing the effectiveness of anti-smoking strategies that have been implemented in Malaysia. We proposed a multi-method modelling framework that served as a basis in understanding the complexity of tobacco epidemic due to the interconnections of multiple elements that may range from qualitative to quantitative aspects. Also, we describe the potential benefits of integrating SD and EAHP in demonstrating the interaction between the smoking causes (initiation factors) and its corrector (anti-smoking strategies).

Keywords: Tobacco control · System dynamics · Enhanced Analytic Hierarchy Process

1 Introduction

Tobacco control has marked several distinguished positive changes in the last 50 years worldwide [1]. This is due to the full implementation of World Health Organization Framework Convention on Tobacco Control (WHO FCTC) which shows positive

© Springer Nature Singapore Pte Ltd. 2017
M.S. Mohamed Ali et al. (Eds.): AsiaSim 2017, Part I, CCIS 751, pp. 345–355, 2017.
DOI: 10.1007/978-981-10-6463-0_30

changes in reducing smoking prevalence. It is believe that tobacco epidemic likely to be ended by today's evidence. Therefore, WHO FCTC sets out to achieve an endgame of tobacco worldwide by the year 2040 [2]. In line with the mission, Malaysia as one of the WHO treaty signatories is obliged to implement various strategies to reduce smoking prevalence as an effort to accelerate the worldwide tobacco-free mission by the year 2040. Policy makers are looking and trying to find an effective ways to achieve the endgame of tobacco. However, difficulties arise when several attempts were made to implement the policies. The difficulties were believed due to the nature of tobacco epidemic which is inherently complex as it involves multi-disciplinary interrelationship among the related elements [3, 4].

The driving forces in tobacco epidemic is the initiation factors [3]. The process of becoming a smoker starts with first trial due to curiosity or initiation which usually occurs at the presence of friends. Along this trial stage, if the individual continues to smoke repeatedly (either on regular basis or non-regular basis), then they are called experimenter smoker. Regular smoker will smoke regularly either daily, weekly or monthly. However, non-regular smoker or social smoker will smoke only during specific situations or specific events. Any initiatives or interventions that aims to discourage the initiation process is considered as prevention of smoking. On the other hand, various correctors (anti-smoking strategies) have been implemented to help reducing smoking habit. WHO FCTC introduced MPOWER strategy to reduce smoking prevalence. MPOWER is an acronym for **M**onitor tobacco use and prevention policies, **P**rotect people from tobacco smoke, **O**ffer help to quit tobacco use, **W**arn about the dangers of tobacco, **E**nforce bans on tobacco advertising, promotion and sponsorship and **R**aise taxes on tobacco [2].

Despite various anti-smoking strategies have been implemented, the statistics shows that the smoking prevalence rate is still high [5]. Hence, when referring to MPOWER, the situation arises a question such as "Which is the most effective strategies to be implemented and should be emphasized in reducing smoking prevalence?". This situation required a specific tool that is able to capture the holistic view of the problem as well as considering the feedback process elements involved in the problem. Therefore, this situation calls for multi-method modelling. One of the effective approach to explore the dynamic complexity of tobacco epidemic is by developing a simulation model that could be used to better understand the holistic structure and its interactions in order to find the solution to the smoking problem. With this model, the causes as well as the correctors are prioritized and the dynamicity of the system are simulated which can assist policy makers to make better decisions.

The remainder of this paper is organized as follows. Section 2 is dedicated to the discussion of previous works related to tobacco modelling using System Dynamics (SD). The following section presents an overview of Enhanced Analytic Hierarchy Process (EAHP). Section 4 describes the proposed framework and followed by explanation of the hypothetical framework. The final section provides a summary of the paper.

2 Tobacco Modelling Using System Dynamics

To date, there are seven SD studies that have been found in the literatures that relevant to various tobacco issues. The earliest study is initiated in 1979 by Roberts et al. [4]. They modelled the complex smoking interactions that focus on the initiation to smoke and motivation to quit. The initiation factors include societal approval, tobacco industry lobbying and promotional expenditures. Accordingly, Ahmad and Billimek developed a model to evaluate the cost-effectiveness of adjusting the state's legal smoking age to 21 [6]. This study focused more on medical care cost. However, a remarkable notion from this study is the measurement of health gains by calculating quality-adjusted life years (QALYS) as the outcome. The QALYS concept combines improvements in length of life and health-related quality of life into a single measure, as recommended by the US Task Force on cost-effectiveness in health and medicine.

However, the study by takes the initiative to develop a tobacco model which provide insights into the overall tobacco control system [7]. This study extends the previous study which only focus on separated components.

In New Zealand, Cavana and Tobias developed an SD model to study the consequences of tobacco control policies [8]. In assessing the best strategies to implement the policies, four scenarios are simulated. These scenarios are business as usual, fiscal strategies which includes less affordable cigarettes, harm minimization that includes less addictive cigarettes and less toxic cigarettes and a combination of all three scenarios.

On the other hand, Hirsch et al. explored the potential impacts of various interventions strategies to reduce the country's cardiovascular burden that is incorporated and track the effects of those risk factors over time on both first-time and recurrent events [9]. This is due to the strenuous efforts in planning and selecting the programs for prevention and treatment of cardiovascular disease. It becomes a challenge to every community to fully-utilized their limited resources.

Studies on tobacco was further explored by a group of tobacco researchers [10]. The developed SimSmoke model simulate the dynamic consequences of smoking, smoking-related mortality and the effects of those policies towards reducing tobacco consumption. The work is applied and has been tested in almost 33 countries. However, the linkages between the smoking causes and the corrector to reduce smoking prevalence were not highlighted.

Finally, another group of tobacco researchers developed a theory of societal life-cycle of smoking by using a parsimonious set of feedback loops to capture historical trends and explore future scenarios [11]. In this study, the time horizon is expanded to be 110 years start from the year 1900 to 2010. They claimed that in order to get the best imitation in SD model, the time horizon should be extended backwards, far enough to capture the real behaviour of the problem. However, previously mentioned tobacco studies used a maximum of 35 years as the time horizon [4, 6–8, 10, 11].

3 The Concept of Enhanced Analytic Hierarchy Process: An Overview

Multi-criteria Decision Making (MCDM) is one of the operation research approach that deals with prioritization issues. These approaches are specifically used for decision making which offers ways to determine the meaningful priority values to multiple decision criteria. Among the examples of MCDM include Analytic Network Process (ANP), Analytic Hierarchy Process (AHP) and Potentially All Pairwise Rankings of All Possible Alternatives (PAPRIKA). These methods are widely used across many disciplines to determine the degree of importance of conflicting criteria in solving complex decision making.

MCDM is widely used due to its systematic decision making in analysing the criteria in highly complex problems [12]. To the best of author's knowledge, there is a limited study on tobacco which employs MCDM approaches. However, there is one relevant study that employed AHP to explore the associated factors and prioritized the factors of smoking among teenagers in Korea [13]. This study used AHP to prioritize the factors of smoking among teenagers as well as prioritizing the anti-smoking strategies.

In AHP, consistency ratio (CR) will measure the degree of consistency of the pairwise comparison judgments provided by the decision maker. It is generally acknowledged that the major drawback of AHP is inconsistency issues, where CR is more than 0.1. If the CR value is more than 0.1, then the decision maker needs to revise the pairwise comparison. Therefore, Balhuwaisl deals with this inconsistency by introducing the pre-evaluation step prior to conducting pairwise comparison procedures in normal AHP by Saaty [14]. The Enhanced Analytic Hierarchy Process (EAHP) suggested approach by Balhuwaisl is believed to produce a CR value of less than 0.1.

4   The Proposed Framework

The basic idea of the proposed framework was derived from the SD methodology as outlined by Sterman comprising problem identification, dynamic hypothesis development, model development, model testing and policy design and evaluation [15]. In tobacco studies, the developed model should incorporate the dynamic relationships among the elements. This is where the SD and EAHP modelling can fit in. Integration of both approaches is able to grasp the importance of the elements in the holistic view simultaneously. The initiation factors as well as the anti-smoking strategies will be prioritized using EAHP. Output from EAHP model will be passed down to SD model to demonstrate the feedback effects of elements in the system. In order to capture the dynamic complexity of tobacco epidemic, the proposed framework named SimPOS-moke, is illustrated in Fig. 1 below.

Stage 1: Problem Identification
There are five main stages in this framework including problem identification, dynamic hypothesis development, model development, model testing and policy design and evaluation. In problem identification stage, EAHP is expected to prioritize the initiation factors and anti-smoking strategies where the output will be used in the simulation model development. Prioritization step starts with problem decomposition. Research problem is decomposed into goal, criteria, sub-criteria and decision alternatives.

Step 1: Problem Decomposition
This step starts with identification of the research problem or initial characterization. Research problem is decomposed into goal, criteria and decision alternatives. Goal is

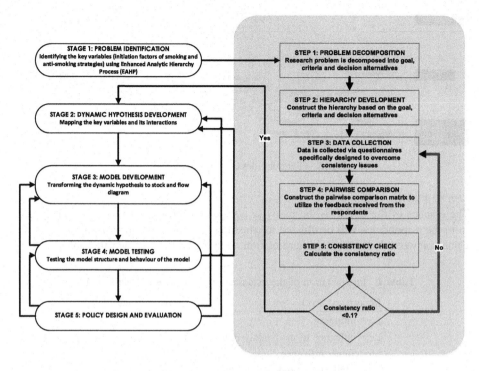

Fig. 1. Proposed framework of SimPOSmoke.

the overall objective to be achieve. There are several options to achieve the goal, the options are called decision alternatives. However, the available decision alternatives can be measured based on several criteria.

Step 2: Hierarchy Development
In this study, the goal is to choose the most effective anti-smoking strategies. There are five anti-smoking strategies have been implemented in Malaysia such as packaging and labelling, increase in pricing and taxation of tobacco products, promote mass media campaign, imposing smoke-free legislation, and promoting education and support. The anti-smoking strategies were set as the decision alternatives. The anti-smoking strategies were measured by the initiation factors of smoking which was leveled as criteria. The identified criteria were personal beliefs and values, personal psychological, family influence, psychosocial influence, culture and legislative. The classification of the criteria was based on the Theory of Triadic Influence as outlined by [3]. The hierarchy can be illustrated as Fig. 2 below.

Step 3: Data Collection
Aset of questionnaire is used to obtain the input data. The respondents are the tobacco experts from Ministry of Health Malaysia. The questionnaire is specifically designed to simplify the tedious pairwise comparison and to overcome inconsistency issues [14].

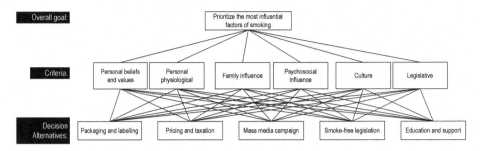

Fig. 2. Hierarchy development of tobacco.

Step 4: Pairwise Comparison
The essence of the EAHP is the pairwise comparison process. The feedback received from the respondents will be utilized to construct the pairwise comparison matrix, with values between 1 and 9. The interpretation of the values are shown in Table 1.

Table 1. Interpretation of the values used in pairwise comparison [14].

Importance level	Numerical value
Less influence	1
Less influence to moderately influence	2
Moderately influence	3
Moderately to strongly influence	4
Strongly influence	5
Strongly to very strongly influence	6
Very strongly influence	7
Very strongly to extremely influence	8
Extremely influence	9

The pairwise comparison is formed to obtain the weights for the criteria. The entry in row $i = 1, 2, ..., j$ and column m of the matrix are labelled with y_{im} to indicate how much more or less important is criterion i as compared to criterion m. Then, the criterion i is rated as a_i and criterion m as a_m. Then,

if $i \leq m$
let $b = a_i - a_m$
if $b < 0$, then $y_{im} = \frac{1}{1-b}$
if $b = 0$, then $y_{im} = 1$
if $b > 0$, then $y_{im} = b + 1$

where, y_{im}, the entries in the matrix.
All the data collected are transformed into a pairwise comparison matrix.

Step 5: Consistency Check
Next, the EAHP provides a measure of consistency for the pairwise comparisons by computing a consistency ratio (CR). This is a crucial process in AHP as this will measure the degree of consistency of the judgments provided by the decision maker.

The values of consistency ratio is determined as follows:

$$CR > 0.10 \longrightarrow \text{inconsistent}$$
$$CR < 0.10 \longrightarrow \text{consistent}$$

The CR should be below 0.1 for a reliable result. However, CR > 0.1 indicates that the pair wise judgments are just about random and are completely untrustworthy.

Stage 2: Dynamic Hypothesis Development

In this stage, the dynamic hypothesis of the tobacco model system is developed prior to the prioritization of the key variables. Sterman defines dynamic hypothesis as the theory on how the problem developed [15]. The dynamic hypothesis is mapped using subsystem diagram since the tobacco epidemic is made of several interrelated sub-system. The subsystem diagram is presented in Fig. 3.

In the subsystem diagram of tobacco model, there are six sectors which are initiation factors of smoking, population, smoking-related diseases, smoking-related mortality, healthcare expenditure and tobacco control strategies. The population in Malaysia was divided into potential smokers, current smokers and ex-smokers. Each types of smokers were further classified into youths and adults. Never smokers were people who never smoke, current smokers were those who were currently smoking and ex-smokers were the ones who had already quit smoking. The direction of the arrow in the diagram indicated that the initiation factors of smoking influenced the population. Similarly, it can be observed that smokers were exposed to smoking-related diseases such as lung cancer, ischaemic heart disease, cerebrovascular disease and chronic lower respiratory. Further observation from the diagram indicates that smoking-related diseases then can led to premature mortality. This implies that any changes in the number of smoking-related diseases cases will affect the number of premature mortality due to smoking. Furthermore, the changes in the number of smokers in the population sector will affect the number of smoking-related diseases and also the healthcare expenditure of those diseases. Generally, the government would allocate certain amount of budget for smoking-related diseases. If the number of people diagnosed with smoking-related diseases increases, the healthcare expenditure and smoking-related mortality will also increase. Therefore, various prevention strategies such as packaging and labelling, pricing and taxation, mass media campaign, smoke-free legislation as well as education and support should be implemented to overcome the problem of growing trend of smoking population in Malaysia.

Stage 3: Model Development

Next, the stock and flow model is developed based on the subsystem diagram that has been developed using SD software. There are several available options regarding software packages to assist SD modeling and analysis, such as Dysmap, Cosmic, Vensim, Stella, Powersim and i-Think. In this study, the SD model will be aided by using the Vensim software package. The Vensim software is deemed as user-friendly, highly flexible and has a visual insight into elements of the developed model. The developed model can also be adjusted and rerun at numerous times. Thus, it provides an interactive process for model construction and it can improves the simulated model. Figure 4 presented a population sector of SimPOSmoke model which consists both of youths and adults that have been developed using Vensim.

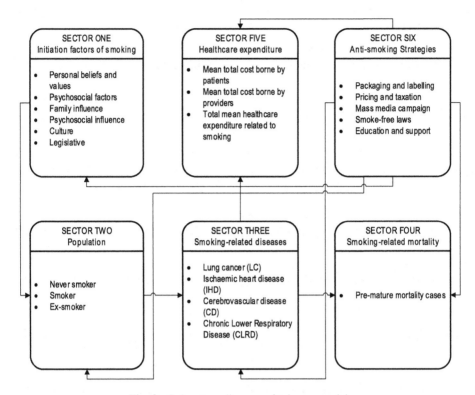

Fig. 3. Subsystem diagram of tobacco model.

Stage 4: Model Testing

The model testing process starts as soon as the SD model has been developed. Model testing is a process to establish the robustness of the developed model [15–18]. The purpose of model testing is to uncover the model flaws and increase model confidence [15]. Generally, model testing is grouped into the structure and behaviour validity tests. The structure validity test aims to directly compare the structure of the real system with the developed model, without examining the relationships and behaviour of the model structure. In addition, the behaviour validity test aims to measure the accuracy of the developed model in order to replicate major behaviour of the real system [17].

Stage 5: Policy Design and Evaluation

Policy design and evaluation is conducted for model improvement after robustness of the model is validated [15]. Generally, model improvement can be categorized into sensitivity test and policy optimization. In this stage, the output from the prioritization stage using EAHP will be used in designing and evaluating policy. Moreover, it is expected that by the time the modellers reach this stage, the linkages between the causes and corrector has been identified.

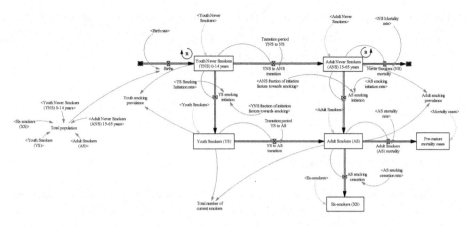

Fig. 4. Population sector of SimPOSmoke model.

5 Initial Results

The initial results obtained from the prioritization revealed that psychosocial influence was perceived as the most important factor associated with the initiation of smoking among adults in Malaysia. This is followed by personal physiological, culture, legislative, family influence and personal beliefs and values. While, the results also revealed that advertising was identified as the most effective strategy in combating tobacco consumption. These results are consistent with the study conducted by the International Tobacco Control Policy Evaluation Project in Malaysia which support that psychosocial influence is the most dominant smoking factor in initiating smoking habits among Malaysians. Meanwhile, the most effective strategy to reduce smoking prevalence is through advertising [5]. The EAHP ranking are illustrated in Tables 2 and 3 below.

In general, people smoke because they consider it sophisticated and socially acceptable supported by smoking habits of their peers. From the initial results obtained, it indicates that government should continue and strengthen mass media campaign strategy in order to cope with smoking habits.

Next, the weights obtained will be passed down to SD model to demonstrate the feedback effects of between interrelated elements in the tobacco system.

Table 2. The rank for the initiation factors of smoking based on the value of weights using EAHP.

Factors	Weights	Rank
Personal beliefs and values	0.0760	6
Personal physiological	0.1845	2
Family influence	0.1116	5
Psychosocial influence	0.2398	1
Culture	0.1303	3
Legislative	0.1156	4

Table 3. The rank for the anti-smoking strategies based on the value of weights using EAHP.

Strategies	Weights	Rank
Packaging and labelling	0.1774	5
Pricing and taxation	0.1889	4
Advertising	0.2216	1
Smoke-free legislation	0.1912	2
Education and support	0.1912	2

6 Conclusion and Future Works

This paper presents an on-going work of a hybrid simulation in tobacco modelling. The SD part is on modelling the stock and flow model and thus only initial part of the model is presented. Once the SD and EAHP models are completely integrated, we hope to see a bigger picture of tobacco modelling with penetration of prioritized key variables. It is expected that the output of the model will assist decision makers in analyzing the most effective anti-smoking strategies to be implemented in order to reach tobacco-free future by 2040.

Acknowledgments. The authors wish to thank the Department of Decision Science, School of Quantitative Sciences and Universiti Utara Malaysia (UUM), Malaysia, for their financial support to carry out this research project. The project was funded under the Fundamental Research Grant Scheme (FRGS) Grant No. 12902.

References

1. Eriksen, M., Mackay, J., Schluger, N., Gomeshtapeh, F.I., Drope, J.: The Tobacco Atlas, 5th edn. (2015)
2. World Health Organization: Tobacco free initiative: why tobacco is a public health priority (2015). http://www.who.int/tobacco/health_priority/en/
3. Flay, B.R., Petraitis, J., Hu, F.B.: The theory of triadic influence: preliminary evidence related to alcohol and tobacco use. In: Fertig, J.B., Allen, J.P. (eds.) Research Monograph No 30 : Alcohol and Tobacco: From Basic to Clinical Practice, pp. 37–59 (1995)
4. Roberts, E.B., Homer, J., Kasabian, A., Varrell, M.: A systems view of the smoking problem: perspective and limitations of the role of science in decision-making. Int. J. Biomed. Comput. **13**(1), 69–86 (1982). https://doi.org/10.1016/0020-7101(82)90051-4
5. ITC Project, & International Tobacco Control: ITC Malaysia National Report. Findings from wave 1 to 4 Surveys (2005–2009) (2012)
6. Ahmad, S., Billimek, J.: Estimating the health impacts of tobacco harm reduction policies: a simulation modeling approach. Risk Anal. **25**(4), 801–812 (2005). https://doi.org/10.1111/j.1539-6924.2005.00647.x
7. Richardson, G.P.: How to anticipate change in tobacco control systems. In: Cancercontrol. Cancer.Gov, pp. 109–114. National Cancer Institute (2007). http://www.cancercontrol.cancer.gov/tcrb/monographs/18/m18_5.pdf

8. Cavana, R.Y., Tobia, M.: Integrated system dynamics: analysis of policy options for tobacco control in New Zealand. In: International System Dynamics Conference, pp. 1–24 (2007). https://doi.org/10.1002/sres.934

9. Hirsch, G.B., Homer, J., Evans, E., Zielinski, A.: A system dynamics model for planning cardiovascular disease interventions. Am. J. Public Health **100**(4), 616–622 (2010). https://doi.org/10.2105/AJPH.2009.159434

10. Levy, D.T., Cho, S.I., Kim, Y.M., Park, S., Suh, M.K., Kam, S.: SimSmoke model evaluation of the effect of tobacco control policies in Korea: the unknown success story. Am. J. Public Health **100**(7), 1267–1273 (2010). https://doi.org/10.2105/AJPH.2009.166900

11. Zagonel, A., Mojtahedzadeh, M., Richardson, G., Brodsky, N.S., Brown, T., Conrad, S., Glass, R.: Developing a theory of the societal lifecycle of cigarette smoking: explaining & anticipating trends using information feedback. In Proceedings of the 29th International Conference of the System Dynamics Society (2011)

12. Aruldoss, M., Lakshmi, M., Ventakesan, P.: A survey on multi criteria decision making methods and its applications. Am. J. Inf. Syst. **1**(1), 31–43 (2013). https://doi.org/10.12691/ajis-1-1-5

13. Matsuda, S.: How do the Japanese medical students evaluate the effectiveness of anti-smoking strategies?- an application of the analytic hierarchy process. Environ. Health Prev. Med. **3**(2), 73–77 (1998). https://doi.org/10.1007/BF02931787

14. Balhuwaisl, M.A.S.: An integration of rank order centroid, modified analytical hierarchy process and 0–1 integer programming in solving a facility location problem. Universiti Utara Malaysia (2013). http://etd.uum.edu.my/3862/

15. Sterman, J.: Business Dynamics: Systems Thinking and Modelling for a Complex World. McGraw-Hill, New York City (2000)

16. Barlas, Y.: Model validation in system dynamics. In: Proceedings of the 1994 International System Dynamics Conference (1994a). https://doi.org/10.1002/(SICI)1099-1727(199623)12:3<183::AID-SDR103>3.0.CO;2-4

17. Barlas, Y.: Model validation in system dynamics **12**(3), 183–210 (1994b). https://doi.org/10.1002/(SICI)1099-1727(199623)12:3<183::AID-SDR103>3.0.CO;2-4

18. Forrester, J.W., Senge, P.M.: Tests for building confidence in system dynamics models (1980)

A Stock Market Trading System Using Deep Neural Network

Bang Xiang Yong$^{(\boxtimes)}$, Mohd Rozaini Abdul Rahim,
and Ahmad Shahidan Abdullah

Faculty of Electrical Engineering, Universiti Teknologi Malaysia,
81310 Skudai, Johor, Malaysia
yongbangxiang@gmail.com, mrozaini.ar@gmail.com,
ashahidan@utm.my

Abstract. The stock market prediction is a lucrative field of interest with promising profit and covered with landmines for the unprecedented. The markets are complex, non-linear and chaotic in nature which poses huge difficulties to predict the prices accurately. In this paper, a stock trading system utilizing feed-forward deep neural network (DNN) to forecast index price of Singapore stock market using the FTSE Straits Time Index (STI) in t days ahead is proposed and tested through market simulations on historical daily prices. There are 40 input nodes of DNN which are the past 10 days' opening, closing, minimum and maximum prices and consist of 3 hidden layers with 10 neurons per layer. The training algorithm used is stochastic gradient descent with back-propagation and is accelerated with multi-core processing. A trading system is proposed which utilizes the DNN forecasting results with defined entry and exit rules to enter a trade. DNN performance is evaluated using RMSE and MAPE. The overall trading system shows promising results with a profit factor of 18.67, 70.83% profitable trades and Sharpe ratio of 5.34 based on market simulation on test data.

Keywords: Deep learning · Stock market prediction · Trading system

1 Introduction

Stock market prediction remains a lucrative field of research with promising profits for investors and researchers. However, there are challenges in predicting the stock markets accurately and precisely as the markets are complex, non-linear and chaotic in nature which calls for more powerful methods to tackle this problem.

Many artificial intelligence methods have been employed to predict stock market prices. Artificial neural networks (ANN) remain a popular choice for this task and are widely studied [1] and have been shown to exhibit good performance [2].

More recently, deep learning has emerged an improved method over conventional neural networks for various applications such as recognition system, natural language processing and medical sciences and has shown astonishing results [3]. It has also been applied in financial markets for prediction of stock prices using textual news data and numerical data [4, 5]. Experiment has been conducted to test its profitability and

© Springer Nature Singapore Pte Ltd. 2017
M.S. Mohamed Ali et al. (Eds.): AsiaSim 2017, Part I, CCIS 751, pp. 356–364, 2017.
DOI: 10.1007/978-981-10-6463-0_31

performance as a trading system in the stock and commodity market [6]. However, there is still a lack of studies conducted on the usage of deep learning as an integral part of a trading system.

In this paper, we propose a trading system for stock market which utilizes the prediction of DNN to generate trading signals, and evaluate its performance in the stock market as an attempt to convert the DNN predictions into a profitable system.

2 Methodology

This section describes the data set, process of training and testing the deep neural network and trading rules applied on the prediction output to test the profitability of the trading system.

2.1 Data Set

The data set used throughout this study consists of historical data of the opening, closing, maximum and minimum prices of FTSE Straits Time Index (STI) which is deemed to be the barometer of Singapore stock market. The opening price is the price at the beginning of the day. The closing price is the price at the end of the day. As the price fluctuates throughout the day, there is a maximum and minimum price which is recorded. Each time series data of stock ranged from 1st January 2010 until 3rd January 2017 with a period of 1769 days where the market is open. They were obtained from Yahoo Finance. The dataset is split into train and test sets with 75–25 ratio whereby evaluations are conducted using the test sets.

2.2 Deep Neural Network

Deep neural network is a special type of artificial neural network characterized by its architecture which consists of higher number of hidden layers and neurons compared to conventional neural network. Higher number of hidden layers exhibits increased capability of high-level features extraction for every added hidden layer [7]. Hence, the raw input data is not required to be pre-processed using features extraction methods compared to conventional neural network.

The principle for forecasting is based on windowing method, that is to use the opening, closing, maximum and minimum prices of $n - 1, n - 2, \dots n - 10$ days as inputs to the DNN to output the predicted closing price of t days ahead. The number of prior working days is selected based on [8] which has shown promising results. Multiple models need to be trained for every forecast of t days ahead.

In this paper, the architecture of DNN comprises of an input layer with 40 input nodes, 3 hidden layers with the composition of 10-10-10 neurons respectively and an output layer with a single node which outputs the stock price in t days ahead. The DNN architecture is depicted in Fig. 1.

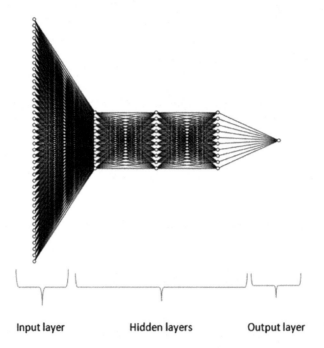

Input layer   Hidden layers   Output layer

Fig. 1. Feed-forward deep neural network architecture used for prediction model of stock price of $n + t$ day.

2.3   Network Training

Stochastic gradient descent and back-propagation is used as the learning algorithm. Training the DNN is an expensive process with 40 input variables and high number of neurons. To address this issue, multi-core processing method is used using Hogwild algorithm [9], which is a lock-free parallelization scheme whereby each core handles separate subsets of the training data. The result of training DNN is a forecast model which can be used to predict the closing price of $n + t$ day.

2.4   Proposed Trading System

The rules of a trading system tell the investor when to buy or sell the stocks which will result in a profitable trade. The proposed trading system uses the results of predicted closing stock prices of n, $n + 1$ and $n + 2$ days.

The proposed trading rules employ the logic of buying stocks when the forecasted closing price is higher than the current opening price, and selling all stocks (if any) in possession if the forecasted closing price is lower than current opening price. The effect of trading rules was investigated using different combination of $n + t$ day forecast. Let $close_t$ be the predicted closing price at $n + t$ day and $open$ be the opening price of n-th day. Trading rules used are divided into entry and exit rules. Different entry rules are proposed to be tested on the trading system to compare its performance. The trading rules used are as follows:

Entry rules:

(1) Buy when $close_0 > open$
(2) Buy when $close_0$ and $close_1 > open$
(3) Buy when $close_0$ and $close_1$ and $close_2 > open$
(4) Buy when $close_0$ and $close_1$ and $close_2$ and $close_3 > open$
(5) Buy when $close_0$ and $close_1$ and $close_2$ and $close_3$ and $close_4 > open$

Exit rule:

(1) Sell all when $close_0 > open$

It is important to note that the proposed trading system do not consider the option of shorting stocks. For each buy signal, an equal amount of stock is bought. Also, the system allows stacking of bought stocks for consecutive buy signals, and sells all stocks in account for any sell signal. If there is no stock in hand when a sell signal is met, the system does nothing.

3   Results

The evaluation is conducted on two components namely the stock prediction model and performance of trading system. All evaluations are performed on the testing set.

3.1   Evaluation of Stock Prediction Model

The predicted closing price for the testing sets are plotted on the graph to visualize the actual versus the predicted price as depicted in Figs. 2, 3, 4, 5 and 6.

Fig. 2. Prediction of STI stock price in n days.

Prediction of STI stock price in n+ 1 days

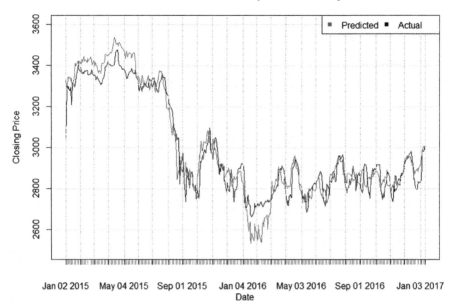

Fig. 3. Prediction of STI stock price in *n + 1* days.

Prediction of STI stock price in n+ 2 days

Fig. 4. Prediction of STI stock price in *n + 2* days.

Prediction of STI stock price in n+ 3 days

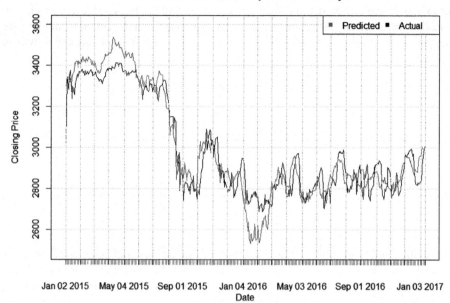

Fig. 5. Prediction of STI stock price in *n + 3* days.

Prediction of STI stock price in n+ 4 days

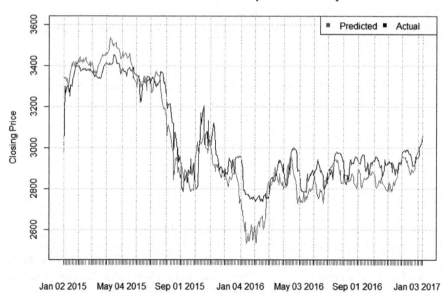

Fig. 6. Prediction of STI stock price in *n + 4* days.

The evaluation metrics used for the prediction models are the conventional root mean square error (RMSE) and mean absolute percentage error (MAPE) which is a statistical measure of prediction accuracy of a forecast model. Different models are compared for closing price of *n, n + 1, n + 2, n + 3, n + 4* days and are shown in Table 1.

Table 1. RMSE of closing stock price prediction models of t days ahead.

t (days)	RMSE	MAPE
0 (Today)	32.77	0.75
1	48.40	1.20
2	51.38	1.26
3	72.00	1.83
4	74.64	1.84

As the number of days increases for the forecast, the generalization error increases as well. This shows that it is less accurate to predict the price further into the future compared to more recent forecasts. Note that since the model uses windowing method, in the beginning of the time series where the past stock prices are not available, the prediction result is not available as well.

3.2   Evaluation of Trading System

The trading system is simulated on the test data using different entry rules as stated in the methodology. The metrics used are profit factor, Sharpe ratio and percentage of profitable trade and results are tabulated in Table 2.

Table 2. Performance of trading system using different entry rules.

Entry rule	Profit factor	Profitable trades (%)	Sharpe ratio
1	2.54	47.37	2.13
2	4.92	52.08	3.21
3	14.32	67.74	4.69
4	15.31	65.52	4.80
5	18.67	70.83	5.34

It is shown that the best performance is exhibited by using the entry rule 5 which enters a buy trade only when the forecasted closing prices of *n, n + 1, n + 2,... n + 4* day are higher than the opening price of n-th day. This can be attributed to the higher chance of entering a profitable trade if there is an upward trend and ultimately increases the profit factor. This shows that the trading system which uses multiple steps of prediction from deep neural network can be profitable for the investors.

The market simulation of the transactions made using the trading system and its cumulative return curve is shown in Fig. 7 where the green triangle depicts a buy signal and the red triangle depicts a sell signal.

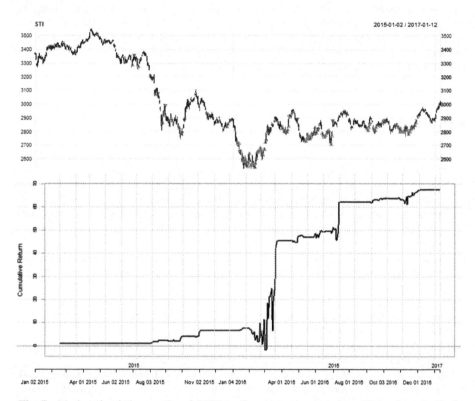

Fig. 7. Market simulation results of DNN trading system on test data. (Color figure online)

4 Conclusion

In this paper, a stock market trading system is proposed which uses deep neural network as part of its core components. The DNN uses historical data prices to forecast stock prices of t days ahead which is incorporated in the trading system to make buy and sell decisions. The effect of varying the number of steps of the forecast model was investigated and it is shown that the forecast further into the future yields less accurate results. The consequences of varying the trading rules were also studied and the trading system with best performance was determined to have a profit factor of 18.67, 70.83% profitable trades and Sharpe ratio of 5.34.

In the future, different types of deep learning algorithm can be investigated such as Deep Boltzmann machine and Deep Q-networks. Better trading rules can also be investigated by using more advanced methods such as evolutionary programming. There is also potential for using different inputs of data such as correlated commodity and currency value, and varying the time frames such as every minute or hourly data. There are huge potential for the expandability of this trading system and its robustness and reliability should also be tested on other stock markets.

Acknowledgement. The authors would like to thank all who contributed toward making this research successful. The authors wish to express their gratitude to Ministry of Higher Education (MOHE), Research Management Center (RMC) for the sponsorship, and Advanced Telecommunication Technology Research Group, Universiti Teknologi Malaysia for the financial support and advice for this project. (VOT number: Q.J130000.2623.12J82).

References

1. Vui, C.S., et al.: A review of stock market prediction with artificial neural network (ANN). In: 2013 IEEE International Conference on Control System, Computing and Engineering (2013)
2. Yetis, Y., Kaplan, H., Jamshidi, M.: Stock market prediction by using artificial neural network. In: 2014 World Automation Congress (WAC) (2014)
3. Soniya, S., Paul, S., Singh, L.: A review on advances in deep learning. In: 2015 IEEE Workshop on Computational Intelligence: Theories, Applications and Future Directions (WCI) (2015)
4. Akita, R., et al.: Deep learning for stock prediction using numerical and textual information. In: 2016 IEEE/ACIS 15th International Conference on Computer and Information Science (ICIS) (2016)
5. Day, M.Y., Lee, C.C.: Deep learning for financial sentiment analysis on finance news providers. In: 2016 IEEE/ACM International Conference on Advances in Social Networks Analysis and Mining (ASONAM) (2016)
6. Deng, Y., et al.: Deep direct reinforcement learning for financial signal representation and trading. IEEE Trans. Neural Netw. Learn. Syst. **PP**(99), 1–12 (2016)
7. Sun, Y., Wang, X., Tang, X.: Deep learning face representation from predicting 10,000 classes. In: Proceedings of the IEEE Conference on Computer Vision and Pattern Recognition (2014)
8. Moghaddam, A.H., Moghaddam, M.H., Esfandyari, M.: Stock market index prediction using artificial neural network. J. Econ. Finance Adm. Sci. **21**(41), 89–93 (2016)
9. Recht, B., et al.: Hogwild: a lock-free approach to parallelizing stochastic gradient descent. In: Advances in Neural Information Processing Systems (2011)

Hemorheology Based Traffic Congestion and Forecasting Model in the Internet of Vehicles

Nurshahrily Idura Ramli[(✉)] and Mohd Izani Mohamed Rawi

University Teknologi MARA, Shah Alam, Selangor, Malaysia
{idura,izani}@tmsk.uitm.edu.my

Abstract. Traffic congestion causes increased vehicular queuing, slower speeds and delay in travel time, continuously claiming many social, economic and environmental problems. While Internet of Vehicles (IoV) advances in equipping vehicles with sensors and actuators that 'communicates', classifying and forecasting traffic congestion in real-time and in fast mobility is a sizzling yet challenging research interest. In hemorheology, hypertension can be classified in stages to indicate severity levels, thus a similar analogy need to be tested in traffic to classify congestion levels. This paper attempts to develop a traffic congestion and forecasting model based on hypertension in hemorheology. Traffic congestion was simulated in the city of Shah Alam's urban area using SUMO urban vehicular mobility simulator. Results show promising and rational adaptation of hemorheology in classifying the severity levels of traffic congestion.

Keywords: Traffic congestion · Internet of Vehicles (IoV) · Hypertension · Hemorheology · SUMO

1 Introduction

Traffic congestion may be defined as a state of capacity demand whereby traffic flow is characterized by high densities and low speeds. Estimated economic losses of RM20 billion per year or RM54 million per day were reportedly caused by traffic congestion in Greater Kuala Lumpur. More than 250 h spent a year in traffic, yielding the total cost of traffic associated with lost productivity, wasted fuel costs and environmental destruction to 1.1–2.2% of GDP in 2014 [1].

Conventional techniques of improving existing roads and facilities are costly, not to mention often involves political, social and environmental issues. Alternately, many researchers are manipulating traffic information acquired from vehicles and infrastructure connected with sensing, actuation, data acquisition and communication systems, termed the Internet of Vehicles (IoV) [2].

While IoV advances, suitable traffic models are utilized to describe the change in the condition of the traffic flow in time and space involving speed, density, velocity and other traffic parameters. These parsed parameters are processed into meaningful traffic information to inform vehicles of the traffic conditions [2, 3].

© Springer Nature Singapore Pte Ltd. 2017
M.S. Mohamed Ali et al. (Eds.): AsiaSim 2017, Part I, CCIS 751, pp. 365–379, 2017.
DOI: 10.1007/978-981-10-6463-0_32

Associations of traffic flow models and continuum mechanics of Newtonian fluids has been well established [2, 4], however, little have been done with Non-Newtonian fluids, such as in hemorheology. In hemorheology, the congestion of blood flow or blood viscosity is a measure of the resistance of blood to flow. An analogy can be made that if blood cells (Non-Newtonian Fluid) are vehicles, then blood flow is traffic flow and blood viscosity is traffic congestion.

The premise of this research is concerned with developing a traffic congestion and forecasting model by means of mimicking hemorheology dynamics. The hypothesis is that if viscosity in blood flow is analogous to congestion in traffic, therefore classification of blood viscosity related diagnosis such as the hypertension levels could also be applied to classifying traffic congestion.

This paper is organized as follows: A review of the traffic flow theory will be provided in Sect. 2. In Sect. 3, we present overview of hypertension classification in hemorheology and in Sect. 4 we relate and present the analogies of traffic and hemorheology. Section 5 discusses the methodology and the simulation in testing the hypothesis of the relation and finally Sect. 6 discusses the results and future direction of this research in IoV.

2   Traffic Flow Theory

The traffic flow modelling involves the knowledge of the fundamental traffic flow dynamics and the associated analytical methods [5]. Fundamental characteristics are independent variables such as speed, density and flow are applied to analytical methods or models [3, 6]. The defined traffic parameters that is used in this work are presented in Table 1.

Table 1. Fundamental traffic parameters.

Traffic parameters	Definition	Expression
Speed	Define the speed of vehicle	$v(x,t)$
	Time-mean speed: The c passing a fixed point (x) over a time interval (t)	
	Space-mean speed: The harmonic mean speed of vehicles passing at a fixed point (x) on a highway over a time interval (t)	
Density	Defined as number of vehicles (ΔN) over a stretch of roadway (L) (in units of vehicles per kilometer)	$\rho(x,t) = Q(x,t)/v(x,t)$
Flow	Defined as the number of vehicles (ΔN) passing location (x) within a time interval (Δt)	$Q(x,t) = \rho(x,t)/v(x,t)$

2.1   Traffic Congestion Classification

The relationship constructed from flow, speed and density as presented in Table 1 forms a fundamental equation of traffic flow. When flow is plotted as a function of density, a fundamental diagram of traffic flow can be formed as depicted in Fig. 1 [3]. Clearly the relationship generates a parabolic synchronization of flow and density. Flow increases in parallel with density during the free flow duration until critical flow-density is reached. Flow will then start to decline proportionately with the inclination of density in critical density. During the declination of flow as opposed to density, the fundamental theory describes that objects in this region is in the unstable, congested state.

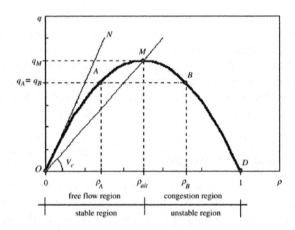

Fig. 1. Flow-density fundamental relationship [3].

The flow-density fundamental relationship as explained in [3] is as follows:

- *Point O refers to the case where both density and flow are zero.*
- *Point D refers to the maximum density, resulting when flow is zero.*
- *Point M refers to maximum flow indicating critical density and critical flow.*
- *Points A and B shows that different densities correspond to the same flow.*
- *The slope of the tangent line ON at point O gives the velocity at which a vehicle can travel when there is no flow.*
- *The slope of line OM gives the velocity Vc for the limit point.*
- *The region with densities lower than critical density is characterized by a constant velocity corresponding to the stable region (free flow region).*
- *The region in which densities are greater than the critical density corresponding to the unstable region (congestion region).*

In the direction of this proposed model, the fundamental relationship of flow-density is used as a base for classifying the traffic congestion levels. The data obtained from intra-vehicle communication will be aggregated and measured to obtain the current congestion level in the vicinity.

Recent works from [7–10] is using the same approach in gathering traffic information, however did not classify the severity of the congestion. A similar approach is proposed by [11] attempts to classify traffic based on three levels using Artificial Neural Network and further recommends a rerouting scheme for the users to take to

avoid traffic congestion. Although there are many researches and studies in manipulating traffic information to mitigate traffic congestion [12–15], calibrating traffic flow
modelling comprehensive of classifying traffic congestion levels in IoV is still rather
scarce, thus in need of much attention.

3 Hemorheology

Hemorheology is a medical field that studies the flow and the formed elements of
blood. Hemorheology also covers the study of deformation behavior of blood and
integrates the dynamic nature of blood flow and fluid flow behavior or fluid mechanics
[16]. Fluid mechanics has shown that for fluid in a pipe with a persistent diameter and
length, flow resistance is influenced by the flow conditions within the pipe. Experimental results yield that pressure is proportional to the speed of flow. It suggests that
resistance to flow would be the cause of slow flow [16, 17].

3.1 Hypertension in Hemorheology

The resistance or pressure in blood is recorded as two numbers; namely systolic blood
pressure and diastolic blood pressure. The systolic blood pressure is the measurement
of pressure when blood is exerting against artery walls whilst the heart is pumping
blood. Diastolic blood pressure is the amount of pressure exerting against the artery
walls while the heart is resting between beats [18, 19].

Measured in units of millimeters of mercury, or mm Hg, blood pressure reading are
categorized in stages implying the level of high blood pressure or hyper-tension [18, 20].
The higher the hypertension level or stages designate a greater need of medical attention.
High blood pressure stage 1 of reading 140/90 is associated with a significant risk of
cardiovascular diseases, and therefore medical attention is warranted [18].

Figure 2 generally presents the measurements of systolic and diastolic in determining the stages of blood pressure to indicate the hypertension level. The stages
evolve from normal to more severe, demanding greater medical attention to avoid
hypertensive crisis that could lead to a condition where the blood could not flow and

Blood Pressure Category	Systolic mm Hg (upper #)		Diastolic mm HG (lower #)
Normal	less than 120	and	less than 80
Prehypertension	120-139	or	80-89
High Blood Pressure (Hypertension) Stage 1	140-159	or	90-99
High Blood Pressure (Hypertension) Stage 2	160 or higher	or	100 or higher
Hypertensive Crisis (Emergency care needed)	Higher than 180	or	Higher than 110

Fig. 2. Hypertension levels in hemorheology [20].

the heart to stop. Blood flow in relation to the circulatory network system shares some similar attributes with traffic flow in vehicular network system. Viscosity in blood can be associated with density in traffic flow. The classification of hypertension therefore could be adapted to the fundamental relationship of flow-density in vehicular traffic to classify and forecast traffic congestion. The analogy of this relationship will be discussed in the following section.

4   The Traffic to Hemorheology Analogy

Although traffic flow and blood flow defines a different underlying physics, a definite similarity between the two is that both involves the movement of objects along a relatively one-dimensional pathway [21]. Mathematical models can be developed based on this similarity, adapting the nature or fundamental relationship of each domain [21]. Specifically in traffic theory and hemorheology, the motion of objects (vehicles or blood cells) is identified as the base of the model. Therefore, a model can be developed utilizing the dynamics of traffic and hemorheology based on the spatial and temporal variables.

In deriving the mathematical model from this basis, vehicles are assigned as the objects and the path as a road or highway. As traffic is a common problem to almost everyone, the mathematical results from the modelling could be easily related with the real-world application. Moreover, *"the theory for traffic flow is still not complete, so there are competing ideas that can be explored. However, it should be remembered that all of this material can be applied to other systems, such as the one dimensional motion of blood cells and molecules"* [21].

Table 2 presents the analogies associated with traffic flow dynamics and hemorheology. The analogies of the attributes in circulatory system of the human body and its similarity are rather clear [22], however its introduction and utilization in classifying traffic congestion or forecasting traffic congestion is rather the opposite (Figure 3).

Table 2. Attributes analogy of hemorheology and traffic flow dynamics.

Hemorheology	Traffic flow dynamics
Circulatory/cardiovascular system	Road networks/system
Blood vessel	Vehicle lane/road
Blood vessel's diameter	Vehicle lane/road's width
Blood vessel's length	Vehicle lane/road's length
Aorta	Freeways/motorways
Artery	Major arterials
Arterioles	Minor collectors
Capillaries	Collectors
Venules	Local streets/roads
Blood cell	Vehicle
Blood flow	Vehicular traffic flow
Heart valves	Traffic controllers
Blood volume	Number of vehicle
Blood viscosity	Vehicular traffic density/slow speed

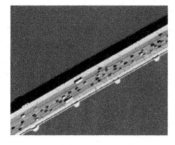
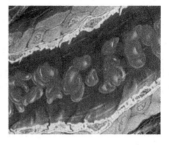

Fig. 3. Similarity of motion in one directional path in vehicular traffic and hemorheology [21].

4.1 Calibration of Traffic Congestion and Hypertension Blood Pressure

The adaptation of hypertension levels in hemorheology to traffic congestion is the base of the development of the Hemorheology based Traffic Congestion and Forecasting Model (HTCFM). Data generated from the On-Board Units (OBU) of each vehicle such as location, speed and velocity will be aggregated. The fundamental traffic flow-density equation is obtained through these parameters to measure the traffic congestion state of a location from all the vehicles in the vicinity.

The two classification from the flow-density relationship illustrated in Fig. 1 is rather broad. On the other hand, adapting the flow-density parabolic curve to hypertension level classification provides more specific and confined classification. Figure 4 illustrates the adaptation of hypertension levels in hemorheology to the fundamental relationship of flow-density.

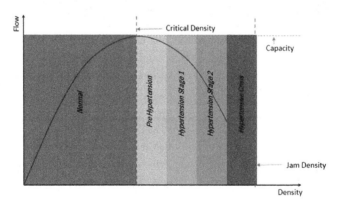

Fig. 4. Adaptation of hypertension stages in hemorheology to traffic congestion.

The normal level of hypertension indicates normal blood flow, and it is equivalently adapted to classify normal traffic flow in vehicular network. As flow slowly decreases with increasing density, the stages of hypertension is parallel to the level of congestion in traffic. Classification can be formed based on this model to classify the levels of traffic congestion. By adapting this model, traffic congestion can also be forecasted following the fundamental relationship of flow and density.

5   The HTCFM Simulation Design

A traffic congestion simulation is conducted using SUMO 0.28.0 to gather the parameters needed in classifying traffic congestion. SUMO is an open source tool that simulates microscopic and continuous road traffic in an urban city [23–25].

The simulation will cover the Persiaran Tunku Ampuan (PTA). A busy road in the city of Shah Alam, Malaysia. Daily weekday traffic along PTA is observed to be in a crawling state towards entering the main highway. A significant traffic congestion along PTA is reported by WAZE in two consecutive days that increases 26 min and 15 min to the traveling time as compared to the usual daily commute.

The two reports obtained from WAVE in the two subsequent days indicates that PTA is a common congested route, however congestion level at the same particular time on different days are not predictable. It is also important to note that reports from WAZE does not consider the current location of the user at the time of the broadcast. In particular, this alert was irrelevant since the alert was received when the user has already reached the destination (Figure 5).

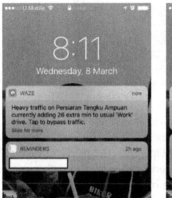

Fig. 5. Reports from WAZE on traffic congestion along Persiaran Tunku Ampuan.

5.1   HTCFM Simulation Setup

The simulation setup starts the first phase in selecting the simulation area. The second phase is to set the traffic generation, third, to generate and run the scenario, and finally the last phase is to generate the output and analyze the results. A similar simulation setup is run three times, with increasing traffic volume to identify the pattern of flow-density relationship.

Simulation Phase 1. PTA route is imported via SUMO Web Wizard to set the parameters for traffic generation. Figure 6 shows the selected area of Shah Alam, and the refined focus area of PTA which the traffic congestion is simulated.

Fig. 6. A map of the city of Shah Alam (*top*) and an extraction of Persiaran Tunku Ampuan route (*bottom*) to be simulated in SUMO.

Simulation Phase 2. The second phase sets the traffic demand to simulate the volume of traffic in the selected area from the OpenStreetMap via OSMWebWizard. It is important to note that the aim of this experiment is only to gather data on the speed, flow and density to observe the formation of traffic congestion.

The "Through Traffic Factor" in the demand generation panel defines how many times that it is more likely for vehicles to depart and arrive at the boundary of the simulation area. The higher the value would simulate a lot of through traffic in the selected area [24]. For this experiment setup, the Through Traffic Factor will be set as the default value of 5.

The "Count" parameter simply defines the number of vehicles generated per hour and kilometer of the road. The count for cars is set to 100. The count will be increased to 150 and 200 in the next following two scenarios to observe the traffic congestion pattern in the effect of increase volume of cars.

Simulation Phase 3. In this phase, the generated scenario is compiled into the sumo configuration file format (*osm.sumocfg*) and run in SUMO Gui. The simulation is set to run for 3600 s and further generation of output data is needed after the simulation time has ended.

Simulation Phase 4. The last phase of the simulation is generating the output file. The output file lists various metrics of the route, departure time, arrival time, trip duration etc., in XML which needed to be parsed. An output file of aggregation time of 300 s (5 min) is generated after the simulation ends and the file is then exported to Microsoft Excel in .xls format.

The output file contains all edges (streets) and all lanes together in the simulation area, with vehicles driving on them for every duration of time set. The vehicles are described by their name, position and speed.

6   Results and Findings

The results obtained in the output file is filtered only to select the PTA route. Traffic parameters relevant to detecting congestion such as time, speed, and velocity of each vehicle are analyzed. Further measurement on flow is needed as it is not automatically generated. The results are analyzed in comparing the density and flow of all three simulations with the increasing count parameters for cars, which were set firstly to 100, subsequently to 150 and finally to 200. Graphs in Figs. 7 and 8 illustrates the increasing pattern of traffic congestion observed from the simulation.

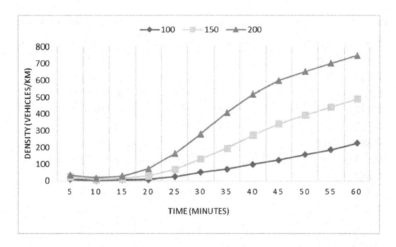

Fig. 7. Traffic density over time for three sets of traffic volume.

Both flow and density obtain from the simulation results of three increasing traffic volume shows an increase in density and decrease in flow throughout the time duration. The result validates the flow density relation as defined in theory that as density increases, flow decreases, forming a parabolic relation of a mathematical function. A further analysis is conducted to analyze only the traffic condition simulated with the most traffic volume, which is set to 200 as the count parameter.

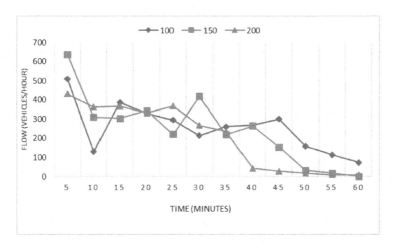

Fig. 8. Traffic flow over time for three sets of traffic volume.

A filtered table consisting parameters relevant only the PTA route for traffic volume of 200 is presented in Table 3.

Table 3. Traffic parameters and data on the most congested scenario simulated

Distance	Number of cars	Density	Speed (km/hr)	Flow (density * speed)
0.882	10	9.23	46.728	431.29944
0.882	9	7.72	47.052	363.24144
0.882	14	12.77	28.728	366.85656
0.882	47	41.48	7.992	331.50816
0.882	109	95.84	3.852	369.17568
0.882	169	148.7	1.8	267.66
0.882	240	211.63	1.116	236.17908
0.882	276	243.29	0.18	43.7922
0.882	294	259.63	0.108	28.04004
0.882	294	259.66	0.072	18.69552
0.882	295	259.95	0.036	9.3582
0.882	295	259.81	0.036	9.35316

Traffic density of Table 3 is illustrated in Fig. 9. The graph shows the density over time from aggregated traffic information collected every 5 min for the duration of 1 h. Similarly, Fig. 10 depicts the traffic flow over time.

The traffic density on the graph clearly shows that traffic congestion increases through time and with no reduction of density. The flow curve however started with a high level and gradually decreases as density intensifies up till the flow stops. Density remains high when flow stops indicates that no additional vehicle are added to the congestion. The scenario confirms on the fundamental relationship of flow-density discussed in Sect. 2, and hence, the result verifies the theory.

Both Figs. 9 and 10 illustrates a similar pattern of the development of congestion observed in all scenarios. A conclusion and verification of the traffic fundamental theory confirms that with the increase in the volume of cars, traffic density increases and the vehicle's velocity or speed fluctuates parallel in time. This will further obstruct flow to a complete stop if the congestion is not resolved quickly.

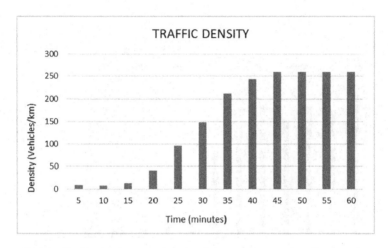

Fig. 9. Traffic density over time for the most congested traffic scenario.

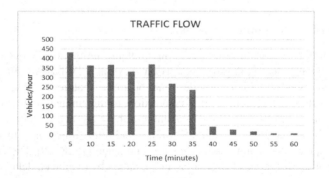

Fig. 10. Traffic flow over time for the most congested traffic scenario.

In modelling HTCFM, the analysis of aggregated data are mapped towards the classification of hypertension in hemorheology. Figure 11 illustrates the adaptation and mapping in HTCFM that shows promising traffic congestion classification approach for further calibration in IoV. The classification of normal traffic flow and levels of congestion within the critical region were clearly categorized. The classification will be used as traffic congestion alert points for Vehicle-to-Vehicle (V2V) communication in IoV. A further construction of mathematical equation or algorithm is required to accommodate this, which will be the next step in our future works.

This study attempts to fill the gap between traffic flow modelling and communication approaches in order to collectively mitigate traffic congestion in urban cities. Although the findings of this paper is a small fraction in the efforts of mitigating traffic congestion, but it is a good representative of theory evaluation and motivation for the future direction of this research domain.

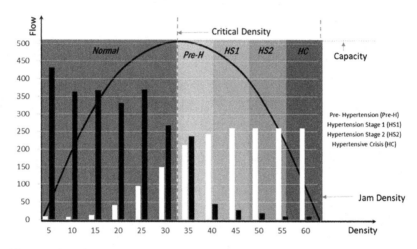

Fig. 11. Mapping of traffic information aggregation with hypertension stage classification for HTCFM.

6.1   Conclusion and Future Direction

Research on traffic congestion and forecasting implementation in V2V communications in IoV has demonstrated good progress thus far. Several V2V-based traffic monitoring techniques are present which provides one or more features such as congestion detection, detection correlation, level of congestion, traffic jam length, limited overhead and dissemination capabilities [26, 27]. Although there are many models available in the study of vehicular traffic to monitor traffic conditions, implying a model in V2V limited communication channel still remains a challenge [7, 28, 29]. Dissemination of traffic information to vehicles is also an issue impacted by overhead, delay and latency, since in IoV, information needs to be disseminated to while is still useful [30]. Therefore, there is a need to calibrate traffic flow modelling and communication approaches for data dissemination in IoV to mitigate the traffic congestion, especially in the urban cities.

The future direction of this study will include the HTCFM architecture proposed for integration in V2V communication within the IoV environment. The proposed architecture of the overall model is presented in Fig. 12.

The architecture starts with the gathering of generated data from the intra-vehicle component such as the OBU and other sensors. Data will then be aggregated and calibrated with HTCFM to measure the mean value flow and density in the next phase. The third phase in the architecture is the dissemination of alerts to inform the on-coming vehicles of the traffic situation ahead.

The approach is aimed to mitigate traffic congestion by alerting oncoming vehicles of the level of congestion ahead and henceforth provide them with a choice of to stay on route or re-route if possible before trapped in critical congestion. Re-routing to avoid being indulged in the traffic congestion would reduce the intensity of congestion and reduce the time-to-clear the congestion to presume to the normal flow of traffic. SUMO simulator will be used to generate traffic demand in the urban area and the IoV network will be designed in network simulators such as OMNeT ++ and Veins. Data aggregation approaches will be evaluated to in order to process the congestion alerts and an appropriate data dissemination technique will be chosen to disseminate the alerts to relevant vehicles through Vehicle-to-Vehicle (V2V) communication.

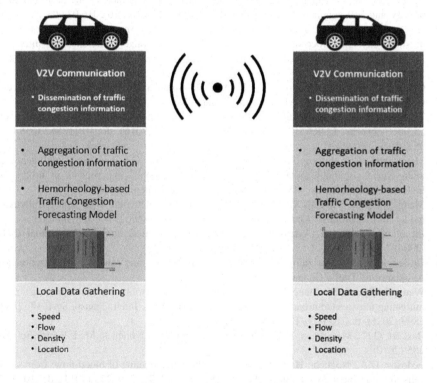

Fig. 12. Architecture of the proposed HTCFM for V2V communication in IoV.

References

1. Gil Sander, F., Blancas Mendivil, L.C., Westra, R.: Malaysia economic monitor: tranforming urban transport, pp. 1–82 (2015)
2. Darbha, S., Rajagopal, K.R., Tyagi, V.: A review of mathematical models for the flow of traffic and some recent results. Nonlinear Anal Theory Methods Appl. **69**, 950–970 (2008). doi:10.1016/j.na.2008.02.123
3. Bonzani, I., Gramani Cumin, L.M.: Critical analysis and perspectives on the hydrodynamic approach for the mathematical theory of vehicular traffic. Math. Comput. Model. **50**, 526–541 (2009). doi:10.1016/j.mcm.2009.03.007
4. Van Wageningen-kessels, F.: Multi-class continuum traffic flow models: analysis and simulation methods. Delft University of Technology (2013). doi:10.4233/uuid:163507af-96df-4804-ad19-2147921b6cb
5. Hoogendoorn, S., Knoop, V.: Traffic flow theory and modelling. Transportation. System and Transport Policy An Introduction, pp. 125–159 (2012)
6. Treiber, M., Kesting, A.: Traffic Flow Dynamics. Springer, Heidelberg (2013). doi:10.1007/978-3-642-32460-4
7. Jia, D., Ngoduy, D.: Enhanced cooperative car-following traffic model with the combination of V2V and V2I communication 90, 172–191 (2016) 10.1016/j.trb.2016.03.008
8. Horng, G.J.: The adaptive recommendation segment mechanism to reduce traffic congestion in smart city. In: Proceedings of - 2014 10th International Conference on Intelligent Information Hiding Multimedia Signal Processing IIH-MSP, pp. 155–158 (2014). doi:10.1109/IIH-MSP.2014.45
9. Cárdenas-benítez, N., Aquino-santos, R., Magaña-espinoza, P.: Traffic congestion detection system through connected vehicles and big data (2016). doi:10.3390/s16050599
10. Wongdeethai, S., Siripongwutikorn, P.: Collecting road traffic information using vehicular ad hoc networks. EURASIP J. Wirel. Commun. Netw. (2016). doi:10.1186/s13638-015-0513-0
11. Meneguette, R.I., Filho, G.P.R., Guidoni, D.L., Pessin, G.: Increasing intelligence in inter-vehicle communications to reduce traffic congestions : experiments in urban and highway environments, 1–25 (2016). doi:10.1371/journal.pone.0159110
12. Meng, J., Qian, Y., Dai, S.: Modeling of urban traffic networks with lattice Boltzmann model. EPL (Europhys. Lett.) **81**, 44003 (2008). doi:10.1209/0295-5075/81/44003
13. Piccoli, B., Tosin, A.: A review of continuum mathematical models of vehicular traffic (2000)
14. Deshmukh, S.M.: Designing an optimized smart device. In: Vehicle For Detection and Avoidance of Traffic Congestion, pp. 33–36 (2016)
15. Wang, S., Djahel, S., Zhang, Z., McManis, J.: Next road rerouting: a multiagent system for mitigating unexpected urban traffic congestion. IEEE Trans. Intell. Transp. Syst. **17**, 2888–2899 (2016). doi:10.1109/TITS.2016.2531425
16. Baskurt, O.K., Meiselman, H.J.: Hemorheology and hemodynamics. Med. Health Sci. **III**, 285 (2010)
17. Fedosov, D.A., Noguchi, H., Gompper, G.: Multiscale modeling of blood flow: from single cells to blood rheology. Biomech. Model. Mechanobiol. **13**, 239–258 (2014). doi:10.1007/s10237-013-0497-9
18. Center for Disease Control: High blood pressure. Sci. Am. **179**, 44–47 (1948)
19. Bighamian, R., Hahn, J.-O.: Relationship between stroke volume and pulse pressure during blood volume perturbation: a mathematical analysis. Biomed. Res. Int. **2014**, 1–10 (2014). doi:10.1155/2014/459269

20. Understanding and Managing High Blood Pressure (2014)
21. Holmes, M.H.: Introduction to the foundations of applied mathematics (2009). doi:10.1007/978-0-387-87765-5
22. Sankar, D.S., Hemalatha, K.: A non-Newtonian fluid flow model for blood flow through a catheterized artery—Steady flow. Appl. Math. Model. 31, 1847–1864 (2007). doi:10.1016/j.apm.2006.06.009
23. Berichte, P.: SUMO 2016 – Traffic, Mobility, and Logistics Berlin-Adlershof (2016)
24. Dkrajzew, N.: Sumo at a Glance. 1 (2014)
25. Krajzewicz, D., Erdmann, J., Behrisch, M., Bieker, L.: Recent Development and Applications of {SUMO - Simulation of Urban MObility}. Int. J. Adv. Syst. Meas. 5, 128–138 (2012)
26. Bassi, A., Bauer, M., Fiedler, M., Kramp, T., van Kranenburg, R., Lange, S., Meissner, S.: Enabling Things to Talk: Designing IoT Solutions with the IoT Architectural Reference Model. Springer, Heidelberg (2013). doi:10.1007/978-3-642-40403-0. Enabling Things to Talk Des IoT Solut with IoT Archit Ref Model 1–349
27. Bauza, R., Gozalvez, J.: Traffic congestion detection in large-scale scenarios using vehicle-to-vehicle communications. J. Netw. Comput. Appl. 36, 1295–1307 (2013). doi:10.1016/j.jnca.2012.02.007
28. Heba El-sersy, A.E.: A survey of traffic congestion detection using VANET. Commun. Appl. Electron. 1, 14–20 (2015)
29. Ilarri, S., Delot, T., Trillo-Lado, R.: A data management perspective on vehicular networks. IEEE Commun. Surv. Tutorials 17, 2420–2460 (2015). doi:10.1109/COMST.2015.2472395
30. Brennand, C.A.R.L., da Cunha, F.D., Maia, G., Cerqueira, E., Loureiro, A.A.F., Villas, L.A.: FOX : a traffic management system of computer-based vehicles FOG (2016)

Self-adaptive Software Simulation: A Lighting Control System for Multiple Devices

Hyunwoo Kim, Euijong Lee, and Doo-kwon Baik$^{(\boxtimes)}$

Department of Computer Science and Engineering, Korea University Seoul,
Seoul, Republic of Korea
{khw0809,kongjjagae,baikdk}@korea.ac.kr

Abstract. In this research, we propose a lighting control system for environments with multiple light sources, including a natural light source and an artificial light source, based on a self–adaptive software control system. We also propose an algorithm for optimization between control devices in a multi-lighting environment, and evaluation methods for self-adaptive software in an Internet of Things environment. Based on these proposals, a simulation is carried out.

Keywords: Self-adaptive software · Software engineering · Simulation

1 Introduction

More than 2 billion people around the world communicate information via the Internet. Advances in network technology have enabled people across the world to exchange and receive a countless amount of information using the Internet. Advances in small network devices have also led to advances in hardware technologies, and have resulted in the creation of the Internet of Things (IoT): an interconnection, via the Internet, of computing devices embedded in everyday objects. Using the IoT, we are able to actively respond to changes in an environment by communicating with the objects in that environment.

Research on the IoT is underway in various fields, including sensors, security, networks, perceptions, etc. [1]. In the field of IoT research, a field based on sensor systems is limited to simple detection and application within a restricted range [1]. Self-adaptive software is software that detects the environment and adapts itself depending on the state of the system. In the real world, many things change in real-time, and thus a self-adaptive software system, enabled by the IoT to able to monitor, adapt, and respond to its environment, has the potential to be very useful. We propose that a multi-lighting control system can be controlled using data gathered from an IoT environment. The self-adaptive software system mentioned above is one that changes itself in a dynamic environment, without user intervention, according to the system requirements [2]. We propose that self-adaptive software be applied to a lighting control system such that it is able to modify the system in response to a dynamically changing environment, in order that the lighting be adjusted and the energy usage of the system managed according to user preference. Existing self-adaptive lighting control systems

© Springer Nature Singapore Pte Ltd. 2017
M.S. Mohamed Ali et al. (Eds.): AsiaSim 2017, Part I, CCIS 751, pp. 380–391, 2017.
DOI: 10.1007/978-981-10-6463-0_33

are limited to a single artificial light source, and are not suitable for environments that contain natural light sources and employ automatic control curtains. Therefore, we also examine multi-lighting scenarios, including artificial light sources and natural light sources. In these scenarios, conflicts between light sources can occur due to the presence of multiple light sources. We need some optimization method for addressing these conflicts, which we suggest in this paper.

Section 2 presents the related works for this research. Section 3 proposes multi-light source scenarios. Section 4 proposes an architectural evaluation criteria for multi-lighting control optimization. Section 5 shows the results of simulating multi-light source scenarios. Finally, Sect. 6 summarizes our research.

2 Related Works

2.1 Self-adaptive Software

Self-adaptive software refers to software that can identify itself and its environment, and handle itself when a violation of requirements occurs [2]. The self-adaptive software described in this paper consists of a MAPE-K loop, a self-adaptive software feedback loop, which has four stages. While the self-adaptive software is running, it continuously cycles through these four stages. Details are below:

- Monitoring stage: The system determines its status using its sensors, which are continuously observing the environment for rule violations. The information obtained from this process is stored in the knowledge base of the self-adaptive system.
- Analysis stage: The analysis stage involves analyzing the patterns of information gathered during the monitoring stage. These patterns of information, retrieved from the knowledge repository, are inspected in order to diagnose symptoms, also stored in the knowledge repository, for future reference.
- Planning stage: The system uses the results of the analysis stage to formulate a strategy for problem solving through its effector(s).
- Execution stage: Change command is issued to the system's effector(s) based on the plan generated during the planning stage. The sensors and the effector(s) may be composed of a plurality of sets external to the system. After the fourth stage execution is complete, the MAPE-K loop repeats, starting over at step one (Fig. 1).

We will explain the above four steps in detail. In previous research, Wuttke et al. [8]. applied self-adaptive software, called ADASIM, to a traffic routing system. In ADASIM, unlike in other self-adaptive software research, the monitoring stage uses the convergence of information from multiple drivers, rather than sensors connected to the system. For example, if some trouble in path which was shortest path from the current location, driver may be delayed beyond the system's expected time. In the analysis stage, ADASIM analyzes data from each driver. If the system finds some problematic patterns in its routing system, then ADASIM will update its traffic information accordingly, and re-compute the current path calculated in the planning stage. As a result, thanks to these traffic information updates, other drivers are better able to find optimal routes.

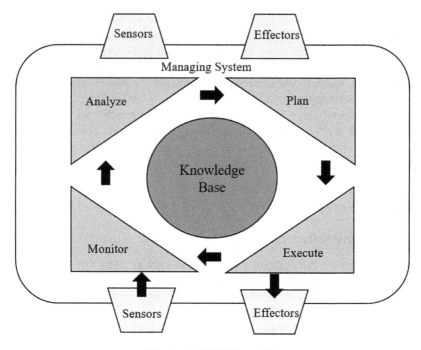

Fig. 1. MAPE-K loop [3].

A number of similar works have been performed to study the effectiveness of self-adaptive software [4, 9, 10]. Anaya et al. [4]. showed that self-adaptive software is more efficient than existing, rule-based sensor systems, by applying such software to a fire detection system, and allowing it to adjust the detection period based on detected data. Garlan et al. [9] proposed a network system framework based on real-time self-adaptive software, and SW Cheng et al. [10] used this framework to implement a hypothetical site called Znn.com, showing that this self-adaptive software framework was more effective than existing systems. In Znn.com, there are three runtime parameters than can be adjusted to adapt the system dynamically: performance, cost, and content fidelity.

Self-adaptive software acquires information about the surrounding environment, and adapts the software based on the information. Therefore, the biggest problem is managing uncertainty related to the information collected from the surrounding environment [3]. Accurate handling of this uncertainty about this information is the key to the completion of self-adaptive software. Many of the current state-of-the-art approaches [12–17] have tackled the different facets of this uncertainty in self-adaptive software, but there are still not enough testbed implementations of self-adaptive software in the Internet of Things environment. Thus, in this research, to address this lack of testbed implementations, we propose a self-adaptive software testbed for an Internet of Things environment.

2.2   Sensor-Based Lighting Control Systems

Existing sensor-based lighting control systems have been studied previously [5, 6]. The intelligent lighting control system described by Singhvi et al. [5] suggests a method of deriving a utility-based strategy that finds the optimal compromise between user convenience and operating cost. However, the method proposed by the study has a limitation: maintenance costs are high, because the system makes changes according to defined rules, and must continuously calculate predictions about the state of the system.

[6] proposed a blind control system based on a fuzzy neural network. The system computes the most efficient angle based on the amount of light, and based on that computation, instructs the user to adjust the angle of the blind to optimize the user's visibility and energy efficiency. Since the study is a blind adjustment system, it is limited to controlling only the natural light source, and is thus difficult to connect to the artificial lighting in the room.

The above-mentioned works have further disadvantages in that their methods make it difficult to adapt to a change of the user's preference in such a way that the system grasps the surrounding environment but controls the light amount using the existing rules and user preferences. [7, 11] propose a light source control system based on self-adaptive software. However, this research addresses only single-source artificial lighting scenarios, and has limitations that make it difficult to apply to a multiple light source environment, as may be found in the Internet of Things.

In this research, the MAPE-K feedback loop technique of self-adaptive software is applied to create a lighting control system that solves the problems of the above mentioned studies. In addition, a multiple light source scenario is proposed that may be easily applied in an Internet of Things environment.

3   Multiple Light Source Scenario

Lighting control systems that use self-adaptive software have been studied [7, 11]. However, since these studies use only a single artificial light source, it is difficult to apply them to situations involving natural light sources. Therefore, the multiple light source scenario of this paper includes a natural light source, equipped with an automatic control curtain that adjusts the amount of light allowed through a window. In this scenario, it is assumed that there is a space containing an artificial light source and a natural light source. Figure 2 shows the scenario flow diagram that occurs when a self-adaptive software-based lighting control system is applied to multiple light source scenarios in MAPE-K order. When the user enters the space, the system reads the current illumination value of the smartphone, using an application loaded on the user's smartphone. If the user's lighting preference is stored in the application, then the artificial light source and the natural light source are each adjusted according to the user's preference, so as to optimize the lighting in the space for that user. When another user comes in, the lighting control system likewise searches for the preferences of that user, and then adjusts the lighting control system to be an average between the preferences of the new and existing users. Next, the system plans an optimal strategy for balancing between the artificial light and the natural light equipped with an automatic

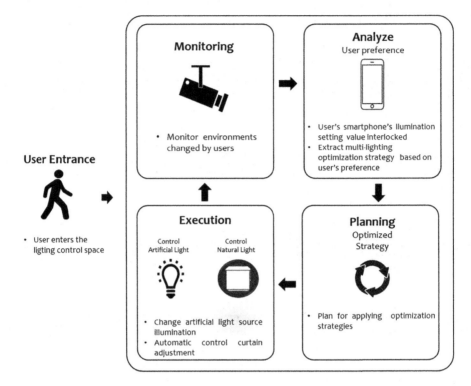

Fig. 2. Multi-lighting scenario flow diagram and MAPE Loop.

control curtain. Finally, in the execution stage, the artificial lighting and natural lighting are set to the illuminance values most suitable for the user(s) preferences, before returning to the monitoring stage.

In the study of lighting control based on existing user preferences [5], the user has a utility function "$\Phi_i\,(a,\,x_i)$" indicating preference, where "x_i" is a user's current location, and "a" is the current illuminance of that user's location. The equation for calculating the maximum value of the utility function can thus be expressed as:

$$argmax_a \sum_{i=1}^{n} \Phi_i(a, x_i) \tag{1}$$

Equation (2) adds an administrator utility function to Eq. (1), which allows the lighting condition to be adjusted when there is no user in the space. The administrator utility function is set lower than the user's preference, so that the amount of illumination generated is reduced when no user is present.

$$U(a,x) = \sum_{i=1}^{n} \Phi_i(a, x_i) + \gamma \Psi(a) \tag{2}$$

3.1 Multi-lighting Optimization Algorithm

Assuming that an artificial light source and a natural light source exist in the same space, the natural light source can be considered to have less energy consumption than the artificial light source. Therefore, if you need to adjust the illumination, by increasing the amount provided by the natural light source, you can give priority to energy efficiency.

Let "*nl*" be the maximum illuminance of the natural light source, and let "*al*" be the maximum illuminance of the artificial light source. In Eq. (3), the total illuminance value is adjusted by adjusting both the natural light source illuminance coefficient "C_n" which is "$0 \leq C_n \leq 1$", and the artificial light source illuminance coefficient "C_a" which is "$0 \leq C_a \leq 1$", in real time. The maximum illuminance of a given natural light source is checked periodically through an external sensor, while the maximum illuminance of the artificial light source is measured before the system begins execution.

$$illumination(lx) = c_n(nl) + l_n(al) \tag{3}$$

For example, if the illumination is lower than the current user preference, the natural light source coefficient should be increased preferentially, since the natural light source has a greater energy efficiency than the artificial light source. Once the natural light source coefficient reaches a value of one, however, the artificial light source coefficient is gradually increased to control the illumination. In the opposite case, if the current illumination is to be lowered, the artificial light source coefficient with low energy consumption efficiency should be lowered first.

4   Architectural Evaluation Criteria

This research is a study on self-adaptive software in an Internet of Things environment. Therefore, we suggest architectural evaluation criteria for self-adaptive software testbeds for such environments, with the intent that these criteria be usable in future works in a similar vein. Our proposed evaluation criteria are based on work performed in Wuttke et al. [8], though our suggestions differ in that they are intended for an Internet of Things environment, rather than an application environment.

Table 1 lists our proposed architectural evaluation criteria, which we next describe. First, Answer Quality is an indicator of whether responses to changes in illumination and user preference are appropriate. Second, Scalability is concerned with how the number of users connected to the system affects its ability to perform. Third, Robustness to Sensor Uncertainty is an assessment of uncertain information in the sensors attached to the system. Fourth, Robustness to effector is a measure of the systems ability to handle effector malfunctions. Fifth, Robustness to churn is about the systems ability to adapt to environmental changes while in the planning stage. Last, Balance is an indicator of whether the balance of user satisfaction and energy efficiency has been taken into consideration. We suggest that these six evaluation criteria be used for self-adaptive software when evaluating applications intended for the Internet of Things, and potentially as testbeds in future works.

Table 1. Architectural evaluation criteria.

Evaluation criteria	Description
Answer quality	Are responses appropriate to each situation variable, including changes in illumination and user preferences?
Scalability	Does the number of users increase the computational complexity?
Robustness to sensor uncertainty	If the sensor's information is uncertain, does it affect the lighting control system?
Robustness to effector	How does it affect the system if the effector, including the lighting, or curtain, fails?
Robustness to churn	Does the planning process reflect changing environmental variables during solution determination?
Balance	Have you considered the balance between energy consumption and user satisfaction?

5   Simulation

This section describes the simulation environment of the multi-lighting control system based on the self-adaptive software we proposed above. We will explain how to apply our proposed algorithm to control multiple light sources, and we will explain the implementation of the simulation in detail.

In the scenario described above, a user with a smartphone enters a place where the multi-lighting system is installed and executes the self-adaptive lighting control application, resulting in a connection between the lighting control system and the user application via the Bluetooth communication protocol. The system receives the user's preferred illumination value, along with the space's current illumination value from the user's smartphone. The system compares the user's preferred level of illumination with the current lighting conditions of the space, and adjusts the lighting conditions to match the user's preference.

Algorithm 1 is a pseudocode listing of the multiple lighting control algorithm described previously. *desiredLux* is the user's preferred illumination value, and *currentlux* is the current illumination value of the space as measured by the user's smartphone. *nc* is the natural light source coefficient controlling the natural light source, while *ac* is the artificial light source coefficient controlling the artificial light source. As mentioned, the system adjusts each light source by using its designated coefficient, which must always be a rational number between 0 and 1.

If the user's preferred illumination is higher than the current illumination, this means that the user wishes to increase the brightness. If possible, the natural light source, with its lower power consumption, is raised until the illumination matches the preference of the user. If it's not possible to adjust the illumination to the user's preference by adjustment of the natural light source alone, then the illumination value is adjusted by raising the coefficient of the artificial light source as well. If the user's preferred illumination value is lower than the current illumination, this means the user desires to lower the illumination. In this case, the artificial light source, having a higher power consumption, is lowered first. If after fully dimming the artificial light the adjustment remains insufficient, then the natural light source coefficient is adjusted as well.

1	**Inputs:**
2	*desiredLux,currentLux*
3	**Loop:**
4	Read *currentLux*
5	Read *desiredLux*
6	**while** *desiredLux > currentLux* **do**
7	*nc*++
8	if(*dL=cL*)
9	**break**
10	else if(*nc* = 1)
11	*ac*++
12	if(*dL = cL*)
13	**break**
14	**while** *desiredLux < currentLux* **do**
15	*ac*--
16	if(*dL = cL*)
17	**break**
18	else if(*ac* = 0)
19	*nc*--
20	if(*dL = cL*)
21	**break**

Algorithm 1. Multi-lighting Control

The lighting control application for a user's smartphone is available for Android 4.3 version or later. The multi-lighting control system based on self-adaptive software is constructed using an Arduino kit. The Arduino Bluno board acts as the main system, and connects the user's smartphone with the Arduino Bluno board using Bluetooth. A 12 V LED strip connected to the Arduino Bluno board serves as the artificial light source, while an HC-06 Bluetooth module, also connected to the Arduino Bluno board, allows Bluetooth communication with other Arduino boards connected to the motor. Another Arduino Uno board equipped with a stepper motor acts as the automatic control curtain, responsible for control the amount of illumination provided by the natural light source. We created a window in the simulation space where the experiment was performed, and placed a stand light behind the window. This light simulated natural sunlight outside the window, and for the purposes of our experiment we did ignored the power consumption of this device.

Figures 3 and 4 are Arduino diagrams for the self-adaptive lighting control system. The connections made in the Arduino diagram are described in Table 2.

Figure 5 is a graph showing the variation of the illumination coefficients along with the current illumination of the space when the user's preferred illumination value was set to 800 lux. Both of the illumination coefficients were set to be 0.5 at the start of the

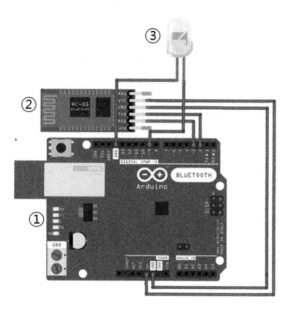

Fig. 3. Arduino diagram for self-adaptive light control system, main system.

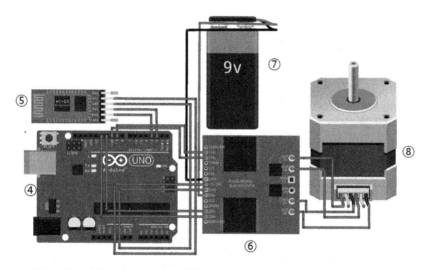

Fig. 4. Arduino diagram for self-adaptive light control system motor part.

experiment. When user's preferred illumination was observed to be bigger than the current illumination of the space, the value of the natural coefficient can be seen to rise first, followed by an increase in the value of the artifical coefficient.

Table 2. Arduino diagram description.

No.	Name	Description
1	Arduino bluno board	Main system of the self-adaptive lighting control system
2	HC-06 bluetooth module	Bluetooth module for communicating with the board that connects the motor
3	LEDs	LED serving as an artificial light source
4	Arduino uno board	Arduino board for motor control
5	HC-06 bluetooth module	Bluetooth module for communicating with the main system board
6	L298N motor drive	Motor drive required to control the stepper motor
7	9 V power supply battery	9 V battery needed to supply power to the motor
8	Stepper motor	Stepper motor serving as a automatic control curtain for controlling natural light source

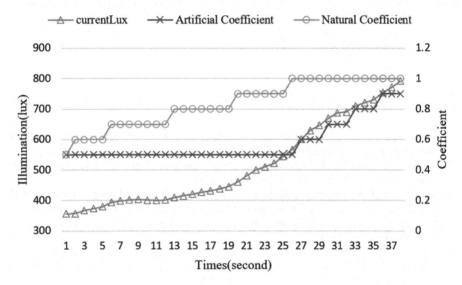

Fig. 5. Result of simulation.

6   Conclusion

In this research, we proposed a self-adaptive software system for controlling multiple light sources, including an artificial light source and a natural light source, using the MAPE-K feedback loop. We also proposed and applied an optimization strategy for balancing the artificial light source with the natural light source. We proposed an evaluation method for the study of self-adaptive software in an Internet of Things environment, which can be used as a testbed for future works. We simulated our proposals using Arduino kits, and showed that the system adjusts the lighting of the space according to user preference.

In this research, we tried to overcome the limitation of existing self-adaptive lighting control system. Unlike previous studies that only considered existing single lighting control devices, we considered an Internet of Things environment in which multiple light sources may exist. Additionally, our proposed evaluation methods can be used to evaluate future self-adaptive software in an Internet of Things environment. In addition, the proposed algorithm can be applied to optimize Internet of Things environments where requirements are in conflict.

Future research will consider the location of users. The reason for this is that the closer the artificial light source is, the better the energy consumption efficiency is. We also need to develop multiple light source optimization algorithms, and fix problems that can occur in the existing algorithm. Because this study targets an Internet of Things environment, we are also considering using additional sensors, as well as lighting control, to create a user-friendly system.

Acknowledgments. This research was supported by the Next-Generation Information Computing Development Program through the National Research Foundation of Korea (NRF) funded by the Ministry of Science, ICT and Future Planning (NRF2012M3C4A7033346) and the Basic Science Research Program through the NRF funded by the Ministry of Education (2016R1D1A1B03936375).

References

1. Miorandi, D., et al.: Internet of things: vision, applications and research challenges. Ad Hoc Netw. **10**(7), 1497–1516 (2012)
2. Salehie, M., Tahvildari, L.: Self-adaptive software: landscape and research challenges. ACM Trans. Auton. Adapt. Syst. (TAAS) **4**(2), 14 (2009)
3. Brun, Y., et al.: Engineering self-adaptive systems through feedback loops. In: Cheng, B.H. C., Lemos, R., Giese, H., Inverardi, P., Magee, J. (eds.) Software Engineering for Self-Adaptive Systems. LNCS, vol. 5525, pp. 48–70. Springer, Heidelberg (2009). doi:10. 1007/978-3-642-02161-9_3
4. Anaya, I.D.P., et al.: A prediction-driven adaptation approach for self-adaptive sensor networks. In: Proceedings of the 9th International Symposium on Software Engineering for Adaptive and Self-managing Systems. ACM (2014)
5. Singhvi, V., et al.: Intelligent light control using sensor networks. In: Proceedings of the 3rd International Conference on Embedded Networked Sensor Systems. ACM (2005)
6. Chen, Y., Li, H., Chen, X.: Venetian blind control system based on fuzzy neural network for indoor daylighting. In: Second International Conference on Computer and Electrical Engineering, ICCEE 2009, vol. 2. IEEE (2009)
7. Lee, J., Lee, E., Baik, D.-K.: Simulation and performance evaluation of the self-adaptive light control system. J. Korea Soc. Simul. **25**(2), 63–74 (2016)
8. Wuttke, J., et al.: Traffic routing for evaluating self-adaptation. In: Proceedings of the 7th International Symposium on Software Engineering for Adaptive and Self-Managing Systems. IEEE Press (2012)

9. Garlan, D., et al.: Rainbow: architecture-based self-adaptation with reusable infrastructure. Computer **37**(10), 46–54 (2004)
10. Cheng, S.-W., Garlan, D., Schmerl, B.: Evaluating the effectiveness of the rainbow self-adaptive system. In: ICSE Workshop on Software Engineering for Adaptive and Self-Managing Systems. IEEE (2009)
11. Lee, J., Lee, E., Baik, D.-K.: Smart lecture room: a case study for self-adaptive software. Korea Inf. Sci. Soc. 490–492 (2015)
12. Whittle, J., Sawyer, P., Bencomo, N., Cheng, B.H.C., Bruel, J.: RELAX: incorporating uncertainty into the specification of self-adaptive systems. In: International Requirements, Engineering Conference, Atlanta, Georgia, pp. 79–88 (2009)
13. Baresi, L., Pasquale, L., Spoletini, P.: Fuzzy goals for requirements-driven adaptation. In: International Requirements Engineering Conference, Sydney, Australia, pp. 125–134 (2010)
14. Elkhodary, A., Esfahani, N., Malek, S.: FUSION: a framework for engineering self-tuning self-adaptive software systems. In: International Symposium on the Foundations of Software Engineering, Santa Fe, New, Mexico, pp. 7–16 (2010)
15. Poladian, V., Sousa, J.P., Garlan, D., Shaw, M.: Dynamic configuration of resource-aware services. In: International Conference on Software Engineering, Scotland, UK, pp. 604–613 (2004)
16. Cooray, D., Malek, S., Roshandel, R., Kilgore, D.: RESISTing reliability degradation through proactive reconfiguration. In: International Conference on Automated Software Engineering, Antwerp, Belgium (2010)
17. Esfahani, N., Kouroshfar, E., Malek, S.: Taming uncertainty in self-adaptive software. In: The Joint Meeting of the European Software Engineering Conference and the ACM SIGSOFT Symposium on the Foundations of Software Engineering, Szeged, Hungary (2011)

Finite Element Analysis for PDMS Based Dual Chamber Bellows Structured Pneumatic Actuator

Tariq Rehman[1,2], Ahmad' Athif Mohd Faudzi[1,3],
Dyah Ekashanti Octorina Dewi[4], and
Mohamed Sultan Mohamed Ali[1(✉)]

[1] Faculty of Electrical Engineering, Universiti Teknologi Malaysia,
81310 Skudai, Johor, Malaysia
rtariq2@live.utm.my, {athif,sultan_ali}@fke.utm.my
[2] Departments of Electronic Engineering,
NED University of Engineering and Technology, Karachi, Pakistan
[3] Center for Artificial Intelligence and Robotics, Universiti Teknologi Malaysia,
Jalan Sultan Yahya Petra, 54100 Kuala Lumpur, Malaysia
[4] Department of Clinical Science, Faculty of Biosciences
and Medical Engineering, Universiti Teknologi Malaysia,
81310 Skudai, Johor, Malaysia
dyah@utm.my

Abstract. In this paper, a polydimethylsiloxane (PDMS) material based pneumatic actuator with a dual chambered square bellows structure was designed and simulated. Using finite element analysis (FEA), the maximum output displacement, bending angle and input pressure requirements for the actuator were analyzed. The simulation analysis revealed that 9 mm^2 square bellows actuator with 17.4 mm length resulted in bidirectional bending. The actuator achieved maximum bending angles of 61° at 38 kPa and 78.5° at 45 kPa under successive and discrete actuation respectively, which makes it suitable for catheter navigation system. The results presented in this work are expected to promote the application of pneumatic based actuators in biomedical application and beyond.

Keywords: Square bellows actuator · Finite element analysis · Soft robotics · Soft actuator · Pneumatic actuator

1 Introduction

The field of soft robotics has strongly cemented its foundations in the robotics domain due to the compatibility in wide range of applications. Subsequently within soft robotics, soft actuators are highly acknowledged by the researchers all over the world. Soft actuators are made up of elastomers materials such as rubber to enhance their operational capabilities and projected motions. As soft actuators have soft and flexible structure, hydraulic and pneumatic are the two suitable sources for their actuation. Soft actuators differ from conventional electric actuators, which are always rigid, heavy and

© Springer Nature Singapore Pte Ltd. 2017
M.S. Mohamed Ali et al. (Eds.): AsiaSim 2017, Part I, CCIS 751, pp. 392–402, 2017.
DOI: 10.1007/978-981-10-6463-0_34

limited in degrees of freedom (DoF). The operations of soft actuators are normally adopted from nature and are normally bio-inspired [1], e.g: A 400 μm pneumatic soft actuator that mimic the locomotion of nematode [2].

Pneumatic soft actuators are commonly made of rubber structure with internal chamber(s) for pneumatic supply and its structure is often reinforced with fiber to improve the actuation [3]. Applying pneumatic pressure to the chamber(s) of the soft actuator causes elastic deformations (extension and contraction) in the rubber structure, which results in actuation [4]. Soft actuator with two chambers can provide bidirectional bending motion [5], while three chambers can offer bending motion up to six different directions [6]. A double-layer, four-channel soft pneumatic actuator was also reported, which can achieve multiple motions in eight directions [7].

Pneumatic soft actuators have found enormous applications in developing medical devices to assist colonoscope [8–12], flexible tip bronchoscope (FOB) for bronchus examination [13] and hand rehabilitation [14]. Furthermore, a soft actuator based propeller system for mimicking gymnotiform swimmers [15] and a three-finger soft grippers [16] was also reported. Some of the soft actuator were developed through micro-electro-mechanical systems (MEMS) fabrication process [17]. The application of MEMS based fabrication processes for developing micro-scaled soft actuator is still a challenging research domain which needs to be explored further.

In this regard, we have designed and simulated a PDMS material based dual chamber pneumatic bellows actuator in square shape. The outline of this paper includes five sections. Starting from the introduction, Sect. 2 discusses the design configuration of square bellows actuator while Sect. 3 highlights the FEA on MARC® software and bending angle calculations. Section 4 is the result and discussion section based on the discrete and sequential actuation of both chambers of square bellows actuator. The last Sect. 5 concludes the paper with quantified results achieved through square bellows actuator.

2   Design Configuration

In this study, we propose to design and analyze a square shaped bellows structured pneumatic soft actuator with dual chambers using finite element analysis (FEA) on MARC®. The objective of this work is to analyze the structural design of this square bellows pneumatic bending actuator and discuss the optimum output bending motion and bending angle achievable through simulation. The simulation analysis was carried out as static analysis using numerical solutions from the FEA software MARC®, that can handle material's nonlinearity and proved good agreement between experimental and simulation results [3, 18, 19].

The design for the proposed pneumatic actuator was selected to have bellows in its structure, to fulfill the aim of developing a fibreless soft actuator with dual chambers for bi-directional bending motion. The selected PDMS material, Dow Corning Sylgard® 184 Part-A/B from Dow Corning-Corporation Midland, Michigan, United States is a type of elastomer which is nonlinear in nature. The SolidWork® based structural design referred in Fig. 1(a) shows the isometric view of the square bellows actuator. Figure 1(b) shows the front view of the actuator along with a node N, marked at the center and

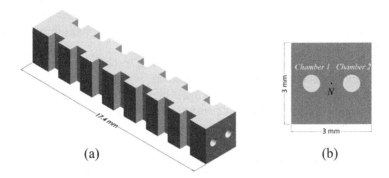

Fig. 1. Structural design (a) Isometric view. (b) Front view with reference node, N.

between the two holes for connecting the pneumatic input to both of its chambers. The node N would be used as a reference node for calculating the bending angle of the square bellows actuator later in Sect. 3.1.

3   Simulation and Analysis

To analyze the nonlinear behavior of PDMS material based dual chamber square bellows actuator, a FEA was performed on MARC®, a software recommended for simulating complex designs made from non-linear materials, such as elastomers and polymers. The simulation analysis was carried out to understand the behavior of dual chamber square bellows actuator in terms of output bending motion against the applied pneumatic supply. To begin with MARC® software, the nodes were connected to form elements, which further combined to forms the overall structure of dual chamber square bellows actuator.

After designing, once the geometrical properties were settled, the values of Young's modulus, $E = 2$ MPa and Poisson's ratio, $\mu = 0.5$ for PDMS were inserted to define the material properties of the square bellows actuator. For the boundary conditions, each of the two chambers were marked with face-load pressures of 38 kPa and 45 kPa for successive and discrete actuation respectively. Each pressure value was applied during simulation through respective contact table at a load-case value of 1000 increments.

A fixed-displacement xyz was set at one end of the designed square bellows actuator to measure the bending motion through reference node, N at the other end of the actuator. By keeping all the above settings of MARC® constant, square bellows actuator was simulated and analyzed under discrete and successive actuation of each chamber to characterize the optimum bending motion and maximum bending angle, θ.

3.1   Bending Angle Calculations

From the simulation results of dual chamber square bellows actuator, the output displacement was resulted in y-z-axes which mainly depends on the axis at which the actuator was designed in MARC® simulation environment. As explained earlier, for tracking the bending motion of the square bellows actuator, a reference node, N was selected at the center of the bending side, as shown in Fig. 1(b). From simulation results, the displacement data of the selected node was considered for bending angle, θ calculations.

As an example; for calculating the θ of PDMS based square bellows actuator, a bending motion simulation profile under discrete chamber actuation at 18 kPa was illustrated in Fig. 2, with a right angled-triangle, marked on it.

Considering the reference node, N as corner of marked right-angled triangle on the bending profile, the side $\overline{ON}$ of the right-angled triangle represents the displacement, Y covered by the square bellows actuator along y-axis. Additionally, while performing the bending motion with respect to the reference node, N the bellows actuator also covered displacement along $-z$-axis, which resulted in reduction in length, $L_{reduced}$ from its total length, L_{total} mentioned in Fig. 2.

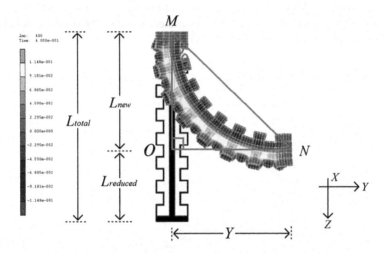

Fig. 2. Simulation profile of Chamber 2 actuation at 18 kPa.

The side $\overline{OM}$ of the right-angled triangle represents the change in the length or new length, L_{new}, which can be determined from the relation; $L_{new} = L_{total} - |L_{reduced}|$. The θ of square bellows actuator was calculated by applying the trigonometric functions expressed in Eqs. (1) and (2):

$$\tan \theta = \frac{Perpendicular}{Base} = \frac{|Y|}{L_{new}} \tag{1}$$

$$\theta = \tan^{-1} \frac{|Y|}{L_{new}} \tag{2}$$

4 Results and Discussion

The simulation results of dual chamber square bellows actuator have shown proportional relation between output displacement and applied pneumatic pressure. The idea was to design and simulate the square bellows actuator in a miniaturized scale (3 mm × 3 mm × 17.4 mm), suitable to be deployed as a catheter navigator. To achieve smooth bending motion, several models of square bellows actuator were designed and simulated by varying side dimension, wall thickness and overall length.

Out of all, two models of square bellows actuator having wall-thickness of 1 mm with dimensions (3 mm × 3 mm × 17.4 mm) and (3 mm × 3 mm × 21.8 mm) resulted in optimum bending motions. Figure 3 shows the simulation results for output bending angle achieved from these two models. Up to a maximum input pressure of 45 kPa, both models resulted in uniform displacement with bending angles of 78.46° and 100.78° respectively. From analysis of Fig. 3, the square bellows actuator with longer length resulted in larger bending angle. However, for selecting the miniaturized design, the square bellows actuator having wall-thickness of 1 mm with dimensions (3 mm × 3 mm × 17.4 mm) was further studied through MARC® simulations to analyze and characterize its bending behavior.

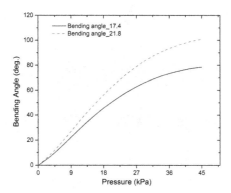

Fig. 3. Bending angle results for 17.4 mm and 21.8 mm long actuators.

Furthermore, in this research, the dual actuation response of the selected square bellows actuator was also studied, which depends on the actuation technique applied for actuating each of the two chambers. In the first simulation case, each of the two chambers were actuated separately at a maximum pressure of 45 kPa to observe the resulted bending motion. In the second simulation case, a maximum sustainable sequential face-load pressure of 38 kPa was applied to both chambers of square bellows actuator to measure the output bending motion.

4.1 Case 1: Discrete Actuation

As mentioned earlier, the discussion on MARC® based simulation results for dual chamber square bellows actuator has been divided in two cases. In case 1, the discussion focusses on the simulation results based on the actuation condition when both chambers were actuated individually through discrete non-sequential pneumatic input pressure, maximum up to 45 kPa. Pressure above this threshold value started to introduce noises in the resulted bending motion. The square bellows actuator has shown uniform output displacement and bending angle along yz-axes against applied pressure. The resulted bending angles from the discrete actuation of both chambers of square bellows actuator are equal and opposite in direction as shown in Fig. 4.

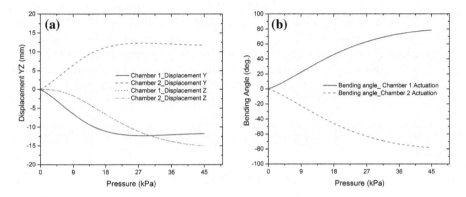

Fig. 4. (a) Displacement in yz direction against discrete chamber actuation. (b) Bending angle results against discrete chamber actuation.

Figure 4(a) illustrated the displacement in yz-direction, while on the other hand Fig. 4(b) shows the output bending angle plot achieved by individual actuation of each chamber of square bellows actuator. The maximum bending angle achieved by the square bellows actuator from individual actuation of each of its chambers was $\pm 78.55°$ at 45 kPa.

Furthermore, the detailed history plot data extracted from selected reference node N, at the bending side of square bellows actuator, which includes: the time, displacement in yz direction, discrete chamber actuation and the resulted output bending angle against the applied input pressure was tabulated in Table 1.

Table 1. Node N based history plot data for discrete actuation of each chamber.

S. no	Pressure (kPa)	Time	Displacement Y (mm)		Displacement Z (mm)		Bending angle (deg.)	
			Chamber 1	Chamber 2	Chamber 1	Chamber 2	Chamber 1	Chamber 2
1	4.5	0.1	−3.010	3.010	−0.322	−0.322	9.996	−9.996
2	9	0.2	−6.489	6.489	−1.708	−1.708	22.467	−22.467
3	13.5	0.3	−9.304	9.304	−3.989	−3.989	34.753	−34.753
4	18	0.4	−11.107	11.107	−6.607	−6.607	45.823	−45.823
5	22.5	0.5	−12.006	12.006	−9.082	−9.082	55.289	−55.289
6	27	0.6	−12.286	12.286	−11.144	−11.144	63.017	−63.017
7	31.5	0.7	−12.230	12.230	−12.712	−12.712	69.031	−69.031
8	36	0.8	−12.050	12.050	−13.829	−13.829	73.495	−73.495
9	40.5	0.9	−11.869	11.869	−14.579	−14.579	76.633	−76.633
10	45	1	−11.760	11.760	−15.018	−15.018	78.551	−78.551

Hence, from the simulation results of square bellows under discrete chamber actuation shown in Fig. 4(a) and (b) along the history plot data in Table 1, it can be concluded that the square bellows actuator shown a symmetrical behavior in terms of displacement and bending angle with equal and opposite magnitude.

4.2   Case 2: Successive Actuation

In this section, the simulation results of square bellows actuator are discussed based on the sequential actuation of both chambers through maximum input pressure up to 38 kPa. Pressure above this threshold value started to produce noises in the resulted bending motion. During MARC® simulation, the sequential input pressure was applied to each chamber of square bellows actuator depending on the values inserted in the contact table. Following the contact table, the pattern developed for applying sequential input pressure to each chamber of square bellows actuator was illustrated in Fig. 5(a).

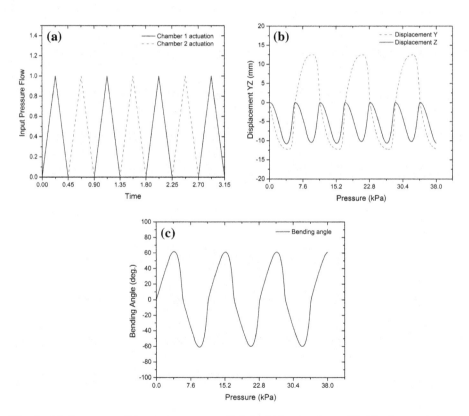

Fig. 5. (a) Sequence of input pressure applied to both chambers. (b) Displacement in yz direction for successive chamber actuation. (c) Bending angle results for square bellows actuator successive chamber.

Using this successive scheme of chamber actuation, the square bellows actuator resulted in a uniform output displacement in yz direction against consecutive actuation of each chamber as shown in Fig. 5(b). While, on the other hand the sinusoidal output response for bending angle, achieved by the square bellows actuator against the sequential input pressure applied to actuate each chamber was presented in Fig. 5(c). The sinusoidal bending angle response against the linear actuation of both chambers of square bellows actuator had resulted in equal and opposite magnitude with a maximum bending angle of $\pm 61°$ at 38 kPa.

Furthermore, the detailed history plot data extracted from simulation of selected reference node N, at the bending side of square bellows actuator, including the time, displacement in yz direction, successive chamber actuation and the resulted bending angle achieved by the square bellows actuator against sequential input pressure was tabulated in Table 2.

Table 2. Node N based history plot data for successive actuation of each chamber.

S. no	Pressure (kPa)	Time	Displacement Y (mm)	Displacement Z (mm)	Bending angle (deg.)
1	3.8	0.3	−12.198	−10.792	61.556
2	7.6	0.6	9.542	−4.182	−35.828
3	11.4	0.9	2.149	−0.150	−7.102
4	15.2	1.2	−12.183	−10.625	60.923
5	19	1.5	9.452	−4.088	−35.377
6	22.8	1.8	2.134	−0.148	−7.053
7	26.6	2.1	−12.183	−10.625	60.923
8	30.4	2.4	9.452	−4.088	−35.377
9	34.2	2.7	2.134	−0.148	−7.052
10	38	3	−12.183	−10.625	60.923

Consequently, from the simulation results of square bellows actuator under sequential chamber actuation presented in Fig. 5(b) and (c) along with the history plot data tabulated in Table 2, it can be concluded that a symmetrical output response was achieved by the square bellows actuator from successive actuation of each chamber.

Following case 2, Fig. 6 shows the simulation results for output bending motion achieved by the square bellows actuator against successive input pressure to actuate both chamber 1 and 2, ranges from 7.6 kPa to 38 kPa. The sequential actuation profile which was followed in Fig. 6 was already illustrated in Fig. 5(a) which resulted in a uniform, symmetrical and sinusoidal bi-direction bending motion with equal and opposite magnitude in response to each chamber actuation.

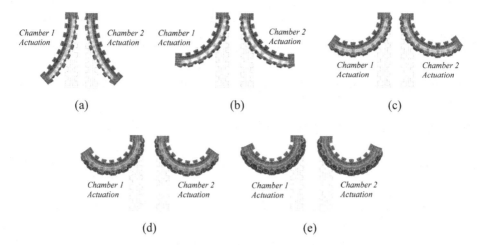

Fig. 6. MARC® simulation results for bending motion of square bellows actuator with successive chamber actuations: (a) 7.6 kPa, (b) 15.2 kPa, (c) 22.8 kPa, (d) 30.4 kPa, (e) 38 kPa.

5   Conclusion

In this study, we designed and simulated a dual chamber square shaped pneumatic bellows actuator using MARC®, a FEA tool. From the simulation analysis of square bellows actuator (3 mm × 3 mm × 1 mm), it can be illustrated that reducing the length of square bellows actuator from 21.8 mm to 17.4 mm, also resulted in reduction in bending angle from 100.78° to 78.46° respectively at maximum input pressure of 45 kPa. Furthermore, the discrete and successive application of input pressure to both chambers of the square bellows actuator also effected the resultant bending angle. The individual or discrete actuation of each chamber of square bellows actuator, resulted in equal and opposite bending angle, maximum up to 78.5° at 45 kPa. Under successive or sequential chamber actuation, the square bellows actuator resulted in sinusoidal bending angles with a maximum bending angle of 61° at 38 kPa. Therefore, it can be concluded that the dual chambered-square shaped pneumatic bellows actuator produced maximum bending angles under sequential and non-sequential chamber actuations. The future direction of this work would focus on the result optimization through metamodeling technique [20], before developing the miniaturized square bellows actuator using MEMS fabrication processes.

Acknowledgements. This work was supported by Universiti Teknologi Malaysia (UTM) under Research University Grant (14H31). Tariq Rehman acknowledges the financial support (M3) from NED University of Engineering & Technology Karachi, Pakistan.

References

1. Faudzi, A.A.M., M.I.A., Fatiha, R., Rusydi, M., Hirooka, D., Wakimoto, S., Suzumori, K.: Application of new braided soft actuator design in biomimetic robot locomotion. In: 15th International Conference on Climbing and Walking Robots and the Support Technologies for Mobile Machines, Baltimore, USA, p. 165 (2012)

2. Yoshioka, R., Wakimoto, S., Suzumori, K., Ishikawa, Y.: Development of pneumatic rubber actuator of 400 μm in diameter generating bi-directional bending motion. In: IEEE International Conference on Robotics and Biomimetics (ROBIO), pp. 1–6. IEEE (2014)

3. Faudzi, A.A.M., Razif, M.R.M., Nordin, I.N.A.M., Suzumori, K., Wakimoto, S., Hirooka, D.: Development of bending soft actuator with different braided angles. In: IEEE/ASME International Conference on Advanced Intelligent Mechatronics (AIM), pp. 1093–1098. IEEE (2012)

4. Ogura, K., Wakimoto, S., Suzumori, K., Nishioka, Y.: Micro pneumatic curling actuator-Nematode actuator. In: IEEE International Conference on Robotics and Biomimetics (ROBIO), pp. 462–467. IEEE (2008)

5. Suzumori, K., Endo, S., Kanda, T., Kato, N., Suzuki, H.: A bending pneumatic rubber actuator realizing soft-bodied manta swimming robot. In: IEEE International Conference on Robotics and Automation, pp. 4975–4980. IEEE (2007)

6. Wakimoto, S., Ogura, K., Suzumori, K., Nishioka, Y.: Miniature soft hand with curling rubber pneumatic actuators. In: IEEE International Conference on Robotics and Automation (ICRA), pp. 556–561. IEEE (2009)

7. Zhang, Q., Zhang, Z.: A novel double-layer, multi-channel soft pneumatic actuator that can achieve multiple motions. In: 23rd International Conference on Mechatronics and Machine Vision in Practice (M2VIP), pp. 1–6. IEEE (2016)

8. Suzumori, K., Hama, T., Kanda, T.: New pneumatic rubber actuators to assist colonoscope insertion. In: IEEE International Conference on Robotics and Automation (ICRA), pp. 1824–1829. IEEE (2006)

9. Onoe, H., Suzumori, K., Kanda, T.: Development of tetra chamber actuator. In: IEEE/RSJ International Conference on Intelligent Robots and Systems (IROS), pp. 777–782. IEEE (2007)

10. Onoe, H., Suzumori, K., Wakimoto, S.: Optimum design of pneumatic multi-chamber rubber tube actuator generating traveling deformation waves for colonoscope insertion. In: IEEE/ASME International Conference on Advanced Intelligent Mechatronics (AIM), pp. 31–36. IEEE (2008)

11. Wakimoto, S., Suzumori, K.: Fabrication and basic experiments of pneumatic multi-chamber rubber tube actuator for assisting colonoscope insertion. In: IEEE International Conference on Robotics and Automation (ICRA), pp. 3260–3265. IEEE (2010)

12. Ozaki, K., Wakimoto, S., Suzumori, K., Yamamoto, Y.: Novel design of rubber tube actuator improving mountability and drivability for assisting colonosocope insertion. In: IEEE International Conference on Robotics and Automation (ICRA), pp. 3263–3268. IEEE (2011)

13. Surakusumah, R.F., Dewi, D.E.O., Supriyanto, E.: Development of a half sphere bending soft actuator for flexible bronchoscope movement. In: IEEE International Symposium on Robotics and Manufacturing Automation (ROMA), pp. 120–125. IEEE (2014)

14. Polygerinos, P., Lyne, S., Wang, Z., Nicolini, L.F., Mosadegh, B., Whitesides, G.M., Walsh, C.J.: Towards a soft pneumatic glove for hand rehabilitation. In: IEEE/RSJ International Conference on Intelligent Robots and Systems (IROS), pp. 1512–1517. IEEE (2013)

15. Razif, M.R.M., Bavandi, M., Nordin, I.N.A.M., Natarajan, E., Yaakob, O.: Two chambers soft actuator realizing robotic gymnotiform swimmers fin. In: IEEE International Conference on Robotics and Biomimetics (ROBIO), pp. 15–20. IEEE (2014)

16. Wang, Z., Chathuranga, D.S., Hirai, S.: 3D Printed soft gripper for automatic lunch box packing. In: IEEE International Conference on Robotics and Biomimetics (ROBIO), pp. 503–508. IEEE (2016)

17. Dahmardeh, M., Ali, M.S.M., Saleh, T., Hian, T.M., Moghaddam, M.V., Nojeh, A., Takahata, K.: High-power MEMS switch enabled by carbon-nanotube contact and shape-memory-alloy actuator. J. Phys. Stat. Sld. (a) **210**(4), 631–638 (2013)
18. Nordin, I.M., Faudzi, A.A.M., Razif, M.R.M., Natarajan, E., Wakimoto, S., Suzumori, K.: Simulations of two patterns fiber weaves reinforced in rubber actuator. J. Teknologi. **3**, 133–138 (2014)
19. Rehman, T., Faudzi, A.A.M., Dewi, D.E.O., Ali, M.S.M.: Design, characterization, and manufacturing of circular bellows pneumatic soft actuator. Int. J. Adv. Manuf. Technol., 1–10 (2017)
20. Ali, M.S.M., Shahrum Shah, A., Osman David, C.: Controllers optimization for a fluid mixing system using metamodelling approach. J. Sim. Mod. **8**(1), 48–59 (2009)

Analysis and Simulation of Wave Power Generation Based on Ship Roll Motion

Tian Xin[1(✉)], Yuying Zhou[2], and Li Liu[1]

[1] School of Automation Science and Electrical Engineering, Beihang University,
Beijing, China
18631370653@163.com
[2] China Shipbuilding Systems Engineering Research Institute, Beijing, China

Abstract. Oceangoing ships produce a roll motion under action of the waves. To absorb and use the energy of roll motion, it's necessary to analyze the movement of the ship. That's of great importance to discuss the feasibility of using the wave activated power generation and evaluate its energy conversion efficiency. In this paper, we choose the ITTC single parameter spectrum and adopt linear superposition method to establish the real-time wave model. Then we simulate the model and verify the correctness of the result according to the spectrum analysis. After that, the roll motion model and energy model of the ship are established. The simulation of the roll motion of ship support for the subsequent study of the energy absorption of the roll motion by basic data.

Keywords: Ship power generation · Hull motion · Real-time wave simulation · Roll simulation

1 Introduction

When ships navigate at sea, with the effect of marine environment like wind and waves, it will have a violent roll motion in the disturbance environment. The violent roll motion reduces the speed of the ship and the equipment on it can't work properly. Furthermore, it makes the staff of ship feel discomfort, which reduces their efficiency and has adverse impact on the boat. In view of this problem, this paper puts forward the idea of absorbing the wave energy of the roll motion of ships to carry out the wave power generation. This can reduce the harm of the roll motion to the hull as well as make the ship's personnel more comfortable, achieving the purpose of reducing. In addition, there are tens of thousands of ships in the world every day, if these vessel can use this renewable energy, the pressure of energy which is getting more and more serious can be alleviate effectively.

The study of wave power generation has been a hundred years of history. The wave energy utilization technology has experienced several stages: device invention, laboratory test and real sea application demonstration. The ultimate goal is reducing the cost of power generation, improving the total efficiency and reliability of the power generation [1]. According to the different ways of energy capture, the existing wave power generation technology include point absorption technology, oscillation water column, oscillating float and so on [2]. The AW-Energy company has developed a tilting

© Springer Nature Singapore Pte Ltd. 2017
M.S. Mohamed Ali et al. (Eds.): AsiaSim 2017, Part I, CCIS 751, pp. 403–412, 2017.
DOI: 10.1007/978-981-10-6463-0_35

expendable wave energy generator—WaveRoller, which has been tested at Peniche in portugal in 2007 [3]. Canada has manufactured an oscillating float wave generator and tested it on the shores of Oregon [4]. The Wavestar is a wave power station consisting of multiple array floats developed by Denmark, which underwent a 1:10 model test in the northern Gulf of Denmark in 2006 [5]. The main equipment of wave energy conversion devices mentioned above are all in the sea and vulnerable to erosion by sea water. Thus they are fragile and difficult to maintain, which means they have lower reliability.

The roll motion of the ship is mainly caused by the wave motion of the sea. The roll motion response of the hull has a great influence on the absorption of wave energy. To research its energy conversion efficiency, it's needed to analyze the roll motion. The interference torque of the waves is mainly related to the wave angle. Analyzing the wave and establishing its mathematical model is the first thing to do. In this paper, the energy that the waves have is calculated. Then we simulate the model of random wave and verify the correctness through frequency spectrum estimation. After that, the mathematic model of the ship with the ideal oceanic disturbance is established. The results of wave angle are taken as the ship roll motion simulation input, getting the roll angle simulation results. Through the analysis of the model, its roll response is studied, helping analyze the energy absorption and motion response.

2 Analysis of Wave Energy

Accurate and reliable wave energy calculation method is the basic prerequisite for researching the conversion efficiency of the wave energy generating device. The wave energy is usually calculated in the form of wave energy flow or wave power. It's the energy of the wave passing through the unit wave width per unit time in the propagation direction [6]. Using the linear wave theory to calculate the wave energy E, the wave surface curve of free water surface can be expressed as follows:

$$\gamma = \zeta_a \cos{(kx - \sigma t)}. \tag{1}$$

In the equation, ζ_a represents the wave height, x represents the distance in the direction of wave propagation, t represents time, k, σ represent the wave number and the fluctuation angle frequency respectively.

There are two kinds of energy carried by wave motion. One is the kinetic energy of the water mass when move at a certain speed. And the other is the potential energy of the water particle vertical displacement relative to the average surface when get away from the equilibrium position. To calculate the energy in the waves, it's necessary to calculate the energy required for all the differential water particles moving from the trough to the crest symmetry. According to the analysis and calculation, the average potential energy generated by the wave motion per unit wavelength is:

$$E_p = \int_0^L \int_0^\gamma \rho g z dx dz = \int_0^L 2\rho g \gamma^2 dx. \tag{2}$$

Substituting γ into the above equation, it turns to:

$$E_p = \frac{1}{4}\rho g \zeta_a^2. \tag{3}$$

where ρ represents the seawater density and g represents the gravitational acceleration.

Similarly, the wave kinetic energy E_k of a single width peak length in a wavelength range can be expressed as:

$$E_k = \int_0^L \int_{-h}^{\gamma} \frac{\rho}{2}\left(u^2 + w^2\right)dxdz. \tag{4}$$

where u, w represents the water particle of the level sub-speed and vertical sub-speed. Then, it becomes:

$$E_k = \frac{1}{4}\rho g \zeta_a^2. \tag{5}$$

The average energy produced by the wave motion of per unit wavelength is:

$$E = E_p + E_k = \frac{1}{2}\rho g \zeta_a^2. \tag{6}$$

The energy contained in the waves is transmitted to the hull in the form of roll motion. For the purpose of studying the energy conversion efficiency, the further analysis of the ship should be carried out.

3   Inertial Wave Energy Generation Absorption Mechanism

In this paper, the inertial wave power generation technology is studied. It's a new type of wave energy generating device based on the gyro effect. The device is composed of a shell part fitted on the hull and a gyro type energy conversion machine inside it. The ship under the action of the waves has roll movement. According to the gyro effect, the internal gyroscope in deflection of the hull maintains the level. This will cause the mechanical transmission mechanism rotation, driving the generator power generation. The energy of the waves is transfer into electricity eventually [7]. In this paper, we do some basic research and focus on the dynamic model of the hull, which may help us analyze its feasibility and energy conversion efficiency (Fig. 1).

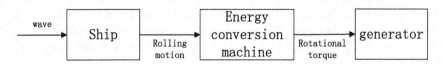

Fig. 1. Wave energy absorption mechanism.

4 Analysis of Ship Roll Motion

The ship absorb energy through the interaction between the waves and the hull. In order to research the movement characteristics of the ship on the waves, the analysis of the characteristics of the waves is needed, which is described by the wave spectrum. And then we take the wave angle as input of the ship roll motion model, completing the simulation of its motion characteristics.

4.1   Random Wave Mathematical Model

1. Random Wave Mathematical Model

The waves are random in time and space. When describing the waves in mathematical models, in order to simplify the problem, it's usually assumed that the waves are two dimension irregular waves. The assumption believe that the waves propagate in a fixed direction. And the crest lines are infinite and parallel to each other. Furthermore, the wave height and the wave period are randomly changed. This kind of irregular waves are also called the long peak irregular waves [8].

According to the theory of linear wave theory, the long peak irregular waves are superimposed by several regular waves of different amplitude, wavelength and random phase [9]. Considering the randomness of the phase, the expression of the waves at one sea level can be written as:

$$\zeta(t) = \sum_{i=0}^{n} \zeta_{ai} \cos(\omega_i t + \varepsilon_i). \tag{7}$$

where ζ_{ai} is the amplitude of the ith harmonic, ω_i is the angular frequency, ε_i is the initial phase angle, evenly distributed between 0 and 2π.

In the practical application of the statistical characteristics of the waves, the concept of wave energy spectrum is used to describe the waves usually. In this paper, the digital simulation of the waves is based on the 12th provisional standard wind wave density formula, that is, the single parameter spectrum. The form of it is:

$$S(\omega) = \frac{A}{\omega^5} \exp\left(-\frac{B}{\omega^4}\right) (m^2 \cdot s). \tag{8}$$

where $A = 8.1 \times 10^{-3} g^2 \approx 0.78$, $B = 3.1/\zeta_{1/3}^2$, ω is the frequency of the waves.

2. Simulation of the Waves

The wave spectrum is a narrow band spectrum, thus the harmonic which frequency is very low or very high has little effect on the amplitude. The simulation of a representative frequency can meet the precision requirements. After selecting the wave spectrum and frequency band to be simulated. The spectrum is discretized by the interval sampling method.

In this paper, the wave height of the selected wave is 2 m, the simulation frequency band is 0.3–3, the number of harmonics is 108, and the corresponding frequency increment is 0.025, simulating the waves of irregular waves in MATLAB and the following results are obtained (Fig. 2).

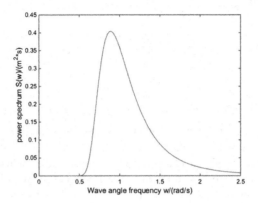

Fig. 2. Wave spectrum simulation.

The results of the simulation need to be tested to determine whether the wave consistent with the requirements. Therefore, we need spectrum analysis of the obtained waves to get its spectrum, which is denoted as $\hat{S}(\omega)$, and compare $\hat{S}(\omega)$ with S(ω) to judge whether the simulation meets the requirements.

3. Spectrum Analysis Verification

The method of power spectrum estimation is used to verify the result of S(ω). The function of Power Spectrum Estimation can estimate the power spectral density of a stationary random signal using a given set of sample data. In this paper, we use the welch algorithm of classical spectral estimation to analyze the spectrum. The main principle is that the data is segmented and windowed to reduce the variance of the spectral estimation, while ensuring that the resolution will not be severely damaged.

According to the spectral estimation theory [10], the power spectrum estimation of the random signal x (n) can be expressed as:

$$S'(\omega) = \frac{1}{2\pi N}|X_N(\omega)|^2. \tag{9}$$

In the formula,

$$X_N(\omega) = X_N(e^{j\omega}) = \sum_{n=0}^{N-1} x(n)e^{-jwn}. \tag{10}$$

where N is the number of points for spectrum analysis. $X_N(\omega)$ is the Fourier transform of the finite length sequence $x(n)$.

The Welch algorithm has improved this method. It divide the length N of the random signal $x(n)$ into segments with the number of p and each segment has M data. It adds the same smooth window $\omega(n)$ and then calculates the Fourier transform. The result is:

$$X_i\left(e^{jw}\right) = \sum_0^{M-1} x_i(n)\omega(n)e^{-jwn}, i = 1, \ldots, M. \tag{11}$$

Calculating the average of the power spectrum of each segment, the result is:

$$S_X\left(e^{jw}\right) = \frac{1}{M}\sum_{i=1}^M \frac{1}{MU}\left|X_i\left(e^{jw}\right)\right|^2. \tag{12}$$

where $U = \frac{1}{M}\sum_0^{M-1}\omega^2(n)$, which means the average power of the window function. Thus $MU = \sum_0^{M-1}\omega^2(n)$ means the energy of the window $\omega(n)$ of length M. The main purpose of windowing function is to extend the signal cycle, so as to get a virtual infinite signal. Then the signal can be Fourier transformed, achieving the goal that convert the signal from the time domain to the frequency domain.

MATLAB provides a function named pwelch which is based on the Welch algorithm. It can complete the power spectrum estimation of the wave random signal. We choose the hamming window as a window function and get the power spectrum as shown in Fig. 2. The shape is similar to the original wave power spectrum. But smoothness of the curve obtained by the power spectrum estimation performance is worse. This may be influenced by the section length, window type or other factors [11].

In order to evaluate the quality of the simulation, we introduce the accuracy evaluation index σ. The expression is as follows:

$$\sigma = \frac{\left|\int_{\omega_1}^{\omega_n}\left(\hat{S}(\omega) - S(\omega)\right)d\omega\right|}{\int_{\omega_1}^{\omega_n} S(\omega)d\omega}. \tag{13}$$

Using the function named trapz in MATLAB to calculate the value of the spectrum. The result is $\sigma = 3.64\%$, which is less than 5%. This meet the simulation accuracy requirements and means that the generated waves and requirements are almost the same (Fig. 3).

4. Wave dip angle simulation

The relationship between wave dip angle amplitude and wave spectrum is:

$$\alpha_{ai} = k\zeta_{ai} = \frac{\omega^2}{g}\sqrt{2S(\omega_i)\Delta\omega_i}. \tag{14}$$

Therefore, the Wave dip angle $\alpha(t)$ at a fixed point in space is:

$$\alpha(t) = \sum_{i=1}^n \sqrt{2Sa\omega_i\Delta\omega_i}\cos\left(\omega_{ei}t + \varepsilon_i\right). \tag{15}$$

The simulation results of a random wave dip angle is as shown in Fig. 4.

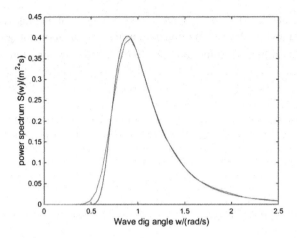

Fig. 3. Wave power spectrum estimation.

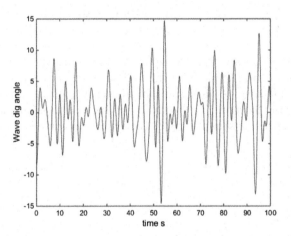

Fig. 4. Wave dip angle simulation results.

4.2   Ship Roll Motion Simulation

The ship navigate at sea has roll motion producing by the waves. According to Connolly's theory, when the ship's roll angle is small, it can be assumed as a linear system with constant time. Using linear rolling theory to research roll motion of the ship, it can be expressed by the linear differential equation with constant coefficients. The core of the problem become determining the response function of the roll frequency [12].

The roll angle of the hull is $\varnothing$. The angular velocity of the roll is $\dot{\varnothing}$. The acceleration of the roll angle is $\ddot{\varnothing}$, the ship roll motion model is:

$$(I_x + \Delta I_x)\ddot{\varnothing} + 2N_\mu\dot{\varnothing} + Dh\varnothing = -(Dh\alpha_m + 2N_\mu\dot{\alpha}_m + \Delta I_x\ddot{\alpha}_m). \tag{16}$$

In the equation above, $(I_x + \Delta I_x)\ddot{\varnothing}$ means the moment of inertia generated by the angular acceleration in the roll motion represents inertia moment generated by the angular acceleration in the roll motion. $2N_\mu\dot{\varnothing}$ means the damping torque generated by the relative action of the ship and the water. $Dh\varnothing$ is the recovery torque generated by the ship's roll. The three terms on the equation's right indicate the wave disturbance torque that causes the ship's roll motion.

The value of the damping disturbance torque $2N_\mu\dot{\alpha}_m$ and the inertia disturbance torque $\Delta I_x\ddot{\alpha}_m$ of wave is much less than the righting perturbed moment $Dh\alpha_m$. So the equation can be written as:

$$(I_x + \Delta I_x)\ddot{\varnothing} + 2N_\mu\dot{\varnothing} + Dh\varnothing = -Dh\alpha_m. \tag{17}$$

Transforming the upper equation, we can get the result as follows:

$$\ddot{\varnothing} + 2\omega_\varnothing\zeta_\mu\dot{\varnothing} + \omega_\varnothing^2\varnothing = -\omega_\varnothing^2\alpha_m. \tag{18}$$

where $\omega_\varnothing = \sqrt{Dh/(I_x + \Delta I_x)}$, $\zeta_\mu = N_\mu/\sqrt{Dh(I_x + \Delta I_x)}$. $\omega_\varnothing$ is the natural angular frequency of roll motion of the ship, which is an important parameter of roll characteristics.

In this paper, we assume that the ship roll motion in the waves is a linear motion. According to the established model of ship roll motion, Laplace transform can get the relationship of roll angle a wave angle in frequency domain, which is called roll frequency response function. By the means of Laplace transform and convolution theorem, we simulate the ship roll angle. The simulation curve is shown in Fig. 5.

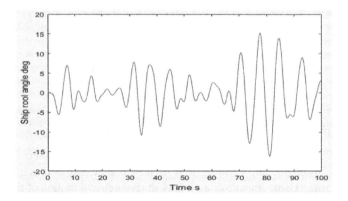

Fig. 5. Ship roll angle simulation.

5 Analysis of Ship Roll Motion

The ship produces the roll motion under the action of the wave and the energy is converted from the wave energy to the mechanical energy of the ship. To absorb this part of the energy, a damper is needed for the roll motion. So the power-take-off device

(PTO) is essential. The energy absorbed by the wave energy generating device is measured on the average power, that is, the energy consumed by the damping of the PTO device per unit time. The total average energy of its absorption in a single wave period is:

$$\bar{P} = \frac{1}{T} \int_0^T B_P \cdot g \cdot \dot{\varnothing}^2 dt. \tag{19}$$

where B_P is the equivalent rotational damping of the PTO.

In the study of energy conversion devices, energy conversion efficiency is an important measure of its ability to work. The energy conversion efficiency is defined as the ratio of the average power obtained by the device to the wave energy generated per unit time. The equation is as follows.

$$\eta = \frac{\bar{P}}{E_S} \times 100\%. \tag{20}$$

Assuming that the effective area of the hull on the waves is S, according to the formula (21), the wave energy per unit time is:

$$\overline{E_S} = \frac{1}{2} \rho g \zeta_a^2 S. \tag{21}$$

Then, the formula (21) can be written as:

$$\eta = \frac{\bar{P}}{E_S} = \frac{\frac{1}{T} \int_0^T B_P \cdot g \cdot \dot{\varnothing}^2 dt}{\frac{1}{2} \rho g \zeta_a^2 S} \times 100\%. \tag{22}$$

Theoretically, the maximum energy can be obtained when the system resonates with the incident wave [13]. The maximum absorption of the wave energy can be achieved by designing the stability of the float and optimizing the energy output part.

6   Conclusion

Based on the engineering application background of ship wave power generation, this paper studies on the wave energy capture technology using energy producing by ship roll motion. Staring from its working mechanism, we establish the ship roll motion model and energy model under random wave.

In this paper, the energy in the waves and the energy absorbed by the ship's roll motion are analyzed and the energy model of wave energy generating device is established. The random wave model is established based on the linear wave theory. The wave dig angle has been simulated by choosing the single parameter spectrum. The result of power spectrum estimated by welch algorithm is compared with the original result and its correctness is verified. Then the model of ship motion is established while the simulation results of wave dip angle is taken as input. The simulation results provide the basic data for the further study of the ship's wave power generation technology, which lays the foundation for the next analysis of its work condition and its energy conversion efficiency.

References

1. Neill, S.P., Hashemi, M.R.: Wave power variability over the northwest European shelf seas (S0306-2619). Appl. Energy **106**(06), 31–46 (2013)
2. Payne, G.S., Taylor, J.R.M., Bruce, T.: Assessment of boundary-element method for modelling a free-floating sloped wave energy device. Part 1: numerical modelling. Ocean Eng. **35**(3–4), 333–341 (2008)
3. AW-EnergyOy.WaveRoller. www.aw-energy.com
4. Vicinanza, D., Margheritini, L., Frigaard, P.: Aquabuoy wave energy converter. J. (2007)
5. Hansen, R.H., Kramer, M.M.: Modelling and control of the wavestar prototype. J. University of Southampton (2011)
6. Wei, M., Bai, Z.: Wave energy resource assessment based on frequency and time domain models (2002)
7. Zhou, Y., Li, B., Cai, Z.: Floating motion and load analysis of gyro - type wave power generating device. Ship Ocean Eng. **45**(3), 90–98 (2016)
8. Wen, S., Yu, Z.: The Theory and Calculation of Waves Theory. Science Press, Beijing (1984)
9. Liang, X., Li, W.: Ship Maneuverability and Wave Resistance. Dalian Maritime University Press, Dalian (2012)
10. Li, Y.: MATLAB to Assist Modern Engineering Digital Signal Processing. Xi'an University of Electronic Science and Technology Press, Xi'an (2002)
11. Hayes, M.H.: Statistical Digital Signal Processing and Modeling. Wiley, New York (1996)
12. Chen, J.: Ship roll motion simulation and fin stabilization system control. Dalian University of Technology (2005)
13. Falcão, A.F.D.O.: Wave energy utilization: a review of the technologies. Renew. Sustain. Energy Rev. **14**(3), 899–918 (2010)

Simulation and Modeling of Free Kicks in Football Games and Analysis on Assisted Training

Zhengqiu Zhu, Bin Chen$^{(\boxtimes)}$, Sihang Qiu, Rongxiao Wang,
and Xiaogang Qiu

College of Information System and Management, National University of Defense
Technology, Changsha 410073, Hunan, People's Republic of China
nudtcb9372@gmail.com

Abstract. Free kick is a common scoring method on football court. Previous study had not yet constructed an effective system assisting players in training free kicks. On basis of studying Dynamic principle, Bernoulli principle and Magnus effect leading to occurrence of such irregular trajectories, stress analysis is conducted to establish the corresponding mathematical model. Based on that, a free-kick simulation and training system is designed to assist daily training of football players in this paper. Experiments are implemented to analyze the effect of parameters such as the kicking point, the kicking force and the kick angle on trajectory of football. Additionally, suggestions are given on how to shoot a goal successfully avoiding the walls and defense of goalkeeper through optimizing the parameters of the kicking point, the kicking force and the kick angle.

Keywords: Free kick · Dynamic principle · Bernoulli principle · Magnus effect · Free-kick simulation and training system

1 Introduction

In football games, the free kick is always fascinating because of its tricky arc, so that goalkeeper often cannot react timely to defense. The world famous football free kicks, for instance, corner kick in the regular season of US Major League by Henry and free kick in the French Four Nations Invitation Tournament by Robert Carlos. The most shocking free kick took place in February 2016, on the Malaysian football field, 28-year-old football player Faiz Soupoli kicked into the most incredible free kick in the history. The arc of the trajectory was so large that all the audience cannot imagine. The football flew toward the left side of the goal, and suddenly changed its direction straight into the right side of the goal. As a result of that, goalkeeper cannot make any judgments, and even camera was cheated. This kind of free kick flies along curved arc, the track of which is similar to a banana, and thus often known as banana ball [1]. The ideal banana ball by virtue of factors of the kick strength, gravity, wind and etc. is formed through different footwork and brilliant technical action.

At present, many scholars have researched and analyzed this strange flight phenomenon of free kick. The main research direction can be broadly divided into three

© Springer Nature Singapore Pte Ltd. 2017
M.S. Mohamed Ali et al. (Eds.): AsiaSim 2017, Part I, CCIS 751, pp. 413–427, 2017.
DOI: 10.1007/978-981-10-6463-0_36

categories. First, the mechanical and aero-dynamical principles were studied [2–6]. Free kicks are considered to be determined by Dynamic principle, Bernoulli principle and Magnus effect. Second, another research direction is on the track offset caused by the initial velocity, the angular velocity and the deformation of football [7–10]. Third, the effects of the kick point, the kick strength and the kick direction on trajectory of football were studied [11–15]. The previous study can reproduce the track of banana ball when initial parameters of the kick point, the kick force and the kick angle are severed as inputs. However, assisting trainings of football players systematically is not the issue of these studies. Besides, complex football stadium environment and the design of wall are also not considered in the previous study.

In light of drawbacks in previous researches, this paper offers remedies to address the challenges of applying principles of free kick into reality with following contributions. First, this paper studies and analyzes related parameters and properties of different types of football because footballs used in different football leagues are various, and the quality, material, size, composition and splicing of which have a great impact on the flight trajectory of free kick. Second, a free-kick simulation and training system is designed based on Dynamic principle, Bernoulli principle and Magnus effect. The system can simulate the Malaysian miraculous free kick and classic free kicks in football history, assisting free kick training of football players and simulation analysis. Finally, this paper offers guidance suggestions on free kicks.

The remainder of this paper is organized as follows. Section 2 presents the main modeling process of free kicks with corresponding solving algorithms. Free kick simulation and training system is designed in Sect. 3. Experiments are conducted in Sect. 4 to analyze the effect of kick point, kick force and kick angle on trajectory of football. Finally, conclusions and future work are discussed in Sect. 5.

2 Model

In this section, the modeling process of free kicks is divided into four steps. The types of football are discussed in Subsect. 2.1; Subsect. 2.2 introduces physical principles of free kicks; the model of kicking phase is given in Subsect. 2.3 while the model of flight phase is constructed in Subsect. 2.4.

2.1 Football Types

Football types have a great impact on stress condition and motion trajectory. Generally speaking, the influence of football itself on the trajectory is mainly reflected in its material, mosaic blocks, mosaic technology, diameter, quality and other factors. In light of statistics of football matches in recent years, types of football are categorized into three classes based on the mosaic blocks. Furthermore, typical types of football of the three classes are listed in Fig. 1: Jabulani football consists of eight blocks; Teamgeist football consists of 14 blocks; Fevernova football consists of 32 blocks.

These three kinds of football are designed by Adidas Sporting Goods Co. Ltd, recognized by International Federation of Association Football which is known as FIFA [2]. Jabulani football was first put into use in the 2010 FIFA World Cup Soccer

Fig. 1. Different types of football (from left to right, Jabulani football, Teamgeist football and Fevernova football respectively).

Tournament; Teamgeist football was first utilized in the 2006 World Cup Soccer Tournament while Fevernova football was first appeared in the 2002 Japan and South Korea World Cup Soccer Tournament. Their physical size and material properties are shown in Table 1.

Table 1. Physical parameters of football.

Types	Jabulani	Teamgeist	Fevernova
Year	2010	2006	2002
Manufacturer	Adidas	Adidas	Adidas
Blocks	8	14	32
Mosaic technology	Thermal bonding	Thermal bonding	Handmade
Surface material	Synthetic materials	Synthetic materials	Synthetic materials
Diameter	220 mm	220 mm	220 mm
Quality	438–441 g	441–444 g	435–450 g

2.2 Physical Principles of Free Kicks

Dynamic Principle. Dynamics is a discipline that studies the relationships between the state of mechanical movement of objects and the forces acted on objects. By studying the movements and forces of objects, general law of mechanical movement is concluded. In essence, the analysis of the trajectory is mainly related to the following principles: the second law of Newton; decomposition theorem of force and basic equations of dynamics.

Bernoulli Principle. The flight of free kicks in the air is a typical aerodynamic problem that will inevitably involve the Bernoulli principle introduced by Daniel Bernoulli [3] in 1738. The principle is that the pressure of object is proportional to its velocity in the flow, which can be formulated in the following formula.

$$p + 0.5\rho V^2 + \rho g h = C. \tag{2.1}$$

where the notation of p represents the pressure of flow; the notation of ρ denotes the density of flow; the notation of g is gravitational acceleration and the notation of h represents the height of flow. The notation of C is a constant, but various to different kinds of flow.

For the phenomenon of banana ball, football not only moves forward, but also rotates around the central axis with high speed at the same time. Due to the viscosity of atmosphere, the rotation of football will drive the surrounding air layer with the same rotation, but the air flows on two sides of football is different. Based on Bernoulli principle, it is easily concluded that the pressure of air on two sides of football would be different in light of air flow, resulting in a transverse pressure difference. Under this transverse pressure difference, football will generate lateral shift deviating from the original trajectory, leading to a curved arc.

Magnus Effect. The Magnus effect is a phenomenon applying the Bernoulli principle to rotational objects. The Magnus effect can be defined as a lateral force in the direction which is perpendicular to the plane consisting of the rotational angular velocity vector and the translational velocity vector when the rotation angular velocity of the object does not coincide with the flight velocity vector. Under this lateral force, the phenomenon of deviation of flight trajectory is named as Magnus effect [4]. As the direction of Magnus force is vertical to the motion direction of football, thus changing the direction of football's trajectory.

2.3   Model of Kicking Phase

This section mainly analyzes the forces at the moment when football is kicked. On the basis of dynamic principles, it is worth noting that the initial velocity and initial angular velocity are generated in virtue of the following factors: the kicking point, the kicking force, the kicking direction, material of football, pressure inside the football and contact time of feet in the kicking phase [5].

Force Analysis in Kicking Phase. Center of football is set as the origin of coordinate system. The spherical coordinate system is shown in Fig. 2. It can be seen that the notation of θ is defined as the counterclockwise rotation angle from the X-axis to the directional line segment of r from the forward view of Z-axis; the notation of ϕ denotes the auxiliary angle from the directional line segment of r to the forward of Z-axis.

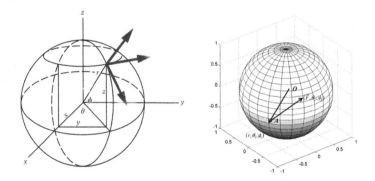

Fig. 2. Spherical coordinate system and force analysis in kicking phase.

We define the action point when football player kicks the ball as point of A. The point can be formulated as $(r \cos \phi_1 \cos \theta_1, r \cos \phi_1 \sin \theta_1, r \sin \phi_1)$ in spherical coordinate system. According to rules of FIFA, the radius of football should be set in the interval of 0.108 and 0.1105 m. If a player wants to play a free kick, the kick point should be located in the lower part of football, that is to say, the value of ϕ_1 ought to be set less than or equal to zero. In addition, due to the limitations in reality, the kicking point could not less than 60°. Therefore, the range of ϕ_1 will be set between zero degree and 60°. We exhibit the force analysis during kicking phase in the right part of Fig. 2. The force of F acting on any direction of football can be expressed as $\vec{F} = (F \cos \phi_2 \cos \theta_2, F \cos \phi_2 \sin \theta_2, F \sin \phi_2)$ in the spherical coordinate system. To determine the initial velocity and initial rotational angular velocity of football, we divide the force of F into two forces: one is the force of $\vec{F}_N$ in the normal direction and another is the force of $\vec{F}_F$ in the tangential direction.

Considering the unit normal vector at point of A can be formulated as the following equation of $\vec{N} = (\cos(-\phi_1) \cos(\theta_1 + \pi), \cos(-\phi_1) \sin(\theta_1 + \pi), \sin(-\phi_1))$, the force of $\vec{F}_N$ in the normal direction can be computed as below.

$$\vec{F}_N = \vec{F} \cdot \vec{N}$$
$$= (-F \cos \phi_1 \cos \theta_1 \cos \phi_2 \cos \theta_2, -F \cos \phi_1 \sin \theta_1 \cos \phi_2 \sin \theta_2, -F \sin \phi_1 \sin \phi_2).$$
$$(2.2)$$

Then, decomposing the force of $\vec{F}_N$ in the direction of X, Y, Z axis, the representation of the force in the Cartesian coordinate system can be formulated as follows.

$$\begin{cases} F_{Nx} = -F \cos \phi_1 \cos \theta_1 \\ F_{Ny} = -F \cos \phi_1 \sin \theta_1 \\ F_{Nz} = -F \sin \phi_1 \end{cases} . \qquad (2.3)$$

Similarly, the force of $\vec{F}_F$ in the tangential direction is shown in equation of 2.4.

$$\begin{cases} F_{Fx} = F \cos \phi_1 \cos \theta_1 (1 - \cos \phi_2 \cos \theta_2) \\ F_{Fy} = F \cos \phi_1 \sin \theta_1 (1 - \cos \phi_2 \sin \theta_2) \\ F_{Fz} = F(1 - \sin \phi_1 \sin \phi_2) \end{cases} . \qquad (2.4)$$

Initial Velocity and Initial Angular Velocity. After determining the force of football in the normal direction and tangential direction, the initial velocity of football could be calculated as the following formula according to momentum conservation law.

$$\begin{cases} V_{0x} = \frac{F_{Nx} + F_{Fx}}{m} t_c \\ V_{0y} = \frac{F_{Ny} + F_{Fy}}{m} t_c \\ V_{0z} = \frac{F_{Nz} + F_{Fz}}{m} t_c \end{cases} . \qquad (2.5)$$

where the notation of t_c is the contact time between feet and football, according to statistical data [5], the value of t_c is generally set as 9.5 ms.

The initial angular velocity of football is mainly determined by the moment it receives. The rotation of football depends mainly on the force of $\vec{F}_F$ in the tangential direction, which generates a moment of $\vec{M}$ determined by the following formula, since the torque in the normal direction is zero.

$$\begin{cases} M_x = r_y F_{Fz} - r_z F_{Fy} \\ M_y = r_z F_{Fx} - r_x F_{Fz} , \\ M_z = r_x F_{Fy} - r_y F_{Fx} \end{cases} \begin{cases} r_x = r \cos \phi_1 \cos \theta_1 \\ r_y = r \cos \phi_1 \sin \theta_1 . \\ r_z = r \sin \phi_1 \end{cases} \tag{2.6}$$

After determining the moment of football in the direction of X, Y, Z axis, the initial angular velocity vector can be calculated as follows. In the formula, we assume that the football is a hollow sphere with uniform mass distribution. The rotary inertia of football is defined as $I = (2/3) \cdot mr^2$.

$$\begin{cases} \omega_{0x} = \frac{M_x t_c}{I} \\ \omega_{0y} = \frac{M_y t_c}{I} . \\ \omega_{0z} = \frac{M_z t_c}{I} \end{cases} \tag{2.7}$$

2.4   Model of Flight Phase

Model Hypothesis. To simplify the modeling process, the following assumptions are made in this paper: (1) ignoring the effects of air buoyancy; (2) the quality of football remains invariant during the game; (3) if football collides with other object in process of flight, its flight velocity is determined by the specular reflection principle after collision; (4) the wind will be set as a constant due to the short flight distance; (5) impact of extreme weather conditions is not considered.

Force Analysis in Flight Phase. Wesson [6] pointed out that movement of football is affected by three forces during flight phase: the gravity $\vec{F}g$, the aerodynamic drag $\vec{F}d$ and the Magnus force $\vec{F}mag$, where the direction of gravity is vertical downward, the direction of aerodynamic drag is opposite to the direction of velocity, and the direction of the Magnus force is perpendicular to the plane consisted of the direction of velocity and the direction of angular velocity, determined by the right-hand Cartesian coordinate system. The detailed force analysis is shown in Fig. 3.

Kreighbaum and Barthels [11] introduced that the aerodynamic drag and the Magnus force are air forces, determined by surface characteristics of football itself, the exposure area in the air, velocity of air flow, pressure and other factors. The corresponding formulas are shown as below.

$$\vec{F}_d = -(1/2) \cdot C_d \rho A |\vec{v}|^2 \cdot (\vec{v}/|\vec{v}|). \tag{2.8}$$

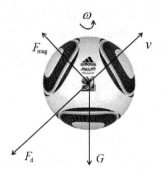

Fig. 3. Force analysis in flight phase.

$$\vec{F}_{mag} = (1/2) \cdot C_m \rho A |\vec{v}|^2 \cdot (\vec{\omega} \times \vec{v} / |\vec{\omega} \times \vec{v}|). \tag{2.9}$$

where the notation of C_d is the coefficient of aerodynamic drag; the notation of C_m is the coefficient of Magnus force; the notation of A denotes project area which is computed as πr^2; the notation of v represents the velocity of football; and density of atmosphere is $\rho = 1.2 kg/m^3$. Since air forces not only slow down the velocity, but also decrease the angular velocity. Thus, both the aerodynamic drag and the Magnus force are varying with time. It is pointed out in [5] that the viscous torque M of rotating football is computed as follows in the fluid where viscous force is defined as μ.

$$M = I \cdot (d\omega/dt) = 8\pi \mu r^3 \omega. \tag{2.10}$$

Integrating both sides of the above formula, the rotating angular velocity of ω at any moment during the flight phase can be represented as below.

$$\omega = \omega_0 e^{-\lambda t}. \tag{2.11}$$

$$\lambda = 8\pi \mu r^3 / I. \tag{2.12}$$

Additionally, football in flight phase will also affected by gravity. In general, acceleration of gravity is set at $9.8\ m/s^2$.

According to [10], the coefficient of aerodynamic drag is determined. Interested readers can refer to this paper. Similarly, the coefficient of Magnus force is determined by Asia in [15].

Acceleration Equations in Flight Phase. Considering the gravity, the aerodynamic drag and the Magnus force, the acceleration equation is defined as below.

$$\vec{a} = \vec{F}_d / m + \vec{F}_{mag} / m + \vec{g}. \tag{2.13}$$

The trajectory in flight phase can be acquired through integrating the above formula. The integration process is implemented in the form of Taylor expansion. In addition, speed of wind should be considered into flight phase. We utilize $\vec{v}_w$ to represent the speed of wind. Therefore, the velocity of football at any moment of flight phase is defined as $\vec{v} \rightarrow \vec{v} + \vec{v}_w$.

$$\begin{cases} \lim_{\Delta t \to 0} x(t + \Delta t) = x(t) + x'(t)\Delta t \\ \lim_{\Delta t \to 0} y(t + \Delta t) = y(t) + y'(t)\Delta t \\ \lim_{\Delta t \to 0} z(t + \Delta t) = z(t) + z'(t)\Delta t \end{cases} \tag{2.14}$$

$$\begin{cases} \lim_{\Delta t \to 0} x'(t + \Delta t) = x'(t) + x''(t)\Delta t \\ \lim_{\Delta t \to 0} y'(t + \Delta t) = y'(t) + y''(t)\Delta t \\ \lim_{\Delta t \to 0} z'(t + \Delta t) = z'(t) + z''(t)\Delta t \end{cases} \tag{2.15}$$

3 Design of Free Kick Simulation and Training System

Based on models discussed in Sect. 2, free kick simulation and training system is implemented by Unity 3D. Unity 3D is a multi-platform and a fully integrated professional game engine developed by Unity Technologies that allows users to easily create interactive content such as 3D video games, architectural visualization, real-time 3D animation and etc. The system realizes functional modules such as classic simulation, free practice and advanced practice procedures. In module of classic simulation, corner kick in the regular season of US Major League by Henry, free kick in the French Four Nations Invitation Tournament by Robert Carlos and shocking free kick on the Malaysian football field by Faiz Soupoli are realized. The free practice module simulates the situation without the defense of other party, users can realize the aims of trajectory prediction, strategy planning and training assistance through setting the initial parameters of the kicking point, the initial velocity, initial angular velocity and shooting location of football. Compared to free practice module, the defense wall is added into advanced practice module, which is a real reduction of the shooting scene. In this module, users can train their free kick techniques under the condition of defensive wall.

3.1 System Interface and Overall Structure

The main interface of free kick simulation and training system is shown in Fig. 4. Entering the operator interface, it can be divided into five parts: parameter setting area, visual angle selecting area, data exporting area, operation controlling area and court displaying area according to function. The detailed division is exhibited in Fig. 5.

Fig. 4. Main interface of system.

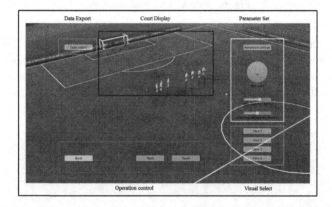

Fig. 5. Operation interface of system.

3.2 Classic Simulation Module

In classic simulation module, corner kick in the regular season of US Major League by Henry, free kick in the French Four Nations Invitation Tournament by Robert Carlos and shocking free kick on the Malaysian football field by Faiz Soupoli are realized. Entering this module, users have to select one of the classis free kicks to simulate. And then, users click on start button, the player is able to complete the entire shooting process based on pre-set parameters while the wall and goalkeeper conduct the defense process based on motion rules. To better exhibit the trajectory of football, uses can switch from four visual angles to observe the shooting process. The free kick of Faiz Soupoli is simulated in Fig. 6.

3.3 Free Practice Module

The free practice module allows users to choose the shooting location in left half of football court. When the shooting location is selected within the restricted area, the system will shoot the football at penalty point by default. In other cases, the shooting

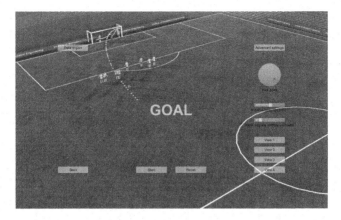

Fig. 6. Free kick of Faiz Soupoli.

location is determined by the users' click position as shown in Fig. 7. Users could acquire trajectory of football through determining parameters of the kicking point, initial velocity and initial angular velocity in parameter setting area or parameters of the kicking point, the kick force and the kicking angle in advanced settings.

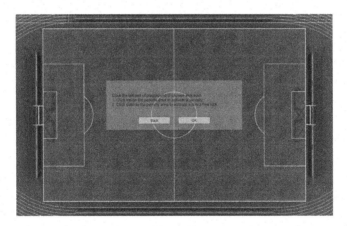

Fig. 7. Entering interface of free practice module.

3.4   Advanced Practice Module

Considering that, it must exist defensive wall of the other party to prevent the goal of free kick in reality. Therefore, the model of defensive wall is added into advanced practice module according to rules of FIFA. The module assists users to play free kicks in the condition of defensive wall. The detailed interface is shown in Fig. 8.

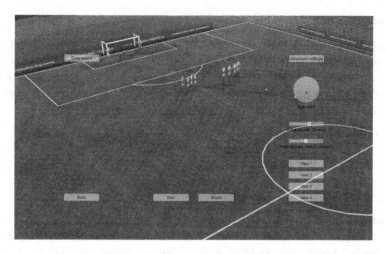

Fig. 8. Influence of θ_1 on trajectory.

4   Experiments

The section firstly studies the effect of kick point, kick force and kick angle on trajectory of football in flight phase. Furthermore, based on the scene of shocking free kick taking place in Malaysian football field, this paper studies how to develop innovative strategies to achieve the purpose of assisting training of players. According to variable-controlling approach, the following three groups of experiments are designed to study the influence of these three factors on trajectory of football. Through the analysis of experimental results, strategies of scoring easily are given to achieve the purpose of assisting training of players and trajectory prediction (Fig. 9).

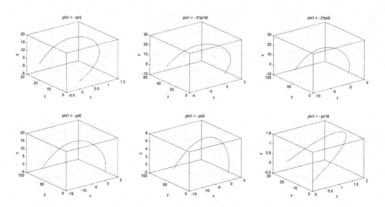

Fig. 9. Influence of φ_1 on trajectory.

4.1   Influence of the Kicking Point

For a certain type of football, the radius of football is a fixed value. Therefore, the influence of kicking point on trajectory is considered as the impact of two parameters of θ_1 and φ_1 in spherical coordinates on trajectory essentially. It can be seen that the value of θ_1 and φ_1 should be set as $\theta_1 \in (-\pi, 0), \phi_1 \in (-\pi/3, 0)$ from the definition of the spherical coordinates and actual kicking regularities.

The Influence of θ_1. In simulations, the actual value of θ_1 is chosen at $-\pi$, $-5\pi/6$, $-2\pi/3$, $-\pi/2$, $-\pi/3$ and $-\pi/6$ when other parameters stay invariant. The simulation results are exhibited in the following figure. By analysis, it is worth noting that the impact of θ_1 on trajectory is reflected in orientation. When the value of θ_1 varies, the orientation of trajectory changes extremely.

The Influence of φ_1. In simulations, the actual value of φ_1 is chosen at $-\pi/3, -5\pi/18, -4\pi/9, -\pi/6, -\pi/9$ and $-\pi/18$ when other parameters stay invariant. The simulation results are exhibited in the following figure. By analysis, it is worth noting that the impact of φ_1 on trajectory is reflected in maximum latitude of positive axis (Z). In conclusion, the maximum height of trajectory grows larger as the value of φ_1 gets smaller.

4.2   Influence of the Kicking Force

Considering the extreme value of the kicking force, the range of kicking force is usually set as $F \in (0, +\infty)$. In simulations, the actual value of F is chosen at 500 N, 1000 N, 1500 N, 2000 N, 2500 N and 3000 N when other parameters are set invariant. The simulation results are shown in the following figure. It is worth noting that when the value of kicking force varies, the orientation of the football track is basically not changed, but the bending degree of trajectory undergoes tremendous changes. Additionally, it is also worth noting that when the value of kicking force is over 2000 N, trajectory of football almost stays invariant (Fig. 10).

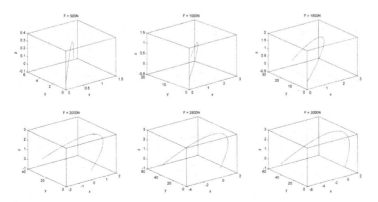

Fig. 10. Influence of the kicking force on trajectory.

4.3   Influence of the Kicking Angle

The kicking angle is reflected by two parameters of θ_2 and ϕ_2 in spherical coordinates. Therefore, the impact of kicking angle on trajectory can be considered as the impact of these two parameters. It can be seen that the value of θ_2 and φ_2 should be set as $\theta_2 \in (0, \pi), \phi_2 \in (0, 2\pi)$ from the definition of the spherical coordinates and actual kicking regularities.

The Influence of θ_2. In simulations, the actual value of θ_2 is chosen at $\pi/6$, $\pi/3$, $\pi/2$, $2\pi/3$, $5\pi/6$ and π when other parameters stay invariant. The simulation results are exhibited in the following figure. Though analyzing the results, it is worth noting that when the value of θ_1 varies, the orientation and bending extent of trajectory changes extremely (Fig. 11).

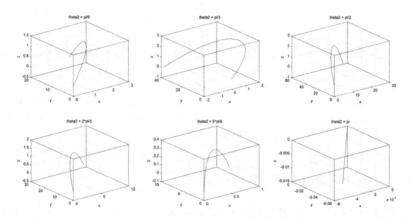

Fig. 11. Influence of θ_2 on trajectory.

The Influence of ϕ_2. In simulations, the actual value of ϕ_2 is chosen at $\pi/18$, $\pi/9$, $\pi/3$, $\pi/6$, $2\pi/9$ and $5\pi/18$ when other parameters stay invariant. The simulation results are exhibited in the following figure. By analysis, it is worth noting that when the value of ϕ_2 varies, the orientation and bending extent of trajectory changes in some extent but not extremely. In addition, when the value of ϕ_2 is over $2\pi/9$, the trajectory of football almost stay invariant. In conclusion, the impact of ϕ_2 on trajectory is reflected in orientation and curvature to some extent in a certain ranges of ϕ_2 (Fig. 12).

4.4   Suggestions on Assisting Training of Players

From point view of a player, if he or she tends to play an effective free kick, the comprehensive impact of the kicking point, the kicking force and the kicking angle should be considered. Based on results and analysis above, some suggestions are given as below. (1) In the moment of kicking football, it is effective to set the kicking force between 2000 and 2500 N; (2) in order to achieve the aim of goal, the choice of kicking

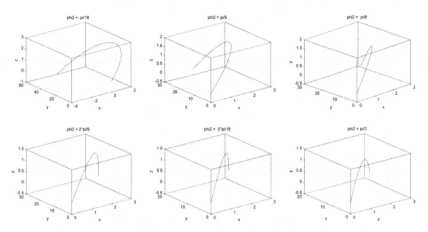

Fig. 12. Influence of ϕ_2 on trajectory.

point should be reasonable. If location of kicking point on football is too high, the maximum of trajectory will be low. Thus the free kick is lack of aggression. If the location of kicking point on football is too low, it is easy to kick the football to the air. Therefore, the suitable kicking point is on the middle lower of football; (3) to avoid the defensive wall, the kicking angle should be well controlled because it directly determines the basic orientation and curvature of football.

5   Conclusions and Future Work

The paper focuses on modeling process of free kicks in football. Then, based on motion model of football, the free kick simulation and training system is designed. Three main modules are implemented in the system, including classic simulation module, free practice module and advanced practice module. Finally, we analyze the impact of kicking point, kicking force and kicking angle on trajectory of football. Results and related analysis illustrates that our system is able to predict the trajectory of football and assist training of players effectively. Additionally, some suggestions are put forward on playing free kicks intelligently. In the future, the impact of weather will be considered in our system. Besides, the impact of the number of defensive players who make up the wall and the combination form of the wall on shooting strategy will also be considered.

Acknowledgments. This study is supported by National Key Research & Development (R&D) Plan under Grant No. 2017YFC0803300 and the National Natural Science Foundation of China under Grant Nos. 71673292, 61503402 and Guangdong Key Laboratory for Big Data Analysis and Simulation of Public Opinion and Shanghai Special Foundation of Software and Integrated Circuit under Grant No. 150312.

References

1. Banana ball. http://baiki.m.sougou.fullLemma.jsp.html
2. Alam, F., Chowdhury, H., Moria, H.: Aerodynamics of contemporary FIFA soccer ball. J. Procedia Eng. **13**, 188–193 (2011)
3. Bernoulli principle. http://m.baike.m.sougou.com/baike/fullLemma.jsp.html
4. Magnus effect. http://m.sougou.com/baike/fullLemma.jsp.html
5. Gupta, G., Panigrahi, P.K.: Curve kick aerodynamics of a soccer ball. In: Proceeding of the Fortieth National Conference on Fluid Mechanics and Fluid Power, Himachal Pradesh (2013)
6. Wesson, J., Mccullen, J.D.: The science of soccer. J. Phys. Today. **56**(6), 64 (2003)
7. Oggiano, L., Santran, L.: Aerodynamics of modern soccer balls. In: 8th Conference of the International Sports Engineering Association, pp. 2473–2479. IEEE Press, Vienna (2010)
8. Alam, F., Chowdhury, H., Moria, H.: A comparative study of football aerodynamics. J. Procedia Eng. **2**, 2443–2448 (2010)
9. Barber, S., Chin, S.B., Carre, M.J.: Sports ball aerodynamics: a numerical study of the erratic motion of soccer balls. J. Comput. Fluids. **38**, 1091–1100 (2009)
10. Alam, F., Ho, H., Chowdhury, H., Subic, A.: Aerodynamics of baseball. J. Procedia Eng. **13**, 207–212 (2011)
11. Krause, J.: Biomechanics: A Qualitative Approach for Studying Human Movement. Macmillan, Basingstoke (1996)
12. Naito, K., Fukui, Y., Maruyama, T.: Multijoint kinetic chain analysis of knee extension during the soccer instep kick. J. Hum. Mov. Sci. **29**, 259–276 (2010)
13. Always, L.W., Hubbard, M.: Experimental determination of baseball spin and lift. J. Sports Sci. **19**, 349–358 (2001)
14. Bray, K., Kerwin, D.G.: Modeling the flight of a soccer ball in a direct free kick. J. Sports Sci. **21**, 75–85 (2003)
15. Asia, T., Seo, K., Kobayashi, O., Sakashita, R.: Fundamental aerodynamics of the soccer ball. J. Sports Eng. **10**, 101–110 (2007)

The Design of Spatial Selection Using CUR Decomposition to Improve Common Spatial Pattern for Multi-trial EEG Classification

Hilman Fauzi[1,2(✉)], Mohd Ibrahim Shapiai[1], Rubiyah Yusof[1],
Gerard B. Remijn[3], Noor Akhmad Setiawan[4], and Zuwairie Ibrahim[5]

[1] Malaysia Japan International Institute of Technology (MJIIT),
Universiti Teknologi Malaysia (UTM), Kuala Lumpur, Malaysia
{md_ibrahim83, rubiyah.kl}@utm.my
[2] Faculty of Electrical Engineering, Telkom University, Bandung, Indonesia
hilmanfauzitsp@telkomuniversity.ac.id
[3] Faculty of Design, Kyushu University, Fukuoka, Japan
remijn@design.kyushu-u.ac.jp
[4] Department of Electrical Engineering and Information Technology,
Universitas Gadjah Mada, Yogyakarta, Indonesia
noorwewe@ugm.ac.id
[5] Faculty of Electrical and Electronic Engineering, Universiti Malaysia Pahang,
26600 Pekan, Pahang, Malaysia
zuwairie@ump.edu.my

Abstract. The most important factor in EEG signal processing is the determination of relevant features in encoding the meaning of the signal. Obtaining relevant features for EEG can be done using a spatial filter. The Common Spatial Pattern (CSP) is known to produce discriminative features when processing EEG signals. Yet, CSP is also sensitive to noise and is channel-dependent, as it is considered to be a spatial filter. However, the disadvantage of CSP is that channels containing only noise are also considered as active channels. In this paper, the design of a filter for spatial selection is proposed using CUR decomposition to select important channels or the time segment of EEG trials in order to improve CSP performance. CUR decomposition can also be used as a noise rejection technique because CUR can be used in factorizing the given EEG signals. In other words, CUR decomposition rejects the non-active channels, which typically contain noise, before spatially filtering the EEG signals. Once the EEG signal is decomposed based on the importance of the channels, time segmentation, and EEG factorization, the decomposed signal can be used as input to the CSP. In general, three approaches were proposed in this framework: (1) channel selection, i.e., C selection; (2) time segment selection, R; and (3) signal factorization, U. Furthermore, the performance accuracy between the original CSP and CSP in which the input was spatially filtered by the proposed framework was validated using datasets IVa of BCI competition III. The test results show that the CSP with spatial selection using C selection and U factorization offers 12% and 9% improvement compared to the original CSP, respectively. Hence, the proposed method in this study can be used as a spatial filter to improve the CSP performance.

© Springer Nature Singapore Pte Ltd. 2017
M.S. Mohamed Ali et al. (Eds.): AsiaSim 2017, Part I, CCIS 751, pp. 428–442, 2017.
DOI: 10.1007/978-981-10-6463-0_37

Keywords: Common spatial pattern · CUR decomposition · Channel selection · BCI

1 Introduction

The Brain Computer Interface (BCI) is an external device that can be used to communicate directly with the brain. Signals generated by brain waves are recorded by electrodes attached to a certain position on the scalp, and connected to an Electroencephalography (EEG) device. BCI does not require the intervention of an external device or muscular organs of the body to produce an interaction [1].

In general, there are two methods to acquire brain signals: invasive and non-invasive. Using invasive technology, electrodes are implanted into or on the surface of the brain. The biggest advantage of this method is its high temporal and spatial resolution, which will improve the quality of the obtained signal and the signal-to-noise ratio. However, invasive, intracranial EEG requires surgical procedures in a clinical environment. Meanwhile, with non-invasive technology, brain activity can be measured using an external sensor [1]. The sensor captures the electrical activity on the surface of the scalp, resulting in brain signals that can be used for further processing and analysis.

Based on various existing studies that have been done, the electrical signal generated from brain activity can be divided into two main approaches: the first approach relates to exploring the effects of various triggered conditions as evoked potentials (EPs). The electrical responses of the nervous system are recorded as a result of a stimulus, which can be subdivided into steady-state evoked potentials (SSEPs) and event-related-potentials (ERPs). Alternatively, other studies aim to detect oscillations, brain signals that are locked to an internal or external stimulus, but not phase-locked to an event, such as in event-related synchronization/synchronization (ERD/ERS). In some ERD/ERS studies it has been found that the changes caused by certain stimulation can discontinue or reduce the power of ongoing EEG signals. The BCI ERD/ERS system does not need external stimuli; extensive training with *internal* stimulation can also induce ERD/ERS. This is done by performing mental tasks, such as motor imagery, mental arithmetics, or mental rotation [1].

Generally, the Brain Computer Interface (BCI) system is divided into three processes: preprocessing, feature extraction, and feature selection. Each process plays a critical role in translating brain signals using EEG. In the preprocessing of BCI, many techniques have been introduced such as spatial filters e.g., Independent Component Analysis (ICA), laplacian, Principal Component Analysis (PCA), Common Spatial Pattern (CSP), Linear Discriminant Analysis (LDA), etc., which are effective in extracting representative brain activity patterns. The motor imagery signal is one of the brain signals for which it is quite difficult to define a good pattern. Therefore, whether it is best still needs to be determined using the CSP method could improve this.

The Common Spatial Pattern (CSP) is commonly used in processing the motor imagery EEG signal because it can discriminate the mental states induced by motor imagery [2]. However, CSP as a spatial filter lacks the ability to drive the data, which makes this method a powerless one. In any case, the method cannot define the true motor imagery of a specific situation. Besides that, CSP still has problems with estimating the class of covariance matrices, which may be negatively influenced by EEG-measurement artifacts such as subject movement or loose electrodes. Furthermore, another problem with CSP is that it assumes all channels to be related to one another even when only noise relationships are evident. Because of these problems, many strategies have been proposed to improve CSP performance.

The various strategies to improve CSP performance include a variety of modifications to the components of the CSP as covariance. A more in-depth discussion of this issue is presented in Sect. 2. In this paper, some other methods to improve the quality of the spatial filter in the BCI process are proposed with no modifications to the components of CSP, which is used as a spatial filtering template. The strategy offered in this study is called spatial selection. In general, spatial selection involves optimization of the quality of the input dataset spatial filtering process through the CUR Decomposition approach.

The variety of strategies for optimizing CSP is not so flexible for application in a multitude of conditions. The strategies vary depending on the data-set. Therefore, the applied method can be applied only in a specific case and is not applicable for other types of datasets. In this paper, a strategy to improve the CSP algorithm was introduced by manipulating the dataset. This work focuses on how to create a new optimal dataset using CUR decomposition without making any changes to the inside mechanics of the CSP algorithm. CSP is only used as a template to optimize the preprocessing process in spatial filtering.

This paper will also discuss similar studies and related works, as well as further discuss the CUR Matrix, Common Spatial Pattern, and Extreme Learning Machine in regard to the techniques employed. The adopted strategy and the proposed method in this study will also be discussed. Furthermore, the testing and analysis phases are presented in the experiment, result, and discussion section.

2 Related Works

The improvement strategies for CSP concern: robust estimation, stationary feature, multi-subject, multi-class, analytics, and local temporal structure. This categorization is based on the methods to improve CSP, which involve all its components. A robust estimation is proposed to improve the estimation of the covariance matrix. Several studies have used the robust estimation strategy, such as Regularized Common Spatial Pattern (RCSP) [3], which modified the covariance estimates using the Minimum Covariance Determinant (MCD) estimator. [4] Masking covariance matrix is introduced based on the functionality of brain region. In [5–7], the improvement to CSP was proposed by selecting channels or imposing the sparsity spatial filter. In [8], the Lp-norm was applied to robustify the variance estimation in the CSP. [9] discussed several methods to minimize noise. The stationary feature involves compensating the non-stationary data pattern. Strategies such as regularizing CSP [10] using the stationary subspaces (sCSP) method aim to increase classification accuracy to solve the non-stationary problem directly. [11, 12] for similar purposes, particle swarm optimization can be proposed to improve CSP. The two-step approach in [13–15] was also suggested to calculate the stationary features. Furthermore, a powerful feature extraction method [16] was proposed to reduce the non-stationarity sessions. Another strategy to improve the CSP is to combine data from another dataset, also known as the multi-subject method. One of the goals of this strategy is for the spatial filter to learn a new subject based on its own data and that of other subjects [17]. A Bayesian method for subject-to-subject information transfer was proposed in [18]. The method used in [19] was part of a multi-subject method, which applied multiple kernel learning to combine information from other subjects. The multi-class strategy involves methods that are specifically designed for modifications or improvements to the multi-class and the optimization of the solutions using a variety of approaches such as information theory [20], joint approximate diagonalization [21], or Kullback-Leibler divergence [22].

Analytic methods are used to analyze the amplitude and phase of an EEG signal to get the best scenario, so as to improve the discriminative capability of CSP [23, 24]. Another method to improve CSP can be conducted by considering the local temporal structure such as in [25–27], which applied this method via observing the samples to improve quality.

3 Employed Technique

3.1 CUR Matrix

CUR is one of the data compression methods, which is appropriately stated in terms of a small part of proper columns and/or proper rows of an original data matrix. CUR is divided into 3 matrices, C, U, and R, as per Eq. (1):

$$\mathbf{A} \approx \mathbf{CUR} \tag{1}$$

where C consists of a selected number of actual columns of A, R consists of a selected number of actual rows of A, and U is a special matrix that ensures the CUR product is as close as possible to $\mathbf{A}$ [28]. This method has been widely used in data analysis such as in computer science.

3.2 Common Spatial Pattern (CSP)

The Common Spatial Pattern (CSP) is a powerful method for feature extraction. It generates a set of spatial filters that can be used to define multi-dimensional data into a set of uncorrelated components [29]. CSP is powerful in distinguishing two classes of EEG data by finding the maximum variances of one multi-channel signal and simultaneously minimizing the other variances.

For simplification purposes, the CSP process can be arranged into six steps:

(1) Obtain sample covariance—assuming a single trial is taken, the sum of sample covariance matrices for that particular trial can be calculated using Eq. (2):

$$C_y = \frac{1}{n_y} \sum \frac{E_j(y)E_j^T(y)}{trace\left(E_j(y)E_j^T(y)\right)} \tag{2}$$

where

E_j = EEG signal for the j-*th* trial
n_y = number of trials for the y class
y = class (e.g. left and right)

(2) Combine sample and obtain eigenvalue. Combine spatial covariance from two classes as per Eq. (3):

$$\mathbf{C_t} = \mathbf{C_1} + \mathbf{C_2} \tag{3}$$

where $\mathbf{C_1}$ is the average spatial covariance for class 1 (left) and $\mathbf{C_2}$ is the average spatial covariance for class 2 (right). After the spatial covariance is combined, the composite spatial covariance will be used to satisfy the factorized formula presented in Eq. (4):

$$\mathbf{C_t} = \hat{\mathbf{U}}\hat{\mathbf{A}}\hat{\mathbf{U}}^{\mathbf{T}} \tag{4}$$

where $\hat{\mathbf{U}}$ is the matrix of the eigenvector and $\hat{\mathbf{A}}$ is the diagonal matrix of the corresponding eigenvalues.

(3) Obtain unity data for both eigenvalues. The obtained eigenvalues are sorted in descending order and then added to the whitened transformation using Eq. (5):

$$\mathbf{P} = \hat{\mathbf{A}}^{-1/2}\hat{\mathbf{U}}^{\mathbf{T}} \tag{5}$$

(4) Separate the data into respective classes. Whiten the signals for both classes using Eqs. (6) and (7);

$$\mathbf{S_1} = \mathbf{P}\mathbf{C_1}\mathbf{P}^{\mathbf{T}} \tag{6}$$

$$\mathbf{S_2} = \mathbf{P}\mathbf{C_2}\mathbf{P}^{\mathbf{T}} \tag{7}$$

and the common eigenvector using Eqs. (8) and (9):

$$\mathbf{S_1} = \mathbf{B}\lambda_1 \mathbf{B}^{\mathbf{T}} \tag{8}$$

$$\mathbf{S_2} = \mathbf{B}\lambda_2 \mathbf{B}^{\mathbf{T}} \tag{9}$$

(5) Take the most and least eigenvalue. The matrix projection is thus formed based on Eq. (10):

$$\hat{\mathbf{W}}_0 = \mathbf{B}^{\mathbf{T}} \mathbf{P} \tag{10}$$

For discriminative patterns, the first and last 3 columns of $\hat{\mathbf{W}}_0$ are kept in form $\hat{\mathbf{W}}$.

(6) Extract feature from the data and simplify it into a single value for each channel. To extract the feature, trial X is projected as per Eq. (11):

$$\hat{Z} = \hat{W}^{T} X \tag{11}$$

Finally, a Q-dimensional feature vector $\hat{y}$ is formed from the variance of $\hat{Z}$, as per Eq. (12):

$$\hat{y}_q = \log \left(\frac{var(\hat{Z}_q)}{\sum_{q=1}^{Q} var(\hat{Z}_q)} \right) \tag{12}$$

where

$\hat{y}_q$ = q-*th* component of $\hat{y}$
$\hat{Z}_q$ = q-*th* row of $\hat{Z}$
$var(\hat{Z}_q)$ = variance of the $\hat{Z}_q$ vector

3.3   Extreme Learning Machine (ELM)

Extreme learning machines are a feedforward neural network for classification or regression with a single layer of hidden nodes. The learning speed in ELM is faster than other traditional feedforward network-learning algorithms because it not only gains the smallest error of training but also the smallest norm of weights [30]. These weights between the hidden nodes and outputs are learned in a single step, which, in principle, amounts to learning a linear model. The ELM equations [31] are presented as per Eqs. (13), (14), and (15):

$$H\beta = T \tag{13}$$

where
$H(w_1, \dots, w_{\tilde{N}}, b_1, \dots b_{\tilde{N}}, x_1, \dots, x_N) =$

$$\begin{bmatrix} g(w_1.x_1 + b_1) & \cdots & g(w_{\tilde{N}}.x_1 + b_{\tilde{N}}) \\ \vdots & \cdots & \vdots \\ g(w_1.x_N + b_1) & \cdots & g(w_{\tilde{N}}.x_N + b_{\tilde{N}}) \end{bmatrix}_{N \times \tilde{N}} \tag{14}$$

$$\beta = \begin{bmatrix} \beta_1^T \\ \vdots \\ \beta_{\tilde{N}}^T \end{bmatrix}_{\tilde{N} \times m}, \text{ and } T = \begin{bmatrix} t_1^T \\ \vdots \\ t_N^T \end{bmatrix}_{N \times m} \tag{15}$$

H is called the hidden layer of the output matrix of the neural network and the *i*th column of H is the *i*th hidden neuron's output with respect to inputs $x_1, x_2, x_3, \dots, x_N$.

4 Proposed Method

In general, the proposed method follows several grooves, which are further divided into two parts: train and test. The train and test parts are based on the needs of the feature extraction process (CSP process) and feature selection, respectively. This work is focused on the process before extraction of features. This process can be seen more clearly in Fig. 1.

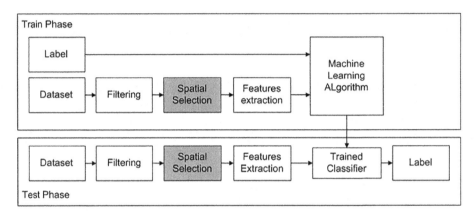

Fig. 1. Flow chart proposed system.

4.1 Dataset

Dataset IIIb in BCI competition III was used in this study. The data was provided by the Laboratory of Brain-Computer Interfaces (BCI-Lab), Graz University of Technology [32]. The dataset consists of five subjects with a different number of trials, which are further separated into training and test phases. In each trial, the training and test phases are divided into motor imagery trials lateralized either to the left or to the right. The distribution of a trial (training or test) on the subject is determined by the possibility of the left and right motor imagery trials.

4.2 Filtering

The filtering stage is the stage in which the EEG signal corresponding to a desired frequency range is selected. In this filtering process, a Butterworth 2nd order filter in the frequency range of 8–14 Hz was used. This frequency range was used to select the signals which actively reflect the alpha waves concerned with the motor imagery.

4.3 Spatial Selection

This study is focused on the spatial selection process. In this part, several steps are undertaken in the CUR decomposition rules to create the R matrix followed by the formation of matrix U and matrix A. More specifically, the CUR decomposition can be divided into the following three steps:

(1) Calculate the importance of each column/row in the network matrix. Each row/column in matrix A is assigned a probability of being selected. In this step, the C and R matrix is created:

    i. Calculate the energy by column in the original matrix to create matrix C and calculate the energy by row to create matrix R

    ii. The result of the energy calculation is then averaged across the dataset trials and dataset row for matrix C and average of the results of energy is used to calculate matrix R on the trial and dataset column

    iii. Sort energy value in descending order by column to get matrix C

    iv. Perform average energy calculations using windowing on rows to get matrix R

The energy calculation, which is meant to get the C and R matrix, is done using Eqs. (16) and (17):

$$\mathbf{C} = c_{pj}, \text{ where } p_i = \frac{\sum_{j=1}^{n} A(i,j)^2}{\sum_{i=1}^{m} \sum_{j=1}^{n} A(i,j)^2} \tag{16}$$

$$\mathbf{R} = r_{pi}, \text{ where } p_j = \frac{\sum_{j=1}^{m} \sum A(i,j)^2}{\sum_{i=1}^{m} \sum_{j=1}^{n} A(i,j)^2} \tag{17}$$

(2) Finding the U Matrix

After getting the C and R matrix, the U matrix is created using Eq. (18):

$$U \cong (W^+)^{\mathbf{T}}, \text{ where } W = \mathbf{C_{pi,}} \tag{18}$$

(+) is the pseudo-inverses and T is the matrix transpose, respectively.

Matrix U is created from the transposed pseudo inverse W matrix. Meanwhile matrix W is created from matrix C, which is calculated based on the energy by row or rule-making matrix R without the windowing process. The dimensional matrix U is heavily influenced by the selection matrix dimensions of the C and R matrix, and this results in the optimization of the performance matrix U depending on both of the matrices.

(3) Estimation of matrix A

After all the components of the CUR matrix (C, R, and U matrix) have been determined, an approximation to matrix A corresponding to Eq. (1) is made.

After the CUR matrix component is created (estimate A matrix, C matrix, U matrix, and R matrix), the components are then used as input to the process of CSP. Its accuracy is calculated so that the components of the CUR matrix that can provide high accuracy can be determined.

4.4   Feature Extraction and Selection

In this study, the training and testing accuracy were set as the performance parameters of the created system. The training and testing accuracy was compared between the original CSP (with original input dataset) and CSP with the CUR components (matrix A, C matrix, R matrix, and U matrix) as input. For the matrix C and R input, some test scenarios were added as follows:

- On the selection of matrix C, the highest energy values of 15, 30, 45, and 59 columns were tested;
- In matrix R, energy use windowing with a row range of 100, 200, 300, and 350 was calculated.

After the implementation of these schemes, the most optimal column and row composition was determined and a matrix U was created based on this information.

For the extraction process features, the CSP method was used as a template to prove the effectiveness of the spatial selection process at an earlier stage. The original CSP was used without any modifications. Likewise, in the feature selection, the ELM was used because of its many advantages.

5   Experiment, Result, and Discussion

This section discusses the results of the series of tests undertaken in this study with accuracy as the parameter. To determine the performance of the system, a series of tests were conducted, which include a test for matrix C accuracy for determining the active channels and intersection in many subjects (datasets), and the accuracy of Matrix R, U, and $\hat{A}$.

5.1   The Accuracy of Matrix C

Modification of the C matrix involves the selection of the columns with the highest average energy points. The matrix column in the dataset presents information about the channel. In other words, the process of modifying the C matrix that was done in this study can be assumed as the process of channel selection imagery. Moreover, the training and accuracy of the selected channels (Channels 59, 45, 30, and 10) were also calculated.

The tabulated results for training and testing accuracy are shown in Table 1 where the testing accuracy is written in bracket i.e. (0.52). The result shows that the most optimal input for matrix C is in column 45 with an average improvement in accuracy of 12.3%. The improvement in testing accuracy is significant for all datasets, except *al* and *aw*. For dataset *al* and *aw*, the point of accuracy gradually reduced by about 1%. Nevertheless, the significant improvements of other datasets can be focused on. Moreover, similar to the number in column 45, in which not all subjects were shown to improve, the number in columns 59 (3%) and 30 (6.1%) for channel selection showed a better average result than the original CSP (see average testing accuracy in Table 1). The result suggests that channel selection through energy calculation using the column matrix can reduce the irrelevant information in the signals before being processed at CSP, so that the accuracy of CSP is significantly improved.

Table 1. Comparison of training and testing accuracy results.

Input	Dataset	Average accuracy					Total average
		aa	al	av	aw	ay	
Matrix C	C118	0.96 (0.52)	0.98 (0.91)	1.00 (0.59)	1.00 (0.63)	1.00 (0.59)	**0.99 (0.65)**
	C59	0.95 (0.53)	**0.97 (0.92)**	0.95 (0.57)	1.00 (0.75)	1.00 (0.56)	**0.97 (0.67)**
	C45	**0.90 (0.62)**	0.96 (0.90)	**0.94 (0.71)**	1.00 (0.62)	**1.00 (0.79)**	**0.96 (0.73)**
	C30	0.86 (0.53)	0.90 (0.84)	0.93 (0.62)	**0.99 (0.82)**	1.00 (0.66)	**0.94 (0.69)**
	C10	0.74 (0.60)	0.73 (0.64)	0.78 (0.61)	0.81 (0.73)	0.99 (0.65)	**0.81 (0.64)**
Matrix R	R401	0.96 (0.52)	0.98 (0.91)	1.00 (0.59)	1.00 (0.63)	1.00 (0.59)	**0.99 (0.65)**
	R350	0.93 (0.52)	0.98 (0.90)	1.00 (0.57)	1.00 (0.62)	1.00 (0.48)	**0.98 (0.62)**
	R300	0.98 (0.52)	0.99 (0.90)	1.00 (0.57)	1.00 (0.59)	1.00 (0.55)	**0.99 (0.63)**
	R200	0.94 (0.52)	0.99 (0.89)	1.00 (0.59)	1.00 (0.65)	1.00 (0.56)	**0.99 (0.64)**
	R100	0.95 (0.55)	0.98 (0.89)	1.00 (0.55)	1.00 (0.58)	1.00 (0.56)	**0.98 (0.63)**
Matrix U	U (C59+R401)	1.00 (0.54)	0.98 (0.81)	1.00 (0.59)	1.00 (0.54)	1.00 (0.58)	**1.00 (0.61)**
	U (C45+R401)	0.90 (0.65)	0.96 (0.80)	0.94 (0.69)	1.00 (0.63)	1.00 (0.79)	**0.96 (0.71)**
	U (C30+R401)	0.89 (0.61)	0.88 (0.76)	0.97 (0.75)	0.99 (0.64)	1.00 (0.57)	**0.94 (0.67)**
	U (C10+R401)	0.73 (0.57)	0.74 (0.66)	0.75 (0.64)	0.85 (0.64)	0.92 (0.67)	**0.80 (0.64)**
Matrix Â	Â	1.00 (0.54)	1.00 (0.50)	1.00 (0.50)	1.00 (0.42)	1.00 (0.25)	**1.00 (0.44)**

The increased levels of CSP accuracy with the highest value in C45 in comparison to the original is due to the selection of appropriate channels with high energy. In C59, the accuracy is higher than the original CSP but this value is not the highest (see Fig. 2). This occurs because in C59 some channels contain artifacts or noise. In another case, in which a higher accuracy for C30 is achieved than the original CSP, the cause is due to the loss in or undefined active channels. In general, it can be concluded that the selection of energy in active channels results in the elimination of channels that contain artifacts or noise. More detailed testing related to the active channels can be seen in the following test process for this study, presented in the next section.

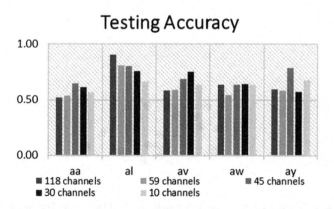

Fig. 2. Comparison of testing accuracy in different number of channels for all datasets.

5.2   The Determination of Active Channels

The determination of active channels is conducted by calculating the amount of the same active channels between one subject and the others in all datasets, which are called the intersection channels. The number of occurrences of the same channel is presented in the form of rankings, where rank 1 means the channels are only active in one subject, rank 2 means that the same active channels are contained in two subjects, rank 3 means the same number of active channels are in three different subjects, and rank 4 and rank 5, means the ideal conditions for which the channels that are in this ranking are assured as an active channel in all subjects.

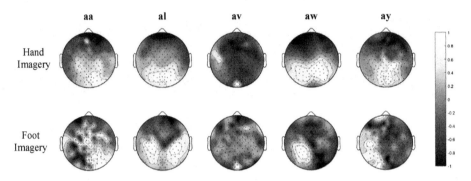

Fig. 3. Power spectrum distribution. The intersection of high-power distribution area (brighter color) in all datasets showed the same area, premotor cortex, especially for the power distribution of hand imagery which is more consistent in active area than the foot imagery. The power distribution is calculated using normalization in range −1 to 1. (Color figure online)

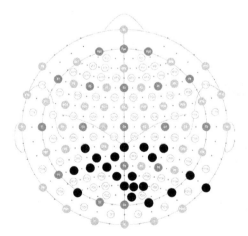

Fig. 4. Intersection active channels on scalp, indicated in black spot. The black spot area is a number of channels which is mostly active in all trials of all datasets. The active channels give an information of active area for motor imagery (hand and foot) on scalp.

The results show that there are no channels in rank 5. Accordingly, the channels in rank 3 and 4 are defined as the active channels. This determination is considered because the intersection opportunity is high. Thus, 22 active channels are obtained, which can be defined as the motor imagery channels (see Fig. 4). The selected channels are confirmed in same region on the scalp with the high-power spectrum distribution in all datasets as shown in Fig. 3.

5.3 Accuracy Test of Matrix R, U, and Â

The determination of the optimal matrix C will affect the quality of the formation of matrix U and Â. The Â matrix, composed by Matrix U and R, was previously defined in Eq. (1).

- *Matrix R*

The way in which the matrix R was created via the energy calculation is not similar to the way the matrix C is defined, because the information in matrix row A contains information across channels such that the average value of the results is not sufficient to represent the desired information, which is based on calculations of energy. Because of this, windowing was done with a range of 100, 200, 300, and 350 rows. The average energy for each shift in windowing was then counted in terms of average totals in all trials to obtain the final value of the windowing scheme.

From the calculations, the matrix R achieved an optimal value in 401 rows, which indicates the original dataset (401×118). The trend of training accuracy versus several windowing R is linear. More detailed information of the accuracy result can be seen in Table 1.

Through this test, it is proven that the information contained in matrix row A is inter-related information, such that when most of the information is removed (with the windowing) important information is also lost, and this can be seen from the trend in accuracy in all schemes, in which the differences are relatively close.

- *Matrix U*

Matrix U is defined as per Eq. (4). The matrix U is formed from the C and R optimal matrix in which the optimal number of columns is 45 and the R optimal is 401 rows. Thus, the dimensions of matrix U and the transposed matrix (U^T) are 45×401 and 401×45, respectively.

The test results of accuracy show that the accuracy of the transposed matrix U (U^T) is 9.2% better than the original CSP (see Table 1) although the results of dataset *al* saw no improvement. Matrix U^T was found to be more optimal than matrix U because of the dimensions of the optimal matrix C. The U matrix (45×401) was obtained using the optimal 45 columns from matrix C, which is used as a row in matrix U, and 401 columns were obtained from the optimum number of rows from matrix R. To restore the columns and rows that optimally match the dimensions of the original dataset, a transpose operation was done on matrix U. The matrix U accuracy matrix, which is higher than the original CSP, is caused by the optimal matrix C.

- *Matrix Â*

Matrix A is a form of the original matrix estimation. It did not provide better accuracy on average, or even close to the original CSP, both for the training and test accuracy. The test results show that the estimation matrix A that was established was not the same or even close to the original data although it was produced using the optimal C and R matrix.

Matrix Â as input to the CSP did not give a better result, and even showed a declining performance for the original CSP. This was caused by matrix operations, which involved the U matrix (no transpose) that changed the matrix dataset pattern, and thus increased the value of deviation and error.

It is possible that the reason why *al* requires more channels compared to the other subjects, *aa, av, aw,* and *ay* is due to the number of available trials. It is assumed that this is due to the non-reproducible brain signal, that is, each dataset has its own character (unique) and therefore it becomes difficult to define them in a similar way as the others. However, the similarities between the datasets can still be determined, albeit not for a large number of trials because this can cause exposure to potentially other channels that can be defined as active channels. However, spatial selection offers a technique for selecting the most important (active) channels. It can also define the active channels, which are less than the entire number of channels, with a better rate of accuracy.

6 Conclusion and Future Works

This work used spatial selection before applying it to CSP as feature extraction in optimizing CSP performance when processing motor imagery EEG datasets. The proposed framework offers better performance accuracy as compared to conventional CSP. Three different approaches in utilizing CUR decomposition as spatial selection were investigated (for datasets). As a result, the channel or *C* selection offered the best performance compared to signal factorization and time segment selection. Also, for high trial subjects, it was found that the EEG signal was non-reproducible, which may have degraded performance accuracy. However, the proposed spatial selection may offer a promising solution through the selection of important channels. In the future, for advanced research, an analysis of the methods can be conducted to determine their impact on other BCI spatial filtering methods with different types of datasets.

Acknowledgement. The authors would like to thanks Universiti Teknologi Malaysia for funding this research through UTM Matching Grant (Q.K130000.3043.00M79) and Centre for Artificial Intelligent and Robotics (CAIRO)-(U.K091303.0100.00000), also to Japan-ASEAN Integration Fund (JAIF) and Telkom University that has provided a scholarship and support to study at Malaysian-Japan International Institute of Technology UTM Kuala Lumpur.

References

1. Abdulkader, S.N., Atia, A., Mostafa, M.-S.M.: Brain computer interfacing: applications and challenges. Egypt. Inform. J. **16**(2), 213–230 (2015)

2. Samek, W., Kawanabe, M., Muller, K.R.: Divergence-based framework for common spatial patterns algorithms. IEEE Rev. Biomed. Eng. **7**, 50–72 (2014)
3. Yong, X., Ward, R.K., Birch, G.E.: Robust common spatial patterns for EEG signal preprocessing. In: Conference Proceedings IEEE Engineering in Medicine and Biology Society, vol. 2008, pp. 2087–2090 (2008)
4. Asyraf, H., Shapiai, M.I., Setiawan, N.A., Wan Musa, W.S.N.S.: Masking covariance for common spatial pattern as feature extraction. J. Telecommun. Electron. Comput. Eng. **8**(11), 81–85 (2016)
5. Lal, T.N., et al.: Support vector channel selection in BCI. IEEE Trans. Biomed. Eng. **51**(6), 1003–1010 (2004)
6. Arvaneh, M., Guan, C., Ang, K.K., Quek, H.C.: Spatially sparsed common spatial pattern to improve BCI performance. In: ICASSP, IEEE International Conference on Acoustics, Speech and Signal Processing - Proceedings, pp. 2412–2415 (2011)
7. Goksu, F., Ince, N.F., Tewfik, A.H.: Sparse common spatial patterns in brain computer interface applications. In: 2011 IEEE International Conference Acoustics Speech Signal Processing, pp. 533–536 (2011)
8. Parra, L.C., Spence, C.D., Gerson, A.D., Sajda, P.: Recipes for the linear analysis of EEG. Neuroimage **28**(2), 326–341 (2005)
9. Samek, W., Vidaurre, C., Müller, K.-R., Kawanabe, M.: Stationary common spatial patterns for brain-computer interfacing. J. Neural Eng. **9**(2), 26013 (2012)
10. Von Bünau, P., Meinecke, F.C., Scholler, S., Müller, K.R.: Finding stationary brain sources in EEG data. In: 2010 Annual International Conference of the IEEE Engineering in Medicine and Biology Society, EMBC 2010, pp. 2810–2813 (2010)
11. Adam, A., Shapiai, M.I., Mohd Tumari, M.Z., Mohamad, M.S., Mubin, M.: Feature selection and classifier parameters estimation for EEG signals peak detection using particle swarm optimization. Sci. World J. **2014**, 1–13 (2014)
12. Li, K.G., Shapiai, M.I., Adam, A., Ibrahim, Z.: Feature scaling for EEG human concentration using particle swarm optimization. In: Proceedings of 2016 8th International Conference on Information Technology and Electrical Engineering: Empowering Technology for Better Future, ICITEE 2016 (2017)
13. Samek, W., Muller, K.R., Kawanabe, M., Vidaurre, C.: Brain-computer interfacing in discriminative and stationary subspaces. In: Proceedings of the Annual International Conference of the IEEE Engineering in Medicine and Biology Society, EMBS 2012, pp. 2873–2876 (2012)
14. Samek, W., Kawanabe, M., Vidaurre, C.: Group-wise stationary subspace analysis - a novel method for studying non-stationarities. In: Proceedings of the 5th International BCI Conference, pp. 3–6 (2011)
15. Arvaneh, M., Guan, C., Quek, C.: EEG data space adaptation to reduce intersession nonstationary in brain-computer interface. J. Neural Comput. **25**, 1–26 (2013)
16. Samek, W., Meinecke, F.C., Muller, K.R.: Transferring subspaces between subjects in brain - computer interfacing. IEEE Trans. Biomed. Eng. **60**(8), 2289–2298 (2013)
17. Devlaminck, D., Wyns, B., Grosse-Wentrup, M., Otte, G., Santens, P.: Multisubject learning for common spatial patterns in motor-imagery BCI. Comput. Intell. Neurosci. **2011** (2011)
18. Kang, H., Choi, S.: Bayesian multi-task learning for common spatial patterns. In: 2011 International Workshop Pattern Recognition NeuroImaging, vol. 1, no. 1, pp. 61–64 (2011)
19. Samek, W., Binder, A., Muller, K.R.: Multiple kernel learning for brain-computer interfacing. In: Annual International Conference of the IEEE Engineering in Medicine and Biology Society, vol. 2013, pp. 7048–7051 (2013)
20. Grosse-Wentrup, M., Buss, M.: Multiclass common spatial patterns and information theoretic feature extraction. IEEE Trans. Biomed. Eng. **55**(8), 1991–2000 (2008)

21. Gouy-Pailler, C., Congedo, M., Brunner, C., Jutten, C., Pfurtscheller, G.: Nonstationary brain source separation for multiclass motor imagery. IEEE Trans. Biomed. Eng. **57**(2), 469–478 (2010)
22. Wang, H.: Harmonic mean of Kullback-Leibler divergences for optimizing multi-class EEG spatio-temporal filters. Neural Process. Lett. **36**(2), 161–171 (2012)
23. Falzon, O., Camilleri, K.P., Muscat, J.: The analytic common spatial patterns method for EEG-based BCI data. J. Neural Eng. **9**, 45009 (2012)
24. Nicolas-Alonso, L.F., Corralejo, R., Alvarez, D., Hornero, R.: Analytic common spatial pattern and adaptive classification for multiclass motor imagery-based BCI. In: International IEEE/EMBS Conference on Neural Engineering, NER, 2013, pp. 1084–1087 (2013)
25. Wang, H., Zheng, W.: Local temporal common spatial patterns for robust single-trial EEG classification. IEEE Trans. Neural Syst. Rehabil. Eng. **16**(2), 131–139 (2008)
26. Wang, H.: Discriminant and adaptive extensions to local temporal common spatial patterns. Pattern Recognit. Lett. **34**(10), 1125–1129 (2013)
27. Wang, H., Xu, D.: Comprehensive common spatial patterns with temporal structure information of EEG data: minimizing nontask related EEG component. IEEE Trans. Biomed. Eng. **59**(9), 2496–2505 (2012)
28. Mahoney, M.W., Drineas, P.: CUR matrix decompositions for improved data analysis. Proc. Natl. Acad. Sci. U.S.A. **106**(3), 697–702 (2009)
29. Blankertz, B., Tomioka, R., Lemm, S., Kawanabe, M., Müller, K.R.: Optimizing spatial filters for robust EEG single-trial analysis. IEEE Sig. Process. Mag. **25**(1), 41–56 (2008)
30. Huang, G.-B., et al.: Extreme learning machine: theory and applications. Neurocomputing **70**(1–3), 489–501 (2006)
31. Huang, G., Zhu, Q., Siew, C.: Extreme learning machine : a new learning scheme of feedforward neural networks. In: IEEE International Joint Conference Neural Networks, vol. 2, pp. 985–990 (2004)
32. BCI Competition III Dataset IVa. http://www.bbci.de/competition/iii/desc_IVa.html

Design of Permanent Magnet Linear Synchronous Motor Stator to Improve Magnetic Flux Density Profile Toward High Thrust Density Performance

Nor Ashikin Mohd Nasir[1], Fairul Azhar Abdul Shukor[1(✉)],
Raja Nor Firdaus Kashfi Raja Othman[1], Hiroyuki Wakiwaka[2],
and Kunihisa Tashiro[2]

[1] Faculty of Electrical Engineering,
Universiti Teknikal Malaysia Melaka, Malacca, Malaysia
{m011620008.student,
fairul.azhar,norfirdaus}@utem.edu.my
[2] Faculty of Engineering, Shinshu University, Nagano, Japan
{wakiwak,tashiro}@shinshu-u.ac.jp

Abstract. The Permanent Magnet Linear Synchronous Motor (PMLSM) is designed in this paper to solve the drawbacks of the previous designed PMLSM. The previous designed PMLSM has magnetic flux density, B saturation at lower rated current, I. Therefore, to overcome the saturation of the magnetic flux density, the stator of the PMLSM is designed. Apart from that, the design of the stator help to increase the ratio of thrust, F to cogging force, F_{cog}. The design of PMLSM is completed in two stages where in the first stage the best model chosen is the model of $t_{y2} = 3$ mm. The thrust of the model has reduced by 14% from the previous designed PMLSM. The model designed and chosen in second stage is compared with the previous designed PMLSM in terms of it performance index. The designed PMLSM has improved in terms of motor constant square density, G compared to the previous designed PMLSM with the increment of 2%.

Keywords: Magnetic flux density profile · PMLSM · Performance index · Slot opening parameter · Stator design

1 Introduction

Linear motor is used to produce direct linear motion can be either AC or DC type. The linear motor can be constructed either in the flat or cylindrical form. The linear motor structure is not much different from rotary motor where it has both rotor and stator, however in linear motor the moving part is called as mover instead of rotor. In the linear motor, instead of producing torque (rotation force) it produced linear force, F as it is moving along its length.

Linear motor has many advantages compare to rotary motor where it has higher dynamic performance, simpler structure, improve reliability by reducing some parts

© Springer Nature Singapore Pte Ltd. 2017
M.S. Mohamed Ali et al. (Eds.): AsiaSim 2017, Part I, CCIS 751, pp. 443–454, 2017.
DOI: 10.1007/978-981-10-6463-0_38

and higher efficiency due to the prevention of the motion translation from rotary to linear motion [1] in a linear motion system. Linear motor extensive usage in many linear motion applications also contributed by their good performances such as high speed high accuracy [2], longer life and maintenance-free operation [3] compared to rotary motor or conventional linear motor.

Despite all the advantages yields by the linear motor, it cannot avoid from being stained by its drawbacks such as high cost and cogging. The cost of the linear motor can be high due to the length of the motor stroke [1] and the permanent magnet used in its structure. The permanent magnet from rare-earth material can be very expensive compare to the other magnets material in the permanent magnet markets [4]. Apart from that, linear motor especially from permanent magnet type produced cogging force as there are interaction between the stator core and the permanent magnet mover [5]. The cogging can decrease the motor efficiency, decline motor controllability and reduced motor average thrust force [5].

2 Basic Principle of the PMLSM

The PMLSM designed in this project is a cylindrical 6-slot, 8-pole types with three phases supply. This motor consists of six stator slot and the Halbach magnetization array of PM on its mover as shown in Fig. 1. The PMLSM has been designed previously [1], however the PMLSM yields weakness where there is unbalanced size between the stator and the coil. The unbalance size made the magnetic flux density, B saturated at lower than targeted rated current hence limit the thrust, F produced [1]. Therefore, in this paper, the stator of the PMLSM was designed to improve the performance characteristics of the PMLSM.

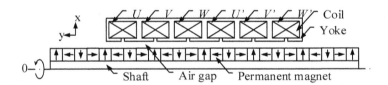

Fig. 1. PMLSM basic structure.

3 Design of the PMLSM Stator

The PMLSM was designed within fixed of outer radius which equal to 25 mm. The structure parameters of the PMLSM is shown in the Table 1. The value of outer radius is fixed because the main purpose of this design is to improve the PMLSM performance by improving its stator part. The general structure of the PMLSM designed in this paper is shown in Fig. 2. During the design, the coil parameters which is coil height, h_c and coil width, w_c were changed accordingly to the changes of the stator yoke thickness, t_{y2} while the other parameters were remain unchanged.

Table 1. PMLSM parameters.

Symbol	Value
PMLSM total radius, r_{total} (mm)	25
Stator height, h_{st} (mm)	11.5
Stator length, l_{st} (mm)	96
Coil height, h_{c} (mm)	4.5–7.5
Coil width, w_{c} (mm)	6–12
Permanent magnet radius, r_{pm} (mm)	13
Shaft radius, r_{s} (mm)	6
Coil pitch, τ_{c} (mm)	16
Permanent magnet pitch, τ_{pm} (mm)	12
Copper wire diameter, $\varnothing$c (mm)	0.337
PM material	NdFeB (N-42)
Stator material	SS400

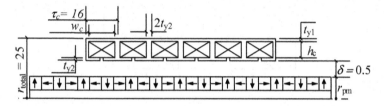

Fig. 2. Design of stator yoke thickness (unit: mm).

The saturation of the magnetic flux density, B affects the saturation of PMLSM thrust, F. Therefore, to avoid the thrust saturation, the magnetic flux density need to be reduced below its saturation level which is $B = 1.8$ T based on the stator material B-H curve. The stator part of the PMLSM was design to reduce the magnetic flux density where the design has been completed within two stages as shown in Fig. 3. The design of PMLSM consists of two stages where the first stage was to design the stator yoke thickness while the second stage was to design the stator slot opening. The models designed were then simulated by using finite element method (FEM) software and the performance characteristics were analysed and evaluated to find the best model.

3.1 Design of Yoke Thickness

Figure 4 shows the magnetic flux density profile of the previous model. Due to the saturated of magnetic flux density, B, the thrust of PMLSM in [1] is saturated at lower aimed rated current. The magnetic flux density, B was observed on specific area as shown in Fig. 4(a). The saturation of the magnetic flux density, B is represented by the line $B = 1.8$ T as shown in the Fig. 4(b) and (c). In the Fig. 4(b) and (c), it shows that the magnetic flux density in the Region 1 is exceeded the saturation line while the

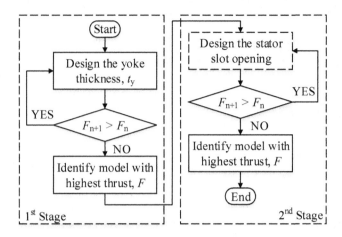

Fig. 3. Flowchart of designing PMLSM stator.

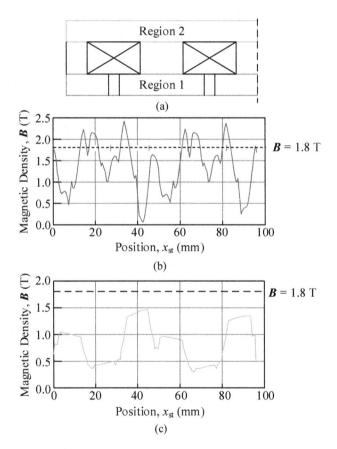

Fig. 4. Magnetic flux density, B of PMLSM. (a) B region of PMLSM stator, (b) B at region 1, (c) B at region 2.

magnetic density, **B** at Region 2 is lower than the saturation line. Region 1 represents the upper yoke thickness, t_{y1} while Region 2 represents the bottom yoke thickness, t_{y2}. Since the magnetic density, **B** at Region 2 is already below the saturation line, the design was focused on t_{y2} to decrease the value of the magnetic flux density, **B** at Region 1.

Figure 5 shows the steps in first stage PMLSM stator design. In the first stage, the designed started by identifying the fixed parameters taken from the previous design [1]. The parameters that were fixed are coil pitch, τ_c, stator height, h_{st} and the upper yoke thickness, t_{y1}. Next was to set the initial value for the variable parameters which is bottom yoke thickness, t_{y2}, coil width, w_c and coil height, h_c to 2 mm, 12 mm and 7.5 mm respectively. The model then was simulated to get the value of thrust, F. The next models were designed by increasing the bottom yoke thickness, t_{y2} by 1 mm for each model until the possible maximum value. The value of coil width, w_c and coil height, h_c were calculated as these parameters were changed accordingly to the changed of bottom yoke thickness, t_{y2}. The models were simulated to capture the thrust, F performance. All the thrust, F obtained from the models designed were evaluated and compared. The final model in first stage was chosen based on the model that produces possible maximum thrust.

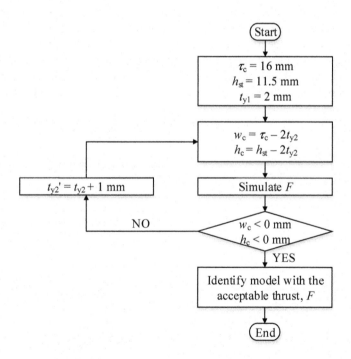

Fig. 5. Flowchart of designing the stator yoke thickness.

3.2   Design of Stator Slot Opening

Model of with yoke thickness, $t_{y2} = 3$ mm has been chosen as the best model from the design in first stage. The model chosen in first stage was used as the initial model in second stage of the PMLSM design. The main objectives of the second stage design is to improve the performance of the models in the first stage design especially in term of cogging force. The best model was determined by choosing the model that can produce the highest thrust, F and the lowest cogging force, F_{cog}. Figure 6 shows the parameters of stator than need to be variable in the second stage.

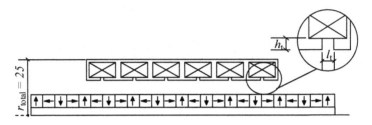

Fig. 6. Design of stator slot opening (unit: mm)

Figure 7 shows the steps taken in second stage of PMLSM design. The second stage design started by identify the structure parameters from the previous stage. In this stage, the parameters identified from the chosen model in previous stage such as yoke thickness, t_y, coil width, w_c, and coil height, h_c were fixed. Next, the initial parameters of stator slot opening which is height of stator slot opening, h_t and length of stator slot

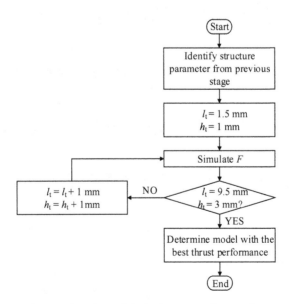

Fig. 7. Flowchart of designing stator slot opening.

opening, l_t were set. The model then simulated to capture the thrust, F. The design was continued by increasing the value of l_t and h_t by 1 mm for each model until the final set value which is $l_t = 9.5$ mm, $h_t = 3$ mm. All the thrust, F obtained from the simulation results were compared to determine the model that satisfy the design's objectives requirement.

4 Analysis of the PMLSM Performance

The design of PMLSM was completed in two stages. The first stage is to design the stator yoke thickness and the second stage is to design the stator slot opening parameters. The performance of the models designed was evaluated based on the magnetic flux density, B, thrust, F characteristics, cogging force, F_{cog} and the thrust ratio of thrust to cogging force. Apart from that, the performance of the PMLSM designed was evaluated based on performance indexes. From the analysis obtained, the PMLSM designed was compared with the previous designed PMLSM and the commercialized PMLSM.

4.1 Effect of Yoke Thickness, t_y to Thrust Characteristics

Figure 8 shows the magnetic flux density, B distribution of the PMLSM designed in first stage. Figure 8 shows that the increment of the stator yoke thickness, t_{y2} (region 1) decreased the value of magnetic flux density, B. Based on the magnetic flux density, B profile in Fig. 8, the corresponding thrust profile of the designed PMLSM is plotted in Fig. 9. Figure 9 shows that the thrust, F decreased as the magnetic flux density, B decreased. However, to choose the best model in first stage, the model with insignificant thrust, F decrement is chosen.

Based on the thrust taken at current, I equal to 3A as shown in Fig. 9(a), the highest thrust was produced by the model of $t_{y2} = 2$ mm with the value of maximum thrust 313 N. The thrust produced by the models were decreased as the thickness of the stator yoke, t_{y2} increased. The decrement of the thrust is represented by the average thrust as shown in the Fig. 9(b) where from the Fig. 9(b), the highest average thrust was produced by the original model, $t_{y2} = 2$ mm with $F_{ave} = 193$ N at current, I equal to 3A. The average thrust of the second model, $t_{y2} = 3$ mm decreased by 14% from the first model with average thrust, F_{ave} value of 166 N while the thrust of third model, $t_{y2} = 4$ mm and fourth model, $t_{y2} = 5$ mm decreased by 45% and 76% respectively from the first model.

4.2 Effect of Stator Slot Opening to Thrust and Cogging Characteristics

Figure 10 shows the thrust characteristics of several models designed taken at current, I equal to 3A. The thrust characteristics consist of thrust, F and cogging force, F_{cog} taken along the PMLSM displacement, x. From Fig. 10(a) it shows that as the length of stator slot opening, l_t increased, the thrust production decreased. From Fig. 10(a), the models that produced the highest thrust are model of $l_t = 2.5$ mm with the maximum thrust value more than 290 N. On the other hand, the models of $l_t = 9.5$ mm produced

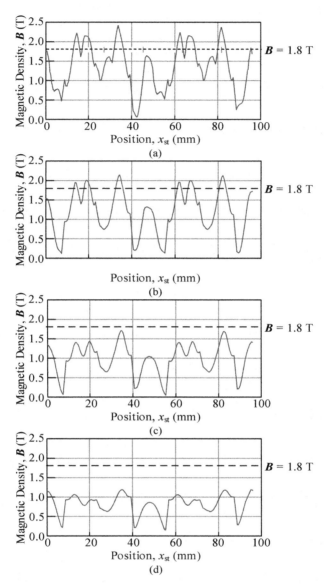

Fig. 8. Magnetic flux density, **B** distribution at region 1. (a) $t_{y2} = 2$ mm, (b) $t_{y2} = 3$ mm, (c) $t_{y2} = 4$ mm, (d) $t_{y2} = 5$ mm.

the lowest peak thrust with the value lower than 100 N. Figure 10(b) shows the cogging force, F_{cog} produced by the models designed. The model of $l_t = 7.5$ mm produced the highest cogging compared with other models with value more than 185 N at peak. Meanwhile, the models of $l_t = 1.5$ mm produced the lowest cogging with value of cogging lower than 100 N at peak. High cogging value influenced the thrust value where the higher the cogging the lower the thrust value and this is shown in Fig. 10.

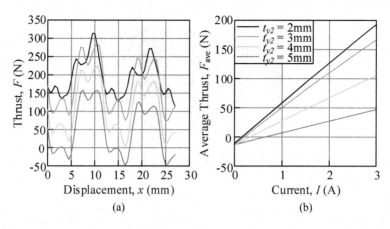

Fig. 9. PMLSM thrust characteristics in stage 1. (a) Thrust at 3A, (b) Average thrust.

Based on the thrust characteristics in Fig. 10, the thrust ratio has been calculated and presented in contour plot as shown in Fig. 11. There are two categories of thrust ratio which is thrust ratio of peak thrust, F_{max} to cogging force, F_{cog} and average thrust, F_{ave} to cogging force, F_{cog}. High thrust ratio designates high thrust, F production with low cogging force, F_{cog}. From Fig. 11 the high ratio value are represents by the red region while the low ratio value represents by dark blue region. The highest ratio of $F_{ave}:F_{cog}$ is 1.8439 whereas the highest ratio of $F_{max}:F_{cog}$ is 3.0469 produced by model $l_t = 1.5$ mm, $h_t = 1$ mm. The model $l_t = 9.5$, $h_t = 2$ mm has the lowest peak thrust to cogging which is $F_{max}:F_{cog}$ equal to 0.9352 while model $l_t = 9.5$ mm, $h_t = 3$ mm has the lowest average thrust to cogging ratio which is $F_{ave}:F_{cog}$ equal to -0.0374. The negative value of ratio produced by the negative average thrust of models $l_t = 9.5$ mm.

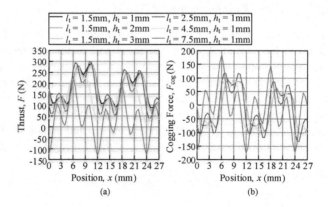

Fig. 10. PMLSM thrust characteristics. (a) Thrust characteristics at 3A, (b) Cogging force at 0A.

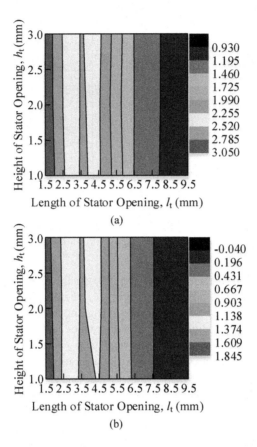

Fig. 11. PMLSM thrust ratio. (a) $F_{\max}$: F_{cog}, (b) F_{ave}: F_{cog}. (Color figure online)

4.3   Performance Index Comparison of PMLSM

Normally, the performance of the PMLSM is evaluated using thrust, F. However, thrust, F is affected by current, I, input power, P and motor volume, V_{mot}. Some researchers are suggesting several other performance characteristics such as spring constant, electrical time constant and mechanical time constant [6]. These parameters are related to dynamic performance. Therefore, in this paper, the performance indexes are implemented to make the comparison between PMLSMs valid. The performance indexes are thrust constant, k_{f} [7], motor constant, k_{m} and motor constant square density, G [8]. These performances indexes are calculated using Eqs. 1, 2 and 3.

$$k_{\text{f}} = \frac{F}{I} \quad (\text{N/A}) \tag{1}$$

$$k_{\text{m}} = \frac{F}{\sqrt{P}} \quad (\text{N/}\sqrt{\text{W}}) \tag{2}$$

$$G = \frac{F^2}{PV_{mot}} \quad (\mathrm{N^2/Wm^3}) \tag{3}$$

where k_f is the thrust constant in (N/A), F is the average thrust in (N), I is the current in each coil in (A), k_m is the motor constant in (N/$\sqrt{W}$), P_{in} is the input power in (W), G is the motor constant square density in (N^2/Wm^3) and V_{mot} is the motor volume in (m^3).

Table 2. Performance indexes comparison of PMLSM.

Model	F_{ave} (N)	$k_f \left(\frac{N}{A}\right)$	$k_m \left(\frac{N}{\sqrt{W}}\right)$	$G \times 10^3 \left(\frac{N^2}{Wm^3}\right)$
Commercialized PMLSM	13	17	3	100
PMLSM as in [1]	193	64	8.52	385
Designed PMLSM	176	59	8.54	387

Table 2 shows the performance indexes comparison of three categories of the PMLSM. They are commercialized PMLSM that has similar volume with the designed PMLSM, the PMLSM as in [1] and the PMLSM designed in this paper.

The commercialized PMLSM with similar volume, V_{mot} has the lowest thrust, F which is 13 N hence produced the lowest thrust constant, k_f. Compared to the PMLSM as in [1], the designed PMLSM produced lower thrust, F hence produced lower thrust constant, k_f. The thrust constant produced by the PMLSM as in [1] and designed PMLSM is 64 N/A and 59 N/A respectively. However, the designed PMLSM produces higher motor constant, k_m and motor constant square density, G compared to the PMLSM as in [1]. Motor constant, k_m produced by PMLSM as in [1] is 8.52 N/$\sqrt{W}$ while the designed PMLSM produced motor constant, k_m equal to 8.54 N/$\sqrt{W}$. Motor constant, k_m represents the thrust sensitivity against input power. This means that the designed PMLSM can produced higher current at lower input power, P compared to the other PMLSM. The designed PMLSM produced the highest motor constant square density, G of 387×10^3 N^2/Wm^3. On the other hand, the factor of linear motor volume, V_{mot} is considered through motor constant square density, G. The motor constant square density, G produced by the designed PMLSM represents that the model produced higher thrust at lower input power, P and smaller volume of the motor, V_{mot} compared with the other two models. However, in this case, since the volume, V_{mot} of the PMLSM as in [1] and the designed PMLSM is the same, the factors considered in the motor constant square density, G is input power, P.

5 Conclusion

The design of the PMLSM stator has been completed in two stages. In the first stage, the stator yoke thickness, t_{y2} has been designed to eliminate the magnetic flux density, B saturation of the PMLSM as in [1]. In the PMLSM as in [1], the magnetic flux density, B saturation occur at current, $I = 1.5A$. In the first stage, the magnetic flux density, B decreased as the yoke thickness, t_{y2} was increased. The decrement of magnetic flux density, B resulted in reduction of the thrust, F produced. Therefore, in the first stage, the best model is chosen based on the model that produced insignificant thrust, F reduction. Model $t_{y2} = 3$ mm has been chosen as the best model in the first stage with the thrust, F production of 269 N at current, $I = 3$A. In the second stage, the PMLSM design was focused on stator slot opening where the parameters involved are length of stator slot opening, l_t and height of stator slot opening, h_t. In the second stage, the aim of the design is to increase the ratio of thrust, F to cogging force, F_{cog}. This ratio performance is presented in the contour plot. Based on the thrust ratio, the model of $l_t = 1.5$ mm, $h_t = 1$ mm was chosen as the final model. The final model then was compared with the PMLSM as in [1] and the commercialized PMLSM in terms of performance index. Based on the comparison, the thrust, F produced by the final PMLSM is lower compared to the PMLSM as in [1]. As the thrust, F is low, the thrust constant, k_f also low correspondingly. However, the designed PMLSM produced higher motor constant, k_m and motor constant square density, G compared to the PMLSM as in [1].

Acknowledgments. The authors would like to thank Ministry of Education & Universiti Teknikal Malaysia Melaka (UTeM) for providing PJP/2016/FKE/HI5/S01478.

References

1. Azhar, F., Wakiwaka, H., Tashiro, K., Nirei, M.: Design and performance index comparison of the permanent magnet linear motor. Prog. Electromagn. Res. M **43**, 101–108 (2015)
2. Omura, M., Shimono, T., Fujimoto, Y.: Thrust characteristics improvement of a circular shaft motor for direct-drive applications. IEEE Trans. Ind. Appl. **51**(5), 3647–3655 (2015)
3. Vărăticeanu, B.D., Minciunescu, P.A.: Modeling and analysis of dual-sided coreless linear synchronous motor. Rev. Roum. Sci. Tech.: Se. **60**, 17–27 (2015)
4. Chen, Q., Liu, G., Zhao, W., Shao, M., Liu, Z.: Design and analysis of the new high-reliability motors with hybrid permanent magnet material. IEEE Trans. Magn. **50**(12), 1–10 (2014)
5. Patel, A.N.: Influence of stator teeth shaping on cogging torque of radial flux permanent magnet brushless DC motor. In: 2016 Biennial International Conference on Power and Energy Systems: Towards Sustainable Energy (PESTSE), pp. 1–4 (2016)
6. Norhisam, M., Firdaus, R.N., Azhar, F., Mariun, N., Aris, I., Abdul, R.J.: The analysis on effect of thrust constant, spring constant, electrical time constant, mechanical time constant to oscillation displacement of slot-less linear oscillatory actuator. In: IEEE 2nd International Power and Energy Conference (PECON), pp. 1076–1081 (2008)
7. Wakiwaka, H., Ninomiya, T., Oda, J., Morimura, T., Yamada, H.: Evaluation of the thrust constant of a linear DC motor for a pen recorder. IEEE Transl. J. Magn. Japan **9**(6), 104–109 (1994)
8. Mizuno, T., Kawai, M., Tsuchiya, F., Kosugi, M., Yamada, H.: An examination for increasing the motor constant of a cylindrical moving magnet-type linear actuator. IEEE Trans. Magn. **41**(10), 3976–3978 (2005)

Achieving Thermal Power System Stability Using Load Frequency Controller

Muhammad Nizam Kamarudin[1,2(✉)], Nabilah Mohd Shaharudin[1,2],
Mohd Hafiz Jali[1,2], Sahazati Md. Rozali[2],
and Mohd Shahrieel Mohd Aras[1,2]

[1] Faculty of Electrical Engineering, Centre for Robotics and Industrial
Automation (CeRIA), Universiti Teknikal Malaysia Melaka (UTeM),
Durian Tunggal, Malaysia
nizamkamarudin@utem.edu.my
[2] Faculty of Engineering Technology, Centre for Robotics and Industrial
Automation (CeRIA), Universiti Teknikal Malaysia Melaka (UTeM),
Durian Tunggal, Malaysia

Abstract. This paper focuses on load frequency control (LFC) of a single area
thermal power system. The purpose of LFC is to minimize the transient varieties
due to frequency deviation by ensuring zero steady state error. The frequency
deviation normally caused by load perturbation. Hence, the primary goal of this
paper is to design LFC for power system stability. Single area thermal power
system comprises of governor framework, non-reheat turbine model and generator with load. The closed loop system performances in term of transient and
steady state are observed and analyzed by injecting multifarious load perturbation. The simulation results are obtained via simulation works using
MATLAB with SIMULINK toolbox.

Keywords: Load frequency control · Thermal power plant · PID

1 Introduction

Electricity is being generated by different types of power generating plants. Power
generating plants are divided into conventional and non-conventional power plants as
shown in Fig. 1. Thermal, hydro, gas, diesel and nuclear are being classified as conventional power plants while for the non-conventional are solar, wind, biogas and
geo-thermal.

Load changes will affect the bus voltages and frequency of the power system. The
reactive power and active power have combined effects on the voltage and frequency
where the normal frequency fluctuation exceeding nominal frequency gives catas-
trophic effect to the power system operation and reliability, including the whole power
system performances. The operating frequency normally disturbed by frequency
deviation due to load perturbation. A large frequency deviation can damage the
equipment, causes the transmission line to be overloaded, ended up in interfere with
system protection schemes and will ultimately lead to power systems instability [1].

© Springer Nature Singapore Pte Ltd. 2017
M.S. Mohamed Ali et al. (Eds.): AsiaSim 2017, Part I, CCIS 751, pp. 455–467, 2017.
DOI: 10.1007/978-981-10-6463-0_39

Any mismatch between generation and demand causes the system frequency and terminal voltage to deviate from the scheduled value [2].

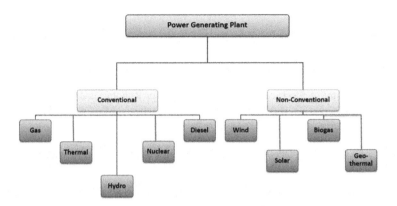

Fig. 1. Block diagram of power generating plant.

Load frequency control (LFC) or Automatic generation control (AGC) [3] is the mechanism augmented to the power system in order to retain system frequency at the scheduled level and control the net tie-line interchange power in a multi area interconnected power system [4–6]. LFC objectives are met by measuring control error signal called area control error (ACE), which represents the real power imbalance between generation and load, and is a linear combination of net power interchanges and frequency deviations [3].

Load frequency controller can be treated a regulation case [7] and tracking case [8] when the tracking control of the demanded frequency is necessary. Until to-date, many approaches in LFC development have been reported such as optimal control [9]; variable structure control [10]; adaptive control [11]; and robust control [12]. Improved performance might be expected from the advance control methods; however, these methods demanded computational burden and require either information on the system states or an efficient on-line identifier thus may be difficult to apply in practice [13].

The objective of this research is to utilized simple three-term controller named Proportional Integral Derivative (PID) with low pass filter (LPF). Beforehand, a single area power system consists of turbine speed governing system, generator and load is modeled. Finally, the transient and steady state performances of the closed loop power system with compensator are analyzed. In other word, the aims of the control scheme is to ensure that the system robust towards frequency deviation due to load perturbation. The results are obtained via the simulation works using MATLAB with SIMULINK toolbox.

The overall structure of this paper takes the form of five sections, including this introductory section. Section 2 discusses power system dynamics. Section 3 presents the methodology of load frequency controller. Section 4 analyses the results. Section 5 concludes the finding.

2 Power System Dynamics

Thermal power system is a power plant in which the heat energy is converted to electric power. In most of the places, the turbine is steam-driven. Water is heated, turns into steam and spins a steam turbine which drives an electrical generator. The thermal power system mainly consists of alternator runs with the help of steam turbine. The steam is obtained from high pressure boiler. Bituminous coal, brown coal and peat are used as fuel of boiler. To increase the thermal efficiency, the coal is used in the boiler in powder form. Governors are the units that are used in power systems to sense the frequency bias caused by the load change and cancel it by varying the input of the turbines. The schematics diagram of a speed governing unit is shown in Fig. 2 where R is the speed regulation characteristic and T_G is the time constant of governor [4].

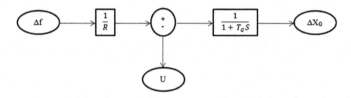

Fig. 2. Block diagram of speed governing unit.

When the load change occurs, part of the change will be compensated by the valve adjustment while the rest of the change is represented in the form of frequency deviation. The goal of LFC is to regulate the frequency deviation in the presence of varying active power load. Thus, the load reference set point can be used to adjust the valve positions so that load changes are canceled by the power generation rather than resulting in a frequency deviation. The dynamic of the governor is expressed as

$$G_T(Ss) = \frac{\Delta X_G}{(u(s) - \Delta f/R)} = \frac{1}{1 + sT_G} \tag{1}$$

A turbine unit in power systems is used to transform the natural energy, such as the energy from steam or water, into mechanical power (ΔP_G) that is supplied to the generator. In LFC model, there are two kinds of commonly used turbines: non-reheat and reheat turbines. Non-reheat turbines are first-order units. A time delay (denoted by T_T) occurs between switching the valve and producing the turbine torque. The transfer function of the non-reheat turbine is represented as

$$G_T(s) = \frac{\Delta P_G}{\Delta X_G} = \frac{1}{1 + T_T s} \tag{2}$$

A generator unit in power systems converts the mechanical power received from the turbine into electrical power. But for LFC, the focus is on the rotor speed output (frequency of the power systems) of the generator instead of the energy transformation.

Since electrical power is hard to store in large amounts, the balance has to be maintained between the generated power and the load demand. The power loads can be decomposed into resistive loads (ΔP_L) which remain constant when the rotor speed is changing, and motor loads that change with load speed [4]. If the mechanical power remains unchanged, the motor loads will compensate the load change at a rotor speed that is different from a scheduled value. Figure 3 shows the block diagram of the generator-load.

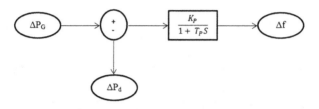

Fig. 3. Block diagram of the generator.

The dynamic of the generator-load is expressed in Eq. (3), where K_P and T_P are the gain constant and time constant of the generator load model respectively. The single area system can be representing by linear model as shown in Fig. 4. The thermal plant is one of the bulk power generators which consist of a speed governor, turbine and a generator as in [1]. The speed governor gives a command u which initiates a sequence of events which leads to the opening and closing of the pilot valve [5, 14–16]. Overall power system dynamic is shown in Eq. (4).

$$G_P(s) = \frac{\Delta f}{\Delta P_G - \Delta P_d} = \frac{K_P}{1 + T_P s} \tag{3}$$

$$G(s) = \frac{K_P}{(T_G s + 1)(T_T s + 1)(T_P s + 1) + K_P/R} \tag{4}$$

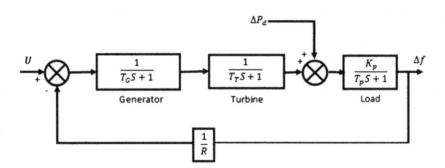

Fig. 4. Linear model of power system.

3 Load Frequency Controller

3.1 System Overview

The parameters of a power system under studies are depicted in Table 1. As such, the numerical system dynamic is shown in Eq. (5). For $K = 1$, step response of uncompensated power system without frequency deviation (ΔP_d) due to load perturbation appeared as in Fig. 5. The performances of uncompensated power system are tabulated in Table 2.

Table 1. Nomencalture [13].

Parameters	Description
T_G	Governor time constant (s)
T_T	Turbine time constant (s)
T_P	Electric system time constant (s)
R	Speed regulation due to governor action (Hz/p.u.MW)
K_P	Electric system gain
ΔX_G	Incremental change in governor valve position
ΔP_G	Incremental change in generator output (p.u.MW)
ΔP_d	Load disturbance (p.u.MW)
Δf	Incremental frequency deviation (Hz)

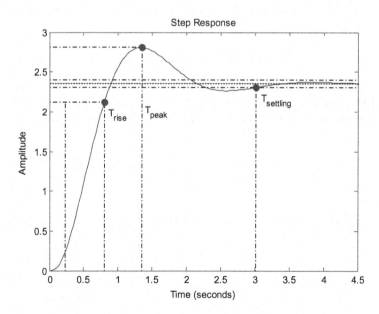

Fig. 5. Step response for power system $G(s)$ with $\Delta P_d = 0$.

$$G(s) = \frac{120K}{0.48s^3 + 7.624s^2 + 20.38s + 51} \tag{5}$$

With the system characteristic $1 + KG(s) = 0$, the range of gain K such that the power system $G(s)$ stable and underdamped is calculated within $-0.425 < K < 2.2125$, with critical gain $K_{critical} = 2.2125$. Hence, the frequency at which the power system dynamic starts to oscillate is recorded at 6.443 rad/s.

Table 2. System performance due to step input.

Transient performance				Steady-state performance
Settling time	Rise time	Peak time	Overshoot	Steady-state error (E_{ss})
3.02 s	0.571 s	1.34 s	19.3%	1.35

3.2   System with Frequency Deviation

When the power system is subjected to frequency deviation (ΔP_d) due to load perturbation, the transient and steady state performance are degrade. Figure 6(a) and (b) show the system performance when subjected to persistent perturbation as expressed in Eq. (6).

$$\Delta P_d = 1\% \quad \forall t > 3 \tag{6}$$

whereas Fig. 7(a) and (b) show the system performance when subjected to pulsed perturbation as expressed in Eq. (7).

$$\Delta P_d = 1\%(\Delta P_d(t-2) - \Delta P_d(t-3)) \tag{7}$$

Note that in Fig. 6(b), frequency deviation occurs every $t > 3$ s. With control facility, LFC should regulate Δf to zero $\Delta f \to 0$, $\forall t \to \infty$. Figure 7(b) shows the frequency deviation pattern where it subsides as the perturbation ceases at $t > 3$ s.

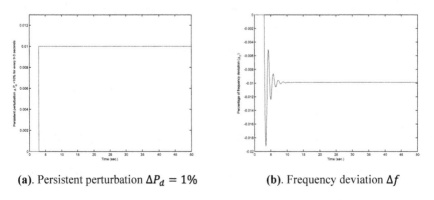

(a). Persistent perturbation $\Delta P_d = 1\%$ (b). Frequency deviation Δf

Fig. 6. Persistent perturbation and its effect towards Δf.

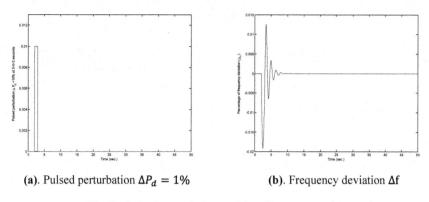

(a). Pulsed perturbation $\Delta P_d = 1\%$ (b). Frequency deviation Δf

Fig. 7. Pulsed perturbation and its effect towards Δf.

3.3   Controller Formulation

Power system dynamic developed in Sect. 2 shows that the system is third-order with type zero family. As such, adding one pole at origin may increase system type and hence, vanishing the steady state error by forcing the position error constant towards ∞. Adding one zero closed to the pole at the origin preserve the desired dominant pole along the locus without affecting the transient. However, with the appearance of frequency deviation (ΔP_d) due to load perturbation, degrades the transient performance and such, new desired dominant pole is therefore required in order to improve the transient when ΔP_d occurs. By removing the real pole of the system $G(s)$, the reduced-order model can be obtained as in Eq. (8a, 8b).

$$G_{red}(s) = \frac{19}{s^2 + 2.593s + 7.995} \tag{8a}$$

$$= \frac{K\omega_n^2}{s^2 + 2\zeta\omega_n s + \omega_n^2} \tag{8b}$$

For the reduced-order model $G_{red}(s)$, the system behavior can be extracted in Table 3. It can be seen that for $K = 2.376$, the reduced-order system preserved under damped behavior. The time responses of $G_{red}(s)$ and $G(s)$ is shown in Fig. 8.

Table 3. Behaviour of reduced-order power system $G_{red}(s)$.

	Gain	Damping ratio	Natural frequency
Numerical value	$K = 2.376$	$\zeta = 0.4584$	$\omega_n = 2.8275$ rad/s

The performance comparison of the reduced-order and original third-order power system is tabulated in Table 4. Therefore, it is clear that the reduced-order model is a good approximation to the original third-order model.

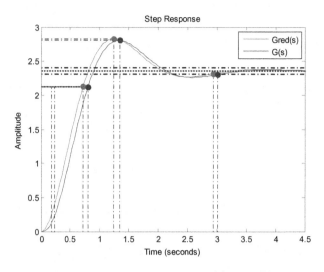

Fig. 8. The time response of $G_{red}(s)$ and $G(s)$.

Table 4. Performance comparison of the reduced-order and original third-order power system.

	Third-order system $G(s)$	Reduced-order system $G_{red}(s)$
Rise time	0.571 s	0.553 s
Settling time	3.02 s	2.94 s
Peak time	1.35 s	1.24 s
Peak amplitude	2.81	2.83
Overshoot	19.2%	19.8%
Steady-state error	1.35	1.36

Load frequency controller $u = -K_f \Delta f$ is designed where K_f takes the three-term control laws cum low pass filter as in Eq. (9).

$$K_f = K_p + K_i \frac{1}{s} + K_d s \left(\frac{N}{Ns+1} \right) \tag{9}$$

By considering reduced-order power system model in Eq. (8a), the control parameters can be tuned by using Lyapunov stability criteria. For the system in Eq. (10),

$$\frac{\Delta f}{u} = \frac{19}{s^2 + 2.593s + 7.995} \tag{10}$$

the state variables can be defined as $x_1 = \Delta f$ and $x_2 = \dot{\Delta f}$. Hence, the system can be expressed in state-space as in Eq. (11).

$$\dot{x} = \begin{bmatrix} 0 & 1 \\ -7.995 & -2.593 \end{bmatrix} x + \begin{bmatrix} 0 \\ 19 \end{bmatrix} u \tag{11}$$

Ignoring low pass filter, let PID control law $u \triangleq K_f$ be defined as in Eq. (12).

$$u(t) = K_p x_1(t) + K_i \int x_1(t)d\tau + K_d \dot{x}_1(t) \tag{12}$$

Then, the existence of Lyapunov function in Eq. (13) yields the control law in Eq. (13).

$$V(x_1, x_2) = \frac{1}{2}x_1^2 + \frac{1}{2}x_2^2 \tag{13}$$

Equation (13) confirms the stability in a sense of Lyapunov as the derivative of (13) renders a negative definite function in Eq. (14)

$$\dot{V}(x_1, x_2) = -C_1 x_1^2 - C_2 x_2^2 \tag{14}$$

where $C_1 > 0$ and $C_2 > 0$. To fulfill Lyapunov stability criteria in Eqs. (13) and (14), the control law can be designed as

$$u = \frac{7.995}{19}x_1(t) + \left[\frac{C_2 + 2.593}{19}\right]\dot{x}_1(t) + C_1 \int x_1(t)d\tau \tag{15}$$

where the proportional constant $K_P = \frac{7.995}{19}$, derivative constant $K_d = \frac{C_2 + 2.593}{19}$ and integral constant $K_i = C_1$. Filter constant N can be chose judiciously. Figure 9 shows the LFC control structure with all control parameters.

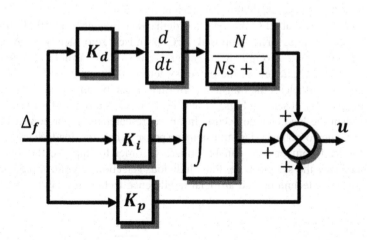

Fig. 9. LFC control structure.

4 Result and Discussion

Figure 10 shows the closed-loop power system with LFC. To observe the effectiveness of the proposed technique, the power system is injected by a frequency deviation due to load perturbation, $\Delta P_d = 1\%$, $\forall t > 3$. The responses are depicted in Figs. 11 and 12.

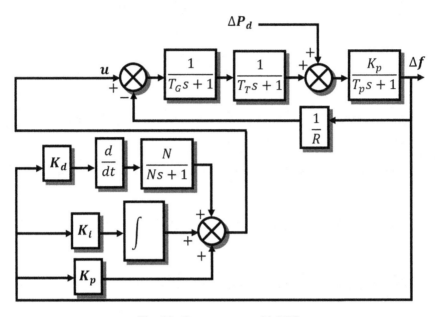

Fig. 10. Power system with LFC.

Figure 11 compares the frequency deviation (in %) when the system is disturbed by persistent perturbation $\Delta P_d = 1\%$ at $t = 3$ s. Without LFC, the 1%-deviation remains for all $t > 3$ s though the oscillation subsides at $t = 14$ s.

Figure 12 shows that LFC preserve the demanded frequency at 50 Hz upon disturbed by load changes. The proposed LFC promises zero steady state error by imposing additional pole at origin due to integral term of the control law, as depicted in Fig. 9. As such, LFC guarantees the power system stability upon perturbation due to load changes. Nevertheless, the transient performance can be improved as the response is rather sluggish. By observing Figs. 11 and 12, LFC takes around 11 s to stabilize the frequency when the load change occurs. In future, researchers might ponder to design control technique to achieve fast transient response when the load changes occurs. Classical lag-lead compensator can be utilizes in order to improve the steady-state without increasing the system type. Plus, judicious selection of control parameters by using optimization technique and artificial intelligence techniques can be suggested.

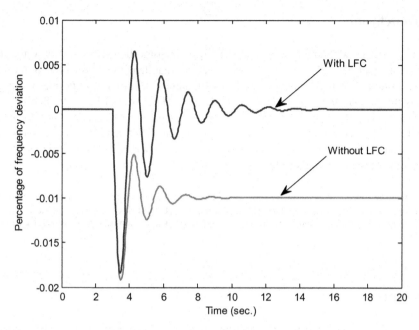

Fig. 11. Percentage of frequency deviation when perturbed by $\Delta P_d = 1\%$ at $t = 3$ s.

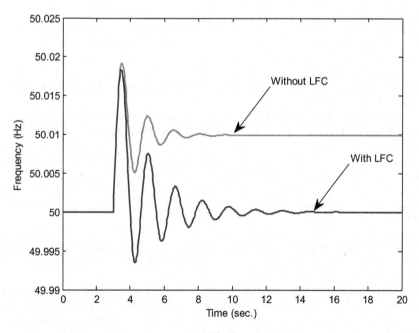

Fig. 12. Load frequency when perturbed by $\Delta P_d = 1\%$ at $t = 3$ s.

5   Conclusion

In this paper, Load frequency control (LFC), or in some literatures stated Automatic generation control (AGC) has been designed to stabilize the frequency of thermal power system. The load change introduces frequency deviation that normally quantified as the *percentage of frequency perturbation*. The aim of LFC is to stabilize the frequency when the perturbation occurs. In this paper, the LFC is designed by using three-term PID controller with low pass filter. The PID parameters are set using Lyapunove stability criteris. The proposed technique guarantees the stabilization even though the transient is rather sluggish.

Acknowledgements. We acknowledge the Center for Robotics and Industrial Automation, Universiti Teknikal Malaysia Melaka (UTeM) for research facilities, research collaboration and research grant funding Vote Nos: FRGS/1/2015/TK04/FKE/03/F00259 and PJP/2015/FKE(21C) S01461.

References

1. Wang, W., Ohmori, H.: Decentralized load frequency control for two-area interconnected power system. Control Theory Technol. **13**(3), 101–114 (2015)
2. Rajaguru, V., Sathya, R.: Effect of SMES unit in a restructured power system considering GDB non-linearity. Int. J. Eng. Res. Technol. **4**(02), 1–12 (2015)
3. Rekhasree, R.L., Abdul Jaleel, J.: Automatic generation control of complex power systems using genetic algorithm: a case study. Int. J. Eng. Res. Technol. **2**(10) (2013)
4. Hore, D.: An analysis of two area load frequency control with different types of feedback controllers. Int. J. Eng. Res. Technol. **3**(03) (2014)
5. Elgerd, O.I.: Electric Energy System Theory: An Introduction, TMH edn. McGraw-Hill, New York City (1971)
6. Jain, D., Bhaskar, M.K., Joshi, S.K., Bohra, D.: Analysis of load frequency control problem for interconnected power system using PID controller. Int. J. Emerg. Technol. Adv. Eng. **4**(11) (2014)
7. Nizam Kamarudin, M., Md. Rozali, S., Rashid Husain, A.: Observer-based output feedback control with linear quadratic performance. Procedia Eng. **53**, 233–240 (2013)
8. Md. Rozali, S., Nizam Kamarudin, M., Fua'ad Rahmat, M., Rashid Husain, A.: Asymptotic tracking position control for nonlinear systems using backstepping technique. Procedia Eng. **53**, 255–263 (2013)
9. Kouba, N.E.Y., Menaa, M., Hasni, M., Boussahoua, B., Boudour, M.: Optimal load frequency control in interconnected power system using PID controller based on particle swarm optimization. In: International Conference on Electrical Sciences and Technologies in Maghreb (CISTEM), pp. 1–8 (2014)
10. Yang, M., Wenlin, L., Yuanwei, J.: Decentralized load frequency variable structure control of multi-area interconnected power system. Chin. Control Decis. Conf. **4**, 666–669 (2011)
11. Pan, C.T., Liaw, C.M.: An adaptive controller for power system load-frequency control. IEEE Trans. Power Syst. **4**(1), 122–128 (1989)
12. AlRifai, M., Zribi, M.: A robust decentralized controller for power system load frequency control. In: Power Engineering Conference, pp. 794–799 (2014)

13. Tan, W.: Tuning of PID load frequency controller for power systems. Energy Convers. Manag. **50**, 1465–1472 (2009)
14. Kothari, M.L., Kaul, B.L., Nanda, J.: Automatic generation control of hydrothermal systems. J. Inst. Eng. **61**, 85–91 (1980)
15. Kiran Kumar, N., Naidu, I.E.S.: Load frequency control for a multi area power system involving wind, hydro and thermal plants. Int. J. Innovative Res. Sci. Eng. Technol. **3**(1) (2014)
16. Silas Stephen, D.: Load frequency control of hybrid hydro systems using tuned PID controller and fuzzy logic controller. Int. J. Eng. Res. Technol. **5**(03) (2016)

Improving Material Handling System Performance in Automotive Assembly Line Using Delmia Quest Simulation

Seha Saffar[1(✉)], Zamberi Jamaludin[2], and Fairul Azni Jafar[2]

[1] Centre of Graduate Studies, Universiti Teknikal Malaysia Melaka,
Hang Tuah Jaya, 76100 Durian Tunggal, Melaka, Malaysia
sehasaffar@yahoo.com
[2] Faculty of Manufacturing Engineering, Universiti Teknikal Malaysia Melaka,
Hang Tuah Jaya, 76100 Durian Tunggal, Melaka, Malaysia

Abstract. This paper presenting an improvement made on material handling system in automotive assembly line in order to investigate the changes or influences that affect the assembly line. Some issues from a case study arose where the current transportation took a long time to supply material at assembly line and a risk of damaging the parts is high. Thus, an improvement is done by changing the current transport equipment into AGV and the storage equipment is changed into semi-automatic pick-to-light system. A method of discrete-event simulation using Delmia Quest software is applied. Based on the simulation result, the total production output increase almost 3 folds from the current output factory can produce. It's concluded that a combined changes give large influences to the manufacturing system. A part of that, Delmia Quest is a useful software to enable decision-making process and improve system effectively without possibility destroying the elements.

Keywords: Simulation · Automated guided vehicle · Pick-to-light system · Automated material handling system · Delmia Quest simulation

1 Introduction

Today ages are current challenges to develop more effective and efficient form of production system. At the same time, to adapt with the competition from all around the world, automation engineering becomes the current age solution for the above problem [1]. In order to achieve tasks in improving efficiency and reduce the cost of human operators, corporate and organizations use automation as an efficient tool in manufacturing plant. Automated guided vehicle (AGV) is one of the transport equipment use in automated material handling system and it's designed mainly to transfer material from one place to another. Nowadays, it's becoming more prevalent in integrating AGV in industrial environment for transporting materials and leads to cost and time reduction at installation and working time [2].

Another material handling equipment that is as importance as transport equipment, is storage equipment. It involves a system of supply and storage in the warehouse. Warehousing is an important part of the material handling system that involves

© Springer Nature Singapore Pte Ltd. 2017
M.S. Mohamed Ali et al. (Eds.): AsiaSim 2017, Part I, CCIS 751, pp. 468–482, 2017.
DOI: 10.1007/978-981-10-6463-0_40

activities like receiving goods, storage, order picking and etc. [3]. One of the major decisions concerning warehouse operation is the equipment selection problem, related to the form of automation to be adopted [4, 5]. To change manual warehouse into automated take a lot of research study time and cost. Thus, this research study recommended semi-automated storage equipment such as pick-to-light system, which is much simple storage equipment in market. Pick-to-light is light-directed order fulfillment system using light indicator mounted in shelving, flow rack or other storage locations. Pick-to-light is ideal for high-speed sortation processes, where a batch of orders is sorted to individual customer orders.

As a case study in actual automotive industry situation, warehouse, which hold function as parts storage area and process dividing the parts, is called supermarket. Each supermarket divides into inventory for each line such as trim line, chassis line and final line in factory plant. All parts will be brought to the assembly line using a manually drive train concept of material handling called tugger train. Meanwhile, the production process during the assembly line is done manually by operators using picking list order system. The process of the assembly is done by semi-auto processes that involve manual and auto system. Studies are focused at assembly shop where it is noticed that the process flow of material from warehouse to the assembly line is done fully manually. Thus, it took time in trafficking the material and high risk of parts damage (either human or material) during the transfer of the material.

A possible solution is by modeling an integration between production system and material supply system using a proper design of material handling system. By investigating the above problem, it is recommended to apply each automated material handling equipment by trial and error in order to see the effect on the production. But to apply it in a real situation is high cost and time-consuming. At the same time, there is a high risk of wasting resources during investigating. Thus, simulation comes in mind, as simulation modeling solutions and tools are effectively used in addressing and challenging new issues to become more flexible, feasible and provide infinite integration of various simulation methods [6].

In recent years, it's possible to develop of automated material handling simulation due to the development of virtual reality technology [7]. Delmia software is used to simulate and optimize the loading and unloading of an air cargo [8]. The Delmia Company was founded in June 2000. The software contains solutions and digital producing method based on the process [9]. Simulation is primarily intended to be useful technique as its integration of Computer-Aided Design and Computer-Aided Manufacturing is the main approach in the decision-making process and improving the quality of products and optimizing the time of production [10, 11].

In Delmia software, there a good discrete-even simulation software suitable to analyze a complete factory system in the various type of industry especially manufacturing industry. The software is named Quest (Queuing event simulation tool), which is a discrete event simulation package and a 3D simulation-based interactive engineering tool for designing and analyzing manufacturing systems. Delmia Quest software able to duplicate appearance, characteristics and features of a real system, without possibility of destroying the elements in factory or disturbing the system, and users enable to experience the process of the target equipment by using simulation method. Knowledge can be enhanced and design cycle can be shortened by using this

method [12]. Thus, the Quest software is a powerful tool in assessing, modeling and
analyzing changes that should be made in a complex manufacturing system [12, 13].

The purpose of this research work is to investigate the influences of automated
material handling system in automotive assembly line by improving the material
handling system using Delmia Quest simulation software. This paper focused on the
effect of automated material handling system in automotive assembly process through
warehouse to assembly line. Delmia Quest V5 is the software used in this project. It
intended to prepare, setup, and perform the simulation for this research work. A design
on the transport system that is comparable to the case study on material handling
system in the automotive industry will be done through simulation and the result will
be analyzed based on the process performance.

2 Case Study

This topic covers the preliminary study to gain data needed in the simulation. The
method flow used to design the simulation is shown in Fig. 1. Phase 1 shows the
preliminary data gathering collected from the case study and acts as the guideline and

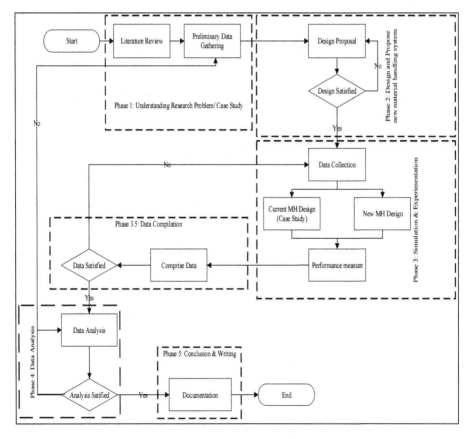

Fig. 1. Process flow in designing material handling system into Delmia Quest.

limitation to design the material handling system in Delmia Quest software. Next, phase 2 is where all the data were taken is translated into input for simulating the design. It focused on explaining all elements needed to design using the software.

Meanwhile, in phase 3, experiments are conducted as to analyze the performance measure of the integration system with the conventional system in the case study. The design of experiment contains 2 models which vary in their transport and storage equipment. As illustrates in Table 1, the variation of factors is used based on the models and noted that model 1 is the similar process used in the case study factory. The improvement is done in model 2 and it is compared with model 1 in order to study the significant effect of changing the actual system. The comparison between both models also acts as a validation of the design to be able to function similarly like the real situation of the factory.

Table 1. Variation of factors and list of models.

Models	MHS configuration		
	Layout	Transport equipment	Storage equipment
Model 1	Loop layout	Tugger train	Picking list system
Model 2		AGV	Pick-to-light system

The preliminary data gathering shows the data collected from a case study of real industry situation. It consists of plant layout from warehouse and assembly line, travel distance, distance between each station, parts involved in the process, and their material handling equipment used during the transfer process. The current layout used in the factory shows the transportation track from warehouse to assembly line which consists of a few workstations. This research work focuses on chassis line that consists of 10 stations with different processes and part supplies.

Figure 2 describes the model 1 layout and the travel distance from warehouse to assembly line. Meanwhile, Fig. 3 illustrates the layout and travel distance for model 2. Both models have the same assembly line. The differences between the two models are their storage and transport equipment. In storage part, model 1 only has 1 load station which represents the point where transport load the part collected manually by operator in warehouse. In the meantime, model 2 applied the semi-automatic pick-to-light system. So, in order to replicate the same action as the real pick-to-light system, model 2 has 7 load stations which represent the 7 type of sources that stored various small parts needed for assembly work. The transport will directly pick up the parts that are automatically ordered by the system.

In assembly line, each process has their owned stations and each station is not fixed with only one process. It involves assembly of 3 to 4 types of different parts for each station. Basically, the travel distance is based on the movement of transportation from pick-up point at the warehouse and return back to its starting point in order to have a total distance traveled in 1 cycle of working hour.

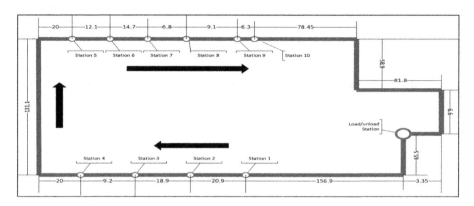

Fig. 2. Model 1 layout for vehicle transport equipment.

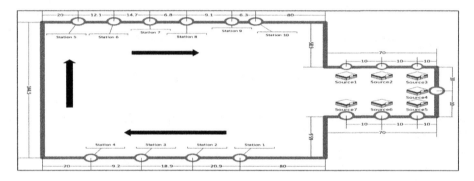

Fig. 3. Model 2 for vehicle transport equipment.

Apart from familiarizing with the assembly line, all parts involved also have been studied in order to know the requirement for parts distribution in every station. 31 parts are required for assembly process of one type of car model. In order to avoid confusion and keep focusing on the objective, only one model of assembled car is put in focus. All the parts data is used in allocating parts to every station in assembly process including positioning in warehouse and logic used in Delmia Quest as the part process flow.

In this case study situation, space has already been fixed and the location of productive and storage space has been decided. So the best improvement in transport equipment is using on-floor transport equipment. From the current tugger train transportation, an AGV is introduced to improve the transportation of the part transfer. Meanwhile, the storage area is divided into sections of rack which stored multiple different parts at the same time. The arrangement of the part is based on the size of the parts in order to ease workers to collect parts based on order from assembly line and put the parts into bins.

As for unit load principle, in the case study real situation, handling system is used to collect parts and transfer them using pallet which is called kit supply bin. The bins are a unit load that can be stored or moved as a single entity at one time. Based on the size of the parts, there are total 7 bins that are transferred into assembly line. The bins contain 4 to 10 parts at the same time and are transferred by a cart, where the cart is pulled by a train. There are no changes in this unit load system due to its ability to effectively achieve the material flow for old layout and is expected to give the same result for the new layout. Material flow for new layout is different due to fewer stations for parts to be transferred. 5 bins contain 4 to 10 parts at one time, and 2 bins contain only 1 part each due to the size of the part is large.

3 Design Using Delmia Quest Software

All elements needed to design the simulation are discussed in this topic. A complete 3D digital factory environment for process flow simulation and analysis is purposely created by Delmia/Quest. Its flexibility, object-based and discrete event simulation environment make engineering and management solution of choice for simulation and analysis. Quest runs on both UNIX (SGI and HP) and Windows NT based systems. It includes the physical model, parts, modeling element, connections and logic that define parts flow through the model.

The simulation is developed in sequence, but the order is not rigid as each step must be completed before running the model. The logical model and interaction of various parts and elements is the point that makes Quest software different from simple CAD approach in laying facility. The physical model is allowed to display the states of the system over time by the application of Quest logical model. This section discusses the major components that created the Quest model for this research work and their relationship. It includes the physical model, parts, modeling elements, element connections, and the logic that define how the parts move through the model. The core of the Quest simulation is the logical model itself, which is made up of two types of logical components; elements and parts.

3.1 Part Creation Elements

Parts are presented in this research work as car components which vary in size. Those parts are the entities in the Quest model that flow through the system, occupying resources and undergoing processing. It is necessary to create parts in the model, no matter what kind of parts in order to represent the model. By creating parts, sources in Quest are existed to produce the parts for processing and consumption by other elements in a model. A source represents the point-of-entry of parts into a model. It's very flexible element that offers a wide range of options by modifying the characteristic.

All models for this research work contain the same quantity of sources and each source has the same parts storage amount and type as shown in Fig. 4. The label of the source also describe for parts arrangement for bins in warehouse, the destination of the parts is already set using the programming method due to a different quantity of parts for every source.

Fig. 4. The list of source in all models.

Source setting for the maximum part count is set to allow the number of parts in source that can be produced and the part creation mode is set to active in order to put the source independently when creating the part for the rest of the model. The normal characteristic is that all sources, in all models are having a maximum part count which is a large default number of 1,000,000 effectively as to assume the supply of part in warehouse has an infinite capacity to produce parts since it particularly questionable that any real model will be called upon to handle so many parts. It is recommended for Quest simulation to use a source specifically when using parts to model entities with a fixed or maximum number and set the maximum part count correctly.

The set up for output type is set to push system to enable the parts available for transfer to downstream elements immediately after they are created. The start offset means that the elements are able to have a time delay for the production of the parts. The research models using default start offset which is zero, that's mean the source will start producing parts the moment the models start to run.

As noted in Fig. 4, there is source named "Main_Car". It's a car's frame function located at assembly line as a dummy part for a worker to assemble all the main parts coming from warehouse. The source characteristic for the "Main-Car" is set to be compatible with the arrival of the first part supplied to the assembly line.

As the real condition happens at the factory, the parts are transferred to transport equipment using bins contain various different parts according to the source classification. The bins used are loaded into the carts that the AGV or tugger train will pull and bring them and other supplied parts into an assembly line. The bins divide parts based on source classification and stored parts safely during the transferred.

3.2   Part Storage Elements

Buffer represent a storage location in warehouse, where the hopper or buffer feeding parts into a machine. It also able to represent the location of stored parts or their access queue to other resources such as machines. In this research work's models, the buffer functions as the hopper or temporary storage for the parts which are to be handled by operators. The buffers are applied at warehouse and also assembly line.

The function of buffer at warehouse is similar as a hopper, where the operator picks up a group of different parts that come from the source and collect them into palettes. As illustrates in Fig. 5, the buffer is shown as a purple palette in the figure, where it collect and store certain parts based on their characteristic from the warehouse and wait until next assignment. Then, it will be pick up by operator or transportation as shown in Fig. 6. This process is not physically applied at real condition of warehouse but as for simulation in Quest, its act as a dummy process as to describe that the parts are already arranged in storage equipment at the real warehouse.

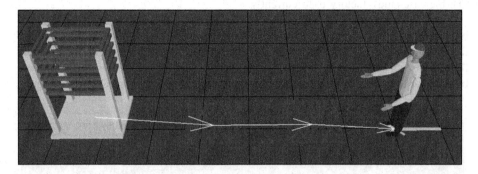

Fig. 5. The buffer connection between source and operator. (Color figure online)

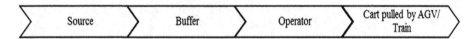

Fig. 6. The process flow of buffer between sources to cart.

As usual, when the buffer button is selected, the buffer dialog box appears and allow the selection of an existing buffer class by name or new. In this model, the list of buffers for both models is shown in Fig. 7. This model has the same buffers quantity and location because they have the same layout which is the old layout. The location of the buffer is divided into warehouse's buffer and assembly line's buffer.

Fig. 7. List of warehouse and assembly line buffers for both model.

There are 10 assembly line buffers due to a number of drop-off stations at assembly line which is 10 stations. Meanwhile, the warehouse has 14 buffers where each source has 2 buffers in order to have a smooth part allocation into the bin. A buffer for pick up station is also created for AGV or tugger train to pick the bins that operator has collected and grouped from warehouse's buffer. The operator will pick up the parts based on the order from the assembly line in order to illustrate the picking list system that the case study factory used currently.

The location of buffers for model 1 and 2 are illustrated as Fig. 8. Each source has 2 buffers together colored as purple in the picture and the pickup station is at the center of the warehouse, allocate together with labor or operator. The 10 buffers at the assembly line are shown as cyan in the figure. The characteristic of all models for warehouse buffers and assembly line buffers are using the default setting from Quest software.

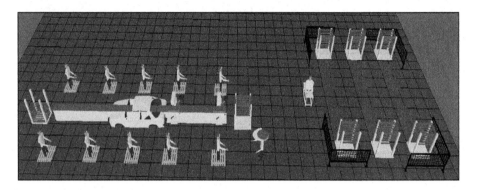

Fig. 8. The location of Buffers at warehouse and assembly line in Quest software. (Color figure online)

The arrival process and production process including a queue implemented in all buffers are created based on a concept of whenever the buffer of the group of workers at assembly line is free, a new part will enter. Such, queuing discipline used in this simulation is called First-In First-Out (FIFO). Thus, the queuing system for the buffer is that the first part to enter the buffer will be the first part to be routed out.

3.3   Material Handling Elements

AGV. Automated Guided Vehicle (AGV) is defined as a vehicle that independently moves around the system, loading and unloading parts at various locations. Quest used AGV as transporters represent for moving the part from those assign locations. Thus, in this research work, AGV and tugger train has the same modeling element. The different between both transport equipment is their speed and quantity.

In modeling the AGVs, a few elements are involved to work together such as, the AGVs itself, the controller that governs the behavior of the AGVs, the decision point where it is a point for loading and unloading points for AGVs to pick up and drop off parts and also the AGVs path system itself. The path system represents the layout of where the AGVs is moving and decision points are located. Individual AGV is created by creating an AGV class that defined the characteristics and behavior. Meanwhile, the behavior of the AGV is defined in its process logic.

Normally, AGV cannot move outside its path system and all the AGVs in the same class have similar characteristic and behavior. However, each element of AGVs can behave differently when logic is written for them. All the characteristics are modeled with or without a controller. In general, all decisions are made by the controller based on the given information and communications on what should be done by the AGV and the executions of the decision. But, the decision making is not restricted to controllers but it can also be done by decision points or the AGV itself.

The information and communications flow between AGVs, decision point and controller, need to be coordinated for correct behavior because unlike others elements such as buffers, machine and sources, whose behavior is dictated by their own logics, AGV behavior is governed by the logics of those 3 elements. The logic behind this command is when the controller gives an AGV command, it waits for notification that the AGV has finished completing the action. When it happen, the AGV respond to the controller by generating the controller event to confirm that the action is completed. Usually, not all commands received by the AGV need to be notified back to the controller for completion of the action.

Labor. Labor is the element that moves around the system, satisfying process requirement, transporting parts, and perform loading and unloading parts at various locations. Labor path system is used as a location for laborers and the path system is the path labors move in the same manner as AGV does. However, labors are free to create their own paths as long as there is labor point, as required. Process logic class defined the behavior of the labor and all labors belonging in the same class have similar characteristic and behavior. But, logic can be written so the labors within the class behave differently. As in this research work, the behaviors of the labors possess the same character and behave similarly as default in Quest.

Modeling the labors involve multiple elements together. Example like the labors themselves, labor controller, labor decision point, labor path system, labor points and labor via paths. When modeling a labor on path system, main elements needed are labor path system and labor decision point. For the simulation in this research work, labor in a warehouse for model 1 used labor path system and decision point because the labor has different depart requirement on every pickup stations in the warehouse. Thus, a decision point is needed for this labor. Meanwhile, labor for an assembly line in all models does not need the path system and decision point because the labor is modeled without explicit path system and the only element in the labor system for this case is the labor itself, without a controller. The labor via path has automatically generated the paths by the labor in this case.

4   Running the Simulation

When appropriate tools and worker are in place, together with the suitable application is selected, the simulation study can be started. A validated simulation is well planned and coordinated as illustrated in Fig. 9. There is no strict rule or process to conduct a simulation project. A general procedure is followed starting from developing the model and conduct the experiment after validation. The simulation is run with a typical Malaysia working day from 8.00 a.m. until 5.00 p.m. (8 h). The rest time for labors is given a total of 1 h which is at 1.00 p.m. for their lunch. The normal working days for the company are 6 days a week based on normal shift. But for the recorded result is only for one day of working. The amount of time the labors take to transfer parts between each assigned station is established at 10 s of constant on the distributions.

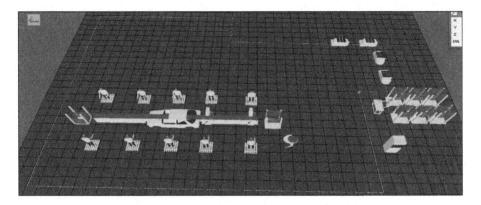

Fig. 9. Simulation figure in Quest software.

5   Improved Material Handling System Performance

The result of the simulation is compiled and presented in the statistical chart as shown in Table 2. The analysis is done by identifying the improvement through a comparison with current system on either the new proposed system is able to increase the performance of the warehouse in the term of production rate, bottleneck decreasing and increment of utilization for both transport and storage equipment.

Simulation is done to observe the improvement of the current manual transportation to automated material handling system. The improvement can be seen noticed from the total part created. The total part created by model 1 is only 14 parts per working hour. From the proposed improvement, model 2 is able to create more than 2 fold value of part created from the current system, which are 36 parts per working hour. As illustrates in Fig. 10, the chart shows the created part for model 2 dominate pie's area more than half compared to model 1. The increment in parts supply is likely due to the AGV's ability effectively transferring part with constant speed. Meanwhile, the throughput rate can be seen at warehouse or source statistic. Figure 11 shows model 2 produce a large area of the part created in every source stations. A significant change

Table 2. Result presentation.

Element class statistic	Formulas
Element class statistic - Total part created - Number of part supply	- Σ total number of part which entered the system in assembly line - Number of parts in system
Sources statistic - Throughput rate	- Number of parts/Simulation runtime
Transport statistic - Number of transport claimed with no wait (Utilization)	- Numbers of transport that did not have to wait in every station
Drop off buffer statistic - Idle time	- Σ total time an element was no executing any processes
Pick up buffer statistic - Average waiting time (WIP)	- Average residence time of any parts that has left the buffer. (Max. waiting time + Min. waiting time)/2

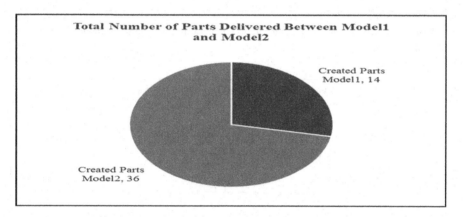

Fig. 10. Pie chart of part delivered from warehouse into assembly line for both models.

can be seen at RC bin source where the rate between both models shows highest difference. This is due to most of the parts coming from RC bin's source and the application of AGV and pick-to-light system is able to produce a large size of supply from RC bin source. The current system by means picking list order and tugger train, cannot do.

Figure 12 represents a graph of idle time comparison in assembly line supply buffer where it is a point for AGV to unload parts. From the figure, there is a large fluctuation point at assembly line buffer 1 and 2. Based on layout configuration, assembly line buffer 1 and 2 are located nearby from each other. Hence, transport is able to transfer part quickly than other assembly line buffers. However, the idle time linearly increasing in other points. Noted that at every drop off stations, transport unloads different parts quantity. Therefore, model 1 gives increasing values of idle time along the stations. On the contrary, model 2 shows a decrement of the idle time, hence shows a nice constant idle time among the stations.

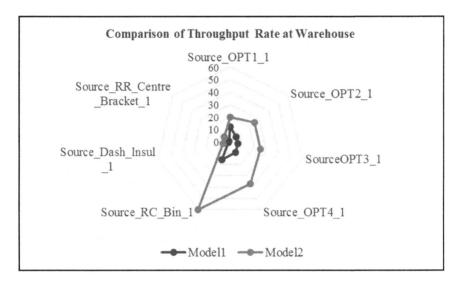

Fig. 11. Chart area of throughput rate in source/warehouse between model 1 and 2.

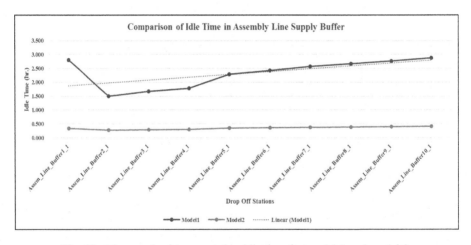

Fig. 12. Line graph of transportation idle time for model 1 and model 2.

Furthermore, Fig. 13 also illustrates the decrement of bottleneck where the average waiting time of AGV in model 2 is reduced as much as 0.28 h during pick up activity instead of 0.716 h (Waiting time of train in model 1). AGV in model 2 able to avoid the waiting time longer by transferring the parts effectively. Lastly, the AGV in model 2 utilized 7 times more than the train in model 1. Furthermore, the average number of AGVs claimed with no waiting time is 78 units rather than train. For train, only 11 units are claimed with no waiting time. This shows a lot of improvement in the transportation system where the system is able to avoid wasting in waiting time.

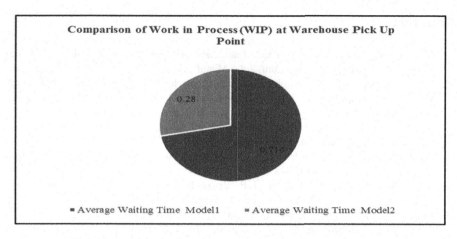

Fig. 13. Pie chart of work in process at warehouse pick up point.

6 Conclusion

Current demand in technology and system of automated material handling is increasing and the study that trending in the optimization of effective and efficient material handling system is arising in order to have better income in the product. Hence, this study aims to expose the benefit and importance application of automated material handling system by investigating their influences in the industry especially in the assembly process of automotive assembly system.

All the preliminary data is translated into simulation elements, and method to design the simulation is explained through this paper. The result presented shown a large significant changed in various areas especially the warehouse and transportation area. Thus, we can conclude that the improvement obtained shows the importance of material handling system in increasing the performance of the automotive assembly factory as well as other manufacturing fields.

Lastly, a large influence can be seen from a combined change into the manufacturing system. At the same time, by using Delmia Quest simulation software, not only one variable can be tested but the software also allows combined changes which affected the system. With the ability to measure the result, an ability to forecast the effect of the changes can be made. Delmia Quest is useful software to enable decision-making process and improve system effectively without possibility of destroying the real elements.

Acknowledgement. First of all, thanks to Allah for allowing us to finish this paper. We would like to thank Universiti Teknikal Malaysia Melaka for giving us the opportunity to develop this study. Special thanks to research grant FRGS/1/2015/TK03/FKP/02/F00277 for funding the research. We also want to thank engineers from Mawea Industries Sdn. Bhd. for support and guide us to conduct a simulation in Delmia Quest software.

References

1. Harisha, S.K.: Design and fabrication of automatic material handling system for engraving machine. Proc. Mater. Sci. Int. Conf. Adv. Manuf. Mater. Eng. **5**, 1540–1549 (2014)
2. Varga, R., Nedevschi, S.: Vision-based autonomous load handling for automated guided vehicles. In: Proceedings of 10th IEEE International Conference on Intelligent Computer Communications and Processing, pp. 239–244. IEEE Press (2014)
3. van den Berg, J.P., Zijm, W.H.M.: Models for warehouse management: classification and examples. Int. J. Prod. Econ. **59**, 219–528 (1999)
4. Gu, J., Goetschalckx, M., McGinnis, L.F.: Research on warehouse operation: a comprehensive review. Eur. J. Oper. Res. **177**, 1–21 (2007)
5. Gu, J., Goetschalckx, M., McGinnis, L.F.: Research on warehouse design and performance evaluation: a comprehensive review. Eur. J. Oper. Res. **203**, 539–549 (2010)
6. Boteanu, E., Zapciu, M.: Improving layout and workload of manufacturing system using delmia quest simulation and inventory approach. Int. J. Innov. Res. Adv. Eng. **1**(6), 52–61 (2014)
7. Long, Y.G., Zhao, H.W.: Gantry crane virtual simulation training system. Comput. Simul. **20**(5), 120–122 (2003)
8. Shi, Y.: Aviation cargo handling process simulation analysis. In: IEEE Symposium on Electrical & Electronics Engineering, pp. 264–267 (2012)
9. Yang, M., Yin, M.D.: Ergonomics simulation and application in virtual assembly. Nanjing University of Aeronautics and Astonautics (2009)
10. Martin, M., Malzahn, D., Whitman, L.: Simulating an aircraft move rate. Int. J. Innov. Educ. http://webs.wichita.edu/depttools/depttoolsmemberfiles/lewhitman/Papers/Pre2007/2005IJIIE Bernbeck_Whitman.pdf
11. Bzymek, Z., Muness, M., Li, M., et al.: Simulation of machining sequence using Delmia/Quest software. Comput. Aided Des. Appl. **5**(4), 401–411 (2008)
12. Saad, N.H., Farouk, M.A.A., Mohamed, Z., Sahab, A.R.M.: Manufacturing plant performance analysis using simulation technique. In: Proceeding of the 2nd International Conference on Mechatronics, pp. 871–878. Kuala Lumpur, Malaysia (2005)
13. Boteanue, G., Zapciu, M., Sindile, M.: Balancing of production line using discrete event simulation model. In: Proceedings of Manufacturing System, pp. 227–232 (2014)

EMF Radiation Effects from 5 × 5 Dipole Array Antenna Towards Human Body for 5G Communication

Nor Adibah Ibrahim[(✉)], Tharek Abd Rahman, and Olakunle Elijah

Faculty of Electrical Engineering, Wireless Communication Center,
Universiti Teknologi Malaysia (UTM), Johor Bahru, Malaysia
adibah_ibrahim19@yahoo.com

Abstract. Electromagnetic Field (EMF) is defined as a physical field produced by electrically charged objects. Nowadays there is an extensive concern about the EMF radiation effects towards human body. In this paper, the effect of EMF radiation is studied using a single dipole and 5 × 5 array dipole antennas. The proposed antenna is designed and simulated by using FEKO software. Results and discussions are explored to scrutinize the EMF performance of the antenna particularly on the distance and the frequency of the antenna with respect to the human body. Subsequently, the results of the SAR and power density at various frequency and distance are presented. It is shown that SAR and power density increases as the frequency increases at a fixed distance. The result of power density for the array antenna at different distances is also presented.

Keywords: 5G · Dipole antenna · Electromagnetic field radiation · Power density · SAR

1 Introduction

Fifth generation (5G) technologies for mobile communications are gaining worldwide attention [1]. Our world today is trying to implement the world's first 5G that will presumably be launched in 2020. The concept of 5G is presented in [2], where a 5G radio access network (RAN) is constructed by using the enhanced LTE-Advanced and the new radio access technologies. In 5G generation, higher frequencies are involved, and more types of antenna designs for telecommunication are required. Antenna in the RF transmission line utilizes several types of transmission tools such as coaxial cable, parallel wire lines and hollow pipe waveguides. In [3], it is stated that the millimetre wave involves 30 to 300 Ghz of frequencies. Antenna has been used, so that as the distance or the frequency rises, the signal loses and the cost of using transmission line increases. For long distance, radio communication using transmit and receive antennas is more appropriate and less expensive compared to using transmission lines.

In [4], in order to conform to the pertinent regulatory requirement on human exposure, all radio-based products emitting radio frequency (RF) electromagnetic fields (EMF) are required to be designed and verified. The power of absorption becomes increasingly superficial at higher frequencies. Furthermore, the International Commission on

© Springer Nature Singapore Pte Ltd. 2017
M.S. Mohamed Ali et al. (Eds.): AsiaSim 2017, Part I, CCIS 751, pp. 483–493, 2017.
DOI: 10.1007/978-981-10-6463-0_41

Non-Ionizing Radiation Protection (ICNIRP) basic restrictions are given free space power density from 10 to 300 Ghz. In radio-based station, there is an electromagnetic field radiation that radiates from array antenna that has been designed by human. Consequently, the person who works in radio-based station will be exposed to EMF radiation. Usually, the antenna commonly need to be used in radio-based station is large array antenna. Due to this reason, the compliance boundary is investigated to ensure that an individual's health will be safe when they are working in RBS area. Illustration of the compliance boundary for radio base station (RBS) can be seen in Fig. 1.

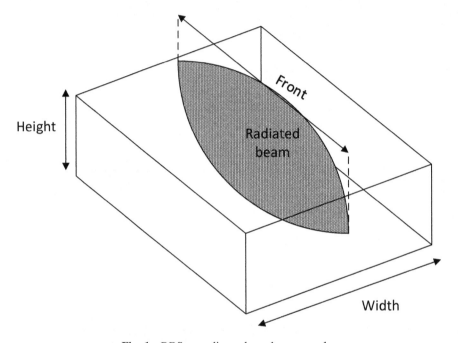

Fig. 1. RBS compliance boundary example.

In [4], a compliance boundary is defined as the specific surface outside of which the RF exposure is below the exposure limits. In this paper, the design of the antenna is designed for single dipole first, and from this design the value of SAR and power density are determined. The SAR is an extremely important parameter for near field at low frequency and when the frequency increases above 6 Ghz, the power density is calculated. Then, the 5 × 5 array dipole antenna is designed and the value of power density is measured with several frequencies. In this paper, we focus on base station array antennas using a 5 × 5 example for 5G systems. The Table 1 shows the limit of SAR and power density that has been decided by worldwide standard bodies [5, 6].

Table 1. Summary of exposure limit.

Body	Metric	Frequency	Public values	Occupational values	Remarks
ICNIRP	SAR	≤ 10 GHz	0.08 W/kg	0.4 W/kg	Whole body averaged over 10 g
	SAR	≤ 10 GHz	2 W/kg	10 W/kg	Localized head/trunk
	SAR	≤ 10 GHz	4 W/kg	20 W/kg	Localized limbs
	Power density	≥ 10 GHz	10 W/m^2	50 W/m^2	Averaged over 20 cm^2
FCC	SAR	≤ 6 GHz	0.08 W/kg	0.4 W/kg	Averaged over 1 g
	Power density	≥ 6 GHz	10 W/m^2		Averaged over 1 cm^2
NRPB	SAR	≤ 10 GHz	0.1 W/kg	0.4 W/kg	Whole body
	SAR	≤ 10 GHz	2 W/kg	10 W/kg	Localized

The equation of SAR is as below. It is a highly significant equation as it is used to calculate how much power absorbed per area [7].

$$SAR = (\sigma_\times E_{rms}2)/\rho \qquad (1)$$

where, σ = conductivity of various human tissues, E_{rms} is RMS of electric intensity of the body and ρ is Density of human tissue.

The equation of power density is expressed as [8],

$$S = \frac{P * G}{4 * \pi * R^2} \qquad (2)$$

where S = power density, P = power input to antenna, G = power gain of antenna and R = distance to center of radiation of antenna.

Manufacturers are not very concerned with higher SAR if it is within the limits, but they are surely concerned with the risk of non-compliance. They are also concerned about publishing SAR values in their user manuals that strongly underestimate the actual SAR value of the device. So yes, they can sometimes be conservative and announce higher SAR values in their manuals in order to cover for potential mass production deviations. There are also possibilities that they voluntarily reduce the transmit power in specific modes. If the telecommunication vendor makers are being too conservative, the device will have a lesser range from the cell-based station, which will then affect the performance. In a competitive environment, this is an extremely critical issue.

Some manufacturers certainly make a lot of testing in production with simple setups like small shield room equipped with couplers enabling an approximate assessment of radiated power. They may then correlate the variations of radiated power with SAR to characterize which sort of SAR dispersion they can expect in their production batches. SAR measurements made with robot systems are done in a limited number of samples picked at defined timesteps from the production lines. Depending on the use, SAR testing may not be required or it perhaps be very limited. The higher the SAR values, the larger the need for testing in cellular bands which have higher nominal transmit powers. All these are still present today and they are mostly operated in phones or tablets. SAR testing is on a critical path in wireless devices development. Especially today, devices are very thin with a large screen so that little volume and degrees of freedom are left to antenna designers. All facets of the devices have to be SAR tested at extremely short distance from human body mannequins.

The broad utilization of mobile phones has been complemented by the concern from the public regarding the possible effects inflicted on human health as the result of constant exposure to RF radiation emitted by the phones. Diverse phone models, head models, and test positions are applied in many studies to study the consequences of the head size on particular absorption rate.

Furthermore, when comparing the SAR values, the references of the electrical sources are also inversely applied. For instance, the fixed current of the phone under the test position is utilized in [9] while the SAR results of [10] are for the fixed conducted power of the phone antenna that gives the desired power of the radiation from the headless phone. Moreover, [11] compares the SAR results for both the continuous current and also the conducted power. In the aforementioned paper, it is decided that the trend in the SAR values can be clarified with the variation of the input resistance of the phone antenna. The authors in [12, 13] investigated the connection between the human head size and the SAR features for handset exposure using an anatomical model and a simple homogeneous model without the pinna. The outcomes depict that the local SAR values are higher approximately in the larger head at 900 MHz but only one source model is utilized in other researches. Then, SARs, in tandem to the antenna power of various phone models are compared in [14].

Furthermore, different assessment methods for antenna array intended for beam-forming applications have been carried out in [12, 15]. The proposed methods in [4, 15–17] focus on straightforward approach which is mainly based on the field combining the embedded assessment outcomes for each element and estimated methods in [18]. The major challenge of the combined and embedded assessment of the array element is that it requires significant amount of simulation time and computer memory which is impractical for large array antenna. To overcome this problem, front compliance approximate methods based on center element and multiple element characteristics are proposed in [18]. Although the approximate method looks promising, it is considered as a general approach for square-shaped array antennas. This method needs to be further investigated and improvised for different shapes of antenna arrays and different array sizes. Furthermore, different array excitations need to be considered for the compliance boundary determination for the array antenna.

Hence, in this paper, a preliminary work is carried out to design and simulate the EMF performance for a single pole dipole antenna and 5×5 array dipole antenna. This paper is organised as follows.

Section 2 is the design of the antenna involved while Sect. 3 discusses the results and the analysis, and finally Sect. 4 concludes this paper.

2 Antenna Design

In this Section, the single dipole and 5 × 5 dipole antenna are introduced. These antennas are designed by using FEKO software. The design of the antennas can be manipulated by using many tools in the FEKO software. Figures 2 and 3 show the design of dipole antenna and the far-field of 2D and 3D view (Fig. 4).

Fig. 2. Dipole antenna.   **Fig. 3.** Far-field in 3D view.

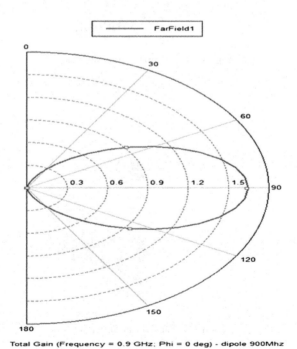

Total Gain (Frequency = 0.9 GHz; Phi = 0 deg) - dipole 900Mhz

Fig. 4. Far-field in 2D view.

Figure 2 is the design of single dipole antenna and Fig. 5 is the design of 5 × 5 array dipole antenna. This array antenna is designed and simulated in FEKO and the performance is determined by using power density at different frequencies and distance. This 5 × 5 dipole array antenna consist of 25 dipole elements in one array antenna (Figs. 6 and 7).

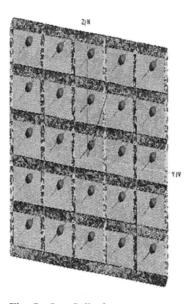

Fig. 5. 5 × 5 dipole array antenna.

Fig. 6. Far-field in 3D view.

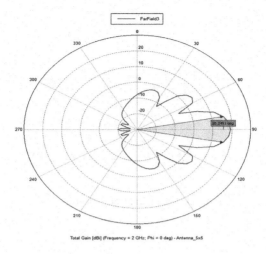

Total Gain [dBi] (Frequency = 2 GHz; Phi = 0 deg) - Antenna_5x5

Fig. 7. Far-field in 2D view.

3   Result and Analysis

The results are achieved from simulation when the frequency is varied from 75 MHz until 10 Ghz at a distance 1 m. The figure below shows the model of the design.

Figures 8 and 9 display the dipole in front of the dielectric cube using the CadFeko and PostFeko, respectively. The dielectric cube represents human body. Normally, in radio-based station, the SAR and power density are specified by the standard body as shown in Table 1 and metrics are used in this simulation. Table 2 shows the SAR and power density obtained when the frequency varies from 75 MHz to 10 Ghz and the distance of 1 m. The result shows that as the frequency increases from 75 MHz until 10 Ghz, the values of SAR and power density increases, respectively.

Table 2. Parameters of 5 × 5 array dipole antenna in FEKO.

Parameters	Values
Frequency	2 and 6 Ghz
Speed of light (c0)	3×10^8
Free space wavelength in millimeters	c0/freq*1000
Lambda	c0/freq
Width	Lambda/2
Length	Lambda/10
Radius	Lambda/1000

Figure 10 shows the simulation of the 5 × 5 dipole antenna, the dielectric cube that represents human body is attached at the dipole 5 × 5 antenna array with the value of the distance being constantly increased starting from 1 m and 10 m. For this design, the frequency used to simulate this model is at 2 Ghz, and 6 Ghz and the distance are 1 m and 10 m, respectively.

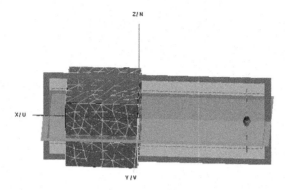

Fig. 8. Dipole in front of dielectric cube.

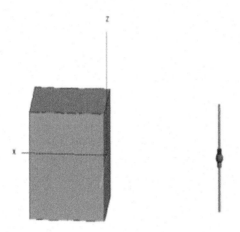

Fig. 9. Design simulated in FEKO.

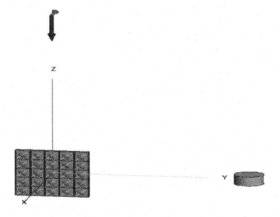

Fig. 10. 5 × 5 dipole array in front of dielectric cube.

Table 3 shows the value of power density when the frequency of the antenna is at 2 Ghz and 6 Ghz. Table 3 is for distance 1 m and Table 4 is for 10 m. The transmitted power is 68 mW and 66 mW for 2 Ghz and 6 Ghz, respectively (Table 5).

Table 3. Single dipole frequency versus SAR and power density.

Frequency	SAR value	Power density
75 MHz	1.6710 μW/kg	0.121119 mW/m^2
900 MHz	1.8670 mW/kg	0.172217 mW/m^2
1.8 Ghz	3.3100 mW/kg	0.188584 mW/m^2
2.4 Ghz	6.2290 mW/kg	0.197789 mW/m^2
2.6 Ghz	8.0607 mW/kg	0.237016 mW/m^2
3 Ghz	10.730 mW/kg	0.339498 mW/m^2
6 Ghz	32.740 mW/kg	0.340877 mW/m^2
10 Ghz	111.25 mW/kg	0.412450 mW/m^2
28 Ghz	213.2 mW/kg	1.2670500 mW/m^2

As shown in Tables 3 and 4, when the distance is 10 m the value of power density decreases when compared to the value of power density when the distance is 1 m. Thus, it can be concluded from this data analysis that the higher the distance of a human body from the antenna at the radio-based station, the safer they are from the EMF radiation. However, there is a need to establish the compliance distance for RBS transmitting at different power due to variation of power density at different distances. The results mentioned in Tables 2, 3 and 4 in the previous section stated that the value of power density for overall data is below the values specified by the standard bodies FCC and ICNIRP defined in Table 1.

Table 4. Frequency versus power density at 1 m distance.

Frequency	Power density
2 Ghz	0.0148662 mW/m^2
6 Ghz	0.0290460 mW/m^2

Table 5. Frequency versus power density at 10 m distance.

Frequency	Power density
2 Ghz	6.74362 μW/m^2
6 Ghz	17.9975 μW/m^2

Apart from that, the measurement of bandwidth and gain has also been measured in this paper for the 2 Ghz and 6 Ghz array dipole antenna. As we can see, the bandwidth value increases parallel to the frequency (Table 6).

Table 6. Bandwidth and gain value for different frequency.

Frequency	Bandwidth (Ghz)	Gain (dBi)
2 Ghz	0.063	20
6 Ghz	0.969	20

4   Conclusion

In this paper, the design and simulation of dipole antenna for 5G is presented. The EMF performance result for single dipole and 5 × 5 array dipole in terms of SAR and power density are presented using FEKO software. The result shows that as the frequency increases, the SAR and power density increases when measured from a fixed distance. However, as the distances increases the values of the power density decreases. This shows that there is a need for compliance distance for 5G RBS where large array of BS antennas is needed. In our future work, we intend to explore on the compliance distances for different array antennas based on the transmitting power needed to meet the regulatory requirements. Higher frequency such as 28 Ghz and 38 Ghz will be considered in our future work and the effect of mutual coupling will also be considered.

Acknowledgments. The authors would like to express utmost gratitude to the Ministry of Higher Education (MOHE) in Malaysia and Universiti Teknologi Malaysia (UTM) for providing the financial support for this research through the HiCOE grant (R.J130000.7809.4J209). The grant is managed by Research Management Centre (RMC) at UTM.

References

1. Oshima, I.: Development of base station antennas for 5G mobile communication systems. In: 2016 IEEE International Workshop on Electromagnetics: Applications and Student Innovation Competition (iWEM), Nanjing, pp. 1–2 (2016)
2. Yoshihara, T., et al.: Five-band base station antennas for introduction of 700 Mhz band services. NTT Docomo Tech. J. **16**(1) (2014)
3. Stutzman, W.L., Thiele, G.A.: Antenna Theory and Design, 3rd edn. Wiley, Hoboken (2013)
4. Degirmenci, E., Thors, B., Törnevik, C.: Assessment of compliance with RF EMF exposure limits: approximate methods for radio base station products utilizing array antennas with beam-forming capabilities. IEEE Trans. Electromagn. Compat. **58**(4), 1110–1117 (2016)
5. ICNIRP: ICNIRP Guidelines for limiting exposure to time varying electric, magnetic and electromagnetic fields (up to 300 GHz). Health Phys. **74**(4), 494–522 (1998)
6. Vecchia, P., Matthes, R.: Exposure to high frequency electromagnetic fields, biological effects and health consequences (100 kHz–300 GHz). ICNIRP (2009)
7. Tharakan, A., Deepthi, J., Gopika, J., Krishna, D.D.: Specific absorption rate reduced (SAR) mobile phone antenna designs. In: 2015 Fifth International Conference on Advances in Computing and Communications (ICACC), Kochi, pp. 250–253 (2015)
8. Pasternack: Power Density Calculator. https://www.pasternack.com/t-calculator-power-density.aspx. Accessed 28 Mar 2017

9. Togashi, T., Nagaoka, T., Kikuchi, S., Saito, K., Watanabe, S., Taka-hashi, M., Ito, K.: FDTD calculations of specific absorption rate in fetus caused by electromagnetic waves from mobile radio terminal using pregnant woman model. IEEE Trans. Microw. Theory Tech. **56**(2), 554–559 (2008)

10. Huang, L., Zhu, G., Du, X.: Cognitive femtocell networks: an opportunistic spectrum access for future indoor wireless coverage. IEEE Wireless Commun. **20**(2), 44–51 (2013)

11. Rappaport, S., Sun, S., Mayzus, R., Zhao, H., Azar, Y., Wang, K., Wong, G.N., Schulz, J.K., Samimi, M., Gutierrez, F.: Millimeter wave mobile communications for 5G cellular: it will work! IEEE Access **1**, 335–349 (2013)

12. Pretorius, J.: Design and manufacture of a ferrimagnetic wave absorber for cellular phone radiations. In: 12th International Symposium on Electron Devices for Microwave and Optoelectronic Applications, EDMO 2004, November 2004, pp. 119–123 (2004)

13. Agyapong, P.K., Iwamura, M., Staehle, D., Kiess, W., Benjebbour, A.: Design considerations for a 5G network architecture. IEEE Commun. Mag. **52**(11), 65–75 (2014)

14. Hossain, E., Rasti, M., Tabassum, H., Abdelnasser, A.: Evolution toward [5G] multi-tier cellular wireless networks: an interference management perspective. IEEE Wireless Commun. **21**(3), 118–127 (2014)

15. Ragha, L., Bhatia, M.: Evaluation of SAR reduction for mobile phone using RF shield. Int. J. Recent Trends Eng. **2**(5), 58–62 (2009)

16. Kelley, D.F.: Embedded element patterns and mutual impedance matrices in the terminated phased array environment. In: 2005 IEEE Antennas and Propagation Society International Symposium, July, vol. 3A, pp. 659–662 (2005)

17. Thors, B., Thielens, A., Fridén, J., Colombi, D., Törnevik, C., Ver-meeren, G., Martens, L., Joseph, W.: Radio frequency electromagnetic field compliance assessment of multi-band and MIMO equipped radio base stations. Bioelectromagnetics **35**(4), 296–308 (2014)

18. Ying, D., Love, D.J., Hochwald, B.M.: Beamformer optimization with a constraint on user electromagnetic radiation exposure. In: 2013 47th Annual Conference on Information Sciences and Systems (CISS), March, pp. 1–6 (2013)

Hazard Source Estimation Based on the Integration of Atmospheric Dispersion Simulation and UAV Sensory System

Rongxiao Wang, Bin Chen$^{(\boxtimes)}$, Sihang Qiu, Zhengqiu Zhu, and Xiaogang Qiu

National University of Defense Technology,
No. 109, Deya Road, 410073 Changsha, China
nudtcb9372@gmail.com

Abstract. Estimating contaminant source has become increasingly important to hazard assessment and emergency management of air contaminant nowadays. In this paper, a source estimation method is proposed to estimate the location and release rate of source. The theoretical basis of this source estimation method is Bayesian inference using the atmospheric dispersion model, Particle Swarm Optimization (PSO) and the observed data. An improved Gaussian dispersion model is proposed to model the continuous emission source. In order to obtain the observed data, a UAV-based air contaminant sensory system is developed consisting of an aerial platform and a sensory system. An experiment is conducted in a chemical industry park to verify the feasibility and credibility of this UAV-based system. Furthermore, the source estimation method proposed recovers the location and release rate of source with a high accuracy, confirming the effectiveness of the method.

Keywords: Source estimation · Bayesian inference · Gaussian dispersion model · UAV · Sensory system

1 Introduction

Owing to the huge economic benefits, increasing number of chemical industry parks are put into use today in some developing countries, associated with the air pollution caused by air contaminant emission. In air contaminant monitoring, the source estimation is an important issue that estimates the source location and release rate.

The various source estimation methods can be divided into forward and backward modeling [1]. Bayesian inference is the typical forward estimation method. By Bayesian inference, the goal of source estimation is to obtain the posterior probability. Huber [2] used an adaptive Gaussian mixture filter to solve the online Bayesian problem. In fact, other filtering techniques are also useful in source estimation, such as Kalman filter [3] and particle filter [4]. Ma et al. [5] used the minimum relative entropy and Particle Swarm Optimization (MRE-PSO) method to locate and quantify the diffusion source with Gaussian model. However, these methods are only for the source with a constant release rate. Neural networks are also useful in source estimation without diffusion model [6]. Wang et al. [7] presented a method for estimating diffusion through a neural network and applied it to the assessment of hazards.

© Springer Nature Singapore Pte Ltd. 2017
M.S. Mohamed Ali et al. (Eds.): AsiaSim 2017, Part I, CCIS 751, pp. 494–504, 2017.
DOI: 10.1007/978-981-10-6463-0_42

The observed data of air contaminant are needed in source estimation. The traditional ways of air contaminant monitoring in chemical industry park mainly depend on the static ground monitoring stations. This kind of station has high precision in contaminant detection and concentration measurement. Unfortunately, the sample interval is too long for the station to obtain enough data in limited time. Moreover, the static location also brings about the possible failure in valid data collection when the station is upwind of the emission source.

The emergence of unmanned aerial vehicle (UAV) has initiated a revolution in this research. UAV provides flexibility in architecture and mobility. It can be constructed according to the demand of the researcher. Thus, UAV has been applied in agriculture and food industry [8, 9], environmental monitoring [10, 11] (e.g. greenhouse gas monitoring in air), precision agriculture [12] (e.g. rationalization of chemical products and optimization of irrigation) and the safety monitoring [13].

In terms of the UAV applications in air contaminant monitoring in chemical industry park, Yang et al. [14] utilized a sensory system based on an unmanned helicopter to monitor the SO_2, NO and CO in a chemical industry park. Hirst et al. [15] proposed a method of locating and quantifying gas emission sources using remotely obtained concentration data collected by UAV. However, the UAV like unmanned helicopter is still too large to carry and operate, so there is an urgent need for a more productive, convenient and flexible air contaminant monitoring system and corresponding method.

In this paper, a hazard source estimation method based on the integration of atmospheric dispersion simulation and UAV sensory system is proposed. The method is based on the Bayesian inference using the atmospheric diffusion model, Particle Swarm Optimization and the observed data collected by the UAV-based sensory system. To verify this method with the sensory system, an experiment was conducted in a chemical industry park in which the air contaminant data was measured by UAV and the source terms are estimated subsequently.

In Sect. 2, the Gaussian dispersion model and the Bayesian inference for source estimation are demonstrated. Section 3 introduces the architecture of the UAV-based sensory system. The deployment and results of the experiment are described in Sect. 4.

2   Source Estimation

This section introduces the Gaussian dispersion model and Bayesian inference. Atmospheric dispersion model is the basis of the source estimation. To model the dispersion of air contaminant caused by the continuous emission source, an improved Gaussian puff model is proposed. Then a method based on the Bayesian inference using the dispersion model is developed for source estimation.

2.1   Atmospheric Dispersion Simulation Model

Gaussian puff and plume models are widely used in atmospheric dispersion simulation. Gaussian plume model is used for the constant and continuous release while the Gaussian puff model is for the situation of instant emission. However, it is inaccurate for these two models to describe the gas dispersion process of time-variant and continuous emission sources in chemical industry park. Therefore, an improved Gaussian puff model is developed combining the characteristics of the two models. The Gaussian plume model is shown as follows:

$$C(x,y,z,t) = \frac{q(t)}{2\pi u \sigma_y \sigma_z} e^{-\frac{y^2}{2\sigma_y^2}} \left(e^{-\frac{(z-H)^2}{2\sigma_z^2}} + e^{-\frac{(z+H)^2}{2\sigma_z^2}} \right) \tag{1}$$

The typical Gaussian puff model is shown as follows:

$$C(x,y,z,t) = \frac{q(t)}{(2\pi)^{\frac{3}{2}}\sigma_x \sigma_y \sigma_z} e^{-\frac{(x-ut)^2}{2\sigma_x^2}} e^{-\frac{y^2}{2\sigma_y^2}} \left(e^{-\frac{(z-H)^2}{2\sigma_z^2}} + e^{-\frac{(z+H)^2}{2\sigma_z^2}} \right) \tag{2}$$

where x, y, z are the coordinates in three-dimensional space respectively. t is the time from the source starts to release, H is the height of source, $q(t)$ is the release rate varying with t, u is the velocity and direction of wind, σ_x, σ_y, σ_z are the dispersion coefficients in axis x, y and z respectively.

The Gaussian plume model only describes the source with constant release rate and the wind fixed direction and speed. In chemical industry park, the atmospheric dispersion usually cannot reach this high requirement, so the traditional Gaussian plume model is unsuitable for the atmospheric dispersion in chemical industry park. The typical Gaussian puff model can describe the dispersion process but the assumption of instant leakage is inappropriate for the usual continuous emission in chemical industry park.

In order to describe the release process of continuous sources, an improved Gaussian puff model named improved Gaussian puff model is developed. We adopt the method of discretization - using the release of multi puffs to approximate release of continuous source. After a period of release, the model will reach the stable state like the typical Gaussian plume model. By adjusting the release time interval, the improved Gaussian puff model can simulate the atmospheric dispersion well. Figure 1 shows the

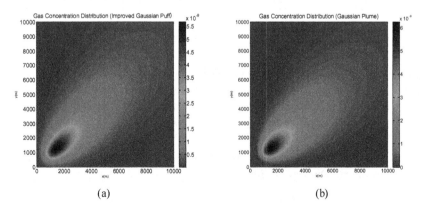

(a)   (b)

Fig. 1. The gas concentration distribution of the improved Gaussian puff model and Gaussian plume model. (a) improved Gaussian puff model; (b) typical Gaussian plume model.

steady state of the improved Gaussian puff model and typical Gaussian plume model ($z = 0$, $H = 83$ m). It can be seen that the improved Gaussian puff model proposed is able to approximate the steady state of the Gaussian plume model well, which proves the effectiveness of this model for the continuous source release.

2.2   Bayesian Inference

Bayesian Inference is a statistical method applied in decision making under uncertain conditions. The notable feature of Bayesian inference is that a prior information and sample information are utilized to obtain a statistical conclusion. In the source estimation using Bayesian inference, we use observed gas concentration data $D = \{\omega_i\}_{i=1}^{m}$ to estimate the location l and release rate $q(t)$ of diffusion source is introduced. The data D is collected by UAV sensory system at location set x in wind field W (wind velocity and wind direction). The source terms are represented as $\theta = \{l, q(t)\}$. Thus, the theoretical concentration at location x and time t can be calculated by $c_z(t) = f(t, x, l, q(t))$, the function f is the improved Gaussian puff model in Sect. 2.1. Moreover, there are m records of observation data corresponding to the trajectory point of the UAV monitoring system. The ith record contains information about location x_i, time t_i and the value of observed concentration c_i. As a result, the following equation can be obtained:

$$c_i = c_{x_i}(t_i) = f(t, x, \theta) + e_i \tag{3}$$

where the observed data are independent with Gaussian errors $e_i \sim N(0, \sigma^2)$.

The goal of source estimation using Bayesian inference is locating and quantifying the most possible source in two-dimensional space. To achieve this aim, the equation of Bayesian inference is utilized to get the posterior probability function (PDF) of θ is computed as:

$$p(\theta|D) = p(\theta)p(D|\theta) \tag{4}$$

where $p(\theta|D)$ means posterior probability density function, $p(\theta)$ is the prior function and $p(D|\theta)$ represents the likelihood function. Moreover, the likelihood function can be expressed as follows:

$$p(D|\theta) = exp\{-\frac{1}{2\sigma_{e^2}}\sum_i [f(t_i, x_i, \theta) - c_i]^2\}. \tag{5}$$

The key of computing posterior PDF is to determine prior PDF and likelihood function. The prior PDF can be obtained from historical data or theoretical assessment. However, there is little information of the diffusion source in this research, so it is feasible to use a uniform distribution as prior PDF. As for the likelihood function, since the release rate is difficult to estimate, it may be more feasible if we use the maximum likelihood estimation of θ: $\theta' = \{l\}$ to substitute θ and estimate $p(\theta'|D)$ instead of $p(\theta|D)$. According to the maximum likelihood estimation (MLE) method, we assume the release rate $q_m(t)$ that maximizes the likelihood function in Eq. (5) as actual release rate. As a result, location l is the only parameter need estimated. Thus, the location l with the highest posterior probability and corresponding release rate $q_m(t)$ constitute the estimated properties of source term. Then PSO is used to find the optimal location with the maximum posterior probability [16].

3   UAV-Based Sensory System

Due to the fixed location, it is inflexible to monitor air contaminant monitoring in chemical industry park by static ground monitoring station. Therefore, the UAV-based sensory system is developed to collect data effectively. This section introduces the system, including the aerial platform, sensors and the integration.

3.1   System Overview

The mini-UAV based sensory system is expected to accomplish the data acquisition and transmission aerially. The architecture and workflow of this system are shown in Fig. 2. It consists of an aerial platform and a sensory system. The aerial platform, which the sensory devices are fixed on, provides the flexible movement ability aerially. The data collection and transmission are executed by the sensory system including microprocessor, gas sensors, GPS and network connection modules. The system collects and stores the data including gas concentration, geo-location and time and transmits them to the database in cloud server. All of these are controlled by the microprocessor and executed automatically once the aerial platform is powered on.

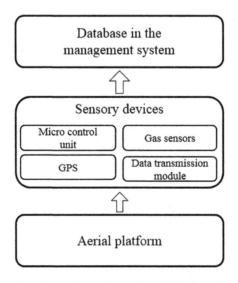

Fig. 2. The architecture and workflow of the UAV-based sensory system.

3.2 Aerial Platform and Sensors

In our work, the DJI M100 quadrotor is selected as the aerial platform. Compared to other larger UAVs such as unmanned fixed wing aircraft and unmanned helicopter. It has the smaller size and simpler structure of 4-rotors, which brings more flexibility in mobility, simpler operation and lower cost. The max duration of hovering flight is 28 min with single battery and 40 min with two batteries. The predominant flight parameters guarantee the effectiveness in the monitoring of large area like the chemical industry park.

The sensory system consists of gas sensors, GPS module, network connection module and the microprocessor. The gas sensors are selected according to the air contaminant categories of the chemical industry park. Then the SGA sensors are selected considering about weight, size, measurement range, precision, and compatibility with quadrotor. SGA sensors are electrochemical pluggable gas sensors with small size, which are convenient for carrying, changing and installing and suitable for gas monitoring consequently. The selected monitoring air contaminant and the corresponding parameters of sensors are listed in Table 1. According to the air contaminant emission level in the chemical industry park, the selected sensors can meet the monitoring request.

Table 1. The selected monitoring air contaminant the parameters of the corresponding sensors (1 ppm = 1000 ppb).

Gas category	Sensor	Measurement range (ppm)	Resolution ratio (ppb)	Accuracy
CO	SGA-700-CO	0–12.5	1	2%
H_2S	SGA-700-H_2S	0–2	1	2%
SO_2	SGA-700-SO_2	0–2	1	2%
NO_2	SGA-700-NO_2	0–2	1	2%
O_3	SGA-700-O_3	0–2	1	2%
CH_4S	SGA-700-CH_4S	0–10	10	2%
Cl_2	SGA-700-Cl_2	0–10	10	2%
HCl	SGA-700-HCl	0–20	10	2%
NH_3	SGA-700-NH_3	0–50	10	2%

3.3 System Integration

The system integration includes construction of sensory system and the whole system. The sensory system must be integrated by gas sensors, GPS, network connection module and microprocessor.

The Single-Chip Microcomputer (SCM) is selected as the microprocessor of the sensory system due to its performance in stability, programmability, connectivity and extendibility. The sensory system is integrated into two circuit boards, shown in Fig. 3

(the upper board is the main board and the lower board is the auxiliary board). The main board contains four sensor interfaces, SCM, power input interface, GPS and network connection module. The sensors (see 1 in Fig. 3) plugged on the interfaces collect gas concentration and send data to the microprocessor (see 2 in Fig. 3) according to the communication protocol. The network connection module (see 3 in Fig. 3) provides the access to the Internet for data transmission. The GPS module (see 4 in Fig. 3) gets the geo-locations and time with preparation time of 45 to 60 s. The program of the sensory system was written into the microprocessor to control the execution of data collection, storage and transmission automatically. The auxiliary board is connected with main board. It only includes six sensor interfaces controlled by the microprocessor on the main board. The power supply of the two boards is provided by the quadrotor's battery. The sensory system therefore starts running once the battery is powered on.

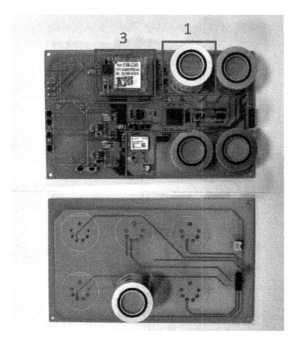

Fig. 3. The integration of system (a) main board; (b) auxiliary board. The upper part is the main board and the lower part is the auxiliary board.

In order to enhance the stability of the sensory system in adverse weather like rainy, a box is made by 3-D printing to hold two circuit boards. The box containing sensory system is installed on the center plate of M100 quadrotor. The fully assembled mini-UAV based polluted gas sensory system is shown in Fig. 4.

Fig. 4. Fully assembled UAV-based aerial sensory system.

4   Experiments and Results

To verify and validate the effectiveness of the UAV-based sensory system and the method of source estimation. An experiment was implemented in a chemical industry park.

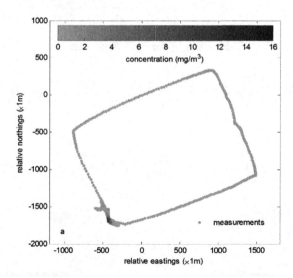

Fig. 5. The concentration of sulfur dioxide (SO_2) along the flight path, the darker region represents higher concentration.

4.1   Data Acquisition

The monitoring area was selected mainly including a petrochemical plant covering about 200 ha. Due to safety concerns, the quadrotor is forbidden to fly into the region of plant. Therefore, the flight trajectory of quadrotor was designed around the area. The quadrotor was flying along the trajectory at approximately 50 m AGL (above ground level) for about 20 min around 3 pm local time, 25th July 2016 during which time the data was collected at a 1 Hz data rate. During the flight, we could get the monitoring gas concentration and the status of quadrotor status including location, height and existing trajectory in the cloud server, which makes us adjust the path of quadrotor according to the monitoring data conveniently. Due to the strict control of air contaminant emission, all kinds of gases maintained at a low level during the experiment except the sulfur dioxide (SO_2), so we only concentrated on SO_2. The SO_2 concentration along the trajectory of this experiment is shown in Fig. 5. In the figure, the darker region represents the higher concentration. It can be seen that the concentration of SO_2 in the southwest of area was relatively higher. Therefore, the quadrotor hovered there to collect more valid data. The maximum concentration is about 10 mg/m³.

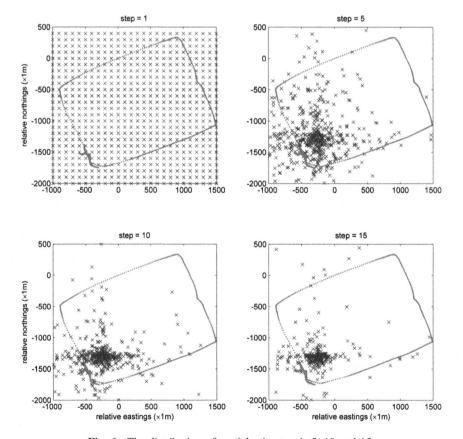

Fig. 6. The distribution of particles in step 1, 5, 10 and 15.

4.2   Source Estimation

Based on the SO_2 concentration data collected from the UAV sensory system, the source location is identified using PSO. Figure 6 displays the distribution of particles in step 1, 5, 10 and 15 with the observed concentration along trajectory. In step 1, 525 particles are initialized uniformly in the searching region of 2500 * 2500 m^2. From step 5 to 15, particles gradually converge to the lower left of the region, which corresponds to the southwest of the monitoring area. The source location could be estimated by computing the weighted average sum of particles, which is (−305.6, −1244.4). After getting the source location, the release rate is estimated as 0.3915 kg/s according to the MLE principle. In the field observation, there was a chimney of sulfuric acid recovery near the location estimated, which roughly verifies the result of source estimation.

5   Conclusions

In this paper, a Hazard source estimation method based on the integration of atmospheric dispersion simulation and UAV sensory system is developed. According to the Bayesian inference, the source location is estimated by seeking the point with the maximum of posterior probability. An improved Gaussian dispersion model is proposed for the simulation of the continuous emission source. In order to obtain the high-quality observed data, an UAV-based air contaminant sensory system composed of an aerial platform and a sensory system is developed. To test the source estimation method with the aerial sensory system, an experiment was implemented in a chemical industry park. During this experiment, the aerial sensory system successfully accomplished the data acquisition and transmission as we had planned. In terms of the collected data, the relatively high concentration of SO_2 was detected in the southwest of monitoring area. Based on the observed data of SO_2, the source was located in the coordinates of (−305.6, −1244.4) with the release rate of 0.3915 kg/s. The experiment verified the effectiveness of the source estimation method and the UAV-based sensory system developed. However, there are still some problems in this method like the relatively low accuracy of the gas sensors. In the future, the autonomous navigation and path planning of UAV will be developed to enhance the efficiency of data collection. Besides, more effective features (e.g. gradient) will be extracted from the concentration distribution for more accurate source estimation.

Acknowledgements. This study is supported by National Key Research & Development (R&D) Plan under Grant No. 2017YFC0803300 and the National Natural Science Foundation of China under Grant Nos. 71673292, 61503402 and Guangdong Key Laboratory for Big Data Analysis and Simulation of Public Opinion and Shanghai Special Foundation of Software and Integrated Circuit under Grant No. 150312.

References

1. Rao, K.S.: Source estimation methods for atmospheric dispersion. Atmos. Environ. **41**(33), 6964–6973 (2007)
2. Huber, M.F.: On-line dispersion source estimation using adaptive gaussian mixture filter. In: IFAC World Congress, pp. 1059–1066 (2014)
3. Zhang, X.L., Su, G.F., Yuan, H.Y., et al.: Modified ensemble Kalman filter for nuclear accident atmospheric dispersion: prediction improved and source estimated. J. Hazard. Mater. **280**, 143 (2014)
4. Chin, T.M., Mariano, A.J.: A particle filter for inverse lagrangian prediction problems. J. Atmos. Oceanic Technol. **27**(2), 371 (2010)
5. Ma, D., Wang, S., Zhang, Z.: Hybrid algorithm of minimum relative entropy-particle swarm optimization with adjustment parameters for gas source term estimation in atmosphere. Atmos. Environ. **94**, 637–646 (2014)
6. So, W., Koo, J., Shin, D., et al.: The estimation of hazardous gas release rate using optical sensor and neural network. Comput. Aided Chem. Eng. **28**(10), 199–204 (2010)
7. Wang, B., Chen, B., Zhao, J.: The real-time estimation of hazardous gas dispersion by the integration of gas detectors, neural network and gas dispersion models. J. Hazard. Mater. **300**, 433–442 (2015)
8. Wang, N., Zhang, N., Wang, M.: Review: wireless sensors in agriculture and food industry-recent development and future perspective. Comput. Electron. Agric. **50**(1), 1–14 (2006)
9. Ruizgarcia, L., Lunadei, L., Barreiro, P., et al.: A review of wireless sensor technologies and applications in agriculture and food industry: state of the art and current trends. Sensors **9**(6), 4728–4750 (2009)
10. Spiess, T., Bange, J., Buschmann, M.: First application of the meteorological Mini-UAV 'M2AV'. Meteorol. Z. **16**(2), 15–169 (2007)
11. D'Oleireoltmanns, S., Marzolff, I., Peter, K.D., et al.: Unmanned aerial vehicle (UAV) for monitoring soil erosion in Morocco. Remote Sens. **4**(11), 3390–3416 (2012)
12. Khan, A., Schaefer, D., Tao, L., et al.: Low power greenhouse gas sensors for unmanned aerial vehicles. Remote Sens. **4**(4), 1355–1368 (2012)
13. Hausamann, D., Zirnig, W., Schreier, G., et al.: Monitoring of gas pipelines – a civil UAV application. Aircr. Eng. Aerosp. Technol. **77**(5), 352–360 (2005)
14. Yang, H., Huang, Y., Center, S.E.: Evaluating atmospheric pollution of chemical plant based on unmanned aircraft vehicle (UAV). J. Geo-Inf. Sci. **17**(10), 126–1274 (2015)
15. Hirst, B., Jonathan, P., Cueto, F.G.D., et al.: Locating and quantifying gas emission sources using remotely obtained concentration data. Atmos. Environ. **74**(2), 141–158 (2012)
16. Qiu, S., Chen, B., Zhu, Z., et al.: Source term estimation using air concentration measurements during nuclear accident. J. Radioanal. Nucl. Chem. **311**, 165–178 (2016)

Delay-Induced Coexistence of Attractors in a Controlled Drill-String

Ibukunolu O. Oladunjoye[✉], James Ing, and Sumeet S. Aphale

University of Aberdeen, Aberdeen, UK
{r01ioo15,j.ing,s.aphale}@abdn.ac.uk

Abstract. The realistic modeling and effective control of drill-strings has been an ongoing research challenge. This has recently come to focus due to the volatility in the oil industry. Owing to the severely nonlinear nature of the drill-string, evolved nonlinear control techniques have recently been proposed to overcome the inherent stick-slip dynamics which are severely detrimental to the drilling performance as well as structural health of any given drill-string. Yet, most of the controller performance is analysed without including the significant delay intrinsic to the overall system. In this paper, the impact of system delay on the overall performance of a controlled drill-string is studied via extensive simulations. The analysis presents the impact of delay on three recently proposed sliding-mode control schemes. A surprising coexistence of attractors is observed from the delayed system on the third controller. This result will potentially impact the design of implementable control schemes proposed in future.

Keywords: Drill-string dynamics · Stick-slip oscillation · Coexistence · Attractors · Sliding-mode controller · Delay

1 Introduction

Stick-slip vibrations are the major cause for concern in an operating drill-string [1–7]. The stick-slip phenomenon can be looked at as a combination of two distinct phases (1) Stick phase (energy absorption) and (2) Slip phase (energy release). These phases are the result of the periodic difference between the static and dynamic friction. During the stick phase the energy gets stored as several turns of twist in the long drill-string. This energy is suddenly released in the form of uncontrolled spin of the drill-string in the slip phase. This uncontrolled spin induces what is known as stick-slip vibrations that are highly detrimental to the drill-string performance and more importantly the structural health of the drill-string [2].

Several mitigation strategies to avoid stick-slip have been proposed over the years. Open-loop mitigation strategies include modification to the drill-bit [8], stabilizes in the borehole assembly [9], optimizing drilling parameters [5] and increasing lubricity [10–12]. The main drawbacks of open-loop strategies are

© Springer Nature Singapore Pte Ltd. 2017
M.S. Mohamed Ali et al. (Eds.): AsiaSim 2017, Part I, CCIS 751, pp. 505–517, 2017.
DOI: 10.1007/978-981-10-6463-0_43

1. Inability to adapt while in operation
2. Difficulty in system integration due to physical design limitations
3. Limited operational range.

To overcome them, closed-loop control strategies have been proposed [1–4, 7, 13, 14]. Owing to the highly nonlinear nature of the drill-string, several nonlinear control schemes that can mitigate stick-slip behaviour of a drill-string have been formulated [2], yet most of these performance simulations do no amount for the significant delay between the drilling motor (actuator) and the drill-bit (end-effector). In this work a detailed analysis of the performance of three proposed sliding-mode control schemes in the presence of variable delay is presented.

The paper is structured as follows. Section 2 presents the 2-DOF drill-string model, the bit-intersection model as well as the drill-string parameters used in this study. The open-loop time histories clearly showing the stick-slip phenomenon are also presented. Section 3 briefly describes the controller design and the 3 switching schemes as reported in [2] and presents the closed-loop system performance analysis in the presence of delay. Section 4 presents the coexistence of attractors seen in this system and motivates it's usage as a possible remedy to the performance degradation issue introduced by the system delay. Section 5 concludes the paper.

2   Two Degree-of-Freedom Drill-String Model

A 2-DOF model of a drill-string is shown in Fig. 1. It consist of the following components: The upper disc denotes the top drive system consisting of the actuator (motor) and rotary table. The key parameters that describe this assembly are: U, c_r, ϕ_b, J_r where,

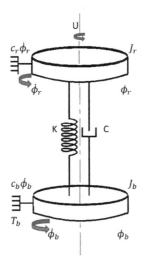

Fig. 1. The 2-DOF lumped-parameter model of the drill-string

1. U is the input torque
2. c_r is the viscous damping coefficient on the top drive
3. ϕ_r is the angular position of the top drive
4. J_r is inertia of the top drive

The drill pipe that connects the top drive assembly to the Bottom Hole Assembly (BHA) is modeled as a connected spring - damper with parameters: C and K where

1. C is the torsional damping
2. K is the torsional stiffness

Lower disc denotes the BHA consisting of the drill-bit and related assembly. The key model parameters are: T_b, J_b, c_r, ϕ_b where

1. T_b is the torque of friction
2. J_b is the inertia of the BHA
3. c_r is the viscous damping coefficient on the BHA
4. ϕ_b is the angular position of the BHA

The simplified equation of motion can be written as

$$J\ddot{\Phi} + C\dot{\Phi} + K\Phi + T = U \tag{1}$$

which can be further parametrized as

$$\ddot{\phi}_r = \frac{U}{J_r} - \frac{C_r + C}{J_r}\dot{\phi}_r + \frac{C}{J_r}\dot{\phi}_b - \frac{K}{J_r}(\phi_r - \phi_b) \tag{2}$$

$$\ddot{\phi}_b = \frac{C}{J_b}\dot{\phi}_r - (C_b + C)\dot{\phi}_b + \frac{K}{J_r}(\phi_r - \phi_b) - T_b \tag{3}$$

Therefore, with the angular displacement and angular velocity given by ϕ_i and $\dot{\phi}_i$ respectively, s.t. $i \in \mathbb{R}$; the new state of the system can be initialized as:

$$x = [\dot{\phi}_r, \phi_r - \phi_b, \dot{\phi}_b] \tag{4}$$

$$= [x_1, x_2, x_3] \tag{5}$$

Using these states, a state-space representation of the system can be formulated as follows:

$$\dot{x}_1 = \frac{U}{J_r} - \frac{C_r + C}{J_r}x_1 + \frac{C}{J_r}x_3 - \frac{K}{J_r}x_2 \tag{6}$$

$$\dot{x}_2 = x_1 - x_3 \tag{7}$$

$$\dot{x}_3 = \frac{C}{J_b}x_1 - \frac{C_b + C}{J_b}x_3 + \frac{K}{J_b}x_2 - T_b \tag{8}$$

This three-state system model will be further combined with the Bit Interaction Model which encapsulates the interaction of the drill-bit with the rock surface.

2.1 Bit Interaction Model

The Bit Interaction Model includes three regimes of drill-surface interaction which can be described as:

1. **The Stick Phase:** In this regime, the drill-bit is stalled in the formation. As seen, the bit velocity is less than the positive constant ζ. Additionally, the reaction torque τ_r is less than or equal to static friction torque τ_s.
2. **Stick-to-Slip Phase:** In this regime, the drill-bit begins to move. The bit velocity is less than the positive constant ζ but reaction torque is greater than the static frictional torque τ_s.
3. **Slip Phase:** In this regime, the drill-bit slips as if the coefficient of friction is negligible. Estimating the frictional torque includes the impact of the W_{ob}, bit radius and the bit dry friction coefficient $\mu_b = \mu_{cb} + (\mu_{sb} - \mu_{cb})e^{(-\gamma_b|\dot{\phi}_b|/\nu_f)}$, the Coulomb friction coefficient is μ_{cb}

The frictional torque during the drill-bit interaction with the rock can be formulated as

$$T_b = \begin{cases} \tau_r, & \text{if } |\dot{\phi}_b| < \zeta \text{ and } |\tau_r| \leq \tau_s \\ \tau_s sgn(\tau_r), & \text{if } |\dot{\phi}_b| < \zeta \text{ and } |\tau_r| > \tau_s \\ \mu_b R_b W_{ob} sgn(\dot{\phi}_b), & \text{if } |\dot{\phi}_b| < \zeta \end{cases} \qquad (9)$$

$\tau_r = C(\dot{\phi}_r - \dot{\phi}_b) + K(\phi_r - \phi_b) - C_b\dot{\phi}_b$ is the Reaction torque, $\tau_s = \mu_{sb}R_bW_{ob}$ is the Friction torque, μ_{sb} is the static friction coefficient, W_{ob} is the Weight on Bit (WOB), R_b is the Bit radius.

From [1,2], a set of drill-string field data was obtained and this data was used to form a set of realistic simulation parameters. These have been presented in Table 1. These parameters are used while simulating the model throughout the work.

Table 1. Realistic drill-string physical parameters used in simulations

Parameters	Values
J_r	$2298 \, \text{kg m}^2$
J_b	$411 \, \text{kg m}^2$
c	$48 \, \text{N m s/rad}$
k	$141 \, \text{N m s/rad}$
C_r	$410 \, \text{N m s/rad}$
C_b	$60 \, \text{N m s/rad}$
μ_{sb}	0.71428
μ_{cb}	0.15178
W_{ob}	$17.5 \, \text{kN}$
γ_b	0.85
ν_f	4
ζ	10^{-2}

The derived model was simulated using the selected set of parameters to ensure that it replicated the expected behavior of the drill-string.

2.2   Open-Loop Model Verification

Figure 2, shows the stick-slip being evident while the system is being simulated for 100 s. The three regimes can be seen from this simulation. The drill-bit sticks, followed by its transition stick to slip phase and finally, the slip phase. The loss in stability is as a result of the Hopf bifurcation [2, 5, 15, 16].

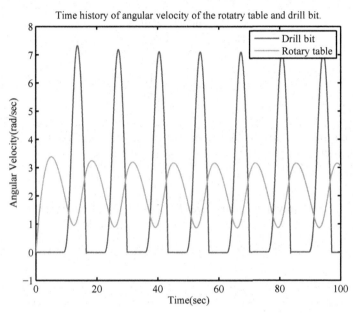

Fig. 2. This shows the time histories of the angular velocities of the rotary table and drill-bit that is being driven by a constant input torque. Simulated for 100 s. Note that the drill-bit is sticking at regular intervals, indicated by the region when drill-bit velocity goes to zero.

3   Effect of Induced Delay

A well-performing sliding surface with three inputs specifically designed to allevi-ate certain dynamic issues was proposed in [2]. The next subsection gives details of the same.

3.1   Sliding-Mode Controller

The sliding surface is of the form:

$$s = (\dot{\phi}_r - \Omega_d) + \lambda \int_0^t (\dot{\phi}_r - \Omega_d)d\tau + \lambda \int_0^t (\dot{\phi}_r - \dot{\phi}_b)d\tau \qquad (10)$$

where we have λ as a positive control parameter. From the equation for the sliding surface, it's time derivative can be computed as:

$$\dot{s} = \ddot{\phi}_r + \lambda(\dot{\phi}_r - \Omega_d) + \lambda(\dot{\phi}_r - \ddot{\phi}_b) \tag{11}$$

The parameters of the proposed sliding-mode controller are tabulated in Table 2.

Table 2. Parameters for the proposed sliding-mode controller

Parameters	Values
M_{jt}	150
M_{kp}	100
M_{cp}	40
M_{crt}	70

$\ddot{\phi}_r$ will be substituted in the equation above to give U_{ideal}. With an aim to eliminate uncertainties in parameter estimation we define the sliding mode controller as below

$$U = U_{eq} + U_{sc} \tag{12}$$

where U_{eq} is the equivalent control and U_{sc} is the switching control. Then, the equivalent control U_{eq} is derived from the ideal controller U_{ideal}:

$$U_{ideal} = (C_p + C_{rt})x_1 - C_p x_3 + K_p x_2 - J_t \lambda(x_1 - \Omega_d) - J_t \lambda(x_1 - x_7) \tag{13}$$

$$U_{eq} = (\hat{C}_p + \hat{C}_{rt})x_1 - C_p x_3 + \hat{K}_p x_2 - \hat{J}_t \lambda(x_1 - \Omega_d) - \hat{J}_t \lambda(x_1 - x_7) \tag{14}$$

the '$\wedge$' in the equation indicates an estimated model parameter.

The paper further proposed three switching control inputs, each with a specific function

$$U_{sc}^1 = -(M_{cp}|\dot{\phi}_t - \dot{\phi}_1| + M_{crt}|\dot{\phi}_t| + M_{kp}|\phi_t - \phi_1| + M_{jt}\lambda|\dot{\phi}_t - \Omega_d| + M_{jt}\lambda|\dot{\phi}_t - \dot{\phi}_b| + \eta)sgn(s) \tag{15}$$

The first switching controller U_{sc}^1 is given in Eq. 15. It forces the system state to 'slide' along a surface that is predefined by 's'. At this stage, the state of the system is being restricted to the surface by tracking the trajectory. High-frequency chattering was observed in simulations and therefore a second control input was designed as an improvement over this one. This input is U_{sc}^2, as shown in Eq. 16

$$U_{sc}^2 = -(M_{cp}|\dot{\phi}_t - \dot{\phi}_1| + M_{crt}|\dot{\phi}_t| + M_{kp}|\phi_t - \phi_1| + M_{jt}\lambda|\dot{\phi}_t - \Omega_d| + M_{jt}\lambda|\dot{\phi}_t - \dot{\phi}_b| + \eta)\frac{s}{|S| + \delta} - ks \tag{16}$$

This controller eliminated the high-frequency chatter but the trajectory of the system cannot reach an acceptable boundary of the sliding surface $s = 0$. The tuning parameter δ had to be carefully selected to ensure that tracking errors were within bounds. To overcome this issue, a third controller was proposed as given in Eq. 17.

$$
U_{sc}^3 = -\frac{M_{cp}|\dot{\phi}_t - \dot{\phi}_1|s}{|s| + \delta_1 exp(-\delta_2 \int |\dot{\phi}_t - \dot{\phi}_1|d_t)}
$$
$$
-\frac{M_{crt}|\dot{\phi}_t|s}{|s| + \delta_1 exp(-\delta_2 \int |\dot{\phi}_t|d_t)}
$$
$$
-\frac{M_{kp}|\phi_t - \phi_1|s}{|s| + \delta_1 exp(-\delta_2 \int |\phi_t - \phi_1|d_t)}
$$
$$
-\frac{M_{jt}\lambda|\dot{\phi}_t - \Omega_d|s}{|s| + \delta_1 exp(-\delta_2 \int \lambda|\dot{\phi}_t - \Omega_d|d_t)}
$$
$$
-\frac{M_{jt}\lambda|\dot{\phi}_t - \dot{\phi}_b|s}{|s| + \delta_1 exp(-\delta_2 \int \lambda|\dot{\phi}_t - \dot{\phi}_b|d_t)} - \kappa s \tag{17}
$$

The third controller U_{sc}^3 effectively suppresses the stick-slip vibrations and at the same time stabilizes the drill-bit and rotary table velocities to the desired values. This controller was then compared with another controller proposed in literature [17] and shown to outperform it.

It must be noted that though each controller performs up to expectation and that the third controller was able to achieve both the performance goals of stick-slip vibration suppression as well as accurate stable tracking of drill-bit and rotary table velocities. However, the simulations did not take into account the substantial delay introduced by the typically long length of the drill-string. This delay changes the problem from instantaneous control to that of delayed control. Thus, the effect of inherent system-induced delay was analyzed for all the three controllers.

3.2   Simulations with Delay

Though only the third controller needed to be analyzed for the induced delay (as it was the best performing of the three), for completeness, all three controllers were simulated for varying induced-delay conditions. Figure 3(a), (b) and (c) plot the angular velocity of the drill-bit for different delay values for the three proposed controllers respectively.

Controller 1: In Fig. 3(a) (for Controller 1: U_{sc}^1), it can be seen that there is high frequency chattering for delay values between 2 s and 2.488 s. From 2.48 s onwards, the controller is deemed ineffective and the drill-bit goes back to experiencing stick-slip vibrations.

Controller 2: In Fig. 3(b) (for Controller 2: U_{sc}^2), it can be seen that the high-frequency chatter is almost non-existent. However, from 2.76 s onwards, the controller is ineffective in suppressing the stick-slip vibrations. A more surprising

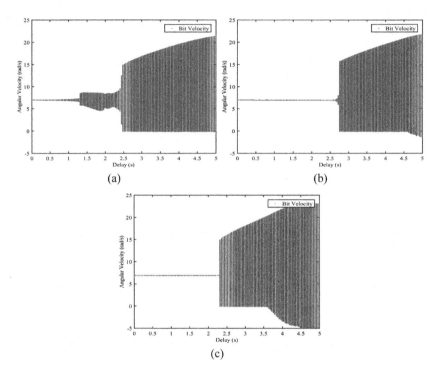

Fig. 3. (a) Plots the steady-state angular drill-bit velocity vs induced delay for Controller 1 (b) plots the steady-state angular drill-bit velocity vs induced delay for Controller 2 (c) plots the steady-state angular drill-bit velocity vs induced delay for Controller 3

observation is that is the induced delay increases to beyond 4.68 s, the drill-bit angular velocity takes on negative values. This suggests that the drill-bit rotates in the opposite direction to that of the rotating table with a realistic chance of warping the drill-string and causing serious structural damage.

Controller 3: The observations made on the behavior of the third controller are even more alarming. As seen in Fig. 3(c) (for Controller 3: U_{sc}^3), the controller suppresses high frequency chattering in the presence of delay. However, the ability of the controller to do this is diminished when compared to that of Controller 2. The system controlled using Controller 3 goes into stick-slip oscillations at delay values lower than that of Controller 2 (2.32 s). More importantly, Controller 3 controlled system experiences negative angular velocity for the drill-bit at a substantially lower delay value of about 3.6 s. Additionally, the magnitude of these negative angular velocities is also much larger than that achieved by Controller 2.

To further explore the behavior of Controller 3, time-domain traces of the drill-bit angular velocity for a system without delay (see Fig. 4(a)) and with a delay of 4 s (see Fig. 4(b)) are plotted. The desired angular velocity is set to 7 rad/s, the WOB is 17.5 kN. Note that the controller is turned on at t = 33 s.

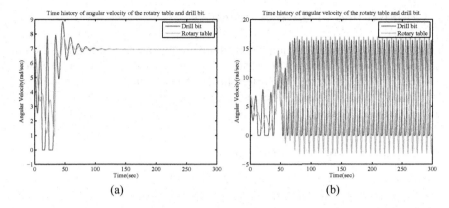

Fig. 4. (a) For the closed-loop controlled drill-string using Controller 3 with no delay. (b) For Closed-loop controlled drill-string using Controller 3 with a delay of 4 s.

The phase plots for the same two cases for Controller 3 plotting the angular displacement between the drill-bit and the rotary table (state x_2) versus the angular velocity of the drill-bit (state x_3 are given in Fig. 5.

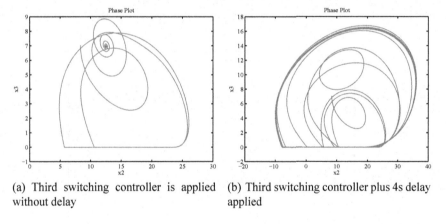

(a) Third switching controller is applied without delay

(b) Third switching controller plus 4s delay applied

Fig. 5. (a) For the closed-loop controlled drill-string using Controller 3 with no delay. (b) For Closed-loop controlled drill-string using Controller 3 with a delay of 4 s.

As can be seen clearly, the introduction of the delay severely degrades the controller performance. This simulation demonstrates the necessity of devising control strategies that can adequately compensate for the effect of induced system delay. A further complication arises from the coexistence of attractors which in turn is a result of the system exhibiting two completely different steady-state behavior for the same set of parameters but different initial conditions. This aspect is explored in the next section.

4 Coexistence of Two Attractors

The occurrence of a phenomenon where there are two attractors having the same parameter values but different starting conditions is checked. The two attractors are stable drilling point and the stick-slip limit cycle. It is seen that depending on the initial conditions of the system, the same set of parameters values could result in different distinct system behaviors, [18].

4.1 Coexistence of Attractors in Open-Loop

Due to the severely nonlinear nature of the drill-string, it is quite natural to expect coexistence of attractors during open-loop operation. That is basically saying that there is a distinct possibility that given two different initial conditions, the open-loop drill-string could either go into stable drilling or get locked in a stick-slip oscillatory cycle. To ascertain that such conditions can occur, the derived model was simulated in open-loop for two initial condition sets where the state vectors are given by:

1. $x = [0, 0, 0]$
2. $x = [4.7086, 9.0042, 4.7103]$

The simulation results are plotted in Fig. 6. As seen, if the system's initial condition is zero i.e., $x = [0, 0, 0]$, then the system reaches a stick-slip limit cycle.

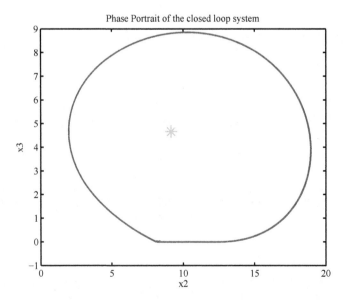

Fig. 6. The open-loop phase plots showing the coexistence of the stick-slip at WOB = 17.5 kN. The stick-slip (red '-') was seen with initial conditions $x = [0, 0, 0]$. The stable drilling (blue '*') was obtained with initial conditions $x = [4.7086; 9.0042; 4.7103]$. (Color figure online)

On the other hand, if the starting state vector is $x = [4.7086, 9.0042, 4.7103]$, the system continues stable drilling.

This clearly shows that if the right initial conditions are selected, stable drilling can be achieved and stick-slip oscillations can be avoided. This could be a way to overcome the issue of the system's delay-induced degradation of performance in closed-loop.

4.2 Coexistence of Attractors in Closed-Loop with Delay

Having confirmed that there lies coexisting attractors in the open loop system, we opt to check if this same possibilities can exist in the system with the third switching control while this system has induced delay. After a basic numerical search, a set of initial conditions were found where the system does indeed give stable drilling even in the presence of a 4 s delay. Initial conditions for the two test cases are:

1. $x = [0, 0, 0]$
2. $x = [7.0289, 8.3525, 7.0285]$

Figure 7 plots the resultant phase plots. At zero initial conditions, the delay-induced closed-loop system experiences stick-slip oscillations. On the other hand, when the right initial conditions ($x = [7.0289; 8.3525; 7.0285]$) are introduced, stable drilling is observed.

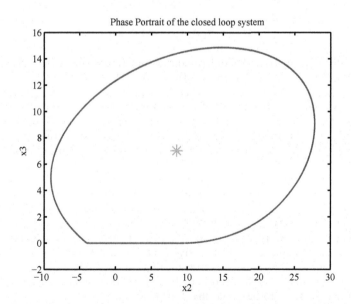

Fig. 7. The closed-loop phase plots showing the coexistence of the stick-slip at WOB = 17.5 kN. The stick-slip (red '-') was seen with initial conditions $x = [0, 0, 0]$. The stable drilling (blue '*') was obtained with initial conditions $x = [7.0289; 8.3525; 7.0285]$. (Color figure online)

5   Conclusions

Delay inherent to the drill-string due to its length is a major factor limiting the performance of any implemented control. This was shown by testing the most recently proposed and well-performing sliding-mode controller in presence of delay. A relatively small delay ($\approx$3 s) was sufficient to not only induce stick-slip back into the closed-loop system but also introduce angular velocities in the reverse direction which have the potential of structurally warping and in severe cases destroying the drill-string. However, it was shown that the inherent system nonlinearity and coexistence of attractors can be exploited to overcome the detrimental effects of the delay. By proper choice of initial conditions, the closed-loop delay-induced system could be brought to operate at a stable drilling point. Future extensions could include automated initial condition computations as well as controller design with the inclusion of a proper delay model.

References

1. Vromen, T.: Control of stick-slip vibrations in drilling systems (2015)
2. Liu, Y.: Suppressing stick-slip oscillations in underactuated multibody drill-strings with parametric uncertainties using sliding-mode control. IET Control Theory Appl. **9**(1), 91–102 (2014)
3. Vaziri Hamaneh, S.V.: Dynamics and control of nonlinear engineering systems. Ph.D. dissertation, University of Aberdeen (2015)
4. Hernandez-Suarez, R., Puebla, H., Aguilar-Lopez, R., Hernandez-Martinez, E.: An integral high-order sliding mode control approach for stick-slip suppression in oil drillstrings. Pet. Sci. Technol. **27**(8), 788–800 (2009)
5. Oladunjoye, I.O., Vaziri, V., Ing, J., Aphale, S.S.: Severity analysis of stick-slip bifurcation in drill-string dynamics under parameter variation. In: IASTED African Conference on Modelling and Simulation, AfricaMS (2016)
6. Navarro-López, E.M., Suárez, R.: Practical approach to modelling and controlling stick-slip oscillations in oilwell drillstrings. In: Proceedings of the 2004 IEEE International Conference on Control Applications, vol. 2, pp. 1454–1460. IEEE (2004)
7. Karkoub, M., Zribi, M., Elchaar, L., Lamont, L.: Robust-synthesis controllers for suppressing stick-slip induced vibrations in oil well drill strings. Multibody Syst. Dyn. **23**(2), 191–207 (2010)
8. Richard Degenhardt, P., Cohen, L.J., Tyczynski, P., Sliwa, R.E., Ostrowski, R.: Analysis of possibilities for modification of drill bit geometrical parameters used to drill holes in composite materials of various composition. Aircr. Eng. Aerosp. Technol.: Int. J. **87**(2), 120–130 (2015)
9. Han, G., Timms, A., Henson, J., Aziz, I.A., et al.: Wellbore stability study: lessons and learnings from a tectonically active field. In: Asia Pacific Oil and Gas Conference & Exhibition. Society of Petroleum Engineers (2009)
10. Livescu, S., Craig, S., et al.: Increasing lubricity of downhole fluids for coiled-tubing operations. SPE J. **20**(02), 396–404 (2015)
11. Abdo, J., Al-Shabibi, A., Al-Sharji, H.: Effects of tribological properties of water-based drilling fluids on buckling and lock-up length of coiled tubing in drilling operations. Tribol. Int. **82**, 493–503 (2015)

12. Marquez, M.B.S., Boussaada, I., Mounier, H., Niculescu, S.-I.: Analysis and control of oilwell drilling vibrations (2015)
13. Serrarens, A., de Molengraft, M.V., Kok, J., den Steen, L.V.: H control for suppressing stick-slip in oil well drillstrings. IEEE Control Syst. 18(2), 19–30 (1998)
14. Canudas-de Wit, C., Corchero, M.A., Rubio, F.R., Navarro-López, E.: D-OSKIL: a new mechanism for suppressing stick-slip in oil well drillstrings. In: 44th IEEE Conference on Decision and Control and 2005 European Control Conference, CDC-ECC 2005, pp. 8260–8265. IEEE (2005)
15. Navarro-López, E.M.: An alternative characterization of bit-sticking phenomena in a multi-degree-of-freedom controlled drillstring. Nonlinear Anal.: Real World Appl. 10(5), 3162–3174 (2009)
16. Rachinskii, D., Schneider, K.: Dynamic Hopf bifurcations generated by nonlinear terms. J. Differ. Eqn. 210(1), 65–86 (2005)
17. Navarro-López, E.M., Licéaga-Castro, E.: Non-desired transitions and sliding-mode control of a multi-dof mechanical system with stick-slip oscillations. Chaos Solitons Fractals 41(4), 2035–2044 (2009)
18. Sprott, J.C., Wang, X., Chen, G.: Coexistence of point, periodic and strange attractors. Int. J. Bifurcat. Chaos 23(05), 1350093 (2013)

Aircraft Motion Model Based on Numerical Integration

Meng Zhang[(⊠)] and Yiping Yao[(⊠)]

College of Computer, National University of Defense Technology,
Changsha, Hunan, China
zhangmeng_sim@163.com, ypyao@nudt.edu.cn

Abstract. The modeling of aircraft motion is very important for aircraft flight performance evaluation, aero-engine design and air-combat modeling and simulation. However, the flight of aircraft is a complex process, and its flight capability is affected by many factors. The existing modeling process is generally based on analytic methods or energy methods, which leads to complex modeling process or lower model accuracy. For this reason, we deduced the coordinate transformation matrix, and on this basis, established a differential equation of aircraft motion with the earth fixed axis system, and finally built an aircraft motion model based on the numerical integration method. Experiments show that the method is simple and high-precision, and can meet the requirements of rapid modeling of warfare simulation.

Keywords: Aircraft motion model · Warfare simulation · Coordinate transformation matrix · Numerical integration

1 Introduction

Since the first use in World War I, the advantage of the aircraft in wars has become increasingly evident [1]. Especially in modern combat, aircraft has been a key factor to victory because of its flexibility, high-speed and three-dimensional features. Aircraft, as a combat platform, its flight function is an important feature to distinguish from other weapons platforms. Aircraft can carry varies of detection equipment, weapons and confrontation facilities which used to be land-based or sea-based into the air to increase their combat capability and improve their operational performance. The most important step to build an aircraft model is to build its motion model. However, the flight process of aircraft in the air is very complex, its flight performance is not only related with physical properties such as engine performance, aerodynamic parameters, weight and so on, but also with the air, terrain, aerodynamic hysteresis effect and other factors [2]. Therefore, it is difficult to establish aircraft motion equations in the geocentric coordinate system directly, and the accuracy of the aircraft motion model is also hard to be guaranteed.

The weight of aircraft is greater than air, so aircraft generates aerodynamic lift to fly through the interaction between wings and air. The flight capability of the aircraft is determined by its own aerodynamic parameters, including the lift coefficient, the drag coefficient and the lateral force coefficient [3]. The surface model of aircraft can be used

© Springer Nature Singapore Pte Ltd. 2017
M.S. Mohamed Ali et al. (Eds.): AsiaSim 2017, Part I, CCIS 751, pp. 518–528, 2017.
DOI: 10.1007/978-981-10-6463-0_44

to calculate the aerodynamic parameters of the aircraft directly, but this surface model is very complex, and needs to take up a lot of computing resources, thus cannot meet the needs of combat simulation. The motion equations of aircraft include full-scale equations and small perturbation equations [4]. The full-scale equations are original equations, and the aircraft motion model established by full-scale equation will have higher precision, but the modeling process and calculation process of this model will be complex. The small perturbation equation is derived based on the full-scale equation for a reference state and ignoring the secondary factors. The small perturbation equation has a good effect on the simulation of constant flight state, which can meet the needs of warfare simulation. In this paper, we derived a small perturbation equation in earth fixed axis system by matrix transformation which can calculate the instantaneous acceleration of aircraft according to the inputted thrust parameters, aerodynamic parameters and environmental parameters. And then we can calculate the instantaneous position and speed of the aircraft by numerical integration method. Experiments show that this model is easy to implement and has high accuracy.

2   Related Work

Aircraft motion simulation is an important aspect of aircraft simulation, thus establishing aircraft motion model is of great significance for warfare simulation, weapon equipment evaluation and tactical theory research. A large number of researchers have carried out this study and put forward many methods and technologies. At present, the methods used to simulate aircraft flight and calculate flight status include analytical method, energy method and numerical integration method [5].

The analytical method establishes the aircraft dynamics equation based on the assumption of moment balance, and then obtains the flight status of the aircraft by solving the dynamics equations. Therefore, it is necessary to consider the force of the aircraft at each moment [6, 7]. The main solutions of dynamics equations are Euler method, four element method [8], second order Runge-Kutta method, fourth order Runge-Kutta method, second order Adams method and Tustin method [9]. The analytic method can solve the force situation and flight status of the aircraft at a certain time accurately, but it needs to establish complex full-scale differential equations, and the solution of the equations needs to consume a lot of computing resources. In addition, the output data of aircraft motion model established by energy method is rough and users cannot get the exact location of the aircraft during flying process [10].

The numerical integration method can calculate the state of the aircraft at the next moment according to the initial state and the inputted state parameters and environmental parameters. This method can establish the aircraft motion model easily and is suitable for computer programming. Using numerical integral method to build motion model can achieve good practical effects. But the selections of dynamic parameters, aerodynamic parameters and movement parameters of existing models are based on the fixed engine performance and aerodynamic characteristic curves or some fixed values, so the precision of models are not high. In literature [11], Johnson gets instantaneous thrust of aircraft by modeling aircraft engine using the similarity method, but the method is not universal and the modeling process is complex. In literature [10], the author uses empirical data to calculate the lift and drag coefficient of taxiing model, which results in low precision.

In this paper, the transformation matrix between the geocentric coordinate system and the body coordinate system is deduced by studying the relationship between the geocentric coordinate system, the earth fixed axis system and the body coordinate system. And we transform the aircraft motion equations in the body coordinate system into the equations in the earth fixed axis system. Then we calculate the instantaneous engine thrust, lift coefficient and drag coefficient by numerical integration method in iteration, so as to obtain the flight state and coordinate position of the aircraft at each moment.

3   Modeling Method

Establishing aircraft motion model according to the aircraft dynamics equation needs to analyze the force situation of aircraft at every moment. Usually, we can only know the force of aircraft in the body coordinate system, as shown in Fig. 1.

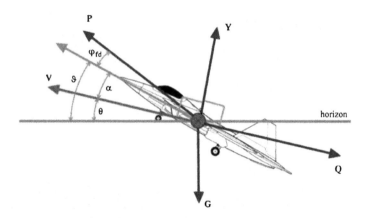

Fig. 1. Force diagram of aircraft in the body coordinate system.

However, the input and output of the aircraft motion model are generally the coordinates of the geocentric coordinate system directly converted from the latitude, longitude and height. Therefore, it is necessary to realize the conversion between the geocentric coordinate system and the body coordinate system. To realize the direct conversion between the body coordinate system and the geocentric coordinate system is difficult, so the earth fixed axis system is needed as the transition coordinate system. The body coordinate system, the geocentric coordinate system and the earth fixed axis system are all right hand system, defined as follows:

1. The body coordinate system S_t is a three-dimensional rectangular coordinate system established on the body of aircraft. The origin O is aircraft centroid, and the X-axis is in the symmetry plane of aircraft, parallel to the aircraft axis and forward to the front.

The Z-axis is perpendicular to the symmetry plane, forward to the right. The Y-axis is perpendicular to the XOZ plane and forward to the up.

2. The geocentric coordinate system S_c is established inside the earth. The origin O is located in the center of the earth, and the X-axis coincides with the intersection of the meridian and the equator, forward to the east. Z-axis coincides with the Earth's rotation axis, forward to the north. The Y-axis is perpendicular to the X-axis and Z-axis and forms the right hand system.

3. The earth fixed axis system S_d is fixed to the surface of the earth, and its origin O can be selected on the surface arbitrarily. Y-axis plumb hammer with ground and forward to the up. The X and Z axes are in the ground and can be selected according to the requirements.

3.1   Coordinate Transformation Matrix

After defining the coordinate system as above, we can think that the earth fixed axis system can be converted from the geocentric coordinate system. The conversion matrix is as follows:

$$B_c^d = B_x(\pi - \text{lat})B_z\left(\text{long} + \frac{\pi}{2}\right) \tag{1}$$

$$B_z\left(\text{long} + \frac{\pi}{2}\right) = \begin{bmatrix} -\sin(\text{long}) & \cos(\text{long}) & 0 \\ -\cos(\text{long}) & -\sin(\text{long}) & 0 \\ 0 & 0 & 1 \end{bmatrix}$$

$$B_x(\pi - \text{lat}) = \begin{bmatrix} 1 & 0 & 0 \\ 0 & -\cos(\text{lat}) & \sin(\text{lat}) \\ 0 & -\sin(\text{lat}) & -\cos(\text{lat}) \end{bmatrix}$$

$$B_c^d = \begin{bmatrix} -\sin(\text{long}) & \cos(\text{long}) & 0 \\ \cos(\text{lat})\cos(\text{long}) & \cos(\text{lat})\sin(\text{long}) & \sin(\text{lat}) \\ \sin(\text{lat})\cos(\text{long}) & \sin(\text{lat})\sin(\text{long}) & -\cos(\text{lat}) \end{bmatrix}$$

Converting the earth fixed axis system into the geocentric coordinate system is the inverse of the above process, so the conversion matrix is as follows:

$$B_d^c = B_x(-(\pi - \text{lat}))B_z\left(-\left(\text{long} + \frac{\pi}{2}\right)\right) \tag{2}$$

$$B_x(-(\pi - \text{lat})) = \begin{bmatrix} 1 & 0 & 0 \\ 0 & -\cos(\text{lat}) & -\sin(\text{lat}) \\ 0 & \sin(\text{lat}) & -\cos(\text{lat}) \end{bmatrix}$$

$$B_z\left(-\left(long+\frac{\pi}{2}\right)\right) = \begin{bmatrix} -\sin(long) & -\cos(long) & 0 \\ \cos(long) & -\sin(long) & 0 \\ 0 & 0 & 1 \end{bmatrix}$$

$$B_d^c = \begin{bmatrix} -\sin(long) & \cos(long)\cos(lat) & \cos(long)\sin(lat) \\ \cos(long) & \sin(long)\cos(lat) & \sin(long)\sin(lat) \\ 0 & \sin(lat) & -\cos(lat) \end{bmatrix}$$

To realize the conversion between the earth fixed axis system and the body coordinate system also needs to know the aircraft drift angle, pitch angle and roll angle, the three angles are defined as follows:

1. The drift angle φ: the angle between the projection line of the body axis X on the horizontal plane XOY and the axis X. If the axis X deviates from the horizontal plane XOY to the left, then φ is positive.
2. The pitch angle ϑ: the angle between the body axis X and the horizontal plane XOZ. ϑ is positive when axis X is tilted upward.
3. The roll angle γ: the angle between the plane symmetry XOY of the aircraft and the plane of the lead hammer containing the axis X. When the right wing tilts down, the left is tilted upward, γ is positive.

Therefore, according to the three angles above, the conversion matrix B_d^t between the earth fixed axis system and the body coordinate system can be derived.

$$B_d^t = B_x(\gamma)B_z(\vartheta)B_y(\varphi) \tag{3}$$

$$B_x(\gamma) = \begin{bmatrix} 1 & 0 & 0 \\ 0 & \cos(\gamma) & \sin(\gamma) \\ 0 & -\sin(\gamma) & \cos(\gamma) \end{bmatrix}$$

$$B_z(\vartheta) = \begin{bmatrix} \cos(\vartheta) & \sin(\vartheta) & 0 \\ -\sin(\vartheta) & \cos(\vartheta) & 0 \\ 0 & 0 & 1 \end{bmatrix}$$

$$B_y(\varphi) = \begin{bmatrix} \cos(\varphi) & 0 & -\sin(\varphi) \\ 0 & 1 & 0 \\ \sin(\varphi) & 0 & \cos(\varphi) \end{bmatrix}$$

$$B_d^t = \begin{bmatrix} \cos(\vartheta)\cos(\varphi) & \sin(\vartheta) & -\cos(\vartheta)\sin(\varphi) \\ -\sin(\gamma)\sin(\vartheta)\cos(\varphi) & & \cos(\gamma)\sin(\vartheta)\sin(\varphi) \\ +\sin(\gamma)\sin(\varphi) & \cos(\gamma)\cos(\vartheta) & +\sin(\gamma)\cos(\varphi) \\ \sin(\gamma)\sin(\vartheta)\cos(\varphi) & & -\sin(\gamma)\sin(\vartheta)\sin(\varphi) \\ +\cos(\gamma)\sin(\varphi) & -\sin(\gamma)\cos(\vartheta) & +\sin(\gamma)\cos(\varphi) \end{bmatrix}$$

3.2 Aircraft Motion Equations

When aircraft is flying in the air, the forces acting on the aircraft include: engine thrust P, aerodynamic R and gravity G. So we can build the aircraft motion model by analyzing the moment generated by the forces on the aircraft to calculate the acceleration vector of each time. The modeling process will describe following:

Usually, the total thrust of the engine is in the aircraft body coordinate plane XOY. Let the thrust line and the body longitudinal axis X constitute the angle φ_p, so the engine thrust component in the body coordinate system is:

$$P_{xt} = P\cos\varphi_p, \quad P_{yt} = P\sin\varphi_p, \quad P_{zt} = 0$$

The aerodynamic force R is usually decomposed into three components in the body coordinate system: resistance Q (negative direction along the axis of the body axis X), lift force Y (along the body axis Y), side force Z (along the body axis Z). So we can get:

$$\begin{bmatrix} R_{xt} \\ R_{yt} \\ R_{zt} \end{bmatrix} = \begin{bmatrix} -Q \\ Y \\ Z \end{bmatrix}$$

Then, we can get the formula of three components of the aerodynamic force using lift coefficient C_y, the drag coefficient C_x and the side force coefficient C_z:

$$Q = C_x \times \tfrac{1}{2} \times \rho \times u^2 \times S$$
$$Y = C_y \times \tfrac{1}{2} \times \rho \times u^2 \times S$$
$$Z = C_z \times \tfrac{1}{2} \times \rho \times u^2 \times S$$

In this formula, lift coefficient C_y, the drag coefficient C_x and the side force coefficient C_z can be obtained by interpolating on the aerodynamic characteristic curve; The air density ρ can be calculated from the atmospheric environment model.

Combined with the gravity $G = mg$ of the aircraft, we can get the aircraft centroid dynamics equation in the earth fixed axis system:

$$m\frac{d}{dt}\begin{bmatrix} v_{xd} \\ v_{xd} \\ v_{xd} \end{bmatrix} = B_t^d \begin{bmatrix} P\cos\varphi_p \\ P\sin\varphi_p \\ 0 \end{bmatrix} + B_t^d \begin{bmatrix} -Q \\ Y \\ Z \end{bmatrix} + \begin{bmatrix} 0 \\ -mg \\ 0 \end{bmatrix}$$

$$\begin{aligned}
m\frac{dv_{xd}}{dt} = {}& P\big[\cos\varphi_p\cos\psi\cos\vartheta + \sin\varphi_p(\sin\psi\sin\gamma - \cos\psi\sin\vartheta\cos\gamma)\big] \\
& - Q\cos\psi_s\cos\theta + Y(\sin\psi_s\sin\gamma_s - \cos\psi_s\sin\theta\cos\gamma_s) \\
& + Z(\sin\psi_s\cos\gamma_s + \cos\psi_s\sin\theta\sin\gamma_s)
\end{aligned} \tag{4}$$

$$m\frac{dv_{yd}}{dt} = P\big[\cos\varphi_p\sin\vartheta + \sin\varphi_p\cos\vartheta\cos\gamma\big] - Q\sin\theta + Y\cos\theta\cos\gamma_s \\ - Z\cos\theta\sin\gamma_s - mg \tag{5}$$

$$m\frac{dv_{zd}}{dt} = P\big[-\cos\varphi_p\sin\psi\cos\vartheta + \sin\varphi_p(\cos\psi\sin\gamma + \sin\psi\sin\vartheta\cos\gamma)\big] \\ + Q\sin\psi_s\cos\theta + Y(\cos\psi_s\sin\gamma_s + \sin\psi_s\sin\theta\cos\gamma_s) \\ + Z(\cos\psi_s\cos\gamma_s - \sin\psi_s\sin\theta\sin\gamma_s) \tag{6}$$

Dividing the time into some small time slice, we can assume that the aircraft is doing uniform flight in every small slice. According to the aircraft centroid dynamics equation, the acceleration of the aircraft in each time slice can be calculated so that the speed and displacement of the aircraft at the end of each time slice can be approximated. The formulas (4) to (5) are the centroid dynamics equations of the aircraft in the earth fixed axis system. The result of the calculation needs to be converted into the acceleration vector in the geocentric coordinate system by using formula (2) derived above.

4 Model Implementation

Through the derivation of the equation, we have obtained the motion differential equations of aircraft in the earth fixed axis system. Using these equations to simulate the flight of aircraft needs to input the instantaneous thrust, aerodynamic parameters and environmental parameters in iteration. For this purpose, an atmospheric environment model based on standard atmosphere parameters is established.

4.1 Atmospheric Environment Model

The magnitude of engine thrust is related to the air pressure at the aircraft's position, and the lift generated by the aircraft flight is also affected by the air density. Therefore, the numerical model of the atmospheric environment needs to be established. The atmospheric environment includes: atmospheric temperature, pressure, air density, etc. The establish of the atmospheric environment model is to calculate the atmospheric characteristics at each instantaneous position.

The instantaneous thrust of the engine is related to the aircraft pressure height H_p and the instantaneous Mach M, where the ambient pressure height H_p is related to the actual air pressure P_s of the airport and is calculated as:

$$H_p = \frac{1 - (P_s/P_0)^{1/5.25588}}{225577} \times 10^5$$

The instantaneous Mach M is the ratio of the instantaneous velocity V of the aircraft to the actual sound velocity v_s, $M = V/v_s$, and v_s is calculated as follows:

$$v_s = \sqrt{1.4 \times 287 \times T_s}$$

Atmospheric temperature is associated with altitude, in general, the higher the altitude, the lower the temperature. The vertical decline rate of temperature is the 1000 m rise of altitude, the temperature dropped $6°$. Reference temperature T_0 can choose the temperature of where the aircraft takeoff, the formula is as follows:

$$T_s = T_0 - 0.006 \times h$$

The lift and drag generated during the flight of the aircraft are related to the air density. The air density ρ_s refers to the mass of per unit volume of air at a given temperature and pressure, and is calculated as follows:

$$\rho_s = \rho_0 \times \frac{P_s}{P_0} \times \frac{T_0}{T_s}$$

Where ρ_0, P_0 and T_0 are the atmospheric density, atmospheric pressure and atmospheric temperature at sea level respectively.

4.2 Model Execution Flow

After the establishment of aircraft differential equations and atmospheric environment model, we have been able to simulate the aircraft's motion function. In order to meet the needs of warfare simulation, we also need to further give the execution flow of aircraft motion model. In warfare simulation, the motion model needs to solve the position of next moment based on the track information and the position at this moment. Therefore, we give the execution flow of the aircraft motion model in this paper, as shown in Fig. 2.

The aircraft motion model first obtains the trajectory information by analyzing scenario and finds its initial position and velocity according to the trajectory information. And according to the current location, call the atmospheric environment model to calculate the atmospheric temperature, pressure, air density and other parameters. Then calculate the instantaneous engine thrust and aerodynamic parameters using two-dimensional interpolation. These parameters are inputted into the aircraft centroid dynamics equation, and the acceleration vector of the aircraft is calculated to get the velocity and position increment of the aircraft in a given minimum time slice. Finally, the new velocity vector and position vector are obtained by vector addition and converted into the coordinates in the geocentric coordinate system through the coordinate transformation matrix. This will be executed cyclically until the simulation end.

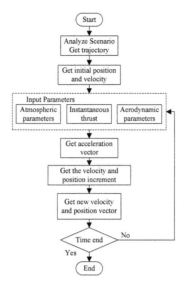

Fig. 2. Aircraft motion model execution flow.

5   Validation

Based on the modeling process above, we uses the C++ programming language to realize the aircraft motion model, which can simulate the actual flight based on the input performance parameters and atmospheric environment parameters. In order to prove the correctness of this model, this paper takes a specific aircraft as an example to compare the running results of this model with the actual measurement data. Figure 3 is the flight path of the aircraft, where (a) is the simulation results of this model; (b) is the actual flight data. By contrast we can find that the two tracks are very similar. Figure 4 is the changing curve of flight distance along with time, and the maximum absolute error between calculation results and measure results is 1417 m, the maximum relative error is 0.7%. Thus, we can prove that the aircraft motion model established in this paper has high accuracy.

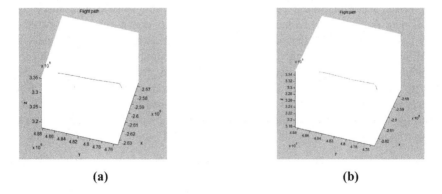

(a)   (b)

Fig. 3. The flight path of the aircraft.

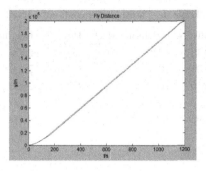

Fig. 4. The changing curve of flight distance along with time.

The physical characteristics of this aircraft are shown in Table 1. Airport environmental data are shown in Table 2. Aerodynamic characteristics and thrust characteristic are shown in Tables 3 and 4.

Table 1. Physical characteristics of aircraft.

Mass	60×10^3 kg
Number of engine	2
Wing area	164.5 m^2
Installation angle	0°
Stop AOA	4°
Takeoff AOA	8°

Table 2. Airport environmental data.

Air pressure	96525 Pa
Temperature	22.3 °C
Wind speed	2.0 m/s
Gravity	9.8 m/s^2
Average slope	−0.0011
Friction	0.025

Table 3. Aerodynamic characteristics of aircraft.

AOA/$^\circ$	Lift coefficient	Drag coefficient
0	0.459	0.052
2	0.623	0.058
4	0.908	0.069
6	0.967	0.080
8	1.171	0.097
10	1.316	0.122
12	1.422	0.151

Table 4. Thrust characteristic of aircraft.

Height/m	Mach	Thrust/N	Height/m	Mach	Thrust/N	Height/m	Mach	Thrust/N
0	0.0	93133	1000	0.0	85762	2000	0.0	77196
0	0.1	88303	1000	0.1	80556	2000	0.1	72793
0	0.2	84870	1000	0.2	77959	2000	0.2	71102
0	0.3	82980	1000	0.3	76244	2000	0.3	69514
0	0.4	82005	1000	0.4	75705	2000	0.4	69423

6 Conclusion

This paper introduces the detailed process of establishing aircraft motion model using numerical integration method. Firstly, the limitations and precision problem of the existing modeling methods and parameter determination methods are summarized. Then the coordinate transformation matrix in the modeling process is deduced, and the differential equation of aircraft motion in the earth fixed axis system is given. After that, the atmospheric environment model is built, and the execution process of the aircraft motion model was described in detail. Finally, the correctness and accuracy of this aircraft motion model are proved by comparing the calculated results with the actual flight data.

References

1. Feng, Z., Yiping, Y., Wenjie, T., et al.: A high performance framework for modeling and simulation of large-scale complex systems. Future Gener. Comput. Syst. **2015**(51), 132–141 (2015)
2. Rolfe, J.M., Staples, K.J.: Flight simulation, pp. 56–89. Cambridge University Press, Cambridge (1986)
3. Li, X., Xing, X.: Design & implementation of civil transport takeoff performance program. J. Civil Aviat. Univ. China **26**(1), 8–13 (2008)
4. Wang, L., Jia, L.: Simulation of aircraft flight system based on motion differential equation. J. China Civil Aviat. Univ. **23**(zl), 82–85 (2005)
5. Hua, Z.: Research on aircraft engine modeling for flight simulation. Nanjing University of Aeronautics and Astronautics (2010)
6. Gu, H.: Dynamic model of aircraft ground handling. Acta Aeronautica et Astronautica Sinica **22**(2) (2001)
7. Shui, Q.-C., Wang, Q.-H.: A mathematical model used to calculate the takeoff performance for an aircraft. Flight Dyn. **19**(4), 70–74 (2001)
8. Wang, J.: Improvement to quaternion-based model of rigid aircraft motion. J. Syst. Simul. **18**(2), 230–232 (2006)
9. Gai, Y., Gu, W., Xu, Y., Li, C.: A method for designing mobile capability simulation system of avion. Comput. Simul. **26**(1), 87–102 (2009)
10. Fang, Z.: Aircraft Flight Dynamics, p. 6. Beijing University of Aeronautics and Astronautics Press, Beijing (2005)
11. Johnson, S.A.: A simple dynamic engine model for use in a real-time aircraft simulation with thrust vectoring. NASA Technical Memorandum, vol. 4240 (1990)

Designing a Biosensor Using a Photonic Quasi-Crystal Fiber with Fan-Shaped Analyte Channel

Suoda Chu[1]([✉]), Nakkeeran Kaliyaperumal[1], G. Melwin[2], Sumeet S. Aphale[1], P. Ramesh Babu Kalivaradhan[2], and Senthilnathan Karthikrajan[2]

[1] School of Engineering, Fraser Noble Building, University of Aberdeen, Aberdeen AB24 3UE, UK
{r05sc15,k.nakkeeran}@abdn.ac.uk
[2] Department of Physics, School of Advanced Sciences, VIT University, Vellore 632 014, Tamil Nadu, India

Abstract. In this research work, we design a biosensor using a six-fold photonic quasi-crystal fiber with a fan-shaped analyte channel based on surface plasmon resonance (SPR). We numerically analyze both the dispersion relations and loss spectra for three different refractive indices of the analyte, n_a, using finite element method. Through optimization of the structure, we find that the proposed biosensor exhibits a maximum refractive index sensitivity of 3200 nm/RIU and a resolution of 3.12×10^{-5} RIU when n_a is increased from 1.41 to 1.43. We infer that the coupling between the core mode and SPR mode can be explained as a complete coupling of the loss matching condition or an incomplete coupling of the phase matching condition. Owing to the ease of fabrication of the proposed biosensor with an average sensitivity of 2250 nm/RIU, we envisage that this biosensor could turn out to be a versatile instrument for detecting the biomolecules.

Keywords: Fan-shaped · Photonic quasi-crystal fiber · Refractive index sensor · Surface plasmon resonance · Sensitivity

1 Introduction

As a surface plasmon resonance (SPR) based senor, photonic biosensors with remarkable advantages such as extremely high sensitivity, fast response, label-free, capability of removable detection, online sensing, etc. give rise to a robust and effective solution for direct sensing application [1]. It is widely studied by a number of researchers in various fields like medical diagnostic, bio-chemical detection and organic chemical detection for the investigation of bio-molecular interaction and the recognition of target analytes [2].

It is well known that SPR is essentially an electromagnetic mode, due to the collective resonant oscillation of free electrons, which is stimulated by incident light at the interface of metal and dielectric material [3]. At a specific wavelength,

© Springer Nature Singapore Pte Ltd. 2017
M.S. Mohamed Ali et al. (Eds.): AsiaSim 2017, Part I, CCIS 751, pp. 529–537, 2017.
DOI: 10.1007/978-981-10-6463-0_45

the coupling will fulfill with the phase matching condition which can be explained by the propagation constants equivalence of a core-guided mode and a plasmonic mode. The first SPR experiment work for bio-sensing and gas detection was presented by Liedberg et al. in 1983 [2]. Conventionally, the SPR biosensors widely available in the market work with the Krechmann configuration which is based on prism-coupling theory. The sensing ability of this kind of prism based SPR sensors is quite good enough to detect even small variation in the refractive index of analyte at the prism-metal interface [2,3]. However, due to their bulk size and complicated design and structure, it is not easy to realize a portable sensor [4,5].

The availability of optical fiber SPR sensor has made a break through in this limitation because of its compact small size and design flexibility. The first optical fiber SPR sensor with a maximum refractive index measurement resolution of 7.5×10^{-4} RIU at 900 nm was proposed by Jorgenson in 1993 [6]. Further, multi-mode fibers were replaced by single mode fibers for higher sensitivity and sharper loss peak [5]. With the development on photonic crystal fibers (PCFs), it is possible to control the optical characteristics of PCF by having different structures and by varying the structural parameters. The sensing ability and sensing range witnessed a further improvement with the optimization of structure [2]. Later on, a lot of PCF-SPR biosensors with different structures such as, multi-core holey fiber in 2012 [1], large size microfluidic channel PCF in 2012 [7], square lattice PCF in 2014 [8], D-shaped PCF in 2015 [9] have been proposed for enhancing the sensitivity. Due to the limitations in the fabrication technology, currently it is quite difficult to coat the metal part onto the air holes. Among these novel designs, the D-shaped PCF was considered as a most promising way to fabricate by side-polishing technology [10]. Besides the common advantages, the D-shaped PCF-SPR biosensor can easily be coated with the metal layer outside the PCF air holes.

Recently, Gandhi et al. proposed a refractive index based biosensor using a photonic quasi-crystal fiber (PQF) [11]. This PQF is a micro-structured fiber with quasi periodicity that has a long-range order with aperiodic arrangement in the cladding region [12]. Based on our previous work on a six-fold PQF biosensor [4], in this work, we propose a six-fold PQF biosensor where a fan-shaped part of the cladding is removed. Here, the cladding material is made of poly methyl methacrylate (PMMA). The structure proposed in this paper is based on the D-shaped fiber. Then, a sector is removed as the resonant wavelength is found to be exceeding the wavelength range for defining the refractive index of PMMA. For a D-shaped PQF biosensor, the matching resonance wavelength is found to be 1.6 μm when the refractive index of analyte is 1.40. The matching resonance wavelength gets increased as the analyte refractive index is increased. As the maximum wavelength used in PMMA refractive index equation is limited to 1.6 μm, for a higher analyte refractive index, say, 1.42, the matching wavelength must be more than the maximum value of the wavelength range. Furthermore, the coupling phenomenon in this SPR sensing system occurs either because of the incomplete coupling of the phase matching condition or the complete coupling of the loss matching condition. This plays a crucial role during the resonant process between the fundamental mode and SPR mode [1]. The paper is laid out as follows. We discuss, a detailed geometrical structure and theoretical modeling in Sect. 2. Section 3 deals with the results and analysis of the proposed work. Finally, we conclude the work in Sect. 4.

2   Simulated Geometrical Structure and Theoretical Modeling

The structure of this designed SPR biosensor is shown in Fig. 1. Unlike the common D-shaped PCF structure, a fan-shaped sector with the central angle of 72° and 6.2 μm in depth is removed from the original circular structure. It is because that the gold layer can be easily coated at the interface between analyte and PMMA cladding. This empty space can be used to fill in with the analyte liquid as a sensor channel. The inter air holes are arranged in a fixed distance of pitch, Λ, of 2 μm. The diameter of all the air holes is kept as 1 μm. The gold layer thickness is fixed as 50 nm. In order to investigate the mode coupling of this sensor, the finite element method (FEM) is used for simulation and a perfectly matched layer (PML) boundary condition is applied for absorbing the radiation power.

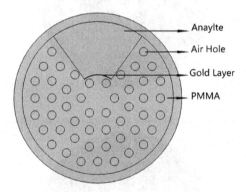

Fig. 1. Cross-section of the proposed six-fold PQF biosensor.

The background material of this sensor is PMMA. For an accurate calculation, the wavelength dependence of the refractive index of PMMA is defined by the following equation which was reported by Beadie et al. [13]:

$$n^2\left(\lambda\right) = a_0 + a_1\lambda^2 + a_2\lambda^4 + a_3\lambda^{-2} + a_4\lambda^{-4} + a_5\lambda^{-6} + a_6\lambda^{-8}, \tag{1}$$

where $a_0 = 2.1778$, $a_1 = 6.1209e{-}3$, $a_2 = -1.5004e{-}3$, $a_3 = 2.3678e{-}2$, $a_4 = -4.2137e{-}3$, $a_5 = 7.3417e{-}4$ and $a_6 = -4.5042e{-}5$. Here, λ represents the incident light wavelength in vacuum. It should be noted that the fit coefficients are valid and can be used in the calculation of refractive index of PMMA when the temperature condition is around 20.1 C with an experimentally verified incident wavelength ranging between 0.4 µm and 1.6 µm. Next, the dielectric constant of gold is characterized by the Drude model [14]. The fan-shaped channel is filled with the analyte liquid sample with the refractive index changing from 1.41 to 1.43.

3 Results and Analysis

Figure 2(a) and (b) illustrate both the distribution of electric field of a fundamental mode and a plasmonic mode of the fan-shaped channel PQF biosensor at 1100 nm. It can be seen clearly from Fig. 2(a) that the power of core-guided mode is almost concentrated in the core area while there is negligible plasmonic mode power existing at the interface between the PMMA and the fan-shaped

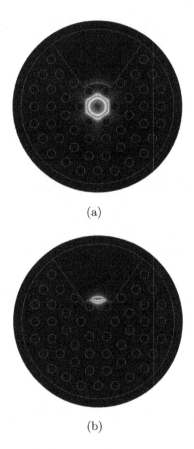

(a)

(b)

Fig. 2. (a) The distribution of electric field of fundamental mode and (b) the distribution of electric field of plasmonic mode at 1100 nm when $n_a = 1.43$.

analyte channel. This indicates that there is no power exchange between those two modes and hence, there is no coupling taking place at this wavelength.

In any plasmonic sensor, it is known that the plasmonic mode arises as a consequence of the energy transfer from the fundamental mode. Figure 3(a) and (b) represent the electric field distribution of the fundamental mode and plasmonic mode at a mode matching wavelength of 1390 nm. As against the case of Fig. 2(a) and (b), one can visualize the power transfer from the fundamental mode as plasmonic which reflects the peak in the loss spectrum. The leaky core mode energy excites the surface plasmon waves (SPWs) at the interface of gold layer. Moreover, it has a maximum loss at this particular wavelength so that we can make use of this confinement loss peak for sensing. Here, the confinement loss α is calculated by [15],

$$\alpha_{loss} = \frac{40\pi}{\lambda \ln 10} Im\left(n_{neff}\right), \tag{2}$$

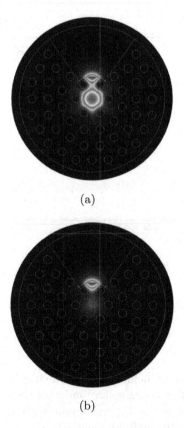

(a)

(b)

Fig. 3. (a) The distribution of electric field of fundamental mode and (b) the distribution of electric field of plasmonic mode at 1390 nm when $n_a = 1.43$.

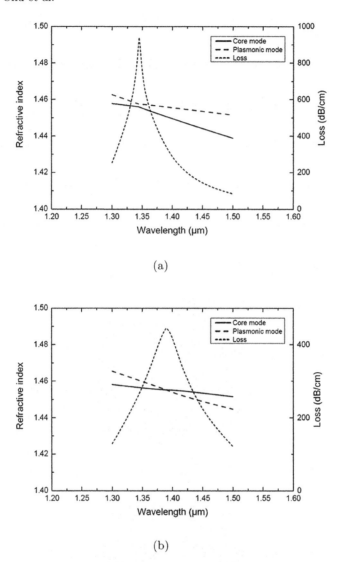

Fig. 4. (a) Dispersion relations of the fundamental mode and SPR mode and confinement loss when $n_a = 1.41$. (b) Dispersion relations of the fundamental mode and SPR mode and confinement loss when $n_a = 1.43$.

where λ is the wavelength of incident light in vacuum and $Im\left(n_{neff}\right)$ represents the imaginary part of effective refractive index of the core-guided mode.

Figure 4(a) and (b) show the dispersion relation of the fundamental mode and plasmonic mode along with the fundamental mode loss when the analyte refractive indices are 1.41 (Fig. 4(a)) and 1.43 (Fig. 4(b)), respectively. It is obvious that, at resonance wavelength, a maximum power loss is reached due to the maximum leakage of fundamental mode. Comparing the real part of effective refractive indices of fundamental mode and SPR mode, there is a crossing between the modes in Fig. 4(b). However, such a crossing is not observed in Fig. 4(a). The real parts of n_{eff} of the fundamental mode and the SPR mode for the increasing values of the analyte refractive index are getting closer to each other. However, for further increase in coupling wavelength they get crossed with a intersection point. This can be explained by the coupled-mode theory [1,3]. In Fig. 4(a), where the imaginary parts are equal to each other, a complete coupling does occur. On the other hand, from the results of Fig. 4(b), when the real parts of effective refractive indices of the two modes are equal, an incomplete coupling occurs [16]. From the detailed numerical results, it is observed that the biosensor works under the complete coupling of the loss matching condition when the analyte refractive index is equal to 1.41. Conversely, there is an incomplete coupling of the phase matching condition when the analyte refractive index is above 1.41. This finding indicates that the SPR phenomenon for this biosensor exhibits a complete coupling with lower analyte refractive indices and then turns into incomplete coupling with the increasing analyte refractive index values.

Figure 5 indicates loss spectra when n_a is increased from 1.41 to 1.43. From the result, it is clear that the loss peak is getting shifted towards the longer wavelength side with the periodical decrement in the loss as and when the refractive of the analyte is increased from 1.41 to 1.43. Based on the sensitivity calculation of the proposed biosensor, for a 0.1 nm peak-wavelength resolution instrument, the maximum sensitivity is 3200 nm/RIU and the average sensitivity is 2250 nm/RIU.

It is well known that the gold layer thickness is a significant parameter in determining the half-width and depth of the resonance peak [17]. Therefore, the impact of different gold layer thickness has also been studied. Figure 6 shows the

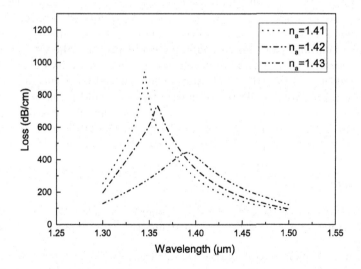

Fig. 5. The loss spectra as a function of wavelength when the refractive index of analyte is varied from 1.41 to 1.43.

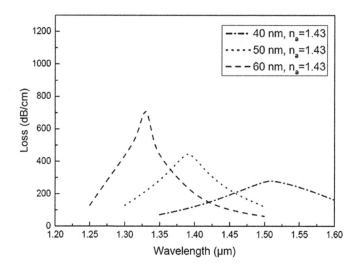

Fig. 6. The loss spectra as a function of wavelength with different thickness of gold layer varying from 40 to 60 nm.

simulated results with the gold layer thickness of 40 nm, 50 nm and 60 nm which indicate that the loss peak decreases and shifts to the longer wavelength side as the gold layer thickness increases.

4   Conclusion

We have proposed a six-fold photonic quasi-crystal fiber biosensor with a fan-shaped analyte channel in this paper. Due to its unique structure, it exhibits two different kinds of coupling conditions, namely, the complete coupling and incomplete coupling. Both these couplings could produce the surface plasmon resonance phenomenon. A maximum refractive index sensitivity of 3200 nm/RIU and a resolution of 3.12×10^{-5} RIU have been achieved for a sensing range from 1.41 to 1.43. It is worthwhile to emphasize that the gold layer coating process in the fan-shaped cavity is easier than coating into the air holes. We are of the opinion that with the existing state of the art of the fabrication technologies, the realization of the proposed biosensor would be a viable one.

References

1. Shuai, B., Xia, L., Zhang, Y., Liu, D.: A multi-core holey fiber based plasmonic sensor with large detection range and high linearity. Opt. Express **20**(6), 5974–5986 (2012)
2. Rifat, A.A., Mahdiraji, G.A., Chow, D.M., Shee, Y.G., Ahmed, R., Adikan, F.R.M.: Photonic crystal fiber-based surface plasmon resonance sensor with selective analyte channels and graphene-silver deposited core. Sensors **15**(5), 11499–11510 (2015)

3. An, G., Li, S., Yan, X., Zhang, X., Yuan, Z., Wang, H., Zhang, Y., Hao, X., Shao, Y., Han, Z.: Extra-broad photonic crystal fiber refractive index sensor based on surface plasmon resonance. Plasmonics **12**(2), 465–471 (2017)

4. Design a Biosensor Using a Stampli Photonic Quasi-Crystal Fiber. ACTA Press (2016)

5. Luan, N., Yao, J.: Surface plasmon resonance sensor based on exposed-core microstructured optical fiber placed with a silver wire. IEEE Photonics J. **8**(1), 1–8 (2016)

6. Zhao, Y., Deng, Z.-Q., Li, J.: Photonic crystal fiber based surface plasmon resonance chemical sensors. Sens. Actuators B: Chem. **202**, 557–567 (2014)

7. Bing, P., Yao, J., Ying, L., Li, Z.: A surface-plasmon-resonance sensor based on photonic-crystal-fiber with large size microfluidic channels. Opt. Appl. **42**(3), 493–501 (2012)

8. Mamun, M.A.A., Islam, M.A., Alam, M.S.: A square lattice photonic crystal fiber based surface plasmon resonance sensor with high sensitivity. In: 2014 International Conference on Electrical Engineering and Information Communication Technology, pp. 1–5, April 2014

9. Wei-Hua, W.J.S., Cheng-Jie, Y.: D-shaped photonic crystal fiber refractive index and temperature sensor based on surface plasmon resonance and directional coupling. Acta Phys. Sin. **64**(22), 224221 (2015)

10. Ying, Y., Si, G.Y., Luan, F.J., Xu, K., Qi, Y.W., Li, H.N.: Recent research progress of optical fiber sensors based on D-shaped structure. Opt. Laser Technol. **90**, 149–157 (2017)

11. Gandhi, M.S.A., Sivabalan, S., Babu, P.R., Senthilnathan, K.: Designing a biosensor using a photonic quasi-crystal fiber. IEEE Sens. J. **16**(8), 2425–2430 (2016)

12. Sivabalan, S., Raina, J.P.: High normal dispersion and large mode area photonic quasi-crystal fiber stretcher. IEEE Photonics Technol. Lett. **23**(16), 1139–1141 (2011)

13. Beadie, G., Brindza, M., Flynn, R.A., Rosenberg, A., Shirk, J.S.: Refractive index measurements of poly (methyl methacrylate) (PMMA) from 0.4–1.6 μm. Appl. Opt. **54**(31), F139–F143 (2015)

14. Hassani, A., Skorobogatiy, M.: Design criteria for microstructured-optical-fiber-based surface-plasmon-resonance sensors. J. Opt. Soc. Am. B **24**(6), 1423–1429 (2007)

15. Zhang, P.-P., Yao, J.-Q., Cui, H.-X., Ying, L.: A surface plasmon resonance sensor based on a multi-core photonic crystal fiber. Optoelectron. Lett. **9**(5), 342–345 (2013)

16. Fan, Z., Li, S., Liu, Q., An, G., Chen, H., Li, J., Chao, D., Li, H., Zi, J., Tian, W.: High sensitivity of refractive index sensor based on analyte-filled photonic crystal fiber with surface plasmon resonance. IEEE Photonics J. **7**(3), 1–9 (2015)

17. Otupiri, R., Akowuah, E.K., Haxha, S., Ademgil, H., AbdelMalek, F., Aggoun, A.: A novel birefrigent photonic crystal fiber surface plasmon resonance biosensor. IEEE Photonics J. **6**(4), 1–11 (2014)

Prediction on the Performance of Helical Strakes Through Fluid-Structure Interaction Simulation

Kee Quen Lee[1(✉)], Aminudin Abu[1], Pauziah Muhamad[1],
Lit Ken Tan[1], Hooi Siang Kang[2], Howe Hing Tang[2],
and Hoong Thiam Toh[1]

[1] Malaysia-Japan International Institute of Technology,
Universiti Teknologi Malaysia Kuala Lumpur, Kuala Lumpur, Malaysia
lkquen@utm.my
[2] Faculty of Mechanical Engineering, Universiti Teknologi Malaysia,
Skudai, Malaysia

Abstract. Fluid-structure interaction (FSI) is used in the study to predict the vortex-induced vibration (VIV) of a cylinder that is fitted with helical strakes. The aims is to predict the characteristic of VIV after the installation of helical strakes on a cylinder. Two-way coupling through commercial fluid and structural solvers is utilized to develop the simulation. Helical strakes of height, $h = 0.10D$ and pitch, $p = 10D$ is used together with cylinder of diameter, $D = 0.018$ m. Three different velocities are tested. The amplitude, frequency, fluctuating lift response and vorticity contour are presented. The present study shows capability of FSI in reproducing the VIV characteristic of cylinder fitted with helical strakes. However, improvement is required especially at low reduced velocity as the values are deviated.

Keywords: Helical strakes · Fluid-structure interaction · Vortex-induced vibration

1 Introduction

Predicting the vortex-induced vibration (VIV) of deepwater risers is one of the critical challenges in the offshore industry. Because of the high current wave, vortex shedding is generated at higher frequencies with higher structural modes. This phenomenon results in great fatigue rate. To reduce the VIV, suppression devices are introduced. Helical strakes are one of the suppression devices that commonly used in the offshore industry [1]. In the past few decades, several laboratory works have been conducted to investigate the effectiveness of helical strakes [2–4]. However, prediction of the behaviour of helical strakes using simulation tools is still scarce.

The challenge that faced by the designers is the accuracy in predicting the VIV response of the cylinder that fitted with helical strakes using numerical simulation tools. The standard tools that are used by the current industry have been found to function inconsistently in predicting certain cases. Empirical models required some basic experimental data as input. However, the data used in this method is only based on

© Springer Nature Singapore Pte Ltd. 2017
M.S. Mohamed Ali et al. (Eds.): AsiaSim 2017, Part I, CCIS 751, pp. 538–547, 2017.
DOI: 10.1007/978-981-10-6463-0_46

experiments of one degree-of-freedom and does not handle non-linearity [5]. Therefore, a more reliable numerical simulation is highly demanded.

Fluid-structure interaction (FSI) is newly introduced recently to address problems dealing with the interaction between fluid and structure. It has been widely used in combustion systems [6, 7] and blood flow [8, 9] applications. Nevertheless, there is still lack of FSI investigation on the helical strakes in suppressing VIV of a cylinder. Pereira Gomes et al. [10] are the few researchers that utilized FSI to simulate the laminar flow over an aluminium cylinder fitted with thin plate in two-dimensional. The outputs were in good agreement with experimental data. However, discrepancy was found in the first swivelling mode. Gustafsson [5] examine the VIV of a short riser using FSI in three-dimension. The author stated that simulation on FSI was stable but conservative. Improvement on computational time was important as FSI is very time consuming. Besides, high level of mesh refining is not recommended as it required longer computational time.

To the best of authors' knowledge, fully three-dimensional FSI simulation on VIV of a cylinder fitted with helical strakes are very limited and not fully addressed. Hence, in this paper, the performance of helical strakes in suppressing the VIV of cylinder is studied using 3D FSI approach. Three different velocities are tested, and the experimental result of a cylinder fitted with helical strakes [11] is used to validate the outputs of the simulation.

2 Methodology

2.1 Computational Equations

It is not an easy task to predict the vortex-induced vibration of a cylinder fitted with helical strakes. The boundary layers and appropriate turbulence model are needed for the prediction. In the present study, fluid-structure interaction is implemented, where it combines structural and fluid solvers for coupling. For the fluid solver, Reynolds-averaged Navier-Stokes equations (RANS) is utilized. Assuming an incompressible Newtonian fluid, the expression of the equation is as follows:

$$\frac{\partial U_i}{\partial x_i} = 0 \tag{1}$$

$$\rho \frac{\partial U_i}{\partial t} + \rho U_j \frac{\partial U_i}{\partial x_j} = -\frac{\partial P}{\partial x_i} + \frac{\partial}{\partial x_j} (2\mu S_{ji} - \overline{\rho u'_j u'_i}) \tag{2}$$

ρ is the density of fluid, P is the pressure, U is the averaged velocity, u' represents the fluctuating velocity, μ as the molecular viscosity and S_{ji} as the rate of strain sensor. The term $-\overline{\rho u'_j u'_i}$ is the Reynolds-stress tensor. The number of unknowns in the RANS equations are more than the number of equations. To close the system, turbulence model is required. In the present study, Shear Stress Transport (SST) k-ω turbulence model is used. The reason of choosing this model is because the turbulent shear stress, which is not reflected in other turbulence model, is included in the calculation. Hence, the separation flow can be estimated more accurately under adverse pressure gradient [12]. The two-equation k-ω SST turbulence model is given by the following transport equation in conservation form:

$$\frac{\partial(\rho k)}{\partial t} + \frac{\partial(\rho u_j k)}{\partial x_j} = P - \beta * \rho \omega k + \frac{\partial}{\partial x_j}\left[(\mu + \sigma_k \mu_t)\frac{\partial k}{\partial x_j}\right] \tag{3}$$

$$\frac{\partial(\rho \omega)}{\partial t} + \frac{\partial(\rho u_j \omega)}{\partial x_j} = \frac{\gamma}{v_t}P - \beta \rho \omega^2 + \frac{\partial}{\partial x_j}\left[(\mu + \sigma_\omega \mu_t)\frac{\partial \omega}{\partial x_j}\right] + 2(1-F_1)\frac{\rho \sigma_{\omega 2}}{\omega}\frac{\partial k}{\partial x_j}\frac{\partial \omega}{\partial x_j} \tag{4}$$

where k is the turbulence kinetic energy and p is the specific dissipation rate. The P is defined as following:

$$P = \tau_{ij}\frac{\partial u_i}{\partial x_j} \tag{5}$$

$$\tau_{ij} = \mu_t\left(2S_{ij} - \frac{2}{3}\frac{\partial u_k}{\partial x_k}\delta_{ij}\right) - \frac{2}{3}\rho k \delta_{ij} \tag{6}$$

and the turbulent eddy viscosity (limiter) is computed from:

$$\mu_t = \frac{\rho a_1 k}{\max(a_1 \omega, \Omega F_2)} \tag{7}$$

The constants β, σ_k, σ_ω, $\sigma_{\omega 2}$, Υ, v_t, a_1, Ω and blending function F_1 and F_2 are as defined in [12].

For the structural solver, the structural dynamic system of a cylinder is represented by equation of motion. By considering a cylinder immersed in water, functions as a spring-damper-mass system encountering external fluid forces, the equation can be described as:

$$m_s\ddot{\chi} + c_s\dot{\chi} + k_s\chi = F_{fluid}(t) \tag{8}$$

$\chi = Xi + Yj + Zk$, where X, Y and Z represent the cylinder instantaneous displacement in x, y and z directions, respectively. $\dot{\chi}$ and $\ddot{\chi}$ are the 1st order-partial derivative and 2nd order-partial derivative of the displacement, respectively to time t. m_s is the mass of the structure, c_s is the damping coefficient, k_s is the spring stiffness, and $F_{fluid}(t)$ is the fluid force acting on the cylinder body. The fluid force is integrated from the body viscous friction and the pressure which is obtained from the Navier-Stokes equation solutions.

A two-way coupling is utilized in the present study, where the structural and fluid equations are solved separately and within one time step, no iteration is applied between the structural and fluid field. The concept of the coupling in one time-step is as following: calculation on fluid equations is performed until it is converged to obtain the force on the cylinder. Then, the forces in fluid interface are interpolated to structural mesh. These forces are treated as boundary conditions in structural domain and the

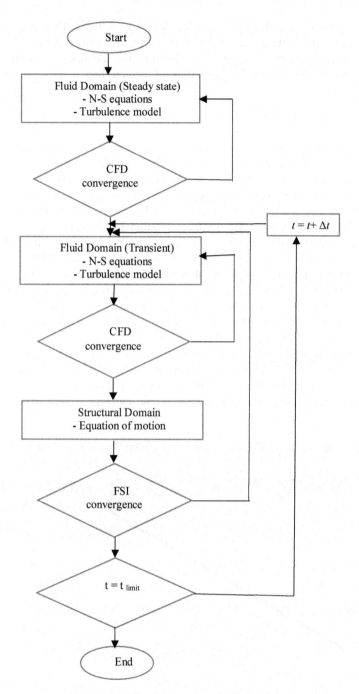

Fig. 1. Flowchart of the coupling procedure.

structural equations are solved to obtain the motion of cylinder. The motion in term of displacement is then interpolated to the fluid mesh, and update the position of mesh point. The same step repeated again by solving the fluid equations on the updated mesh until convergence is reached. The procedure of the coupling is shown in Fig. 1.

2.2 Boundary Condition

In the numerical simulation, physical system in general is very complex to analyse. Therefore, the model is constructed to retain the essential features to the real experimental condition. In the present study, the experimental data of Quen et al. [11] is used as benchmark for validation. In the paper, a pre-tensioned (147 N) flexible cylinder with 2.92 m length and 0.018 m diameter is used where both ends are connected with universal joints. To generate the similar condition in simulation, both ends of the cylinder are constrained in terms of displacement. To allow the motion of universal joint, rotation is allowed in x and y directions, but rotation in z direction is constrained. At one end of the cylinder, an axial force of 147 N is applied to produce the pre-tensioned effect. A standard gravity in −Y direction is also applied on the cylinder fitted with strakes to represent the gravity effect of the cylinder. Besides, Fluid Solid Interface is implemented on the surface of the cylinder to create the force and displacement integration between fluid and structural domains.

For the fluid domain, seven boundaries are defined, to be exact the upper and lower boundaries, left and right boundaries, upstream and downstream boundaries and the wall of cylinder. To avoid the effect of boundaries towards the simulation calculation of the cylinder, the distance between boundaries and cylinder is very important. Borch

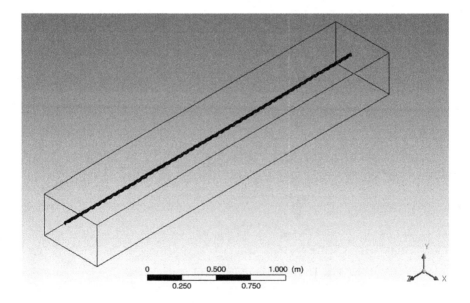

Fig. 2. The cylinder model fitted with helical strakes.

and Rodi [13] stated that at least 4.5D (D = diameter of cylinder) of the distance is required to escape the influence of velocity and pressure. However, they recommended that 10D of the boundary distance was more suitable to eliminate the effect. Therefore, in the present study 10D is set as the distance between cylinder and the upstream, upper and lower boundaries. 20D, on the other hand, is applied between cylinder and downstream boundary to capture the vortices of the cylinder. Grid independence study was conducted to test the meshing size. Medium meshing is selected after a series of run. Detail information on the grid independence study can be referred to [19]. In the present study, cylinder with length of 2.92 m and diameter of 0.018 m is used, while the helical strakes is designed to have height, $h = 0.10D$ and pitch, $p = 10D$, as shown in Fig. 2.

3   Results and Discussions

The simulation is conducted to identify the possibility of Fluid-structure interaction (FSI) software in predicting the response of a flexible cylinder fitted with helical strakes. In the present study, only synchronization (lock-in) region is examined because it is the most critical region where the structural shedding frequency is driven by its oscillation. Based on the previous study [11], lock-in occurs from $V_r = 3.2$ to 11.5 (3000 < Re < 11000). Therefore, three difference Reynolds numbers ($Re \approx 5300$, 9000,12500) are selected to be tested in the study and the results are compared to the existing experimental results of similar configuration.

The simulation and the experimental results of amplitude ratio are shown in Fig. 3. The reduced velocity is used to characterize the fluid speed based on the natural frequency and the diameter of a cylinder. It is defined as

$$V_r = \frac{U}{f_n D} \tag{9}$$

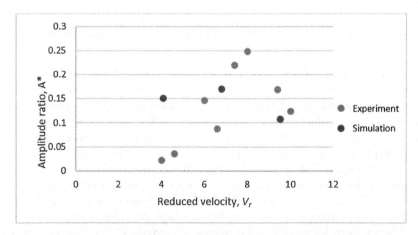

Fig. 3. Amplitude ratio of cylinder fitted with helical strakes.

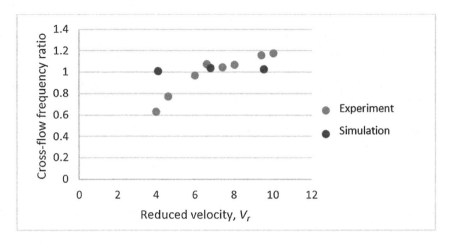

Fig. 4. Cross-flow (CF) frequency ratio of cylinder fitted with helical strakes.

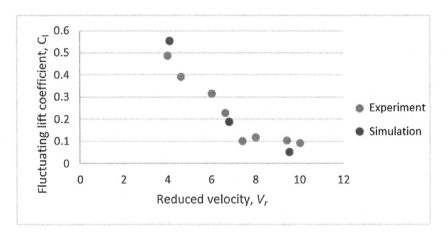

Fig. 5. Fluctuating lift coefficient of cylinder fitted with helical strakes.

where f_n is the natural frequency, D as the diameter of cylinder and U is the flow velocity. Figure 3 shows that the simulation is able to predict the amplitude response of a cylinder fitted with helical strakes as the trend of the simulated data of amplitude ratio is similar to the experimental data, except for $V_r \approx 4$. The large discrepancy on the low reduced velocity ($Re \approx 5300$) may be due to the use of turbulent model in the present study is not suitable for that particular velocity range. According to Williamson [14], shear-layer transition is from Re = 1000 to 200,000. However, at $Re \approx 5000$, transition from KH-instability in shear layer into subcritical range occurs, where significant changes of the wake are noticed [15]. This transition may not be simulated by the current turbulent model, and hence result in the large deviation. Further investigation should be given in identifying more appropriate turbulent model for this transition.

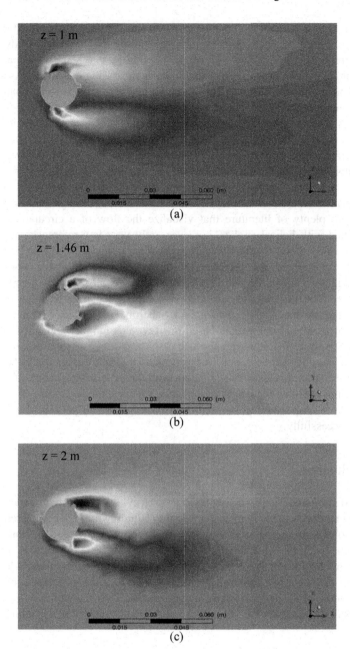

Fig. 6. Vorticity contour of cylinder fitted with helical strakes on X-Y plane at $V_r \approx 6.8$, (a) Z = 1 m; (b) Z = 1.46 m; (c) Z = 2 m.

Similar circumstance is also found in the cross-flow frequency ratio (Fig. 4). The simulated data is in good agreement with the experimental data for high reduced velocities, except for $V_r \approx 4$. The CF frequency ratios are obtained by taking the CF frequency response divided with the natural frequency of the cylinder fitted with helical strakes. Focus is given on the dominant frequency only. In the present study, deviation of the CF frequency ratio as low as 3.6% is found at $V_r \approx 6.8$ and 11.4% at $V_r \approx 9.5$.

The vortex shedding is the origin that induces the oscillating forces. As the current flows around a cylinder, the vortices are shed, and result in periodic changes of the pressure around the cylinder. The varying of the pressure causes the periodic variation of the forces. The forces can be defined in term of fluctuating force coefficient ($C_{1\ \text{fluct}}$). In the present study, the $C_{1\ \text{fluct}}$ is indicated in Fig. 5 to identify the intensity if the oscillation in CF direction. Based on Fig. 5, the simulated $C_{1\ \text{fluct}}$ follow very well the experimental data, where it is reduced as the reduced velocity increased. It is important to identify the fluctuating force of a cylinder as its oscillation intensity will affect the stress concentration along the structure and the fracture possibility of the structure [16].

There are plenty of literature that visualize the flow of a circular cylinder. For cylinder fitted with helical strakes, however, only very few references are available. The present study shows the flow visualization of the cylinder fitted with helical strakes in order to understand the mechanism of strakes in suppressing vortex-induced vibration. Figure 6 shows the vorticity contour at different positions along the helical strakes. At each of the positions (z = 1, 1.46 and 2 m), it can be seen that separation is clearly caused by the strakes. Sadeh and Saharon [17] reported that the point of separation of a circular cylinder is based on Reynolds number and turbulence condition, from 85° to 130°. However, the use of helical strakes in the present study has successfully control the separation of the flow as the flow separation is based on the position of the strakes. This is in agreement with the experimental work of Korkischko and Meneghini [18] that the height of the strakes control the separation of shear layers. By changing the separation point of the flow, the generated periodical vortex can be disrupted successfully.

4   Conclusions

The 3D FSI simulation in predicting the VIV of a cylinder fitted with helical strakes is conducted in the present study by using two-way coupling through commercial fluid and structural solvers. In overall, the present study is able to reproduce the vortex-induced vibration characteristic of a flexible cylinder fitted with helical strakes in terms of amplitude, frequency and fluctuating lift responses. Although the values at low reduced velocity are deviated, they have the same trends with the experimental outputs. The vorticity contour of the helical strakes suggests that the flow separation is depends on the strakes position. Changing the separation point reduces the vortex shedding.

References

1. Allen, D.W., Lee, L., Henning, D.L.: Fairings versus helical strakes for suppression of vortex-induced vibration: technical comparisons. Offshore Technology Conference, OTC 19373 (2008)

2. Frank, W.R., Tognarelli, M.A., Slocum, S.T.: Flow-induced vibration of a long, flexible, straked cylinder in uniform and linearly sheared currents. Offshore Technology Conference, May 3–6, Houston, Texas, USA (2004)
3. Tognarelli, M.A., Slocum, S.T., Frank, W.R., Campbell, R.B.: VIV response of a long flexible cylinder in uniform and linearly sheared currents. Offshore Technology Conference, OTC 16338, Houston, Texas, USA (2004)
4. Huse, E., Saether, L.K.: VIV excitation and damping of straked risers. Proceeding of 20th International Conference on Offshore Mechanics and Artic Engineering, OMAE 2001, Brazil, ASME (2001)
5. Gustafsson, A.: Analysis of vortex-induced vibrations of risers. Master thesis. Chalmers University of Technology, Sweden (2012)
6. Khatir, Z., Pozarlik, A.K., Cooper, R.K., Watterson, J.W., Kok, J.B.W.: Numerical study of coupled fluid-structure interaction for combustion system. Int. J. Numer. Meth. Fluids **56**(8), 1343–1349 (2008)
7. Pozarlik, A.K., Kok, J.B.W.: Fluid-structure interaction in combustion system of a gas turbine – effect of linear vibrations. Journal of Engineering for gas turbines and power 136, Issue 9, 091502 (2014)
8. Bukac, M., Canic, S., Glowinski, R., Tambaca, J., Quaini, A.: Fluid-structure interaction in blood flow capturing non-zero longitudinal structure displacement. J. Comput. Phys. **235**, 515–541 (2013)
9. Torii, R., Oshima, M., Kobayashi, T., Takagi, K., Tezduyar, T.E.: Fluid-structure interaction modeling of blood flow and cerebral aneurysm: Significance of artery and aneurysm shapes. Comput. Methods Appl. Mech. Eng. **198**(45–46), 3613–3621 (2009)
10. Gómez, F., Quesada, J.H., Gómex, R., Theofilis, V., Carmo B., Meneghini, J.: Stability analysis of the flow around a cylinder fitted with helical strakes. 43rd AIAA Fluid Dynamics Conference, San Diego, CA, June 24–27 (2013)
11. Quen, L.K., Abu, A., Kato, N., Muhamad, P., Sahekhaini, A., Abdullah, H.: Investigation on the effectiveness of helical strakes in suppressing VIV of flexible riser. Appl. Ocean Res. **44**, 82–91 (2014)
12. Menter, F.R.: Two-equation eddy-viscosity turbulence models for engineering applications. AIAA Journal **32**(8), 1598–1605 (1994)
13. Bosch, G., Rodi, W.: Simulation of vortex shedding past a square cylinder with different turbulence models. Int. J. Numer. Meth. Fluids **28**, 601–616 (1998)
14. Williamson, C.H.K.: Vortex dynamics in the wake of a cylinder. Annual Review of Fluid mechanic **28**(1), 477–539 (1996)
15. Fey, U., Konig, M., Eckelmann, H.: A new Strouhal-Reynolds-number relationship for the circular cylinder in the range $47 < Re < 2x10^5$. Phys. Fluids **10**, 1547 (1998)
16. Huang, C.: Structural health monitoring system for deepwater risers with vortex-induced vibration: Nonlinear modeling, blind identification, fatigue/damage estimation and vibration control. Doctor of Philosophy. Rice University, Texas (2012)
17. Sadeh, W.Z., Saharon, D.B.: Turbulence effect on crossflow around a circular cylinder at subcritical Reynolds numbers. NASA Contractor Report **3622**, 48–52 (1982)
18. Korkischko, I., Meneghini, J.R.: Experimental investigation of flow-induced vibration on isolated and tandem circular cylinders fitted with strakes. J. Fluids Struct. **26**, 611–625 (2010)
19. Lee, K.Q., Abu, A., Muhamad, P., Sahekhaini, A., Tan, L.K., Kang, H.S.: Prediction of vortex-induced vibration of bare cylinder and cylinder fitted with helical strakes. MATEC Web of conference **95**, 04001 (2017)

EEG Brain Symmetry Index Using Hilbert Huang Transform

Fathrul Azarshah Abdul Aziz[1(✉)], Mohd Ibrahim Shapiai[1],
Aznida Firzah Abdul Aziz[2], Fairuz Ali[2], Ayman Maliha[1],
and Zuwairie Ibrahim[3]

[1] Electronic System Engineering,
MJIIT Center of Artificial Intelligence and Robotics (CAIRO),
UTM Kuala Lumpur, Kuala Lumpur, Malaysia
atoy92zx@gmail.com, md_ibrahim83@utm.my,
amaliha@iugaza.edu.ps
[2] Department of Family Medicine, UKM Medical Centre Kuala Lumpur,
Kuala Lumpur, Malaysia
draznida@ppukm.ukm.edu.my, pherel@gmail.com
[3] Faculty of Electrical and Electronic Engineering, Universiti Malaysia Pahang,
Gambang, Malaysia
zuwairie@ump.edu.my

Abstract. Electroencephalography (EEG) monitoring is known to be techni-
cally feasible and possibly clinically relevant to determine patients with acute
ischemic hemispheric stroke. The EEG is very useful tool in understanding
neurological dysfunction of stroke plausible improving the treatment and
rehabilitation. Most of the existing techniques to diagnose stroke from the EEG
signal is mainly based on Fourier Transform (FT). For instance, the Brain
Symmetry Index (BSI) employed Fast Fourier Transform (FFT) as coefficients
to measure symmetrical of blood flow between left and right brain hemisphere.
The symmetrical index ranges between zero and one where one indicates the
highest asymmetrical of blood flow. It is known that the conventional FFT has
limitation in analyzing non-linear and non-stationary signal. Therefore, the
existing BSI and its variations may also suffer from this transformation properties. In this study, we propose BSI based on Hilbert Huang Transform
(HHT) which defined as BSI-HHT. HHT is a way to decompose a signal into
so-called intrinsic mode functions (IMF) along with a trend, and obtain
instantaneous frequency data. The HHT will be used as coefficients instead off
FFT in calculating the BSI index. An experiment to validate the performance of
BSI-HHT is conducted in this study as to compare with the existing BSI
technique. The EEG signal of Middle Cerebral Artery (MCA) subjects and
healthy subjects are used for this investigation. The proposed BSI-HHT has
offered better interpretation as it correlates to the stimulation procedure on the
gathered data especially at specific frequency band. Also, through the analysis,
the HHT coefficient is able to capture the non-stationary and non-linear of the
interest electrode.

Keywords: Electroencephalography · Hilbert huang transform · Ischemic
stroke

© Springer Nature Singapore Pte Ltd. 2017
M.S. Mohamed Ali et al. (Eds.): AsiaSim 2017, Part I, CCIS 751, pp. 548–560, 2017.
DOI: 10.1007/978-981-10-6463-0_47

1 Introduction

Stroke disease causes long-term cognitive state and health condition of patient affected. The study of Electro-neurophysiology in cortical electroencephalogram (EEG) analysis has been gain much interest of research on understanding of neurological dysfunction of stroke plausible improving the treatment and rehabilitation [1].

There is two type of stroke, first type is Ischaemia can arise slowly from the progression of atherosclerotic disease (stable angina, claudication) or acutely in the case of vascular (atherosclerotic plaque rupture) or intracardiac (atrial fibrillation, mechanical valve prostheses) thromboembolisation. The resulting blockage causes reduction of blood supply to the certain region in the brain i.e. the lack of oxygen (or ischaemia) causes death of brain cells in the affected area. Stroke or also known as 'brain attack' is the result. The second type of stroke is the haemorrhagic stroke type. This type occurs when there is bleeding or haemorrhage because of a blood vessel in or around the brain has ruptured [2]. Raw EEG signal are mostly only can be determined or interpreted by medical experts and a doctor with continuous review and very delicate procedure with time consuming to analyse [3]. In this study, investigate on ischemia stroke diseases.

Using the state of calm consciousness were used as baseline of data which is easier to conduct data acquisition for patients with less interruption as possible. Many studies have been carried out and discovered that human brain waves undergo a significant changes when a person is in a state of concentration compared to a relaxed state [4, 5]. EEG records electrical activity of the brain from the scalp. The recorded waveforms reflect the cortical electrical activity. EEG offers high temporal information in real time which can be used to diagnose epilepsy, seizures, Alzheimer's disease, cerebral dysfunctions, degenerative diseases of the brain and stroke [6]. To achieve the goal of real-time detection of critical brain events, raw EEG would require continuous expert review. This limitation remains very subjective which requires expert interpretation. However, by applying a fast Fourier transform (FFT), EEG can be quantified in terms of its amplitude, power, frequency, and rhythmicity to generate numerical values, ratios, or percentages; graphically display arrays or trends; and set thresholds for alarms. EEG has improved detection and localization of pathophysiology of brain ischemia [7].

In research study about ischaemic stroke, the EEG signal activities are slow in the delta frequency range and fast in the alpha frequency range [8]. Thalamus and cells in layer II–IV cortex generate slower frequency in delta (0.5–3 Hz) and theta (4–7) whereas cell layer IV and V cortex generate faster frequency in alpha (8–12 Hz). Thus, these leads to abnormal changes for EEG pattern in ischemia have sensitive to have low oxygen level of their pyramidal neurons at layer III, V, and VI [3]. In related study, Brain Symmetry Index (BSI) method have shown promising results in analysing stroke by determining the magnitude of asymmetry power spectra between right and left hemisphere of brain. The exploitation of the method also derived in ischemic changes of stroke patient [9].

However, applying Fourier Transform (FT) method generally suffers from the window averaging of the signal. FT was fundamentally not possible to correctly determine the spindle onset and offsets accurately due its limitation implicitly assume a periodic signal, and requires sufficient samples for spectrum estimation. This study presents a method of analysing stroke patient with Middle Cerebral Artery (MCA) infarcted and compared with healthy condition of human EEG signals. The proposed method of BSI is calculated between bilateral of right and left hemisphere of brain based on Hilbert Huang Transform (HHT). HHT technique has the advantages of processing non-stationary and non-linear signals and requires no prior knowledge of understanding the technique.

The outline in this study, second section is related work, shared previous research had been done related in this study investigation. Third section methodology, this chapter explained how this study conducted and used of purposed method applied for the problem investigated. Forth section result, the results of the data are analyzed and discussed the effectiveness of proposed method compared to existed method. Final section conclusion, the discussion of understanding finding in this study investigation and future work to exploit better resolution in this fields research.

2 Related Works

There are various techniques to extract brain information such as spatial filtering [10], and temporal information [11], spectral information and Event Related Potential (ERP) [12]. However, spectral analysis have been commonly used by the researcher as an alternative tool instead of using functional magnetic resonance imaging (fMRI) [13]. Different perspectives of spectral analysis have been used in different research areas to provide useful information like the difference of power band and relative power of the band. The spectral analyses include in Relative Power Ratio (RPR) and BSI.

2.1 Event Related Potential (ERP)

Instead of using fMRI, ERP was alternative to measure brain activations [13]. It commonly used as a monitor brain activation with millisecond precision and provide very detail resolution of EEG data on-line [14]. ERP localizes low-dimensional EEG with associated specific region of the brain [12]. However, most analysis in EEG stroke are quantitative pattern analysis [12]. These only confirm by monitoring only and not by its feature.

2.2 Spectral Analysis

Spectral Analysis is a standard method that is used to analyze EEG signal. The power spectrum (power spectral) reveal the 'frequency content' of EEG signal or the distribution of power by the frequency. Power spectrum is very useful to differentiate in the EEG signal behavior [15]. Such as FT to compute Power Spectral Density (PSD) [6]. FT assumption may give misleading results in its harmonic component globally and uses linear superposition of trigonometric function [16].

2.3 Relative Potential Ratio (RPR)

Previous research had studied the EEG signal pattern level in cognitive or thinking ability of the stroke patients. The method of Relative Potential Ratio (RPR) is used to investigate the characteristics groups of stroke patients. RPR is compute based on power spectrum density (PSD) which in turn is calculated using FT between right and left hemisphere pair of channel by [17]:

$$RPR = \frac{PowerLeftChannel + PowerRightChannel}{\sum (PowerLeftChannel + PowerRightChannel)} \tag{1}$$

2.4 BSI for EEG

BSI is created to assist visual interpretation of the EEG and method can process the detection of focal seizure activity and monitoring stroke patient [18]. The BSI captures asymmetry in spectral power between the two cerebral hemispheres. The calculated value is normalized to be between 0 for perfect symmetry and 1 for maximal asymmetry. The original definition of sBSI [18–21] is given below in Eq. (1). Fourier coefficient belonging frequency i = 1...N and Hemispheric bipolar derivations j = 1...M. Both R_{ij} (right part of channel pair) and L_{ij} (left part of channel pair) are the input channel of the signal.

$$BSI = \frac{1}{MN} \sum_{j=1}^{M} \left| \sum_{i=1}^{N} \frac{R_{ij}(t) - L_{ij}(t)}{R_{ij}(t) + L_{ij}(t)} \right| \tag{2}$$

There also have different type of BSI, such as BSIphase, $_{temporal}$BSI, $_{revise-standard}$BSI, $_{revise-temporal}$BSI, pdBSI these was modified variously changes of parameter [18]. However, these BSI are identical and no significant changes [22].

3 Hilbert Huang Transform

In previous research, proposed Hilbert Marginal Spectrum used the spectral entropy and energy features corresponding EEG frequency for seizure detection. The research method provide better classification than FFT analysis [23]. HHT gives more advantages as nonstationary signal processing in form of time-frequency analysis and also has similarity based on Fourier theory without given a new definition of frequency mathematically [23].

The first step in getting HHT is Empirical Mode Decomposition (EMD); this method consists of the decomposition of a time series into a finite number of components known as IMF. IMF is an oscillation mode embedded inside the data [16, 24]. Each component needs to follow certain conditions: the mean value of the two envelopes defined respectively by local maxima and local minima must be zero and the number of extrema and the zero-crossing must be either equal or differ at most by one

[16, 24]. The extraction of IMFs by original signal is called the sifting process. The proto IMF can be expressed from the mean of the upper and lower envelope m1(t) as follows:

$$h_1(t) = x(t) - m_1(t) \tag{3}$$

$h_1(t)$ is proto IMF because it does not necessarily satisfy the rigorous constraints that define an IMF. Therefore, the sifting process is applied again on $h_1(t)$:

$$h_1(t) - m_{11}(t) = h_{1k}(t) \tag{4}$$

where $m_{11}(t)$ is the mean of the upper and lower envelopes of $h_1(t)$. This process is generally reiterated k times until eventually $h_{11}(t)$ obtained as:

$$h_{1(k=1)}(t) - m_{k1}(t) = h_{1k}(t) \tag{5}$$

The iteration of k allows $h_{1k}(t)$ to satisfy the stoppage criterion of the sifting process [25]. Once the first IMF $c1(t)$ finish extraction from the original signal $x(t)$, the residual part $r(t)$ will be obtained:

$$x(t) - c_1(t) = r_1(t) \tag{6}$$

Thus, the $r_1(t)$ can be treated as new time series to be sifted to get next IMF. This whole process will be continued until the residue $r_n(t)$ is a monotonic function with only single extremum. The originated signal $x(t)$ can be represented as the sum of all IMFs with adding residue such as [25]:

$$x(t) = \sum_{i=1}^{n} c_1(t) - r_{n1}(t) \tag{7}$$

Obtain IMF component then is possible to apply Hilbert Transform to each component as:

$$H[x(t)] = x * \frac{1}{\pi t} = y \tag{8}$$

The marginal spectrum represents accumulated energy over entire data span [26], can define as:

$$h(w) = \int_0^T H(w, t) dt \tag{9}$$

A thorough theoretical discussion on this definition of frequency is given by Huang et al. [16]. By using EMD together with HT, it is possible to calculate time by time the frequency (i.e. the instantaneous frequency) of a non-stationary signal (TMS–EEG evoked potentials) generated by a non-linear system (the cerebral cortex). Since both frequency and amplitude are a function of time, the Hilbert Spectrum $H(w,t)$ can be obtained by plotting the amplitude (or the energy, i.e. amplitude square) in the time–frequency plane [25].

4   Methodology

This section will discuss about the experimental procedure of this study from data acquisition to result analysis as Fig. 1 shown the work flow of the study to analyze the processed data of stroke patient.

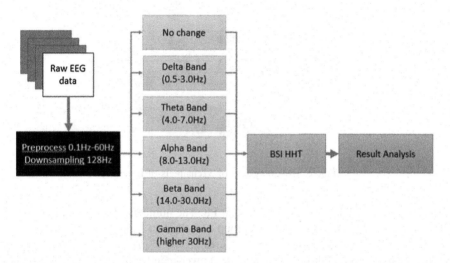

Fig. 1. Framework design, the raw EEG data were band passed into 0.1 Hz to 60.0 Hz and downsampling 128 Hz. The signal then process another band passed into several sub band of Delta band, Theta band, Alpha band, Beta band and Gamma band. All band featured extracted into BSI-HHT to be analyze.

4.1   Data Acquisition

All procedure performed in this study involving human participant were accordance with ethical standard of the institutional and research ethics committee of Hospital Univerisiti Kebangsaan Malaysia (HUKM). For this study, formal consent is required for patients willing to participate. In this prospective study, the patient was selected by HUKM staff. A stroke survivor male and female with more than 20 years old and have severe post-stroke after 6 month on set. EEG data are recorded with BR32i consist of 32 channel (FP1, FP2, AF3, AF4, F7, F3, FZ, F4, F8, FT7, FC3, FCZ, FC4, FT8, T7, C3, CZ, C4, T8, TP7, CP3, CPZ, CP4, TP8, P7, P3, PZ, P4, P8, O1, OZ and O2) as shown in Fig. 2 in compliance with international 10–20 system with reference and ground with adjusted sampling rate of 256 Hz and 50 Hz notch filter by the device itself.

From all 32 channels, 10 pair of channel were used following the area affected of MCA infarct territory stroke which is F7, F8, FT7, FC3, FC4, FT8, T7, C3, C4, T8,

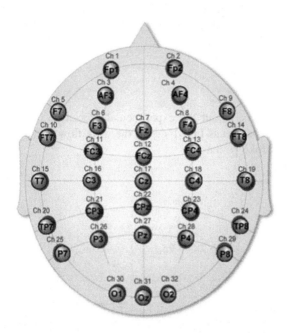

Fig. 2. 10–20 system of 32channels of BRi32.

TP7, CP3, CPZ, CP4, TP8, P7, P3, P4, and P8. The numbers of stroke patients within these study criteria were selected and group of volunteer healthy people for comparison. Data subject is taken under "awake + resting state". Awake state of the brain is useful for reference condition [1]. Thus, the power manifesting EEG in alpha band is confirmed as index of little or no ongoing functional activity [2]. A session of EEG recording consist of 6 trial, each trial took 5 s ready or resting and 30 s trial data. The subject required to close their eyes during 30 s trial data are taken.

4.2   BSI-HHT

The proposed method used similar fundamental of BSI technique with HHT spectrum analysis. Standard BSI used spectral power to compute the index value which basically taken from FFT method preprocessing. However, the Hilbert Marginal Spectral energy is very alike Fourier case data from stationary and linear process but the frequency in $H(w,t)$ and $h(w)$ giving different meaning than Fourier spectral analysis and more accurately [23]. The BSI HHT given the HMS with $h(w)$ in form of:

$$R_{ij} = \sum_{i=1}^{k} h_t(w) \tag{10}$$

And used same representation of R_{ij} or L_{ij} in BSI similarly in as Eq. 2.

5   Experiment Result and Discussion

5.1   Experiment Setup

From this study data acquisition, a group of 8 patients with Right or Left MCA territory infarct were used for this analysis and compared with 10 healthy people which have similar range of ages. These channels were selected base from affected region of MCA infract territory based from medical fundamental as shown in Fig. 3.

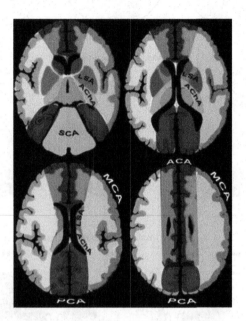

Fig. 3. Labels of stroke territory region.

From the acquired data from the data collection procedure, a group of 8 patients with Right or Left MCA territory infarct were used for this analysis and compared with 10 healthy people which have similar range of ages. Figure 4 depict the power spectrum of the subject condition based on the specific bilateral pair of channels.

From this mapping, by using the standard EEG power spectrum, the healthy (i.e. Fig. 4(a)) subject has symmetrical power spectrum as compared to the stroke patients (i.e. Fig. 4(b) and (c)). In general, for the stroke patient, the power spectrum is found to be asymmetrical between left and right hemisphere. However, the actual value of the power spectrum may subject noise from the limitation of FFT in providing information to non-linear and non-stationary of the EEG signal.

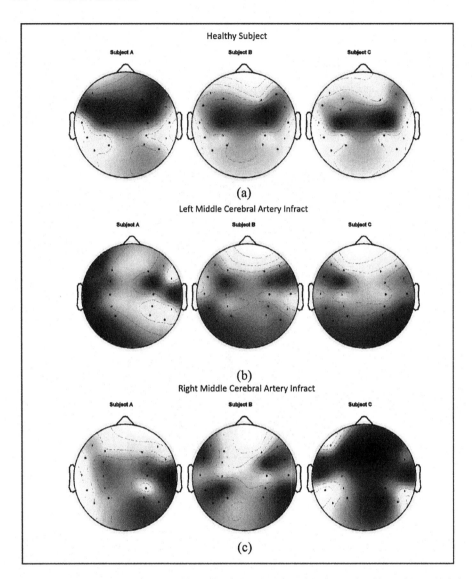

Fig. 4. Power spectrum between right and left hemisphere of brain (a) healthy subject (b) left MCA and (c) right MCA.

5.2 Result

Both experiment used same data and same computational preprocessing as mention before. The Table 1 (standard BSI result) and Table 2 (BSI with HHT feature result) shown the different value in mean, standard deviation, minimum and maximum from Fig. 5 result analysis of standard BSI and Fig. 6 result analysis BSI with HHT feature.

Both analysis shown that stroke index had higher value than healthy BSI. With standard BSI given the analysis shows that every component of band had similar result

Table 1. Statistic of conventional BSI index.

	Max		Min		Mean (Standard deviation)	
	Stroke	Healthy	Stroke	Healthy	Stroke	Healthy
Fullband	0.6406	0.5975	0.4711	0.4113	0.5787 (0.0430)	0.5444 (0.0375)
Delta	0.7762	0.7357	0.5488	0.5025	0.6599 (0.0514)	0.6357 (0.0523)
Theta	0.7440	0.6729	0.5219	0.5108	0.6276 (0.0523)	0.5988 (0.0408)
Alpha	0.6878	0.6737	0.5019	0.4366	0.6038 (0.0449)	0.5662 (0.0529)
Beta	0.6380	0.6074	0.4770	0.4949	0.5694 (0.0488)	0.5558 (0.0258)
Gamma	0.6254	0.5910	0.4209	0.4179	0.5481 (0.0579)	0.5355 (0.0284)

Table 2. Statistic of BSI-HHT index.

	Max		Min		Mean (Standard deviation)	
	Stroke	Healthy	Stroke	Healthy	Stroke	Healthy
Fullband	0.3939	0.4441	0.2781	0.2454	0.3308 (0.0252)	0.3086 (0.0412)
Delta	0.4084	0.4106	0.1981	0.2089	0.3022 (0.0419)	0.3023 (0.0482)
Theta	0.2338	0.2421	0.1208	0.1153	0.1679 (0.0244)	0.1671 (0.0250)
Alpha	0.2595	0.2272	0.1427	0.1487	0.1835 (0.0201)	0.1772 (0.0148)
Beta	0.3179	0.3102	0.2336	0.2243	0.2782 (0.0207)	0.2583 (0.0177)
Gamma	0.4358	0.4272	0.3251	0.3261	0.3794 (0.0281)	0.3695 (0.0283)

from delta to gamma band. These conclude that FT have no significant behavior of index value between pairs of channel due the FT relies on sin and cosine that limits the FFT. However, BSI with HHT seen more likely have better comparison of stroke and healthy during alpha band and beta band. As for gamma band, have not much different since the gamma band just mostly noise in EEG and the delta band theta band also partially differ. The HHT was empirical basis feature it can analysis the EEG data in form of non-stationary and non-linear. Because the experiment was conducted in awake and resting with eyes close condition are more focusing in alpha band therefore these two bands delta band and theta band not effect much.

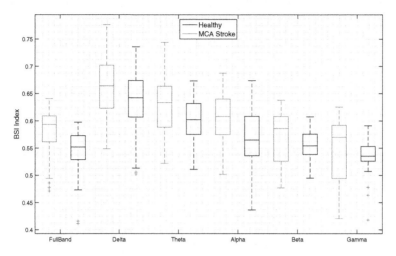

Fig. 5. Statistical of conventional BSI index for each frequency band.

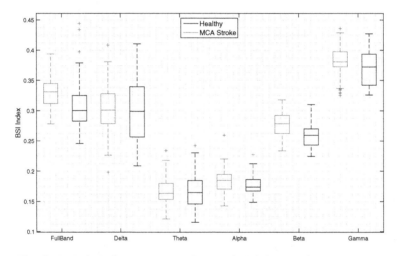

Fig. 6. Statistical of conventional BSI-HHT index for each frequency band.

6 Conclusion

In general, BSI with HHT technique extract better information resolution than standard BSI by replaced FT with HHT. This investigation was recorded under awake and resting state with eye closed condition therefore, the alpha band would be most effective finding in this analysis. Due close eye condition, most of subject may increase their level of concentrate or alertness triggered. This could be the cause of existed respond in beta band information. HHT can extract better information than FFT in frequency domain and time domain. HHT could give more specific of behavior in spectral analysis that FFT cannot find due its limitation processing. In future, different approach of HHT will be conducted by the selected EMD used to determine best analytic of signal behavior of its IMFs given. Each IMF also can determine different findings of the EEG signal data since the EMD are given the sub components of its signal from each IMFs.

Acknowledgment. The authors would like to thank Universiti Teknologi Malaysia for funding this research project through a research university Grant (Q.K130000.2543.13H71) titled "Mask Covariance of Common Spatial Pattern for Brain Computer Interface" and also Centre for Artificial Intelligent and Robotics (CAIRO) (U.K091303.0100.00000) for funding this work.

References

1. Wu, W., Jin, Z., Qiu, Y., Zhu, Y., Li, Y., Tong, S.: Influences of bilateral ischemic stroke on the cortical synchronization. In: Proceedings of the 31st Annual International Conference of the IEEE Engineering in Medicine and Biology Society: Engineering the Future of Biomedicine, EMBC 2009, pp. 2216–2219 (2009)
2. Wang, L., Guo, X., Sun, J., Jin, Z., Tong, S.: Cortical networks of hemianopia stroke patients: a graph theoretical analysis of EEG signals at resting state. In: Conference Proceedings of IEEE Engineering in Medicine and Biology Society 2012, pp. 49–52 (2012)
3. Foreman, B., Claassen, J.: Quantitative EEG for the detection of brain ischemia. Crit. Care **16**, 216 (2012)
4. Liu, N.H., Chiang, C.Y., Chu, H.C.: Recognizing the degree of human attention using EEG signals from mobile sensors. Sensors (Switzerland) **13**, 10273–10286 (2013)
5. Li, K.G., Shapiai, M.I., Adam, A., Ibrahim, Z.: Feature scaling for EEG human concentration using particle swarm optimization. In: Proceedings of 2016 8th International Conference on Information Technology and Electrical Engineering Empowering Technology for Better Future, ICITEE 2016 (2017)
6. Wijaya, S.K., Badri, C., Misbach, J., Soemardi, T.P., Sutanno, V.: Electroenchephalography (EEG) for detecting acute ischemic stroke. In: 2015 4th International Conference on Instrumentation, Communications, Information Technology, and Biomedical Engineering Bandung, 2–3 November 2015, vol. 4, pp. 42–48 (2015)
7. Suman, B., Xiao-ning, Z., Tuerhong, T.: EEG and SPECT changes in acute ischemic stroke. J. Neurol. Neurophysiol. **5**, 190 (2014)
8. Finnigan, S., Wong, A., Read, S.: Defining abnormal slow EEG activity in acute ischaemic stroke: delta/alpha ratio as an optimal QEEG index. Clin. Neurophysiol. **127**, 1452–1459 (2016)
9. Yuvaraj, R., Murugappan, M., Sundaraj, K.: EEG dynamics in neurological disorders: Parkinson's disease and stroke. In: 2012 IEEE Student Conference on Research and Development, pp. 32–37 (2012)
10. Asyraf, H., Shapiai, M.I., Setiawan, N.A., Musa, W.S.N.W.: Masking covariance for common spatial pattern as feature extraction. J. Telecommun. Electron. Comput. Eng. **8**, 1–6 (2016)
11. Adam, A., Shapiai, M.I., Mohd Tumari, M.Z., Mohamad, M.S., Mubin, M.: Feature selection and classifier parameters estimation for EEG signals peak detection using particle swarm optimization. Sci. World J. **2014**, 1–13 (2014)

12. Molnár, M., Osman-Sági, J., Nagy, Z., Kenéz, J.: Scalp distribution of the dimensional complexity of the EEG and the P3 ERP component in stroke patients. Int. J. Psychophysiol. **34**, 53–63 (1999)
13. Barbancho, M.A., Berthier, M.L., Navas-Sánchez, P., Dávila, G., Green-Heredia, C., García-Alberca, J.M., Ruiz-Cruces, R., López-González, M.V., Dawid-Milner, M.S., Pulvermüller, F., Lara, J.P.: Bilateral brain reorganization with memantine and constraint-induced aphasia therapy in chronic post-stroke aphasia: an ERP study. Brain Lang. **145–146**, 1–10 (2015)
14. Friederici, A.D.: The brain basis of language processing: from structure to function. Physiol. Rev. **91**, 1357–1392 (2011)
15. Dressler, O., Schneider, G., Stockmanns, G., Kochs, E.F.: Awareness and the EEG power spectrum: analysis of frequencies. Br. J. Anaesth. **93**, 806–809 (2004)
16. Huang, N.E., Shen, Z., Long, S.R., Wu, M.C., Shih, H.H., Zheng, Q., Yen, N.-C., Tung, C. C., Liu, H.H.: The empirical mode decomposition and the Hilbert spectrum for nonlinear and non-stationary time series analysis. In: Proceedings of the Royal Society of London A: Mathematical, Physical and Engineering Sciences, pp. 903–995. The Royal Society (1998)
17. Omar, W.R.W., Taib, M.N., Jailani, R., Mohamad, Z., Jahidin, A.H., Sharif, Z.: Application of discriminant function analysis in ischemic stroke group level discrimination. In: Proceedings of 2014 IEEE 10th International Colloquium on Signal Processing and Its Applications, CSPA 2014, pp. 229–232 (2014)
18. van Putten, M.J.A.M.: The revised brain symmetry index. Clin. Neurophysiol. **118**, 2362–2367 (2007)
19. van Putten, M.J.A.M.: Extended BSI for continuous EEG monitoring in carotid endarterectomy. Clin. Neurophysiol. **117**, 2661–2666 (2006)
20. Van Putten, M.J.A.M., Tavy, D.L.J.: Continuous quantitative EEG monitoring in hemispheric stroke patients using the brain symmetry index. Stroke **35**, 2489–2492 (2004)
21. Van Putten, M.J.A.M., Kind, T., Visser, F., Lagerburg, V.: Detecting temporal lobe seizures from scalp EEG recordings: a comparison of various features. Clin. Neurophysiol. **116**, 2480–2489 (2005)
22. Yan, M., Hou, Z., Gao, Y.: A bilateral brain symmetry index for analysis of EEG signal in stroke patients. In: Proceedings of 2011 4th International Conference on Biomedical Engineering and Informatics, BMEI 2011, vol. 1, pp. 8–11 (2011)
23. Fu, K., Qu, J., Chai, Y., Zou, T.: Hilbert marginal spectrum analysis for automatic seizure detection in EEG signals. Biomed. Signal Process. Control **18**, 179–185 (2015)
24. Huang, N.E., Wu, Z.: A review on Hilbert-Huang transform: method and its applications to geophysical studies. Rev. Geophys. **46**, 1–23 (2008)
25. Pigorini, A., Casali, A.G., Casarotto, S., Ferrarelli, F., Baselli, G., Mariotti, M., Massimini, M., Rosanova, M.: Time-frequency spectral analysis of TMS-evoked EEG oscillations by means of Hilbert-Huang transform. J. Neurosci. Methods **198**, 236–245 (2011)
26. Stork, M.: Hilbert-Huang transform and its applications in engineering and biomedical signal analysis, pp. 188–195. Wseas.Us (2012)

Experimenting Patient Flow Using Computer Simulation

Rania Al-Ashwal$^{(\boxtimes)}$, Fatimah Al Zahra Binti Ayoep,
and Nashuha Binti Omar

Clinical Science Department, Faculty of Biosciences and Medical Engineering,
University of Technology, Malaysia, 81310 Skudai, Malaysia
rania@utm.my, fazahraayoep@gmail.com,
nashuhaomar@gmail.com

Abstract. The patient flow in the health centres is one of contributing factors to the dissatisfaction and delay in the delivery of healthcare service. This study aims to explore the pattern of dental patient flow in one centre and to solve the delay reason using computer simulation. Three different scenarios has been experimented using FlexSim 4.0 software to simulate the patient's flow. Three proposed solutions have been experimented, and the best-proposed scenario successfully improved three from seven observed variables: the patient throughput, fasten service in the dental clinic and the length of stay. The length of stay from real data and from simulation output has been compared. The explored times was the longest at registration area for receiving the service from receptionist. The finding shows that we can customise safe interventions without interfering with the operational system using the simulation software.

Keywords: Waiting times · Patient flow and FlexSim simulation

1 Introduction

The waiting time used to be the highest priority and most highlighted factor contributing to the patient's satisfactions [1–4]. The exact reasons for waiting time problem remain unclear and varied with different hospitals scales. Some researchers have identified prolonged waiting time determinant factors such as poor appointment scheduling, busier practice at the location, decision-making delay, insufficiency of patient's transportation and others [1, 5–9]. Rezaian *et al.* found that majority of UTM students were not satisfied with services in university health centre and long waiting time is one of the reasons in the outpatient clinic [10].

Computer simulation is beneficial in health care sector as it is an efficient approach to study the complex system. It is suitable for almost any analysis types to be performed and also every kind of performance measurement to be computed. Moreover, from previous studies, improvements in health care has been made with computer simulation applications such as reducing wait times, the workload of staffs, reduce delays in treatment and service performances enhancement [12–14]. Therefore, this study aims to observe the patient flow inside dental clinic and design simulation model

© Springer Nature Singapore Pte Ltd. 2017
M.S. Mohamed Ali et al. (Eds.): AsiaSim 2017, Part I, CCIS 751, pp. 561–569, 2017.
DOI: 10.1007/978-981-10-6463-0_48

for determining the waiting times during patient care process. This study also involved the experimentation on simulation model with creating different scenarios and checking the optimal scenario for better flow model.

2   Method

2.1   Study Design

This study has adopted observational study design for data collection. Prior permission has been obtained to conduct the study at the dental clinic during operation hours. The data has been modelled and experimented using FlexSim 3.0 software. The flow of dental care process has been constructed to study the actual process in reality. The constructed flow of dental care process output and performance of flow has been analyzed statistically. The following subsection further details the stages of the study.

Flow Mapping of Dental Care Process. In general, the flow that patient might have experienced are include (1) registration; (2) waiting que; (3) vital sign and examination by doctor; (4) treatment; (5) intra oral x-ray; (6) dispensary; (7) treatment; (8) payment; and lastly (9) departure. The AutoCAD drawing for the clinic has been obtained from the clinic and used for the software graphic constructions.

Various kinds of services has been observed by following on real time and record the steps as the patient's experience which found to variant with several pathways in the dental care process. The patient flow process map in dental was redrawn and presented according to the simple understanding of dental care process itself. Besides that, the number of resources such as staff and equipment used also observed, On the other hand, patient que numbers were used to mark the patient to avoid confusion and prevent data missing once patient leave without being noticed.

From the direct observations on dental care process, the time intervals at each location or activity were measured manually by using a digital watch and recorded into checklist form. The times at the moment of patient arrival at registration counter until their departure from the clinic also has been recorded as well as the processing periods of each activity.

The time unit is an essential element for simulation input data during data collection other than count on the type of data input collected [15]. This study required discrete data which is a positive integer value because of the time always measured in positive value. ExpertFit from FlexSim Healthcare software used for statistical distribution fitting.

Model Development. The collected information have been input to the model such as time patient arrivals, type of services provided by dental clinic and duration of the activities in operation process. Dental Clinic flow model was constructed based on the movement of patients during dental care procedures.

The raw data provided from observations were fitted by using Expert Fit in FlexSim HC software. The patient pathway has been designed under various patient track. Each track of patients has different processing times, the best fit model candidates were chosen by graphical comparison among mathematical models (Fig. 1).

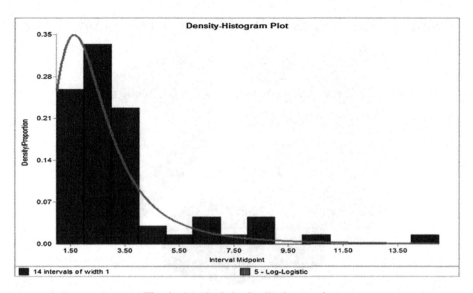

Fig. 1. Log-logistic distribution graph.

3   Results and Discussion

3.1   Observational Result

There are 160 patients observed for a total of 26 days follow-up. The patients classified into six groups according to the type of the procedure 'scaling, filling, intra-oral x-ray, abscess, dental check-up', and others minority numbers like tooth extraction or root canal treatment, and minor oral surgery as illustrated in the pie chart in Fig. 2.

3.2   Simulation Model

The constructed layout for the clinic has been simulated as shown in Fig. 3. This layout was useful to run the patient flow and check the waiting times from the output results of simulation model as well as the length of stay and patient throughput in the dental clinic.

The output results show the waiting times, the locations and activities that have waiting times were identified which is shown in Table 1.

The registration area has achieved the longest waiting times which is 7.59 min as the patients has to que with other patients who seek for the services other than dental service. This situation can be a result of the times patient spent in waiting for receptionist which is 6.38 min to complete serving the other patients. Other than that, patients also has faced waiting times while queueing to provide the medicine from the pharmacist (6.89 min) or servants as there are also que with other patients in healthcare centre. Meanwhile, waiting for being serviced at bill counter area in 5.59 min seems not uncommon situations; the patient has to que while settling their payment. However,

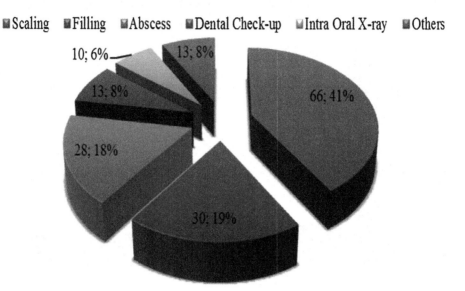

Fig. 2. Percentage of patient groups observed.

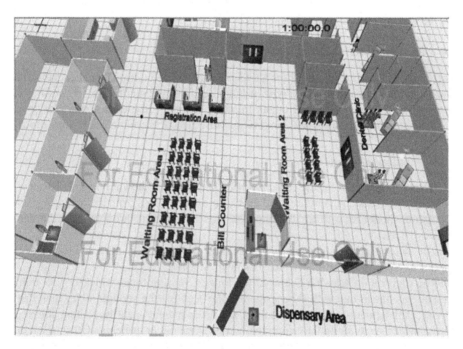

Fig. 3. Simulation model of health centre.

waiting times at bill counter might prolong their length of times to remain stayed in the healthcare centre. Moreover, patients spent 3.83 min for waiting in dental chair area before being serviced by the dental care provider.

Table 1. Waiting times in dental care process.

Objects	Waiting times (minutes)
Receptionist	6.38
Dentists	2.50
X-ray area	2.60
Bill counter area	5.59
Dental chair area	3.83
Dispensary counter area	6.89
Registration area	7.59

Furthermore, there is waiting time exists in x-ray (intra-oral) area which is 2.60 min where patients probably wait for staff or nurse makes preparation for an x-ray procedure. Lastly, the patient takes 2.50 min waiting for dentist service/task. Najmuddin *et al.* [4] has proposed the model of improvement that involves the changes number of input variables for the simulation model to evaluate whether the model can reduce waiting times and service time or not.

The suggested improvement was made based on the results of each scenario in this model [11]. For this study, the length of stay also recorded and considered since the most of the patient in healthcare centre are consists of students. Hence, simulation also is being used to measure the length of stay of the patient in dental care process as illustrated in Table 2.

Table 2. The length of stay in clinic.

Group	Length of stay (minutes)
PCI 1	59.85
PCI 2	37.26
PCI 3	25.01
PCI 4	28.61
PCI 5	28.23
PCI 6	44.86

3.3 Designing Different Scenarios in Simulation Model

An experiment was performed on the flow patterns to determine the response of the model on the changes in variables, resources allocated and how it is significant to the behaviour of system operation. The output results from experiments were presented in Fig. 4 to all scenarios. The resources in-charged for each experimented scenarios are:

(i) The actual scenario includes: 2 receptionists; 2 dentists; 3 dental nurses; 1 Cashier 1 pharmacist; 2 registration counter used; and 2 dental chair.
(ii) The experimental scenario 1: Add one receptionist, one dental nurse and one Registration counter used.
(iii) The experimental scenario 2: Add only one dentist.
(iv) The experimental scenario 3: Add one pharmacist and one dental chair used.

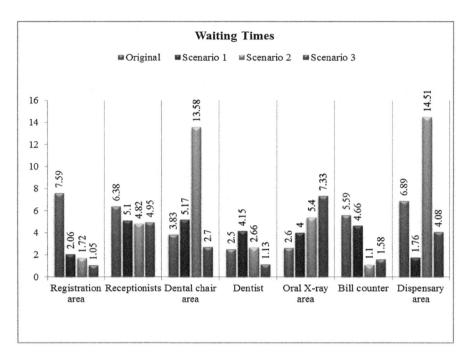

Fig. 4. Changes of waiting times corresponding to different scenarios.

Then, the optimised performance of dental services was evaluated with optimised scenario results which can be described based on which locations/activity have the positive impacts in waiting times; how many patients served by dental care are increased, and which patient group have the reducing length of stay in the clinic.

Figure 4 illustrates the significance of customised the staff allocation on process flow. The performance inside dental clinic is highly concerned when evaluating the scenarios and deciding the optimised model scenario. In scenario 1, a dentist, a dental nurse and one registration counter have been added. The effects on variables of the experiment in scenario one has resulted in reduced wait times at registration area, receptionists' task, bill counter and dispensary area. However, wait times in dental clinic has increased after experiments. Wait times for dentist rose to 4.15 min meanwhile wait times at dental chair rose to 5.17 min as well as wait times for oral x-ray is 4 min.

Overall, the operational performance in clinics were mainly concerned on times and number of patients. The observed patient flow is reflecting the need of health care service delivery to more resources. The effectiveness of performance of resources and patient flow can be measured with high patient throughput, prompt service from healthcare, low patient wait times as well as the length of stay in the clinic and also utilisation of staff [11, 16]. Hence, the performances for each scenario are evaluated by the number of patients served and also the length of stay in the clinic (Fig. 5).

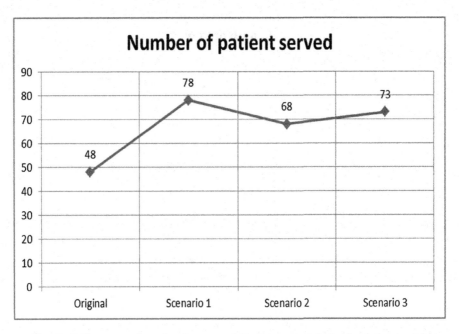

Fig. 5. Different number of patient served for every scenario in simulation model.

In Fig. 5, one more registration counter is open and available as well as the number of dentists and dental nurse and there is 78 patients has been served in the dental clinic in scenario one. The number of patients waiting for dental services increased and have the highest number of patient arrived at the dental clinic based on scenario one.

Meanwhile, scenario three has utilised the maximum capacity of resources where another two resources added which a staff for dispensary counter and a dental chair used. Even though the maximum capacity of resources was allocated, but there is the delay during an oral x-ray. The probability of patients seeking for oral x-ray increased as all dental chairs are fully utilised. So, the wait time for receiving is longer than that of original scenario. Still, the performance of operations also can be evaluated from the length of stay for each scenario as in Fig. 5.

Based on results in Fig. 6, patient group PCI 1 have experienced the longest length of stay than other patient groups because dental treatment process in this group of the patient might take much time besides they had to come at early in the morning to avoid other patients to wait.

In scenario 3, additional a pharmacist allocated and one dental chair used has given positive impacts on the length of stay among patient group PCI 2, PCI 4, PCI 5 and PCI 6 too. The duration of the stay of patient group PCI 2 was reduced to 31.36 min, save 5.90 min after edition of resources. In the meantime, the time for patient group PCI 4 stayed in clinic become shorter than original scenario, which is from 28.61 min reduced to 25.51 min. Another group is PCI 5 also has reduced the length of stay in the clinic to 20.74 min, which the least time. Meanwhile, the duration of residence among patient group PCI 6 reduced from 44.86 min to 36.86 min. The patient group PCI 1

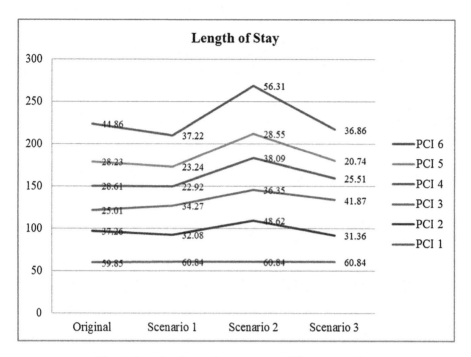

Fig. 6. Length of stay changes among different scenarios.

duration of residence has increased to slightly more than 1 h (60.84 min) while group PCI 3 has risen time for staying to 41.87 min. The output results of experiments show that scenario 1 and scenario 3 have improvements in waiting times, patient throughput, and length of stay.

Therefore, the waiting time has been improved in all type of patients groups by adding scenario three. This experiments that was conducted in desk without intervention to the real situation but the simulation actually based on the real situation collected data. The waiting time depends on the length of time of each activity in the entire process. We have been able to simulate and experiment new solutions and scenarios for the dental clinic under study in short time.

4   Conclusions

From this study, Improvement in resources shows improvement in time. We have been able to see and conclude that 3D simulation technique to analyse the patient flows and identified contribute to flow management in safe interventions without interfering in the real situation of the operational system could be achieved. It is recommended to follow this type of simulation as an effective Improvement tool. Moreover, pilot study to the suggested scenario is the second step and it should include investigating the perceptions of patient and their satisfactions on the dental services so that the solution to the problem becomes more concrete.

Acknowledgment. We appreciate the support by Ministry of higher education Malaysia MOHE transdisciplinary grant TRGS grant number 4L843.

References

1. Ho, E.T.L.: Improving waiting time and operational clinic flow in a tertiary diabetes center. BMJ Open Quality **2**(2) (2014). doi:10.1136/bmjquality.u201918.w1006
2. Wu, X.-D., Khasawneh, M.T., Yue, D.-M., Chu, Y.-N., Gao, Z.-T.: A simulation study of outpatient scheduling with multiple providers and a single device. Int. J. Compute. Intell. Syst. **7**(suppl. 2), 15–25 (2014)
3. Mielczarek, B., Uziałko-Mydlikowska, J.: Application of computer simulation modeling in the health care sector : a survey. Simul. Trans. Soc. Model. Simul. Int. **88**(2), 197–216 (2010)
4. Najmuddin, A.F., Ibrahim, I.M., Ismail, S.R.: A simulation approach: improving patient waiting time for multiphase patient flow of obstetrics and gynecology department (O&G Department) in local specialist center. WSEAS Trans. Math. **9**(10), 778–790 (2010)
5. Al-Ashwal, R.H., Supriyanto, E., Andriantoro, H.: Design standard in health care to follow or not? An insight from clinical pathway. Jurnal Teknologi. **78**(9), 161–167 (2016)
6. Jaakkimainen, L., Glazier, R., Barnsley, J., Salkeld, E., Lu, H., Tu, K.: Waiting to see the specialist: patient and provider characteristics of wait times from primary to specialty care. BMC Fam. Pract. **15**(1), 16 (2014)
7. Sreekala, P., Dan, A., Varghese, E.M.: Patient waiting time in emergency department. Int. J. Sci. Res. Publ. **5**(5), 8–10 (2015)
8. Green, J., Dawber, J., Masso, M., Eagar, K.: Emergency department waiting times: do the raw data tell the whole story? Aust. Heal. Rev. **28**, 65–69 (2014)
9. Chen, B.L., Li, E.D., Yamawuchi, K., Kato, K., Naganawa, S., Miao, W.J.: Impact of adjustment measures on reducing outpatient waiting time in a community hospital: application of a computer simulation. Chin. Med. J. (Engl) **123**(5), 574–580 (2010)
10. Rezaian, S., Selamat, H.: Patient satisfaction in a university health center: a malaysian study. J. Health Inform. Dev. Ctries. **8**(2), 104–114 (2014)
11. Bhattacharjee, P., Ray, P.K.: Patient flow modelling and performance analysis of healthcare delivery processes in hospitals: a review and reflections. Comput. Ind. Eng. **78**, 299–312 (2014)
12. Tako, A.A., Kotiadis, K., Vasilakis, C., Miras, A., Le Roux, C.W.: Improving patient waiting times: a simulation study of an obesity care service. BMJ Qual. Saf. **23**(5), 373–381 (2014)
13. Best, A.M., Dixon, C.A., Kelton, W.D., Lindsell, C.J., Ward, M.J.: Using discrete event computer simulation to improve patient flow in a Ghanaian acute care hospital. Am. J. Emerg. Med. **32**(8), 917–922 (2014)
14. Aboueljinane, L., Sahin, E., Jemai, Z., Marty, J.: A simulation study to improve the performance of an emergency medical service: application to the French Val-de-Marne department. Simul. Model. Pract. Theory **47**, 46–59 (2014)
15. Ungureanu, D., Sisak, F., Kristally, D.M., Moraru, S.: Simulation modeling. Input data collection and analysis (2005)
16. Koo, H., Nielsen, K.B., Jang, J., Kolker, A.: Simulation-based patient flow analysis in an endoscopy unit. In: 2010 IEEE Workshop on Health Care Management (WHCM), pp. 1–6 (2010)

Factors that Increase Web 2.0 Adopting Within an Enterprise Environment

Nada Hassan Sharafuddin[(✉)]

Asia Pacific of Technology and Innovation, Kuala Lumpur, Malaysia
nada.sharafuddin@gmail.com

Abstract. New forms of collaboration in business world have emerged with the developments of the recent technologies. The success of Web 2.0 usage encouraged business companies to adopt enterprise 2.0 technology. Enterprise 2.0 that use emergent social software platforms (ESSPs) have been adopted by companies around the world. However, although the huge advantages of this technology, the adoption of enterprise 2.0 process is regularly facing end-client resistance due to the lack of empirical evidence of how Enterprise 2.0 is supporting the business objectives. The purpose of this study is to highlight on how successful company like IBM use ESSPs to achieve collaborative efforts that lead to achieve the enterprises strategy goals. Theory of planned behavior has been picked to recount the operation of building awareness and trust to open and share experiences of sharing information and ideas through Enterprise 2.0 platforms. This theory has been applied on a case study that uses social network strategy within IBM Company. The results show that strategies of knowledge sharing, providing resources for instance time and effort, distributing trust, social influence and the use of technology are factors that increase the Enterprise 2.0 adoption in companies and it proof that collaborate, communicate and connection are the most important factors that should be achieved through Enterprise 2.0 to meet a business objectives.

Keywords: Web 2.0 · Enterprise 2.0 · ESSPs · Theory of planned behavior · Collaborative efforts · Knowledge share · Social software

1 Introduction

The quick development of the collaborative and Information Technology infrastructure has changed the communication method and strategies of communication in enterprises environment. The expression 'collaboration' inside the enterprise can be define as "a process whereby two or more individuals, groups or enterprises work together to achieve a common goal" [7]. Intelligent systems are employed in the information and knowledge gathering that are imperative to increase the collaborative and communication in enterprises. A good example of that is the web analytics that gets the market intelligence on a service that is sold in any place of the world [1]. To understand the concept of web 2.0 we should understand what the web 1.0 is first. Basically, web 1.0 is any static website which means "read-only web." In other words, it is any website that allowed users to search for information and read it only. No interaction or

© Springer Nature Singapore Pte Ltd. 2017
M.S. Mohamed Ali et al. (Eds.): AsiaSim 2017, Part I, CCIS 751, pp. 570–579, 2017.
DOI: 10.1007/978-981-10-6463-0_49

information interchanges in this type of technology. But the web 2.0 is a dynamic website which means "read and write web". It allows users to read and write comments. It can be saying there is a data exchange and there is more interaction in web 2.0 than web 1.0.

The use of web 2.0 technologies like wikis, mashups, blogs, and other social networks that its applications are designed in a manner that they merge various Web 2.0 innovations have made huge progressions in giving clients the tool which is needed for embrace and promote collaboration inside the enterprise. For more understanding of Web 2.0, there are few samples for each tool. Blogspot.com is based on blogs, Wikipedia is a good example of wikis, Twitter is social networking software, and YouTube is a social media. "Those Web 2.0 sites such as Facebook, MySpace, YouTube, Google, Wikipedia, blog, etc. are examples of emergent social software platforms (ESSPs)" [2]. ESSPs include wikis, social media, blogs, forums and social network software. It can be saying that web 2.0 is new strategy to knowledge management [3].

Using the technology of web 2.0 in the enterprise environment is known as "Enterprise 2.0". Enterprise 2.0 is community-based-user technology that supports collective intelligent which is cheaper, flexible and easier to apply. Enterprise 2.0 is a group based system; the more workers embrace it, the better the chance for this framework to success. McAfee defines Enterprise 2.0 as "the use of emergent social software platforms by organizations in pursuits of their goals" [2]. The term Enterprise 2.0 means using the Web 2.0 tools by enterprises [4]. However, both terms are different from each other. McAfee (2006), tried to distinguish the term enterprise 2.0 from web 2.0, he argues that Enterprise 2.0 is related only to companies' platforms that are bought or built to improve outputs of employee's knowledge [9]. According to Bidgoli, Professor Andrew McAfee describes Enterprise 2.0 as "the use of (ESSP) emergent social software platforms within enterprises, or between enterprises and their partners or customers" [5]. According to "the term 'Enterprise 2.0' is the utilization of Web 2.0 technologies inside the enterprise environment, to permit workers to team up, collaborate, communicate, share ideas and create content" [6]. Despite the different definitions, all of them have one meaning that is, Enterprise 2.0 main purposes is to improve employees' knowledge and to support them to share information to achieve collaboration which is required to company success.

According to Ducker and Payne, there are increases numbers of enterprises that are using this new technological development to make different in the way they handle data and carry out various transactions [8]. Enterprises are currently interested in the use of Web 2.0 primarily in two areas: within the enterprise to improve the operations and efficiency and outside the organization to the clients to improve revenue and the clients' satisfaction.

1.1 Problem Statement

Despite the huge number of Enterprise 2.0 benefits, some companies are still encountering significant difficulties that related to adopting the use of Enterprise 2.0 collaboration technologies in the enterprise section. The adoption of enterprise 2.0

process is regularly faced end-client resistance and this is resulting in a long adoption process. This low willingness to embrace the system among elder employees is because of the fear of cultural change [10] and the lack of empirical evidence of how Enterprise 2.0 is supporting the business objectives [11].

2 Conflicting Attitudes of Adopting Enterprise 2.0

Some researchers stated that using Enterprise 2.0 within enterprises offers many advantages by encouraging collaboration among suppliers, customers and employees. It is eventually adding more value towards enterprise-intellectual capital [12]. Furthermore, according to McAfee, the biggest advantage of Enterprise 2.0 is self-organization which means "the ability of users to build valuable communities and resources and shape them over time without having to rely on guidance from any center or headquarters" [2]. The unexpected high quantity of companies' embrace Web 2.0 was a proof to their perspective [13], this happens because it helps companies achieve unique collaborative environments [9]. Enterprise 2.0 technology adoption is increasing, especially for corporate issues [14, 15]. Social media can be considered as a revolutionary orientation for online business and communication. Tapscott believes that enterprise 2.0 can improve enterprises products and services and solve the big problems as well [16]. On the other hand, some researchers believe that there is lack of understanding about what can be gained from social network [17]. It is because there are some kinds of worries about the utilization of the Enterprise 2.0 inside the organization. Besides, it doesn't fit companies whose privacy is critical and data security is basic.

Furthermore, some organizations appear to be uncomfortable to embrace social media, because users can use it to speak freely among others. Patel stated that, the use of the technology can lead to the loss of productivity since the employees tend to waste lots of their time playing with the features of the social networks, instead of using the sites for the productive benefit [18]. It is also predicted that there may be some bias of adoption among different segments of age. The younger ones are more likely to become active on the social network platforms while older employees may be reluctant in the use of the computers since they show less enthusiasm for the computer [8]. The implementation of an enterprise 2.0 system has to take into account a balance between information openness and data protection into consideration. The Enterprise 2.0 is a defunct tool without data sharing. A balance should be addressed between being properly relaxing and being productive.

3 Research Methodology

Secondary data method has been chosen for this study. Studying the case of International Business Machines (IBM) due to its adopting of old platforms which is IBM Connection Lotus Notes that enterprise has designed for collaboration and knowledge sharing purposes. Achieving collaboration and knowledge sharing at IBM is not only an administrative purpose, IBM also provide collaboration and knowledge sharing to external clients by selling IT solutions as well.

International Business Machines or IBM is a multinational PCs corporation. IBM headquarter is in New York, US. IBM has a big history since the 19th century. The main product in IBM is offering hardware, software and frameworks services. IBM considered as one of the world's biggest PC organizations that has a big history, epically lately. It has over 400,000 workers around the world. IBM has over 34 million employees, speaking 165 languages across 75 countries and serving clients in 174 countries [19]. IBM is a globally integrated company and it provides some services regarding to the social networking to enhance lots of thing within the enterprise. For example, improving the way that employees search, helps employees to find answers for their problem with short time and effort, provide an expertize category for instant questions, and other office tools like the ability to share documents and templates that are required daily.

For IBM case the theory of planned behavior will be used because this theory has been used many times to explain people behavioral intentions toward technology.

According to Ajzen, theory of TPB is a theory that links beliefs and behavior [20]. The TPB explains the user perception that affects the behavior not only according to the behavior characteristics, but according to the user general attitude about the behavior, subjective norms and behavior control [21]. Thus, theory of planed behavior (TPB) can be used in this research to explore the adoption factors which are associated with user attitude toward using such technology, subjective norms and behavioral control of adopting enterprise 2.0.

4 Discussion

4.1 IBM Social Media Strategy

The policy at IBM is embracing and applying the social business within the company. The IBM manager for Lotus solutions, James Ek, thinks of social media as the future way to communicate. He also believes that, IBM strategy of adopting social business can be achieved by changing all company applications to be 'social'. According to James Ek, the more and quick use of information by many people in a valuable way is the way to the success. He also believes that, social awareness mixing with a great need of collaboration technology are making companies achieve more communicates internally and externally [22].

IBM now is aware that individuals are all more socially mindful today. But rather than utilizing social media for relaxation purpose, IBM effectively utilize it at the work place to improve profitability. Another accomplished issue through social media in the enterprises is achieving "Collaboration". Along these lines, the common motto among workers at IBM is: "When team IBM comes together, we are unbeatable" [22]. In order to gain and cultivating more collaboration inside IBM, they adopted the open information culture through their platform which calls "Connection". The Connection system is an open platform created for inward utilize at IBM. Now it is much easier to access to information and resources. IBM makes it possible by adopting social network throughout the enterprise. According to Zaffar and Ghazawneh, James EK states that: "Social media flattens the organization and facilitates access to the right information and resources" [22]. The company empowers the workers to share their information with everybody. With social media, IBM makes progress toward an all-inclusive incorporated organization, one which expands the capacity of outreach of its workers. That is why the IBM's CEO decided to create important tools to support collaboration. They were success to design and create the tools that they dream about to achieve collaboration within the enterprise. This tool calls IBM Lotus Connections. The purpose of it is to build a strong network for all IBMers generation to collaborate social computing inside or outside the organization.

4.2   IBM Connections Platform

A set of ESSP's (the emerging social software platforms) has been coordinated and merged to create one site with Social Networking pattern named IBM Connections. It is a Web 2.0 enterprise social software platform created by IBM to offer online social networking tools for employees who are associated with the company. IBM connections incorporate a wide range of various platforms over the company. This system is created to enable smoothly integration with the current frameworks at the company. In a commonplace internet framework, the chiefs and IT managers choose which data can be accessed; they also choose the person who is able to access them, and what time they can access. In contrast, IBM Connections gives clients opportunity to choose the type of information they want to share, whom to share it with and how to share with them. IBM Connections main purpose is to create collaboration and knowledge sharing inside the organization. Seven categories are forming the IBM's Connections services: profiles, communities, blogs, bookmarks, activities, files, and wikis [23].

4.3   Theories Related to the Adopting of Enterprise 2.0

Investigating the user intention to adopt Enterprise 2.0 and its tools like wiki, blogs, social networking websites and bookmarking is a big concern not only in industrial environment but in academia as well. Hester and Scott reviewed the adoption theories as well as Web 2.0 tools and develop a conceptual theory/model for Wiki diffusion [24]. They come up with some possible wiki adoption factors includes relative advantage, critical mass, complexity, organizational culture and organizational compatibility.

A conceptual model has been built by Chiu et al. based on the theory of Reasoned Action to proof that, Technology Acceptance components which are perceived usefulness, perceived ease of use are required for user acceptance and participation towards Enterprise 2.0 to be successful [25]. Theories like Social Exchange Theory [26], leadership and behavioral science, assumption from perceived organizational support theory [27], Time frame adopted, Culture of sharing information and ideas adopted [28] and many other theories are used to recount the operation of building awareness and trust to open and share experiences of sharing information and ideas through Enterprise 2.0 platforms. In addition, Louw and Mtsweni argued that, top administration should support users to switch towards using Enterprise 2.0 collaboration technologies through applying motivation, communication, training and support [10]. And that is all cannot be achieved through using models like, Technology Acceptance Model, Value-added model and diffusion of innovations theory. Instead, they suggested a four critical adoption factors which is going to form part of any Enterprise 2.0 collaboration technology adoption strategy. According to them, these factors can be concluded as following: the adoption strategy of the enterprise, alignment, communication, governance, and training and support.

Some researchers see another element based on Louw and Mtswen elements. They believe that applying TPB theory on studies can fit the Enterprise 2.0 environment and web in general. This theory states that attitude toward behavior, subjective norms, and perceived behavioral control, together shape an individual's behavioral intentions and behaviors. Theory of Planned Behavior has been used lately by many researchers for many web purposes. Liaw has a research in the impact of behavioral intentions in using search engines as a learning tool; he applied the TPB on his study [29]. Studying the purchaser studies using the TPB is winning power among the researches of behavior toward digital technologies. Another researcher as Goby used TPB on his study that is regarding to online purchasing [30], Hsu and Chiu studied electronic service continuance by using a disintegrated version of the TPB [31]. Hsu et al. (2006) tried to study the expectation of the people's behavior toward online shopping using the TPB model [25]. This theory is much flexible than others. Some studies have changed the TPB to particular settings. For example, Consumers' acceptance of broadband web [32] or bases of social impacts in online environments [37]. It can be saying that, in this theory, the more positive that subjective standard is, the more excellent the perceived control, the stronger ought the person's intention to perform the behavior in question [33].

4.4   TPB Theory and IBM Strategies

There are some strategies that IBM uses to increase the Enterprise 2.0 adoption. This study is highlighting on the method that IBM followed based on TPB theory variables as following:

4.4.1   Attitude to Behaviour (Behavioural Beliefs)

– Knowledge sharing

It refers to the action of exchanging ideas, thoughts and information among individuals [25]. Knowledge must be shared among co-workers, group team, it is because companies face difficulties with knowledge loss that happen when a particular employee leaves the company [34]. Employees' willingness to share in IBM is a determent for the success adoption of enterprise 2.0. Through the IBM Connection system, users can quickly locate people, content, expertise and activate the workforce.

Knowledge share can be also from outside to inside the company because through this system, it can be learned what customers are thinking about by gaining customer insights. Moreover, enabling a wider knowledge reach to build a smarter workforce to the employees. IBM doesn't want its employees to waste their time searching for information and knowledge. Wiki option that IBM provides through its system is a good tool for such thing.

– Resources for instance time and effort

Employees voluntarily participate and share their knowledge. All applications on IBM platform are accurately linked together to facilities the process of finding right resources in less time and efforts. IBM BluePages is an employee directory that makes employees find each other easily by allowing people to search for other employees based on their areas of expertise. Finding expertise for employees' questions is the vital purpose for IBM Connections. Not only this but providing category for specific problems makes it much easier for employees and it saves their time and effort as well. Moreover, IBM Connection is available globally because the platform is fully integrated in the web and can be accessed through the Internet from any point around the world. And this is a really good sign for its success.

4.4.2 Subjective Norm

– Trust

It could be defined as "The subjective assessment of one party that another party will perform a particular transaction according to his or her confident expectations, in an environment characterized by uncertainty." [35]. In the context of this study, trust includes trust the quality of the content generated, trust employees to recognize each other contributions and trust others so they can share their own knowledge. Moreover, Trust leads to more openness. Adopting openness policy at IBM through its globally platform means to be transparent company which are permeable to external ideas.

– Social influence

Since the social related to relationship, not to personal thing, IBM create its policy to provide financial reward to the employee to share information. In another word, IBM provide social motivation to encourage connect workers with their colleges for socializing or work purpose. To be digitally linked to a diverse and huge number of social contacts through participation in different virtual group activities, support the concept of the social influence on IBM social network. IBM provides many tools to make the social influence support the employee especially the elder to be more active. IBM's Beehive Social Network gives IBM'ers a rich connection to the people they work with wither they are professionally or personally. Using this platform, workers can create new connections, track exist co- workers, and re-contact with individuals they have worked with them before.

4.4.3   Perceived Behavioural Control

– Technology

There are some technological characteristics which have an impact on employees to accept enterprise 2.0 in IBM. These characterizes might be general attributes for any technology like ease of use and trainability. Moreover, because IBM enterprise 2.0 technologies have no access costs for users, youth generation of 17–33 years old adopted this technology faster than others (Fig. 1).

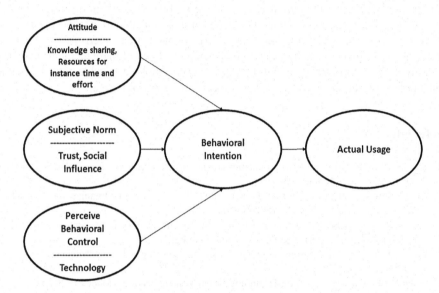

Fig. 1. Theory of planned behavior [21] mixing with IBM strategies.

5   Conclusion

IBM has been aggressively using social media to tie its far-flung and enormous workforce together and also with a mind towards selling these technologies as part of its service offering. IBM Company is reliant on a great enterprise 2.0 adoption. For Enterprise 2.0 successful, it is a crucial thing that employees accept it. Applying the TPB theory to measure the acceptance of enterprise 2.0 at IBM showed how IBM succeeded to encourage its employees to adopt it and it shows much benefits companies can get when adopting it. By adopting Enterprise 2.0 in an enterprise, end-users are able to establish community networks inside and outside the enterprise environment, thereby enabling end-users to establish relationships with customers, suppliers and partners [36]. Furthermore, Enterprise 2.0 should not only be viewed from a technology perspective, but also from a people perspective.

As explained earlier, Enterprise 2.0 is the use of the technology web 2.0 inside the enterprise and the key role of these tools is to support knowledge management enterprise 2.0, facilitates the sharing of the employees in the company, sharing knowledge and ideas in a collaborative manner. In other words, the benefits of Enterprise 2.0 are conditioned by the user's acceptance and adoption. The adoption of this technology may be affected by several factors. Thus, a case study of IBM using Enterprise 2.0 as a business strategy has been reviewed. The results show that IBM strategies like knowledge sharing, providing resources for instance time and effort, trust, social influence and the use of technology are factors that increase the Enterprise 2.0 adoption in companies.

Enterprise 2.0 technology works with various resources to improve three over-lapping informal organization skills which are: Collaboration (which means, gathering of individuals working mutually towards solving problems), Communication (which is exchanging of data through existing contacts that have social pattern) And Connection (which is creating a new relationship and links inside the enterprise or between enterprise's employees and the external environment). Each of these elements does not work by itself. It can be saying that, Enterprise 2.0 is employees inside enterprises that collaborate, communicate and connect to meet a business objective.

References

1. Stobbe, A.: Enterprise 2.0: how companies are tapping into the benefits of web 2.0. Deutsche Bank Research, September 2010
2. McAfee, A.: Enterprise 2.0: New Collaborative Tools for Your Organization's Toughest Challenges. Harvard Business Press, Boston (2009)
3. Keyes, J.: Knowledge Management, Business Intelligence, and Content Management: the IT Practitioner's Guide. Taylor & Francis Group, Abingdon (2006)
4. Levy, M.: WEB 2.0 implications on knowledge management. J. Knowl. Manag. 13(1), 120–134 (2009)
5. Bidgoli, H.: The Handbook of Technology Management. Wiley, Hoboken (2010)
6. Ramirez-Medina, J.A.: Enterprise 2.0 readiness index. In: Portland International Conference on Management of Engineering & Technology, PICMET 2009. IEEE, pp. 2677–2684 (2009)
7. Turban, E., Liang, T.P., Wu, S.P.: A framework for adopting collaboration 2.0 tools for virtual group decision making. Group Decis. Negot. 20(2), 137–154 (2011)
8. Ducker, M., Payne, J.: Information communication technology as a catalyst to enterprise competitiveness. Business Growth Initiative (2010)
9. McAfee, A.: Enterprise 2.0: the dawn of emergent collaboration. MIT Sloan Manag. Rev. 47(3), 22–28 (2006)
10. Louw, R., Mtsweni, J.: The quest towards a winning Enterprise 2.0 collaboration technology adoption strategy. Int. J. Adv. Comput. Sci. Appl. (IJACSA) 4(6) (2013)
11. Wong, D., Bosua, R., Chang, S., Kurnia, S.: Exploring the use of enterprise 2.0 and its impact on social capital within a large organisation (2016). arXiv preprint arXiv:1606.02486
12. Bruno, A., Marra, P., Mangia, L.: The enterprise 2.0 adoption process: a participatory design approach. In: 2011 13th International Conference on Advanced Communication Technology (ICACT), Proceedings , pp. 1457–1461. IEEE (2011)
13. Libert, B., Spector, J.: We Are Smarter Than Me. Wharton School Publishing, New Jersey (2008)
14. Grossman, M., McCarthy, R.: Web 2.0: is the enterprise ready for the adventure. Issues Inf. Syst. VIII(2), 180–185 (2007)

15. Hideo, S., Shinichi, K.: KM 2.0: business knowledge sharing in the web 2.0 age. NEC Tech. J. **2**(2), 50–54 (2007)
16. Tapscott, D.: Grown Up Digital: How the Net Generation is Changing Your World. McGraw-Hill Professional, New York (2008)
17. Kaplan, A.M., Haenlein, M.: Users of the world, unite! the challenges and opportunities of social media. Bus. Horiz. **53**(1), 59–68 (2010)
18. Patel, M.: The Roles of IS-IT in Transforming Enterprises: With the use of the Web, E-commerce & Mobile Applications. GRIN Verlag, Munich (2012)
19. Philip, T.: Enterprise 2.0 Adoption in Italian Companies: Analysis of the Maturity Level. Ph. D. diss., polo regionale di como, 2009/2010. politecnico di Milano: department of management, economics and industrial engineering (2010)
20. Ajzen, I.: From intentions to actions: a theory of planned behavior. In: Kuhl, J., Beckmann, J. (eds.) Action Control. SSSP Springer Series in Social Psychology. Springer, Heidelberg (1985). doi:10.1007/978-3-642-69746-3_2
21. Ajzen, I.: The theory of planned behavior. Organ. Behav. Hum. Decis. Process. **50**, 179–211 (1991)
22. Zaffar, F., Ghazawneh, A.: Objectified knowledge through social media. Int. J. Inf. Commun. Technol. Hum. Devel. **5**(3), 1–17 (2013)
23. Zaffar, F., Ghazawneh, A.: Enterprise 2.0: Knowledge -sharing and collaboration through emergent social software platforms (ESSP) (The case of IBM). Jonkoping University Business School, p. 2 (2011)
24. Hester, A.J., Scott, J.E.: A conceptual model of Wiki technology diffusion. In: Proceedings of the 41st Annual Hawaii International Conference on System Sciences (HICSS 2008) (2008)
25. Chiu, C.M., Hsu, M.H., Wang, E.T.G.: Understanding knowledge sharing in virtual communities: an integration of social capital and social cognitive theories. Decis. Support Syst. **42**, 1872–1888 (2006)
26. Forsyth, D.R.: Group Dynamics. Cengage Learning, Boston (2009). (Fifth edit., p. 680)
27. Eisenberger, R., Huntington, R., Hutchison, S., Sowa, D.: Perceived organizational support. J. Appl. Psychol. **71**(3), 500–507 (1986)
28. Ruppel, C., Harrington, S.: Sharing knowledge through intranets: A study of organizational culture and intranet implementation. IEEE Trans. Prof. Commun. **44**(1), 37–52 (2001)
29. Liaw, S.: The theory of planned behaviour applied to search engines as a learning tool. J. Comput. Assist. Learn. **20**, 283–291 (2004)
30. Goby, V.P.: Online purchases in an infocomm sophisticated society. Cyber Psychology Behav. **9**, 423–431 (2006)
31. Hsu, M.H., Yen, C.H., Chiu, C.M., Chang, C.M.: A longitudinal investigation of continued online shopping behavior: an extension of the theory of planned behavior. Int. J. Hum. Comput. Stud. **64**(9), 889–904 (2006)
32. Oh, S., Ahn, J., Kim, B.: Adoption of broadband Internet in Korea: The role of experience in building attitudes. J. Inf. Technol. **18**(4), 267–280 (2003)
33. Gollwitzer, P.M.: Implementation intentions: Strong effects of simple plans. Am. Psychol. **54**, 493–503 (1999)
34. Sharafuddin, N.: The role of knowledge management in achieving sustainable competitive advantage in business. J. Educ. Soc. Sci. **6**(2), 137–142 (2017)
35. Ba, S., Pavlou, P.A.: Evidence of the effect of trust building technology in electronic markets: price premiums and buyer behavior. MIS Q. **26**, 243–268 (2002)
36. Christidis, K., Mentzas, G., Apostolou, D.: Supercharging enterprise 2.0. IT Prof. **13**(4), 29–35 (2011)
37. Bagozzi, R.P., Dholakia, U.M., Mookerjee, A.: Individual and group bases of social influence in online environments. Media Psychol. **8**, 95–126 (2006)

Modelling of Application-Centric IoT Solution for Guard Touring Communication Network

Amirul Hazeim Faizul, Rozeha A. Rashid[(✉)],
Abdul Hadi Fikri Abdul Hamid, Mohd Adib Sarijari, Alias Mohd,
and Ahmad Shahidan Abdullah

Department of Telecommunication Engineering,
Faculty of Electrical Engineering, Universiti Teknologi Malaysia,
Skudai, Johor Darul Takzim, Malaysia
hazeimfaizul@gmail.com, hadifikri@gmail.com,
{rozeha,madib,aliasmohd,ashahidan}@utm.my

Abstract. Internet of Things (IoT) enables advance digital services by utilizing data acquisition and controlling device remotely across wireless network infrastructure. It is a primary catalyst for an increasing numbers of application in the fields of cyber-physical systems. In this project, an IoT based guard touring system is proposed. A traditional guard touring system devices lacks the abilities to provide a real-time data acquisition, integration of security related functionalities, summoning features and also a low cost to benefit ratio. Therefore, the proposed IoT based guard touring system provides a solution to the existing systems' pitfalls at a cost effective price. The system consists of an Android based application for real-time interaction and also an admin monitoring webpage for communication management. The proposed system provides the smart connection and data to information conversion that could be used easily for data mining and subsequent data cognition process.

Keywords: Internet of Things (IoT) · Near Field Communication (NFC) · Graphical User Interface (GUI) · Guard Touring System (GTS) · MQ Telemetry Transport (MQTT) and Radio Frequency Identification (RFID)

1 Introduction

The state of the art of Internet of Things (IoT) is already evolving traditional devices that used to operate in silos without any connectivity into smart devices that are connected on a world-wide network. IoT is a network of physical objects that can interact with each other to share information and make a decision. Furthermore, IoT based devices have network connectivity, allowing them to collect and transmit data. Utilization of mobile information and communication technologies in home monitoring applications is becoming more and more common [1].

The conventional guard touring system require more man power, error prone and extra time to organize the collected information. Other than that, the price for conventional guard touring system device is too expensive. Furthermore, manually updating and extracting information from the collected data is inefficient due the

© Springer Nature Singapore Pte Ltd. 2017
M.S. Mohamed Ali et al. (Eds.): AsiaSim 2017, Part I, CCIS 751, pp. 580–590, 2017.
DOI: 10.1007/978-981-10-6463-0_50

amount of data being generated daily [2]. The main objectives of the proposed smart Guard Touring System (GTS) are to develop a model of application-centric IoT solution for guard touring communication network that provides audio and image communication, integrated database management equipped with GPS technology as well as an integrated database using cloud services.

The proposed system performance will be investigated in terms of latency and accuracy utilizing NFC technology embedded in the smartphone as the medium for collecting patrol data. An android based application software will be designed together with a web application software for human interaction. The system performance will be investigated in term of network delay tolerance and precision of accuracy to guarantee it is within acceptable time limit and distance limit. This paper is organized as follows. In Sect. 2, the project background which include the related works are discussed. Subsequently in Sect. 3, the proposed architecture for the IoT based GTS is introduced. Section 4 presents the results and discussion. Finally the conclusion is drawn in the last section.

2 System Background

In this section, the review on related works that form the basis of the proposed system as well as the fundamental system modules are given.

2.1 Related Works

Related research works on a GTS based on IoT technology and the cellular networking system are presented. These works form the basis of the proposed system design. The author in [6] highlighted that mobile technology has grown rapidly for the past centuries. Network planning and optimization has been the central focus in this paper. However, when there are multiple calls or activities regarding the carrier network occur simultaneously, it will overload the network thus leading to the failure of the system [6].

Research works on the usage of smartphones as gateways has brought some challenges due to the lack of continuous network connectivity [7]. This issue is presented in several projects involving delay tolerant networking where the tradeoffs of delay tolerant networks in energy, latency, and storage while improving technology are addressed [7].

GPS tracking system proposed in [8] uses a technique known as differential GPS (DGPS) which claimed the accuracy of GPS tracking could be improved greatly. It requires operating a GPS receiver around familiar location. The receiver is used to compute satellite pseudo range correction data using stored knowledge of the correct satellite pseudo ranges, which is then broadcasted to users around the same geographic area. The pseudo range corrections are integrated into the navigation solution of another GPS receiver to correct the observed satellite pseudo range measurements, thereby improving the accuracy of the position determination [8].

IoT based Smart uses a NFC reader to obtain the identification of the guards and WiFi Access Point which utilizes IoT technology to upload the collected data to the cloud database. However, the usage of a standalone custom device is rather high in cost in comparison to its limited functionalities [9]. IoT based Home Intercom System in [10] proposed IoT based home intercom system with notification and video which is developed to provide a solution for issues of remote home and home security by identifying people at the front door via a smart phone. The communication protocols used in the proposed system provides a basis for GTS communication protocols, however, the GUI lacks features and there are no server and database involved [10].

The work in [11] developed and implemented tracking application on a smartphone and establishes M2M communication between GPS transceiver and server over 3G network and HTTP protocol. However, the interface is not user friendly, and does not provide a panic state function as well as lack of real-time data update. Another location tracking application for cyclist based on Android application implemented a similar architecture [12]. In this system, wireless sensor nodes are assigned to collect the required data such as cyclist's heart rate and cadence. However, the system lacks server's GUI webpage that could ease the data storage and monitoring via website.

2.2   Guard Touring System

GTS optimizes the security of target sites or patrol route coverage which are managed by an admin or officer that analyzes and makes a decision based on the collected data in real-time. The management software is responsible for capturing all the data generated by patrol guards on a daily basis. It is used to ensure that the guards perform their daily touring routine and records are uploaded real time and kept as evidence.

2.3   Near Field Communication (NFC) Technology

Near Field Communication (NFC) is a short-range wireless communication protocols which are adapted from Radio Frequency Identification (RFID) technology [3]. It uses ISO 14443 standard where the operating frequency is 13.56 MHz. It works in a similar manner with RFID technology with the exception of a shorter range of approximately 10 cm. Reader/writer mode allows NFC tags information to be read or write into the tags embedded memory chips. This technology is adopted into this project due to its wide spread availability in the smartphones models as well as its inherent security features. Figure 1 shows the components of NFC technology framework.

The NFC tags are used at checkpoints where a smartphones equipped with NFC readers carried by a patrol guards would log the checkpoints and uploaded into the cloud service in real-time.

2.4   Java Integrated Development Environment (IDE)

An IDE is basically a programming environment that has been integrated as an application programming software, typically consisting of a code editor, compiler, debugger, and graphical user interface (GUI) builder. This Java-based framework is made up of two components: The Android SDK Platform, a runtime library that provides the basic IDE elements such as an application's data presentation, configuration, and template

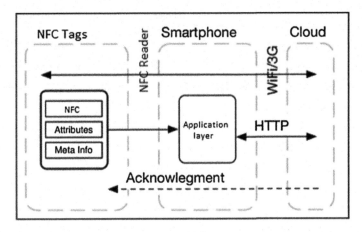

Fig. 1. NFC framework.

coding that are mainstream to be used by users or programmers and user interface; and the IDE itself, which provides controls, such as editing and version control, for the platform's functionality [4]. The Android development architecture are tailored for ease of use and rapid application development [5].

2.5   Mobile Network

Mobile network operator plays a huge role in this project where nearly 80% of the functionalities of this project depends on the network carrier. This is because this project requires functionalities such as sending text messages, notification in terms of email and location tracking that require internet connection that is provided by the mobile carrier in addition to the basic function such as making and receiving a phone call. The critical aspect of these functionalities such as delay, coverage and signal strength are highly dependent on service provider quality of service.

2.6   Cloud Services and Communication Networking

Cloud services are the central service station where the data collected are stored and processed as well as responding to end user queries. An advance data analytics service could also be deployed in the cloud to perform data mining and cognition service. For example, a patrol touring pattern could be discovered and optimized in maximizing the efficiencies of patrol routes. The communication network allows the smart devices as well as the end users to push and pull data from the cloud services. Socket.io and REST protocols are used to facilitate these communications. In particular, socket.io allows a stateful connection between a client and server and where the data can be push and pull asynchronously. For example, a notification service requires a stateful connection for a real-time response while login and non-critical data updates are more suitable for REST protocols. Figure 2 shows the network model used in the proposed GTS.

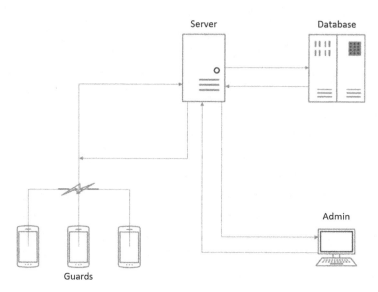

Fig. 2. Data transition on cloud structure.

3 System Architecture

This section discusses in detail about the system architecture in design and development of the IoT based GTS and an Android-based application. The methodology includes the overall system and the programming flowchart.

3.1 Methodology

The proposed GTS will be used by the guard or employee and it is connected to the internet via GSM/3G/4G network from the smartphone. It also can be connected via Wi-Fi network as an alternative to send and receive data.

In this system, the embedded NFC reader in the smartphone acts as the sensor, while the web application serves as the end-users interface. The data collected by the NFC reader then will be uploaded to cloud services through the internet to be retrieved by the admin on the management side.

3.2 System Flowchart

Figure 3 shows the flowchart of the developed Android application.

As shown in Fig. 3, the user of the smart phone (in this case, the guard) needs to log into the system using a username, password and tapping the NFC embedded authorized card to the phone. From the application home page, the user may start his or her tour by tapping the back of the phone at the designated checkpoints. Other functions include, making/receiving a phone call, sending a text messages, issuing summons, view patrol log map, log in a report as well as activating panic button in case of emergency.

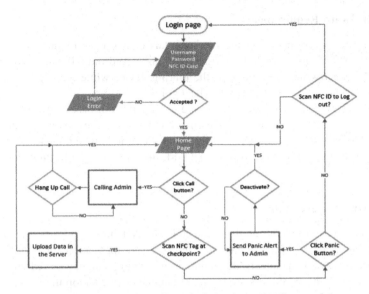

Fig. 3. Flowchart of the NFC reading, panic button and call part of the system.

Figure 4 shows the details of each functionality work flow.

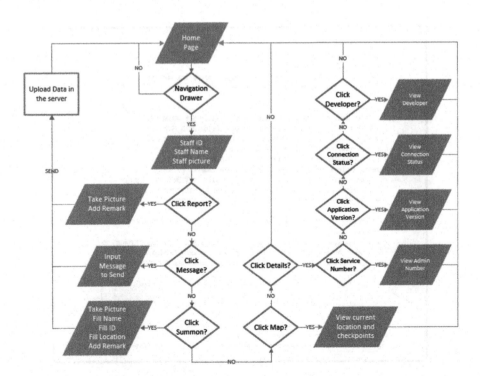

Fig. 4. Flowchart of the report, summons, message and map part of the system.

3.3   Hardware Requirements

The hardware requirements are the fundamentals components required to implement the proposed GTS. In general, a smartphone running Android 6.0 and above equipped with NFC reader/writer is required as the touring device while NFC tags with unique serial number are used on the touring checkpoints.

The NFC tags have to be weathered and tampered proof based on the location it is being deployed. The smartphone on the other hand also requires a sturdy casing as well as tempered proof applications, specifically on user identification/authentication. In addition, a reliable and wide coverage network must be selected to prevent data from being dropped.

3.4   Software Development

The software development for this project is divided into two parts which are the development of the Android application and the web application for monitoring and management. Java language is the main programming language used for Android application while html and .css are the main languages to develop the web application frontend together with Twitter Bootstrap framework.

Android Studio is the official IDE for Android Apps platform development. Android Studio includes ubiquitous tools that are needed to build an app, such as a code editor, code analysis tools emulators, quick debugging and more. There are three

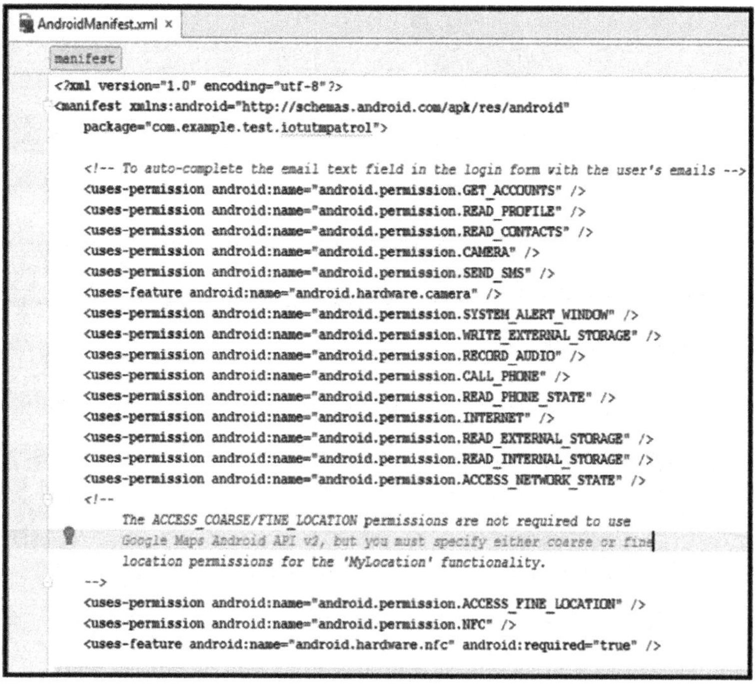

```
AndroidManifest.xml ×

manifest

<?xml version="1.0" encoding="utf-8"?>
<manifest xmlns:android="http://schemas.android.com/apk/res/android"
    package="com.example.test.iotutmpatrol">

    <!-- To auto-complete the email text field in the login form with the user's emails -->
    <uses-permission android:name="android.permission.GET_ACCOUNTS" />
    <uses-permission android:name="android.permission.READ_PROFILE" />
    <uses-permission android:name="android.permission.READ_CONTACTS" />
    <uses-permission android:name="android.permission.CAMERA" />
    <uses-permission android:name="android.permission.SEND_SMS" />
    <uses-feature android:name="android.hardware.camera" />
    <uses-permission android:name="android.permission.SYSTEM_ALERT_WINDOW" />
    <uses-permission android:name="android.permission.WRITE_EXTERNAL_STORAGE" />
    <uses-permission android:name="android.permission.RECORD_AUDIO" />
    <uses-permission android:name="android.permission.CALL_PHONE" />
    <uses-permission android:name="android.permission.READ_PHONE_STATE" />
    <uses-permission android:name="android.permission.INTERNET" />
    <uses-permission android:name="android.permission.READ_EXTERNAL_STORAGE" />
    <uses-permission android:name="android.permission.READ_INTERNAL_STORAGE" />
    <uses-permission android:name="android.permission.ACCESS_NETWORK_STATE" />
    <!--
        The ACCESS_COARSE/FINE_LOCATION permissions are not required to use
        Google Maps Android API v2, but you must specify either coarse or fine
        location permissions for the 'MyLocation' functionality.
    -->
    <uses-permission android:name="android.permission.ACCESS_FINE_LOCATION" />
    <uses-permission android:name="android.permission.NFC" />
    <uses-feature android:name="android.hardware.nfc" android:required="true" />
```

Fig. 5. Android manifest coding for app's permission.

parts in Android Studio that need to be programmed to create and design the application interface which are java part to configure the function, xml part to configure GUI and android manifest to configure permission for the android system within the smartphone. Figure 5 shows the list of permissions required for the GTS application.

Figure 6 shows the snapshot of frontend development using HTML5 and Twitter Bootstrap framework.

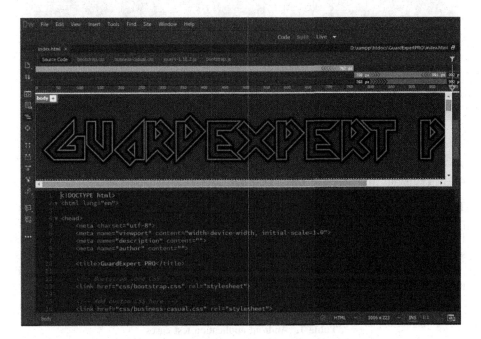

Fig. 6. HTML coding for web page.

These two applications communicate via a cloud service that is developed using PHP and node.js framework where MySQL database is used to store the data. A set of Application Programming Iinterfaces (APIs) was developed on the cloud service to facilitate the functionalities of GTS.

4 Result and Discussion

This chapter presents the results achieved from the trial run of the developed system. Additionally, an analysis is made on the data collected to investigate the factors that influence the communication delay. Figure 7 shows the login page of the web application on the end-user side.

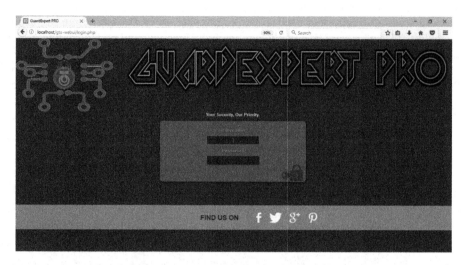

Fig. 7. Login page of the web application hosted on cloud service.

4.1 Transmit and Receive Data Testing

There are four activities that will be tested, which are test cases, pre-condition, post-condition and result. Test cases are the activity for each function being tested. Pre-condition column is for the condition before the test was conducted and the result is stated in the post-condition column. The result column is to state whether the test cases pass or fail. Table 1 below shows the test cases on the Android App of the guard touring system.

Table 1. Android application test cases.

No	Test case	Pre-condition	Post-condition	Result
1	Panic button	Home page	Sends panic alert to admin number	Pass
2	Call button	Home page	Direct calling admin number	Pass
3	Camera	Navigation drawer	Sends e-mail of the image reporting to admin	Pass
4	Summons	Navigation drawer	Sends summons details to admin number	Pass
5	Messaging admin	Settings	Sends informing message to admin number	Pass
6	Map	Navigation drawer	Views on the checkpoint within pre setup map	Pass

Figure 8 shows the results of activated Panic state as well as the patrol log marked on the map.

On the left is the Android application interface showing the activated panic state while the middle screen display shows the notification received on the administrator's

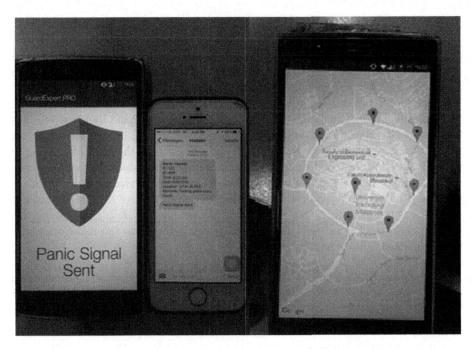

Fig. 8. Transmitting and receiving panic signal and marker location on map in the application.

phone. The notification also include the location of the device that generate the signals. On the right is the snapshot of patrol log of the current tour.

4.2 Network Delay

As for the latency test that have been conducted, on average the result for the delay are tolerable as it has five second of maximum delay in receiving data after transmitting it via cellular network. Figure 9 below shows the result for latency test between two network carriers which are Digi and U-mobile throughout several locations within UTM compound.

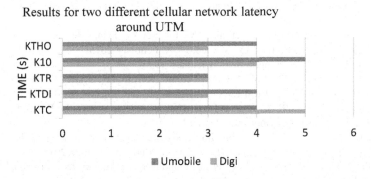

Fig. 9. Comparison of network latency between two cellular operators within UTM campus.

5 Conclusion

IoT is the key enabling technology for the next generation of digital services composed of billions of connected smart devices. The aim of the proposed system is to transform a conventional GTS into internet-connected system that enables ubiquitous and wireless deployment, uploads data real time and provides a cloud based platform where the data can be mined and analyzed. The system eases the guards' patrolling activities just by using the developed apps on their smartphones anywhere and anytime without the hassle of carrying extra device with them. In order to establish the connection between the GTS apps and the cloud-based database management or administrative personnel, IoT technology in the form of internet connection from service provider or Wi-Fi network is utilized to provide real-time communication protocol to send and receive data as it is designed for a two-way communication system. It is foreseen that the proposed IoT based smart GTS can provide a promising solution to the existing systems' pitfalls at a low cost to benefit ratio.

Acknowledgement. The authors wish to express their gratitude to Ministry of Higher Education (MOHE), Malaysia and Research Management Center (RMC), Universiti Teknologi Malaysia for the financial support of this project under GUP research grant no: Q.J130000.2523.14H35.

References

1. Sandeep, V., Gopal, K.L., Naveen, S., Amudhan, A., Kumar, L.S.: Globally accessible machine automation using raspberry pi. In: International Conference on Advances in Computing, Communications and Informatics (ICACCI), pp. 1144–1147 (2015)
2. Chen, T.-L., Hsiao, T.-C., Chen, S.-C., Chung, Y.-F., Huang, Y.-M., Chen, T.-S.: Patrol management system applying RFID to petrochemical industry. In: 2013 IEEE International Conference of IEEE Region 10 (TENCON 2013)
3. Mareli, M., Rimer, S., Paul, B., Ouahada, K., Pitsillides, A.: Experimental evaluation of NFC reliability between an RFID tag and a smartphone, Africon (2013)
4. Vaughan-Nichols, S.J.: The battle over the universal Java IDE, Technology News. April 2003
5. Symth, N.: Android studio 2.2 development essentials - Android 7 edition, July 2016
6. Mishra, A.R.: Fundamentals of cellular network planning and optimization: 2G/2.5G/3G/4G, April 2004
7. Zachariah, T., Klugman, N., et al.: The Internet of Things has a gateway problem. HotMobile 2015, Santa Fe, New Mexico, USA, February 2015
8. Brown, A.K.: GPS tracking system, 3 January 1995
9. Hau, T.J., Rashid, R.A., et al.: IoT based smart guard touring system (T-REC System). In: Proceedings of 2016 Electrical Engineering Symposium, December 2016
10. Azman, N.Z., Rashid, R.A., et al.: IoT based home intercom system. In: Proceedings of 2016 Electrical Engineering Symposium, December 2016
11. Zakariya, N.I., Rashid, R.A. et al.: Implementation of mobile tracking application using GPS/3G. In: Android Smartphone, Tesis Sarjana Muda UTM, June 2015
12. Latiffa, N.M.A., Mohamad, M.M., et al.: Training monitoring system for cyclist based on android application development. Jurnal Teknologi (Sci. Eng.) (2013)

Common Spatial Pattern with Feature Scaling (FSc-CSP) for Motor Imagery Classification

Yohanes de Britto Hertyasta Prathama[1(✉)], Mohd Ibrahim Shapiai[1,2],
Siti Armiza Mohd Aris[3], Zuwairie Ibrahim[4], Jafreezal Jaafar[5],
and Hilman Fauzi[1,6]

[1] Department of Electronic Systems Engineering, Malaysia-Japan International
Institute of Technology, Universiti Teknologi Malaysia, Jalan Sultan Yahya
Petra, 54100 Kuala Lumpur, WP Kuala Lumpur, Malaysia
hertyasta.prathama@gmail.com
[2] Centre for Artificial Intelligence and Robotics, Universiti Teknologi Malaysia,
Jalan Sultan Yahya Petra, 54100 Kuala Lumpur, WP Kuala Lumpur, Malaysia
[3] Razak School of Engineering and Advanced Technology,
Universiti Teknologi Malaysia, Jalan Sultan Yahya Petra, 54100 Kuala Lumpur,
WP Kuala Lumpur, Malaysia
[4] Faculty of Electrical and Electronic Engineering,
Universiti Malaysia Pahang, 26600 Pekan, Pahang, Malaysia
[5] Department of Computer and Information Sciences,
Faculty of Science and Information Technology,
Universiti Teknologi Petronas, Seri Iskandar, Malaysia
[6] Faculty of Electrical Engineering, Telkom University, Bandung, Indonesia

Abstract. Brain-Computer Interface (BCI) is a way to translate human
thoughts into computer commands. One of the most popular BCI type is
Electroencephalography (EEG)-based BCI, where motor imagery is considered
one of the most effective ways. Previously, to extract useful information, various
filters are introduced, such as spatial, temporal, and spectral filtering. A spatial
filtering algorithm called Common Spatial Pattern (CSP) was developed and
known to have excellent performance, especially in motor imagery for BCI
application. In general, there are several approaches in improving CSP such as
regularization approach, analytic approach, and frequency band selection. In
general, the existing techniques for band selection is either to select or reject the
band by ignoring the importance of the band. For example, Binary Particle
Search Optimization Common Spatial Pattern (BPSO-CSP) was proposed to
choose multiple possible best bands to be used in processing the data. In this
paper, we propose an algorithm called Feature Scaling Common Spatial Pattern
(FSc-CSP) to overcome the problem of feature selection. Instead of selecting
features, the proposed algorithm employs a feature scaling system to scale the
importance of each band by using Genetic Algorithm (GA) altogether with
Extreme Learning Machine (ELM) as classifier, with 1 signifying the most
important bands, declining until 0 for the unused bands, as opposed to the 1 and
0 selection system used in BPSO-CSP. Conducted experiments show that by
employing feature scaling, better results can be achieved especially compared to
vanilla CSP and feature selection with 100 hidden nodes in three from five BCI
Competition III datasets IVa, namely *aa*, *aw* and *ay*, with around 5–8% better
results compared to vanilla CSP and feature selection.

© Springer Nature Singapore Pte Ltd. 2017
M.S. Mohamed Ali et al. (Eds.): AsiaSim 2017, Part I, CCIS 751, pp. 591–604, 2017.
DOI: 10.1007/978-981-10-6463-0_51

Keywords: EEG · Common Spatial Pattern · Motor imagery · Genetic Algorithm · Feature scaling

1 Introduction

Brain-computer interface (BCI) is a system that translates human thoughts into commands, which enables humans to interact with their surroundings, without the involvement of peripheral muscles and nerves. BCI based on electroencephalography (EEG) uses control signals from the EEG activity as input/commands. BCI creates an alternative non-muscular pathway for relaying a person's intentions to external devices such as computers, neural prostheses, and other different assistive peripherals [1]. Generally, BCI could be divided into three types; invasive, partially invasive, and non-invasive. Non-invasive BCI is the most risk-free, subject-wise, type of BCI, because it doesn't involve any surgery to be implemented to the subject. However, it has one trade-off: intervention from the scalp and skull decreases the resolution and provides noise to the brain signal, compared to the invasive and partially-invasive BCI. Some of the most popular modalities are Magnetic Resonance Imaging (MRI), Magnetoencephalography (MEG), and Electroencephalography (EEG).

Despite its worst spatial resolution compared to the other types of BCI, BCI through EEG is one of the most modern modality and most studied field of BCI, mainly because of its non-invasive, portable, and low-cost nature. But BCI through EEG is not without its weakness; it is susceptible to noises and artifacts, mostly from unwanted movements such as eye blinks, or poor contact surface [2]. This problem mostly solved by trying to reduce artifacts and noises by utilizing reference electrodes placed in locations where there is little cortical activity and attempting to filter out correlated patterns [3, 4]. Other precautions are done by applying filtering and defining the right information to the EEG signals [5].

EEG architecture basically can be divided into four blocks; signal acquisition, preprocessing, feature extraction, and classification. One of the most proponent algorithm of BCI feature extraction is Common Spatial Pattern (CSP) [6]. This algorithm focuses in maximizing the variance ratio of two classes of an EEG data [8]. However, CSP is not without its limitations; CSP needs a fine-tuning of its filtering band for each subject because it can only process one band and solely designed for two-classes use.

Several approaches have been done to overcome the limitations of CSP, which can be categorized into five approaches: Improvement of estimation robustness [6, 7], regularization [9, 10], multi-subject implementation [10, 11], kernel-based algorithm [13, 14], and frequency band selection [14, 15]. There is an algorithm proposed to address the limitation of CSP which belongs to the frequency band selection approach called Binary Particle Swarm Optimization Common Spatial Pattern (BPSO-CSP) [16]. BPSO-CSP can use features from multiple bands it deems important, through the usage of feature selection. With this algorithm, the important band is defined as 1 and the unimportant or unused band is defined as 0. The classifier will then only process the bands marked as 1. However, despite its ability to solve the fine-tuning problem of CSP, BPSO-CSP only uses the selected bands and rejects the rest, despite the probability of usable information within the rejected band.

In this paper, we propose an alternative approach to BPSO-CSP, especially to overcome the selection problem of both algorithms. Instead of selecting or rejecting the feature, we scale the feature through importance of it between zero and one by using Genetic Algorithm (GA). Through this approach, the bands with less significance will have a chance to be processed due to the probability of having several usable information within them.

This manuscript is divided into part 1 as introduction, part 2 to present works related to this paper, part 3 to explain the research methodology, part 4 to present the findings and discussion, and part 5 serves as conclusion. Introduction explains about the issue of BCI through EEG, and more specifically, the potential of CSP-derived algorithms for its significance. And then, the related works discusses about the previously done studies in CSP, especially those with the significance regarding the topics of multi-band-related CSP. In the methodology part, the dataset used and the systematic methodology is explained. In the findings and discussion part, the result of experiment is presented, and by that result, opens a discussion on possible future improvements and current milestone on improvements. Finally, the conclusion summarizes the point of the whole proposal.

2 Related Works

2.1 Common Spatial Pattern

CSP produces a set of spatial filters that can be used to decompose multi-dimensional data into a set of uncorrelated components [6]. CSP maximizes the variance-ratio of two conditions or classes. In other words, CSP finds a transformation basis that maximizes the variances of one multi-channel signal and simultaneously minimizes the variances of the other multi-channel signal. For instance, CSP for BCI is employed to distinguish between the variance or power of the associated left-hand and right-hand motor imagery classification from brain signal. This features particularly useful tool for the discrimination of EEG data obtained during different mental states in BCI system. In general, CSP is considered among the best performing algorithm for BCI community. CSP is categorized as supervised learning method as it requires not only the training samples but also the information of the classes of the signal, e.g. left-hand signal.

CSP is an algorithm that maximizes the variance of one class and minimize the variance of other class to discriminate between two classes of EEG data. The multi-channel EEG signal separated into two mental tasks (A and B) can be described as two spatiotemporal signal matrices of X_A and X_B, with dimension ($N \times T$), where N signifies few number of channels and T signifies few number of samples. Then, the covariance matrices of these signals are calculated by

$$R_n = \frac{X_n X_n^t}{trace(X_n X_n^t)} \tag{1}$$

where n signifies the respective classes (A or B), M^t signifies the transpose of the matrix M, and $trace(M)$ signifies the sum of the diagonal elements of matrix M.

The matrices X_A and X_B contain different mental task records; however, they share the same condition and therefore can be modeled as follows:

$$X_n = [C_n C_c]\begin{bmatrix} S_n \\ S_c \end{bmatrix} \tag{2}$$

where S_n and C_n signifies the specific source component and corresponding spatial pattern for each mental task, while S_c and C_c signifies the source component and spatial pattern for the common condition.

CSP algorithm is created with the purpose of designing two spatial filters, so the source component S_n can be extracted with

$$S_n = F_n X_n \tag{3}$$

where F_n refers to the spatial filters corresponding to each task. From these information, CSP applies principal component and spatial subspace analysis to the diagonalized covariance matrices using training data to estimate the spatial filters. A more detailed explanation and calculation of CSP can be found at its corresponding research [6].

CSP is known to be yielding bad results when applied to unfiltered EEG data or EEG data filtered with poor frequency band [15], which, in turn, leads a different problem of the need of fine-tuning in order to achieve optimum results. There are several CSP derived methods which have been proposed in the literature to deal with various limitations of CSP. It is generally divided into binary-class [11, 15, 17–19] and multi-class [20, 21]. Binary-class, as its name states, solves the problem of CSP with its own basic characteristics of maximizing and minimizing two covariance matrices for two classes, meanwhile the multi-class tries to implement CSP to data with more than two classes.

The binary-class method can then be divided into five means, which specifies the solution. The first means is to enhance the estimation of the robustness [7], which also faces the inherent fine-tuning problem of CSP; the second one is applying regularization [9, 10], which has a susceptible selection of regularization parameter which may result in underfitting or overfitting of the solution; the third one is through addressing a multi-subject problem [11, 12], which causes differentiation of the acquired brain signal from multiple subject may differ much, leading to irreproducible results; the fourth one is through the kernel-based solution [13, 14], which subjects the result to the kernel selection and the parameter; and the last category is a multi-band solution [15, 16], which, mostly, suffers from information negligence due to the nature of band selection methods.

2.2 Binary Particle Swarm Optimization Common Spatial Pattern

BPSO-CSP is an improvement of CSP algorithm proposed by [16]. This methodology employs Binary Particle Swarm Optimization (BPSO) [22] to select the suitable bands to process the brain signals. This algorithm selects the bands to be used according to acceptance and rejection of each band by BPSO.

The methodology of BPSO-CSP can be concluded into 4 steps: Initialization of each particles which correspond with a vector of 1 s and 0 s, where 1 means accepted band and 0 means rejected band; computing fitness values for each particle which is derived from the classification accuracy of each sub-band; updating the velocity and position of the iteration based on the previous best velocity and position (given that there has been a previous iteration); and mutation, in which a mutation operator is employed in order to get the optimal points out of the BPSO algorithm. The steps are repeated from updating until a certain threshold of maximum iteration which is pre-defined before is reached. In this paper, for comparison, we employ a similar algorithm, which is called Feature Selection. The procedure is shown in Fig. 1.

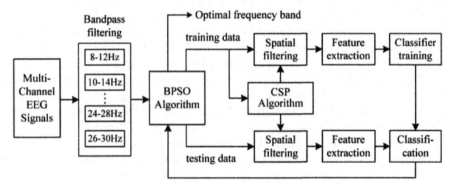

Fig. 1. BPSO-CSP framework [16].

3   Methodology

In brief, our proposed methodology of FSc-CSP is shown in Fig. 2. The data-set was preprocessed with Butterworth filter with sliding windows of 17 bands, next processed by CSP at respective bands, and then scaled by GA-ELM, which finally passed onto classifier for testing. Extreme Learning Machine (ELM) will be used as the classifier.

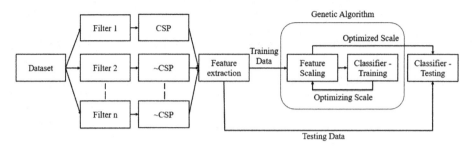

Fig. 2. FSc-CSP framework.

3.1 Preprocessing

The data were first preprocessed by using sliding window and Butterworth filters. Sliding Window is a method of choosing/splitting a lengthy band into several small bands. It works by splitting an individual length of bands, e.g. 4–40 Hz, into several bands based on windows, determined by variables called width and step. Width means the range of the band, e.g. width of 4 means the band is four values long, minus the starting value (e.g. a window that starts from 4 Hz with a width of 4 will have a length of 4–8 Hz). Step means the margin between the starting point of one window to the other, e.g. with a step of 2 and width of 4, with the band ranging from 4–12 Hz, the windows will consist of 4–8 Hz, 6–10 Hz, and 8–12 Hz. In this experiment, the actual length of the band is 4–40 Hz, with the width of 4 and step of 2, and 17 bands in total. This range encompasses the theta, alpha, mu and beta bands.

The Butterworth filter is a type of signal processing filter designed to have as flat frequency response as possible in the passband. In this experiment, third-order bandpass filter is used, meaning that the signal is filtered only at a certain range of length. The value for the low pass (lowest threshold of the length) and high pass (highest threshold of the length) of the bandpass filter is the value of the sliding window. For example, if the current window is 6–10 Hz, then the low pass is 6 Hz and the high pass is 10 Hz. The example representation of sliding window can be seen in Fig. 3 below.

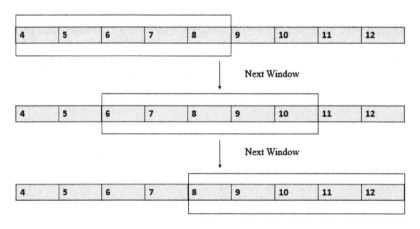

Fig. 3. Example representation of sliding window.

3.2 Feature Scaling for Proposed Framework

GA is an optimization method process that tries to mimic biological evolution. The algorithm creates a population of random solutions for the function, and at each generation, the algorithm is aimed to move toward an optimal solution of the function. The flowchart can be seen in Fig. 4. In this FSc-CSP algorithm, GA is used to find an optimized scale for the classifier. The scale signifies the importance of the combination; The higher the classifier accuracy with that scale, more important that scale is. The number of the scale is the same as the number of bands, and then the scale is replicated for each feature in that band.

As pictured in Fig. 4, the GA will first initialize a set of populations of the scale, and then these scales will be applied to the ELM classifier. And then GA will try to crossover all the members of the initial sets to produce children scales, in which will be passed again to the ELM classifier. Throughout the iterations, GA will try to optimize the scale so that the classifier will reach the best result. The scale that gives zero or closest to zero error percentage during training with ELM compared with other scale sets is the one that is selected as the best scale for the data. As for the process in ELM itself can be seen in Fig. 5.

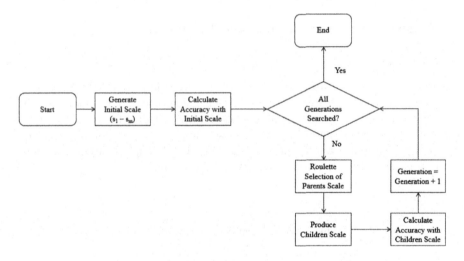

Fig. 4. Genetic Algorithm flowchart.

In Fig. 5, features encompass all the features from every bands, with m representing the number of bands, and n representing the number of features. s_1 until s_m is the scale the GA is trying to find in order to reach the optimal scale combination, which is valued between zero to one depending on the importance of the band, and replicated for the number of n for each m. For example, if there are 17 bands and each band has 8 features, then the scale will be replicated 8 times for each band. h represents the number of the predetermined hidden nodes. The criteria for the optimal scale combination tuning is based on the training accuracy of a certain scale combination. The combination of the scaling which yields the best training accuracy will then be passed into testing to validate the result of the algorithm.

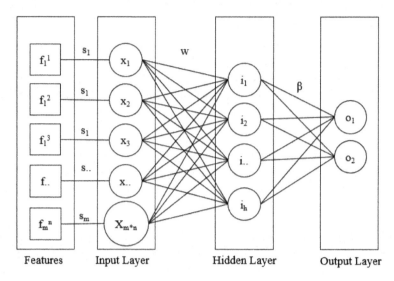

Fig. 5. Extreme learning machine.

4 Experiments Setup, Results and Discussion

4.1 Experiments Setup

To test our method, we use dataset IVa *aa*, *al*, *av*, *aw*, and *ay* from BCI Competition III [23]. For the Genetic Algorithm, we use 50 Generations and 50 Populations. The band is split into 17 sub-bands, ranging from 4–40 Hz, with a width of 4 and a step of 2. We generate ten random samples from each dataset, and split them as follows: 60% of the sample is used as the training sample and 40% of the sample is used as the testing sample. Detailed explanation can be seen in Tables 1 and 2.

Table 1. Dataset partitioning with 60:40 ratio.

Dataset	# of trials	# of class 1 data	# of class 2 data
Subject *aa*	168	80	88
Subject *al*	224	112	112
Subject *av*	84	42	42
Subject *aw*	56	30	26
Subject *ay*	28	18	10

Table 2. Parameter setup for conducted experiment.

Parameter setup	
# of GA generations	50
# of GA populations	50
# of hidden nodes	5/10/68/100
# of runs	10
# of sub-bands	17
# of features	8
# of window steps	2
# of window width	4
Window range	4–40 Hz
Filter type	Third-order butterworth
ELM activation function	Sigmoid
# of input nodes	136 (Bands × Features = 17 × 8)
# of output nodes	2

4.2 Performance Evaluation

The performance of the algorithms is evaluated through the Mean Squared Error (MSE) of the algorithm, which can be represented as

$$\frac{1}{n}\sum_{i=1}^{n}\left(Y_i' - Y_i\right)^2 \tag{4}$$

where n represents the number of prediction, Y' represents the predictions itself and Y is the predictor. The evaluation is done per hidden nodes basis to attune the underfitting or overfitting problem of neural network.

4.3 Results and Discussion

In this test, we conduct tests using vanilla CSP, with a bandwidth of 8–12 Hz, or the alpha band, and Feature Selection to represent the BPSO-CSP, to give a comparison to our proposed algorithm. Each algorithm is tested using different numbers of hidden nodes for the classifier. The number of hidden nodes is decided randomly, except for 68, which is half of the total number of training and testing data of dataset *aa*. ELM is used as the classifier. 10-fold cross validation is used to validate each data. These tests were done in order to validate the result of our proposed algorithm.

Table 3 shows the testing performance of FSc-CSP algorithm. The performance of feature scaling compared to Feature Selection yields some performance improvement for at least three data sets, namely *aa*, *aw* and *ay* for 100 hidden nodes configuration, while for a lower number of hidden nodes, Feature Selection yields better performance, albeit with lower accuracy compared to FSc-CSP with higher hidden nodes.

There is an anomaly, however, with dataset *al* as the only dataset which performance with both algorithms yield not an objectively bad result, but compared to the

Table 3. Testing performance validation of the FSc-CSP.

# of HN	Type	aa	al	av	aw	ay
5	FSc-CSP	**0.52**	0.60	0.48	0.50	0.48
	Feature selection	0.50	0.59	**0.52**	**0.56**	**0.50**
	Vanilla CSP	0.48	**0.71**	0.47	0.45	0.43
10	FSc-CSP	0.48	0.65	**0.49**	0.48	0.48
	Feature selection	0.47	0.60	0.45	**0.52**	0.48
	Vanilla CSP	**0.52**	**0.74**	0.47	0.48	0.48
68	FSc-CSP	**0.53**	0.60	0.53	**0.68**	0.48
	Feature selection	0.49	0.70	0.53	0.57	**0.50**
	Vanilla CSP	0.52	**0.84**	**0.57**	0.52	0.47
100	FSc-CSP	**0.58**	0.64	0.53	**0.61**	**0.55**
	Feature selection	0.53	0.68	**0.55**	0.53	*0.55*
	Vanilla CSP	0.53	**0.82**	0.54	0.52	0.48

*Note: **Bold** means the best result for the dataset compared to other algorithms with respective hidden nodes configuration*

vanilla CSP, the performance is much worse, and compared to other datasets, should we put vanilla CSP results aside and only put FSc-CSP and Feature Selection into consideration, dataset al yields a reversed result: FSc-CSP yields better performance for lower hidden nodes, while Feature Selection yields better performance for higher hidden nodes.

In Fig. 6, we present an example of scale distribution of FSc-CSP for 100 Hidden Nodes. It is seen that the algorithm can distinct between the most important bands with the less important bands, evident in the results. Some bands, namely band 11 (24–28 Hz), 12 (26–30 Hz) and 13 (28–30 Hz), are deemed less important due to the

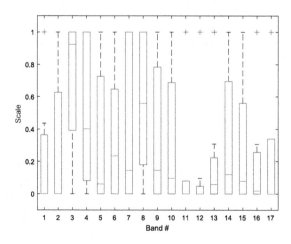

Fig. 6. Dataset *aa* scale distribution for 100 hidden nodes.

range of the scale. The outliers from these bands are occasions where the algorithm deem the band as important enough, however, compared to significant bands like band 3, where the most evident range of importance is equal or above 0.4, these bands seem to contain not so many useful information.

In Fig. 7(a) and (b), we present the power spectrum distribution of two of the most significant bands with the closest range, namely band 3 (8–12 Hz) and band 4 (10– 14 Hz). From the figures, it is seen that both bands can distinguish between the hand imagery and foot imagery, which is evident from the gradient difference in both sides. We can also see that the 10–14 Hz band, which was deemed less important by the scale in Fig. 7, albeit able to distinct the signals, the spread of the gradient is less distinct and has more overlapping gradients compared to 8–12 Hz.

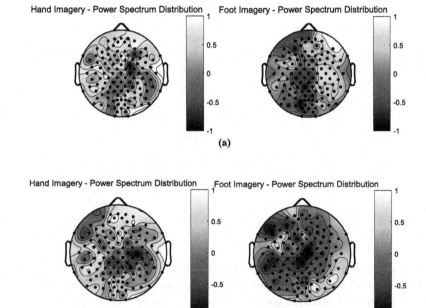

Fig. 7. EEG Power spectrum for (a) band 8–12 Hz (b) band 10–14 Hz.

In Fig. 8(a) and (b), we present the eigenvalue pairing of both bands, and it is seen that the results are in accordance with the scale. 8–12 Hz can distinguish both classes in a good manner, evident in EV Pair 1 and 2 for class 1 and EV Pair 5 for class 2. As for the 10–14 Hz band, it can distinguish for EV Pair 1 and 2 for the first class, but not so much for the second class.

In Fig. 9(a) and (b), the results of CSP filtering are presented for Channel C5 and C6. Both channels were selected because of its position as the center position of both left and right side of the head, thus providing the most representative signal for the

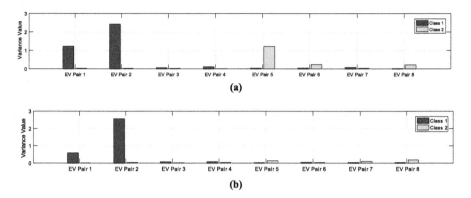

Fig. 8. Eigenvalue pairing for (a) band 8–12 Hz (b) band 10–14 Hz.

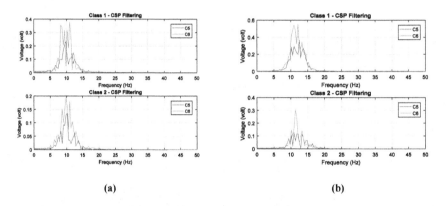

Fig. 9. CSP class distinction for (a) band 8–12 Hz and (b) band 10–14 Hz.

distinction of left and right brain signal. Figure 9(a) shows the result of CSP filtering for 8–12 Hz, which shows good distinction with some spike overlaps in Class 1, but a clean distinction in Class 2. A good distinction can also be seen in Fig. 9(b); however, 10–14 Hz has more overlaps compared to the 8–12 Hz, which means the scale of the features can predict the importance of the bands.

5   Conclusion

In this paper, we present a new algorithm developed to overcome the fine-tuning problem of CSP. The fine-tuning problem is one of the most significant problem faced in BCI research due to its time-consuming nature and its fine-tuned nature causes difficulty for other researchers to replicate the results for benchmarking purposes.

We propose a Feature Scaling Common Spatial Pattern (FSc-CSP) algorithm, which is benchmarked using datasets from BCI Competition III datasets IVa. In the experiment, we also include the vanilla CSP algorithm and From the results, it is seen that FSc-CSP could provide better result spreads compared to Feature Selection. Feature Selection tends to have better results at a very low hidden nodes number compared to FSc-CSP, whilst FSc-CSP has a better spread across different numbers of hidden nodes compared to Feature Selection, even at the lower ones, as evidenced by the result of dataset *aa*. FSc-CSP is also proven to be able to determine the importance of each band through the scaling system.

The only exception for both algorithm is in dataset *al*, where in all hidden nodes spread, dataset *al* is consistent in providing best result by using only one specific band range, which is 8–12 Hz or the alpha wave.

In the future works, several improvements can be made based on these findings; for example, an improvement of the algorithm through the improvement of the vanilla CSP algorithm itself to overcome the limitation of the vanilla CSP algorithm, or the improvement of feature scaling algorithm to include the probability of using single sub-band, as evidenced by the result of dataset *al* where best results can only be seen by using single sub-band.

Acknowledgment. The author would like to express gratitude to JAIF (Japan ASEAN Integration Fund) for all the supports and CAIRO (Centre for Artificial Intelligence and Robotics) laboratory of Malaysia-Japan International Institute of Technology Faculty of Universiti Teknologi Malaysia for the grant (Grant Number: U.K091303.0100.00000).

References

1. Falzon, O., Camilleri, K.P., Muscat, J.: The analytic common spatial patterns method for EEG-based BCI data. J. Neural Eng. **9**, 45009 (2012)
2. Szafir, D.J.: Non-invasive BCI through EEG (2009)
3. Ludwig, K.A., Miriani, R.M., Langhals, N.B., Joseph, M.D., Anderson, D.J., Kipke, D.R.: Using a common average reference to improve cortical neuron recordings from microelectrode arrays. J. Neurophysiol. **101**, 1679–1689 (2009)
4. Adam, A., Ibrahim, Z., Mokhtar, N., Shapiai, M.I., Mubin, M.: Evaluation of different peak models of eye blink EEG for signal peak detection using artificial neural network. Neural Netw. World. **26**, 67–89 (2016)
5. Adam, A., Shapiai, M.I., Mohd Tumari, M.Z., Mohamad, M.S., Mubin, M.: Feature selection and classifier parameters estimation for EEG signals peak detection using particle swarm optimization. Sci. World J. **2014**, 1–13 (2014)
6. Ramoser, H., Müller-Gerking, J., Pfurtscheller, G.: Optimal spatial filtering of single trial EEG during imagined hand movement. IEEE Trans. Rehabil. Eng. **8**, 441–446 (2000)
7. Lemm, S., Blankertz, B., Curio, G., Müller, K.R.: Spatio-spectral filters for improving the classification of single trial EEG. IEEE Trans. Biomed. Eng. **52**, 1541–1548 (2005)
8. Asyraf, H., Shapiai, M.I., Setiawan, N.A., Wan Musa, W.S.N.S.: Masking covariance for common spatial pattern as feature extraction. J. Telecommun. Electron. Comput. Eng. **8**, 81–85 (2016)
9. Lu, H., Plataniotis, K.N., Venetsanopoulos, A.N.: Regularized common spatial patterns with generic learning for EEG signal classification. In: Proceedings of 31st Annual International Conference of the IEEE Engineering in Medicine and Biology Society: Engineering the Future of Biomedicine, EMBC 2009, pp. 6599–6602 (2009)

10. Thang, L.Q., Temiyasathit, C.: Regularizing multi-bands common spatial patterns (RMCSP): a data processing method for brain-computer interface. In: International Symposium on Medical Information and Communication Technology (ISMICT), May 2015, pp. 180–184 (2015)
11. Kang, H., Choi, S.: Bayesian multi-task learning for common spatial patterns. In: 2011 International Pattern Recognition in NeuroImaging, vol. 1, pp. 61–64 (2011)
12. Devlaminck, D., Wyns, B., Grosse-Wentrup, M., Otte, G., Santens, P.: Multisubject learning for common spatial patterns in motor-imagery BCI. Comput. Intell. Neurosci. **2011**, 8 (2011)
13. Samek, W., Binder, A., Muller, K.R.: Multiple kernel learning for brain-computer interfacing. In: 2013 Proceedings of Annual International Conference on IEEE Engineering in Medicine and Biology Society, pp. 7048–7051 (2013)
14. Albalawi, H., Song, X.: A study of kernel CSP-based motor imagery brain computer interface classification. In: 2012 IEEE Signal Processing in Medicine and Biology Symposium, SPMB 2012 (2012)
15. Novi, Q., Guan, C., Dat, T.H., Xue, P.: Sub-band common spatial pattern (SBCSP) for brain-computer interface. In: Proceedings of 3rd International IEEE EMBS Conference on Neural Engineering, pp. 204–207 (2007)
16. Wei, Q., Wei, Z.: Binary particle swarm optimization for frequency band selection in motor imagery based brain-computer interfaces. Biomed. Mater. Eng. **26**, S1523–S1532 (2015)
17. Zhang, H., Chin, Z.Y., Ang, K.K., Guan, C., Wang, C.: Optimum spatio-spectral filtering network for brain-computer interface. IEEE Trans. Neural Netw. **22**, 52–63 (2011)
18. Lu, H., Eng, H.L., Guan, C., Plataniotis, K.N., Venetsanopoulos, A.N.: Regularized common spatial pattern with aggregation for EEG classification in small-sample setting. IEEE Trans. Biomed. Eng. **57**, 2936–2946 (2010)
19. Benoît, F., van Heeswijk, M., Miche, Y., Verleysen, M., Lendasse, A.: Feature selection for nonlinear models with extreme learning machines. Neurocomputing **102**, 111–124 (2013)
20. Grosse-Wentrup, M., Buss, M.: Multiclass common spatial patterns and information theoretic feature extraction. IEEE Trans. Biomed. Eng. **55**, 1991–2000 (2008)
21. Gouy-Pailler, C., Congedo, M., Brunner, C., Jutten, C., Pfurtscheller, G.: Multi-class independent common spatial patterns: exploiting energy variations of brain sources. In: 2008 Proceedings of 4th International Brain-Computer Interface Workshop and Training Course, pp. 20–25 (2008)
22. Yuan, X., Nie, H., Su, A., Wang, L., Yuan, Y.: An improved binary particle swarm optimization for unit commitment problem. Expert Syst. Appl. **36**, 8049–8055 (2009)
23. BCI Competition III Dataset IVa. http://www.bbci.de/competition/iii/desc_IVa.html

Gravitational Search Algorithm with a More Accurate Newton's Gravitational Principle

Nor Azlina Ab. Aziz[1]([⊠]), Mohamad Nizam Aliman[2],
Muhammad Sharfi Najib[2], Norazian Subari[2],
Aminurafiuddin Zulkifli[1], Mohd Ibrahim Shapiai[3],
and Zuwairie Ibrahim[2]

[1] Faculty of Engineering and Technology,
Multimedia University, 75450 Melaka, Malaysia
azlina.aziz@mmu.edu.my
[2] Faculty of Electrical and Electronics Engineering,
Universiti Malaysia Pahang, 26600 Pekan, Pahang, Malaysia
[3] Department of Electronic Systems Engineering,
Malaysia-Japan International Institute of Technology,
54100 Kuala Lumpur, Malaysia

Abstract. Gravitational search algorithm (GSA) is a metaheuristic population-based optimization algorithm inspired by the Newtonian law of gravity and law of motion. However, GSA has a fundamental problem. It has been reported that the force calculation in GSA is not genuinely based on the Newtonian law of gravity. Based on the Newtonian law of gravity, force between two masses in the universe is inversely proportional to the square of the distance between them. However, in the original GSA, R has been used. In this paper, a modification is done to GSA by considering the square of the distance between masses, which is R^2. The CEC2014 benchmark functions for real-parameter single objective optimization problems are employed in the evaluation. An important finding is that by considering the square of the distance between masses, significant improvement over the original GSA is observed provided a large gravitational constant should be used at the beginning of the optimization process.

Keywords: Gravitational search algorithm · PureGSA · Newtonian law of gravity · Law of motion

1 Introduction

Gravitational search algorithm (GSA) has been firstly introduced by Rashedi *et al.* in 2009 [1]. It is a metaheuristic population-based optimization algorithm which is inspired by the Newtonian law of gravity and law of motion. In GSA, fitness is translated into mass and interaction between agents is simulated based on these laws.

The GSA has been modified extensively. For example, to apply the GSA algorithm to multi-objective optimization problems, several variants of GSA algorithms have been reported. In solving multi-objective optimization problems, Nobahari *et al.* have proposed a Non-Dominated Sorting GSA (NSGSA) [2]. Also, a novel approach for

© Springer Nature Singapore Pte Ltd. 2017
M.S. Mohamed Ali et al. (Eds.): AsiaSim 2017, Part I, CCIS 751, pp. 605–614, 2017.
DOI: 10.1007/978-981-10-6463-0_52

handling multiple objectives using GSA, which is called Vector Evaluated GSA (VEGSA) [3], has been reported.

In solving combinatorial optimization problems, Binary GSA (BGSA) has been introduced by Rashedi et al. [4]. The BGSA preserves the fundamental concept of the GSA except that each agent of a swarm consists of binary string representing an agent's position vector. The BGSA updates each agent's mass velocity using the original velocity update equation but each agent's position is updated as either 1 or 0 based on a probabilistic equation. Instead of using GSA with binary representation for solving combinatorial optimization problems, Ibrahim et al. introduced multi-state GSA [5] in which a state representation has been employed.

Even though GSA has a good potential in solving continuous, multi-objective, and combinatorial optimization problems and has been employed to solved real-world problems, Gauci et al. [6] has pointed out that an inconsistency used in gravitational formulation in GSA. They have proved theoretically that GSA was indeed not genuinely based on Newtonian law of gravity. Specifically, in the calculation of force, distance R is employed instead of R^2. Therefore, this paper presents the reformulated GSA to be as close as possible to the Newtonian law of gravity and law of motion. The performance of the modified GSA, which is called PureGSA, is analyzed and compared to the original GSA algorithm by varying the value of initial gravitational constant, G_o.

2 Gravitational Search Algorithm

In GSA, agents are considered as an object and their performance are expressed by their masses. The position of particle is corresponding to the solution of the problem. Consider a population consisted N quantity of agents, so the position of i-th agent can be presented by:

$$X_i = \left(x_i^1 \ldots x_i^d \ldots x_i^n\right) \text{ for } i = 1, 2, \ldots, N. \tag{1}$$

The mass of i-th particle at time t is derived from Eqs. (2) and (3), denoted as $M_i(t)$.

$$m_i(t) = \frac{fit_i(t) - worst(t)}{best(t) - worst(t)}. \tag{2}$$

$$M_i(t) = \frac{m_i(t)}{\sum_{j=1}^{N} m_j(t)}. \tag{3}$$

where N is a population size, $m_i(t)$ is an intermediate variable in agent mass calculation, $fit_j(t)$ is the fitness value of i-th agent at time t, $best(t)$ and $worst(t)$ denote the best and the worst fitness value of the population at time t. The best and the worst fitness for the case of minimization problem are defined as follows;

$$best(t) = \min_{j \in \{1,...,N\}} fit_j(t)$$
$$worst(t) = \max_{j \in \{1,...,N\}} fit_j(t) \cdot$$

(4)

whereas for maximization problem,

$$best(t) = \max_{j \in \{1,...,N\}} fit_j(t)$$
$$worst(t) = \min_{j \in \{1,...,N\}} fit_j(t) \cdot$$

(5)

At specific time t, the force acting on agent i from agent j in d-th dimension can be represented as the following:

$$F_{ij}^d(t) = G(t) \frac{M_i(t) \times M_j(t)}{R_{ij}(t) + \varepsilon} \left(x_j^d(t) - x_i^d(t) \right).$$

(6)

where $M_i(t)$ is the gravitational mass of agent i, $M_j(t)$ is the gravitational mass of agent j, $G(t)$ is the gravitational constant, ε. a small constant, and $R_{ij}(t)$ is the Euclidian distance between agent i and j. The distance is calculated as follows:

$$R_{ij}(t) = \left\| X_i(t), X_j(t) \right\|_2.$$

(7)

while gravitational constant is defined as a decreasing function of time, which is set to G_0 at the beginning.

$$G(t) = G_0 \times e^{-\alpha \frac{t}{t_{max}}}.$$

(8)

To give a stochastic characteristic to GSA, the total force acted on agent i in d dimension is a randomly weighted sum of d-th components of the forces exerted from other agents;

$$F_i^d(t) = \sum_{j=1, j \neq i}^{N} rand_i F_{ij}^d(t).$$

(9)

where, $rand_i$ is a random number in the interval of $[0, 1]$.

According to law of motion, the current velocity of any mass is equal to the sum of the fraction of its previous velocity and the variation in the velocity. Variation or acceleration of any mass is equal to the force acted on the system divided by mass of inertia, which is shown in the following formula.

$$a_i^d(t) = \frac{F_i^d(t)}{M_i(t)}.$$

(10)

Therefore, the new agent's velocity and position are calculated using these equations:

$$v_i^d(t+1) = rand_i \times v_i^d(t) + a_i^d(t) \ . \tag{11}$$

$$x_i^d(t+1) = x_i^d(t) + v_i^d(t+1) \ . \tag{12}$$

Finally, the next iteration is executed until the maximum number of iterations t_{max}, is reached. In summary, the principle of standard GSA is shown in Fig. 1.

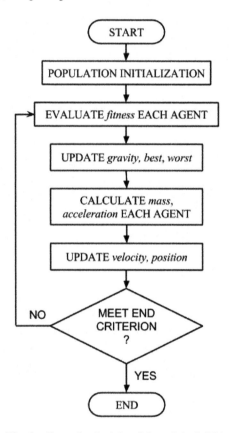

Fig. 1. General principle of the original GSA.

3 Modification to GSA

Following the definition of gravitational force based on the Newton's gravitational principle:

$$F = G\frac{M_1 M_2}{R^2} \ . \tag{13}$$

In GSA, the calculation of force supposedly based on this equation. However, as shown in Eq. (6), distance R, is used as the denominator. Let $\varepsilon = 0$, then

$$F_{ij}^d(t) = G(t) \frac{M_i(t) \times M_j(t)}{R_{ij}(t)} \left(x_j^d(t) - x_i^d(t) \right). \tag{14}$$

since $R_{ij}(t) = x_j^d(t) - x_i^d(t)$, therefore,

$$F_{ij}^d(t) = G(t) \times M_i(t) \times M_j(t). \tag{15}$$

which clearly shows that the force F_{ij}^d is not influenced by the distance between agent i and j. Thus, the original GSA is not genuinely follows the Newtonian gravitational law.

In the proposed PureGSA, the use of R^3 as the dominator in Eq. (14) is suggested. Hence, the Eq. (14) can be rewriten as:

$$F_{ij}^d(t) = G(t) \frac{M_i(t) \times M_j(t)}{R_{ij}^3(t) + \varepsilon} \left(x_j^d(t) - x_i^d(t) \right). \tag{16}$$

Similarly, let $R_{ij}(t) = x_j^d(t) - x_i^d(t)$, therefore,

$$F_{ij}^d(t) \simeq G(t) \frac{M_i(t) \times M_j(t)}{R_{ij}^2(t) + \varepsilon} \simeq G(t) \frac{M_i(t) \times M_j(t)}{\left(x_j^d(t) - x_i^d(t) \right)^2 + \varepsilon}. \tag{17}$$

which shows that the calculation of force can be formulated based on the Newton's gravitational principle, as shown in Eq. (13), and thus, the force can be influenced by the distance between agents.

4 Experiment, Results and Discussion

The parameter setting for all experiments is tabulated in Table 1. In this study, thirty standard benchmark functions from CEC2014 test functions [7] have been used throughout the experiment. These benchmark functions consist of the shifted, rotated, expanded, and combined classical test function.

Table 1. Parameter setting used in all experiments.

Parameter	Value
Number of agents, N	100
Number of iterations, t_{max}	2000
Number of dimensions, D	50
Search range	$[-100,100]$
α	20

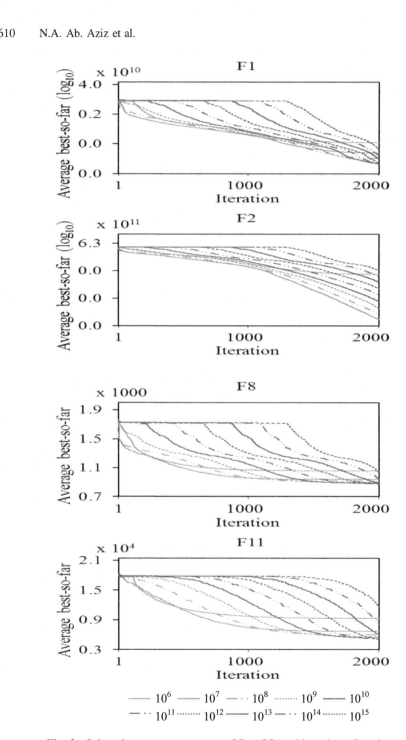

Fig. 2. Selected convergence curves of PureGSA with various G_o values.

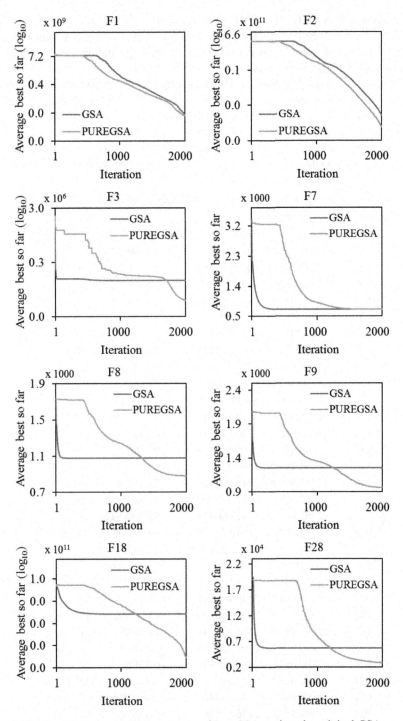

Fig. 3. Selected convergence curves of PureGSA against the original GSA.

Different values of G_o, $G_o = 10^6$ until $G_o = 10^{19}$ were tested in experiments for PureGSA. Figure 2 shows selected convergence curves of PureGSA with various G_o value. Obviously, trade-off between exploration and exploitation can be improved if different values of G_o were used.

Then, PureGSA result with $G_o = 10^{11}$ was subjected to comparison with the original GSA. Figure 3 shows selected convergence curves of PureGSA with $G_o = 10^{11}$ against the original GSA. According to the result of the Wilcoxon test shown in Table 2, by using p-value equal to 0.05, the Z-value obtained is -2.1288. Based on normal distribution curve it shows p-value for -2.1288 is equal to 0.03318, which is smaller than 0.05. Hence, it can be concluding the PureGSA is significantly better than the original GSA.

Table 2. Wilcoxon test of GSA and the proposed PureGSA. Average results of 50 runs are used in this analysis.

Function	GSA	PureGSA	Sign	Abs	R	Sign R
F1	14775830.9	12883470.66	1	1892360.26	28	28
F2	22443764.2	4968937.554	1	17474826.68	29	29
F3	138080.202	59465.40302	1	78614.7992	25	25
F4	878.734707	615.689502	1	263.0452	15	15
F5	519.999717	521.1891105	−1	1.1894	7	−7
F6	647.955355	612.9128535	1	35.0425	10	10
F7	702.097125	701.0457413	1	1.0514	5	5
F8	1076.49811	879.3150936	1	197.183	13	13
F9	1250.69963	961.3578655	1	289.3418	16	16
F10	8193.16657	5469.131576	1	2724.035	19	19
F11	9275.68745	4727.836415	1	4547.851	21	21
F12	1200.00289	1200.217911	−1	0.215	2	−2
F13	1300.47788	1300.504456	−1	0.0266	1	−1
F14	1400.29839	1400.570478	−1	0.2721	3	−3
F15	1765.90409	1516.062916	1	249.8412	14	14
F16	1622.52317	1621.368509	1	1.1547	6	6
F17	2181643.85	1247794.934	1	933848.912	27	27
F18	69338904.1	7594.924638	1	69331309.14	30	30
F19	1944.0205	1975.554168	−1	31.5337	9	−9
F20	59215.9615	31845.97477	1	27369.9867	23	23
F21	1844950.35	1897721.523	−1	52771.171	24	−24
F22	4133.86178	3546.484171	1	587.3776	17	17
F23	2500	2657.698759	−1	157.6988	12	−12
F24	2600.09343	2664.497601	−1	64.4042	11	−11
F25	2700	2707.254295	−1	7.2543	8	−8
F26	2800.08141	2800.362955	−1	0.2815	4	−4
F27	4789.01228	3224.517002	1	1564.4953	18	18
F28	6083.88723	3243.136466	1	2840.7508	20	20
F29	3100.15831	14569.2538	−1	11469.0955	22	−22
F30	3200.01244	109137.5661	−1	105937.5537	26	−26

5   Conclusion

The original GSA algorithm was not genuinely follows the Newtonian gravitational law. In this paper, by correcting the force of calculation in original GSA and investigating various initial gravitational constants, G_o, PureGSA algorithm has been proposed. In conclusion, the PureGSA algorithm not only superior to the original GSA, but most importantly, PureGSA algorithm follows more closely to the Newtonian gravitational law.

The impact of this finding is substantial. The GSA has been applied in solving many problems and good results have been reported, for examples, in feature selection [8], power system [9], control system [10], and digital filter design [11]. Better results might be observed if this enhanced GSA is employed in solving those problems. This could be a good direction of this study. Also, application of PureGSA to new problem such as DNA sequence design [12, 13] will be undertaken soon.

Acknowledgement. This research is funded by the Fundamental Research Grant Scheme (FRGS/1/2015/ICT02/MMU/03/1), which is awarded by Ministry of Higher Education Malaysia to Multimedia University.

References

1. Rashedi, E., Nezamabadi-pour, H., Saryazdi, S.: GSA: a gravitational search algorithm. Inf. Sci. **179**(13), 2232–2248 (2009)
2. Nobahari, H., Nikusokhan, M., Siarry, P.: Non-dominated sorting gravitational search algorithm. In: International Conference on Swarm Intelligence (2011)
3. Ibrahim, Z., Muhammad, B., Ghazali, K.H., Lim, K.S., Nawawi, S.W., Yusof, Z.M.: Vector evaluated gravitational search algorithm (VEGSA) for multi-objective optimization problems. In: Fourth International Conference on Computational Intelligence, Modelling and Simulation, pp. 13–17 (2012)
4. Rashedi, E., Nezamabadi-pour, H., Saryazdi, S.: BGSA: binary gravitational search algorithm. Nat. Comput. **9**(3), 727–745 (2009)
5. Ibrahim, I., Ahmad, A., Ibrahim, Z., Yusof, Z.M.: A novel multi-state gravitational search algorithm for discrete optimization problems. Int. J. Simul. – Syst. Sci. Technol. **16**(6), 15.1–15.8 (2015)
6. Gauci, M., Dodd, T.J., Groß, R.: Why 'GSA: a gravitational search algorithm' is not genuinely based on the law of gravity. Nat. Comput. **11**(4), 719–720 (2012)
7. Liang, J.J., Qu, B.Y., Suganthan, P.N.: Problem definitions and evaluation criteria for the CEC 2014 special session and competition on single objective real-parameter numerical optimization. Technical report 201311, Computational Intelligence Laboratory, Zhengzhou University (2013)
8. Wang, H.-Q., Niu, Z.-W., Liang, L.-J: Feature selection based on rough set and gravitational search algorithm. In: Proceedings of 20th International Conference on Industrial Engineering and Engineering Management: Theory and Apply of Industrial Engineering, pp. 409–418 (2013)

9. Li, P., Xu, W., Zhou, Z., Li, R.: Optimized operation of microgrid based on gravitational search algorithm. In: 2013 International Conference on Electrical Machines and Systems, pp. 338–342 (2013)

10. De Moura Oliveira, P.B., Solteiro Pires, E.J., Novais, P.: Gravitational search algorithm design of posicast PID control systems. In: Snášel, V., Abraham, A., Corchado, E. (eds.) SOCO 2012. AISC, vol. 188, pp. 191–199. Springer, Heidelberg (2013). doi:10.1007/978-3-642-32922-7_20

11. Saha, S.K., Mukherjee, S., Mandal, D., Kar, R., Ghoshal, S.P.: Gravitational search algorithm in digital FIR low pass filter design. In: 2012 3rd International Conference on Emerging Applications of Information Technology, pp. 52–55 (2012)

12. Mustaza, S.M., Zainal Abidin, A.F., Ibrahim, Z., Shamsudin, M.A., Husain, A.R., Ahmed Mukrid, J.A.: A modified computational model of ant colony system in DNA sequence design. In: 2011 IEEE Student Conference on Research and Development (SCORED 2011), pp. 187–191 (2011)

13. Kurniawan, T.B., Khalid, N.K., Ibrahim, Z., Khalid, M., Middendorf, M: Evaluation of ordering methods for DNA sequence design based on ant colony system. In: Asia International Conference on Modeling and Simulation, pp. 905–910 (2008)

Simulation of Electromagnetic Actuated Valveless Micropump for Bidirectional Flow

Mohd Qamarul Arifin Rusli[1], Pei Song Chee[2], and Pei Ling Leow[1(✉)]

[1] Faculty of Electrical Engineering, Universiti Teknologi Malaysia,
81310 Skudai Johor, Malaysia
leowpl@utm.my
[2] Lee Kong Chian, Faculty of Engineering and Science,
Universiti Tunku Abdul Rahman, 43000 Kajang Selangor, Malaysia

Abstract. In this work, a theoretical analysis on the electromagnetic actuated valveless micropump for bidirectional flow is reported. The microchannel module is optimized to increase the smoothness of stream flow inside the chamber by modified the tangential angle to an optimum angle of 79.80°, with microchannel specifications of 10 mm chamber diameter and 1 mm channel width. In addition, the numerical simulation study determines the best shape selection of the micropump actuator: NdFeB magnet involved in membrane displacement. It is observed that cylindrical shaped magnet gives the lowest membrane stress when a force is applied. The obtained optimum geometrical parameters and best magnet shape were then being used for the dual chamber design for bidirectional flow micropump. From the analysis obtained, the micropump was capable for bidirectional flow application. Hence, the optimized design geometry for the microchannel and the best NdFeB magnet size can serve as a design guideline for bidirectional flow micropump without a complex structure.

Keywords: Dual chambers · Bidirectional flow · Valveless micropump

1 Introduction

Microfluidics device is a miniature laboratory platform that processes or manipulates small amounts of fluids using channels with the dimensions of tens to hundreds of micrometres [1–3]. For the past few decades, the microfluidic devices or the Lab on Chip (LOC) has gained rapid research interest in various fields such as chemical analysis, environmental analysis and biomedical diagnosis [4–6]. The idea was first introduced by Manz et al. [7], and is accelerated in the early of the 21th century [6, 8, 9] due to the emergence of nanotechnology. Micropump, an element in fluids flow controlled, has become prominent in microfluidics devices [10, 11]. Integration of microfluidics system that able to dispense small dose of liquids (drug) into the patient's body with the controlled amount has long been a goal in the micropump development [11–13]. For instance, the micropump able to control the insulin delivery level to maintain the diabetics' blood sugar level instead frequent needle injections.

© Springer Nature Singapore Pte Ltd. 2017
M.S. Mohamed Ali et al. (Eds.): AsiaSim 2017, Part I, CCIS 751, pp. 615–627, 2017.
DOI: 10.1007/978-981-10-6463-0_53

With the diversity of lab on a chip (LOC) applications, various micropumps are needed to provide a wide range of flow that is compatible to different LOC' needs [2, 3, 14]. It is hard to have a commercial micropump that is versatile and robust enough to fit for various type of LOC applications that able to provide variety of flow rate [9]. In addition, most of the designed micropump focus on single flow and consists of expensive build up. Often due to the diversity of the LOC applications, the use of a single micropump is very limited and often several micropumps will be needed in order to cope with the LOC applications. For different LOC application, integration of multiple micropumps in a LOC is required. As the pumping chamber is permanently attached to the micropump that causes it to be difficult to be cleaned, furthermore the actuation unit is often shared by various applications, therefore special care is highly needed in order to ensure the pumping chamber is 100% free of contamination.

In this study, an electromagnetic actuated valveless micropump for bidirectional fluid flow is studied using a finite element analysis method. The deflection of magnet (actuator) is the important element in this study to relate the flow properties of the valveless pump. In addition, the construction of the actuator device must be parallel with the chamber design, so that, the system can pump to generate a flow. The microchannel design was more focusing on the aspect of fixed geometry valveless micropump. The availability of new microfabrication techniques has made smaller size micropump system more feasible and achievable. The fabrication for miniature device can be designed for mobile device purpose for example in drug dosing application [10, 15, 16]. In contrast, when designing a complex system, the drawback is the cost for fabrication is very high.

2   Design Overview and Working Principle

An electromagnetic actuated micropump has been developed in an effort to meet the needs in the microfluidics field's application, for example in fluid mixing, liquid cooling and modern drug treatments [13, 17]. The new design offers a low voltage supply (1.5 V_{dc} input supply [18]), miniature (dimension), bidirectional flow and constructed in a modular basis. The pump parameters and design requirements are based on the simulated result prior before fabrication. The geometrical layout is shown in Fig. 1, drawn by SolidWorks® 3D CAD software (Dassault SystèmesSolidWorks Corp, USA).

Figure 1 shows the micropump setup, comprises a moving diaphragm (membrane sheet), dual chambers valveless microchannel, an electromagnetic actuator, an external controller and reservoirs. The working fluid is supplied via the reservoirs to the microchannel inlet/outlet and the fluid flow is in bidirectional mode. The membrane sheet is bonded on top of the microchannel module. The microchannel chip consists of two chambers with a diameter of 10 mm. To maximize the membrane displacement, the NdFeB magnets were positioned at centre of the chambers coincide with the vertical centreline of the power inductors respectively. The ratio between the chambers to the NdFeB magnet is 10:1. Two power inductors (Coilcraft Inc., Illinois, USA) were placed at the bottom of the microchannel module in series with the NdFeB magnets. The electromagnetic actuator module is controlled by an external controller. The controller controls the input supply of the actuator to attract and repel the working

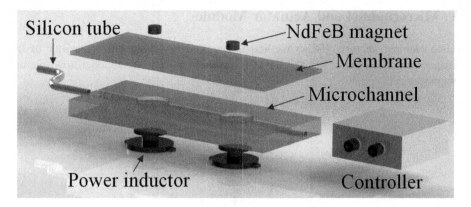

Fig. 1. The complete electromagnetic actuated micropump system with a controller module.

magnet on the membrane at a desired frequency. Each power inductor commands its own fluid direction either to flow in forward or in reversed direction. Figure 2 shows the operation of a power inductor in steady state mode, repel and attract operation based on the induced voltage supply.

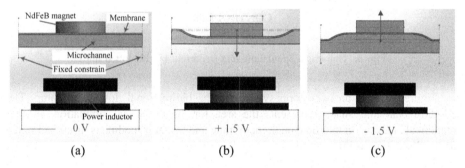

Fig. 2. Electromagnetic actuator working principle (a) Rest mode (b) magnetized condition induced by positive voltage (c) repelled condition induced by negative voltage.

Figure 2 illustrates the operation of the micropump in three conditions: rest mode, upward motion and downward motion. The oscillation of NdFeB magnet was influenced by the polarity of the supplied voltage from the power inductor to attract and repel the magnet [19, 20]. In rest mode (Fig. 2(a)) no supply voltage, and hence, there is no membrane movement. When the positive polarity voltage is induced (Fig. 2(b)), the magnet is attracted towards the power inductor. The membrane is deflected to expel fluid through the channel. On the other hand, negative polarity (Fig. 2(c)) repelled the magnet and inflates the membrane, thus the fluid will enter into the chamber. The continuous cycle of changing voltage polarities to attract and repel the magnet create a net fluid flow. Different frequency gives different flow rate [19, 21].

3   Microchannel and Actuator Module

Finite element analysis (FEA) method is required to predict the behaviour of the designed device. Figure 3 shows the element involve in a bidirectional flow microp-ump system.

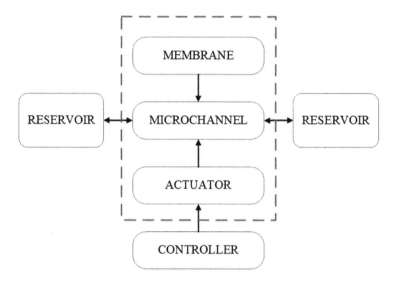

Fig. 3. Numerical simulation area (represent by the dotted line).

Figure 3 shows an open loop system for the bidirectional flow micropump. The dashed-rectangular shape represents the area for the numerical simulation. Further numerical analysis on microchannel, membrane and actuator module is discussed in the next subsections in this section.

3.1   Microchannel Modules

To ensure the micropump delivers optimum flow performance, the physical parameters of the actuator device: the membrane thickness and shape, and the design of the microchannel have been studied for the FEA method by using COMSOL Multi-physics® (COMSOL Inc., Burlington, USA). Numerical simulation parameters required for FEA are shown in Fig. 4.

As shown in Fig. 4, the microfluidics device consists of two pump chambers, a single channel and a membrane sheet. The density, Young's modulus and Poisson's ratio of the PDMS material are 965 kgm^{-3} [22], 1.32×10^6 Pa [23] and 0.499 [23] respectively. To reduce the fluid flow resistance on the wall and increase the smoothness of the fluid stream when the fluid enters inside or exit the chamber, a curvature radius was introduced. The geometrical illustration on a curvature radius is shown in Fig. 5.

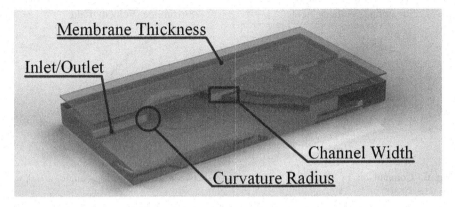

Fig. 4. Simulation parameter for microchannel and membrane modules.

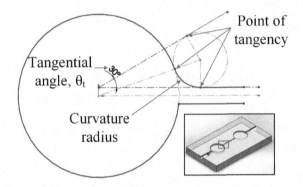

Fig. 5. The curvature radius and tangential angle for a microchannel.

The curvature radius is situated between the chamber and straight channel as shown in Fig. 5. The radius is determined by the opening of tangential angle, θ_t. Tangential angle is where the two points of tangencies touches or make contact with the channel and chamber wall to form a circle. The curve intersection between the channel and chamber is called a curvature radius. The tangential angle for this design specification is 79.80° for a 10 mm chamber diameter and 1 mm channel width. The distance between outlet and centre chamber is 15 mm. The streamlines pattern and the average velocity as respect to the curvature radius opening were studied. The input pressure was applied at 1×10^{-3} Nm^{-2} at the inlet channel. The streamline results for minimum and maximum tangential angles are shown in Fig. 6.

Figure 6 shows the streamline flow pattern between two tangential angles when fluid enter the straight channel from the chamber. The streamline flow on the maximum tangential angle was very smooth as compared to the 0° of tangential angle. The full simulation result from 0° to 79.80° of tangential angle is presented in Fig. 7.

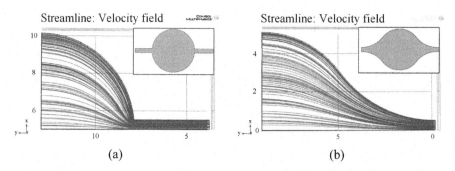

Fig. 6. Comparison of streamline velocity field between two tangential angle (a) $\theta_t = 0°$ (b) $\theta_t = 79.80°$.

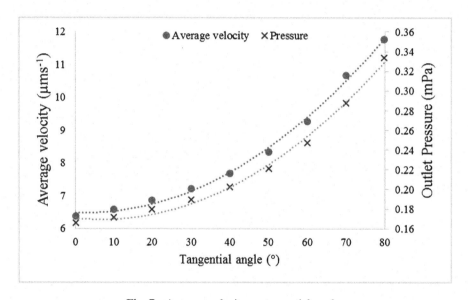

Fig. 7. Average velocity vs tangential angle.

Figure 7 shows average velocity inside the microchannel at different tangential angle design. The graph shows that when the opening of tangential angle increased, the flow became smooth, thus increase the fluid velocity to flow inside the microchannel. From the unmodified angle until to the maximum tangential angle, the velocity at the outlet is increasing. Based on the input pressure of 1×10^{-3} Nm^{-2} at the inlet channel, among the simulated tangential angle, the maximum average velocity at the outlet is 11.27 μms^{-1} with 79.80° of the tangential angle. In addition, the pressure at the outlet is increased from 0.17 mPa ($\theta_t = 0°$) to 0.33 mPa ($\theta_t = 79.80°$). Therefore, to reduce the streamline resistance on the wall and increase the smoothness of the fluid flow to the optimum is by modifying the tangential angle to maximum of 79.80° for the design specification of 10 mm chamber diameter and 1 mm channel width.

3.2   Electromagnetic Actuator

The micropump involves permanent magnets as the actuating element. The numerical simulation study was to determine the best magnet in term of membrane stress and displacement. There are two types of permanent magnets available in the market; neodymium iron boron (NdFeB) and samarium-cobalt (SmCo). SmCo magnet can be found only in a powder and huge block forms only, whereas NdFeB magnet is produced in many forms. For this work, the only parameter to be emphasized is the magnet shape and its availability in the market, meanwhile compressive and tensile strength were in low priority. In term of cost, NdFeB is cheaper than SmCo. The available NdFeB magnet shapes are triangle, cylindrical, rectangular and ball shaped magnet. The density, Young's modulus and Poisson's ratio of the NdFeB magnet are 7500 kgm^{-3}, 1.6×10^{11} Pa and 0.24 respectively (Taiwan Magnetic Corporation Ltd, China).

Each shape gives different magnetic strength that is resulting to different membrane displacement. The magnet was bonded on top centre of the membrane. The thin membrane was made from a polydimethysiloxane (PDMS) material. The membrane was a round flat sheet with thickness of 1 mm. shows the magnet shape and type that was being used for the numerical simulation. From Table 1, there are five types of magnet size range from 3 mm to 7 mm. At initial state, there are no force is acting on

Table 1. NdFeB magnet shape and type.

NdFeB magnet		
Shape	Type	Size
Cylindrical shape	1	3 mm
	2	4 mm
	3	5 mm
	4	6 mm
	5	7 mm
Rectagular shape (length × width)	1	3 mm × 3 mm
	2	4 mm × 4 mm
	3	5 mm × 5 mm
	4	6 mm × 6 mm
	5	7 mm × 7 mm
Triagle shape	1	3 mm × 3 mm × 3 mm
	2	4 mm × 4 mm × 4 mm
	3	5 mm × 5 mm × 5 mm
	4	6 mm × 6 mm × 6 mm
	5	7 mm × 7 mm × 7 mm
Ball shape (diameter)	1	3 mm
	2	4 mm
	3	5 mm
	4	6 mm
	5	7 mm

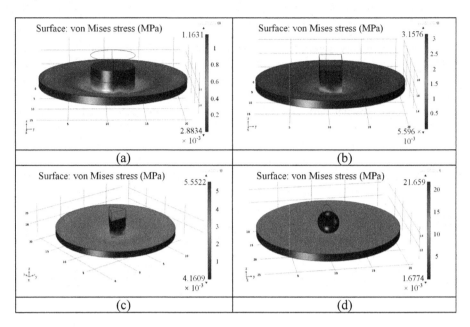

Fig. 8. Membrane displacement from Type 1 on each magnet shape (a) cylindrical shape (b) rectangular shape (c) triangular shape (d) ball shape.

the NdFeB magnet. After that, the force is applied at 1 N in −z direction on the top centre of the magnet. Therefore, displacement is observed in downward direction on the membrane. The shape of the membrane and thickness were constant. Only the size of the magnet was changed and the responding variables are the membrane displacement and Von Mises Stress. So, there are 20 simulations were being conducted. Figure 8 shows the 3D visualization results from the simulation for the smallest size of each magnet shape.

Figure 8 shows that the membrane displacement at different force. Result was taken in form of Von Mises stress. By definition, Von Mises stress is widely used by designers to check whether their design can withstand from a given load condition. The design will break if the stress exceed the maximum tensile strength of a material. For the type 1, it is observed that cylindrical shape magnet gives the lowest stress when force applied as compared to the other three shapes. Meanwhile, the ball shape magnet gives the highest stress to the membrane. This is because the surface contact ratio between the cylindrical magnet and membrane is larger among the other three magnets. The relation of the data is plotted in Fig. 9.

As reported by Johnston et al., the ultimate strength (fracture strength) for PDMS at 25 °C curing temperature is 5.13 ± 0.55 MPa [23]. If the stress limit of the membrane is on or above this limit, the membrane will break and fail to operate. The fracture strength limit of 5.13 MPa was added to the plot. As observed in Fig. 9, the cylindrical shape is within the stress limit. As a result, the best magnet shape for the membrane in this actuating operation is the cylindrical shape. In addition, in all the shape types, cylindrical shape gives the lowest stress among the rest.

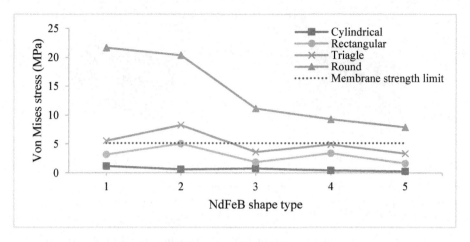

Fig. 9. Von Mises stress *vs* NdFeB magnet type.

4   Dual Chamber Design for Bidirectional Flow

FEA is further extended to investigate on the dual chambers design. The design criterias for the dual chambers is based on the optimum parameter from the previous analysis. The geometrical design is illustrated in Fig. 10.

As shown in Fig. 10, there are two types on microchannel; Type 1 and Type 2 microchannel design. The Type 2 microchannel is the modified version from Type 1 by adding the curvature radius. Two chambers were being designed and a magnet was placed on top of the chamber respectively. The size ratio between the chamber and magnet was 1:0.4 where 5 mm for chamber radius and 2 mm for cylindrical shape

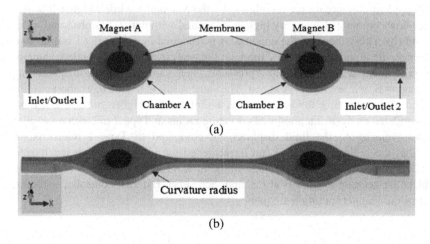

Fig. 10. The dual chamber design with a membrane and two magnets (a) Type 1 microchannel design (b) Type 2 microchannel design.

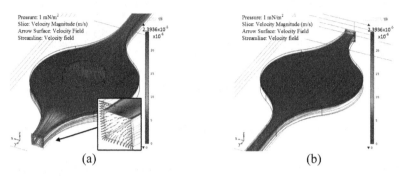

Fig. 11. Streamline comparison on Type 2 between chamber A and B when 1×10^{-3} Nm^{-2} pressure is applied on the magnet A (a) Chamber A with magnet (b) Chamber B.

magnet radius. The channel is in rectangular shape with 1 mm height and width. The total channel length from the outlet 1 to outlet 2 was 60 mm. There were two steps in performing the simulation: apply a pressure on top of Magnet A while Magnet B at rest. The reading on outlet A and B were taken, while the second step is to repeat the method on step one with the pressure applied on Magnet B while Magnet A at rest. The pressure was applied in parametric sweep between the values of 0.2×10^{-3} Nm^{-2} to 1×10^{-3} Nm^{-2} with a 0.2×10^{-3} Nm^{-2} increment. The pressure was applied in $-z$ direction (downward). The simulated result on Type 2 is shown on Fig. 11.

Figure 11 illustrates the simulated result on Type 2 microchannel when Magnet A is applied with a 1×10^{-3} Nm^{-2} pressure. The flow velocity occurred at the outlet A was 12.39 μms^{-1} meanwhile at the outlet B is only 2.70 μms^{-1}. Maximum flow rate occurs is noted at 23.94 μms^{-1}. The simulated result with different input pressures on both magnets are plotted in Fig. 12.

Figure 12 shows the average velocity comparison between Type 1 and Type 2 at the two outlets when the pressure was applied on Magnet A and Magnet B respectively. In all applied pressure on the membrane by the Magnet A while Magnet B at rest, the water flows on outlet 1 was very high as compared with outlet 2 as observed in Fig. 12 (a) and (b). This is because the chamber A is designed near to outlet 1 but far to outlet 2. Hence, the liquid tends to flow more on the nearest outlet. Both outlets velocity was observed linear at all applied input pressure. Then, same input pressures were applied on Magnet B, while Magnet A at rest. The same result is obtained, as shown in Fig. 12 (c) and (d) but this time the velocity flow at outlet 2 was higher that outlet 1. Based on the simulated analysis, the modified curvature radius at Type 2 microchannel gives the highest velocity to the fluid displacement compared to Type 1 microchannel. In addition, the bidirectional flow can be achieved by controlling both the magnets to vibrate the membrane; fluid will flow in the forward direction when only magnet A is induced by keeping magnet B at rest and vice versa. External controller is required to control the magnet vibration frequency.

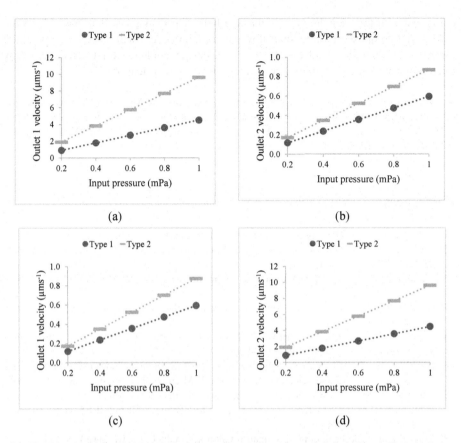

Fig. 12. Simulated result (a) velocity on outlet 1 when Magnet A is induced (b) velocity on outlet 2 when Magnet A is induced (c) velocity on outlet 1 when Magnet B is induced (d) velocity on outlet 2 when Magnet B is induced.

5   Conclusion

In this study, finite element analysis of the bidirectional micropump has been reported. This study proposes the mechanism to design a bidirectional micropump actuated by an electromagnetic actuator. Simulation using Comsol Multiphysics reveals the modification of curvature radius between the chamber and straight channel gives a significant effect to the working fluid to flow. The modification advantageous a better streamline without the usage of a moving valve, which is easily to break and contaminate the working fluid. When the curve opening is increased, the fluid flow resistance is reduced, thus smoothen the streamline flow. In this study, the maximum tangential angle for curvature radius is 79.80° with 1 mm channel width and 10 mm chamber radius. The input pressure of $1 \times 10^{-3} \, \mathrm{Nm}^{-2}$ is applied to the working fluid at the inlet channel, producing $\sim 11.27 \, \mathrm{\mu m s^{-1}}$ maximum flow velocity. In addition, the interaction between NdFeB cylindrical magnet and membrane gives an optimum displacement compared with the triangle, rectangular and ball shaped magnets that available in the market. The proposed bidirectional flow micropump design will have a vast potential for future development and could serve as a design guideline for bidirectional flow micropump without a complex structure and low cost fabrication.

Acknowledgement. The authors would like to acknowledge the Ministry of Higher Education of Malaysia for sponsoring this research study through the MyPhD scholarship. This research study is also funded by Research University Grant (Q.J130000.2523.05H29), UTARRF (IPSR/RMC/UTARRF/2017-C1/C01) Vote: 6200/CC8 and FRGS (R.J130000.7823.4F462).

References

1. Whitesides, G.M.: The origins and the future of microfluidics. Nature **442**, 368–373 (2006)
2. Woias, P.: Micropumps—past, progress and future prospects. Sens. Actuators B: Chem. **105**, 28–38 (2005)
3. Laser, D.J., Santiago, J.G.: A review of micropumps. J. Micromech. Microeng. **14**, R35 (2004)
4. Cima, M.J.: Microsystem technologies for medical applications. Annu. Rev. Chem. Biomol. Eng. **2**, 355–378 (2011)
5. West, J., Becker, M., Tombrink, S., Manz, A.: Micro total analysis systems: latest achievements. Anal. Chem. **80**, 4403–4419 (2008)
6. Bell, D.J., Lu, T.J., Fleck, N.A., Spearing, S.M.: MEMS actuators and sensors: observations on their performance and selection for purpose. J. Micromech. Microeng. **15**, S153 (2005)
7. Manz, A., Graber, N., Widmer, H.M., Terry, S.C., Jerman, J.H., Angell, J.B.: Miniaturized total chemical analysis systems: a novel concept for chemical sensing. IEEE Trans. Electron Devices **26**, 244–248 (1979)
8. Mirkin, C.A.: The beginning of a small revolution. Small **1**, 14–16 (2005)
9. Nabavi, M.: Steady and unsteady flow analysis in microdiffusers and micropumps: a critical review. Microfluid. Nanofluid. **7**, 599 (2009)
10. Foroutan, P., Djadid, A.D., Nadafi, R., Barazandeh, F., Mahdiabadi, A.M.: Process design and microfabrication of a novel lab on a chip. In: 2011 Symposium on Design, Test, Integration & Packaging of MEMS/MOEMS (DTIP), pp. 372–374 (2011)
11. Wikswo, J.P., Block, F.E., Cliffel, D.E., Goodwin, C.R., Marasco, C.C., Markov, D., et al.: Engineering challenges for instrumenting and controlling integrated organ-on-chip systems. IEEE Trans. Biomed. Eng. **60**, 682–690 (2013)
12. Thomas, L.J., Bessman, S.P.: Prototype for an implantable insulin delivery pump. Proc. West. Pharmacol. Soc. **18**, 393–398 (1975)
13. Hamie, A., Ghafar-Zadeh, E., Sawan, M.: An implantable micropump prototype for focal drug delivery. In: 2013 IEEE International Symposium on Medical Measurements and Applications (MeMeA), pp. 278–281 (2013)
14. Bartel, S., Trawiński, T.: Design issues of electromagnetic micropump. In: 15th International Workshop on Research and Education in Mechatronics (REM), pp. 1–7 (2014)
15. Liguo, C., Yaxin, L., Lining, S., Dongsheng, Q., Jijiang, M.: Intelligent control of piezoelectric micropump based on MEMS flow sensor. In: 2010 IEEE/RSJ International Conference on Intelligent Robots and Systems, pp. 3055–3060 (2010)

16. Goffredo, R., Pecora, A., Maiolo, L., Ferrone, A., Guglielmelli, E., Accoto, D.: A swallowable smart pill for local drug delivery. J. Microelectromech. Syst. **25**, 362–370 (2016)
17. Zhi, C., Shinshi, T., Saito, M., Kato, K.: Planar-type micro-electromagnetic actuators using patterned thin film permanent magnets and mesh type coils. Sens. Actuators, A: Phys. **220**, 365–372 (2014)
18. Rusli, M.Q.A., Ling, L.P., Song, C.P.: Characterization of electromagnetic valveless micropump. In: International Conference on Electrical, Electronic, Communication and Control Engineering (ICEECC 2016), Faculty of Electrical Engineering, Universiti Teknologi Malaysia, Johor Bahru Malaysia, pp. 771–777 (2016)
19. Shen, M., Yamahata, C., Gijs, M.A.M.: Miniaturized PMMA ball-valve micropump with cylindrical electromagnetic actuator. Microelectron. Eng. **85**, 1104–1107 (2008)
20. Ni, J., Wang, B., Chang, S., Lin, Q.: An integrated planar magnetic micropump. Microelectron. Eng. **117**, 35–40 (2014)
21. Ke, M.-T., Zhong, J.-H., Lee, C.-Y.: Electromagnetically-actuated reciprocating pump for high-flow-rate microfluidic applications. Sensors **12**, 13075–13087 (2012)
22. Selvaraj, H., Tan, B., Venkatakrishnan, K.: Maskless direct micro-structuring of PDMS by femtosecond laser localized rapid curing. J. Micromech. Microeng. **21**, 075018 (2011)
23. Johnston, I.D., McCluskey, D.K., Tan, C.K.L., Tracey, M.C.: Mechanical characterization of bulk Sylgard 184 for microfluidics and microengineering. J. Micromech. Microeng. **24**, 035017 (2014)

Aspen Plus® Simulation Studies of Steam Gasification in Fluidized Bed Reactor for Hydrogen Production Using Palm Kernel Shell

Maham Hussain[✉], Lemma Dendena Tufa, Suzana Yusup,
Haslinda Zabiri, and Syed A. Taqvi

Department of Chemical Engineering,
Universiti Teknologi PETRONAS, Seri Iskandar, Malaysia
maham.hussain@gmail.com

Abstract. In this paper, a steady state simulation for hydrogen production from steam gasification of Palm kernel shell was developed and studied. The gasification pilot plant process has been modelled in Aspen Plus® using Gibbs reactor (R-Gibbs). The effects of different operating parameters using sensitivity analysis, including gasification temperature 600–900 °C and steam flow rate (1 to 2 kg/hr.), on hydrogen yields and Syngas composition were investigated. The simulation results have shown the main gas components in Synthesis gas were H_2, CO, CO_2, CH_4. The product gas hydrogen yield increases with the increase in temperature. The hydrogen concentration improved from 22.52 vol. % to 36.06 vol.%, but the CO concentration decreased from 37.53 vol.% to 28.37% with increasing temperature from 650–900 °C under the operating parameters of the steam flow rate of 1.56 kg/hr.

Keywords: Biomass gasification system · Palm kernel shell · Steady state simulation · Aspen plus software

1 Introduction

With the increasing world energy demands and depleting oil and natural gas reserves, biomass is considered as the most promising alternative to fossil fuels owing to its abundant availability and carbon neutral nature [1–4]. In a sustainable energy system hydrogen is likely to be the most significant energy source for future [5–8]. Presently, there are a number of energy sources and technologies to produce hydrogen but about 99% comes from fossil fuel. It is mainly by steam reforming of natural gas which is the fossil fuel based process that could not address above serious concerns to meet the renewable and sustainable hydrogen production. There is potential in biomass to increase the production of hydrogen and a primary source of energy [5, 9]. More recent attention has focused on the provision of using hydrogen as an energy resource. It is reported that the use of hydrogen has a number of attractive features such as clean fuel because hydrogen combustion yields water rather than greenhouse gases though combustion of hydrogen gives heat and energy which can than used to drive turbine for

© Springer Nature Singapore Pte Ltd. 2017
M.S. Mohamed Ali et al. (Eds.): AsiaSim 2017, Part I, CCIS 751, pp. 628–641, 2017.
DOI: 10.1007/978-981-10-6463-0_54

electricity production [8]. Particularly, oil palm is abundantly available in Malaysia and Indonesia approximately 87% of the worldwide capacity [10]. It is estimated that at about 85.5% of biomass waste is in the form of palm kernel shell, oil palm trunks and fronds and empty fruit bunches in Malaysia. Palm kernel shell is reported as a preferred feedstock in gasification process due to its characteristics like high fixed carbon proportion and volatile matter, low ash and moisture content [11]. Among thermochemical conversion technologies, biomass gasification provides distinctive attributes of efficiency, product flexibility and emission control in comparison to combustion and pyrolysis [12]. Biomass materials can be successfully converted into energy by using circulating fluidized bed biomass gasifier owing to the features of adequate gas-solid contact, improved temperature control, considerable heat capacity, a favorable turbulence condition etc. [5, 10]. Even though CFB gasification commenced with rapid commercialization for biomass, but still there is need of fundamental and pilot studies to scale-up and for its optimum design [13]. Currently, studies and development have shown the potential of producing more and cleaner hydrogen from biomass steam gasification by using catalyst and adsorbent [14]. However, there are many shortcomings while producing hydrogen from biomass gasification technologies [10]. A lot of research and efforts relevant to the catalyst and CO_2 adsorbent usage has been carried out to minimize the biomass gasification process shortcomings. A limited work has been done by using palm oil wastes gasification for hydrogen production in fluidized bed gasifier. The modeling and simulation of biomass gasification is a developing area of research. By far several models with different complexity of biomass gasification process have been proposed [15–26]. Aspen gasifier model can be useful for design, analysis of gasifier behavior and operational condition predictions during start up and shut down. It is reported that experiments are usually expensive and complicated, when performed at a larger scale [27–29]. However, modelling can save time as well as money and also have the ability for the optimization and preparation of experiments in real time [18].

Biomass-based conversion process has been simulated by many researchers using Aspen Plus® [30–48]. Cohce et al. [49] presented flow sheet simulation for biomass gasification for Syn gas production. The minimization of Gibbs free energy along with mass and energy balance approach has been used. It is assumed that catalyst effects are negligible, only char is present which consists of carbon, ash and tar were ignored during the assessment.

The effect of temperature on product gas composition has been studied. The maximum hydrogen predicted from biomass is 41.85 g/kg [49]. Mansaray et al. simulate rice husk gasification process using commercial software Aspen Plus® for the calculation of material, energy, and chemical equilibrium [50]. Nikoo and Mahinpey have also developed Aspen plus reactor model by using FORTRAN subroutines for kinetics and hydrodynamics data generation. The effects of different operating conditions were used to validate the model [10]. Ramzan et al. [45] demonstrate steady-state simulation model for the gasification process [8]. It is reported that simulation model can be used for optimization and behavioural study of the gasifier. The optimization was done in terms of equivalence ratio, the temperature of the gasifier, air preheating effects on gas composition and heating value [45]. Atnaw et al. used Aspen plus for the simulation of downdraft gasification of oil palm fronds [51].

The aim of this paper is to develop a steady state Aspen plus simulation model of palm kernel shell gasification process for hydrogen production. A parametric analysis has been done to predict the steady state performance of fluidized bed gasifier and the gasifier temperature along with the steam to biomass ratio on Syngas composition, hydrogen yield is analyzed.

1.1 Chemical Reactions

The reaction kinetics that is used in gasification process is as shown in Table 1:

Table 1. Reaction scheme for PKS steam gasification.

Sr #	Process reactions	Reaction	ΔH (kJ/mol)
	Overall reaction	Biomass $\rightarrow$ H_2O, CO, CO_2, CH_4, C_2H_4 and C	
1	Char gasification	$C + H_2O \rightarrow CO + H_2$	+131.5
2	Boudouard	$C + CO_2 \rightarrow 2C$	+172
3	Water-gas shift	$CO + H_2O \rightarrow CO_2 + H_2$	−41
4	Methanation	$C + 2H_2 \rightarrow CH_4$	−74.8
5	Methane reforming	$CH_4 + H_2O \rightarrow CO + 3H_2$	+206

1.2 Process Model

A steady state equilibrium model has been developed for the gasification process using Aspen Plus.

1.2.1 Assumptions
The main assumptions considered in the simulation are as follows:

- The process is carried out at steady state conditions and atmospheric pressure.
- The devolatilization process occurs spontaneously produces synthesis gas contains H_2, CO, CO_2, CH_4 and H_2O.
- The reaction takes place at isothermal and constant volume conditions.
- A constant temperature inside the gasifier and intimate mixing.
- The heat losses are negligible.
- The pressure drop in the gasifier is neglected.
- The particles are assumed to be of spherical and of uniform size and the average diameter remains constant during the gasification.

1.2.2 Thermodynamic Property Package
In aspen plus several property methods are available together with activity coefficient methods and equation of state (EOS) methods [43]. In this study, the PENG-ROBINSON equation of state has been used to estimate all physical properties of conventional components in Aspen Plus steady-state simulation. PENG–ROBIN-SON equation itself is the particular version of the general cubic equation of state. At high temperature, this package improves the correlation of pure component vapor pressure which makes it suitable for gasification process [45].

1.2.3   Biomass Feedstock Properties

The biomass including palm kernel was considered as possible feedstock for syngas production in the gasification process. An instrumented controlled pilot plant of bio-mass gasification situated in Block-P University Teknologi PETRONAS that can be sufficiently run using feedstock PKS as shown in Fig. 1. Palm kernel shell has been reported as a prominent feedstock due to its properties for the gasification of biomass [12]. The ultimate analysis and proximate analysis on a dry free basis along with higher heating values of PKS can be found in Table 2. The calorific value of palm kernel shell is 20.40 MJ kg^{-1}, it contains 17.5% moisture which is less in comparison with other biomass such as coconut shell (18.5 wt%), sugarcane residue (52.20 wt%) and empty fruit bunch (66.26 wt%). Palm kernel Shell holds 14.87% fixed carbon and 81.03% volatile matter. The efficiency of gasification process would be more due to a higher percentage of these matters results in the better ignition and gasifying properties. Ng et al. [13] has also reported that gasification of palm kernel shell results in highest hydrogen production (28.48 g H_2/kg palm kernel shell) in contrast to rice husk, bagasse and coconut shell.

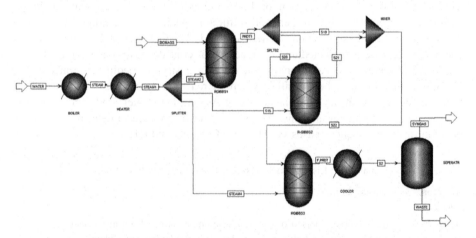

Fig. 1. Simulation flow sheet for the fluidized bed gasification process.

1.2.4   Simulation Description

The schematic flow sheet of PKS gasification process (developed in Aspen Plus®) is shown in Fig. 1. This flow sheet represents a typical setup used in biomass experimental studies [53]. The unit operations block data along with the operating conditions are taken from an actual plant given in Table 3. The overall gasification stages comprise of feed decomposition, de-volatilization and gas-solid separation in the simulation model. Biomass (Palm kernel shell) as a feedstock (on a wt% dry basis) is regarded as a non-conventional component fed at 1.35 kg/hr and (defined as a heterogeneous solid in Aspen Plus®). Aspen Plus ®incorporate R-YIELD reactor block to decompose it into elementary conventional components (C, H_2, O_2, N_2, Cl, S). The Aspen plus R-GIBBS Reactor was used to perform the decomposition and gasification of PKS with the

Table 2. Properties of palm kernel shell [52].

Palm kernel shell	
Molecular equation	$CH_{1.283}O_{0.594}N_{0.031}$
Moisture (%)	9.61
Volatile matter (wt% dry basis)	80.92
Fixed carbon (wt% dry basis)	14.67
Ash content	4.31
C (wt% dry basis)	49.74
H (wt% dry basis)	5.68
N (wt% dry basis)	1.02
S (wt% dry basis)	0.27
O (by difference)	43.36
Higher heating value	18.46
Calorific value (MJ/kg^{-1})	20.40

assumption that these reactions follow the Gibbs free energy minimization calculations. This step employs decomposition of PKS into constituting components including carbon, hydrogen, oxygen, nitrogen, and sulfur at a specified temperature and pressure. The combustible substance from R-GIBBS include H_2, CO, CO_2, CH_4, and SO_2. The catalytic effects were neglected and the reactor was considered to operate at isothermal and isobaric conditions. Additionally, steam as a gasifying medium supplied to the bottom of the fluidized bed gasifier, where it reacts with biomass. The steam has produced at 300 °C in the super heater using Aspen plus Heater model. Some part of the gas is further sent for analysis. An analyzer has been used to determine the composition of the subsequent gases i.e. H_2, CO, CO_2, N_2 and CH_4.

Table 3. List of block in biomass gasification simulation.

Reactor block	Description
R-Gibbs	This model is based on single phase chemical equilibrium works on minimization of Gibbs free energy; This model has significance under known temperature and pressure with unknown stoichiometry
Heater	Thermal and phase state changer. Increase the temperature of water to make it superheated steam
Split	Feed splitter. Divide feed based on splits specified by outlet streams
Mixer	Mixes two or more stream. It can also combine material, heat and work streams
Flash	It is generally known as two-outlet flash. this model works on the principle of rigorous vapor-liquid or vapor-liquid-liquid equilibrium

Additionally, the gas product supplied further to Gasfier-2 and Gasifier-3. The final product from Gasifier-3. Furthermore, the product stream is cooled to 40 °C in a cooler and later will go to adsorption column system. A gas-liquid absorber was used for the separation of liquid and gas (syn. gas) products at atmospheric conditions. The equipment involve are summarized in Table 4.

Table 4. List of equipment in biomass gasification system.

Equipment	Parameters			
	Temperature °C	Pressure barg	Flow rate m^3/hr	Capacity m^3/hr
Cooling water pump	25	1	0.6	2
Boiler	150	6	0.0082	0.1
Super heater	400	6.9	0.00196	5.0
Fluidized bed gasifier	700	6	0.17	0.044
Guard bed gasifier	700	6	0.15	0.044
Gas polisher reactor	700	6	0.26	0.044
Adsorption column system	40	12	5	0.008

2 Results and Discussion

The developed simulation model is evaluated by synthesis gas composition variation with temperature and steam to biomass ratio in Aspen Plus®.

2.1 Effect of Gasification Temperature

The effects of gasifier temperature on Syngas production using PKS and steam as gasifying agents in interconnected fluidized bed gasifiers was analyzed and reported. The gasifier temperature was varied from 650–900 °C, at 2.1 bars constant pressure, with steam to biomass ratio of 0.6. Then composition of product Syngas as a function of gasifier temperature is presented, as shown in Fig. 2.

The result indicates that temperature has significant effects on hydrogen yield. The production of H_2 and CO increases as the temperature increase. Conversely, the composition of CO_2 and CH_4 decrease respectively. The hydrogen production enhanced with the increase in gasifier temperature and then kept nearly constant at about 800 °C. This further demonstrates that within the gasifier temperature range of 650–900 °C. H_2 content was about 50–70 mol%. It is clear from the Fig. 2 that the favorable operating temperature for the gasifier lies between 750–850 °C to maintain higher hydrogen content in the product gas.

A series of reactions involve for PKS gasification, which results in syngas production, as mentioned in Table 1. The first two reactions are endothermic processes whereas water gas shift reaction (3) is an exothermic reaction. Consequently, higher temperature favors the reactants in the exothermic and products in the endothermic reactions. Therefore, endothermic reactions 1, 2, 5 were promoted with an increase in gasifier temperature. This results in an increase of H_2, CO, and decrease in CO_2 and CH_4 content.

It is apparent from the results that hydrogen was much higher than CO and there exist a constant difference between the two gases concentrations. Due to the water gas shift reaction activity CO and H_2 composition changes within the temperature range of 650–900 °C. Moreover, the water gas shift reaction increases the hydrogen production

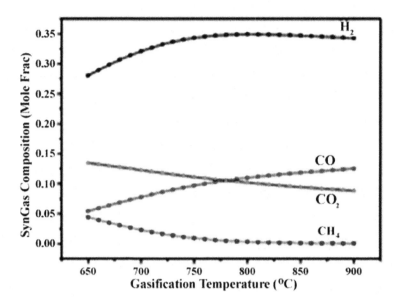

Fig. 2. Effect of gasifier temperature on product gas composition (steam/biomass ratio = 2.0).

in the presence of steam. The hydrogen production was further enhanced due to the methane reforming reaction in the presence of steam.

Even though, water gas shift reaction produces CO_2 which further decrease with increase in temperature. This was due to boudouard reaction (2), which becomes dominant and consumes CO_2, The results showed an increase of CO content and decrease in CO_2 with the increase in temperature. In the current study, it is clear that as the temperature increase water gas shift reaction becomes dominant in the range of 600–675 °C. This give rise to an increase in CO content up to 750 °C due to the high reactivity of steam methane reforming reaction. Furthermore, the hydrogen yield efficiency was analyzed within the gasifier temperature effects.

The H_2 yield efficiency of biomass can be defined by the given formulas, respectively.

$$H_2 \text{ Yield efficiency} = \frac{H_2 \text{ yield in the gasifier(g)}}{Biomass(dry, \; ashfree) \, fed \, into \, the \, system \, (kg)} \quad (1)$$

The effect of the gasifier temperature on the H_2 yield is as shown in Fig. 3. The results, as shown in Fig. 3, indicates that hydrogen yield increased as the gasifier temperature increased. The favorable operating temperature range is 750–850 °C, corresponding to the high hydrogen yield. There is no increase beyond the temperature 850 °C, as higher temperature further facilitates the side product formation. Furthermore, it was observed that increase in steam content, shifts the water gas reaction towards the product formation direction. Overall more steam produces more hydrogen but of consumes higher energy.

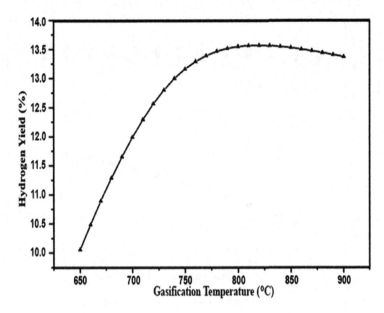

Fig. 3. Effect of gasifier temperature on product gas yield.

2.2 Effect of Steam/Biomass Ratio

This study has examined the effect of steam/biomass on syngas production from PKS gasification in inter-connected fluidized beds. For steam/biomass ratio, the analysis was done by varying the steam flow under a constant flow rate of biomass.

The steam/biomass ratio effect on product gas composition at gasifier temperature of 650 °C is shown in the Fig. 5. The findings of current study support the published experimental data which showed that the steam/biomass holds a complex effect on the product gas composition. The results of this study indicates that by increasing steam/biomass ratio H_2 and CO content increased well, whereas CO_2 content decrease constantly and decrease in CH_4 was much less. Furthermore, this can be understood by the chemical equilibrium achieved during water-gas shift reaction.

For the simulation results, hydrogen yield corresponds to the maximum for a steam/biomass ratio of 0.74 and the gasifier temperature of 800–850 °C as illustrated in Fig. 4. It is demonstrated that a maximum value of Hydrogen yield can be achieved as the S/B ratio increased. It is established that for steam/biomass ratio around 0.74 gasifiers could achieve equilibrium conditions along with the gasifier temperature of 800 °C in relation to the influencing reactions.

It can be concluded from the results that steam/biomass of about 0.74 can be considered and suggested for future work as an optimized value for H_2 yield efficiency as well as for gas composition.

It is, therefore, likely that at a lower value of steam/biomass ratio of 0.74, there was less steam present to react with the biomass, subsequently, it desists water-gas shift reaction and steam reforming reaction. Therefore, H_2 yield increase with an increase in steam/biomass ratio.

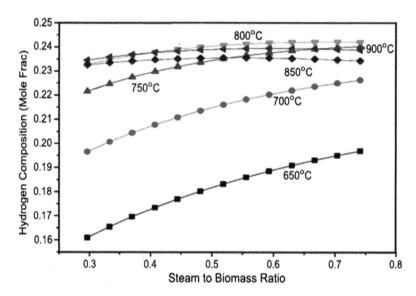

Fig. 4. Effect of steam to biomass ratio on hydrogen gas yield.

At a maximum point, H_2 yield decreases with the increase of steam/biomass ratio. The steam to biomass ratio value correspond to maximum hydrogen yield declined from 0.8–0.5 with the gasifier temperature increase (Fig. 5).

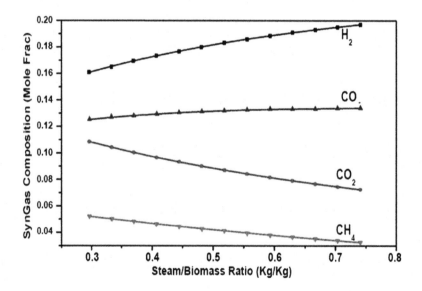

Fig. 5. Effect of steam to biomass ratio on product gas yield.

3   Comparison and Validation

The developed simulation model was validated using measured experimental data of PKS gasification for lab scale gasifier published by Ramzan et al. [45]. The experimental and simulation results are shown in the Fig. 6. Experimental results are compared and presented with error bars which indicate that the simulation data are within 96% confidence level.

A detailed investigation of hydrogen composition comparison with the literature is as shown in the Fig. 6. In the research, hydrogen composition of 60.07 vol.% (dry N2 free) was observed at 750 °C, S/B ratio of 2.0wt/wt. The experimental study reported by Khan et al. [53] on the same pilot plant observed hydrogen composition of 67.40 vol.% at 750 °C, S/B ratio of 2.0wt/wt and adsorbent to biomass ratio of 1.0wt/wt which yields zero carbon dioxide relatively. This study utilized the same feedstock palm kernel shell under steam gasification with nickel catalyst in fluidized bed gasifier. Han et al. [54] reported hydrogen composition of 69 vol.% at a relatively higher temperature of 850 °C utilizing char (from empty fruit bunch) under air gasification in the fluidized bed gasifier. Han et al. [54] produced H_2 composition of 58 vol.% at S/B ratio of 2.55wt/wt in steam gasification with CO_2 adsorbent in fluidized bed gasifier.

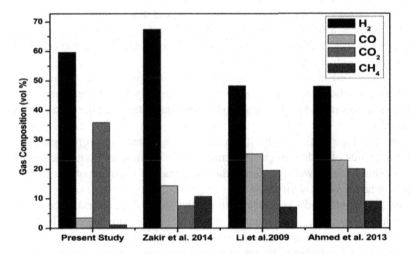

Fig. 6. Comparative study of product gas composition.

The existing study verifies the previous findings from the literature and experimental studies on the similar pilot plant and contributes additional evidence that suggests that air-steam gasification in fluidized bed produced adequate hydrogen amount in product gas but at the cost of the high temperature of 850 °C. Consequently, the use of Cao as an adsorbent reduces the carbon dioxide in the overall product gas which is suggested as future work. Furthermore, steam gasification produced relatively favorable hydrogen at a lower reaction temperature between 630 and 675 °C in the present study, highest hydrogen concentration of 60.1 vol.% with the presence of CO_2

in the product gas at temperature 750 °C is produced. Contrary experimental studies inferred carbon dioxide capture favored low reactor temperature. At lower temperature CO_2 adsorption is the high activity of steam methane reforming along with water gas shift reaction is high which leads to increase hydrogen composition in the product gas. Overall, present study validates the experimentally reported findings with the optimum gas composition in comparison to reported literature. For future work, it is suggested that combination of catalyst and adsorbent in the process provides improved product gas heating values in comparison to only biomass catalytic steam gasification and steam gasification with in situ CO_2 adsorption processes.

4   Conclusion

A simulation model was developed for the gasification of biomass in an atmospheric fluidized bed gasifier using aspen plus® simulator. A sensitivity analysis was carried out in order to evaluate gasifier performance as a function of gasifier temperature and steam to biomass ratio. The simulation results for the product gas composition and product gas yield versus temperature and steam to biomass ratio is reported.

The higher temperature improves both the gasification process as well as product gas yield. The increase in temperature shows that hydrogen and CO content increase and a product gas composition of 70% was achieved at a medium gasifier temperature 675 °C, whereas a lowest composition of 67.32 vol.% is attained at a highest temperature of 800 °C caused by reverse carbonation reaction, the absence of CO_2 was observed at a temperature range of 600–675 °C.

It is concluded from the results that H_2 yield increase with an increase in gasifier temperature Furthermore, hydrogen composition and hydrogen yield were favored by steam to biomass ratio. Despite steam to biomass ratio effects higher than 2.0wt/wt. was not significant.

From the comparative study, it can thus be suggested that current study gives the significant value of hydrogen gas in comparison to biomass steam gasification. Finally, the simulation model well represents the experimental behavior of the biomass gasification, when it is fed with PKS.

The simulation model is adequate to predict the gasifier performance over a range of operating conditions. This model is also suitable for simulation of PKS and other feedstock such as wood, green waste, sugar cane bagasse etc. Therefore, it can be used fully to support the design of the experimental campaigns. Further study is being under taken for modelling performance by considering in situ-catalytic gasification.

Acknowledgment.   The authors gratefully acknowledge financial grant **FRGS:** 0153AB-K40 by Universiti Teknologi PETRONAS.

References

1. Singh, R., Krishna, B.B., Kumar, J., Bhaskar, T.: Opportunities for utilization of non-conventional energy sources for biomass pretreatment. Bioresour. Technol. **199**, 398–407 (2016)

2. Henkel, C., Muley, P.D., Abdollahi, K.K., Marculescu, C., Boldor, D.: Pyrolysis of energy cane bagasse and invasive Chinese tallow tree (Triadica sebifera L.) biomass in an inductively heated reactor. Energy Convers. Manag. **109**, 175–183 (2016)
3. Lim, C.H., Lam, H.L.: Biomass supply chain optimisation via novel biomass element life cycle analysis (BELCA). Appl. Energy **161**, 733–745 (2016)
4. Sharma, S., Sheth, P.N.: Air–steam biomass gasification: experiments, modeling and simulation. Energy Convers. Manag. **110**, 307–318 (2016)
5. Shen, L., Gao, Y., Xiao, J.: Simulation of hydrogen production from biomass gasification in interconnected fluidized beds. Biomass Bioenergy **32**, 120–127 (2008)
6. Göllei, A., Görbe, P., Magyar, A.: Measurement based modeling and simulation of hydrogen generation cell in complex domestic renewable energy systems. J. Cleaner Prod. **111**, 17–24 (2016)
7. Meng, L., Tsuru, T.: Hydrogen production from energy carriers by silica-based catalytic membrane reactors. Catal. Today **268**, 3–11 (2016)
8. Dutta, S.: A review on production, storage of hydrogen and its utilization as an energy resource. J. Ind. Eng. Chem. **20**, 1148–1156 (2014)
9. Holladay, J.D., Hu, J., King, D.L., Wang, Y.: An overview of hydrogen production technologies. Catal. Today **139**, 244–260 (2009)
10. Nikoo, M.B., Mahinpey, N.: Simulation of biomass gasification in fluidized bed reactor using aspen plus. Biomass Bioenergy **32**, 1245–1254 (2008)
11. Abdullah, S.S., Yusup, S.: Method for screening of Malaysian biomass based on aggregated matrix for hydrogen production through gasification. J. Appl. Sci. (Faisalabad) **10**, 3301–3306 (2010)
12. Rezaiyan, J., Cheremisinoff, N.P.: Gasification technologies: a primer for engineers and scientists. CRC Press, Boca Raton (2005)
13. Ng, R.T., Tay, D.H., Ghani, W.A.W.A.K., Ng, D.K.: Modelling and optimisation of biomass fluidised bed gasifier. Appl. Thermal Eng. **61**, 98–105 (2013)
14. Khan, Z., Yusup, S., Ahmad, M.M., Rashidi, N.A.: Integrated catalytic adsorption (ICA) steam gasification system for enhanced hydrogen production using palm kernel shell. Int. J. Hydrogen Energy **39**, 3286–3293 (2014)
15. Shabbar, S., Janajreh, I.: Thermodynamic equilibrium analysis of coal gasification using Gibbs energy minimization method. Energy Convers. Manag. **65**, 755–763 (2013)
16. Barman, N.S., Ghosh, S., De, S.: Gasification of biomass in a fixed bed downdraft gasifier–a realistic model including tar. Bioresour. Technol. **107**, 505–511 (2012)
17. Azzone, E., Morini, M., Pinelli, M.: Development of an equilibrium model for the simulation of thermochemical gasification and application to agricultural residues. Renew. Energy **46**, 248–254 (2012)
18. Saravanakumar, A., Hagge, M.J., Haridasan, T., Bryden, K.M.: Numerical modelling of a fixed bed updraft long stick wood gasifier. Biomass Bioenergy **35**, 4248–4260 (2011)
19. Kaushal, P., Proell, T., Hofbauer, H.: Application of a detailed mathematical model to the gasifier unit of the dual fluidized bed gasification plant. Biomass Bioenergy **35**, 2491–2498 (2011)
20. Xie, J., Zhong, W., Jin, B., Shao, Y., Liu, H.: Simulation on gasification of forestry residues in fluidized beds by Eulerian-Lagrangian approach. Bioresour. Technol. **121**, 36–46 (2012)
21. Baggio, P., Baratieri, M., Fiori, L., Grigiante, M., Avi, D., Tosi, P.: Experimental and modeling analysis of a batch gasification/pyrolysis reactor. Energy Convers. Manag. **50**, 1426–1435 (2009)
22. Deydier, A., Marias, F., Bernada, P., Couture, F., Michon, U.: Equilibrium model for a travelling bed gasifier. Biomass Bioenergy **35**, 133–145 (2011)

23. Nilsson, S., Gómez-Barea, A., Fuentes-Cano, D., Ollero, P.: Gasification of biomass and waste in a staged fluidized bed gasifier: modeling and comparison with one-stage units. Fuel **97**, 730–740 (2012)
24. Duan, W., Yu, Q., Wang, K., Qin, Q., Hou, L., Yao, X., et al.: ASPEN Plus simulation of coal integrated gasification combined blast furnace slag waste heat recovery system. Energy Convers. Manag. **100**, 30–36 (2015)
25. Bassyouni, M., ul Hasan, S.W., Abdel-Aziz, M.H., Abdel-hamid, S.M.S., Naveed, S., Hussain, A., et al.: Date palm waste gasification in downdraft gasifier and simulation using ASPEN HYSYS. Energy Convers. Manag. **88**, 693–699 (2014)
26. Castello, D., Fiori, L.: Supercritical water gasification of biomass: a stoichiometric thermodynamic model. Int. J. Hydrogen Energy **40**, 6771–6781 (2015)
27. Loha, C., Chattopadhyay, H., Chatterjee, P.K.: Three dimensional kinetic modeling of fluidized bed biomass gasification. Chem. Eng. Sci. **109**, 53–64 (2014)
28. Gómez-Barea, A., Leckner, B.: Modeling of biomass gasification in fluidized bed. Progress Energy Combust. Sci. **36**, 444–509 (2010)
29. Patra, T.K., Sheth, P.N.: Biomass gasification models for downdraft gasifier: a state-of-the-art review. Renew. Sustain. Energy Rev. **50**, 583–593 (2015)
30. Ahmed, T.Y., Ahmad, M.M., Yusup, S., Inayat, A., Khan, Z.: Mathematical and computational approaches for design of biomass gasification for hydrogen production: a review. Renew. Sustain. Energy Rev. **16**, 2304–2315 (2012)
31. Detournay, M., Hemati, M., Andreux, R.: Biomass steam gasification in fluidized bed of inert or catalytic particles: comparison between experimental results and thermodynamic equilibrium predictions. Powder Technol. **208**, 558–567 (2011)
32. Tan, W., Zhong, Q.: Simulation of hydrogen production in biomass gasifier by ASPEN PLUS. In: Power and Energy Engineering Conference (APPEEC), 2010 Asia-Pacific, pp. 1–4 (2010)
33. Ahmad, M.M., Inayat, A., Yusup, S., Sabil, K.M.: Production from empty fruit bunch. J. Appl. Sci. **11**, 2171–2178 (2011)
34. Ahmad, M.M., Chiew, C.K., Inayat, A., Yusup, S.: Hydrogen production using iCON. J. Appl. Sci. **11**, 3593–3599 (2011)
35. Inayat, A., et al.: Flowsheet development and modelling of hydrogen production from empty fruit bunch via steam gasification. Chem. Eng. Trans. **21**, 427–432 (2010)
36. Inayat, A., Ahmad, M.M., Abdul Mutalib, M., Yusup, S.: Process Design of Enriched Hydrogen Gas Production from Empty Fruit Bunch via Steam Gasification with In-Situ CO_2 Capture (2010)
37. Adeyemi, I., Janajreh, I.: Modeling of the entrained flow gasification: kinetics-based ASPEN Plus model. Renew. Energy **82**, 77–84 (2015)
38. Kuo, P.-C., Wu, W.: Thermodynamic analysis of a combined heat and power system with CO_2 utilization based on co-gasification of biomass and coal. Chem. Eng. Sci. **142**, 201–214 (2016)
39. Damartzis, T., Michailos, S., Zabaniotou, A.: Energetic assessment of a combined heat and power integrated biomass gasification–internal combustion engine system by using Aspen Plus®. Fuel Process. Technol. **95**, 37–44 (2012)
40. Jana, K., De, S.: Biomass integrated combined power plant with post combustion CO_2 capture – performance study by ASPEN Plus®. Energy Procedia **54**, 166–176 (2014)
41. Gopaul, S.G., Dutta, A., Clemmer, R.: Chemical looping gasification for hydrogen production: a comparison of two unique processes simulated using ASPEN Plus. Int. J. Hydrogen Energy **39**, 5804–5817 (2014)

42. Doherty, W., Reynolds, A., Kennedy, D.: Computer simulation of a biomass gasification-solid oxide fuel cell power system using Aspen Plus. Energy **35**, 4545–4555 (2010)
43. Louw, J., Schwarz, C.E., Knoetze, J.H., Burger, A.J.: Thermodynamic modelling of supercritical water gasification: investigating the effect of biomass composition to aid in the selection of appropriate feedstock material. Bioresour. Technol. **174**, 11–23 (2014)
44. Begum, S., Rasul, M.G., Akbar, D.: A numerical investigation of municipal solid waste gasification using Aspen Plus. Procedia Eng. **90**, 710–717 (2014)
45. Ramzan, N., Ashraf, A., Naveed, S., Malik, A.: Simulation of hybrid biomass gasification using Aspen Plus: a comparative performance analysis for food, municipal solid and poultry waste. Biomass Bioenergy **35**, 3962–3969 (2011)
46. Tushar, M.S.H.K., Dutta, A., Xu, C.: Simulation and kinetic modeling of supercritical water gasification of biomass. Int. J. Hydrogen Energy **40**, 4481–4493 (2015)
47. Hunpinyo, P., Narataruksa, P., Tungkamani, S., Pana-Suppamassadu, K., Chollacoop, N.: Evaluation of techno-economic feasibility biomass-to-energy by Using ASPEN Plus®: a case study of Thailand. Energy Procedia **42**, 640–649 (2013)
48. Hammer, N.L., Boateng, A.A., Mullen, C.A., Wheeler, M.C.: Aspen Plus® and economic modeling of equine waste utilization for localized hot water heating via fast pyrolysis. J. Environ. Manag. **128**, 594–601 (2013)
49. Cohce, M., Dincer, I., Rosen, M.: Energy and exergy analyses of a biomass-based hydrogen production system. Bioresour. Technol. **102**, 8466–8474 (2011)
50. Mansaray, K., Al-Taweel, A., Ghaly, A., Hamdullahpur, F., Ugursal, V.: Mathematical modeling of a fluidized bed rice husk gasifier: part I-model development. Energy Sources **22**, 83–98 (2000)
51. Atnaw, S.M., Sulaiman, S.A., Yusup, S.: A simulation study of downdraft gasification of oil-palm fronds using ASPEN PLUS. J. Appl. Sci. **11**, 1913–1920 (2011)
52. Kotowicz, J., Sobolewski, A., Iluk, T.: Energetic analysis of a system integrated with biomass gasification. Energy **52**, 265–278 (2013)
53. Khan, Z., Yusup, S., Ahmad, M.M., Chin, B.L.F.: Hydrogen production from palm kernel shell via integrated catalytic adsorption (ICA) steam gasification. Energy Convers. Manag. **87**, 1224–1230 (2014)
54. Han, L., et al.: Hydrogen production via CaO sorption enhanced anaerobic gasification of sawdust in a bubbling fluidized bed. Int. J. Hydrogen Energy **36**(8), 4820–4829 (2011)

A Hardware and Software Integration Approach for Development of a Non-invasive Condition Monitoring Systems for Motor-Coupled Gears Faults Diagnosis

Muhammad Irfan[2], Nordin Saad[1(✉)], Rosdiazli Ibrahim[1],
Vijanth S. Asirvadam[1], Nursyarizal Mohd Nor[1], Abdullah Alwadie[2],
and Muhammad Aman Sheikh[1]

[1] Electrical and Electronics Engineering Department,
Universiti Teknologi PETRONAS, 32610 Bandar Seri Iskandar, Perak, Malaysia
nordiss@utp.edu.my
[2] Faculty of Engineering, Electrical Engineering Department, Najran University,
King Abdul Aziz Road, P.O.BOX 1988, Najran, Saudi Arabia

Abstract. A non-invasive condition monitoring system for diagnosis of faults is vital for induction motors to operate safely and reliably. The currently used invasive techniques need direct access to the motor to collect and analyze data. Furthermore, the sensors used in invasive techniques are relatively expensive. This paper presents the development of hardware and software integrations for non-invasive diagnostic system to monitor specifically motor-coupled gear defects. The proposed system employs instantaneous power analysis, a unique technique for diagnostic condition monitoring which allows real-time non-stop tracking as well as assesses the severity of the defects. This technique can be adopted for decision-making that is not only fast but reliable. The severity of different gear defects have been studied experimentally, and the results were analyzed. The effectiveness of the proposed method has been verified through experimentation from the actual hardware implementation through the system-design platform and development environment software tool, LabVIEW.

Keywords: System-design platform and development environment · Condition monitoring · Instantaneous power analysis · Fault diagnosis · Gear faults

1 Introduction

In industry, induction motors are encompassing up to 95% of the prime movers [1, 2]. Several applications utilize these motors that include paper mills, power plants, mining plants and process industry. Even though induction motors need simple maintenance, faults may occur incidentally [2, 3]. These faults may in turn cause production loss. Therefore, it is necessary to detect these emerging failures to avoid unexpected breakdowns [2, 4]. By avoiding induction motor breakdowns, unpredicted downtime and plant maintenance cost can be decreased [5].

© Springer Nature Singapore Pte Ltd. 2017
M.S. Mohamed Ali et al. (Eds.): AsiaSim 2017, Part I, CCIS 751, pp. 642–655, 2017.
DOI: 10.1007/978-981-10-6463-0_55

For applications based on electro-mechanical power transmission, gears play a major role. In the case of wound rotor induction generators (WRIG) based wind turbine, downtime depends greatly on multistage gearbox which connects the rotor blades to the generator [6]. For railway traction systems, gearboxes link traction motors to the wheels. Thus, proper working of gears is important to ensure reliability and security [7]. Early fault detection in gear performance can avoid unpredicted break-downs and in turn decreasing downtime and maintenance cost. Consequently, the development of an efficient fault diagnosis and condition monitoring system is necessary [8–10].

Notably, a non-invasive method for gear failure diagnosis will have the benefits of easy installation and lower cost. It is because of these advantages that several researchers have focused on non-invasive gear failure diagnosis methods [12–17].

Stator current monitoring was used for diagnosis of mechanical fault-related load torque oscillations in induction motors, [18]. However, the theoretical model presented in the work did not take into account the influence of gear stiffness on the stator current. According to a study of gearbox specific frequencies in stator current, three different shaft frequencies along with mesh frequencies emerge in the electromagnetic torque spectrum. These sideband frequencies around the electric supply frequency of stator current in the multi-stage gearbox are related to input, output and layer shafts. Some of these frequencies are related to the gear tooth fault [11, 19, 20]. The effects of motor coupled gear on stator current spectrum were studied in [21, 22]. This study has shown that for healthy gears, harmonics occur at the mesh and mesh-related frequencies. On the other hand, supplementary harmonics associated with fault-induced mechanical effects appear at the rotational frequency for faulty gears.

In order to investigate the effect of gear torsional vibrations on a motor current spectrum, a simplified dynamic model was used by taking into consideration the realistic behavior of a gear under the minimum number of mechanical parameters for the gear [23, 24]. The influence caused by the transmission error in the gear was found to have a relation to the wheel and pinion eccentricities as well as the tooth profile abnormalities. This had developed the sideband frequencies of the pinion and wheel rotation around the fundamental and mesh frequencies in the spectrum of the stator current. In [25], the same technique was used to investigate how the torsional vibrations of the planetary gear box influence the electrical signatures of a generator with a wound rotor induction. In [26], an attempt was made to join the experimental work with the numerical simulations so that the tooth pitting defect in a gear that is multi-staged could be detected. A model with a low-degree of freedom was used for the gear dynamic modeling which was comparable to the one employed in an earlier work [24]. The results in [27] verified that it is possible for the gear teeth faults to produce mechanical effects which are observable in the torque and thus, are noticeable in the electrical signatures of the machine. In a recent work, [28] has focused on extracting operating point independent fault signatures by using a kinematic error observer, spatial domain sampling methods, and spatial domain signal filtering methods for gear fault diagnostics of electromechanical actuators. The identification of mechanical vibrations due to backlash phenomena appearing between the pinion gear and the girth gear rim of the kiln using the motor current stator analysis (MCSA) was reported in [29]. The proposed diagnostic method was tested on under-scale laboratory test rig. It was shown that due to fault in pinion gear, the pinion rotation frequencies appear around fundamental supply frequency.

Although the MCSA technique has been proven to be non-invasive and economical for the motor gear fault detection, however, the amplitudes changes at characteristic defect frequencies are affected by highest amplitude peak at fundamental frequency especially when fault frequencies lie in a region near to the fundamental frequency. This factor could influence the reliability of the on-line fault diagnosis system and could lead to wrong decisions. As related to this, the instantaneous power analysis (IPA) carries three characteristic defect frequencies two side band components and one component directly at vibration frequency. The amplitude of this extra frequency component is not affected by the highest peak at the fundamental frequency and thus could be utilized to enhance the decision making capability of the on-line fault diagnosis system. The usage of the IPA method for analysis of gear defects in induction motors has not being investigated previously, and this paper addresses this new approach for the analysis of various gear defects for on-line condition monitoring of motors. This technique provides continuous real-time tracking of faults and estimates the severity through visual indication [33–38].

In this work, a real condition monitoring system are integrated with the system-design platform and development environment software tool, LabVIEW, for analysis and design of a non-invasive condition monitoring systems. This has involved in brief the work undertaken in developing the program routine in LabVIEW, engineering analyses, system data, and all other qualitative and quantitative engineering data related to conditioning and monitoring operation, focusing on motor-coupled gear defects fault detections.

This paper first highlights the issues in induction motor fault diagnosis and thus Sect. 1 gives an overview of motor-coupled gears fault analysis techniques. Section 2 discusses the software and hardware for the system. Section 3 highlights the experimental procedures of the proposed non-invasive fault diagnosis system and gives the mathematical formulation of gear defect frequencies. Section 4 presents the implementation of the proposed technique to analyze various gear defects. Finally, Sect. 5 presents the conclusions of this paper.

2 Software and Hardware for the On-Line Condition Monitoring System

This section provides an overview of the software and hardware module used in the development of experimental test rig for the non-invasive diagnostic condition monitoring system. The experimental test rig has been developed using the commonly used firm-wares in industry i.e. induction motor, current and voltage transducers, data acquisition module (DAQ) and LabVIEW software. The DAQ is interfaced with LabVIEW to acquire and process the data coming from the transducers. LabVIEW was interfaced with power switching circuit to turn-off the motor if a fault exceeds some threshold values.

The experimental test rig is developed that allows performing 3-phase currents and voltage measurements and can be used as the data to analyze and detect any faults as defined in the study. From these experimental data, the mathematical equation or the algorithm representing instantaneous power analysis (IPA) can be realized and evaluated. The IPA technique has been employed to recognize the characteristic frequencies related to gears defects. The amplitude at characteristic frequencies utilized as the indices to indicate faulty or healthy conditions of the motor. In this work, a code was created in LabVIEW so that the fault frequencies from the instantaneous power spectrum could be identified. The LabVIEW block diagram window was used to write the code for the acquisition of real time data from the current (SCT-013-005) and voltage transducers (LF-AV12-T4A25-0.5/400 V). The main purpose for this software is to collect real time data, perform analysis and display results on the screen. The data coming from the current and voltage transducers was read by the LabVIEW program and processed to record the instantaneous power spectrum. The hanning window was applied to avoid spectral leakages. The spectrum was normalized with respect to the highest peak (fundamental element). The noise and DC bias variations have been calculated based-on the design thresholds for reliable decision on the existence of fault signatures.

The data acquisition system consist of an electronic device designed to acquire data from sensors and transducers and to monitor parameters such as voltage and current, by conversion of physical analog quantities into digital data and rescaling them into physical quantities according to the transducers sensitivities. A DAQ has two parts: hardware and software. The hardware consists of the data acquisition card and a host PC computer with control software and data storage space. Complementary, the software controls the data collection process and has basic data analysis tools such as spectrum calculation for on-line data inspection. The data acquisition and processing system used in this work consists of National Instruments data acquisition card NI 6281, AC current and voltage transducers and LabVIEW.

Sampling is an essential process of data acquisition system in which the continuous analog signal is converted to a discrete signal. The output of any transducer is a continuously varying voltage. The ADC samples the analog signal as discrete values and stores it in the computer. LabVIEW has the configuration utility known as Measurement Automation Explorer (MAX) for the configuration and installation of all external data acquisition devices. MAX reads the information from device manager windows registry and assigns it specific device name from which the information is collected. The relation between the MAX and data acquisition device is shown in Fig. 1, [39].

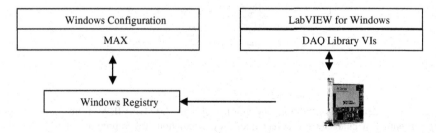

Fig. 1. Relation between DAQ and MAX.

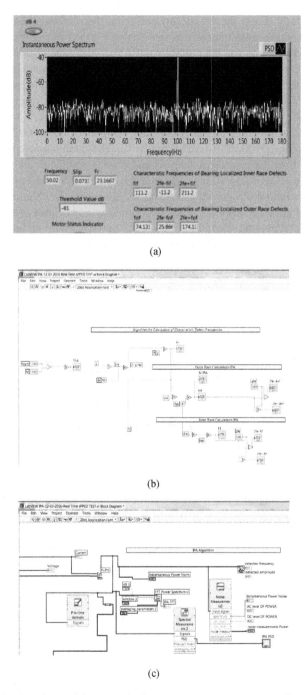

(a)

(b)

(c)

Fig. 2. The developed condition monitoring system (a) LabVIEW front panel display (b) Subroutine of characteristic defect frequency calculations (c) Subroutine of IPA algorithm (d) Subroutine for tracking amplitude values (e) Subroutine of threshold design algorithm.

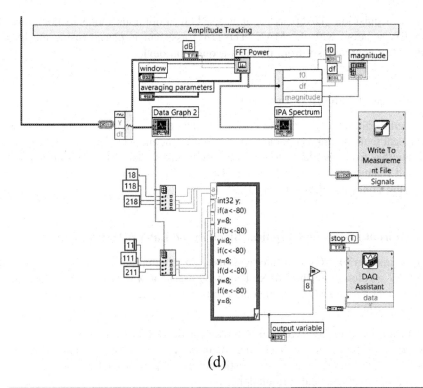

(d)

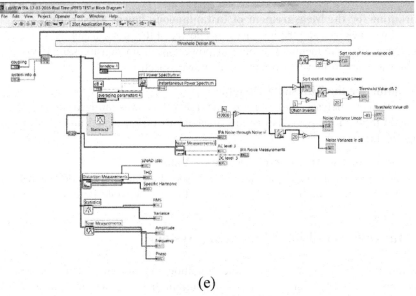

(e)

Fig. 2. (continued)

Data acquisition (DAQ) assistant is used in continuous mode to configure the LabVIEW window with the MAX. The DAQ assistant is placed inside the loop to acquire data continuously from the data acquisition device.

2.1 Design of LabVIEW Program

This section discusses briefly the design of LabVIEW program for the diagnosis of mechanical fault at various operating conditions of the induction motor. The developed algorithm has five subroutines to perform various tasks related to condition monitoring and fault diagnosis of induction motor. The LabVIEW front panel window and program subroutines are shown in Fig. 2.

2.2 Subroutines of the Graphical Block in the LabVIEW Program

Data acquisition (DAQ) assistant was used in continuous mode to configure the LabVIEW window with the MAX. The DAQ assistant was placed inside the loop to acquire data continuously from the data acquisition device. A brief description of each subroutines are as follows:

Subroutine for the Calculation of Characteristic Defect Frequencies:
This program subroutine collects the stator current and voltage data from DAQ assistant and calculates the characteristic defect frequencies related to gear defects based on the mathematical formulation.

Subroutine for the Measurement of Instantaneous Power Spectrum:
This subroutines measure the instantaneous power of the motor using the stator current and voltage measurements. The built-in power spectrum density sub.vi inside LabVIEW was used to plot the instantaneous power spectrum.

Subroutine for the Threshold Design:
The statistical analysis sub.vi inside the LabVIEW was utilized to calculate the threshold through the analysis of the instantaneous power signal under various operating conditions.

Subroutine for the Tracking of Amplitude Values:
This subroutine track the amplitude values at specific characteristic defect frequencies and set an alarm if amplitude value increases the set threshold limits.

3 On-Line Condition Monitoring System

The test rig developed for the on-line condition monitoring system consists of an induction motor, data acquisition device, a current and a voltage transducer and LabVIEW®. The schematic diagram of the experimental set-up is shown in Fig. 3. A gear assembly has been used for the analysis of gear teeth faults.

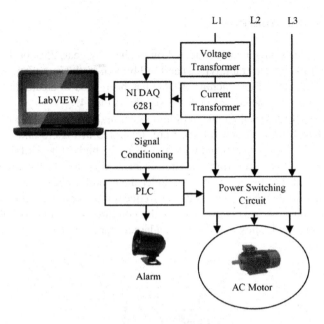

Fig. 3. The block diagram of the developed experimental test rig.

Table 1. Expected pinion gear defect frequencies under various loading conditions.

Load conditions	Motor speed (rpm)	Characteristic defect frequency (Hz)		
		f_{g1}	$\left\|2f_e - f_{g1}\right\|$	$\left\|2f_e + f_{g1}\right\|$
No load	1480	24.6	75.4	124.6
Full load	1390	23.2	76.8	123.2

In normal situations, both gears have a smooth surface so contact of pinion with wheel does not create any impact. However, fluctuations of air-gap are produced due to presence of gear defect. Due to these fluctuations, gear defect frequencies (f_g) are induced in motor electric supply and could be calculated using (1) and are shown in Table 1.

$$f_{es} = \left|f_e \pm mf_g\right| \tag{1}$$

where:

f_e,   is the electric supply frequency
m,   is the modulation index
f_g,   is the gear characteristic defect frequency

4 Results and Analysis

A total of eight tests have been conducted on the healthy gear, 25% broken teeth (fault type 1), 50% broken teeth (fault type 2) and full broken teeth (fault type 3) of the pinion gear. The electric discharge machine (EDM) has been used to create faults in the gear teeth. The healthy and defected gears are shown in Fig. 4.

The IPA spectrums of the defected pinion gear and the healthy pinion gear for the conditions of both no-load and full-load are illustrated in Figs. 5 and 6, respectively. Each spectrum has been normalized with regards to the highest peak of the fundamental power element. In each spectrum, the highest peak is related to the fundamental element of 100 Hz. It has been noticed that under the condition of no-load, the change in amplitude value at the characteristic defect frequency is very small for fault type 1 as compared to fault type 3. However, under the condition of a full-load, the change in values of the amplitude shown to have much larger increased at the characteristic defect frequency.

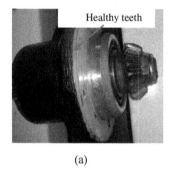

(a)

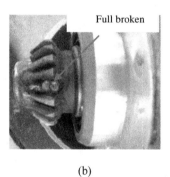

(b)

Fig. 4. Example (a) healthy gear (b) full broken teeth in pinion.

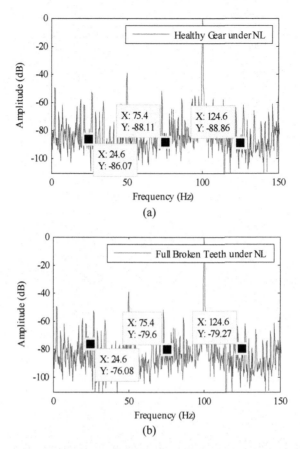

Fig. 5. The normalized instantaneous power spectrum of the motor for pinion gear defects under no-load condition (a) Healthy motor (b) 100% broken teeth.

The analysis of the spectrums of the frequencies for all three types of defects under a variety of loading conditions has been summarized in Table 2. The results show that at the characteristic fault frequencies, the values of the amplitude grow larger as the fault size of the gear teeth increased. Moreover, it has been observed that the increased in the values of the amplitude was even more prominent under the conditions of full-load.

It has been demonstrated that the IPA technique provides stronger fault frequencies components. This implies that the IPA is a better alternative for diagnosing motor coupled gear faults. This is due to the fact that the IPA has an additional element of the characteristic vibration frequency, f_{g1}, (other than just the two sideband elements). This gives a bit of additional data for enhanced fault detection in an on-line diagnostic system for defect determination.

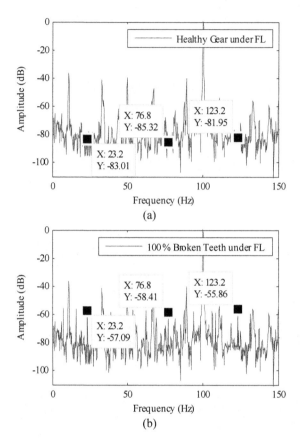

Fig. 6. The instantaneous power spectrum of the motor for pinion gear defects under full-load condition (a) Healthy motor (b) 100% broken teeth.

Table 2. Summary of change in amplitude values at various defects levels.

Defect type (broken tooth)	Characteristic defect frequency (Hz)		Change in amplitude (dB)	
	No load	Full load	No load	Full load
25%	24.6	23.2	3	10
50%	75.4	76.8	5	16
100%	124.6	123.2	9	26

5 Conclusions

This paper presents the development of a non-invasive condition monitoring system using system-design platform and development software tool for fault diagnostic of gears faults in induction motors. The fault analysis software created in LabVIEW is used for the identification of the fault frequencies of the induction motor. The test rig is designed to be flexible that facilitate the acquisition of experimental data in the form of the 3-phase currents and voltages measurements containing information about the fault types. The LabVIEW program has been designed and coded to represent the IPA algorithm. As a demonstration platform and 'proof-of-concept', the on-line non-invasive system for condition monitoring has been able to determine the various motor-coupled gears defects using the IPA technique. A significant level of amplitude (dB) value changes is observed at specific fault frequencies for both the no-load and full-load conditions, which verifies the viability of the proposed method. In the IPA spectrum, the additional information with regards to the characteristic vibration frequency element (f_{g1}) has given the relevant information on the detection of the gearing fault. This has resulted in enhancement of the accuracy and the reliability of the detection and diagnosis of the defects in motor-coupled gears.

Acknowledgement. The authors acknowledge the support from the Universiti Teknologi PETRONAS Malaysia for the award of University Research Internal Fund (URIF) and the Ministry of Higher Education (MOHE) Malaysia for the awards of the Exploratory Research Grant Scheme (ERGS) ERGS/1/2012/TK02/UTP/02/09, and the Prototype Research Grant Scheme (PRGS) PRGS/1/2016/TK04/UTP/02/8.

References

1. Irfan, M., Saad, N., Ibrahim, R., Asirvadam, V.S.: A non invasive method for condition monitoring of induction motors operating under arbitrary loading conditions. Arab. J. Sci. Eng. **41**(9), 3463–3471 (2016)
2. Irfan, M., Saad, N., Ibrahim, R., Asirvadam, V.S.: Condition monitoring of induction motors via instantaneous power analysis, J. Intell. Manuf. doi:10.1007/s10845-015-1048-2, February 2015
3. Irfan, M., Saad, N., Ibrahim, R., Asirvadam, V.S.: An intelligent diagnostic condition monitoring system for ac motors via instantaneous power analysis. Int. Rev. Electr. Eng. **8**(2), 664–672 (2013)
4. Irfan, M., Saad, N., Ibrahim, R., Asirvadam, V.S., Hung, N.T., Magzoub, M.: Analysis of bearing surface roughness defects in induction motors. J. Fail. Anal. Prev. **15**(5), 730–736 (2015)
5. Irfan, M., Saad, N., Ibrahim, R., Asirvadam, V.S.: An online condition monitoring system for induction motors via instantaneous power analysis. J. Mech. Sci. Technol. **29**(4), 1483–1492 (2015)
6. Irfan, M., Saad, N., Ibrahim, R., Asirvadam, V.S.: An intelligent fault diagnosis of induction motors in an arbitrary noisy environment, J. Nondestr. Eval. **35**(12) doi:10.1007/s10921-015-0327-3, March 2016
7. Kia, S.H., Henao, H., Capolino, G.-A.: Development of a test bench dedicated to condition monitoring of wind turbines, IEEE-IECON, Dallas (TX, USA), 28 October–1 November 2014
8. Dalpiaz, G., Rivola, A., Rubini, R.: Effectiveness and sensitivity of vibration processing techniques for local fault detection in gears. Mech. Syst. Signal Process. **14**(3), 387–412 (2000)

9. Baydar, N., Ball, A.: Case study-detection of gear failures via vibration and acoustic signals using wavelet transform. Mech. Syst. Signal Process. **17**, 787–804 (2003)

10. Loutas, T.H., Sotiriades, G., Kalaitzoglou, I., Kostopoulos, V.: Condition monitoring of a single-stage gearbox with artificially induced gear cracks utilizing on-line vibration and acoustic emission measurements. Appl. Acoust. **70**, 1148–1159 (2009)

11. Mohanty, A.R., Kar, C.: Monitoring gear vibrations through motor current signature analysis and wavelet transform. Mech. Syst. Signal Process. **20**(1), 158–187 (2006)

12. Feki, N., Clerc, G., Velex, P.: An integrated electro-mechanical model of motor-gear units - applications to tooth fault detection by electric measurements. Mech. Syst. Signal Process. **29**, 377–390 (2012)

13. Strangas, E.G.: Response of electrical drives to gear and bearing faults - diagnosis under transient and steady state conditions. In: Proceedings of Workshop on Electrical Machines Design Control and Diagnosis (WEMDCD), invited paper, Paris (France), pp. 289–297, 11–12 March 2013

14. Henao, H., Kia, S.H., Capolino, G.-A.: Torsional vibration assessment and gear fault diagnosis in railway traction system. IEEE Trans. Ind. Electron. **58**(5), 1707–1717 (2011)

15. Bogiatzidis, I., Safacas, A., Mitronikas, E.: Detection of backlash phenomena appearing in a single cement kiln drive using the current and the electromagnetic torque signature. IEEE Trans. Ind. Electron. **60**(8), 3441–3453 (2013)

16. Trajin, B., Regnier, J., Faucher, J.: Comparison between stator current and estimated mechanical speed for the detection of bearing wear in asynchronous drives. IEEE Trans. Ind. Electron. **56**(11), 4700–4709 (2009)

17. Ibrahim, A., El-Badaoui, M., Guillet, F., Bonnardot, F.: A new bearing fault detection method in induction machines based on instantaneous power factor. IEEE Trans. Ind. Electron. **55**(12), 4252–4259 (2008)

18. Blödt, M., Chabert, M., Regnier, J., Faucher, J.: Mechanical load fault detection in induction motors by stator current time-frequency analysis. IEEE Trans. Ind. Appl. **42**(6), 1454–1463 (2006)

19. Mohanty, A.R., Kar, C.: Fault detection in a multistage gearbox by demodulation of motor current waveform. IEEE Trans. Ind. Electron. **53**(4), 1285–1297 (2006)

20. Kar, C., Mohanty, A.R.: Vibration and current transient monitoring for gearbox fault detection using multiresolution Fourier transform. J. Sound Vib. **311**(1/2), 109–132 (2008)

21. Kia, S.H., Henao, H., Capolino, G.-A.: Analytical and experimental study of gearbox mechanical effect on the induction machine stator current signature. IEEE Trans. Ind. Electron. **45**(4), 1405–1415 (2009)

22. Kia, S.H., Henao, H., Capolino, G.A.: Gear tooth surface damage fault detection using induction machine stator current space vector analysis. IEEE Trans. Ind. Electron. **62**(3), 1866–2001 (2015)

23. Kia, S.H., Henao, H., Capolino, G.-A.: Torsional vibration effects on induction machine current and torque signatures in gearbox-based electromechanical system. IEEE Trans. Ind. Electron. **56**(11), 4689–4699 (2009)

24. Feki, N., Clerc, G., Velex, P.: Gear and motor fault modeling and detection based on motor current analysis. Electric Power Syst. Res. **95**, 28–37 (2013)

25. Daneshi-Far, Z., Henao, H., Capolino, G.-A.: Planetary gearbox effects on induction machine in wind turbine: modeling and analysis, In: Proceedings of International Conference on Electrical Machines (ICEM), Marseille (France), pp. 1790–1796, 2–5 September 2012

26. Ottewill, J.R., Orkisz, M.: Condition monitoring of gearboxes using synchronously averaged electric motor signals. Mech. Syst. Signal Process. **38**(2), 482–498 (2013)

27. Girsang, I.P., Dhupia, J.S., Muljadi, E., Singh, M., Pao, L.Y.: Gearbox and drive train models to study of dynamic effects of modern wind turbines. IEEE Trans. Ind. Appl. **50**, 3777–3786 (2014)
28. Huh, K.-K., Lorenz, R.D., Nagel, N.J.: Gear fault diagnostics integrated in the motion servo drive for electromechanical actuators. IEEE Trans. Ind. Appl. **48**(1), 142–150 (2012)
29. Bogiatzidis, I.X., Safacas, A.N., Mitronikas, E.D.: Detection of backlash phenomena appearing in a single cement kiln drive using the current and the electromagnetic torque signature. IEEE Trans. Ind. Electron. **60**(8), 3441–3453 (2013)
30. Kia, S.H., Henao, H., Capolino, G.-A.: A real-time platform dedicated to on-line gear tooth surface damage fault detection in induction machines. In: International Conference on Electrical Machines (ICEM), Berlin, 2–5 September 2014
31. Kia, S.H., Henao, H., Capolino, G.-A.: Gear tooth surface damage fault detection using induction machine stator current space vector analysis. IEEE Trans. Ind. Electron. **62**(3), 1866–1878 (2015)
32. Fournier, E., et al.: Current-based detection of mechanical unbalance in an induction machine using spectral kurtosis with reference. IEEE Trans. Ind. Electron. **62**(3), 1879–1887 (2015)
33. Irfan, M., Saad, N., Ibrahim, R., Asirvadam, V.S., Hung, N.T.: Analysis of bearing outer race defects in induction motor. In: The 5th IEEE International Conference on Intelligent and Systems (ICIAS), Kuala Lumpur, Malaysia, June 2014
34. Irfan, M., Saad, N., Ibrahim, R., Asirvadam, V.S.:An intelligent diagnostic system for condition monitoring of ac motors. In: The 8th IEEE Conference on Industrial Electronics and Applications, Melbourne, Australia, June 2013
35. Irfan, M., Saad, N., Ibrahim, R., Asirvadam, V.S., Hung, N.T.: A non-invasive fault diagnosis system for induction motors in noisy environment. In: IEEE International Conference on Power and Energy (PECon), Kuching, Malaysia, pp. 271–276, December 2014
36. Irfan, M., Saad, N., Ibrahim, R., Asirvadam, V.S.: An approach to diagnose inner race surface roughness faults in bearings of induction motors. In: IEEE International Conference on Signal and Image Analysis (ICSIPA), Kuala Lumpur, Malaysia, October 2015
37. Irfan, M., Saad, N., Ibrahim, R., Asirvadam, V.S.: An online fault diagnosis system for induction motors via instantaneous power analysis, Tribol. Trans. doi:10.1080/10402004. 2016.1190043, May 2016
38. Irfan, M., Saad, N., Ibrahim, R., Asirvadam, V.S.: Development of an intelligent condition monitoring system for AC induction motors using PLC. In: 2013 IEEE Business Engineering and Industrial Applications Colloquium (BEIAC) (2013)
39. Bishop, R.H.: Learning with LabVIEW 8, Pearson/Prentice Hall (2007)

Application of Brushless Motor Speed Control System in Wave Power Generation Technology

Xiao-hu Fan$^{(\boxtimes)}$, Yu-ying Zhou, and Zhou Yan

School of Automation Science and Electrical Engineering,
Beihang University, Beijing, China
373630348@qq.com

Abstract. In the development of new energy, a new type of marine gyro power plant has a higher wave energy conversion efficiency in the field of wave energy, the key component of which is the gyroscope speed control system, but designing a motor system for a heavy inertia gyro rotor is rare, it is a challenge for engineering design methods under limited output power and other design conditions. In this paper, we design the dual-loop speed control system by using the engineering method, and aim at the problem of the proportional integral coefficient caused by the heavy moment of inertia. Analyzing the design principle and the MATLAB simulation results, we propose a method for parameter modification using the Bode diagram. In ensuring the overshoot, stability at the proper adjusting range, we not only effectively reduce the proportional integral coefficient, but also provide a reference for engineering design ideas.

Keywords: Marine gyro power · Heavy moment of inertia · Speed control system · PI controller · Gyro rotor · Bode

1 Introduction

Marine energy in the development of new energy has been taken seriously, because of its rich energy reserves, a variety of energy forms, sustained and stable utilization [1].

A new type of marine gyro power plant has a higher wave energy conversion efficiency, the key component of which is the gyroscope speed control system. The system provides a stable speed for the gyro device, ensuring that the power plant in the sea wave was in a power generation state.

The system requires that the moment of inertia of the gyro rotor is large. At limited output power, the motor that drove the heavy moment of inertia gyro rotor is barely, so it need to carry out a special design. The scale factor of speed control system designed by using the engineering method is too big and the setting time is too long. In this design, we propose a new method of theoretical analysis and simulation, and provide a new idea of engineering design.

2 Simulation Models

The marine gyro power plant is an inertial wave power generation, which includes an inertial conversion device of wave power, a transmission system and a generator. When the inertial wave power generation works, it is separated from wave by a closed shell.

© Springer Nature Singapore Pte Ltd. 2017
M.S. Mohamed Ali et al. (Eds.): AsiaSim 2017, Part I, CCIS 751, pp. 656–667, 2017.
DOI: 10.1007/978-981-10-6463-0_56

This design avoids the generation is corroded by sea water, and reduces material production requirements (Fig. 1).

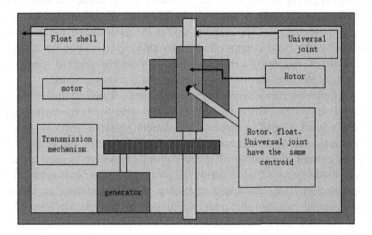

Fig. 1. The profile of the inertial wave power generation.

The inertial conversion device of wave power has precession characteristic, it can make a sensitive reaction to wave force and convert the wave energy into mechanical power. In response to the rapid changes in wave force caused by complex ocean fluctuation, the gyroscope speed control system adjusts the speed of the rotor which is in the inertial conversion device, to ensure the conversion efficiency.

The gyro speed control system contains permanent magnet brushless DC motor, the design of system bases on the open-loop frequency domain method. By simplifying the double closed-loop speed control structure, the system is transformed into a typical system, then completing the design according to the relationship between typical system parameters and performance indicators.

The engineering parameters given: Power is 2 kW, Moment of inertia is 16 N.m/s^2, range of rotation speed is 3000–6000 r/min.

The transfer function of motor torque, load torque and moment of inertia is as fallows,

$$T_e = J\frac{d\omega}{dt} + B\omega + T_l \tag{1}$$

Annotation:

T_e - motor torque
T_l - load torque
J - moment of inertia
B - damping coefficient
ω - angular velocity of rotor

The value of $B\omega$ compared with the value of T_e and T_l is very small, it can be ignored. Because the value of the moment of inertia is large, so the angular acceleration is little, the rotating speed growth is very slow in the speed control process. That is why the responding speed is one of the main indicators in the choice of control strategy.

As we know, in the field of traditional PI control, double closed-loop DC motor control system is widespread applications, and is the most classic control program [2].

For the motor, the good control effect under rated speed is one basic requirements. The test standard of measuring a motor system includes the range of speed control, the speed of rising or decline, the stability of maintain a constant speed.

Double closed-loop motor control system contains a speed control subsystem and a current control subsystem, when the speed control subsystem exists individually, the system doesn't have a good control of the current dynamic process and the motor appears the over-current phenomenon. These two subsystems respectively adjust the speed and the current, the output of speed control subsystem is used as input of the current control subsystem which controls the power electronic converter [3]. From the closed-loop structure side, the speed control subsystem becomes an external speed loop, and the current control subsystem becomes an internal current loop which also is a part of the external speed loop (Fig. 2).

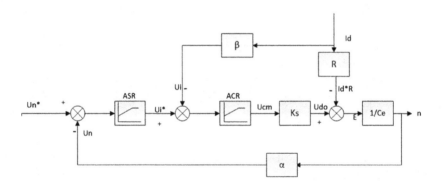

Fig. 2. The steady-state structure image.

The output limited voltage (U_i^*) of ASR (the rotate speed regulator) determines the maximum value of the current, and the output limit voltage (U_{cm}) of ACR (the current regulator) limits the maximum output voltage (U_{do}) of the power electronic converter, the limited values ensured that the components are safe to operate [4].

Engineering design of the speed and current control subsystem accords to the principle, the outer loop is after the inner loop. First, to transform and approximate the current loop, and then accord to the requirement of current loop control, correct into what kind of typical system, finally determine the type of current regulator and calculate the related parameters. Like that, current loop as part of the speed loop involves in the design of the speed loop (Fig. 3).

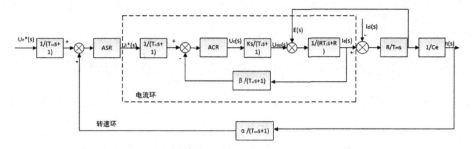

Fig. 3. Equivalent of the double closed loop speed regulation system.

2.1   The Design of Current Regulator (ACR)

The speed change of Motor speed regulation system is much more slowly than the current change. In one or several current cycles, Speed is considered to be constant, therefore we could ignore the influence of the counter electromotive force [5]. In order to meet the needs of current loop with performance, we choose the typical type I system and draw a simplified dynamic structure of current loop (Fig. 4).

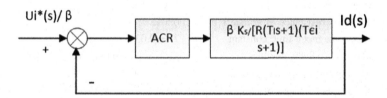

Fig. 4. The simplified dynamic structure diagram of current loop

The transfer function of ACR is as follows,

$$W_{ACR}(S) = \frac{K_i(\tau_i s + 1)}{\tau_i s} \tag{2}$$

where K_i means the proportion of current regulator coefficient, then τ_i means lead time constant current regulator.

The open loop transfer function of current loop was as follows,

$$W_{opi}(s) = \frac{K_i(\tau_i s + 1)}{\tau_i s} \frac{\beta K_s / R}{(T_l s + 1)(T_{\varepsilon i} s + 1)} \tag{3}$$

where τ_i is equal of T_l , $W_{opi}(s)$ was correct for typical type I system which was as follows (Fig. 5),

$$W_{opi}(s) = \frac{K_i \beta K_s / R}{\tau_i s (T_{\varepsilon i} s + 1)} = \frac{K_I}{s(T_{\varepsilon i} s + 1)} \tag{4}$$

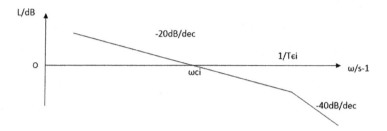

Fig. 5. Logarithmic amplitude-frequency characteristics of current loop.

$$K_I = \frac{K_i K_s \beta}{\tau_i R} = \frac{K_i K_s \beta}{T_l R} \tag{5}$$

The output voltage limited value of ASR is 5 V, the parameters of Current regulator are worked out (Table 1).

Table 1. The parameters of current regulator.

Power source	220 V Dc
The total resistance of armature circuit	0.5 Ω
Electromagnetic time constant	$T_l = 0.03$ s
Current feedback coefficient	$\beta = \frac{5}{1.5*50} = 0.0667$ V/A
The current filter time constant	$T_{oi} = 0.003$ s
Small time constant of current loop	$T_{\varepsilon i} = T_s + T_{oi} = 0.005$ s
Electromotive force coefficient	$C_e = \frac{U_N - I_N R_a}{n} = 0.0333$ V/(r/min)
The torque coefficient	$C_m = \frac{30}{\pi} C_e = 0.3183$ N.m/A
Electromechanical time constant	$T_m = \frac{GD^2}{375} \frac{R_\varepsilon}{C_e C_m} = 78.83$ s

All the indexes are in the acceptable ranges by querying related statistics. The output voltage limited value of ACR is 25 V, then

$$K_s = 9.25$$

$$K_I = \frac{0.5}{T_{\varepsilon i}} = \frac{0.5}{0.005} s^{-1} \approx 100 s^{-1} \tag{6}$$

$$K_i = \frac{K_I \tau_i R}{K_s \beta} = \frac{100 * 0.03 * 0.5}{9.25 * 0.0667} = 2.43 \tag{7}$$

The K_i is the proportion of current regulator coefficient. We can use the MATLAB software to set up the simulation block diagram (Fig. 6), set the simulation time is 0.5 s, then we get the simulation result of current loop (Fig. 7).

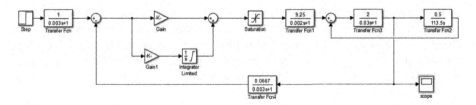

Fig. 6. The simulation diagram of current loop.

Fig. 7. The simulation result of current loop.

It can be obtained that the current keeps at around 75 A after overshoot, and remain stably until the speed meet the rated speed.

2.2 The Design of Speed Regulator (ASR)

We list part of the constant time of speed regulator in the Table 2.

Table 2. Part of the time constant of speed regulator.

Equivalent time constant of the current loop	0.01 s
Speed filtering time constant	0.02 s
Small time constant of speed loop	$T_{\varepsilon n} = 2T_{\varepsilon i} + T_{on} = 0.03\ \text{s}$
Speed feedback coefficient	$\alpha = \frac{U_{nm}^*}{n_N} = \frac{120}{6000} = 0.02$
The current filter time constant	$T_{oi} = 0.003\ \text{s}$
Small time constant of current loop	$T_{\varepsilon i} = T_s + T_{oi} = 0.005\ \text{s}$

Both overshoot of speed and dynamic fall-speed can be measured by immunity index. In this regard, the typical type II system is better than the typical type I system. Therefore we choose the better one and put the speed loop correction as a typical type II system [6]. The design of the speed control loop bases on the Minimum order peak M_p method [7], and draw the figure of log magnitude-frequency characteristics of speed open-loop (Fig. 8).

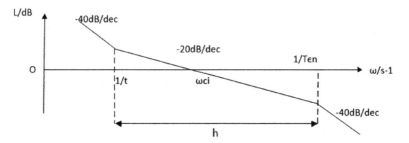

Fig. 8. Log magnitude-frequency characteristics of Speed open-loop.

When the intermediate frequency width is 5, we calculate the lead time constant of speed regulator is as follows,

$$\tau_n = hT_{en} = 5 * 0.03s = 0.15s \tag{8}$$

The speed open-loop gain is as follows,

$$K_N = \frac{h+1}{2h^2 T_{en}^2} = \frac{6}{2 * 25 * 0.03^2} s^{-2} = 133.3s^{-2} \tag{9}$$

The proportion coefficient of ASR is as follows,

$$K_n = \frac{(h+1)\beta C_e T_m}{2h\alpha R T_{en}} = \frac{6 * 0.0667 * 0.0333 * 78.83}{2 * 5 * 0.02 * 0.5 * 0.03} = 350.5 \tag{10}$$

Using the MATLAB software to set up the simulation diagram (Fig. 9), and set the simulation time is 0.5 s, we get the simulation results of speed loop (Figs. 10, 11 and 12).

We can obtain from Fig. 7, current rapidly reaches steady state after the initial overshoot, and the value of current is 1.5 times the rated current, which provides stably stalling torque; the figure of speed slowly rises at a certain acceleration. In Fig. 12, the current fells to the rated current at a breakneck speed and with shock when the speed reaches the rated speed (Fig. 11). The process last for a short, less than 1 s.

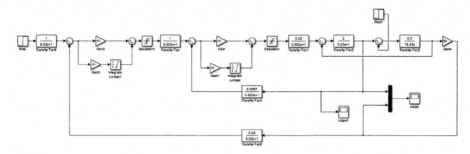

Fig. 9. The simulation diagram of the system.

Fig. 10. The simulation results of the system. (........: speed;-:current)

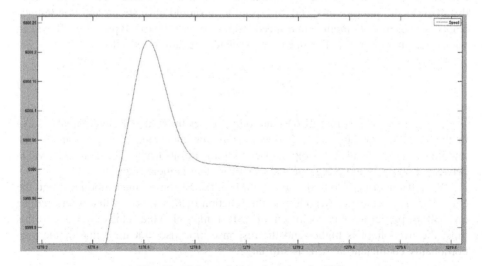

Fig. 11. Enlarge figure when time is 1278.

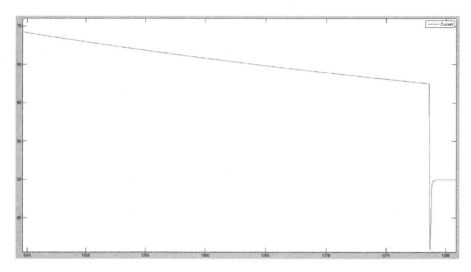

Fig. 12. The simulation results of the current when time is 1278.

3 Simulation and Discussion

In the Sect. 2, we design ACR and ASR by using engineering design methods. In the current loop, the input value is be limited, which definitely limits the rang of the proportionality coefficient of ACR in a way; In the speed loop, the input value is smaller than feedback, which cause that Feedback proportionality coefficient is also small, therefore, it must increase the proportionality coefficient of speed regulator to improve speed in forward channel. It is why that we get a high proportionality coefficient of ASR.

The current loop is simplified into the transfer function of typical type I and is equivalent to a module when we design ASR. Irregular disturbance of flexible load disturbances the stability of speed, the speed loop should have strong anti-interference ability, so it is a better mothed that speed loop is corrected into a typical type II system with better immunity [7]. The open-loop transfer function is as follows,

$$W(s) = \frac{K(\tau s + 1)}{s^2 (Ts + 1)} \tag{11}$$

In Fig. 8, the slope of 20 dB/Dec not only crosses the 0 dB/Dec line, but also stays in the middle-frequency band. It makes sure that the value of ω_n belong to the middle-frequency band, the simplified conditions are also met. The difference value between τ and T is more big, the stability of system is more high.

When the intermediate frequency width is 5, the response time is optimum, and the over-shoot is reasonable. Accoding to the function of K_n, we know that it will reduce one half the proportionality coefficient of ASR if improving the value of h to 10. At this time, the over-shoot is higher and the response time rise, but the value of the proportionality coefficient of ASR is still large.

We presents a novel method in the aspect of stability. The advantage of engineering design method is higher stability. the stability can be controled within a certain range, if not out, the system is still good. So we can reduce the proportionality coefficient of ASR under the premise of better stability. In Fig. 13, The first half of the image is the amplitude-frequency characteristic figure, the lower part is phase angle margin figure. We get the information that when the value of the proportionality coefficient of ASR turns lower (higher), the slope line shift to the left (right), then the value of ω_{cn} and phase margin reduces (rises). The value range of ω_{cn} is from $1/\tau_n$ to $1/T_{\varepsilon n}$.

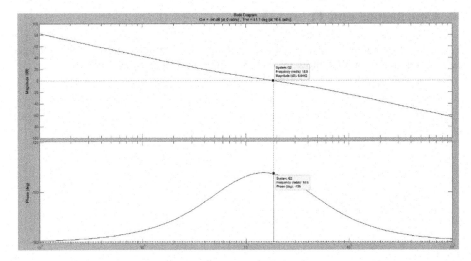

Fig. 13. Bode diagram.

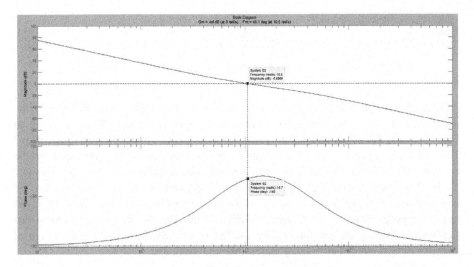

Fig. 14. New Bode diagram.

While the value of proportionality coefficient of ASR reduces 20 each time, we observe the bode diagram to check the value of ω_{cn} and phase margin, several times like this. When the value of the proportionality coefficient of ASR is 163.5, we get the Fig. 14. In the image, the value of ω_{cn} is little more than $1/\tau_n$, and the value of phase margin is flat pro.

Comparatively speaking, the new value of the proportionality coefficient is significantly less than pro, the result is acceptable. The only drawback is that the setting time becomes longer.

4   Conclusions and Future Work

According to the new values, we adjust the figure of the simulation model (Fig. 9), get new simulation diagrams, draw up the collation map (Figs. 15 and 16).

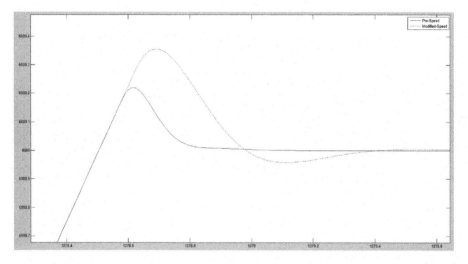

Fig. 15. The collation map of speed. (-: pre-speed; ....: modified-speed)

We observe that the current recovers to rated current after a gently shock, the oscillation process last almost 50 s. And we analyze the result of speed curve in Fig. 15, when the speed reaches the rated value, it shows almost no overshoot. Why? The closer the speed is to the rated speed, the smaller the torque provided by the current, and the slower the rate of speed growth, so the overshoot is not obviously.

In this study, we design the gyroscope speed control system, drawing on the engineering design method, finding that if the moment of inertia of the gyro rotor is too large, the proportionality coefficient of ASR rise quickly. So we propose a new idea that we can reduce the proportionality coefficient of ASR by adjusting the range of stability. It is proved that the way is feasible and verifiable.

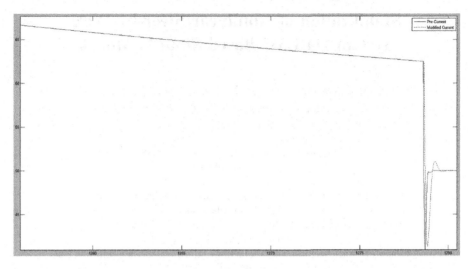

Fig. 16. The collation map of current. (-: pre-current; ....: modified-current)

In future work, we will introduce the fuzzy control technology, improve performance of ASR, optimize the structure of the speed regulation system of gyro.

References

1. Liu, Y.-C.: Gyro wave power generation system. Electr. World **2**, 109 (2015)
2. Jing, W.: Research of high-performance permanent magnet brushless DC motor speed control system. **06**, 3–5 (2013) Mongolian university
3. Li, Z.-X., Yang, Y.-l.: AC / DC speed control system. **02**, 58–60 (2013) Publishing House Of Electronics Industry
4. Pan, Y.-D., Qing, L., Li, H,-D.: Electric drag automatic control system. **11**, 104–110 (2013) CHINA MACHINE PRESS
5. Yu, A.-F.: Digital research brushless DC motor-vehicle turret system. **11**, 24–26 (2011) Chinese Academy of Sciences
6. Wei, F., Hui, Z.: Design of Double Closed Loop Control System for Brushless DC Motor. J. Power Supply **02**(03), 38–39 (2014)
7. Zhang, H.-R., Jin, W.-P., Huai, G.: Automatic control technology and engineering application **10**, 157-162 (2013) TSING HUA UNIVERSITY PRESS
8. Chung, S.K., Lee, J.H., Ko, J.S.: Robust speed control of brushless direct-drive motor using integral variable structure control. Electr. Power Appl. **142**(6), 361–370 (1995)

Stabilization of Nonlinear Steer-by-Wire System via LMI-Based State Feedback

Muhammad Iqbal Zakaria[1,2(✉)], Abdul Rashid Husain[1],
Zaharuddin Mohamed[1], Mohd Badril Nor Shah[3],
and Fernando Augusto Bender[4]

[1] Faculty of Electrical Engineering, Universiti Teknologi Malaysia,
Johor Bahru, Malaysia
csiqbal.z7@gmail.com
[2] Faculty of Electrical Engineering, Universiti Teknologi MARA,
Shah Alam, Malaysia
[3] Faculty of Engineering Technology, Universiti Teknikal Malaysia Melaka,
Durian Tunggal, Malaysia
[4] Center of Exact Sciences and Technology, Universidade de Caxias do Sul,
Caxias do Sul, Brazil

Abstract. An effective state feedback stabilizing controller plays an important role to ensure the reliability and robustness of nonlinear steer-by-wire (SbW) system. This paper addresses a new state feedback controller designed to ensure stability of SbW system. The SbW systems modeling is further studied where the additive of nonlinearities and disturbance need to be taken into account and compensated effectively. The state feedback control law can be designed based on the bound information of nonlinearity in the system in the sense that not only the robustness with respect to nonlinearity can be obtained but also the front steering wheel angle can converge to the hand-wheel reference angle asymptotically. The state feedback controller K is obtained by solving a linear matrix inequality (LMI) condition which formulated based on Lyapunov functional candidate. The efficacy of the proposed method is verified by applying the theorem on the SbW system simulated on Matlab/Simulink. The simulation work validated that the proposed controller results in excellent system performance.

Keywords: Steer-by-wire system · Nonlinear · State feedback · Stabilization · Linear matrix inequalities

1 Introduction

Recently, the automobile industry is working on a new technology called Drive-by-Wire (DbW) systems where electronic sensors, controllers and actuators are replacing hydraulic and mechanical subsystems such as steering, suspension and braking. Steer-by-wire (SbW) systems are part of DbW systems that are recognized as the succeeding generation of steering systems. The benefits of using SbW systems in road vehicles are to improve the overall steering performance, lower the power consumption, and enhance the safety and comfort of the passengers [1–3]. The modern SbW

© Springer Nature Singapore Pte Ltd. 2017
M.S. Mohamed Ali et al. (Eds.): AsiaSim 2017, Part I, CCIS 751, pp. 668–684, 2017.
DOI: 10.1007/978-981-10-6463-0_57

systems have the following dissimilar characteristics: First, the conventional mechan-. ical link in the traditional vehicles used to connect the hand-wheel to the steered the front wheels, through the rack and pinion gearbox, is removed. Second, the steering column is equipped with the hand-wheel angle sensor to provide the reference signal for the front-wheel steering angle to follow. Third, coupled to the rack and pinion gearbox, the steering motor is implemented to steer the front wheels based on the reference information provided by the hand-wheel angle sensor. Figure 1 shows comparison of conventional steering system and SbW system.

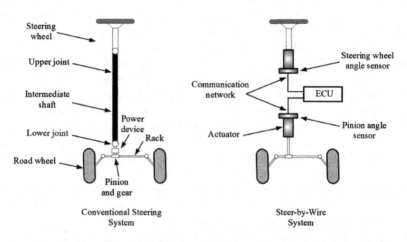

Fig. 1. Comparison of conventional steering system and SbW system.

Many researches on the SbW systems modeling have been carried out over the past few years. In [4], the dynamics of the test vehicle's SbW system was described with a simple second-order model based on the observation of the experimental results by ignoring tire forces and considering tire-to-road contact. In [5] and [6], two second-order models considering the effect of tire forces and vehicle dynamics were utilized in both the steered-wheel side and the hand-wheel side, respectively. Never-theless, from the aforementioned work, the dynamics of the motors are not contained within modeling of the SbW system. In [7, 8], the hand-wheel with the front-wheel directional assembly described by the rack motion were represented by two second-order models. Based on the relationship between the rack displacement and the hand-wheel rotational angle, the complete closed-loop SbW system is developed. The weaknesses of this SbW modeling structure, however, the tire dynamics, particularly the tire self-aligning torque, were not considered, and the effect of the self-aligning torque on the steering performance cannot be compensated efficiently in the controller design of SbW system.

In most existing SbW control systems, a number of control methods realization have been used to perfect steering characteristics. In [4, 5, 7–10], the conservative proportional-derivative (PD) control practice was commonly used with the objective of allowing front wheels to narrowly follow the driver's command. In [11, 12], a state feedback controller using the linear quadratic control technique was developed, targeting at driving the rolling angle of the SbW motorcycle to track the reference angle. As proposed in [13], an adaptive control method was applied through the estimation of the front tire cornering stiffness to control the front-wheel actuators. Furthermore, the adaptive online estimation method was used in [14] to classify the uncertain parameters of the vehicle directional-control.

Furthermore, the stabilization problem of SbW system is a present issue under consideration by many researchers [15–17]. The work in [15] proposed a two-wheel steering bicycle with the front wheel is controlled by a SbW system. The stabilization of the system and the controller are designed using linear-quadratic control method. Stabilization of SbW systems with bounded time delays in the control input and system states is proposed in [16] where the stability condition is expressed in linear matrix inequalities (LMIs). In [17], a μ-synthesis robust controller is developed based on linear fractional transformation theory for SbW system that aims to prevent instability from the effect of model uncertainty and external disturbance. However, all of the mentioned works in the literature review not considered the nonlinearity of the SbW system. In [18, 19], a nonlinear state feedback control law is proposed for systems containing Lipschitz nonlinearities. The work in [20] presented a robust quadratic stabilization of nonlinear systems within the framework of LMIs. In [21], a specific attention is paid to improve the transient performance of steering system using the composite nonlinear feedback (CNF) method. To the best of the author's knowledge, there is little work undertaken on the problem of stabilization state feedback controller for nonlinear SbW system, which is still open in the literature.

In this paper, the development of state feedback controller methodologies for the SbW systems with nonlinearity is presented. The controller is obtained by solving an LMI condition which is developed based on Lyapunov candidate function. In this work, the design specification for the proposed control objective of this system is to ensure that the front steering wheel angle can converge to the reference angle input asymptotically. This paper consists of 5 sections and is presented as follows: Sect. 2 describes the problem formulation on the nonlinear SbW system with vehicle dynamics. In Sect. 3, the state feedback stability condition for nonlinear SbW system is derived. Section 4 provides an extensive analysis of simulation work developed in Matlab/Simulink to investigate the efficacy of the proposed method. The conclusions are drawn in Sect. 5.

2   Nonlinear SbW System Modeling with Vehicle Dynamics

The basic principle of an SbW system with vehicle dynamics model is shown in Fig. 2 [4, 5, 22]. It can be seen that the physical parts of the SbW system can be separated into two: First, the upper part includes the hand-wheel and the hand-wheel angle sensor, respectively. Second, the lower part is composed of the DC motor, the pinion angle sensor, the rack and pinion gearbox, and the steered front wheels. The electronic control unit (ECU) is where controller algorithm is executed.

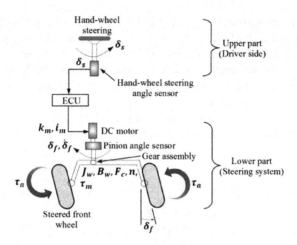

Fig. 2. Physical parts and state variables of SbW system.

In this work, the steered front wheel in Fig. 2 can be treated as the load of the steering motor and rotates about the vertical axis crossing the wheel centre. Hence, the rotation of the front wheel satisfies the dynamic equation as follows [22]:

$$J_w \ddot{\delta}_f + B_w \dot{\delta}_f + F_c \text{sign}\left(\dot{\delta}_f\right) + \tau_a = n\tau_m \qquad (1)$$

where J_w is moment of inertia of the steering wheel, B_w is viscous damping coefficient, F_c is torque due to Columb friction force, τ_a is self-aligning torque, n is number of steering wheel motors and δ_f is steering wheel angle.

Assuming that a single SbW motor is in operation in the system (i.e. $n = 1$), therefore, the SbW motor torque can be calculated as a function of the current i_m, where k_m is the motor constant as follows:

$$\tau_m = k_m i_m \qquad (2)$$

Equation (1) can be rearranged such that:

$$\ddot{\delta}_f = -\frac{B_w}{J_w}\dot{\delta}_f - \frac{1}{J_w}F_c \text{sign}\left(\dot{\delta}_f\right) - \frac{1}{J_w}\tau_a + \frac{k_m}{J_w}i_m \qquad (3)$$

Torque due to Columb friction force is the nonlinearity of the system and is defined as follows:

$$f(x(t)) = \left[\begin{matrix} 0 \\ -\frac{F_c}{J_w}\text{sign}\left(\dot{\delta}_f\right) \end{matrix} \right] \qquad (4)$$

Based on the symmetry of vehicle geometry a single-track vehicle dynamics model or a bicycle model [22, 23], the forces acting on the steered front wheel and rear wheel during a handling maneuver is illustrated in Fig. 3. F_F^y and F_R^y are the lateral forces of the front wheel and rear wheel, respectively, F_F^x and F_R^x are the longitudinal forces of the front wheel and rear wheel, respectively, v is the vehicle velocity at the centre of gravity (CoG), δ_f is the steering wheel angle of the front wheel, v_F^w and v_R^w are the velocities of the front wheel and rear wheel, respectively, a and b are the distances of the front wheel and rear wheel from the CoG of the vehicle, respectively, α_F and α_R are the tire sideslip angles of the front wheel and rear wheel, respectively and β and r are the vehicle-body sideslip angle and yaw rate at CoG, respectively.

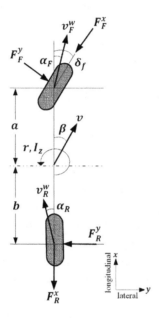

Fig. 3. Single-track vehicle model.

The self-aligning torque is the disturbance of the system occurs due to the tire contact forces on the steering system to resist steering away from the straight-ahead position. Figure 4 shows the tire contact forces and self-aligning torque at the front wheel. From the figure, the pneumatic trail is the distance between the tire centre and the point where lateral force is applied, whereas, the mechanical trail is the distance between the tire centre and the point on the ground where the tire pivots as a result of caster angle.

The equation to calculate the self-aligning torque is given as follows [22]:

$$\tau_a = (t_p + t_m)F_F^y \tag{5}$$

where t_p is pneumatic trail, t_m is mechanical trail and F_F^y is the lateral forces of the front wheel.

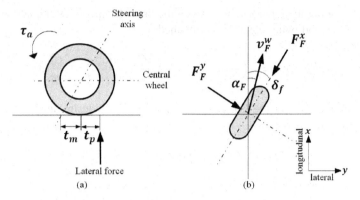

Fig. 4. (a) Tire contact forces. (b) Self-aligning torque at the front central wheel.

At a small slip angle, such as $4°$ or less, the lateral forces F_F^y and F_R^y varies linearly with the tire sideslip angles.

$$F_F^y = -C_F^\alpha \alpha_F$$
$$F_R^y = -C_R^\alpha \alpha_R$$

(6)

where C_F^α and C_R^α are the tire cornering coefficients of the front wheel and rear wheel and α_F and α_R are the tire sideslip angles of the front wheel and rear wheel.

Furthermore, the tire sideslip angles of the front wheel and rear wheel can be approximated to the vehicle-body sideslip angle, the yaw rate and steering wheel angle by the following relationship:

$$\alpha_F = \beta + \frac{a}{v}r - \delta_f$$
$$\alpha_R = \beta - \frac{b}{v}r$$

(7)

By substituting (7) into (6), the lateral forces equations now become:

$$F_F^y = -C_F^\alpha \beta - \frac{aC_F^\alpha}{v}r + C_F^\alpha \delta_f$$
$$F_R^y = -C_R^\alpha \beta + \frac{bC_R^\alpha}{v}r$$

(8)

Recalling single-track vehicle model in Fig. 3, the following equation can be used to describe the dynamics of the vehicle-body sideslip angle for the vehicle [22]:

$$v\left(\dot{\beta} + r\right) = \frac{1}{m}(F_F^y + F_R^y)$$

(9)

By substituting the relationship between the tire sideslip angles and lateral forces in (8) into (9), the following equation is obtained as

$$v\left(\dot{\beta}+r\right) = -\left(\frac{C_F^\alpha + C_R^\alpha}{m}\right)\beta + \left(\frac{bC_R^\alpha - aC_F^\alpha}{mv}\right)r + \frac{C_F^\alpha}{m}\delta_f \tag{10}$$

Then, by rearranging the Eq. (10), the vehicle-body sideslip angle of the vehicle dynamics can be obtained as:

$$\dot{\beta} = -\left(\frac{C_F^\alpha + C_R^\alpha}{mv}\right)\beta + \left(\frac{bC_R^\alpha - aC_F^\alpha}{mv^2} - 1\right)r + \frac{C_F^\alpha}{mv}\delta_f \tag{11}$$

Next, the dynamics of the yaw rate for the vehicle can be described as the following equation [22]:

$$I_z\dot{r} = aF_F^y - bF_R^y \tag{12}$$

Then, substituting (8) into (12), the following equation is obtained:

$$I_z\dot{r} = -\left(aC_F^\alpha - bC_R^\alpha\right)\beta - \left(\frac{a^2 C_F^\alpha + b^2 C_R^\alpha}{v}\right)r + aC_F^\alpha\delta_f \tag{13}$$

Furthermore, the equation yaw rate for the vehicle dynamics in (13) can be rearranged as follows:

$$\dot{r} = -\left(\frac{aC_F^\alpha - bC_R^\alpha}{I_z}\right)\beta - \left(\frac{a^2 C_F^\alpha + b^2 C_R^\alpha}{I_z v}\right)r + \frac{aC_F^\alpha}{I_z}\delta_f \tag{14}$$

Now, combining (11) and (14) in a state-space form, the vehicle model is completed with vehicle-body sideslip angle and yaw rate as the states.

$$\dot{x}(t) = Ax(t) + Bu(t)$$

where

$$x(t) = \begin{bmatrix} \beta & r \end{bmatrix}^T, u(t) = \delta_f,$$

$$A = \begin{bmatrix} -\left(\frac{C_F^\alpha + C_R^\alpha}{mv}\right) & \frac{bC_R^\alpha - aC_F^\alpha}{mv^2} - 1 \\ -\left(\frac{aC_F^\alpha - bC_R^\alpha}{I_z}\right) & -\left(\frac{a^2 C_F^\alpha + b^2 C_R^\alpha}{I_z v}\right) \end{bmatrix}, B = \begin{bmatrix} \frac{C_F^\alpha}{mv} \\ \frac{aC_F^\alpha}{I_z} \end{bmatrix} \tag{15}$$

By substituting (8) into (5), the self-aligning torque can be represented as a function of the vehicle states; the vehicle-body sideslip angle, the yaw rate and steering wheel angle as follows:

$$\tau_a = -\left(t_p + t_m\right)C_F^\alpha \beta - \frac{a\left(t_p + t_m\right)C_F^\alpha}{v} r + \left(t_p + t_m\right)C_F^\alpha \delta_f \tag{16}$$

Then, substituting (16) into (3), the steering dynamics can be rewritten in the function of the vehicle states as:

$$\ddot{\delta}_f = -\frac{B_w}{J_w}\dot{\delta}_f - \frac{1}{J_w}F_c\mathrm{sign}\left(\dot{\delta}_f\right) + \frac{\left(t_p + t_m\right)C_F^\alpha}{J_w}\beta + \frac{a\left(t_p + t_m\right)C_F^\alpha}{J_w v} r$$
$$- \frac{\left(t_p + t_m\right)C_F^\alpha}{J_w}\delta_f + \frac{k_m}{J_w}i_m \tag{17}$$

Combining (17) and (15) in a state-space form, the steering dynamics system model is completed with the vehicle dynamics model where steering wheel angle, steering rate angle, vehicle-body sideslip angle and yaw rate as the states. The system where the motor current as the input and the steering wheel angle as the output include the nonlinearity term as presented in the following equation:

$$\dot{x}(t) = Ax(t) + Bu(t) + f(x(t))$$
$$y(t) = Cx(t)$$

where

$$x(t) = \begin{bmatrix} \delta_f & \dot{\delta}_f & \beta & r \end{bmatrix}^T, u(t) = i_m,$$

$$A = \begin{bmatrix} 0 & 1 & 0 & 0 \\ -\dfrac{\left(t_p + t_m\right)C_F^\alpha}{J_w} & -\dfrac{B_w}{J_w} & \dfrac{\left(t_p + t_m\right)C_F^\alpha}{J_w} & \dfrac{a\left(t_p + t_m\right)C_F^\alpha}{J_w v} \\ \dfrac{C_F^\alpha}{mv} & 0 & -\left(\dfrac{C_F^\alpha + C_R^\alpha}{mv}\right) & \dfrac{bC_R^\alpha - aC_F^\alpha}{mv^2} - 1 \\ \dfrac{aC_F^\alpha}{I_z} & 0 & -\left(\dfrac{aC_F^\alpha - bC_R^\alpha}{I_z}\right) & -\left(\dfrac{a^2 C_F^\alpha + b^2 C_R^\alpha}{I_z v}\right) \end{bmatrix},$$

$$B = \begin{bmatrix} 0 \\ \dfrac{k_m}{J_w} \\ 0 \\ 0 \end{bmatrix}, f(x(t)) = \begin{bmatrix} 0 \\ -\dfrac{F_c}{J_w}\mathrm{sign}\left(\dot{\delta}_f\right) \\ 0 \\ 0 \end{bmatrix}, C = \begin{bmatrix} 1 & 0 & 0 & 0 \end{bmatrix} \tag{18}$$

3 LMI-Based State Feedback Stabilization for Nonlinear SbW System

Consider the SbW system with the nonlinearity function described by the following differential equation:

$$\dot{x}(t) = Ax(t) + Bu(t) + f(x(t))$$
$$y(t) = Cx(t) \tag{19}$$

where for every $t > 0$, $x(t) \in \Re^n$, $u(t) \in \Re^m$, $y(t) \in \Re^p$ represent the state, the input and the output of the system, respectively. The nonlinearity function $f(x(t))$ is a time-varying vector and is a piecewise-continuous function in both arguments t and x. The matrices A, B and C are known real constant matrices.

The state feedback control law to ensure the stability of the closed-loop SbW system is given as follow:

$$u(t) = Kx(t) \tag{20}$$

where the controller gain K is designed in the form of LMIs.

By substituting (20) into (19), the following equation is obtain.

$$\dot{x}(t) = (A + BK)x(t) + f(x(t)) \tag{21}$$

In order to propose the controller which serves as the main result of this work, the following lemmas will be used.

Lemma 1 [20, 24]. The function $f(x(t))$ is uncertain in the domain of continuity and it satisfies the following quadratic inequality.

$$f^T(x(t))If(x(t)) \le x^T(t)H^T Hx(t) \tag{22}$$

where H is a constant matrix to bound the nonlinearity function and I is identity matrix.

Lemma 2 [18, 19, 25]. The function $f(x(t))$ is Lipschitz for all $x(t) \in \Re^n$ and $\bar{x}(t) \in \Re^n$, and satisfies:

$$\|f(x(t)) - f(\bar{x}(t))\| \le \|Lx(t) - \bar{x}(t)\|, \tag{23}$$

where L is a Lipschitz constant matrix. The inequality (24) can be written as

$$f^T(x(t))If(x(t)) \le x^T(t)L^T Lx(t) \tag{24}$$

The study of system stability will be carried out using Lyapunov candidate function. An LMI-based sufficient condition is developed to determine the controller gain K in (20), which guarantees the asymptotic stability of the system.

Theorem 1. Consider the nonlinear SbW system (19) and the control law (20). If there exist positive definite symmetric matrix $Y = Y^T > 0$ and positive definite diagonal matrix L with appropriate dimensions such that

$$\begin{bmatrix} AY + YA^T + BL + L^T B^T & * & * \\ I & -I & * \\ HY & 0 & -I \end{bmatrix} \le 0 \tag{25}$$

is satisfied, then the control law (20) ensures the asymptotic stability of the system states and the controller gain K in (20) can be obtained as $K = LY^{-1}$.

Proof. Construct Lyapunov candidate function as follows:

$$V(t) = x^T(t)Px(t) \tag{26}$$

where P is symmetric positive definite matrix such that $P = P^T > 0$.

Taking the derivative of (26) with respect to time using the trajectories of (21), the following equation is obtained:

$$\dot{V}(t) \leq \left(A^T + K^T B^T\right)Px(t) + x^T(t)P(A+BK) + f^T(x(t))Px(t) \\ + x^T(t)Pf(x(t)) \tag{27}$$

By adding Lemma 1 on the $\dot{V}(t)$, the time derivative of the Lyapunov function becomes:

$$\dot{V}(t) \leq x^T(t)\left(A^T P + PA + K^T B^T P + PBK\right)x(t) + f^T(x(t))Px(t) \\ + x^T(t)Pf(x(t)) - f^T(x(t))If(x(t)) + x^T(t)H^T Hx(t) \tag{28}$$

The inequality (28) can be further written as:

$$\dot{V}(t) \leq \Psi^T(t)\Omega\Psi(t) \tag{29}$$

where $\Psi^T(t) = \begin{bmatrix} x^T(t) & f^T(x(t)) \end{bmatrix}$ and

$$\Omega = \begin{bmatrix} PA + A^T P + PBK + K^T B^T P + H^T H & * \\ P & -I \end{bmatrix} < 0 \tag{30}$$

By applying the Schur complement in (30) yields,

$$\begin{bmatrix} PA + A^T P + PBK + K^T B^T P & * & * \\ P & -I & * \\ H & 0 & -I \end{bmatrix} < 0 \tag{31}$$

By introducing the change of variable $Y = P^{-1}$, $L = KY$, premultiplying and postmultiplying (31) by diag (Y, I, I), LMI (25) is obtained.   □

Theorem 2. Consider the SbW system in (19) with Lipschitz nonlinearity and the control law (20). If there exist positive definite symmetric matrix $X = X^T > 0$ and positive definite diagonal matrices S and Y with appropriate dimensions such that

$$\begin{bmatrix} AX + XA^T + BS + S^T B^T & * & * \\ I & -I & * \\ Y^T & 0 & -I \end{bmatrix} < 0 \tag{32}$$

is satisfied, then the control law (20) ensures the asymptotic stability of the system states and the controller gain K in (20) can be obtained as $K = SX^{-1}$.

Proof. Take the following Lyapunov candidate function:

$$V(t) = x^T(t)Px(t) \tag{33}$$

where P is symmetric positive definite matrix such that $P = P^T > 0$.

Taking the derivative of (33) with respect to time using the trajectories of (21), the following equation is obtained:

$$\dot{V}(t) \le (A^T + K^T B^T)Px(t) + x^T(t)P(A + BK) + f^T(x(t))Px(t) \\ + x^T(t)Pf(x(t)) \tag{34}$$

By adding Lemma 2 on the $\dot{V}(t)$, the time derivative of the Lyapunov function becomes:

$$\dot{V}(t) \le x^T(t)(A^T P + PA + K^T B^T P + PBK)x(t) + f^T(x(t))Px(t) \\ + x^T(t)Pf(x(t)) + x^T(t)L^T Lx(t) - f^T(x(t))If(x(t)) \tag{35}$$

The inequality (35) can be further written as:

$$\dot{V}(t) \le \Sigma^T(t)\phi\Sigma(t) \tag{36}$$

where $\Sigma^T(t) = \begin{bmatrix} x^T(t) & f^T(x(t)) \end{bmatrix}$ and

$$\phi = \begin{bmatrix} PA + A^T P + PBK + K^T B^T P + L^T L & * \\ P & -I \end{bmatrix} < 0 \tag{37}$$

By applying the Schur complement in (37) yields

$$\begin{bmatrix} PA + A^T P + PBK + K^T B^T P & * & * \\ P & -I & * \\ L & 0 & -I \end{bmatrix} < 0 \tag{38}$$

By introducing the change of variable $X = P^{-1}$, $S = KX$, $Y = XL^T$, premultiplying and postmultiplying (38) by diag (X, I, I), LMI (32) is obtained.   □

Remark 1. It is noted from the system stability that the steps in deriving the Theorems 1 and 2 are almost the same except that in the step to solve the controller gain K. In Theorem 1, the nonlinearity term is assigned by a matrix H, whereas, in Theorem 2, the nonlinearity term is assigned as one of the LMI variable which is Y and later the change of variable is introduced as $Y = XL^T$. These two different approaches will resulted different controllers gain as presented in the next section.

4 Simulation Results and Discussions

In this section, the performance of the proposed control theorems will be evaluated where simulations of a nonlinear SbW system with vehicle dynamic are conducted in Matlab/Simulink. Consider the SbW system with vehicle dynamic model in (18). Some key parameters for the SbW system and the vehicle have been considered for preliminary simulation runs and are listed in Table 1 [22, 26]:

Table 1. SbW system and vehicle model parameters.

Parameter	Value (Unit)
J_w	3.5 (kg m^2)
B_w	70 (N.m.s/rad)
k_m	0.2
t_p	0.0381 (m)
t_m	0.04572 (m)
F_c	2.68 (N.m)
m	1961 (kg)
I_z	3136 (kg m^2)
a	1.05 (m)
b	1.71 (m)
C_F^α	23,000 (N/rad)
C_R^α	46,000 (N/rad)
v	13.4 (m/s)

Then, from these parameters the Eq. (18) can be calculated as:

$$\dot{x}(t) = \begin{bmatrix} 1 & 0 & 0 & 0 \\ 550.81 & -20 & -550.81 & -43.16 \\ -1.75 & 0 & 46003.50 & -1.30 \\ 15.40 & 0 & -48350.16 & -50708.59 \end{bmatrix} x + \begin{bmatrix} 0 \\ 0.0571 \\ 0 \\ 0 \end{bmatrix} u$$

$$+ \begin{bmatrix} 0 \\ -0.7657\,\mathrm{sign}\left(\dot{\delta}_f\right) \\ 0 \\ 0 \end{bmatrix} \tag{39}$$

Solving the LMI problem (25) and bound the uncertain nonlinearity matrix $H = I$ using the LMI Toolbox [27, 28], the following feedback gain controller is obtained

$$K = \begin{bmatrix} 0.9678 & 3.8822 & 0.1705 & 0.5084 \end{bmatrix} \times 10^3 \tag{40}$$

Similarly, by using the LMI Toolbox, the LMI problem in (32) is solved and the following feedback gain controller is obtained as:

680   M.I. Zakaria et al.

$$K = [0.2751 \quad 5.4681 \quad 0.1967 \quad 0.3145] \times 10^3 \tag{41}$$

The performance of the SbW system is evaluated using integral of the absolute of the error (IAE) index function [29], which is defined as

$$IAE = \int_0^L |r_s(t) - c_s(t)| dt \tag{42}$$

where $r_s(t)$ is reference signal or steering wheel angle input of driving maneuver and $c_s(t)$ is the parameters that need to measure their performance. For this case, $c_s(t)$ is the steering wheel angle δ_f. The lower value of IAE indicate a better control system performance.

In this study, the driving maneuver ramp steering which usually adopted in a J-turn maneuver is considered [30]. The driver model gives steering wheel angle input for the driving maneuver as shown in Fig. 5. The simulation is performed until time $t = 8$ s. The desired steering wheel angle input is initially at 0 rad for 2 s and the ramp maneuver takes effect from 2 s until the end of simulation time. The control objective of this system is to ensure that the front steering wheel angle can converge to the reference angle input asymptotically.

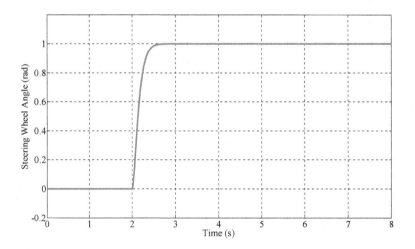

Fig. 5. Steering wheel angle of simulation using ramp steering maneuver [30].

The comparative results of the steering performance of a ramp maneuver implemented controller gain from Theorems 1 and 2 are shown in Fig. 6 to Fig. 8. It is seen from the result in Fig. 6 that both of the proposed controllers using Theorems 1 and 2 have driven the front steering wheel angle δ_f to track the reference angle input satisfactorily, but the controller using Theorem 1 exhibits better performance in terms of rise time and IAE of steering wheel angle error. The rise time for controller using

Theorems 1 and 2 are $T_{r(Theorem1)} = 2.36$ s and $T_{r(Theorem2)} = 5.26$ s, respectively, which indicate the controller using Theorem 1 has faster response. The IAE of steering wheel angle error for controller using Theorems 1 and 2 are $IAE_{Theorem1} = 0.01019$ and $IAE_{Theorem2} = 0.5021$, respectively. Moreover, the analysis of the vehicle stability results as shown in Figs. 7 and 8 show that, the vehicle-body sideslip angle and yaw rate are remain stable without oscillation on both controllers using Theorem 1 and 2.

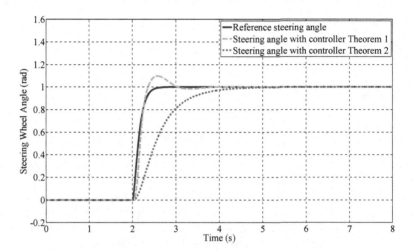

Fig. 6. The response of steering angle of SbW system.

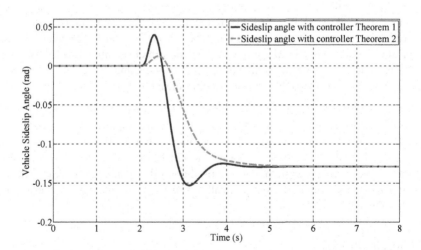

Fig. 7. The response of vehicle-body sideslip angle of SbW system.

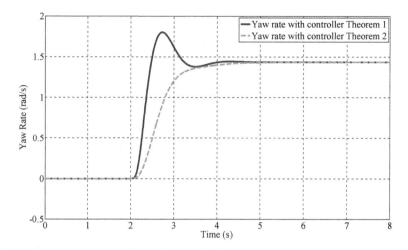

Fig. 8. Vehicle yaw rate response of SbW system.

Remark 2. It has been noted that the tracking performances in the simulations using controller in Theorem 1 is better as compared to the controller in Theorem 2 as the rise time of the steering wheel angle of the SbW system is faster and the value of performance index IAE is lower. In term of stability aspect, controller in Theorem 2 showed a better result that controller in Theorem 1 as it produced less overshoot but need longer settling time to reach steady state. In real implementation of SbW system, controller in Theorem 1 is more favorable as it offers faster response that desirable in SbW time-critical application.

Remark 3. In this work, the vehicle velocity at the centre of gravity v is set at relatively low which is 13.4 (m/s) [22, 26]. As noted in [31], for safety considerations, the longitudinal velocity is selected in the range of 1–10 (m/s) which adequately reflected of typical safe maneuvers. Furthermore, in [32], the vehicle equipped with SbW system is set to two different velocities which are 5 and 30 (m/s), and the results shown that at high velocity $v = 30$ (m/s), the vehicle become unstable.

Remark 4. In this work, the limit of the steering angle input for ramp driving maneuver is set to 1 rad as shown in Fig. 5 [30]. Similar driving input maneuver also implemented in [33] where the maximum steering angle input is 60° which approximately equivalent to 1 rad. Since the controller is design based on the SbW system model, when the input excite the system, the proposed controller is able to track the reference input trajectory and converge asymptotically even when the maximum steering angle input has changed.

5 Conclusion

This paper discussed a new state feedback controller which designed to ensure the reliability and robustness of a nonlinear SbW system. The SbW system modeling has been further explored where the Coulomb friction and tire self-aligning torque are

considered in order to compensate the effect of nonlinearities and disturbance efficiently. The state feedback control law has been proposed which derived based on the
Lyapunov theory and the stability condition is expressed in the form of LMIs. The
simulation results have verified the exceptional steering performance of the proposed
controller. The further work on designing a LMIs-based anti-windup compensator
subjected to time delays and actuator saturation is under the authors' investigation.

References

1. Fukao, T., et al.: Active steering systems based on model reference adaptive nonlinear
   control. Veh. Syst. Dyn. **42**(5), 301–318 (2004)
2. Kazemi, R., Janbakhsh, A.A.: Nonlinear adaptive sliding mode control for vehicle handling
   improvement via steer-by-wire. Int. J. Automot. Tech. **11**(3), 345–354 (2010)
3. Segawa, M., et al.: Vehicle stability control strategy for steer by wire system. Jsae Rev.
   22(4), 383–388 (2001)
4. Yih, P., Gerdes, J.C.: Modification of vehicle handling characteristics via steer-by-wire.
   IEEE Trans. Control Syst. Technol. **13**(6), 965–976 (2005)
5. Bertoluzzo, M., Buja, G., Menis, R.: Control schemes for steer-by-wire systems. IEEE Ind.
   Electron. Mag. **1**(1), 20–27 (2007)
6. Baviskar, A., et al.: An adjustable steer-by-wire haptic-interface tracking controller for
   ground vehicles. IEEE Trans. Veh. Technol. **58**(2), 546–554 (2009)
7. Park, T.J., Han, C.S., Lee, S.H.: Development of the electronic control unit for the
   rack-actuating steer-by-wire using the hardware-in-the-loop simulation, system. Mechatronics **15**(8), 899–918 (2005)
8. Setlur, P., et al.: A trajectory tracking steer-by-wire control system for ground vehicles. IEEE
   Trans. Veh. Technol. **55**(1), 76–85 (2006)
9. Kim, G.J., et al.: Development of a control algorithm for a rack-actuating steer-by-wire
   system using road information feedback. Proc. Inst. Mech. Eng. Part D-J. Automobile Eng.
   222(D9), 1559–1571 (2008)
10. Oh, S.W., et al.: The design of a controller for the steer-by-wire system. Jsme Int. J. Series
    C-Mech. Syst. Mach. Elem. Manufact. **47**(3), 896–907 (2004)
11. Marumo, Y., Nagai, M.: Steering control of motorcycles using steer-by-wire system. Veh.
    Syst. Dyn. **45**(9), 877 (2007). (vol 45, pg 445, 2007)
12. Marumo, Y., Katagiri, N.: Control effects of steer-by-wire system for motorcycles on
    lane-keeping performance. Veh. Syst. Dyn. **49**(8), 1283–1298 (2011)
13. Yamaguchi, Y., Murakami, T.: Adaptive control for virtual steering characteristics on
    electric vehicle using steer-by-wire system. IEEE Trans. Ind. Electron. **56**(5), 1585–1594
    (2009)
14. Cetin, A.E., et al.: Implementation and development of an adaptive steering-control system.
    IEEE Trans. Veh. Technol. **59**(1), 75–83 (2010)
15. Nakagawa, C., et al.: Stabilization of a bicycle with two-wheel steering and two-wheel
    driving by driving forces at low speed. J. Mech. Sci. Technol. **23**(4), 980–986 (2009)
16. Zakaria, M.I., et al.: Lyapunov-Krasovskii stability condition for system with bounded delay
    - an application to steer-by-wire system. In: 2015 IEEE International Conference on Control
    System, Computing and Engineering (ICCSCE), pp. 543–547 (2015)
17. Wang, C.Y., et al.: Stability control of steer by wire system based on mu synthesis robust
    control. Sci. China-Technol. Sci. **60**(1), 16–26 (2017)

18. Rehan, M., Hong, K.S., Ge, S.S.: Stabilization and tracking control for a class of nonlinear systems. Nonlinear Anal.-Real World Appl. **12**(3), 1786–1796 (2011)
19. Mobayen, S.: Optimal LMI-based state feedback stabilizer for uncertain nonlinear systems with time-varying uncertainties and disturbances. Complexity **21**(6), 356–362 (2016)
20. Siljak, D.D., Stipanovic, D.M.: Robust stabilization of nonlinear systems: The LMI approach. Math. Probl. Eng. **6**(5), 461–493 (2000)
21. Ramli, L., et al.: Optimal composite nonlinear feedback controller for an active front steering system. In: Sidik, N.A.C. (ed.) Mechanical and Materials Engineering, pp. 526–530. Trans Tech Publications Inc., Zürich (2014)
22. Anwar, S., Chen, L.: An analytical redundancy-based fault detection and isolation algorithm for a road-wheel control subsystem in a steer-by-wire system. IEEE Trans. Veh. Technol. **56**(5), 2859–2869 (2007)
23. Anwar, S.: Generalized predictive control of yaw dynamics of a hybrid brake-by-wire equipped vehicle. Mechatronics **15**(9), 1089–1108 (2005)
24. Boyd, S., et al.: Linear matrix inequalities in system and control theory. SIAM (1994)
25. Mathiyalagan, K., Park, J.H., Sakthivel, R.: Exponential synchronization for fractional-order chaotic systems with mixed uncertainties. Complexity **21**(1), 114–125 (2015)
26. Wang, H., et al.: Sliding mode control for steer-by-wire systems with AC motors in road vehicles. IEEE Trans. Indust. Electron. **61**(3), 1596–1611 (2014)
27. Sturm, J.F.: Using SeDuMi 1.02, a MATLAB toolbox for optimization over symmetric cones. Optim. Methods Softw. **11–2**(1–4), 625–653 (1999)
28. Lofberg, J.: YALMIP: a toolbox for modeling and optimization in MATLAB. In: 2004 IEEE International Conference on Robotics and Automation (2004)
29. Shah, M.B.N., et al.: Error handling algorithm and probabilistic analysis under fault for CAN-based steer-by-wire system. IEEE Trans. Ind. Inform. **12**(3), 1017–1034 (2016)
30. Shuai, Z.B., et al.: Combined AFS and DYC Control of Four-Wheel-Independent-Drive Electric Vehicles over CAN Network with Time-Varying Delays. IEEE Trans. Veh. Technol. **63**(2), 591–602 (2014)
31. Zhang, H., Wang, J.M.: Active steering actuator fault detection for an automatically steered electric Gnd Veh. IEEE Trans. Veh. Technol. **66**(5), 3685–3702 (2017)
32. Shah, M.B.N., et al.: An analysis of CAN-based steer-by-wire system performance in vehicle. IEEE International Conference on Control System, Computing and Engineering, pp. 350–355 (2013)
33. Diao, X.Y., et al.: Composite active front steering controller design for vehicle system. IEEE Access. **5**, 6697–6706 (2017)

Determination of Modeling Parameters for a Low Cost Air Pollution Measurement System Using Feedforward Neural Networks

Nur Azie Dahari and Herman Wahid[(⊠)]

Faculty of Electrical Engineering, Universiti Teknologi Malaysia, 81310 Skudai,
Johor, Malaysia
nazie2@live.utm.my, herman@utm.my

Abstract. Air pollution model is commonly used to predict the pollutant level in the air for the upcoming days based on the previous data. In this paper, a new model for predicting ozone, nitrogen dioxide and sulphur dioxide will be developed using the previous data of pollutants agents such as carbon monoxide, sulphur dioxide, nitrogen dioxide, ozone, particulate matter and the meteorological data includes wind speed, temperature and humidity. It is developed to improve the estimation values for a low cost setup of air pollution measurement system. The models are constructed using the Levenberg-Marquardt training algorithms in the neural network tool. Different input parameters are investigated to develop better performance model for predicting air pollution. The proposed model is capable to predict the air pollution level with high accuracy and the meteorological data are dominantly influenced the accuracy of the model.

Keywords: Modeling · Air pollutant · Levenberg-Marquardt · Feedforward networks · Pollutant agent · Meteorological data

1 Introduction

Air pollution is currently an on-going issue in Malaysia. This is due to rapid growth in industrial site, factories, and suspended hazardous materials from the vehicles and numerous residential units. Every day, the air that enter into the lung is not pure, which contains lots of pollutants and mostly toxic [1–3]. There are five major pollutants found in the air which are sulphur dioxide, carbon monoxide, particulate matter, nitrogen dioxide and ozone [4]. These pollutants can give negative effects on human health and also environment.

Exposure to the polluted air can cause diseases of respiratory system such as asthma, chronic obstructive pulmonary disease, allergies, runny nose, cough and sore throat. In addition, exposure to air pollution can have permanent health effect in nervous system such as problems with memory, concentration, more frequent depressive behaviour, faster aging of the nervous system, and increased risk of Alzheimer's disease [5]. Exposure to air pollutant also can lead to skin irritant [6] and premature death [7].

© Springer Nature Singapore Pte Ltd. 2017
M.S. Mohamed Ali et al. (Eds.): AsiaSim 2017, Part I, CCIS 751, pp. 685–696, 2017.
DOI: 10.1007/978-981-10-6463-0_58

Furthermore, air pollution can lead to environment problem such as rain acid and global warming. The environment problem can harm the buildings, lakes, plants and animal by increasing the temperature surrounding, higher the sea levels and changes in forest composition.

Basically, neural networks are trained so that input data will leads to a specific target output and neural network which are applied in a various fields of application such as pattern recognition, identification, classification and control systems to perform complex functions [8].

This paper will focus on forecasting the concentration levels of pollutant using a neural network model. The model is a function of carbon monoxide, sulphur dioxide, nitrogen dioxide, ozone, particulate matter, time, wind speed, temperature and humidity data that collected by a low cost air quality monitoring system that we have developed. The choice of its architecture such as the number of neurons and selection of a learning algorithm can significantly affect the model performance and have to be studied individually for each case.

Up to now, many studies have developed neural network models to predict the air pollution. For example, a neural network model are developed to predict the tropospheric (surface or ground) ozone concentrations as a function of meteorological conditions and various air quality parameters and their results showing that the Artificial Neural Network (ANN) is a promising method for air pollution modeling [9].

In another study, neural network models are developed to predict the carbon monoxide (CO) level air the air [10]. In 2009, an ANN model is developed to predict the concentration of pollutants in Delhi, India. Their result showing that the concentration of sulphur dioxide (SO_2) can be predicted with maximum accuracy using nonlinear perceptron and that the non-linear perceptron is better for forecasting the concentration of sulphur dioxide, carbon monoxide, suspended particulate matter (SPM) and ozone (O_3) and delta learning is better for forecasting nitrogen dioxide (NO_2) [11].

In Malaysia, the ANNs model is developed for carbon dioxide emissions forecast by investigating the performances of Levenberg-Marquardt and gradient descent algorithms of back propagation. The model are trained using the Malaysian data of energy use, gross domestic product per capita, population density, combustible renewable and waste and carbon dioxide intensity. As the results, the Levenberg-Marquardt was outperformed the gradient descent in carbon dioxide emissions forecast [12].

2 Methodology

The study area is located in the southern part of Peninsular Malaysia in Johor Bahru. The area is bounded by the latitudes 1.559274°N and longitudes 103.641968°E. The geographical map for the air pollution monitoring locations is shown in Fig. 1.

The daily data are recorded by a low cost air quality monitoring system that placed at the top of building of Faculty of Electrical Engineering, Universiti Teknologi Malaysia. A low cost air quality monitoring system is an arduino based device which is consisting of carbon monoxide sensor, ozone sensor, dust sensor, sulphur dioxide sensor, nitrogen dioxide sensor, temperature and humidity sensor and anemometer as

Fig. 1. The study area is marked with blue dot (circle). (Color figure online)

shown in Fig. 2(a). The internal looks of the system are shown in Fig. 2(b). The data are collected from 16 March–19 April 2017. The sensor monitor the air quality almost 9 h every day, start from 8.00 a.m. until 5.00 p.m.

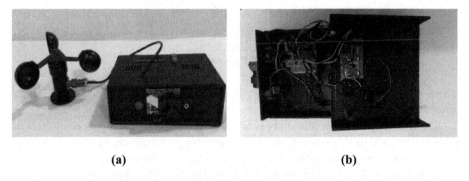

(a)   (b)

Fig. 2. (a) A low cost air monitoring system; (b) Internal look of the system.

The ANN network is divided by three layers, defined as input layer, hidden layer and output layer [13], which is discussed in details as follows:

Input Layer: There are seven independent variables were selected as inputs: carbon monoxide (CO), nitrogen dioxide (NO_2), sulphur dioxide (SO_2), ozone (O_3), particulate matter, wind speed, time, temperature and relative humidity.

The model is built using neural network toolbox in MATLAB. The data are divided into three groups for training the network (70% of data), validating (15% of data), and testing (15% of data).

Hidden Layer: Next, the number of hidden neuron is selected. The predictable accuracy of the model also depends on hidden neuron. If the number of neuron is too low, the capability of the model will be reduced and if the number of neuron is too high, phenomena of over-fitting will occur [14]. For this reason, basically the number of hidden neuron is selected based on experience and practical necessity [15].

There are many optimized algorithms in neural network such as orthogonal least square learning algorithms, linear least square algorithms and Levenberg-Marquardt algorithms [16]. However, Levenberg-Marquardt algorithm is applied in this work because of fast response and better performance [17].

Output Layer: The mean absolute error (MAE), the root mean square error (RMSE) and determination correlation (R^2) and index of agreement (d_2) are used to evaluate the model. The formula for calculating the mean absolute error (MAE), the root mean square error (RMSE) and determination correlation (R^2) and index of agreement (d_2) as shown as below [18, 19]:

$$\text{MAE} = \frac{\sum_{i=1}^{n_i} |P_i - O_i|}{n}. \tag{1}$$

$$\text{RMSE} = \sqrt{\frac{\sum_{i=1}^{n_i} (O_i - P_i)^2}{n}}. \tag{2}$$

$$R^2 = 1 - \frac{\sum_{i=1}^{n_i} (O_i - P_i)^2}{\sum_{i=1}^{n_i} (O_i - \overline{O})^2}. \tag{3}$$

$$d_2 = 1 - \frac{\sum_{i=1}^{n_i} |P_i - O_i|^2}{\sum_{i=1}^{n_i} (|P_i - \overline{O}| - |O_i - \overline{O}|)^2}. \tag{4}$$

where O_i is observed concentration, P_i is the predicted concentration and $\overline{O}$ is the observation mean.

The main objectives of this study is to investigate the suitable inputs candidates for air pollutant models that offering the best predicting performance, by means of giving accurate inputs-output mapping. The targeted pollutants' models are: ozone, nitrogen dioxide, sulphur dioxide and carbon monoxide. The general architecture of the specific model is as depicted in Fig. 3 where x_i are the possible inputs and y_j is the predicted pollutant.

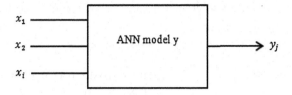

Fig. 3. The model architecture of the specific air pollutant model.

3   Results and Analysis

In this study, we performed 32 simulation of difference combination of input as shown in Tables 1, 2, 3 and 4 to find the best performance model for ozone, nitrogen dioxide, sulphur dioxide and carbon monoxide using the proposed algorithms.

Table 1. Performance of the test set by difference combination of inputs for ozone model.

Set	Inputs	RMSE	MAE	R^2	d_2	Hidden neuron
1	Time, SO_2, NO_2, PM_{10}	1.9840	1.1852	0.8740	0.9685	16
2	Time, SO_2, NO_2, PM_{10}, temp	1.7934	0.9884	0.8971	0.9743	17
3	Time, SO_2, NO_2, PM_{10}, temp, hum	1.7533	1.0542	0.9016	0.9754	18
4	Time, SO_2, NO_2, PM_{10}, temp, hum, WSP	1.3078	0.7890	0.9453	0.9863	20
5	SO_2, NO_2, PM_{10}	2.2760	1.1442	0.8342	0.9586	16
6	SO_2, NO_2, PM_{10}, temp	1.7917	1.0303	0.8973	0.9743	17
7	SO_2, NO_2, PM_{10}, temp, hum	1.7011	1.0428	0.9074	0.9768	18
8	SO_2, NO_2, PM_{10}, temp, hum, WSP	1.6993	1.0094	0.9076	0.9769	20

Table 2. Performance of the test set by difference combination of inputs for nitrogen dioxide model.

Set	Inputs	RMSE	MAE	R^2	d_2	Hidden neuron
1	Time, SO_2, O_3, PM_{10}	2.2932	1.3007	0.9126	0.9782	12
2	Time, SO_2, O_3, PM_{10}, temp	1.2280	0.7604	0.9750	0.9937	12
3	Time, SO_2, O_3, PM_{10}, temp, hum	1.0907	0.6754	0.9802	0.9951	12
4	Time, SO_2, O_3, PM_{10}, temp, hum, WSP	1.0651	0.6717	0.9812	0.9953	12
5	SO_2, O_3, PM_{10}	3.2551	1.8530	0.8240	0.9560	12
6	SO_2, O_3, PM_{10}, temp	1.6531	1.0841	0.9546	0.9887	12
7	SO_2, O_3, PM_{10}, temp, hum	1.4191	0.9567	0.9665	0.9916	12
8	SO_2, O_3, PM_{10}, temp, hum, WSP	1.2184	0.7794	0.9753	0.9938	12

Table 3. Performance of the test set by difference combination of inputs for sulphur dioxide model.

Set	Inputs	RMSE	MAE	R^2	d_2	Hidden neuron
1	Time, NO_2, O_3, PM_{10}	0.0795	0.0510	0.9214	0.9803	10
2	Time, NO_2, O_3, PM_{10}, temp	0.0489	0.0331	0.9702	0.9926	11
3	Time, NO_2, O_3, PM_{10}, temp, hum	0.0481	0.0312	0.9713	0.9928	12
4	Time, NO_2, O_3, PM_{10}, temp, hum, WSP	0.0465	0.0310	0.9731	0.9933	14
5	NO_2, O_3, PM_{10}	0.1172	0.0754	0.8291	0.9573	10
6	NO_2, O_3, PM_{10}, temp	0.0793	0.0472	0.9218	0.9804	11
7	NO_2, O_3, PM_{10}, temp, hum	0.0649	0.0381	0.9476	0.9869	12
8	NO_2, O_3, PM_{10}, temp, hum, WSP	0.0946	0.0536	0.8886	0.9722	14

Table 4. Performance of the test set by difference combination of inputs for carbon monoxide model.

Set	Inputs	RMSE	MAE	R^2	d_2	Hidden neuron
1	Time, SO_2, NO_2, O_3, PM_{10}	0.1397	0.0845	0.8990	0.9747	10
2	Time, SO_2, NO_2, O_3, PM_{10}, temp	0.1406	0.0946	0.8977	0.9744	12
3	Time, SO_2, NO_2, O_3, PM_{10}, temp, hum	0.0637	0.0442	0.9790	0.9948	13
4	Time, SO_2, NO_2, O_3, PM_{10}, temp, hum, WSP	0.0953	0.0519	0.9530	0.9883	14
5	SO_2, NO_2, O_3, PM_{10}	0.2073	0.1489	0.7775	0.9444	10
6	SO_2, NO_2, O_3, PM_{10}, temp	0.1512	0.1027	0.8817	0.9704	12
7	SO_2, NO_2, O_3, PM_{10}, temp, hum	0.1344	0.0934	0.9065	0.9766	13
8	SO_2, NO_2, O_3, PM_{10}, temp, hum, WSP	0.1141	0.0749	0.9326	0.9831	14

First, for the ozone model first simulation was performed using the information of time, SO_2, NO_2 and PM_{10}. For the next three set, we added the first set with meteorological information that includes temperature, humidity and wind speed and for the next four set, we are removed the information of time.

By referring to Table 1, the best combination for ozone model with the highest accuracy is given by the inputs in the set number 4. The good combination of the number of hidden neuron and selected variables inputs in ozone model presented the best results. The number of hidden neuron used for this model is 18. The number of hidden neuron is increasing regularly with the number of input variables as depending on the complexity of the training process. Besides, it can be noticed that the temperature, humidity and wind speed effect much on the performance of the model. For example, set 4 constructed with the metrological data obtained determination correlation R^2 of 0.9453 and the set 1 which are constructed without meteorological data obtained determination correlation R^2 of 0.8740.

Moreover, by referring to Table 1, it can be observed that the inputs set number 5 until 8, the input of time are excluded from the dataset. Unfortunately, the performances of the model are affected as the value of RMSE and MAE become higher and value for determination correlation R^2 decreased. So, it can be concluded that time also influence much on the accuracy of the model.

Figure 4 shows the prediction and observed level of ozone in one week correlation. As we can observe, predicted patterns are mostly follow the observed pattern that measured by our low cost air quality monitoring system. However, some predicted data cannot follow the observed data especially when the observed data are peaking data. From the graph, it is also shown that the decreasing trend in one week with the rate of about −0.0054 ppm/min using the linear fit line.

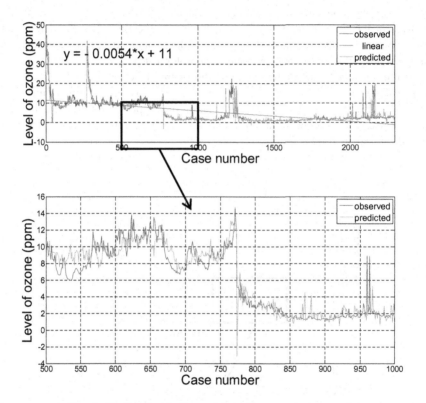

Fig. 4. Predicted and observed data for ozone in one week.

Next, for the nitrogen dioxide model the first simulation was performed using the information of time, SO_2, O_3 and PM_{10}. For the next three set, we added the first set with meteorological information that includes temperature, humidity and wind speed. For the next four set, the simulation are performed without input of time.

According to Table 2, it shows that the nitrogen dioxide model are constructed using a fixed number of hidden neuron. The number of hidden neuron is selected based on performance of the model. All set of data are constructed with range of 10–20 number of hidden neuron and the number of hidden neuron 12 gives a better results with highest accuracy. Hence, all set of the data are developed using 12 number of hidden neuron.

By referring to Table 2, it is also shown that the best combination with the higher accuracy is given by the inputs in the set number 4. Again, meteorological parameter such as wind speed, temperature and humidity are determined to influence the model performance. For example, set number 4 that are constructed with all the metrological data are produced errors as derived by the RMSE and MAE are lowest than other set of data. Furthermore, the determination correlation R^2 is 0.9812, also the highest compare with other set of data. However, without the good performance from the time data, the set number 4 also cannot form the best combination with the higher accuracy. As we can observe, the inputs in the set number 8 are same with the inputs in the set number 4 but without the time input. Because of excluded of the time data the determination correlation R^2 are decreasing to 0.9753. It can be concluded, the performance of set number 4 are influence by the time and meteorological data.

Figure 5 shows the prediction and the observation level of nitrogen dioxide in one week correlation. As we can notice, most of predicted pattern are approximately following the observed pattern with error deviation of ±5 ppm. From the graph, we also can demonstrate the increasing trend in one week with the rate of about 0.01 ppm/min using the linear fit line.

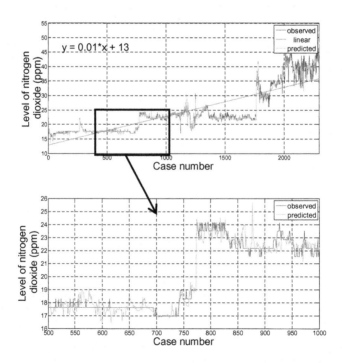

Fig. 5. Predicted and observed data for nitrogen dioxide in one week.

Next, for the sulphur dioxide model, the first simulation was performed using the information of time, NO_2, PM_{10} and O_3. For the next three set, we added the first set with meteorological information that includes temperature, humidity and wind speed. The last four set, we removed the time input.

By referring to Table 3, the best combination for sulphur dioxide model with highest accuracy is given by the inputs in the set number 4. The number of hidden neuron used for this model is 14. The number of hidden neuron is increasing gradually with the complexity of the training process. Besides, it can be stated that time, temperature, humidity and wind speed affect much in the accuracy and the performance of the model. The excellent combinations of the inputs give the lowest value of RMSE and MAE that are 0.0465 and 0.0310 respectively. This is the best model that has been constructed in this work.

The prediction and observation level of sulphur dioxide in one week is shown in Fig. 6. From the graph, we can observe most of predicted pattern are following the observation pattern with error deviation of ±2 ppm. In addition, the graph also represented the increasing trend in one week with the rate of about 0.00037 ppm/min using the linear fit line.

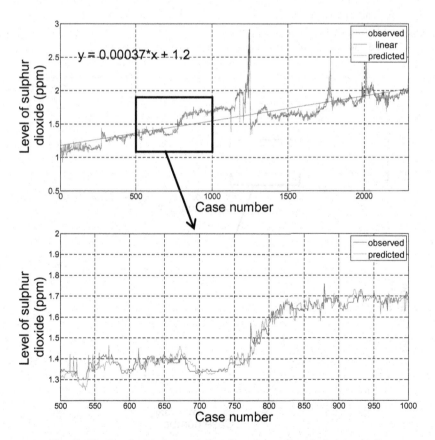

Fig. 6. Predicted and observed data for sulphur dioxide in one week.

Finally, for the carbon monoxide model, the first simulation was performed using the information of time, SO_2, NO_2, O_3 and PM_{10}. For the next three set, we added the first set with meteorological information that includes temperature, humidity and wind speed. The last four set, we removed the time. The data are collected during the haze phenomenon. It can be spotted that the level of pollutant are increasing dramatically especially for PM_{10}. The level of temperature surrounding also faced significant increasing especially at early in the morning and noon.

By referring to the Table 4, the best combination for carbon monoxide model is given by the inputs in the set number 3. The model is constructed without the input of wind speed. The number of hidden neuron applied for this model is 13. The number of hidden neuron is increasing steadily with the complexity of the training process. We expect that the wind speed will give an influence on the model performance. Unfortunately, the results do not support the statement. It is due to small variation of the recorded wind speed level. Hence, wind speed has minor influence to the model performance. The performance and the accuracy of the model majorly depended on time, temperature and humidity.

The prediction and observation level of carbon monoxide is shown in Fig. 7. From the graph, we can detect most of predicted pattern follows the observed pattern. Besides, we can obviously detect the levels of carbon monoxide are higher at the early minutes and middle minutes. Furthermore, the graph also represents the increasing trend with the rate of about 0.0014 ppm/min using the linear fit line.

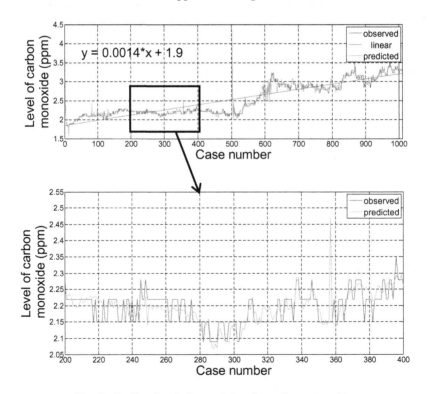

Fig. 7. Predicted and observed data for carbon monoxide.

4   Conclusion

As a conclusion, new models for predicting the ozone, nitrogen dioxide, sulphur dioxide and carbon monoxide have been presented. The several combination of the input variables have been used to develop the model as the input variables would influence the accuracy and the performance of the constructed model. The considered inputs such are time, meteorological data, particulate matter and pollutant agents included O_3, NO_2 and SO_2. It has been noticed that time and meteorological data, especially temperature and humidity dominantly affect the model performance. It is also noticed that the presented of pollutant agents are not give much effect on the model performance. For future work, we would apply the current methodology for long term prediction of the ozone, nitrogen dioxide, sulphur dioxide and carbon monoxide.

Acknowledgement. The authors would like to acknowledge the UTM-GUP Grant from Universiti Teknologi Malaysia (UTM) and Malaysian Government with vote number Q.J130000.2523.11H49 for supporting this work.

References

1. Asghari, M., Nematzadeh, H.: Predicting air pollution in tehran: genetic algorithm and back propagation neural network. J. Al. Data Min. **4**(1), 49–54 (2016)
2. Fleischer, N.L., Merialdi, M., Van Donkelaar, A., Vadillo-Ortega, F., Martin, R.V., Betran, A.P.: Outdoor air pollution, preterm birth, and low birth weight: analysis of the world health organization global survey on maternal and perinatal health. Environ. Health Perspect. **122**(4), 425–430 (2014)
3. Khader, Y., Abdelrahman, M., Abdo, N., Awad, S., Al-Sharif, M., Elbetieha, A., Malkawi, A.: Exposure to air pollution and pregnancy outcomes in the east mediterranean region: a systematic review. Int. J. Pediatr. **4**(1), 1255–1271 (2016)
4. Zallaghi, E., Geravandi, S., Haddad, M.N., Goudarzi, G., Valipour, L., Salmanzadeh, S., Soltani, F.: Estimation of health effects attributed to nitrogen dioxide exposure using the airq model in tabriz city, Iran. J. Health Scope **4**(4), 31–37 (2015)
5. Pawul, M., Śliwka, M.: Application of artificial neural networks for prediction of air pollution levels in environmental monitoring. J. Ecol. Eng. **17**(4), 190–196 (2016)
6. Lakey, P.S., Wisthaler, A., Berkemeier, T., Mikoviny, T., Pöschl, U., Shiraiwa, M.: Chemical Kinetics of Multiphase Reactions Between Ozone and Human Skin Lipids: Implications for Indoor Air Quality and Health Effects. Indoor Air (2016)
7. Khafaie, M.A., Yajnik, C.S., Salvi, S.S., Ojha, A.: Critical review of air pollution health effects with special concern on respiratory health. J. Air Pollut. Health **1**(2), 123–136 (2016)
8. Demuth, H., Beale, M., Hagan, M.: Neural network toolbox: for use with MATLAB: user's guide: version 5. MathWorks, Natick, MA (2007)
9. Abdul-Wahab, S.A., Al-Alawi, S.M.: Assessment and prediction of tropospheric ozone concentration levels using artificial neural networks. Environ. Modell Softw. **17**(3), 219–228 (2002)
10. Sabah, A., Al-Rubiei, R., Al-Shamsi, A.: A statistical model for predicting carbon monoxide levels. Int. J. Environ. Pollut. **19**, 209–224 (2003)

11. Chaudhuri, S., Acharya, R.: Artificial neural network model to forecast the concentration of pollutants over delhi: skill assessment of learning rules. Asian J. Water Environ. Pollut. **1**, 71–81 (2012)
12. Pauzi, H.M., Abdullah, L.: Neural network training algorithm for carbon dioxide emissions forecast: a performance comparison. In: Sulaiman, H.A., Othman, M.A., Othman, M.F.I., Rahim, Y.A., Pee, N.C. (eds.) Advanced Computer and Communication Engineering Technology. LNEE, vol. 315, pp. 717–726. Springer, Cham (2015). doi:10.1007/978-3-319-07674-4_67
13. Li, W., Wu, X., Jiao, W., Qi, G., Liu, Y.: Modeling of dust removal in rotating packed bed using artificial neural networks (ANN). Appl. Therm. Eng. **112**, 208–213 (2017)
14. Feng, X., Li, Q., Zhu, Y., Hou, J., Jin, L., Wang, J.: Artificial neural networks forecasting of PM2.5 pollution using air mass trajectory based geographic model and wavelet transformation. Atmos. Environ. **107**, 118–128 (2015)
15. Swingler, K.: Applying Neural Networks: A Practical Guide. Academic Press, London (1996)
16. Saha, D.: Prediction of mass transfer coefficient in rotating bed contactor (Higee) Using artificial neural network. Heat Mass Transfer. **45**, 451–457 (2009)
17. Lashkarbolooki, M., Vaferi, B., Mowla, D.: Using artificial neural network to predict the pressure drop in a rotating packed bed. Sep. Sci. Technol. **47**, 2450–2459 (2012)
18. Memarianfard, M., Hatami, A.M.: Artificial neural network forecast application for fine particulate matter concentration using meteorological data. Global J. Environ. Sci. Manag. **3**(3), 333–340 (2017)
19. Wahid, H., Ha, Q.P., Nguyen-Duc, H.: A Metamodel for background ozone level using radial basis function neural networks. In: Control Automation Robotics and Vision (ICARCV), pp. 958–963 (2010)

Simplifying the Auto Regressive and Moving Average (ARMA) Model Representing the Dynamic Thermal Behaviour of iHouse Based on Theoretical Knowledge

Shamsul Faisal Mohd Hussein[1(✉)], Mohd Anuar Abu Bakar[1],
Yoshiki Makino[3], Hoaison Nguyen[2], Shahrum Shah Abdullah[1],
Yuto Lim[3], and Yasuo Tan[3]

[1] Biologically Inspired System and Technology (Bio-iST) iKohza,
Department of Electronic Systems Engineering (ESE),
Malaysia – Japan International Institute of Technology (MJIIT),
Universiti Teknologi Malaysia (UTM) Kuala Lumpur,
Jalan Sultan Yahya Petra (Jalan Semarak), 54100 Kuala Lumpur, Malaysia
foxfaisal@yahoo.co.uk, mohdanuar.abubakar@gmail.com,
shahrum@fke.utm.my
[2] Faculty of Information Technology,
Department of Networks and Computer Communications,
VNU University of Engineering and Technology,
Building E3, 144 Xuan Thuy, Cau Giay, Hanoi, Vietnam
hsnguyen@jaist.ac.jp
[3] School of Information Science,
Japan Advanced Institute of Science and Technology (JAIST),
1-1 Asahidai, Nomi, Ishikawa Prefecture 923-1211, Japan
{m-yoshi, ylim, ytan}@jaist.ac.jp

Abstract. Modelling and simulation is an alternative way of testing the dynamic behaviour of a real system – in some situation, testing the real system are expensive, time consuming, not comfortable, and dangerous. Mathematical model describing the dynamic behaviour of a system can be represented by using white, black, or grey box model. This study focuses on developing a simplified Auto Regressive Moving Average (ARMA) model (a type of linear black model) to represent the dynamic thermal behaviour of iHouse – simplification is done based on the theoretical knowledge of the building. The performance of the simplified ARMA model developed in this study is compared with the performance of the models developed in previous studies, which are: (1) House Thermal Simulator; (2) and ARMA model. Result shows that the simplified ARMA model developed in this study consists of simpler set of mathematical equations, but can still simulate the dynamic thermal behaviour of iHouse with the accuracy that is almost on par with the models developed in previous studies.

Keywords: Modelling and simulation · Black box modelling · Building temperature simulation · Building temperature prediction

© Springer Nature Singapore Pte Ltd. 2017
M.S. Mohamed Ali et al. (Eds.): AsiaSim 2017, Part I, CCIS 751, pp. 697–711, 2017.
DOI: 10.1007/978-981-10-6463-0_59

1 Introduction

Mathematical model is used to represent the dynamic behaviour of a system for simulation purpose. Mathematical model can be categorised as white, black and grey box model.

White box model is also known as theoretical model [1] and is developed based on the fundamental knowledge in science and engineering [2]. The value of unknown parameters in the white box model representing the dynamic behaviour of a system can be obtained through measurement in the actual system, referring to datasheet/manual of the system etc. [2]. Complex models can be simplified by making assumptions [2]. The advantage of white box model is it gives insight to the user on how the system behaves according to the fundamental law of science and engineering [1]. Since the model is constructed based on fundamental law of science and engineering, the model can be simulated over a wide range of operating point [1]. However, the white box model also has some weaknesses – in some situations, the value of unknown parameters contained in the system that is going to be modelled is difficult or even impossible to be measured or obtained [1]. In addition, assumptions made to simplify complex model may cause the model to be inaccurate [2].

Black box model is also known as empirical model [1] or data driven model [3], is developed by tuning the parameters in a set of linear or non-linear equations to map the relationship between the input(s) and output(s) of a system. Example of linear black box models are Auto Regressive (AR) model, Moving Average (MA) model, Auto Regressive Moving Average (ARMA) model etc. Example of non-linear black box model is Artificial Neural Network (ANN). Black box model is a purely data driven model – it maps the relationship between input(s) and output(s) of a system without describing the physical theory behind it. One of the advantages of the black box model is that it is suitable to be implemented when only the recorded input(s) and output(s) produced by the system that is going to be model are available, but the theoretical knowledge describing the system is unknown [1, 3]. Shamsul et al. [4] developed a black box model to simulate the air temperature of one of the rooms in iHouse, a smart house testbed (shown in Fig. 1) belongs to Japan Advanced Institute of Science and Technology (JAIST) with minimal physical knowledge of iHouse. Mustafaraj et al. in [5] predicted the room temperature and relative humidity of visa building in London using the following models: (1) autoregressive model with external inputs (ARX); (2) and neural network- based nonlinear auto regressive model with external inputs (NNARX) – results shows that both ARX and NNARX performed reasonably good, but the NNARX outperformed ARM. Mustafaraj et al. in [6] investigated the performance of the following models to predict the thermal behaviour of an open-plan office (room) in Portman House, located in central London: (1) a neural network-based non-linear autoregressive model with external inputs (NNARX); (2) a non-linear autoregressive moving average model with external inputs (NNARMAX); (3) and a non-linear output error model (NNOE) to predict the thermal behaviour of an open-plan office (room) in Portman House, central London – results showed that all models performed reasonably good, but the NNARX and NNARMAX models outperformed the NNOE model. Hazyuk et al. in [7] uses physical knowledge to decide the structure of the model, then uses black box modelling to represent the dynamic behaviour of the indoor temperature of a typical detached house in France, which is used as one of the reference building by *Centre Scientifique et Technique du Bâtiment* (CSTB)/Building Scientific and Technical Centre for performance evaluation. Even though black box model can be implemented with minimal theoretical knowledge of the system, knowing more theoretical knowledge will be more advantageous during the model development [3]. Like other models, the black box model also has disadvantage – it cannot be simulated within the operating condition that is outside the range of the data that is used to train/regress the black box model [1, 3] and it doesn't give physical insight regarding the theoretical knowledge of the system.

Fig. 1. The photo of iHouse, the smart house testbed belongs to Japan Advanced Institute of Science and Technology (JAIST).

Grey box model is also known as semi-empirical model [1] or hybrid model [3], is the combination of both white box model and black box model – the set of mathematical equations describing the dynamic behaviour of the model is constructed based on the knowledge of science and engineering while the unknown parameters in these equations are estimated based on the input(s)-output(s) relationship data produced by the system. The mathematical equations constructed based on fundamental knowledge of science and engineering gives physical insight to the system like the white box model, but the value of the unknown parameters in the equations that are difficult or impossible to be obtained can be estimated based on the input(s)-output(s) relationship data produced by the system that is going to be modelled [1]. Unlike black box model, the grey box model can be simulated (with caution) within the operating range that is outside the range of the data that is used to train/regress the grey box model [1]. Nguyen et al. [8] built a SIMULINK® toolbox named House Thermal Simulator to simulate the dynamic indoor temperature of iHouse, JAIST (shown in Fig. 1) based on a set of large quantity of equations that describe how the controlled inputs and disturbances affect the indoor air temperature of iHouse – the unknown parameters in these equations were estimated based on the real recorded data in iHouse using Simulink Design Optimization toolbox in MATLAB®.

A mathematical model is just a set of mathematical equations that represents the dynamic behaviour of a system [1]. Depending of the application of the model, care must be taken before and during the development process to maintain the balance between accuracy and complexity of the model [1]. Too accurate models will increase its complexity and consume lots of resources (in terms of time, budget, etc.) during the model development while too simple model will decrease its accuracy [1].

This study focuses on simplifying the ARMA model developed in [4] to represent the dynamic indoor air temperature behaviour of iHouse belongs to JAIST (shown in Fig. 1) based on theoretical knowledge – simpler model leads to simpler implementation and faster simulation. There are 2 previous studies that modelled the dynamic thermal behaviour of iHouse: (1) the first study developed a grey box model called House Thermal Simulator [8], which was developed using a set of many detailed mathematical equations describing the dynamic thermal behaviour of iHouse; (2) and the second study developed a black box model which was based on a purely data driven auto regressive and moving average (ARMA) model with minimal theoretical knowledge regarding the heat transfer properties of iHouse [4]. This study simplify the model developed in [4] based on some of the theoretical knowledge learnt in [8] and other sources.

2   Methodology

Since this study is related to the previous work in [4], the scope of this study is also similar with the previous work. First, only one out of fifteen rooms available in iHouse is modelled in this study. The modelled room is Bedroom A, which is the same room modelled in previous work in [4] and is shown in the iHouse floor plan shown in Fig. 2.

Fig. 2. The floorplan of iHouse.

Second, only the weather-related inputs (disturbances) without control-related input (s) are considered for this study. Even though thermal comfort devices such as air conditioner and motor-operated windows are installed in iHouse, the available historical data that are recorded when these thermal comfort devices are operated by the time this study is done are still not sufficient to develop model with control-related inputs using black box and grey box modelling. Therefore, it is still unable to develop a grey box or black box model that is capable to simulate control-related input by the time this study is done.

Third, all the walls of the room that is going to be modelled is assumed to be consisted of plain wall without doors or windows – these door and windows are assumed to be part of the wall to maintain the simplicity of the model and reduce time taken to develop it. Including the equations describing how the weather-related inputs affect the room's air temperature through the door and windows will increase the total number or length of the mathematical equations in the model and will increase the development duration.

2.1 Data Collection

Due to time constrain, available historical data that were used in previous study in [4] are used again in this study. These selected data were recorded with the following conditions: (1) the air conditioner was switched off; (2) and the motor-operated windows were closed.

Two groups of historical data that were recorded with same conditions (as mentioned previously) and were recorded on the date that are as close with each other as possible are identified and assigned as training and testing data set. The reason why the training and testing data set must be recorded on the date that are as close as possible is to reduce the variation of weather related inputs, especially in four-season countries.

The first group of historical data were recorded from the 1st of August 2012 until the 3rd of August 2012 (assigned as train data set) while the second group of historical data were recorded from the 10th of August 2012 until the 19th of August 2012 (assigned as test data set).

Different types of sensors in iHouse record different data at different time intervals. To simplify the model development process, the interval for all recorded data is standardized at every 90 s – this means that there will be 960 recorded input-output relationship data for every day if the data is recorded at the interval of every 90 s. Training data set (recorded from the 1st of August 2012 until the 3rd of August 2012) has 2880 recorded inputs-outputs relationships while testing data-set (recorded from the 10th of August 2012 until the 19th of August 2012) has 9600 recorded inputs-outputs relationships.

2.2 Data Selection

In previous work in [4], the ARMA model representing the dynamic indoor thermal behaviour of iHouse was created based on minimal (almost zero) theoretical knowledge regarding the physical thermal characteristic of iHouse. By the time this study is done, more theoretical knowledge regarding the thermal characteristic of iHouse (and other buildings) has been learnt.

Like the ARMA model developed in previous study in [4], the simplified ARMA model developed in this study is a multi-input single-output (MISO) system. However, the number of inputs has been reduced after having more information regarding the theoretical knowledge of iHouse (and other buildings). The output assigned for this model is the future temperature of bedroom A, (T_{BedA}). Unlike in the previous work in [4], the inputs assigned for this model has been revised based on the physical insight regarding how the weather related inputs affect the indoor air temperature of iHouse, which are: (1) the past temperature of bedroom A itself (T_{BedA}); (2) the differences between the past temperatures of the spaces surrounding bedroom A and the temperature of bedroom A itself – based on Fig. 2, bedroom A is surrounded by bedroom B and staircase from the North $(\Delta T_{BedB-BedA}$ and $\Delta T_{Stair-BedA})$, outdoor from the East and South $(\Delta T_{Out-BedA})$, master bedroom from the West $(\Delta T_{MBed-BedA})$, roof attic from the top $(\Delta T_{Attic-BedA})$ and Japanese-style room from the bottom $(\Delta T_{JRoom-BedA})$; (3) the past heat emitted from residence(s) and electronic device(s) in bedroom A $(Q_{ResDevBedA})$; (4) the past heat radiation from outside air and ground onto the outer walls of bedroom A $(Q_{OutAirRad})$; (5) the past solar radiations – only 2 types of solar radiations data are considered in this study, which are direct solar radiation on eastern and southern outer wall surface of bedroom A $(\varphi_{DirEastWall}$ and $\varphi_{DirSouthWall})$ and diffuse solar radiation on both eastern and southern outer wall surface of bedroom A $(\varphi_{DiffEastWall}$ and $\varphi_{DiffSouthWall})$; (6) and the past heat gain due to convection between outside air and both eastern and southern outer wall surface of bedroom A $(Q_{ConvEastWall}$ and $\varphi_{ConvSouthWall})$. This model with the determined inputs and output is illustrated in Fig. 3.

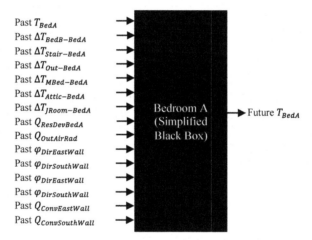

Fig. 3. The illustration of model for the thermal behaviour of bedroom A with listed possible inputs.

2.3 Model Construction

Let's say that the ARMA model has k past input(s), which is from $i = 0$ until $i = k - 1$. After the inputs that may have the potential to influence the temperature in bedroom A are determined and listed in Sect. 2.3 and depicted in Fig. 3, the simplified ARMA model equation with k past input(s) describing the air temperature in bedroom A is written, which is shown below:

$$
\begin{aligned}
T_{BedA}[n+k] =\ & \sum_{i=0}^{k-1} A_i T_{BedA}[n+i] + \sum_{i=0}^{k-1} B_i \Delta T_{BedB-BedA}[n+i] \\
& + \sum_{i=0}^{k-1} C_i \Delta T_{Stair-BedA}[n+i] + \sum_{i=0}^{k-1} D_i \Delta T_{Out-BedA}[n+i] \\
& + \sum_{i=0}^{k-1} E_i \Delta T_{MBed-BedA}[n+i] + \sum_{i=0}^{k-1} F_i \Delta T_{Attic-BedA}[n+i] \\
& + \sum_{i=0}^{k-1} G_i \Delta T_{JRoom-BedA}[n+i] + \sum_{i=0}^{k-1} H_i Q_{ResDevBedA}[n+i] \\
& + \sum_{i=0}^{k-1} I_i Q_{OutAirRad}[n+i] + \sum_{i=0}^{k-1} J_i \varphi_{DirEastWall}[n+i] \\
& + \sum_{i=0}^{k-1} K_i \varphi_{DirSouthWall}[n+i] + \sum_{i=0}^{k-1} L_i \varphi_{DiffEastWall}[n+i] \\
& + \sum_{i=0}^{k-1} M_i \varphi_{DiffSouthWall}[n+i] + \sum_{i=0}^{k-1} N_i Q_{ConvEastWall}[n+i] \\
& + \sum_{i=0}^{k-1} O_i Q_{ConvSouthWall}[n+i].
\end{aligned}
\tag{1}
$$

Equation (1) can also be written in an expanded form as shown below:

$$
\begin{aligned}
T_{BedA}[n+k] =\ & A_{k-1} T_{BedA}[n+k-1] + A_{k-2} T_{BedA}[n+k-2] + \cdots \\
& + A_1 T_{BedA}[n+1] + A_0 T_{BedA}[n] + B_{k-1} \Delta T_{BedB-BedA}[n+k-1] \\
& + B_{k-2} \Delta T_{BedB-BedA}[n+k-2] + \cdots + B_1 \Delta T_{BedB-BedA}[n+1] \\
& + B_0 \Delta T_{BedB-BedA}[n] + C_{k-1} \Delta T_{Stair-BedA}[n+k-1] + C_{k-2} \Delta T_{Stair-BedA}[n+k-2] + \cdots \\
& + C_1 \Delta T_{Stair-BedA}[n+1] + C_0 \Delta T_{Stair-BedA}[n] \\
& + D_{k-1} \Delta T_{Out-BedA}[n+k-1] + D_i \Delta T_{Out-BedA}[n+k-2] + \cdots \\
& + D_1 \Delta T_{Out-BedA}[n+1] + D_0 \Delta T_{Out-BedA}[n] + E_{k-1} \Delta T_{MBed-BedA}[n+k-1] \\
& + E_{k-2} \Delta T_{MBed-BedA}[n+k-2] + \cdots + E_1 \Delta T_{MBed-BedA}[n+1] \\
& + E_0 \Delta T_{MBed-BedA}[n] + F_{k-1} \Delta T_{Attic-BedA}[n+k-1] + F_{k-2} \Delta T_{Attic-BedA}[n+k-2] + \cdots \\
& + F_1 \Delta T_{Attic-BedA}[n+1] + F_0 \Delta T_{Attic-BedA}[n] \\
& + G_{k-1} \Delta T_{JRoom-BedA}[n+k-1] + G_{k-2} \Delta T_{JRoom-BedA}[n+k-2] + \cdots \\
& + G_1 \Delta T_{JRoom-BedA}[n+1] + G_0 \Delta T_{JRoom-BedA}[n] + H_{k-1} Q_{ResDevBedA}[n+k-1] \\
& + H_{k-2} Q_{ResDevBedA}[n+k-2] + \cdots + H_1 Q_{ResDevBedA}[n+1] \\
& + H_0 Q_{ResDevBedA}[n] + I_{k-1} Q_{OutAirRad}[n+k-1] + I_{k-2} Q_{OutAirRad}[n+k-2] + \cdots \\
& + I_1 Q_{OutAirRad}[n+1] + I_0 Q_{OutAirRad}[n] + J_{k-1} \varphi_{DirEastWall}[n+k-1] \\
& + J_{k-2} \varphi_{DirEastWall}[n+k-2] + \cdots + J_1 \varphi_{DirEastWall}[n+1] \\
& + J_0 \varphi_{DirEastWall}[n] + K_{k-1} \varphi_{DirSouthWall}[n+k-1] + K_{k-2} \varphi_{DirSouthWall}[n+k-2] + \cdots \\
& + K_1 \varphi_{DirSouthWall}[n+1] + K_0 \varphi_{DirSouthWall}[n] \\
& + L_{k-1} \varphi_{DiffEastWall}[n+k-1] + L_{k-2} \varphi_{DiffEastWall}[n+k-2] + \cdots \\
& + L_1 \varphi_{DiffEastWall}[n+1] + L_0 \varphi_{DiffEastWall}[n] + M_{k-1} \varphi_{DiffSouthWall}[n+k-1] \\
& + M_{k-2} \varphi_{DiffSouthWall}[n+k-2] + \cdots + M_1 \varphi_{DiffSouthWall}[n+1] \\
& + M_0 \varphi_{DiffSouthWall}[n] + N_{k-1} Q_{ConvEastWall}[n+k-1] \\
& + N_{k-2} Q_{ConvEastWall}[n+k-2] + \cdots + N_1 Q_{ConvEastWall}[n+1] \\
& + N_0 Q_{ConvEastWall}[n] + O_{k-1} Q_{ConvSouthWall}[n+k-1] \\
& + O_{k-2} Q_{ConvSouthWall}[n+k-2] + \cdots + O_1 Q_{ConvSouthWall}[n+1] \\
& + O_0 Q_{ConvSouthWall}[n].
\end{aligned}
\tag{2}
$$

S.F.M. Hussein et al.

2.4 Model Regression

'Regression' is defined as the process of estimating the unknown parameter(s) in ARMA model. In Artificial Neural Network, this process is known as 'training'.

Let's say that the training data-set is recorded from $t = 0$ until $t = p$. Therefore, the number of available sampled data recorded from $t = 0$ until $t = p$ are $p + 1$. The value of $p + 1$ in this study is equal to the number of data recorded from the 1st of August 2012 until the 3rd of August 2012, which is 2880 (as mentioned earlier in Subsect. 2.2 – Data Collection). When the data from k previous steps are used to estimate the temperature of bedroom A (from $t = 0$ until $t = k - 1$), the input-output pairs are equal to $p + 1 - k$. This can be illustrated by the matrices in Eq. (3) below:

$$\mathbb{Y} = \mathbb{X}\mathbb{M}. \tag{3}$$

where:

$$\mathbb{Y} = \begin{bmatrix} T_{BedA}[n+k] \\ T_{BedA}[n+k+1] \\ \vdots \\ T_{BedA}[n+p-1] \\ T_{BedA}[n+p] \end{bmatrix},$$

$$\mathbb{X} = \begin{bmatrix} \mathbb{X}_{(1,:)} \\ \mathbb{X}_{(2,:)} \\ \vdots \\ \mathbb{X}_{(p-k,:)} \\ \mathbb{X}_{(p+1-k,:)} \end{bmatrix},$$

$$\mathbb{X}_{(1,:)} = \begin{bmatrix} T_{BedA}[n+k-1] \\ T_{BedA}[n+k-2] \\ \vdots \\ T_{BedA}[n+1] \\ T_{BedA}[n] \\ \Delta T_{BedB-BedA}[n+k-1] \\ \Delta T_{BedB-BedA}[n+k-2] \\ \vdots \\ \Delta T_{BedB-BedA}[n+1] \\ \Delta T_{BedB-BedA}[n] \\ \vdots \\ Q_{ConvSouthWall}[n+k-1] \\ Q_{ConvSouthWall}[n+k-2] \\ \vdots \\ Q_{ConvSouthWall}[n+1] \\ Q_{ConvSouthWall}[n] \end{bmatrix}^T,$$

$$
\mathbb{X}_{(2,:)} =
\begin{bmatrix}
T_{BedA}[n+k] \\
T_{BedA}[n+k-1] \\
\vdots \\
T_{BedA}[n+2] \\
T_{BedA}[n+1] \\
\Delta T_{BedB-BedA}[n+k] \\
\Delta T_{BedB-BedA}[n+k-1] \\
\vdots \\
\Delta T_{BedB-BedA}[n+2] \\
\Delta T_{BedB-BedA}[n+1] \\
\vdots \\
Q_{ConvSouthWall}[n+k] \\
Q_{ConvSouthWall}[n+k-1] \\
\vdots \\
Q_{ConvSouthWall}[n+2] \\
Q_{ConvSouthWall}[n+1]
\end{bmatrix}^{T} ,
$$

$$
\mathbb{X}_{(p-k,:)} =
\begin{bmatrix}
T_{BedA}[n+p-2] \\
T_{BedA}[n+p-3] \\
\vdots \\
T_{BedA}[n+p-k] \\
T_{BedA}[n+p-1-k] \\
\Delta T_{BedB-BedA}[n+p-2] \\
\Delta T_{BedB-BedA}[n+p-3] \\
\vdots \\
\Delta T_{BedB-BedA}[n+p-k] \\
\Delta T_{BedB-BedA}[n+p-1-k] \\
\vdots \\
Q_{ConvSouthWall}[n+p-2] \\
Q_{ConvSouthWall}[n+p-3] \\
\vdots \\
Q_{ConvSouthWall}[n+p-k] \\
Q_{ConvSouthWall}[n+p-1-k]
\end{bmatrix}^{T} ,
$$

$$\mathbb{X}_{(p+1-k,:)} = \begin{bmatrix} T_{BedA}[n+p-1] \\ T_{BedA}[n+p-2] \\ \vdots \\ T_{BedA}[n+p+1-k] \\ T_{BedA}[n+p-k] \\ \Delta T_{BedB-BedA}[n+p-1] \\ \Delta T_{BedB-BedA}[n+p-2] \\ \vdots \\ \Delta T_{BedB-BedA}[n+p+1-k] \\ \Delta T_{BedB-BedA}[n+p-k] \\ \vdots \\ Q_{ConvSouthWall}[n+p-1] \\ Q_{ConvSouthWall}[n+p-2] \\ \vdots \\ Q_{ConvSouthWall}[n+p+1-k] \\ Q_{ConvSouthWall}[n+p-k] \end{bmatrix}^{T},$$

$$\mathbb{M} = \begin{bmatrix} A_{k-1} \\ A_{k-2} \\ \vdots \\ A_1 \\ A_0 \\ B_{k-1} \\ B_{k-2} \\ \vdots \\ B_1 \\ B_0 \\ \vdots \\ O_{k-1} \\ O_{k-2} \\ \vdots \\ O_1 \\ O_0 \end{bmatrix}.$$

In this study, the least square method is used to regress the simplified ARMA model. The purpose of regression is to estimate the values of the unknown constants in matrix $\mathbb{M}$ for the ARMA model in Eq. (3). The least square equation used for regressing the model is represented by Eq. (4) is written below:

$$\mathbb{M} = \left(\mathbb{X}^T\mathbb{X}\right)^{-1}\mathbb{X}^T\mathbb{Y}. \tag{4}$$

After the values of the unknown constants in matrix $\mathbb{M}$ are estimated using least square method, the model is then simulated again using the training data set to check its ability to fit the data-set. Then, the model can be tested and optimized with new data set that has never been 'seen' by the model, which will be discussed in the next sub-section.

2.5 Model Testing

In this process, the regressed simplified ARMA model is simulated with a new data-set that has never been 'seen' by the model. This data-set is called testing data-set. The purpose of this process is to ensure that the regressed model can produce accurate result when the model is simulated using different data-set (other than the training data-set).

Let's say that the testing data-set is recorded from $t = 0$ until $t = q$. Therefore, the number of available sampled data recorded from $t = 0$ until $t = q$ are $q + 1$. The value of $q + 1$ in this study is equal to the number of data recorded from the 10th of August 2012 until the 19th of August 2012, which is 9600 (as mentioned earlier in Subsect. 2.2 – Data Collection).

2.6 ARMA Model Parameter Estimation

The only parameter that needs to be tuned to optimize the ARMA model is the number of past input(s), which is the value of k. Bigger value of k leads to more quantity of constants available in matrix $\mathbb{M}$ (and vice versa). A MATLAB® script is written to try the possible values of k one by one (instead of assigning the value of k randomly and manually using trial and error method). Due to time constraint however, the value of k in this research is tried one by one only from $k = 1$ until $k = 200$. The percentage of fitness, %Fit is calculated for each tested value of k and its formula is shown below:

$$\%Fit = 1 - \frac{norm\left(T_{BedA} - \hat{T}_{BedA}\right)}{norm\left[T_{BedA} - mean(T_{BedA})\right]}. \tag{5}$$

3   Results

The performance of the optimized simplified ARMA model in this study is compared with the performance of the previous works, which are: (1) the optimised ARMA model [4]; (2) the optimized House Thermal Simulator [8]. The parameters in both ARMA model [4] and House Thermal Simulator [8] are also estimated and optimized by using their own parameter estimation and optimization methods, but using the same training and testing data-sets as those used in this study. The simulation results for the simplified ARMA model in this study, the ARMA model in previous study [4], and House Thermal Simulator [8] are plotted and displayed in Fig. 4 for comparison. Meanwhile, the value of percentage of fitness, %Fit for the simplified ARMA model in this study, the ARMA model in previous study [4], and House Thermal Simulator [8] are summarized in Table 1 for comparison.

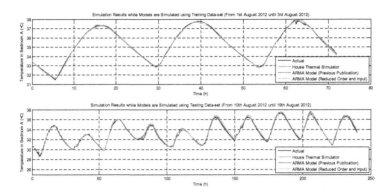

Fig. 4. The simulation result comparison for all three optimized models when simulated with training data set and testing data set.

Table 1. The %*Fit* values for all optimized models during simulation are presented in.

Model	%*Fit* (Train data set)	%*Fit* (Test data set)
House Thermal Simulator [8]	94.824	88.0188
ARMA Model [4]	97.6667	91.6101
Simplified ARMA Model	95.071	87.4575

4 Discussion

From the result displayed on Fig. 4 and Table 1, the accuracy of the simplified ARMA model obtained in this study in terms of percentage of best fit, %*Fit* is slightly less compared to the previous works in [8] and [4]. However, the differences are not big.

Even though the accuracy of the simplified ARMA model done in this study is slightly less compared to the previous works [4, 8], it's development and implementation is simpler. The ARMA model developed in previous study [4] has 19 types of inputs – when the model's number of order (which is also the number of past inputs) is tuned from $k = 1$ until $k = 200$, the model is accurate the most when $k = 26$. Meanwhile the simplified ARMA model developed in this study has 15 types of inputs – when the model's number of order is tuned in this study (from $k = 1$ until $k = 200$), the model is accurate the most when $k = 1$. Lesser types of inputs increase model's simplicity and reduces the time taken during model's regression process while model with lower order number (or lesser number of past inputs) reduces computation time during simulation. Meanwhile, the model developed in this study is also simpler to be implemented compared to House Thermal Simulator even though the accuracy of the model developed in this study is slightly lower than the accuracy of House Thermal Simulator because the simplified ARMA model developed in this study has lesser and simpler mathematical equations.

House Thermal Simulator [8] is a grey box model – it was developed based on fundamental knowledge of science and engineering while the unknown parameters in the model are estimated based on recorded inputs-output data relationship recorded in iHouse, which provide insight regarding how each input cause increment/decrement to the air temperature in iHouse. The set of equations used in House Thermal Simulator [8] are in large quantities to describe the relationship between the inputs and output vividly base on theoretical knowledge. This makes the House Thermal Simulator suitable to be used by the advanced researchers who would like to get a very detail insight on how the inputs affect the output. However, utilizing large quantity of equation is time consuming and requires more powerful computers for simulation. Meanwhile, the ordinary ARMA model that was developed [4] is a purely data driven model and was developed with minimal theoretical knowledge – ARMA model is just a single equation with parameters tuned to map the value of inputs versus output of a system. This make a black box model suitable to be used by beginner researchers because it can be constructed with minimal physical knowledge describing the system. Model with single equation (or a set of equation in small quantity) can be simulated in less powerful computers. Knowing more theoretical knowledge of a system while developing black box models will be more advantageous [3]. Compared to the ARMA model developed previously in [4], the number of inputs and model's order in this study is managed to be reduced based on the theoretical knowledge. In previous work, the only inputs that provide the insight regarding how they affect the air temperature increment/decrement in iHouse are: (1) the past temperature of bedroom A (T_{BedA}); (2) the past temperature difference between the surrounding spaces and bedroom A $(\Delta T_{BedB-BedA}, \Delta T_{Stair-BedA}, \Delta T_{Out-BedA}, \Delta T_{MBed-BedA}, \Delta T_{Attic-BedA},$ and $\Delta T_{JRoom-BedA})$; (3) the heat generated by residence(s) and electrical device(s) in bedroom A $(Q_{ResDevBedA})$; (4) and heat radiation from outside air and ground onto the outer walls of bedroom A $(Q_{OutAirRad})$. Meanwhile the rest of the inputs utilised in previous study [4] did not give insight on how they affect the air temperature gain/loss in iHouse – these inputs are: (1) the relative humidity of bedroom A (RH_{BedA}); (2) the solar altitude (Z_{Solar}); (3) the solar azimuth (θ_{Solar}); (4) and the wind speed blowing from all 4 directions $(V_{NorthWind}, V_{EastWind}, V_{SouthWind},$ and $V_{WestWind})$. Instead of being used directly as one of the inputs in the previous study, the relative humidity of bedroom A (RH_{BedA}) should be used to calculate the heat capacity of the air in bedroom A. However, neither the relative humidity of bedroom A (RH_{BedA}) nor the heat capacity of the air in bedroom A are used as the inputs of the simplified ARMA model in this study. Then, instead of being used directly as some of the inputs in the previous study, the value of solar position (Z_{Solar}) and solar azimuth (θ_{Solar}) are used to calculate the amount of direct and diffuse solar radiation that hit both the eastern and southern outer wall surfaces of bedroom A $(\varphi_{DirEastWall}, \varphi_{DirSouthWall}, \varphi_{DiffEastWall}, \varphi_{DiffSouthWall})$, which are used as the inputs of the simplified ARMA model in this study – these values are calculated based on solar altitude, solar azimuth wall slope angle, and wall azimuth. Finally, the wind speed (v_{Wind}) and direction (θ_{Wind}) in the previous research were resolved using trigonometric method into wind velocities that are coming from 4 directions, which are the wind velocity blowing from all 4 directions $(v_{NorthWind}, v_{EastWind}, v_{SouthWind},$ and $v_{WestWind})$. However, the values of v_{Wind} and θ_{Wind} should be used to calculate heat gain due to convection between outside air and both eastern and southern outer wall surface of bedroom A ($Q_{ConvEastWall}$ and $Q_{ConvSouthWall}$), which are used as the inputs of the simplified ARMA model in this study – these values are calculated based on outdoor air temperature (T_{Out}), the wind speed (v_{Wind}), and wind direction (θ_{Wind}).

5 Suggestion for Future Work

The simplified ARMA model developed in this study is the improvement of the basic ARMA model developed in the previous study in [4] and will be used in the future as a platform to test any proposed control system and strategy to maintain the thermal comfort in iHouse. Like the ARMA model developed in the previous study [4], the simplified ARMA model developed in this study only considers weather-related inputs during the model development due to the unavailability of historical data that was recorded when thermal comfort devices were operated. The next step is to include the control-related input(s) produced by thermal comfort device(s) so that the developed model can be used to simulate any proposed control system and strategy to maintain the thermal comfort in iHouse. New data will be recorded in iHouse while the thermal comfort devices (air conditioner and motor operated window) are operated. The study in this area is in progress and will be published once it is completed.

The equation of the model can be improved to increase the model's accuracy. One of the suggestion is to include the mathematical equations to represent the heat transfer through the door and windows. Due to time constrain, all the walls of bedroom A in this study is assumed to be plain walls (without window and door) to simplify the model development. Investigation should be done on the model's performance when the model is expanded to have mathematical equations describing the heat transfer through door and windows.

In addition, additional mathematical equations describing the heat transfer through the envelope of bedroom A can be investigated and added.

6 Conclusion

The main goal of this study is to simplify the ARMA model describing the thermal behaviour of iHouse developed in [4] based on fundamental knowledge in science and engineering. Through this study, it is shown that the simplified ARMA model with lesser inputs and model's order can still perform almost on par compared to the ARMA model in [4] and House Thermal Simulator in [8]. This is supported by the results presented in Sect. 3 which show that the accuracy of the simplified ARMA model developed in this study is slightly less compared to the other models of the previous studies, but the accuracy differences are not big. In addition, the model developed in this study is simpler to be implemented and faster to be simulated due to the lower number of inputs and model's order. The main contribution from this finding is in the simplification of ARMA model based on theoretical knowledge that can be implemented easier and simulated faster.

Acknowledgement. We would like to express our gratitude to the Japan Student Services Organization (JASSO) for their financial support and the Malaysia-Japan International Institute of Technology (MJIIT), Universiti Teknologi Malaysia (UTM) for their well-managed attachment program.

References

1. Seborg, D.E., Mellichamp, D.A., Edgar, T.F., Doyle, F.J.: Process Dynamics and Control. Wiley, Hoboken (2010)
2. Nise, N.S.: Control Systems Engineering, 6th edn. Wiley, Hoboken (1995)
3. Atam, E., Helsen, L.: Control-Oriented thermal modeling of multizone buildings: methods and issues: intelligent control of a building system. IEEE Control Syst. **36**, 86–111 (2016). doi:10.1109/MCS.2016.2535913
4. Mohd Hussein, S.F., Nguyen, H., Abdullah, S.S., et al.: Black box modelling the thermal behaviour of iHouse using auto regressive and moving average (ARMA) model. J. Teknol. **78**, 51–58 (2016). doi:10.11113/jt.v78.9272
5. Mustafaraj, G., Lowry, G., Chen, J.: Prediction of room temperature and relative humidity by autoregressive linear and nonlinear neural network models for an open office. Energy Build. **43**, 1452–1460 (2011). doi:10.1016/j.enbuild.2011.02.007
6. Mustafaraj, G., Chen, J., Lowry, G.: Thermal behaviour prediction utilizing artificial neural networks for an open office. Appl. Math. Model. **34**, 3216–3230 (2010). doi:10.1016/j.apm.2010.02.014
7. Hazyuk, I., Ghiaus, C., Penhouet, D.: Optimal temperature control of intermittently heated buildings using model predictive control: part I - building modeling. Build. Environ. **51**, 379–387 (2012). doi:10.1016/j.buildenv.2011.11.009
8. Nguyen, H., Makino, Y., Lim, A.O., Tan, Y., Shinoda, Y.: Building high-accuracy thermal simulation for evaluation of thermal comfort in real houses. In: Biswas, J., Kobayashi, H., Wong, L., Abdulrazak, B., Mokhtari, M. (eds.) Inclusive Society: Health and Wellbeing in the Community, and Care at Home, pp. 159–166. Springer, Heidelberg (2013)

Multirate Output Feedback Based Discrete Integral Sliding Mode Control for System with Uncertainties

Rafidah Ngadengon[1(✉)], Yahaya Md. Sam[2], Rohaiza Hamdan[1],
Mohd Hafiz A. Jalil[1], and Herdawatie Abdul Kadir[1]

[1] Advanced Mechatronics Research Group (ADMIRE),
Department of Mechatronics and Robotics Engineering,
Faculty of Electrical and Electronic Engineering,
Universiti Tun Hussein Onn Malaysia,
86400 Parit Raja, Batu Pahat, Johor, Malaysia
rafida@uthm.edu.my
[2] Department of Control and Instrumentation Engineering,
Faculty of Electrical Engineering, Universiti Teknologi Malaysia,
81310 Skudai, Johor, Malaysia

Abstract. This paper presents the design approach of Multirate Output Feedback (MROF) based Discrete Integral Sliding Mode Control (DISMC) for system with uncertainties. Firstly, the state representing the MROF has to be identified. The discrete integral sliding surface were selected in order to design the controller. The MROF that used output feedback with two different sampling times which are slow and fast rate is then combined with the DISMC to control the uncertain system. The reachability condition and stability are also considered and presented. Through extensive computer simulation, it shows that the proposed controller's capable to track the reference input even though uncertainties present in the system. The findings demonstrated that the MROF based DISMC provided better system response as compared to the Discrete Linear Quadratic Regulator (DLQR) and discrete Proportional Integral Derivative (PID).

Keywords: Multirate Output Feedback · Sliding Mode Control · Discrete integral · Inverted pendulum system

1 Introduction

In practical applications, systems are commonly operated under uncertain conditions for examples modelling error, measurement error and external disturbance. The existence of uncertainties will affect the performances, responses of the system and may lead the system to be unstable. An uncertainty that exists in the system is difficult to track and control. Sliding Mode Control (SMC) was proposed in the 1960's is a special nonlinear control strategy with discontinuous property [1]. SMC is a robust nonlinear control technique which has been applied widely for many applications that are involved with uncertainties [2–6]. The advantages of SMC among other controllers are external disturbance rejection, guarantee stability and insensitivity to system

© Springer Nature Singapore Pte Ltd. 2017
M.S. Mohamed Ali et al. (Eds.): AsiaSim 2017, Part I, CCIS 751, pp. 712–722, 2017.
DOI: 10.1007/978-981-10-6463-0_60

parameters variation especially after the system is driven to sliding surface as discussed by Edwards and Spurgeon [7]. These characteristics have made the SMC a suitable controller to control an uncertain system.

Nowadays the trend has been changed to discrete, as well as the SMC. That is due to the rapid development of digital computer and digital equipment. In general, digital control systems have many advantages over analog control system. Some of the advantages include low power consumption, high accuracy and high reliability and ease of making software and design changes [8]. For that reason, the discrete-time system representation is more justifiable for controller design compared to continuous-time. The brief idea of Discrete Sliding Mode Control (DSMC) was firstly appeared in the control literature during mid-80s by Milosavljevi´c followed by increasing list of publications [9, 10]. The new discrete integral sliding surface that can eliminate the reaching law was designed in [11]. Then a combination of equivalent control and integral control replacing the switching control was implemented by [12]. The matched and unmatched uncertainties were considered when designing the DISMC [13]. Normally, most of the SMC strategies are based on state feedback. But not all of the system states are available in practical, this situations would demand the need for some observers or dynamic compensators. However the used of observer would make the overall system more complex.

Meanwhile, the output feedback is always available all the time, so output feedback can be used to design the controller. In [14, 15] a concept known as Multirate Output Feedback (MROF) was introduced. The algorithm makes use of only the output samples for designing the controller. In MROF two sampling time were used, the system output sampled at faster rate and the control input is sampled at the slower rate. Several researchers have successfully implemented the concept of MROF to control various nonlinear plant [16–18].

In this paper, the controller is designed by combining MROF and DISMC in order to deal with the uncertain system. Then, the designed controller is implemented to inverted pendulum system. Inverted pendulum is selected because it is known as a highly nonlinear and unstable system.

2   Controller Designed

The system in continuous time can be represented as follows:

$$\dot{x}(t) = (A + \Delta A)x(t) + (B + \Delta B)u(t) + Be(t) \tag{1}$$

where $x(t) \in R^n$ is the state vector, $u(t) \in R^n$ is the control input, $y(t) \in R^n$ is the output vector, A and B are the nominal constant matrices, ΔA is the uncertainties present in the system, ΔB denote the uncertainties that exist in the input matrices and $e(t)$ is the external disturbance. The output of the inverted pendulum system in continuous time can be described as

714   R. Ngadengon et al.

$$y(t) = Cx(t) = \begin{bmatrix} C_1 \\ C_2 \end{bmatrix} x(t) = \begin{bmatrix} 1 & 0 & 0 & 0 \\ 0 & 1 & 0 & 0 \end{bmatrix} x(t) \qquad (2)$$

In order to have the reference tracking in the system, a new error state variable, z has to be added, where $z(t) = r(t) - C_1 x(t)$ and $r(t)$ is the desired reference. The C_1 is chosen because the system only consider the first state as a desired reference. By using Eqs. (1) and (2) with the reference tracking, the continuous time system can be

$$\dot{x}_p(t) = (A_p + \Delta A_p)x_p(t) + (B_p + \Delta B_p)u(t) + B_p e(t) + R_p r(t)$$
$$y_p(t) = C_p x_p(t) \qquad (3)$$

where

$$x_p = \begin{bmatrix} z \\ x \end{bmatrix} \quad A_p = \begin{bmatrix} 0 & -C_1 \\ 0_{n\times 1} & A \end{bmatrix} \quad \Delta A_p = \begin{bmatrix} 0 & 0 \\ 0_{n\times 1} & \Delta A \end{bmatrix}$$
$$B_p = \begin{bmatrix} 0 \\ B \end{bmatrix} \quad \Delta B_p = \begin{bmatrix} 0 \\ \Delta B \end{bmatrix} \quad C_p = \begin{bmatrix} 1 & 0_{1\times n} \\ 0 & C \end{bmatrix} \quad R_p = \begin{bmatrix} 1 \\ 0_{n\times 1} \end{bmatrix} \qquad (4)$$

The $x(t) \in R^n$ is the state vector, $u(t) \in R^n$ is the control input, $y(t) \in R^n$ is the output vector, A_p and B_p are the nominal constant matrices, ΔA_p is the uncertainties present in the system, ΔB_p denote the uncertainties that exist in the input matrices and R_p is the reference. If the condition in Eq. (3) is satisfied, then the matching condition holds, where:

$$rank([B_p \vdots \Delta A_p \vdots \Delta B_p \vdots B_p]) = rank(B_p) \qquad (5)$$

The pair (A_p, B_p) is controllable and the following match conditions are satisfied [19].

$$\Delta A_p = B_p \Delta \bar{A}_p (\Delta \bar{A}_p \text{ is a vector}) \quad \text{and} \quad \Delta B_p = B_p \Delta \bar{B}_p \quad (\Delta \bar{B}_p \text{ is a scalar}) \qquad (6)$$

The system in Eq. (7) is obtained by substituting (6) into (3). It can be rewritten in the following equation:

$$\dot{x}_p(t) = A_p x_p(t) + B_p u(t) + B_p(\Delta \bar{A}_p + \Delta \bar{B}_p + e(t)) + R_p r(t)$$
$$= A_p x_p(t) + B_p u(t) + B_p d(t) + R_p r(t) \qquad (7)$$

where

$$d(t) = \Delta \bar{A}_p + \Delta \bar{B}_p + e(t) \qquad (8)$$

Since the controller is in discrete time, the continuous time system in Eq. (7) is sampled using zero order hold (ZOH) at a slow rate as $\tau = 0.004$ s. Then discrete time of the system is given as

$$x(k+1) = \Phi x(k) + \Gamma u(k) + \Gamma f(k) + Hr(k)$$
$$y(k) = C_p x(k) \tag{9}$$

where $\Phi = e^{A_p \tau}$, $\Gamma = \int_0^\tau e^{A_p \tau} B_p d\tau$, $f = \int_0^\tau e^{A_p \tau} B_p ((k+1)\tau - \tau) d\tau$.

The discretization of Eq. (8) is obtained by applying *ZOH* sampling over time interval $(k\tau, (k+1)\tau)$ where τ is a sampling period [20]. The fast output sampling time, η can be obtained by dividing τ with N, where N is an integer and the value of N must be larger or the same as the observability index of (Φ, C). Using the fact that $u(k)$ is unchanged in the interval $\tau \le t \le (k+1)\tau$. The previous N fast sampled outputs be denoted as the N-element column as

$$y_k = \begin{bmatrix} y(k-1)\tau \\ y(k-1)\tau + \eta \\ y(k-1)\tau + 2\eta \\ \vdots \\ y(k\tau - \eta) \end{bmatrix} \tag{10}$$

The system in Eq. (9) can be represented in a faster sampling time of $\eta = 0.001$ s as

$$x(k+1) = \Phi_\eta x(k) + \Gamma_\eta u(k) + \Gamma_\eta f(k) + H_\eta r(k)$$
$$y_{k+1} = C_0 x(k) + C_u u(k) + C_u f(k) + C_r r(k) \tag{11}$$

where the value of C_0, C_u and C_r can be expressed as

$$C_0 = \begin{bmatrix} C_p \\ C_p \Phi_\eta \\ C_p \Phi_\eta^2 \\ \vdots \\ \vdots \\ C_p \Phi_\eta^{N-1} \end{bmatrix}, \quad C_u = \begin{bmatrix} 0 \\ C_p \Gamma_\eta \\ C_p(\Phi_\eta \Gamma_\eta + \Gamma_\eta) \\ \vdots \\ \vdots \\ C_p \sum_{i=0}^{N-2} \Phi_\eta^i \Gamma_\eta \end{bmatrix}, \quad C_r = \begin{bmatrix} 0 \\ C_p H_\eta \\ C_p(\Phi_\eta H_\eta + H_\eta) \\ \vdots \\ \vdots \\ C_p \sum_{i=0}^{N-2} \Phi_\eta^i H_\eta \end{bmatrix} \tag{12}$$

By considering Eqs. (11) and (12), the state $x(k)$ can be expressed as

$$\begin{bmatrix} x(k) \\ f(k) \end{bmatrix} = ([C_0 \quad C_u]^T [C_0 \quad C_u])^{-1} [C_0 \quad C_u]^T (y_{k+1} - C_u u(k) - C_r r(k))$$
$$= \Psi(y_{k+1} - C_u u(k) - C_r r(k)) \tag{13}$$

where

$$\Psi = ([C_0 \quad C_u]^T [C_0 \quad C_u])^{-1} [C_0 \quad C_u]^T \tag{14}$$

Substituting Eqs. (12) and (13) into Eq. (11), will gives

$$\begin{bmatrix} x(k+1) \\ f(k) \end{bmatrix} = \begin{bmatrix} \Phi_\eta & \Gamma_\eta \\ 0 & I \end{bmatrix} (\Psi y_{k+1} - \Psi C_u u(k) - \Psi C_r r(k)) + \begin{bmatrix} \Gamma_\eta \\ 0 \end{bmatrix} u(k) + \begin{bmatrix} H_\eta \\ 0 \end{bmatrix} r(k)$$

(15)

Then, the state $x(k+1)$ can be represented as in Eq. (16)

$$x(k+1) = [\Phi_\eta \quad \Gamma_\eta]\Psi y_{k+1} + (\Gamma_\eta - [\Phi_\eta \quad \Gamma_\eta]\Psi C_u)u(k)$$
$$+ (H_\eta - [\Phi_\eta \quad \Gamma_\eta]\Psi C_r)r(k))$$

(16)

If $Q = [\Phi_\eta \quad \Gamma_\eta]$ then the state $x(k)$ can be expressed using the output y_k as

$$x(k) = Q\Psi y_k + (\Gamma_\eta - Q\Psi C_u)u(k-1) + (H_\eta - Q\Psi C_r)r(k-1)$$

(17)

The discrete integral sliding surface is defined as

$$\sigma_{imrof}(k) = G_{imrof}x(k) - G_{imrof}x(0) + h(k)$$

(18)

where $h(k)$ is computed as

$$h(k) = h(k-1) - (G_{imrof}\Phi - G_{imrof}\Gamma K)x(k-1)$$

(19)

where $\sigma_{imrof} \in R^n$ is the sliding surface for MROF based DISMC, $h \in R^n$ is the integral vectors, $x(0)$ is the initial condition, $G_{imrof} \in R^{m \times n}$ and $K \in R^{m \times n}$ are the constant matrices. The matrix K is chosen such that $\Phi + \Gamma(G_{imrof} \Phi)^{-1}G_{imrof} + \Gamma K$ is lie within unit circle. The forward expression of the integral sliding surface can be simplified when considering Eqs. (18), (19) and (9) such that:

$$\sigma_{imrof}(k+1) = G_{imrof}[\Gamma u(k) + \Gamma f(k) + Hr(k) - x(0) + \Gamma Kx(k)] + \varepsilon(k)$$

(20)

By consider Eqs. (9), (17) and (20), the control input of the system can be represented in the output feedback as follows

$$u_{imrof}(k) = -(G\Gamma)^{-1}(G_{imrof}\Gamma K - G_{imrof})[Q\Psi y_k + (\Gamma_\eta - Q\Psi C_u)u(k-1)$$
$$+ (H_\eta - Q\Psi C_r)r(k-1)] - (G\Gamma)^{-1}[G_{imrof}Ff(k) + G_{imrof}Hr(k)$$
$$+ \rho|\sigma_{imrof}(k)|sign(\sigma_{imrof}(k))]$$

(21)

Different from the continuous time system where the disturbance can be taken directly, in discrete time system the Eq. (21) cannot be implemented because the current value of disturbance $f(k)$ is unknown. To overcome this problem, according to [21], if the updated value is not available, the estimation value can be used in which the last value of a disturbance signal can be taken as the estimate of its current value. Then $f(k)$ will be replaced by the estimated disturbance $\bar{f}(k) = f(k-1)$. Therefore, the control input in output feedback is given as:

$$u_{imrof}(k) = -(G_{imrof}\Gamma)^{-1}(G_{imrof}\Gamma K - G_{imrof})[Q\Psi y_k + (\Gamma_\eta - Q\Psi C_u)u(k-1)$$
$$+ (H_\eta - Q\Psi C_r)r(k-1)] - (G_{imrof}\Gamma)^{-1}[G_{imrof}\Gamma\bar{f}(k) + G_{imrof}Hr(k)$$
$$+ \rho|\sigma_{imrof}(k)|sign(\sigma_{imrof}(k))]$$

$$(22)$$

2.1 Stability Analysis

The stability condition for the designed controller in Eq. (22) is necessary to be proven to make sure that it is reachable and stable. The stability condition can be proven by using the Sarpturk stability condition as in Eqs. (23) and (24). The first part of Sarptuk stability condition can be described as

$$(\sigma_{imrof}(k+1) - \sigma_{imrof}(k))\text{sgn}(\sigma_{imrof}(k))$$
$$= -\rho|\sigma_{imrof}(k)| < 0 \tag{23}$$

The condition above is only true if the value of $\rho > 0$. Meanwhile the second part of Sarpturk stability condition can be expressed as:

$$(\sigma_{imrof}(k+1) + \sigma_{imrof}(k))\text{sgn}(\sigma_{imrof}(k)) > 0$$
$$= (2 - \rho)|\sigma_{imrof}(k)| > 0 \tag{24}$$

Equation (24) is only true if the value of $2 - \rho > 0$. From both conditions as stated in Eqs. (23) and (24), which $\rho > 0$ and $2 - \rho > 0$, it can be concluded that the designed controller is stable when the value of ρ is in the range of $0 < \rho < 2$.

3   Result and Discussion

The designed controller as Eq. (22) is implemented to inverted pendulum system. An inverted pendulum model is selected due to its characteristics which is under actuated nonlinear system, unstable and owns more than one degree of freedom. Therefore, it is a challenge to stabilize the unstable inverted pendulum system. The inverted pendulum consists of a single rod mounted on a linear cart in which the axis of rotation is right angles to the direction of the cart motion. The cart is constrained to only move in the horizontal direction, while the pendulum can only rotate in the x–y plane. The system state for inverted pendulum system as in Eq. (1) is fourth order system. Thus the observability index of the system is 4, hence the value of N is chosen as 4. In this work, the output is sampled at slow rate of $\tau = 0.004$ s. The inverted pendulum system that discretized in fast sampling time with $\eta = 0.001$ s as in Eq. (11) is shown as below:

$$\Phi_\eta = \begin{bmatrix} 1 & -0.001 & 0 & 0 & 0 \\ 0 & 1 & 0 & 0.0010 & 0 \\ 0 & 0 & 1.000 & -0.0000 & 0.0010 \\ 0 & 0 & 0.0009 & 0.9881 & 0 \\ 0 & 0 & 0.0462 & -0.0513 & 0.9995 \end{bmatrix} \quad \Gamma_\eta = \begin{bmatrix} 0 \\ 0 \\ 0.0000 \\ 0.0016 \\ 0.0067 \end{bmatrix}$$

$$F_\eta = \begin{bmatrix} 0 \\ 0 \\ 0.0000 \\ 0.0016 \\ 0.0067 \end{bmatrix}, \quad H_\eta = \begin{bmatrix} 0.001 \\ 0 \\ 0 \\ 0 \\ 0 \end{bmatrix}$$

$$C_f = 1.0e - 004 * \begin{bmatrix} 0 & 0 & 0 & 0 & 0 & 0 & 0 & 0.0160 & 0.0670 & 0 & 0.0478 & 0.2002 \end{bmatrix}^T$$
$$C_r = \begin{bmatrix} 0 & 0 & 0 & 0.0010 & 0 & 0 & 0.0020 & 0 & 0 & 0.0030 & 0 & 0 \end{bmatrix}^T$$

The MROF based DISMC has been simulated to demonstrate the ability of cart to move to desired position and at the same time maintain the inverted pendulum in upright position. In this condition, the initial cart position is zero meter and the measured pendulum angle is also zero radian. The cart position then is forced to move to reference tracking which is the unit step input. The switching surface is designed as G_{imrof} = [0.6819 0.1779 0.5724 −0.4204 −0.4950] and the matrix K is defined as K = [− 35.9282 −22.6932 −8.3910 12.8303 35.7651]. The selection of switching surface is via Particle Swarm Optimization (PSO). Based on stability analysis, the value of ρ must be between $0 < \rho < 2$, therefore ρ is selected as 1.995. For the comparison purpose, the performance of the MROF were compared with the discrete linear quadratic regulator (DLQR) and discrete Proportional-Integral-Derivative (PID). The value of DLQR control gain, K_{dlqr} is set as K_{dlqr} = [945.9 1415.5 −560.1 1530.3]. Meanwhile, there are two PID controllers used in the investigation to control the inverted pendulum system. PID controller 1 is used to control the position and PID controller 2 controls the angle of the inverted pendulum system. The parameter values of K_p, K_i and K_d for PID controller 1 and the PID controller 2 are −20, −0.1, −25 and 100, 4, 12 respectively.

The simulation results of the inverted pendulum's cart position for MROF based DISMC, DLQR and PID is displayed in Fig. 1. Meanwhile, details of the comparison is shown in Table 1. Based on this comparison, the MROF based DISMC gives the lowest settling time and lowest overshoot among the rest. Although the difference in settling time for the DLQR is only 0.7 s from the MROF based DISMC, the maximum voltage for the control input is very high which is near to 4 V compared to DISMC which is less than 2 V. Meanwhile the PID controller provides the highest overshoot and slowest settling time compared to the MROF based DISMC and DLQR controllers. The simulation result for the angle of the inverted pendulum system for all controllers are shown in Fig. 2. The angle of the inverted pendulum for MROF based DISMC is moved to −0.56 rad, then it moves to positive 0.18 rad before maintaining at 0 rad when the steady state is achieved. The result of control input for three difference types of controller is shown in Fig. 3. Meanwhile Fig. 4 shows the sliding surface for the MROF based DISMC. The system state slides onto sliding surface and remains on that surface thereafter at $\sigma_{imrof}(k + 1) = 0$.

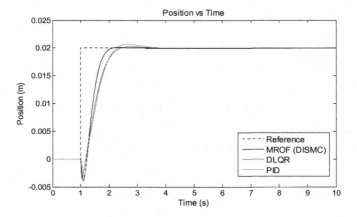

Fig. 1. Position of the cart.

Table 1. Comparison of the cart position with different types of controller.

Characteristic	MROF (DISMC)	DLQR	PID
Rise time (s)	0.6489	0.7493	0.7202
Settling time (s)	2.6682	3.3545	3.5971
Percentage of overshoot (%)	0.3572	1.1322	3.1241

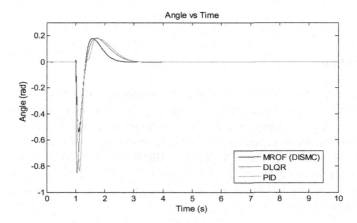

Fig. 2. Angle of the inverted pendulum.

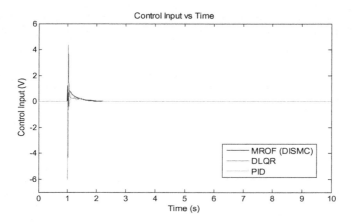

Fig. 3. Control input.

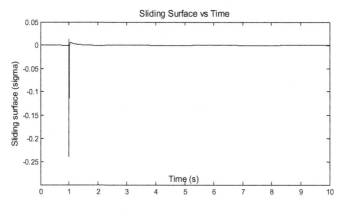

Fig. 4. Sliding surface.

4 Conclusion

The performance of the designed controller was demonstrated to prove that the MROF based DISMC is invariant to the uncertainties that are present in the system and guarantee the stability. Only by the usage of output state, the system is able to be controlled, follow the reference tacking and not depending on the state feedback. The comparison between the PID, DLQR and MROF based DISMC shows that the designed controller has achieved the best capability in providing desired functional and better system response in term of its fast settling time and less overshoot when compared to the others.

Acknowledgments. The authors would like to thank to University Tun Hussein Onn Malaysia (UTHM) and Research, Innovation, Commercialization, Consultancy Office (ORICC), UTHM for supporting this research.

References

1. Young, K.D., Utkin, V.I., Özgüner, Ü.: A control engineer's guide to sliding mode control. IEEE Trans. Control Syst. Technol. **7**(3), 328–342 (1999)
2. Abed, E.H.: Output regulation of DC-DC switching converters using discrete-time integral control. In: Proceedings of the 1999 American Control Conference, pp. 1052–1056 (1999)
3. Lai, N.O., Edwards, C., Spurgeon, S.K.: An implementation of an output tracking dynamic discrete-time sliding mode controller on an aircraft simulator. In: Proceedings of the 2006 International Workshop on Variable Structure Systems, pp. 35–40 (2006)
4. Herrmann, G., Edwards, C., Hredzak, B., Venkataramanan, V., Spurgeon, S.K.: A novel discrete-time sliding mode technique and its application to a HDD dual-stage track-seek and track-following servo system. In: 22nd IEEE International Symposium on Intelligent Control, pp. 283–288 (2008)
5. Majidabad, S.S., Shandiz, H.T.: Discrete time based sliding-mode control of robot manipulators. Int. J. Intell. Comput. Cybernet. **5**(3), 340–358 (2012)
6. Behnamgol, V., Vali, A.R.: Terminal sliding mode control for nonlinear systems with both matched and unmatched uncertainties. Iran. J. Electr. Electron. Eng. **11**(2), 109–117 (2015)
7. Edwards, C., Spurgeon, K.S.: Sliding Mode Control: Theory and Applications. Taylor and Francis Group/CRC Press, Boca Raton/Didcot (1998)
8. Wang, B.: On discretization of sliding mode control systems. Ph.D. thesis, RMIT University (2008)
9. Gao, W.B., Wang, Y.F., Homaifa, A.: Discrete time variable structure control systems. IEEE Trans. Industr. Electron. **42**(2), 117–122 (1995)
10. Govindaswamy, S., Floquet, T., Spurgeon, S.K.: Discrete time output feedback sliding mode tracking control for systems with uncertainties. Int. J. Robust Nonlinear Control **24**(5), 2098–2118 (2013)
11. Abidi, K., Xu, J., Xinghuo, Y.X.Y.: On the discrete-time integral sliding mode control. In: International Workshop on Variable Structure Systems, pp. 29–34 (2006)
12. Xi, X.C., Hong, G.S., Poo, A.N.: Improving CNC contouring accuracy by integral sliding mode control. Mechatronics **20**(4), 442–452 (2010)
13. Xi, Z., Hesketh, T.: Discrete time integral sliding mode control for system with matched and unmatched uncertainties. IET Control Theory Appl. **4**(10), 2071–2081 (2010)
14. Janardhanan, S., Bandyopadhyay, B.: Output feedback sliding-mode control for uncertain systems using fast output sampling technique. IEEE Trans. Industr. Electron. **53**(5), 1677–1682 (2006)
15. Janardhanan, S., Satyanarayana, N.: Sliding mode control of uncertain systems using multirate output feedback functional observer. In: 12th International Workshop on Variable Structure Systems, pp. 314–318 (2012)
16. Waterman, D.M., Nonami, K.: Hydraulic cylinder velocity tracking with multirate output feedback sliding mode control. J. Syst. Des. Dyn. **3**(5), 717–729 (2009)
17. Prem, K.R., Siva, K.M., Srinivasa, R.D.: Control of nonlinear inverted pendulum system using PID and fast output sampling based discrete sliding mode controller. Int. J. Eng. Res. Technol. (IJERT) **3**, 1000–1006 (2014)

18. Ngadengon, R., Sam, Y.M., Osman, J.H.S., Tomari, R., Wan Zakaria, W.N.: Stabilization of inverted pendulum: a multirate output feedback based discrete time sliding mode control. In: Ibrahim, H., Iqbal, S., Teoh, S.S., Mustaffa, M.T. (eds.) 9th International Conference on Robotic, Vision, Signal Processing and Power Applications. LNEE, vol. 398, pp. 419–426. Springer, Singapore (2017). doi:10.1007/978-981-10-1721-6_45
19. Yu, F.I.: High precision motion control based on a discrete-time sliding mode approach. Ph. D. thesis, Royal Institute of Technology (2001)
20. Shaocheng, Q., Xiaohua, X., Jiangfeng, Z.: Dynamics of discrete-time sliding-mode-control uncertain systems with a disturbance compensator. IEEE Trans. Industr. Electron. **6107**, 3502–3510 (2014)
21. Su, W.C., Drakunov, S.V., Ozguner, U.: An O(T2) boundary layer in sliding mode for sampled-data systems. IEEE Trans. Autom. Control **45**(3), 482–485 (2000)

Erratum to: Multi-loop Damping and Tracking Strategy Emulating a Butterworth Pattern for Accurate Nanopositioning

Mohammed Altaher and Sumeet S. Aphale[✉]

University of Aberdeen, Aberdeen, UK
{mohammed.altaher, s.aphale}@abdn.ac.uk

Erratum to:
Chapter "Multi-loop Damping and Tracking Strategy Emulating a Butterworth Pattern for Accurate Nanopositioning" in: M.S. Mohamed Ali et al. (Eds.), Modeling, Design and Simulation of Systems, Part I, CCIS 751, https://doi.org/10.1007/978-981-10-6463-0_2

The initially published versions of Figs. 4 and 5 are incorrect. These are the correct versions:

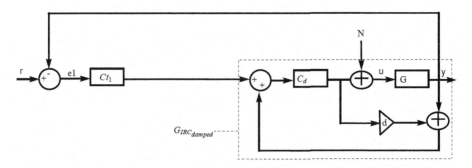

Fig. 4. Schematic of the traditional damping + tracking control scheme

---

The updated online version of this chapter can be found at
https://doi.org/10.1007/978-981-10-6463-0_2

© Springer Nature Singapore Pte Ltd. 2017

M.S. Mohamed Ali et al. (Eds.): AsiaSim 2017, Part I, CCIS 751, pp. E1–E2, 2017.
https://doi.org/10.1007/978-981-10-6463-0_61

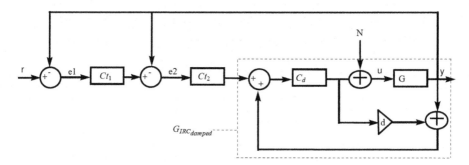

Fig. 5. Schematic of the proposed control scheme with dual-loop tracking + damping

Author Index

Printed in the United States
By Bookmasters

Printed in the United States
By Bookmasters